Fourth Edition

Standard Catalog of U.S. Paper Money

By Chester L. Krause and Robert F. Lemke

Pricing Editor: Robert E. Wilhite

krause publications

700 E. State St., Iola, WI 54990

Special Consultants:
☆ Frederick J. Bart
☆ Colin R. Bruce II
☆ Kevin Foley
☆ Len Glazer
☆ Alan Herbert
☆ John T. Hickman
☆ Harry Jones
☆ Tom Knebl
☆ Dean Oakes
☆ Russell Rulau
☆ R.B. White

Contributions to earlier editions by the late **Carl Allenbaugh** *are gratefully remembered.*

Library of Congress Catalog Card Number: 81-81876
International Standard Book Number: 0-87341-078-5

INDEX

Introduction

Though paper media representing gold or other intrinsic-value stores of wealth have been issued in the United States and its predecessor colonies and territories since 1690, the widespread acceptance of paper currency by the American people is a comparatively recent development and came only grudgingly.

Paper money emissions by the British colonies in New England, the earliest paper currency within the borders of what is now the U.S.A., circulated alongside other untraditional exchange media such as Indian wampum shells and musket balls during chronic periods of shortages of "real" — coined — money.

Even though the first issues of an organized central government, the Continental Congress' currency notes, promised to pay the bearer face value in "Spanish milled dollars, or the value thereof in gold or silver," these notes circulated at a heavy discount — if they were acceptable at all. The fledgling government's final solution for the Continental Currency problem, accepting them in 1787 at 1% of face value in exchange for interest bearing bonds, did nothing to bolster public confidence in paper money.

Neither did the often larcenous "banking" practices of the various elements of the private sector to whom the note-issuing prerogative fell. With states denied the power to issue money by the Constitution of the United States, and the powers of the Federal Government to do so left unspecified; various private issues of banks, railroads, utilities, and even individual citizens, cropped up, with varying resources to guarantee their value, until the Government halted the practice in 1863.

By the late 19th Century, U.S.-issued paper money had become a viable part of the nation's commerce as people recognized that such notes were, indeed, redeemable on demand for gold or silver. By 1963, paper currency was such an ingrained part of the American economy that the Government was able to remove all specie-redemption quality from its currency issues, raising only minimal objections from strict interpretationists of the Constitution.

Now, ironically, paper money may be on the way out as a circulating medium of exchange. The growth of demand deposits (checking accounts), electronic fund transfers and the arrival of the home computer age may one day soon put an end for the need for physical symbols of wealth to pass from hand to hand.

Scope of this catalog

It is not the intention of this catalog to provide a reference to every type of official and unofficial paper currency which has circulated in the United States. Indeed, such a project between the covers of one volume represents an impossible, though intriguing, challenge.

Rather, this catalog will provide a guide to those paper money issues since 1812 of the Government of the United States of America, along with several related currency issues which are traditionally collected by paper money hobbyists in conjunction with the regular issues of the U.S.

Such a scope is intended, therefore, to provide the collector of U.S. paper money with a catalog reflective of the current state of the hobby.

Since it is not intended that this book serve as a definitive history of paper money in the United States, the reader will be provided with sufficient background information to facilitate and illuminate the building of a collection, without being subjected to fiscal, legislative or historical data that would be of interest to only a small minority of readers.

History of Pre-Federal Paper Money in the U.S.

To better understand the forces which shaped the United States Government's issues of paper currency since 1861, it is necessary to look backward to the many and varied public and private currency issues which preceded them in this country.

The use of paper money in the area which would become the United States actually predates its use in many parts of Western Europe and in most of the rest of the world. While paper currencies had been in use in China since the 7th Century, when it was known as "flying money" because of its light weight and ability to circulate widely with ease, it was not until the late 17th Century that the western world began experiments with non-metallic circulating currencies.

Surprisingly quickly, the North American continent had its first "paper money" issues in 1685, when the Intendant of New France (Canada) issued promissory notes hand-printed on pieces of playing cards, to circulate as money until the delayed arrival of the paymaster.

The Massachusetts Bay Colony followed suit soon after, issuing in December, 1690, £7,000 worth of the first publicly authorized paper money notes in the western world to pay expenses of a border war with Canada (previous paper money issues in Europe and North America had been either issued by banks, or were emergency measures not authorized by any public body).

Following that precedent, by the turn of the 18th Century, other colonies were emitting paper currencies as needed to run their specie-short economies. By the end of the War for Independence, all 13 colonies had issued some form of paper currency.

Beginning in May, 1775, the Congress of the newly unified former colonies began the issue of Continental Currency to finance its fight for freedom.

The Continental Currency was plagued, though, by increasing public distrust. The Continental paper dollar was able to hold its value at par with a specie dollar only until October, 1777, by which time widespread counterfeiting by British, Tories and opportunists conspired with the natural inflation of a printing press economy and increasing uncertainty as to the outcome of the war to push the exchange ratio of the Continental Currency to $11 in paper for $10 in specie.

After that point, the devaluation accelerated. By the next year, October, 1778, the ratio was 4.66 to 1.

The low point was reached in April, 1780, when a dollar in silver or gold was worth $40 Continental. And these were the *official* exchange ratios adopted by the Congress and many of the states, to offset the rampant inflation. In actual commerce, the Continentals were all but worthless. George Washington himself lamented that it took a wagonful of Continental Currency to purchase a wagonload of supplies for his army. A truer measure of the value of the Government paper currency could be found in the fact that by October, 1787, amid speculation that the Continental Currency might never be redeemable, it was selling at the rate of $250 paper for $1 specie. Eventually, the Government issued 6% interest bearing bonds at the rate of $1 for every $100 of Continental Currency turned in.

Issued current with the Colonial and Continental currencies were numerous privately-sponsored paper monies emitted by banks (as early as 1732 in Connecticut), utilities, merchants, individuals and even churches.

These issues continued after the Revolutionary War, and proliferated in the 19th Century. Today, lumped together under the generic, if not altogether correct, label of "broken bank notes," these colorful, historic notes and their collectible adjuncts make up a significant portion of the paper money hobby's interest.

The ten of thousands of privately-issued bank and scrip notes of the 1800s ranged in denomination from one-half cent to several thousand dollars. While today their collector value depends on a combination of rarity, condition and demand; their value when issued was solely dependent on the reputation of the issuing authority — be it bank, railroad or Main Street apothecarian. In those days, when a note might be worth every cent of its face value or might be worth nothing more than the paper on which it was printed, an entire industry sprang up to supply banks and merchants with accurate, timely information about which notes would pass current, which should be accepted only at a discount, and those from an issuer who had gone "broken." In addition, because of the wealth of larcenous talent available for changing broken bank notes into "good" notes through the alteration of a bank or city name, or raising the denomination of a note from $1 to $10 by deft penmanship; those who handled the dizzying variety of paper money in circulation in the mid 19th Century needed books which listed and described the genuine issues of a particular bank. (It is, incidentally, from the common name of these paper money reporting services that the name *Bank Note Reporter* was derived for the monthly paper money newspaper published by the publisher of this catalog.)

The only restraints on the issue of paper money at that time were those which the individual states cared to apply, and such restraints were infrequent and ineffective.

The Federal Government put an effective end to these halcyon days of currency free-for-all in 1863, by imposing a 10% tax on outstanding notes; and later through the 14th Amendment to the Constitution, forbidding the private issue of circulating media of exchange altogether.

With that the Government of the United States of America attained a monopoly on the note-issuing function which it has maintained, except in localized emergency situations, to this day.

Pre-Civil War (1812-1861) United States Treasury Notes

Compiled by Russell Rulau

The first paper money issued by the United States Government was not, as is often thought, the Interest Bearing Treasury Notes of 1861, the so-called "7-30's." Issued as a result of the Civil War, these 1861 notes were actually the last in a long series of Treasury notes that commenced in 1812 as a consequence of the financial condition of the nation in the War of 1812.

The U.S. Treasury issued five separate series of notes between 1812-1815 with denominations ranging from $3 to $1,000. Though originally intended as loans to the government, they soon began to circulate since they were receivable for debts, taxes and duties due the federal government. Neither the 1812-1815 notes nor later Treasury notes until 1861 were ever actually legal tender for all debts, public and private, however — an important distinction between them and the legal tender notes beginning in the Civil War.

The panic and depression of 1837-1843 brought about eight more series of Treasury notes in those years. These notes differed from the earlier issues in that they were signed by the Treasurer of the U.S. (the 1812-1815 issues had been signed by appointed commissioners).

The Mexican War was responsible for the next two series of Treasury notes in 1846-1847. These also were signed by the Treasurer of the U.S.

The severe financial conditions surrounding the panic of 1857 brought about the next series of Treasury notes, issued from December, 1857, through March, 1861. These notes were issued at competitive interest rates rather than predetermined interest rates. Confidence in the government was lacking, though, and of the $10 million in 6% notes offered in December, 1860, only $70,200 was taken up. The remainder of the notes was issued at rates above 6%, with the largest numbers going at 10, 10¾, 11 and 12%. (Bids were received as high as 36% but the Treasury rejected all bids over 12%.)

The final issue of Treasury notes was the Interest Bearing Notes of July, 1861, to 1865. Issued to help finance the Civil War, they were not the first government notes but merely the continuation of a long series begun a half-century earlier.

Most of the pre-Civil War Treasury notes bear the date of the Act which authorized them, and an issue date (in ink) as well. The catalog is arranged by authorization (not issue) dates.

All pre-Civil War Treasury notes are rare and seldom met with. Many are unique or exist only in museum collections, and a number of them exist only as specimens or as proofs. Pricing is really not possible; such prices as are given are mainly auction results. The only series of notes usually met with as issued, signed notes, is the Series of 1815.

The catalog which follows lists the various issues of pre-Civil War Treasury notes. The information herein comes from several sources:

United States Notes, by John Knox, 1888.

An Illustrated History of U.S. Loans 1775-1898, by Gene Hessler, BNR Press, 1985.

Author Sheds Light on 1812 Treasury Notes, by Donald Kagin, in Coin World for July 9, 1980.

Important United States Paper Money (Alexandre Vattemare collection auction), by Christie Manson & Woods International, Sept. 17, 1982.

Paper Money Issued by the U.S. Government prior to the Civil War, by Bruce W. Smith, unpublished manuscript, 1977.

Photos and notes from Larry Stevens, Eric P. Newman, Walter Breen.

There is a very interesting tale regarding the circulation of the July, 1861, series (the "7-30's"). Much of the loot taken in Jesse James' first bank robbery, the Clay County Savings Bank in Liberty, Missouri, on Feb. 13, 1866, consisted of 7-30 notes. A few thousand dollars of the money soon turned up in Ohio, Tennessee and Kentucky, but most of the money is said to have been exchanged in England. To the James boys, at least, Treasury bonds were as good as gold.

U.S. TREASURY NOTES June, 1812 - March, 1861

WAR OF 1812 NOTES

ACT OF 30 JUNE 1812

1 year notes at 5 2/5% interest. $5,000,000 authorized and issued.

KL#	Denom.		Fine
P1	$100	Eagle on branch at right.	—

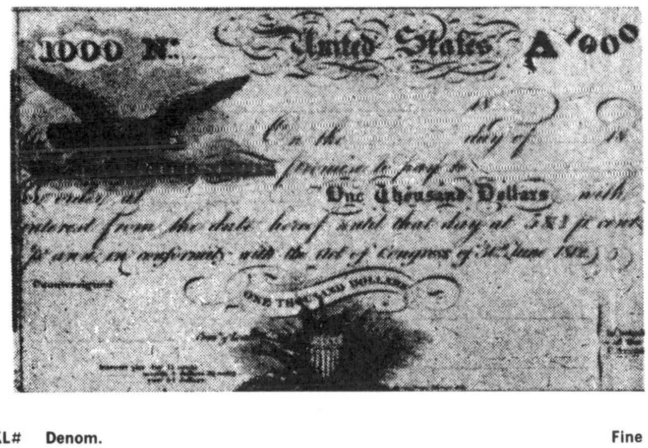

KL#	Denom.		Fine
P2	$1,000	Eagle on branch at left.	—

ACT OF 25 FEBRUARY 1813

1 year notes at 5 2/5% interest. $5,000,000 authorized and issued.

KL#	Denom.		Fine
P3	$100	No description available.	—

ACT OF 4 MARCH 1814

1 year notes at 5 2/5% interest. $10,000,000 authorized and issued.

KL#	Denom.		Fine
P4	$20	No description available.	—
P5	$50	No description available.	—
P6	$100	No description available.	—

ACT OF 26 DECEMBER 1814

1 year notes at 5 2/5% interest. $8,318,400 issued.

KL#	Denom.		Fine
P7	$20	Eagle on shield at left. Imprint: MDF	Rare
P8	$50	No description available.	—
P9	$100	Eagle on branch at right. Imprint: MDF	Rare

ACT OF 24 FEBRUARY 1815

(Called "Small Treasury Notes) $3 to $50 notes - no interest. $100 notes - indefinite at 5 2/5% interest. $3,392,994 issued in $3 to $50 notes; $1,969,400 issued in $100 notes.

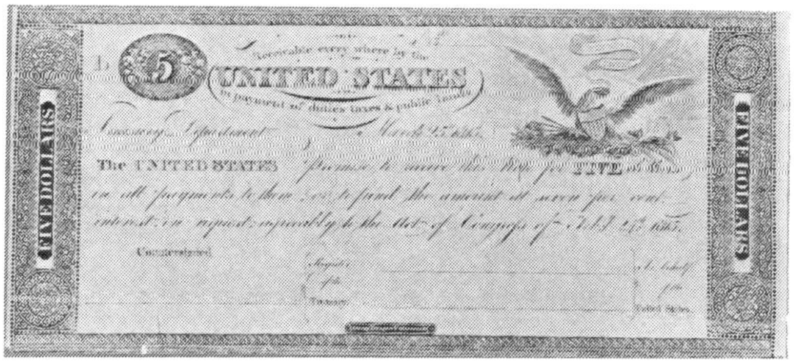

KL#	Denom.		Fine
P10	$3	U.S. shield at center. Imprint: MDF	—

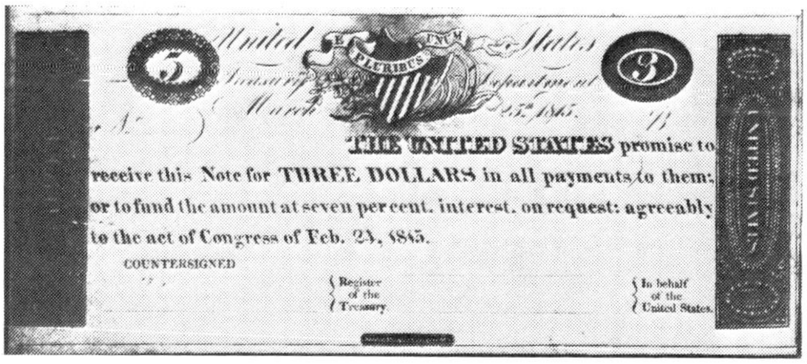

KL#	Denom.		Fine
P11	$5	Eagle on branch at right. Imprint: MDF	—

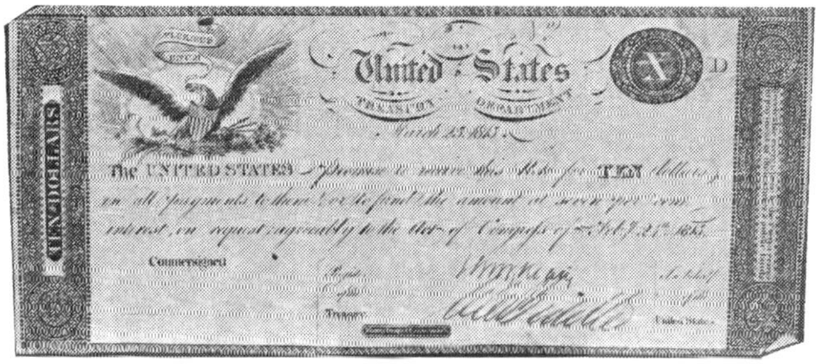

KL#	Denom.		Fine
P12	$10	Type 1. Eagle on branch at left. Text at right. Imprint: MDF	—

KL#	Denom.		Fine
P13	$10	Type 2. Similar, but TEN DOLLARS at right.	—

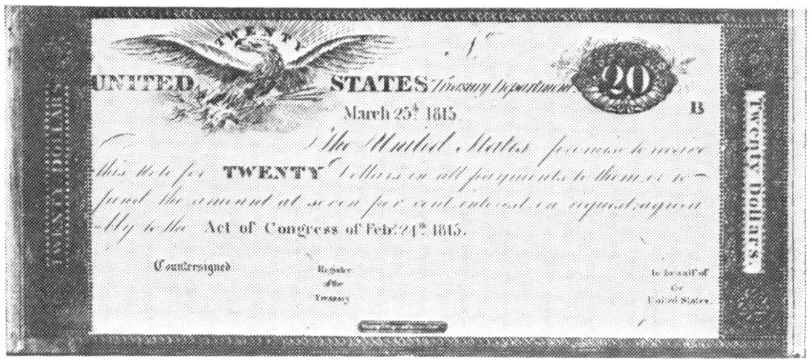

KL#	Denom.		Fine
P14	$20	Eagle at left. Imprint: MDF	—

KL#	Denom.		Fine
P15	$50	Eagle on branch at right. Imprint: MDF	—

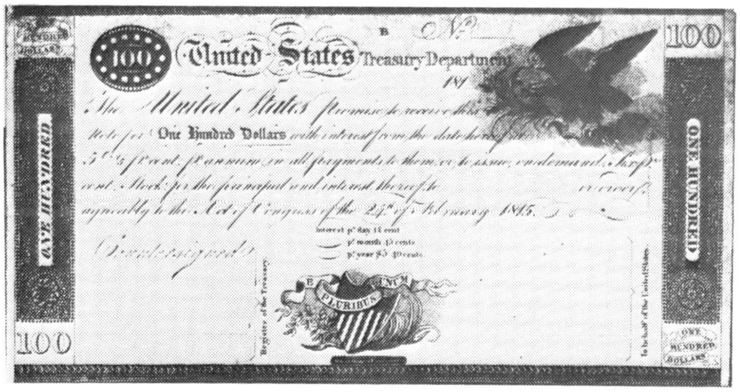

KL#	Denom.		Fine
P16	$100	Eagle at right, shield at lower center. MDF	—

NOTE: The issue of February 1815 actually circulated as currency, though not a legal tender for all debts.

PANIC OF 1837 NOTES

ACT OF 12 OCTOBER 1837

1 year notes issued at four different rates of interest - 1 mill, 2%, 5% or 6%, the rate written in ink at time of issue. The 1-mill rate, which was nominal, was used on notes intended to circulate as currency. $10,000,000 authorized and issued (6% notes are rarest)

KL#	Denom.		Fine
P17	$50	No description available.	Specimens only
P18	$100	No description available.	Specimens only
P19	$500	No description available.	Specimens only
P20	$1,000	No description available.	Specimens only

ACT OF 21 MAY 1838

1 Year notes at 6% interest. $6,888,809 issued.

KL#	Denom.		Fine
P21	$50	No description available.	—
P22	$100	No description available.	—
P23	$500	No description available.	—
P24	$1,000	No description available.	—

ACT OF 2 MARCH 1839

1 year notes at 2% or 6% interest. $3,857.276 issued.

KL#	Denom.		Fine
P25	$50	No description available.	—
P26	$100	No description available.	—
P27	$500	No description available.	—
P28	$1,000	No description available.	—

ACT OF 31 MARCH 1840

1 year notes at 2%, 5%, 5 2/5% or 6% interest, the rate written in by ink at time of issuance.

KL#	Denom.		Fine
P29	$50	No description available.	Specimens only

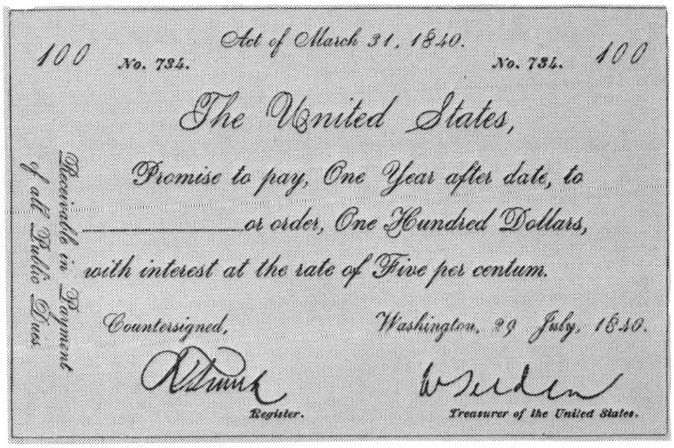

KL#	Denom.		Fine
P30	$100	Knox drawing only available.	Specimens only
P31	$500	No description available.	Specimens only
P32	$1,000	No description available.	Specimens only
P33	$10,000	No description available.	Specimens only

ACT OF FEBRUARY 1841

NOTE: Records indicate $7,529,062 was issued in notes of this issue, but no specimens are known.

ACT OF 31 JANUARY 1842

1 year notes at 2% or 6% interest. $7,959,994 issued (including reissues).

KL#	Denom.		Fine
P34	$50	No description available.	Specimens only
P35	$100	No description available.	Specimens only
P36	$500	No description available.	Specimens only
P37	$1,000	No description available.	Specimens only

ACT OF 31 AUGUST 1842

1 year notes at 2% or 6% interest. $3,025,554 issued.

KL#	Denom.		Fine
P38	$50	Mercury at left, female at right. Imprint: RW&H	—
P39	$100	No description available.	Specimens only
P40	$500	No description available.	Specimens only
P41	$1,000	No description available.	Specimens only

ACT OF 3 MARCH 1843

1 year notes at 1 mill or 4% interest. $1,806,950 issued.

KL#	Denom.		Fine
P42	$50	Female at left, eagle at center, female at right. Imprint: RW&H	—

SPECIAL NOTE: In 1887 there were only $83,425 outstanding in all Treasury Notes issued under acts prior to 1846!

MEXICAN WAR NOTES

ACT OF 22 JULY 1846

1 year notes at 1 mill or 5 2/5% interest. $7,687,800 issued. NOTE: In 1887, only $5,900 was outstanding!

KL#	Denom.		Fine
P43	$50	No description available.	Specimens only

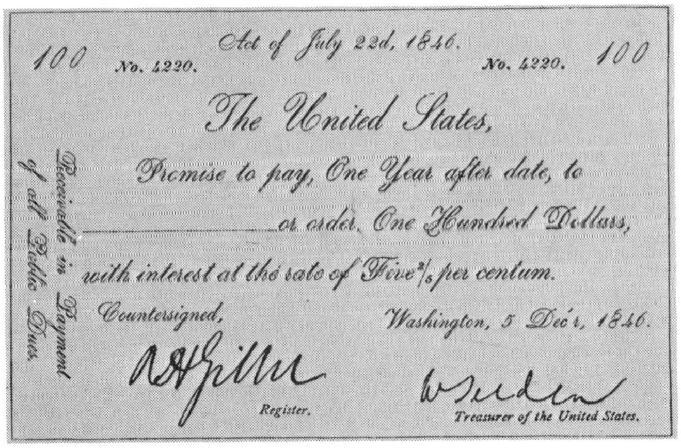

KL#	Denom.		Fine
P44	$100	Knox drawing only available.	Specimens only
P45	$500	No description available.	Specimens only
P46	$1,000	No description available.	Specimens only

ACT OF 28 JANUARY 1847

60 day or 1 or 2 year notes at 5 2/5% or 6% interest. $26,122,100 issued (including reissues). NOTE: In 1887, only $950 of 6% notes were still outstanding!

KL#	Denom.		Fine
P47	$50	No description available.	Specimens only
P48	$100	Knox drawing only available.	Specimens only
P49	$500	No description available.	Specimens only
P50	$1,000	No description available.	Specimens only

KL#	Denom.		Fine
P51	$5,000	Type 1. Girl at left, eagle at center, lady at right. 2-year notes. Imprint: RWH&E	Specimens only

KL#	Denom.		Fine
P52	$5,000	Type 2. Female at left, eagle and Washington at center, warrior female at right. Imprint: TC	Specimens only

PANIC OF 1857 NOTES

ACT OF 23 DECEMBER 1857

1 year notes at 3 to 6% interest. $20,000,000 authorized. NOTE: In 1887, only $700 of all these notes were outstanding!

KL#	Denom.		Fine
P53	$100	Knox drawing only available. Imprint: TC	—
P54	$500	No description available.	—
P55	$1,000	No description available.	—

ACT OF 17 DECEMBER 1860

1 year notes at 6% to 12% interest. $15,000,000 issued (most at rates of 10¾, 11 or 12%)

KL#	Denom.		Fine
P56	$50	No description available.	—
P57	$100	No description available.	—
P58	$500	No description available.	—
P59	$1,000	No description available.	—

ACT OF 2 MARCH 1861

1 or 2 year notes at 6% interest. $35,364,450 issued ($22.4 million in 2-year notes)

KL#	Denom.		Fine
P60	$50	Jackson at left, Webster at right. Black & orange; blue back. Imprint: NBNC	10,000.

KL#	Denom.		Fine
P61	$100	Seated female at left, eagle in center. Black & orange; green back.	2,500.

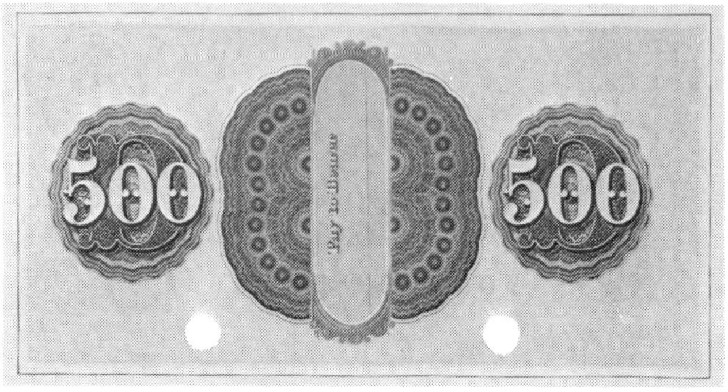

KL#	Denom.		Fine
P62	$500	Type 1. Washington at left, females at center, eagle at right. Black & green; brown back. 60-day note. Imprint: ABNC and RWH&E	Specimens only

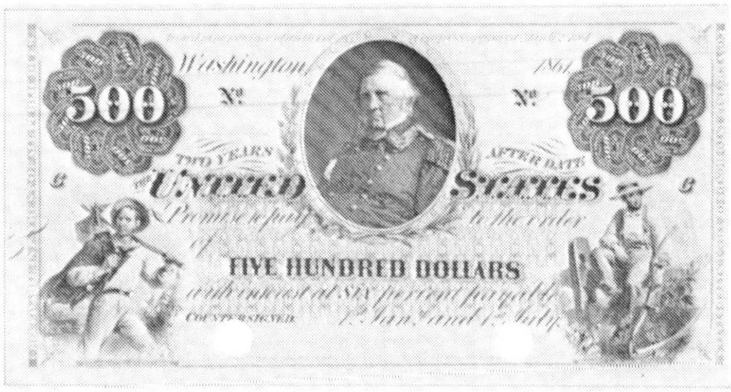

KL#	Denom.		Fine
P63	$500	Type 2. Winfield Scott at center. 2-year note.	2,500.

LIST OF PRINTERS ABBREVIATIONS

ABNC	American Bank Note Company
MDF	Murray Draper Fairman & Co.
NBNC	National Bank Note Co.
RW&H	Rawdon Wright & Hatch
RWH&E	Rawdon Wright Hatch & Edson
TC	Toppan Carpenter & Co.

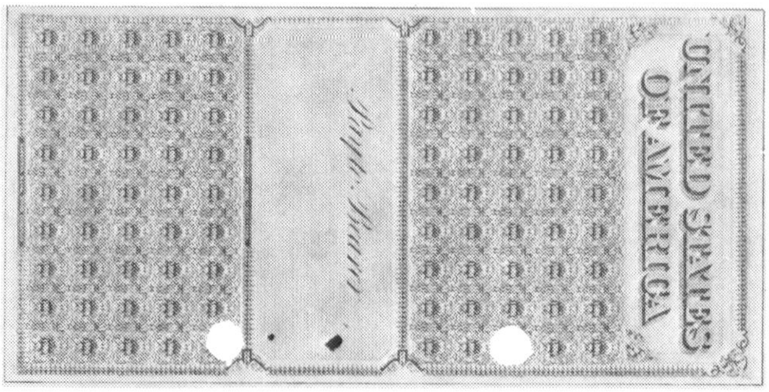

KL#	Denom.		Fine
P64	$1,000	Washington at left, female at center. Black & green; rust back.	5,000.
P65	$5,000	No description available.	—

ESSAYS FOR ACTS NOT APPROVED

LOAN OF 1848

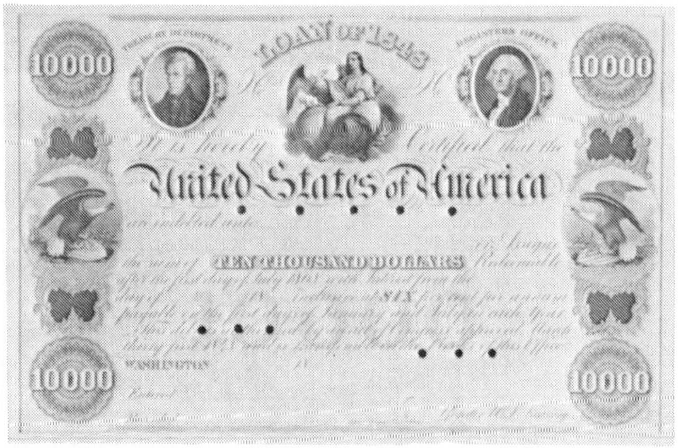

KL#	Denom.		Fine
P71	$10,000	Rust color. Jackson, female and Washington at top center. Imprint: TC	1,500.

ACT OF JUNE 14, 1858

KL#	Denom.		Fine
P72	$5,000	Rust color. Ceres, eagle and Ceres at top center, Franklin at bottom.	750.

ACT OF JUNE 22, 1860

KL#	Denom.		Fine
P73	$1,000	Eagle on rock at center. Imprint: ABNC	350.
P74	$5,000	Similar. Imprint: ABNC	350.

Large Size Notes

For the convenience of the reader, brief and basically historical backgrounds have been provided for each of the major types of U.S. currency. No great amount of fiscal or legislative data has been provided, except where it might serve to clarify some aspects of the notes themselves or their collectibility.

Demand Notes

Despite two issues of interest-bearing Treasury notes in 1860-1861, the opening guns of the Civil War found the United States Government short of the necessary funds to put down the rebellion in a protracted war.

Congress moved swiftly in the national emergency to provide legislation authorizing the issue of $60,000,000 by Acts of July 17, and Aug. 5, 1861.

It is generally believed among numismatists today that the Demand Notes were backed by faith in the Government alone; but this was not entirely the case. By the terms of the authorizing legislation, the Demand Notes were not payable in gold. But, in a circular from the Secretary of the Treasury sent out before the suspension of specie payments on Dec. 21, 1861, they were declared payable in coin, and the Government redeemed them as such in order to sustain its credit. Thus, for a short time in 1861, the Demand Notes were quoted on a par with gold. However, as the war progressed, in most parts of the country the Demand Notes — and all other paper money of the U.S. Government — were acceptable only at a discount, even though they were receivable for all payments to the Goverment, including duties.

The Demand Notes took their famous "Greenback" nickname from the color of their back designs (back designs in themselves were scarce on paper money in the U.S. prior to the Civil War). The name was subsequently applied to virtually every other form of U.S. currency and remains current today.

Because the United States Government was not prepared to be in the note-printing business in 1861, the work of producing the Demand Notes was contracted to the American Bank Note Company and National Bank Note Company. Working with essentially stock currency elements, the private contractors turned out more than 7.25 million $5, $10 and $20 Demand Notes.

The actual "issuing" of the notes required that they be signed by the Treasurer of the United States (Francis E. Spinner) and the Register of the Treasury (Lucius E. Chittenden), or persons designated by them.

Accordingly, platoons of clerks within the Treasury Department were put to work autographing Demand Notes. However, on the very earliest specimens, the engraved blanks on the face of the notes indicated only the office of the signer, and the clerks were required to pen in the words "for the" on each note as they signed it, a most laborious process that was eliminated with the addition of "for the" on the engraved face plates themselves. The Demand Notes which survive today with the hand-signed "for the" on the face are much scarcer than the engraved version, and command a significant price premium.

Rarity and value of the Demand Notes is also affected by the engraved location on the face of the note indicating where the notes were issued and, therefore, payable.

The obligation on the notes reads: "The United States promises to pay to the bearer five dollars (or ten dollars or twenty dollars) on demand . . . payable by the Assistant Treasurer of the United States at . . ."

One of five cities was then engraved. Those notes payable at New York are far and away the most common among the survivors, with Philadelphia second and Boston third. Specimens which promise redemption in Cincinnati and, especially, St. Louis, are extremely rare and seldom encountered.

United States Notes (Legal Tender Notes)

The longest-lived type of U.S. paper money, the United States Notes (called interchangeably Legal Tender Notes because of the wording of the obligation) was first authorized in 1862 and is still current today, though none have been issued since 1969.

The subject of major Constitutional debate at the time of their issue, the notes did much to pave the way for future issues of U.S. currency backed only by the credit of the Government.

While there are five official "issues" of large size Legal Tender Notes, as well as the small size series, they are generally collected today by type (major design) and, occasionally, by signature combination.

The First Issue of United States Notes, dated March 10, 1862, was issued in denominations of $5, $10, $20, $50, $100, $500 and $1,000.

Two different varieties of notes, bearing different obligation wording on the backs, are popularly collected among the First Issue notes.

The earliest First Issues bear what is known as the First Obligation on back, reading: "This note is a legal tender for all debts, public and private, except duties on imports and interest on the public debt, and is exchangeable for U.S. six per cent twenty year bonds, redeemable at the pleasure of the United States after five years."

The Second Obligation, much rarer, reads as follows: "This note is a legal tender for all debts, public and private, except duties on imports and interest on the public debt, and is receivable in payment of all loans made to the United States."

These First Issue notes do not carry the large face inscriptions "United States Note" or "Treasury Note," which are found on later Legal Tender issues.

Dated Aug. 1, 1862, and issued only in denominations of $1 and $2, the Second Issue U.S. Notes carry the Second Obligation on back.

The Third Issue U.S. Notes, dated March 10, 1863, were issued in denominations from $5 through $1,000, again using the Second Obligation.

Fourth Issue Legal Tenders were authorized by an Act of Congress dated March 3, 1863, and issued in denomination from $1 through $10,000 in the various Series of 1869, 1874, 1878, 1880, 1907, 1917 and 1923. Those notes in Series 1869 bear the label "Treasury Notes" on face, with all later issues carrying the "United States Notes" designation.

Back obligation on all series is the same: "This note is a legal tender at its face value for all debts public and private, except duties on imports and interest on the public debt."

The Fifth Issue Legal Tenders consisted solely of the Series 1901 $10 note (the popular Bison design), issued under the authority of the Legal Tender Acts of 1862-1863. A new face obligation was introduced: "This note is a legal tender for ten dollars subject to the provisions of Section 3588 R.S.," on back, the obligation reads: "This note is a legal tender at its face value for all debts public and private except duties on imports and interest on the public debt."

Legislation remains in force requiring that the amount of Legal Tender Notes in official circulation be maintained at $346,681,016, which is done, on paper at least, through the continuing "circulation" of the small size Red Seal $100s.

Compound Interest Treasury Notes

Circulating currency notes which grew in face value each six-month period they remained in circulation were just one of the innovations to which the Federal Government turned to finance the protracted Civil War.

Authorized by Congressional Acts of March 3, 1863, and June 30, 1864, these notes were intended to circulate for three years, bearing interest at the then-attractive rate of six percent a year, compounded semi-annually. The backs of each note carry a table spelling out the actual interest earned and current face value of the note through maturity. Theoretically, a note that was acquired when issued at face value, could be spent a year later as $10.60; although little is known as to whether this theory worked in practice. It is known, though, that those persons holding the notes at maturity generally took their profit, leaving very few surviving specimens for today's collectors.

Neither should it be assumed that the surviving notes continue to earn interest. The interest payments ended at maturity (if interest had been allowed to accumulate, the $10 note, as of June, 1985, would have a "face value" in excess of $11,000 — even more than the numismatic value of the note — with corresponding denominations — $20, $50, $100, $500 and $1,000 — worth multiples thereof).

The face of each note bears a surcharge in large gold letters, reading "Compound Interest Treasury Note," along with corresponding numerals of issue value. Unfortunately, the gold ink used for these overprints contributed greatly to the demise of the notes themselves, for it is highly acidic and attacks the rather fragile paper to the point where many examples are found with this surcharge "burned" into and through the paper. Additionally, the $50 and $100 notes, the highest values which could practically be said to have circulated, were extensively counterfeited and the Treasury was forced to withdraw them in the face of such "competition."

In any denomination, the Compound Interest Treasury Notes are scarce in better than Fine condition.

Examples are known with a number of different issue dates on face. The $10-$50 notes with the June 10 or July 15, 1864, dates are the rarest, with dates from Aug. 15, 1864, through Oct. 16, 1865, being more common; while in the $100 notes, the June 10, 1864, date is most common, followed by the Aug. 15, 1864-Sept. 1, 1865, dates. No July 15, 1864-dated $100 Compound Interest Treasury Notes are known, nor are there any reported survivors among the $500 and $1,000 denominations, though the Treasury reports several examples still officially outstanding.

Interest Bearing Notes

As a group, probably the rarest type of U.S. paper money is the Interest Bearing Note issues of the Civil War era. Like the Compound Interest Treasury Notes and the Refunding Certificates (also interest bearing), they were something of a desperation currency issue by the Federal Government to bolster the Union war chest.

The Interest Bearing Notes were issued in a trio of distinctive types, all of which are very rare, or unknown to have survived.

The first issue was a series of One-Year Notes, issued under authority of the Act of March 3, 1863, and paying interest of five percent for one year. Face designs of the one-year issue were similar to the Compound Interest Treasury Notes, without the gold surcharges. Backs were significantly different, lacking the tabular interest-figuring chart. A face inscription reads: "One year after date the United States will pay to the bearer with five per interest — dollars." On back, the obligation was worded: "This note is a legal tender at its face value, excluding interest, for all debts public and private, except duties on imports and interest on the public debt."

Denominations of the One-Year Notes ranged from $10 through $5,000, with no specimens of the $500, $1,000 or $5,000 known. Each note bears an individually stamped date of issue on the face. One year from that date, the notes were redeemable for face value plus interest.

Two-Year Notes were also authorized by the March 3, 1863 Act of Congress. Issued only in the $50, $100, $500 and $1,000 denominations, and paying five percent interest per year for a two-year term, they are naturally much scarcer because of the high return they offered the holder near the end of the Civil War. Designs were completely different from the One-Year Notes, although the face and back inscriptions are similar.

Like the Interest Bearing Notes themselves, the Three-Year Notes are comprised of three separate issues, due to three different authorizing Acts of Congress; July 17, 1861, June 30, 1864, and March 3, 1865. Again issued in the higher denominations, from $50 through $5,000, the notes paid interest at the rate of 7-3/10 percent a year; the highest rate the Government paid on circulating notes. Like the Compound Interest Treasury Notes, the actual amount of interest is spelled out on the notes, though in this case it is expressed in terms of interest per day. Thus, the $50 note expresses a promise to pay interest of one cent per day, while the $5,000 bill paid interest at the rate of $1 per day.

That the notes were not intended to circulate widely is indicated by the fact that they are payable to the order, not to the bearer. That is, there is a blank on the face of every Three-Year Interest Bearing Note for the name of the original holder, and a corresponding blank on back for endorsement at the time of maturity.

Another feature which makes the Three-Year Notes unusual among U.S. paper money issues was the original attachment of five coupons to each note. Each coupon indicated the interest payable for a six-month period, and was removed from the note when that interest was collected semi-annually. The final interest payment was made when the note itself was presented for redemption at the end of the three-year period. This arrangement is spelled out on the face of each note.

As mentioned earlier, these notes are of the greatest rarity, most of them unknown to survive, existing only in proof form or existing in a unique, or nearly so, issued example.

Refunding Certificates

More of a government security than circulating medium of exchange, the Refunding Certificates authorized by Congress in the Act of Feb. 26, 1879, brought these interest bearing instruments within the reach of more Americans in that they were denominated at $10.

The authorizing legislation intended that these notes bear interest of four percent annually in perpetuity. However, in 1907 Congress passed a law stopping interest payments as of July 1, forever fixing the "face" value of these notes at $21.30. Presumably at that time the incentive for the public to hold these notes was removed, and their redemption accelerated.

The $10 Refunding Certificates were issued in two different forms, one type payable to the bearer, the other to the order of the original purchaser. Like the Three-Year Interest Bearing Notes, the Refunding Certificates payable to order had spaces on face and back for the owner and endorser. The "pay to order" type is far rarer than the "pay to bearer" variety.

Rather than being redeemable for specie, per se, these notes, in amounts of $50 or more, were convertible into four percent bonds.

Silver Certificates

Among the most popular of U.S. notes due to their wealth of design excellence and challenging, but not impossible, rarity, the Silver Certificates of 1878-1963 comprise five major issues of large size notes, and the various series of small size notes.

Authorizing legislation for all issues were the Congressional Act of Feb. 28, 1878, and Aug. 4, 1886.

The First Issue Silver Certificates consist of Series 1878 and 1880 notes in denominations from $10-$1,000. The notes of 1878, besides bearing the engraved signatures of G.W. Scofield, Register of the Treasury, and James Gilfillan, Treasurer of the U.S., have on their face an engraved or autographed countersignature of the Assistant Treasurers in New York, Washington, D.C., and San Francisco, attesting that the requisite amount of silver dollars had been deposited in their offices to cover the face value of the notes. In addition to the Series 1878 countersigned notes, several $20 Series 1880 Silver Certificates are known bearing the engraved countersignature of T. Hillhouse, Assistant Treasurer at New York.

The silver bills' Second Issue was made up of notes from $1 through $1,000 in the Series of 1886, 1891 and 1908, although not all denominations were issued in all series.

The "Educational" notes, $1, $2, and $5 Silver Certificates of Series 1896, are the sole component of the Third Issue.

Similarly, the Fourth Issue Silver Certificates are made up of $1, $2 and $5 notes of the Series of 1899.

The Silver Certificates of the Fifth Issue are the Series 1923 $1 and $5 notes.

The obligation on the First Issue notes reads: "This certifies that there have been deposited with the Treasurer of the U.S. at Washington, D.C. (or Assistant Treasurers at New York and San Francisco) payable at his office to the bearer on demand — silver dollars. This certificate is receivable for customs, taxes and all public dues and when so received may be reissued."

Obligation on the last four issues of silver notes was worded: "This certifies that there have been deposited in the Treasury of the United States — silver dollars payable to the bearer on demand. This certificate is receivable for customs, taxes and all public dues and when so received may be issued."

Treasury or Coin Notes

Pushed through Congress by the silver mining industry, the authorizing legislation of July 14, 1890, which created the Treasury Notes carefully did not specify that they be redeemable in silver; only that they be issued to pay for silver bullion purchased by the Treasury and that they be payable "in Coin" (hence the more commonly encountered name Coin Notes). With the co-operation of Treasury officials, silver sellers were able to turn their bullion in at artificially high official prices, receive the Coin Notes in payment, and redeem them immediately for gold coin and a tidy profit.

In denominations of $1, $2, $5, $10, $20, $100 and $1,000, the Coin Notes were issued in Series 1890 and 1891 form, the 1890 issue bearing ornately engraved green back designs that filled the print area. The $50 was issued only in Series of 1891, and the $500 note, which had been designed and a plate prepared with the portrait of Gen. William T. Sherman, was not issued at all. It was felt that even as late as 25 years after the Civil War, the use of Sherman's portrait on a currency note would inflame passions in the South. The 1890 notes are much scarcer and in greater demand than the Series 1891 issue, especially in new condition.

Face and back obligations of the Coin Notes are interesting and unique. They read: "This United States of America will pay to bearer — dollars in coin." And, "This note is a legal tender at its face value in payment of all debts public and private except when otherwise expressly stipulated in the contract."

National Gold Bank Notes

Gold and the American West have been inseparably linked as part of this nation's history since the discovery of gold at Sutter's Mill in 1848. The unique, but short-lived National Gold Bank Note series was a contemporary part of "The Golden West," and today trades on that romantic image — and the inherent rarity of the notes themselves — as one of the most sought-after types of U.S. paper money.

The National Gold Bank Notes were authorized under the provisions of the Currency Act of July 12, 1870, and are very much analogous to the regular National Currency issue.

The principal difference, besides design, is that the National Gold Bank Notes were payable — and prominently said so — in gold coin. This was a concession to the traditional mistrust of Western America in paper currency and the California area's long history of gold use as the principal medium of exchange, whether in the form of gold dust, nuggets, private-issue coinage or genuine coins of the United States Mint.

Under the general provisions of the National Bank Act of 1863, the National Gold Banks had to secure the issue of their currency with the deposit of bonds with the Treasurer of the United States. However, the conditions for the N.G.B.N. issues were a bit more stringent. The Gold Banks could issue notes only to the value of 80% of their deposited bonds, while the other National banks could issue to 90%. Additionally, the Gold Banks were required to have on hand in their vaults gold coinage equal to 25% of the value of their note issue. The responsibility of redeeming these notes *in gold,* lay with the issuing banks, not the Federal Government, which did not resume specie payments until 1879, nearly a decade after the N.G.B.N. issues began. The Treasury would, of course, redeem National Gold Bank Notes for other lawful currency.

This gold redemption property gave the N.G.B.Ns, the necessary credibility, and they circulated at par with the precious metal. They circulated so extensively that surviving notes are generally found in conditions which many collectors would find unacceptable in other U.S. currency types. No strictly uncirculated National Gold Bank Note is known today, and the average condition found is Good to Very Good. Specimens in Fine or better condition command attractive premiums in the infrequent times when they become available.

Though authorized in denominations from $5-$1,000, National Gold Bank Notes were issued to circulation only as high as $500. The face of each note was similar to corresponding denominations in the First Charter National Bank Note series, while the backs had as their central feature a photo-like engraving of a stack of U.S. gold pieces, representing $211.50 face value in $1 through $20 denominations.

In all, 10 National Gold Banks were chartered, nine in California and The Kidder National Gold Bank in Boston, Mass. Notes were actually printed for the Kidder N.G.B., and delivered, but the bank eventually returned them all for cancellation, never issuing them to circulation. The Kidder was the only National Gold Bank to have $1,000 notes prepared.

Because of the relatively small size of the issue, much can be determined about the issue and survivability of the National Gold Bank Notes.

In the period 1870-1878, exactly 196,849 notes, with a face value of $3,267,420, were issued. Treasury records indicate a total of 6,639 notes remain outstanding (including four $500 examples, none of which are known to collectors). A recent comprehensive survey of known notes accounted for fewer than 275 in all denominations.

Like the other National Bank Notes, National Gold Bank Notes are known in both Original Series and Series of 1875 issues, although all nine California banks did not issue all denominations in both series. Indeed, the Series 1875 notes are somewhat scarcer than the Original notes.

Federal Reserve Bank Notes

Often confused with the Federal Reserve Notes, which are currency issues of the Federal Reserve System itself, Federal Reserve Bank Notes were issued by the 12 individual Federal Reserve Banks, much like the National Bank Notes.

Indeed, Federal Reserve Bank Notes, large and small size, carry the "National Currency" inscription.

In the large size note-issuing period, the similarity of Federal Reserve Bank Notes to Federal Reserve notes extended to nearly identical back designs in the $5-$50 denominations. FRBNs were also issued in $1 and $2 denominations, while the FRNs were issued in value from $5 through $10,000.

Two separate issues of Federal Reserve Bank Notes comprise the large size issue, while there was a single issue in small size.

The Series 1915 FRBNs were authorized under the terms of the Federal Reserve Act of Dec. 23, 1913. Issued only in denominations of $5-$20, only the banks in Atlanta, Chicago, Kansas City, Dallas and San Francisco participated, with the Frisco bank issuing only $5s.

Like the National Bank Notes, the obligation to pay the bearer on the FRBNs is made by the issuing bank, rather than the Fed system or U.S. Government. The security notice on the 1915 issue reads: "Secured by United States bonds deposited with the Treasurer of the United States."

That obligation was changed for the Series 1918 FRBNs, issued under authority of a Congressional Act of April 23, 1918. The modification reads: "Secured by United States certificates of indebtedness or United States one-year gold notes, deposited with the Treasurer of the United States."

The Series 1918 FRBNs consist of all denominations from $1 through $50, though again, not all 12 banks issued all denominations. For instance, only the Atlanta and St. Louis banks issued $20 Series 1918 FRBNs, while only St. Louis issued $50s.

Spurred initially by demand for the attractive "Battleship" back design of the $2, and the defiant eagle on the $1 (symbols of America's defense posture in World War I), all large size FRBNs are actively collected today, especially in new condition. A wealth of combinations of U.S. Government signatures combined with signatures of the various Governors and Cashiers of the individual issuing banks, creates myriad varieties to keep the series challenging.

Also contributing to the challenge is the sheer scarcity of surviving specimens. Treasury sources indicate just over $2 million worth of FRBNs outstanding, from a total issue of more than $760 million.

Federal Reserve Notes

Authorized by the Federal Reserve Act of Dec. 23, 1913 and first issued in 1914, the Federal Reserve Note is the only type of U.S. paper money which continues in production today.

The large size issues of FRNs are in two series, 1914, in denominations from $5-$100, and 1918, in denominations from $500-$10,000. Additionally, two distinctive varieties of 1914 notes exist, those with red Treasury seal and serial number, and those with the elements in blue. The Red Seal 1914 FRNs are considerably scarcer than the blue.

While they are issued to circulation through the 12 Federal Reserve Banks, the FRNs are an obligation of the United States Government, rather than bank named thereon (unlike the Federal Reserve Bank Notes). Neither are Federal Reserve Notes secured by government bonds, precious metals or other reserves. The obligation on FRNs simply states that: "The United States of America will pay to the bearer on demand — dollars."

On back, the redemption qualities of the large size FRNs was spelled out thus: "This note is receivable by all National and member banks and Federal Reserve Banks and for all taxes, customs and other public dues. It is redeemable in gold on demand at the Treasury Department of the United States in the city of Washington, District of Columbia or in gold or lawful money at any Federal Reserve Bank."

This redeemable-in-gold clause continued in use on the Series 1928 small size FRNs, but was revoked with the passage of the Gold Reserve Act of 1933. The obligation, beginning with the Series 1934 notes, was modified to read: "This note is legal tender for all debts, public and private, and is redeemable in lawful money at the United States Treasury, or at any Federal Reserve Bank."

Beginning with Series 1963, the obligation was changed to its present form: "This note is legal tender for all debts, public and private."

Wide variances in the number of notes printed for each bank in any particular series of a denomination have created many challenging issues within the Federal Reserve Note series, both large and small size.

NOTE: Three interesting, if not altogether popular among collectors, varieties exist within the large size FRNs bearing the White-Mellon Federal signature combination, and two within the Burke-McAdoo combination notes. The variations deal with the size and placement of the numeral-letter combination designating the bank through which the notes were issued, and appearing in the lower left corner of the face. The earliest variety has a large size combination, matching that in the upper right corner of the note. The second variety has the combination greatly reduced (compared to that in the upper right). The third reverts to the larger size, but the combination has been moved higher and more to the left, while the Treasury and Fed Bank seals on each end of this variety have been moved closer to center. Not all three varieties exist on every bank in every combination. While the second and third varieties command some premium from interested collectors, the demand for them is not such as to greatly influence the market for the type as a whole, and they are, therefore, not cataloged individually.

Gold Certificates

With their bright orange back designs (though some early gold notes are uniface), the large size Gold Certificates issued from 1865 through 1928 are a popular and tangible reminder of the days when U.S. paper currency was "as good as gold."

While many of the earlier Gold Certificate issues were not designed to be used in general circulation, due to their high face value, later types did enter the channels of commerce, circulating alongside the myriad other currency issues of the late 19th and early 20th Centuries.

Nine separate issues of Gold Certificates were created in the large size series, several of which were used almost exclusively in inter-bank channels to transfer and settle gold accounts.

The first issue goldbacks were authorized by the Currency Act of March 3, 1863, and consisted of notes in denominations of $20, $100, $500, $1,000, $5,000 and $10,000. While examples of the two lowest denominations survive, they are extremely rare.

No known examples of the second issue Gold Certificates are known today. Issued pursuant to the same act, and countersigned and dated by hand in the 1870-71 period, they were in denominations of $100-$10,000 only.

Third issue gold notes, bearing the impression "Series of 1875," were also issued in limited denominations: $100, $500, and $1,000. Uniface, the issue is represented today by only a few examples of the $100 note.

With the fourth issue, Gold Certificates entered general circulation, and the type begins to be known by its series designation. Ten-dollar goldbacks were issued in Series 1907 and 1922; $20 in Series 1882, 1905, 1906 and 1922; $50 in Series 1882, 1913 and 1922; $100 in Series 1882 and 1922; $500 in Series 1882; $1,000 in Series 1882, 1907 and 1922; $5,000 in Series 1882 and 1888; and, $10,000 in Series 1882, 1888 and 1900. Naturally, the notes in denominations above $100 are very rare, though not unknown.

To correspond the various issues to the series in these post-1875 notes; the fourth issue consisted of the Series 1882 notes; the fifth issue comprises the 1888 Series, the sixth is the 1900 $10,000 notes; the seventh issue Gold Certificates are the Series 1905, 1906 and 1907 $10 and $20 notes; the eighth is the $1,000 of Series 1907; and, the ninth issue of large size Gold Certificates are the Series 1913 ($50 only) and 1922 goldbacks in $10-$1,000 denominations.

U. S. Large Size Currency Valuations

Note: National Bank Notes issued between 1863-1928 will be found in a separate section, Pages 38-129.

One Dollar

United States Notes

KL#	Series	Signatures	Seal	Fine	XF	CU
Red Numeral "1" "2" "3" vertically in center.						
1	1862	Chittenden-Spinner	Small red	85.00	200.	500.
National Bank Note Co. American Bank Note Co., lower border. No monogram.						
2	1862	Chittenden-Spinner	Small red	85.00	155.	500.
As above with monogram ABN Co. upper right.						
3	1862	Chittenden-Spinner	Small red	85.00	155.	500.
National Bank Note Co., twice in border. No monogram.						
4	1862	Chittenden-Spinner	Small red	95.00	175.	500.
As above, with monogram ABN Co. upper right.						

KL#	Series	Signatures	Seal	Fine	XF	CU
Red serial numbers.						
5	1869	Allison-Spinner	Large red	95.00	225.	700.
National Bank Note Co., lower portion back design.						

KL#	Series	Signatures	Seal	Fine	XF	CU
Red Serial numbers. Red ornamentation at right, face design.						
6	1874	Allison-Spinner	Small red	50.00	120.	450.
Face, micro at right, "Engraved & Printed at the Bureau Engraving & Printing". Back, Columbian Bank Note Co., twice in lower portion.						
7	1875	Allison-New	Small red	45.00	80.00	300.
8	1875 Series "A"	Allison-New	Small red	90.00	200.	650.
9	1875 Series "B"	Allison-New	Small red	80.00	200.	600.
10	1875 Series "C"	Allison-New	Small red	80.00	275.	800.
11	1875 Series "D"	Allison-New	Small red	110.	275.	800.
12	1875 Series "E"	Allison-New	Small red	150.	400.	1000.
13	1875	Allison-Wyman	Small red	45.00	70.00	175.
14	1878	Allison-Gilfillan	Small red	40.00	100.	275.
"Series 1878" top margin, back design. "Printed by Bureau of Engraving & Printing" lower margin, back design.						

KL#	Series	Signatures	Seal	Fine	XF	CU
Ornamentation removed. Large seal introduced.						
15	1880	Scofield-Gilfillan	Large brown	30.00	65.00	250.
16	1880	Bruce-Gilfillan	Large brown	30.00	65.00	200.
17	1880	Bruce-Wyman	Large brown	30.00	65.00	200.
Blue serial numbers						
18	1880	Rosecrans-Huston	Large red	150.	300.	550.
19	1880	Rosecrans-Huston	Large brown	150	300.	625.
20	1880	Rosecrans-Nebeker	Large brown	150.	300.	625.
21	1880	Rosecrans-Nebeker	Small red	30.00	65.00	200.
22	1880	Tillman-Morgan	Small red	30.00	65.00	235.
Serial number panel dropped.						
23	1917	Teehee-Burke	Small red	20.00	42.00	135.
24	1917	Elliott-Burke	Small red	20.00	42.00	125.
25	1917	Burke-Elliott	Small red	40.00	100.	275.
26	1917	Elliott-White	Small red	20.00	42.00	125.
27	1917	Speelman-White	Small red	20.00	42.00	125.

KL#	Series	Signatures	Seal	Fine	XF	CU
28	1923	Speelman-White	Small red	22.00	50.00	200.

Silver Certificates

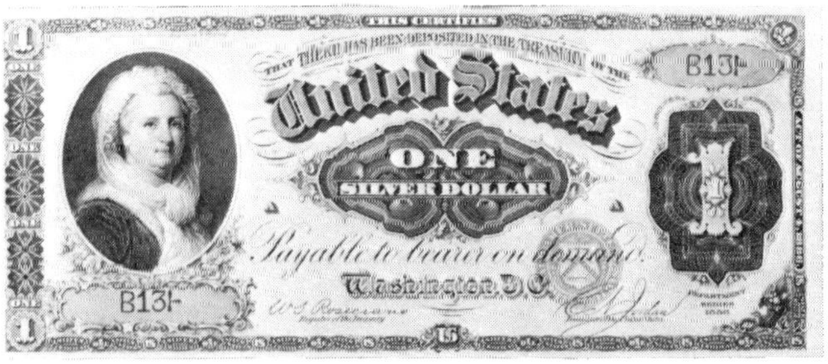

KL#	Series	Signatures	Seal	Fine	XF	CU
		Blue Serial numbers on all Silver Certificates.				
29	1886	Rosecrans-Jordan	Small red	80.00	250.	500.
30	1886	Rosecrans-Hyatt	Small red	65.00	225.	875.
31	1886	Rosecrans-Hyatt	Large red	75.00	250.	500.
32	1886	Rosecrans-Huston	Large red	60.00	225.	875.
33	1886	Rosecrans-Huston	Large brown	75.00	250.	500.
34	1886	Rosecrans-Nebeker	Large brown	60.00	225.	875.
35	1886	Rosecrans-Nebeker	Small red	100.	300.	875.

KL#	Series	Signatures	Seal	Fine	XF	CU
36	1891	Rosecrans-Nebeker	Small red	75.00	250.	400.
37	1891	Tillman-Morgan	Small red	70.00	150.	750.

KL#	Series	Signatures	Seal	Fine	XF	CU
38	1896	Tillman-Morgan	Small red	85.00	300.	750.
39	1896	Bruce-Roberts	Small red	85.00	250.	850.

KL#	Series	Signatures	Seal	Fine	XF	CU
		Series date above serial number, upper right.				
40	1899	Lyons-Roberts	Small blue	27.50	40.00	100.
		Series date below serial number.				
41	1899	Lyons-Roberts	Small blue	23.00	35.00	150.
42	1899	Lyons-Treat	Small blue	23.00	35.00	150.
43	1899	Vernon-Treat	Small blue	23.00	35.00	150.
44	1899	Vernon-Mc Clung	Small blue	23.00	35.00	150.
		Series date vertically right, on the following:				
44A	1899	Vernon-Mc Clung	Small blue	—	—	—
45	1899	Napier-Mc Clung	Small blue	23.00	35.00	125.
46	1899	Napier-Thompson	Small blue	75.00	115.	475.
47	1899	Parker-Burke	Small blue	23.00	35.00	125.
48	1899	Teehee-Burke	Small blue	23.00	35.00	125.
49	1899	Elliott-Burke	Small blue	23.00	35.00	125.
50	1899	Elliott-White	Small blue	23.00	35.00	125.
51	1899	Speelman-White	Small blue	23.00	35.00	125.

52	1923	Speelman-White	Small blue	10.00	20.00	40.00
53	1923	Woods-White	Small blue	10.00	15.00	40.00
54	1923	Woods-Tate	Small blue	35.00	50.00	200.

Treasury or Coin Notes

KL#	Series	Signatures	Seal	Fine	XF	CU
55	1890	Rosecrans-Huston	Large brown	95.00	350.	1000.
56	1890	Rosecrans-Nebeker	Large brown	90.00	300.	1500.
57	1890	Rosecrans-Nebeker	Small red	85.00	300.	900.

KL#	Series	Signatures	Seal	Fine	XF	CU
58	1891	Rosecrans-Nebeker	Small red	65.00	125.	400.
59	1891	Tillman-Morgan	Small red	65.00	125.	400.
60	1891	Bruce-Roberts	Small red	65.00	125.	400.

Federal Reserve Bank Notes
Series 1918

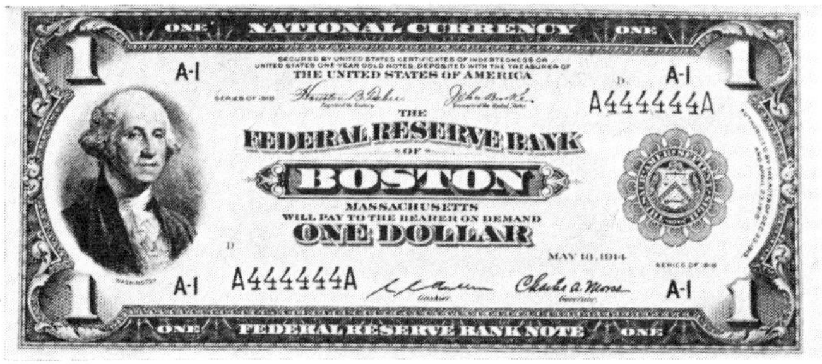

KL#	Bank	Federal Sigs.	Bank Sigs.	Fine	XF	CU
61	Boston	Teehee-Burke	Bullen-Morss	25.00	60.00	150.
62	Boston	Teehee-Burke	Willett-Morss	60.00	100.	300.
63	Boston	Elliott-Burke	Willett-Morss	25.00	60.00	150.
64	New York	Teehee-Burke	Sailer-Strong	25.00	60.00	150.
65	New York	Teehee-Burke	Hendricks-Strong	25.00	60.00	150.
66	New York	Elliott-Burke	Hendricks-Strong	25.00	60.00	150.
67	Philadelphia	Teehee-Burke	Hardt-Passmore	25.00	60.00	150.
68	Philadelphia	Teehee-Burke	Dyer-Passmore	25.00	60.00	150.
69	Philadelphia	Elliott-Burke	Dyer-Passmore	25.00	60.00	150.
70	Philadelphia	Elliott-Burke	Dyer-Norris	25.00	60.00	150.
71	Cleveland	Teehee-Burke	Baxter-Fancher	25.00	60.00	150.
72	Cleveland	Teehee-Burke	Davis-Fancher	25.00	60.00	150.
73	Cleveland	Elliott-Burke	Davis-Fancher	25.00	60.00	150.
74	Richmond	Teehee-Burke	Keesee-Seay	25.00	60.00	150.
75	Richmond	Elliott-Burke	Keesee-Seay	25.00	60.00	150.
76	Atlanta	Teehee-Burke	Pike-Mc Cord	25.00	60.00	150.
77	Atlanta	Teehee-Burke	Bell-Mc Cord	25.00	60.00	150.
78	Atlanta	Teehee-Burke	Bell-Wellborn	25.00	60.00	150.
79	Atlanta	Elliott-Burke	Bell-Wellborn	25.00	60.00	150.
80	Chicago	Teehee-Burke	Mc Cloud-Mc Dougall	25.00	60.00	150.
81	Chicago	Teehee-Burke	Cramer-Mc Dougall	25.00	60.00	150.
82	Chicago	Elliott-Burke	Cramer-Mc Dougall	25.00	60.00	150.
83	St. Louis	Teehee-Burke	Attebery-Wells	25.00	60.00	150.
84	St. Louis	Teehee-Burke	Attebery-Biggs	25.00	60.00	150.
85	St. Louis	Elliott-Burke	Attebery-Biggs	25.00	60.00	150.
86	St. Louis	Elliott-Burke	White-Biggs	25.00	60.00	150.
87	Minneapolis	Teehee-Burke	Cook-Wold	40.00	75.00	225.
88	Minneapolis	Teehee-Burke	Cook-Young	300.	550.	900.
89	Minneapolis	Elliott-Burke	Cook-Young	50.00	80.00	225.
90	Kansas City	Teehee-Burke	Anderson-Miller	25.00	60.00	150.
91	Kansas City	Elliott-Burke	Anderson-Miller	25.00	60.00	150.
92	Kansas City	Elliott-Burke	Helm-Miller	25.00	60.00	150.
93	Dallas	Teehee-Burke	Talley-Van Zandt	25.00	60.00	150.
94	Dallas	Elliott-Burke	Talley-Van Zandt	60.00	125.	200.
95	Dallas	Elliott-Burke	Lawder-Van Zandt	25.00	60.00	150.
96	San Francisco	Teehee-Burke	Clerk-Lynch	25.00	60.00	150.
97	San Francisco	Teehee-Burke	Clerk-Calkins	25.00	60.00	150.
98	San Francisco	Elliott-Burke	Clerk-Calkins	25.00	60.00	150.
99	San Francisco	Elliott-Burke	Ambrose-Calkins	25.00	60.00	150.

Two Dollars
United States Notes

KL#	Series	Signatures	Seal	Fine	XF	CU
		Red Numerals "1" "2" "3" vertically in center.				
100	1862	Chittenden-Spinner	Small red	100.	250.	1100.
		American Bank Note Co., vertically at left, face design.				
101	1862	Chittenden-Spinner	Small red	100.	250.	1250.
		National Bank Note Co., vertically at left, face design.				

Patented April 23, 1860, National Bank Note Co., in lower border, on both types.

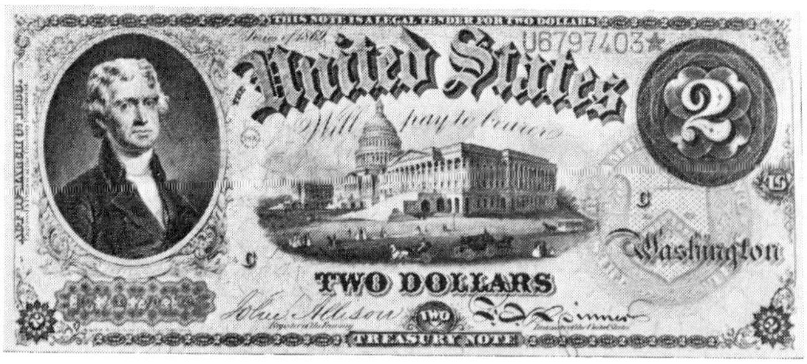

KL#	Series	Signatures	Seal	Fine	XF	CU
		Red Serial numbers				
102	1869	Allison-Spinner	Large red	125.	400.	1500.
		"Engraved and printed at the Treasury Department", vertically at left, face design.				
		American Bank Note Co. bottom left, face design and twice below back design.				
		Red Serial numbers. Red ornamentation at right.				
103	1874	Allison-Spinner	Small red	75.00	200.	500.

KL#	Series	Signatures	Seal	Fine	XF	CU
104	1875	Allison-New	Small red	45.00	95.00	325.
		Issued in two additional series, same design.				
105	1875 Series A, lower right of face design.			135.	400.	550.
106	1875 Series B			135.	400.	550.
107	1875	Allison-Wyman	Small red	45.00	95.00	375.
108	1878	Allison-Gilfillan	Small red	65.00	160.	500.
109	1878	Scofield-Gilfillan	Small red	1900.	(Very rare)	
		Red Serial numbers. Ornamentation removed.				
110	1880	Scofield-Gilfillan	Large brown	30.00	75.00	275.
111	1880	Bruce-Gilfillan	Large brown	27.50	75.00	300.
112	1880	Bruce-Wyman	Large brown	27.50	75.00	300.
		Blue serial numbers				
113	1880	Rosecrans-Huston	Large red	80.00	175.	400.
114	1880	Rosecrans-Huston	Large brown	80.00	225.	500.
115	1880	Rosecrans-Nebeker	Small red	35.00	75.00	250.
116	1880	Tillman-Morgan	Small red	35.00	75.00	275.
		Red serial numbers				
117	1917	Teehee-Burke	Small red	30.00	60.00	175.
118	1917	Elliot-Burke	Small red	20.00	40.00	150.
119	1917	Elliot-White	Small red	20.00	40.00	150.
120	1917	Speelman-White	Small red	20.00	40.00	150.

Silver Certificates

KL#	Series	Signatures	Seal	Fine	XF	CU
121	1886	Rosecrans-Jordan	Small red	125.	350.	850.
122	1886	Rosecrans-Hyatt	Small red	90.00	185.	1000.
123	1886	Rosecrans-Hyatt	Large red	125.	350.	850.
124	1886	Rosecrans-Huston	Large red	90.00	185.	1000.
125	1886	Rosecrans-Huston	Large brown	125.	350.	850.

KL#	Series	Signatures	Seal	Fine	XF	CU
126	1891	Rosecrans-Nebeker	Small red	140.	350.	1200.
127	1891	Tillman-Morgan	Small red	140.	350.	1500.

KL#	Series	Signatures	Seal	Fine	XF	CU
128	1896	Tillman-Morgan	Small red	135.	525.	2250.
129	1896	Bruce-Roberts	Small red	135.	525.	2500.

KL#	Series	Signatures	Seal	Fine	XF	CU
130	1899	Lyons-Roberts	Small blue	50.00	120.	400.
131	1899	Lyons-Treat	Small blue	65.00	85.00	275.
132	1899	Vernon-Treat	Small blue	65.00	85.00	275.
133	1899	Vernon-Mc Clung	Small blue	65.00	85.00	275.
134	1899	Napier-Mc Clung	Small blue	65.00	85.00	275.
135	1899	Napier-Thompson	Small blue	100.	300.	1200.
136	1899	Parker-Burke	Small blue	65.00	85.00	275.
137	1899	Teehee-Burke	Small blue	65.00	85.00	275.
138	1899	Elliott-Burke	Small blue	65.00	85.00	275.
139	1899	Speelman-White	Small blue	65.00	125.	450.

Treasury or Coin Notes

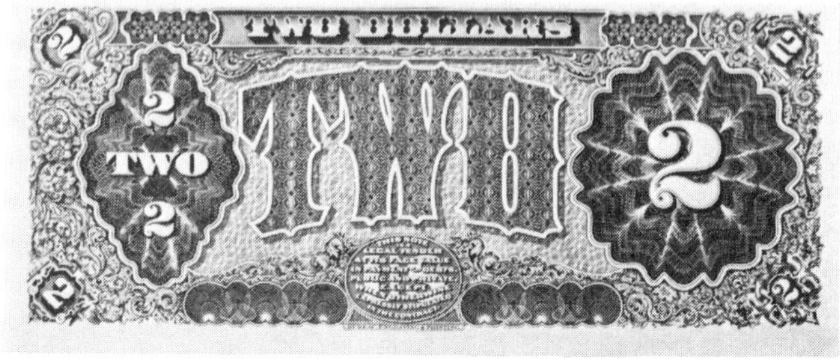

KL#	Series	Signatures	Seal	Fine	XF	CU
140	1890	Rosecrans-Huston	Large brown	120.	500.	1750.
141	1890	Rosecrans-Nebeker	Large brown	175.	600.	2300.
142	1890	Rosecrans-Nebeker	Small red	100.	500.	1750.

KL#	Series	Signatures	Seal	Fine	XF	CU
143	1891	Rosecrans-Nebeker	Small red	90.00	175.	600.
144	1891	Tillman-Morgan	Small red	100.	200.	625.
145	1891	Bruce-Roberts	Small red	100.	200.	625.

Federal Reserve Bank Notes Series 1918

KL#	Bank	Federal Sigs.	Bank Sigs.	Fine	XF	CU
146	Boston	Teehee-Burke	Bullen-Morss	70.00	140.	400.
147	Boston	Teehee-Burke	Wilett-Morss	70.00	140.	400.
148	Boston	Elliott-Burke	Willett-Morss	70.00	140.	400.
149	New York	Teehee-Burke	Sailer-Strong	70.00	140.	400.
150	New York	Teehee-Burke	Hendricks-Strong	70.00	140.	400.
151	New York	Elliott-Burke	Hendricks-Strong	70.00	140.	400.
152	Philadelphia	Teehee-Burke	Hardt-Passmore	70.00	140.	400.
153	Philadelphia	Teehee-Burke	Dyer-Passmore	70.00	140.	400.
154	Philadelphia	Elliott-Burke	Dyer-Passmore	70.00	140.	400.
155	Philadelphia	Elliott-Burke	Dyer-Norris	70.00	140.	400.
156	Cleveland	Teehee-Burke	Baxter-Fancher	70.00	140.	400.
157	Cleveland	Teehee-Burke	Davis-Fancher	70.00	140.	400.
158	Cleveland	Elliott-Burke	Davis-Fancher	70.00	140.	400.

KL#	Bank	Federal Sigs.	Bank Sigs.	Fine	XF	CU
159	Richmond	Teehee-Burke	Keesee-Seay	70.00	140.	400.
160	Richmond	Elliott-Burke	Keesee-Seay	70.00	140.	400.
161	Atlanta	Teehee-Burke	Pike-Mc Cord	70.00	140.	400.
162	Atlanta	Teehee-Burke	Bell-Mc Cord	70.00	140.	400.
163	Atlanta	Elliott-Burke	Bell-Wellborn	70.00	140.	400.
164	Chicago	Teehee-Burke	Mc Cloud-Mc Dougal	70.00	140.	400.
165	Chicago	Teehee-Burke	Cramer-Mc Dougal	70.00	140.	400.
166	Chicago	Elliott-Burke	Cramer-Mc Dougal	70.00	140.	400.
167	St. Louis	Teehee-Burke	Attebery-Wells	70.00	140.	400.
168	St. Louis	Teehee-Burke	Attebery-Biggs	70.00	140.	400.
169	St. Louis	Elliott-Burke	Attebery-Biggs	70.00	140.	400.
170	St. Louis	Elliott-Burke	White-Biggs	70.00	140.	400.
171	Minneapolis	Teehee-Burke	Cook-Wold	70.00	140.	400.
172	Minneapolis	Elliott-Burke	Cook-Young	70.00	140.	400.
173	Kansas City	Teehee-Burke	Anderson-Miller	70.00	140.	400.
174	Kansas City	Elliott-Burke	Helm-Miller	70.00	140.	400.
175	Dallas	Teehee-Burke	Talley-Van Zandt	70.00	140.	400.
176	Dallas	Elliott-Burke	Talley-Van Zandt	70.00	140.	400.
177	San Francisco	Teehee-Burke	Clerk-Lynch	70.00	140.	400.
178	San Francisco	Elliott-Burke	Clerk-Calkins	70.00	140.	400.
179	San Francisco	Elliott-Burke	Ambrose-Calkins	70.00	140.	400.

Five Dollars
Demand Notes

Type One: "For the" autographed
Type Two: "For the" engraved

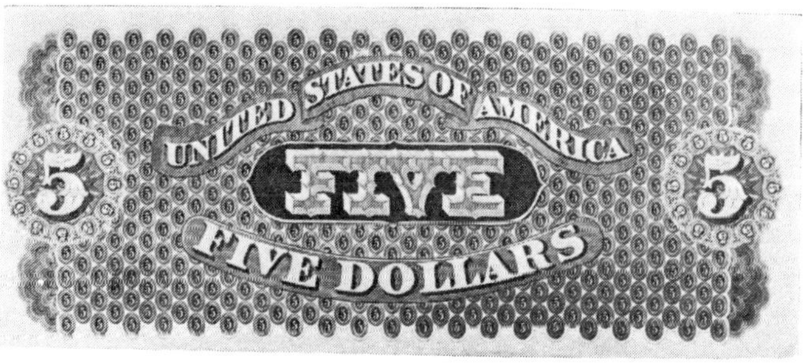

KL#	Payable at:		Good	VG
180	Boston	Type One	400.	800.
181	Boston	Type Two	325.	500.
182	New York	Type One	400.	800.
183	New York	Type Two	325.	500.
184	Philadelphia	Type One	400.	800.
185	Philadelphia	Type Two	325.	500.
186	St. Louis	Type One	1500.	3000.
187	St. Louis	Type Two	1250.	2000.
188	Cincinnati	Type One	2500.	4000.
189	Cincinnati	Type Two	2000.	3000.

United States Notes

KL#	Series	Signatures	Seal	Fine	XF	CU
		First Obligation inscription on back. Red Serial numbers.				
190	1862	Chittenden-Spinner	Small red	110.	250.	500.
		American Bank Note Co. in top border face design.				
		Second Obligation inscription. Red Serial numbers.				
191	1862	Chittenden-Spinner	Small red	100.	200.	900.
		American Bank Note Co. National Bank Note Co. lower border face design.				
192	1863	Chittenden-Spinner	Small red	100.	200.	500.
		American Bank Note Co., twice in lower border face design. One serial number.				
193	1863	Chittenden-Spinner	Small red	100.	200.	900.
		American Bank Note Co., twice in lower border. Two serial numbers.				
		Red serial numbers				

KL#	Series	Signatures	Seal	Fine	XF	CU
194	1869	Allison-Spinner	Large red	100.	165.	400.

Face: Bureau, Engraving & Printing, upper left, face design.
Back: American Bank Note Co., upper and lower margin.
Red Serial numbers. Large "V" in red ornamentation at right.

KL#	Series	Signatures	Seal	Fine	XF	CU
195	1875	Allison-New	Small red	50.00	100.	275.
		Issued in two additional series, same design.				
196	1875 Series A in lower right of face design.			80.00	110.	500.
197	1875 Series B			80.00	110.	500.
198	1875	Allison-Wyman	Small red	80.00	110.	500.
199	1878	Allison-Gilfillan	Small red	85.00	150.	400.
		Red serial numbers				
200	1880	Scofield-Gilfillan	Large brown	35.00	65.00	225.
201	1880	Bruce-Gilfillan	Large brown	35.00	65.00	225.
202	1880	Bruce-Wyman	Large brown	35.00	65.00	225.
		Blue serial numbers				
203	1880	Bruce-Wyman	Large red	45.00	95.00	400.
204	1880	Rosecrans-Jordan	Large red	45.00	95.00	450.
205	1880	Rosecrans-Hyatt	Large red	45.00	95.00	450.
206	1880	Rosecrans-Huston	Large red	70.00	150.	550.
207	1880	Rosecrans-Huston	Large brown	50.00	105.	250.
208	1880	Rosecrans-Nebeker	Large brown	70.00	105.	350.
209	1880	Rosecrans-Nebeker	Small red	30.00	65.00	200.
210	1880	Tillman-Morgan	Small red	30.00	65.00	250.
211	1880	Bruce-Roberts	Small red	30.00	65.00	250.
212	1880	Lyons-Roberts	Small red	30.00	65.00	250.

KL#	Series	Signatures	Seal	Fine	XF	CU
		Red Serial numbers. Ornamental "V" at left.				
213	1907	Vernon-Treat	Small red	25.00	50.00	175.
214	1907	Vernon-Mc Clung	Small red	25.00	50.00	200.
215	1907	Napier-Mc Clung	Small red	25.00	50.00	200.
216	1907	Napier-Thompson	Small red	100.	300.	500.
217	1907	Parker-Burke	Small red	25.00	50.00	200.
218	1907	Teehee-Burke	Small red	25.00	50.00	200.
219	1907	Elliott-Burke	Small red	25.00	50.00	200.
220	1907	Elliott-White	Small red	25.00	50.00	200.
221	1907	Speelman-White	Small red	25.00	50.00	200.
222	1907	Woods-White	Small red	25.00	50.00	200.

National Gold Bank Notes

KL#	Series	Issuing Bank	Location	Good	Fine
223	Orig.	First Nat'l Gold Bank	San Francisco	550.	1200.
224	Orig.	Nat'l Gold Bank & Trust Co.	San Francisco	550.	1200.
225	Orig.	Nat'l Gold Bank of D.O. Mills	Sacramento	750.	1750.
226	Orig.	First Nat'l Gold Bank	Stockton	750.	1750.
227	Orig.	First Nat'l Gold Bank	Santa Barbara	750.	1750.
228	Orig.	Farmers' Nat'l Gold Bank	San Jose	750.	1750.

Silver Certificates

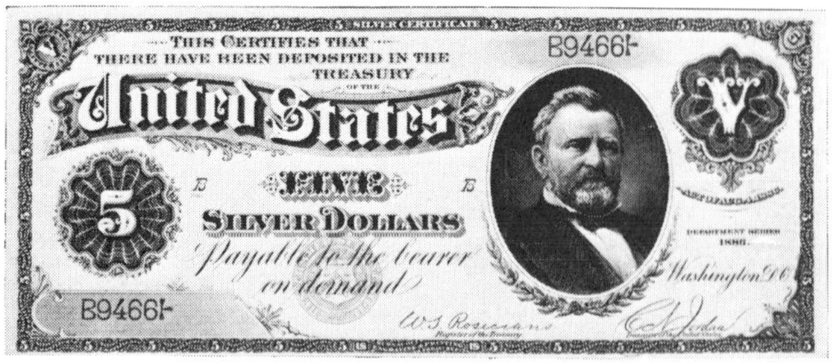

KL#	Series	Signatures	Seal	Fine	XF	CU
		Blue serial numbers				
229	1886	Rosecrans-Jordan	Small red	200.	450.	1800.
230	1886	Rosecrans-Hyatt	Small red	200.	500.	2000.
231	1886	Rosecrans-Hyatt	Large red	225.	500.	2000.
232	1886	Rosecrans-Huston	Large red	250.	550.	2300.
233	1886	Rosecrans-Huston	Large brown	225.	500.	2000.
234	1886	Rosecrans-Nebeker	Large brown	275.	600.	2300.
235	1886	Rosecrans-Nebeker	Small red	200.	500.	2000.

KL#	Series	Signatures	Seal	Fine	XF	CU
236	1891	Rosecrans-Nebeker	Small red	150.	400.	1500.
237	1891	Tillman-Morgan	Small red	150.	1000.	3500.

KL#	Series	Signatures	Seal	Fine	XF	CU
238	1896	Tillman-Morgan	Small red	300.	750.	3500.
239	1896	Bruce-Roberts	Small red	300.	750.	3500.
240	1896	Lyons-Roberts	Small red	300.	750.	3500.

KL#	Series	Signatures	Seal	Fine	XF	CU
241	1899	Lyons-Roberts	Small blue	75.00	240.	650.
242	1899	Lyons-Treat	Small blue	75.00	240.	650.
243	1899	Vernon-Treat	Small blue	75.00	240.	650.
244	1899	Vernon Mc Clung	Small blue	75.00	240.	650.
245	1899	Napier-Mc Clung	Small blue	75.00	240.	650.
246	1899	Napier-Thompson	Small blue	100.	450.	2500.
247	1899	Parker-Burke	Small blue	75.00	240.	650.
248	1899	Teehee-Burke	Small blue	75.00	240.	650.
249	1899	Elliott-Burke	Small blue	75.00	240.	650.
250	1899	Elliott-White	Small blue	75.00	240.	650.
251	1899	Speelman-White	Small blue	75.00	240.	650.

KL#	Series	Signatures	Seal	Fine	XF	CU
252	1923	Speelman-White	Small blue	75.00	200.	1000.

Treasury or Coin Notes

KL#	Series	Signatures	Seal	Fine	XF	CU
253	1890	Rosecrans-Huston	Large brown	125.	300.	1500.
254	1890	Rosecrans-Nebeker	Large brown	150.	400.	1750.
255	1890	Rosecrans-Nebeker	Small red	150.	400.	1750.

KL#	Series	Signatures	Seal	Fine	XF	CU
256	1891	Rosecrans-Nebeker	Small red	100.	200.	650.
257	1891	Tillman-Morgan	Small red	115.	225.	800.
258	1891	Bruce-Roberts	Small red	115.	225.	800.
259	1891	Lyons-Roberts	Small red	115.	400.	900.

Federal Reserve Notes
Series 1914

KL#	Bank	Red Seals Signatures	Fine	XF	CU
260	Boston	Burke-Mc Adoo	32.50	65.00	250.
261	New York	Burke-Mc Adoo	32.50	65.00	250.
262	Philadelphia	Burke-Mc Adoo	32.50	65.00	250.
263	Cleveland	Burke-Mc Adoo	32.50	65.00	250.
264	Richmond	Burke-Mc Adoo	32.50	65.00	250.
265	Atlanta	Burke-Mc Adoo	32.50	65.00	250.
266	Chicago	Burke-Mc Adoo	32.50	65.00	250.
267	St. Louis	Burke-Mc Adoo	32.50	65.00	250.
268	Minneapolis	Burke-Mc Adoo	32.50	65.00	250.
269	Kansas City	Burke-Mc Adoo	32.50	65.00	250.
270	Dallas	Burke-Mc Adoo	32.50	65.00	250.
271	San Francisco	Burke-Mc Adoo	32.50	65.00	250.

KL#	Bank	Blue Seals Signatures	Fine	XF	CU
272	Boston	Burke-Mc Adoo	15.00	30.00	100.
273	Boston	Burke-Glass	15.00	30.00	100.
274	Boston	Burke-Houston	15.00	30.00	100.
275	Boston	White-Mellon	15.00	30.00	100.
276	New York	Burke-Mc Adoo	15.00	30.00	100.
277	New York	Burke-Glass	15.00	30.00	100.
278	New York	Burke-Houston	15.00	30.00	100.
279	New York	White-Mellon	15.00	30.00	100.
280	Philadelphia	Burke-Mc Adoo	15.00	30.00	100.
281	Philadelphia	Burke-Glass	15.00	30.00	100.
282	Philadelphia	Burke-Houston	15.00	30.00	100.
283	Philadelphia	White-Mellon	15.00	30.00	100.
284	Cleveland	Burke-Mc Adoo	15.00	30.00	100.
285	Cleveland	Burke-Glass	15.00	30.00	100.
286	Cleveland	Burke-Houston	15.00	30.00	100.
287	Cleveland	White-Mellon	15.00	30.00	100.
288	Richmond	Burke-Mc Adoo	15.00	30.00	100.
289	Richmond	Burke-Glass	15.00	30.00	100.
290	Richmond	Burke-Houston	15.00	30.00	100.
291	Richmond	White-Mellon	15.00	30.00	100.
292	Atlanta	Burke-Mc Adoo	15.00	30.00	100.
293	Atlanta	Burke-Glass	15.00	30.00	100.
294	Atlanta	Burke-Houston	15.00	30.00	100.
295	Atlanta	White-Mellon	15.00	30.00	100.

KL#	Bank	Signatures	Fine	XF	CU
296	Chicago	Burke-Mc Adoo	15.00	30.00	100.
297	Chicago	Burke-Glass	15.00	30.00	100.
298	Chicago	Burke-Houston	15.00	30.00	100.
299	Chicago	White-Mellon	15.00	30.00	100.
300	St. Louis	Burke-Mc Adoo	15.00	30.00	100.
301	St. Louis	Burke-Glass	16.00	32.00	100.
302	St. Louis	Burke-Houston	15.00	30.00	100.
303	St. Louis	White-Mellon	15.00	32.00	100.
304	Minneapolis	Burke-Mc Adoo	17.00	33.00	100.
305	Minneapolis	Burke-Glass	17.00	33.00	100.
306	Minneapolis	Burke-Houston	15.00	30.00	100.
307	Minneapolis	White-Mellon	15.00	30.00	100.
308	Kansas City	Burke-Mc Adoo	16.00	32.00	100.
309	Kansas City	Burke-Glass	17.00	33.00	100.
310	Kansas City	Burke-Houston	15.00	30.00	100.
311	Kansas City	White-Mellon	15.00	30.00	100.
312	Dallas	Burke-Mc Adoo	19.00	35.00	100.
313	Dallas	Burke-Glass	18.00	39.00	100.
314	Dallas	Burke-Houston	15.00	30.00	100.
315	Dallas	White-Mellon	15.00	30.00	100.
316	San Francisco	Burke-Mc Adoo	15.00	30.00	100.
317	San Francisco	Burke-Glass	19.00	40.00	100.
318	San Francisco	Burke-Houston	15.00	30.00	100.
319	San Francisco	White-Mellon	15.00	30.00	100.

Federal Reserve Bank Notes
Series 1915

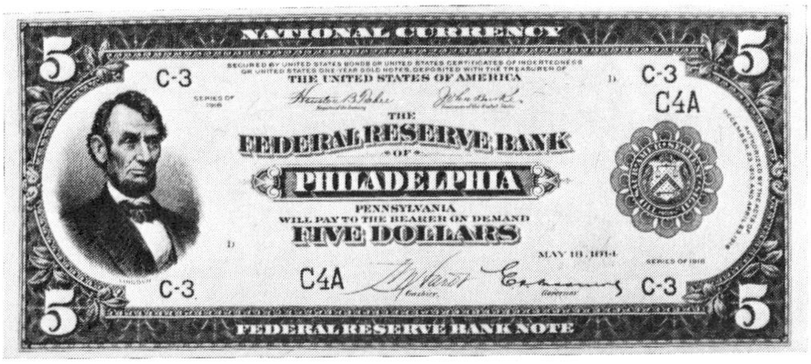

KL#	Bank	Federal Sigs.	Bank Sigs.	Fine	XF	CU
320	Atlanta	Teehee-Burke	Bell-Wellborn	55.00	150.	500.
321	Atlanta	Teehee-Burke	Pike-Mc Cord	55.00	150.	500.
322	Chicago	Teehee-Burke	Mc Lallen-Mc Dougal	55.00	150.	500.
323	Kansas City	Teehee-Burke	Anderson-Miller	55.00	150.	500.
324	Kansas City	Teehee-Burke	Cross-Miller	55.00	150.	500.
325	Kansas City	Teehee-Burke	Helm-Miller	55.00	150.	500.
326	Dallas	Teehee-Burke	Hoopes-Van Zandt	55.00	150.	500.
327	Dallas	Teehee-Burke	Talley-Van Zandt	65.00	175.	550.
328	San Francisco	Teehee-Burke	Clerk-Lynch	65.00	175.	550.

Series 1918

KL#	Bank	Federal Sigs.	Bank Sigs.	Fine	XF	CU
329	Boston	Teehee-Burke	Bullen-Morss	750.	1200.	2000.
330	New York	Teehee-Burke	Hendricks-Strong	50.00	100.	400.
331	Philadelphia	Teehee-Burke	Hardt-Passmore	50.00	100.	400.
332	Philadelphia	Teehee-Burke	Dyer-Passmore	50.00	100.	400.
333	Cleveland	Teehee-Burke	Baxter-Fancher	50.00	100.	400.
334	Cleveland	Teehee-Burke	Davis-Fancher	50.00	100.	400.
335	Cleveland	Elliott-Burke	Davis-Fancher	50.00	100.	400.
336	Atlanta	Teehee-Burke	Pike-Mc Cord	50.00	100.	400.
337	Atlanta	Teehee-Burke	Bell-Wellborn	50.00	100.	400.
338	Atlanta	Elliott-Burke	Bell-Wellborn	50.00	100.	400.
339	Chicago	Teehee-Burke	Mc Cloud-Mc Dougal	50.00	100.	400.
340	Chicago	Teehee-Burke	Cramer-Mc Dougal	50.00	100.	400.
341	St. Louis	Teehee-Burke	Attebery-Wells	50.00	100.	400.
342	St. Louis	Teehee-Burke	Attebery-Biggs	50.00	100.	400.
343	St. Louis	Elliott-Burke	White-Biggs	50.00	100.	400.
344	Minneapolis	Teehee-Burke	Cook-Wold	50.00	100.	400.
345	Kansas City	Teehee-Burke	Anderson-Miller	50.00	100.	400.
346	Kansas City	Elliott-Burke	Helm-Miller	50.00	100.	400.
347	Dallas	Teehee-Burke	Talley-Van Zandt	50.00	100.	400.
348	San Francisco	Teehee-Burke	Clerk-Lynch	50.00	100.	550.

San Francisco notes dated May 20, 1914. One issue dated May 18, 1914. Scarce.

Ten Dollars
Demand Notes

Type One: "For the" autographed
Type Two: "For the" engraved

KL#	Payable at:		Good	VG
349	Boston	Type One	700.	1200.
350	Boston	Type Two	500.	800.
351	New York	Type One	700.	1200.
352	New York	Type Two	500.	800.
353	Philadelphia	Type One	700.	1200.
354	Philadelphia	Type Two	500.	800.
355	St. Louis	Type One	2500.	4500.
356	St. Louis	Type Two	2000.	3000.
357	Cincinnati	Type One	2500.	4500.
358	Cincinnati	Type Two	2000.	3000.

United States Notes

KL#	Series	Signatures	Seal	Fine	XF	CU
First Obligation inscription on back. One red serial number.						
359	1862	Chittenden-Spinner	Small red	200.	350.	1100.
American Bank Note Co. upper border.						

KL#	Series	Signatures	Seal	Fine	XF	CU
Second Obligation on back. One red serial number.						
360	1862	Chittenden-Spinner	Small red	200.	350.	1100.
American Bank Note Co. upper border. National Bank Note Co. lower border.						
Second Obligation on back. Two red serial numbers.						
361	1863	Chittenden-Spinner	Small red	200.	325.	1100.
American Bank Note Co. upper and lower borders.						

KL#	Series	Signatures	Seal	Fine	XF	CU
Red serial numbers						
362	1869	Allison-Spinner	Large red	125.	375.	1000.

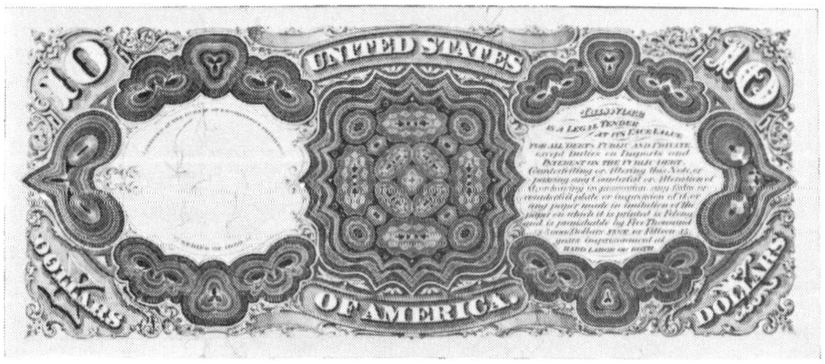

KL#	Series	Signatures	Seal	Fine	XF	CU
Face: Bureau of Engraving and Printing. Back: National Bank Note Co.						
363	1875	Allison-New	Small red	95.00	275.	950.
Issued in one additional series, same design.						
364	1875 Series A in lower right of face design.			125.	300.	1000.
365	1878	Allison-Gilfillan	Small red	150.	265.	1250.
Red serial numbers						
366	1880	Scofield-Gilfillan	Large brown	90.00	175.	950.

KL#	Series	Signatures	Seal	Fine	XF	CU
367	1880	Bruce-Gilfillan	Large brown	90.00	175.	950.
368	1880	Bruce-Wyman	Large brown	90.00	175.	950.
		Blue serial numbers				
369	1880	Bruce-Wyman	Large red	90.00	180.	900.
370	1880	Rosecrans-Jordan	Large red	90.00	180.	1000.
371	1880	Rosecrans-Hyatt	Large red	90.00	180.	1000.
372	1880	Rosecrans-Hyatt	Red spikes	90.00	180.	900.
373	1880	Rosecrans-Huston	Red spikes	90.00	180.	1000.
374	1880	Rosecrans-Huston	Large brown	90.00	180.	1000.
375	1880	Rosecrans-Nebeker	Large brown	90.00	180.	1000.
376	1880	Rosecrans-Nebeker	Small red	85.00	160.	600.
377	1880	Tillman-Morgan	Small red	85.00	160.	600.
378	1880	Bruce-Roberts	Small red	85.00	160.	600.
379	1880	Lyons-Roberts	Small red	85.00	160.	600.

KL#	Series	Signatures	Seal	Fine	XF	C
		Red Serial numbers. Large "X" at left.				
380	1901	Lyons-Roberts	Small red	110.	350.	950.
381	1901	Lyons-Treat	Small red	100.	350.	1100.
382	1901	Vernon-Treat	Small red	100.	350.	1100.
383	1901	Vernon-Mc Clung	Small red	100.	350.	1100.
384	1901	Napier-Mc Clung	Small red	100.	350.	1100.
385	1901	Parker-Burke	Small red	100.	350.	1100.
386	1901	Teehee-Burkee	Small red	100.	350.	1100.
387	1901	Elliott-White	Small red	100.	350.	1100.
388	1901	Speelman-White	Small red	100.	350.	1100.

KL#	Series	Signatures	Seal	Fine	XF	C
		Red Serial numbers. Large "X" at right.				
389	1923	Speelman-White	Small red	150.	550.	1750.

Compound Interest Treasury Notes

KL#	Act	Overprint Date	Signatures	Fine	XF	CU
390	1863	June 10, 1864	Chittenden-Spinner	1200.	5000.	—
391	1864	July 15, 1864	Chittenden-Spinner	1200.	5000.	—
392	1864	Aug. 15-Dec. 15,1864	Colby-Spinner	1200.	5000.	—

Interest Bearing Notes

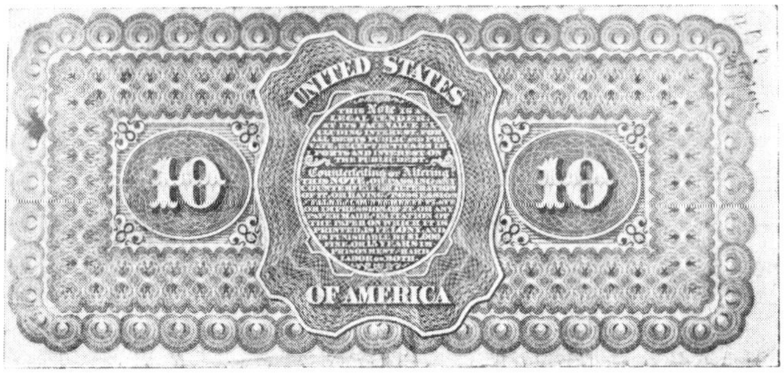

KL#	Act	Signatures	Fine	XF	CU
393	1863	Chittenden-Spinner	3000.	6500.	—

Refunding Certificates

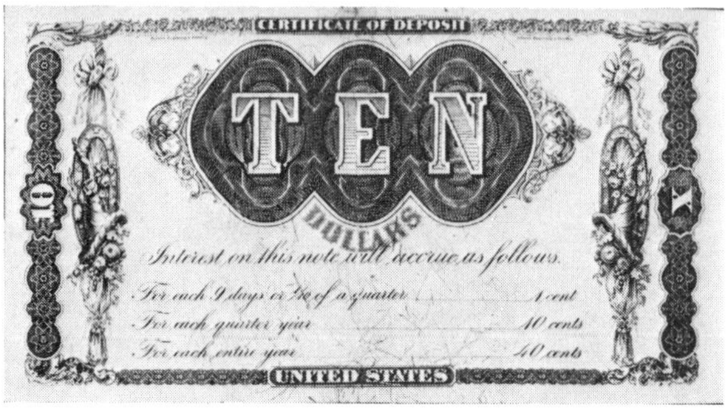

KL#	Signatures	Payable to...	Fine	XF	CU
394	Scofield-Gilfillan	Order	—	—	—
395	Scofield-Gilfillan	Bearer	1250.	1800.	—

National Gold Bank Notes

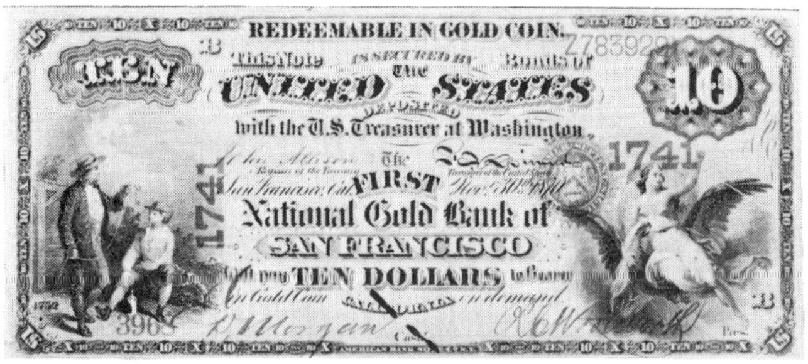

KL#	Series	Issuing Bank	Location	Good	Fine
396	Orig.	First Nat'l Gold Bank	San Francisco	600.	2200.
397	1872	Nat'l Gold Bank & Trust Co.	San Francisco	600.	2200.
398	Orig.	Nat'l Gold Bank of D.O. Mills	Sacramento	850.	2750.
399	Orig.	First Nat'l Gold Bank	Stockton	850.	2750.
400	Orig.	First Nat'l Gold Bank	Santa Barbara	950.	2750.
401	Orig.	Farmers' Nat'l Gold Bank	San Jose	850.	2750.
402	Orig.	First Nat'l Gold Bank	Petaluma	850.	2750.
403	1875	First Nat'l Gold Bank	Petaluma	850.	2750.
404	1875	First Nat'l Gold Bank	Oakland	850.	2750.
405	1875	Union Nat'l Gold Bank	Oakland	900.	2750.
406	1875	First Nat'l Gold Bank	Stockton	800.	2750.

Silver Certificates

The Countersigned Series
Scofield-Gilfillan signatures. Blue serial numbers.
Types 1, 2 4 and 5, place of deposit: New York.
Type 3 place of deposit: Washington, D.C.
Series 1878 Large red seal and large red "ten" below seal.
Series 1880 Large brown seal and large "X" below seal.

KL#	Series	Countersigned by:	Type	VG	VF
407	1878	J.C. Hopper, Asst. U.S. Treas.	1	3750.	Rare
408	1878	W.G. White, Asst. U.S. Treas.	2	3750.	Rare
409	1878	A.V. Wyman, Asst. U.S. Treas.	3	3750.	Rare
410	1878	T. Hillhouse, Asst. U.S. Treas.	4		Very Rare
411	1880	T. Hillhouse, Asst. U.S. Treas.	5	3500.	Rare

KL#	Series	Signatures	Seal	Fine	XF	CU
		Blue serial numbers, without large "X" below center seal.				
412	1880	Scofield-Gilfillan	Large brown	325.	675.	3000.
413	1880	Bruce-Gilfillan	Large brown	325.	675.	3000.
414	1880	Bruce-Wyman	Large brown	325.	675.	3000.
		Blue serial numbers, without large "X" below center seal.				
415	1880	Bruce-Wyman	Large red	400.	900.	2600.

KL#	Series	Signatures	Seal	Fine	XF	CU
416	1886	Rosecrans-Jordan	Small red	195.	550.	2250.
417	1886	Rosecrans-Hyatt	Small red	195.	550.	2500.
418	1886	Rosecrans-Hyatt	Large red	195.	550.	2250.
419	1886	Rosecrans-Huston	Large red	195.	550.	2500.
420	1886	Rosecrans-Huston	Large brown	195.	550.	2250.
421	1886	Rosecrans-Nebeker	Large brown	225.	600.	2500.
422	1886	Rosecrans-Nebeker	Small red	300.	650.	2500.
423	1891	Rosecrans-Nebeker	Small red	110.	225.	1250.
424	1891	Tillman-Morgan	Small red	110.	190.	1500.
425	1891	Bruce-Roberts	Small red	110.	190.	1500.
426	1891	Lyons-Roberts	Small red	110.	190.	1500.
427	1908	Vernon-Treat	Small blue	100.	300.	1000.
428	1908	Vernon-Mc Clung	Small blue	100.	190.	1000.
429	1908	Parker-Burke	Small blue	100.	190.	1000.

Treasury or Coin Notes

KL#	Series	Signatures	Seal	Fine	XF	CU
430	1890	Rosecrans-Huston	Large brown	245.	400.	2200.
431	1890	Rosecrans-Nebeker	Large brown	275.	500.	3000.
432	1890	Rosecrans-Nebeker	Small red	225.	450.	1750.

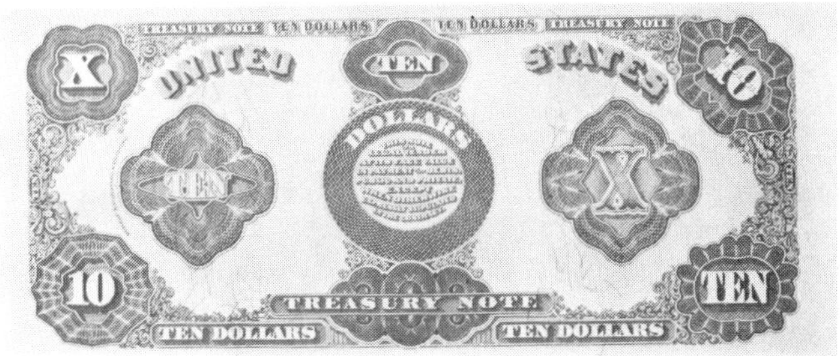

433	1891	Rosecrans-Nebeker	Small red	125.	250.	750.
434	1891	Tillman-Morgan	Small red	125.	250.	800.
435	1891	Bruce-Roberts	Small red	125.	250.	800.

Gold Certificates

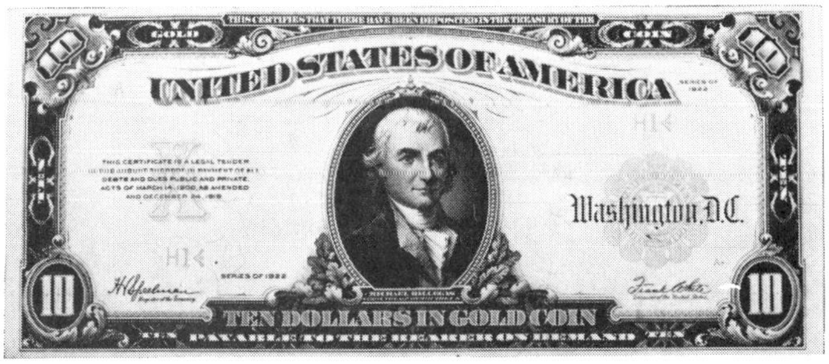

KL#	Series	Signatures	Fine	XF	CU
436	1907	Vernon-Treat	45.00	95.00	275.
437	1907	Vernon-Mc Clung	45.00	95.00	350.
438	1907	Napier-Mc Clung	45.00	95.00	350.
439	1907	Napier-Thompson	75.00	150.	900.
440	1907	Parker-Burke	45.00	95.00	350.
441	1907	Teehee-Burke	45.00	95.00	350.
442	1922	Speelman-White	35.00	85.00	225.

Federal Reserve Notes Series 1914

Red Seals

KL#	Bank	Signatures	Fine	XF	CU
443	Boston	Burke-Mc Adoo	35.00	75.00	375.
444	New York	Burke-Mc Adoo	35.00	75.00	375.
445	Philadelphia	Burke-Mc Adoo	35.00	75.00	375.
446	Cleveland	Burke-Mc Adoo	35.00	75.00	375.
447	Richmond	Burke-Mc Adoo	35.00	75.00	375.
448	Atlanta	Burke-Mc Adoo	35.00	75.00	375.
449	Chicago	Burke-Mc Adoo	35.00	75.00	375.
450	St. Louis	Burke-Mc Adoo	35.00	75.00	375.
451	Minneapolis	Burke-Mc Adoo	35.00	75.00	375.
452	Kansas City	Burke-Mc Adoo	35.00	75.00	375.
453	Dallas	Burke-Mc Adoo	35.00	75.00	375.
454	San Francisco	Burke-Mc Adoo	35.00	75.00	375.

Blue Seals

455	Boston	Burke-Mc Adoo	20.00	40.00	125.
456	Boston	Burke-Glass	20.00	40.00	125.
457	Boston	Burke-Houston	20.00	40.00	125.
458	Boston	White-Mellon	20.00	40.00	125.
459	New York	Burke-Mc Adoo	20.00	40.00	125.
460	New York	Burke-Glass	20.00	40.00	125.
461	New York	Burke-Houston	20.00	40.00	125.
462	New York	White-Mellon	20.00	40.00	125.
463	Philadelphia	Burke-Mc Adoo	20.00	40.00	125.
464	Philadelphia	Burke-Glass	20.00	40.00	125.
465	Philadelphia	Burke-Houston	20.00	40.00	125.
466	Philadelphia	White-Mellon	20.00	40.00	125.
467	Cleveland	Burke-Mc Adoo	20.00	40.00	125.
468	Cleveland	Burke-Glass	20.00	40.00	125.
469	Cleveland	Burke-Houston	20.00	40.00	125.
470	Cleveland	White-Mellon	20.00	40.00	125.
471	Richmond	Burke-Mc Adoo	20.00	40.00	125.
472	Richmond	Burke-Glass	20.00	40.00	125.
473	Richmond	Burke-Houston	20.00	40.00	125.
474	Richmond	White-Mellon	20.00	40.00	125.
475	Atlanta	Burke-Mc Adoo	20.00	40.00	125.
476	Atlanta	Burke-Glass	20.00	40.00	125.
477	Atlanta	Burke-Houston	20.00	40.00	125.
478	Atlanta	White-Mellon	20.00	40.00	125.
479	Chicago	Burke-Mc Adoo	20.00	40.00	125.
480	Chicago	Burke-Glass	20.00	40.00	125.
481	Chicago	Burke-Houston	20.00	40.00	125.
482	Chicago	White-Mellon	20.00	40.00	125.
483	St. Louis	Burke-Mc Adoo	20.00	40.00	125.
484	St. Louis	Burke-Glass	20.00	40.00	125.
485	St. Louis	Burke-Houston	20.00	40.00	125.
486	St. Louis	White-Mellon	20.00	40.00	125.
487	Minneapolis	Burke-Mc Adoo	20.00	40.00	125.
488	Minneapolis	Burke-Glass	20.00	40.00	125.
489	Minneapolis	Burke-Houston	20.00	40.00	125.
490	Minneapolis	White-Mellon	20.00	40.00	125.
491	Kansas City	Burke-Mc Adoo	20.00	40.00	125.
492	Kansas City	Burke-Glass	24.00	55.00	160.
493	Kansas City	Burke-Houston	20.00	40.00	125.
494	Kansas City	White-Mellon	20.00	40.00	125.
495	Dallas	Burke-Mc Adoo	20.00	40.00	125.
496	Dallas	Burke-Glass	20.00	40.00	125.
497	Dallas	Burke-Houston	20.00	40.00	125.
498	Dallas	White-Mellon	20.00	40.00	125.
499	San Francisco	Burke-Mc Adoo	20.00	40.00	125.
500	San Francisco	Burke-Glass	25.00	60.00	240.
501	San Francisco	Burke-Houston	20.00	40.00	125.
502	San Francisco	White-Mellon	20.00	40.00	125.

Federal Reserve Bank Notes
Series 1915

KL#	Bank	Federal Sigs.	Bank Sigs.	Fine	XF	CU
503	Atlanta	Teehee-Burke	Bell-Wellborn	300.	600.	2250.
504	Chicago	Teehee-Burke	Mc Lallen-Mc Dougal	175.	390.	1000.
505	Kansas City	Teehee-Burke	Anderson-Miller	175.	390.	1000.
506	Kansas City	Teehee-Burke	Cross-Miller	175.	390.	1000.
507	Kansas City	Teehee-Burke	Helm-Miller	175.	390.	1000.
508	Dallas	Teehee-Burke	Hoopes-Van Zandt	175.	390.	1000.
509	Dallas	Teehee-Burke	Gilbert-Van Zandt	350.	700.	2250.
510	Dallas	Teehee-Burke	Talley-Van Zandt	175.	390.	1000.

Series 1918

KL#	Bank	Federal Sigs.	Bank Sigs.	Fine	XF	CU
511	New York	Teehee-Burkee	Hendricks-Strong	200.	425.	2500.
512	Atlanta	Elliott-Burke	Bell-Wellborn	200.	425.	2500.
513	Chicago	Teehee-Burke	Mc Cloud-Mc Dougal	175.	390.	2500.
514	St. Louis	Teehee-Burke	Attebery-Wells	225.	450.	2500.

Twenty Dollars
Demand Notes

Type One: “For the” autographed
Type Two: “For the” engraved

KL#	Payable at:		Good	VG
515	Boston	Type One		(VERY RARE)
516	Boston	Type Two		(VERY RARE)
517	New York	Type One	3300.	5500.
518	New York	Type Two	3300.	5500.
519	Philadelphia	Type One	3300.	5500.
520	Philadelphia	Type Two	3000.	5500.
521	Cincinnati	Type One		(VERY RARE)
522	Cincinnati	Type Two		(VERY RARE)

United States Notes

KL#	Series	Signatures	Seal	Fine	XF	CU
		First Obligation inscription on back. One red serial number.				
523	1862	Chittenden-Spinner	Small red	300.	650.	2750.
		American Bank Note Co. lower border.				
		Second Obligation on back. One red serial number.				
524	1862	Chittenden-Spinner	Small red	300.	650.	2750.
		National Bank Note Co. American Bank Note Co.				
		Second Obligation on back. Two red serial numbers.				
525	1863	Chittenden-Spinner	Small red	300.	650.	2500.
		American Bank Note Co. lower border.				

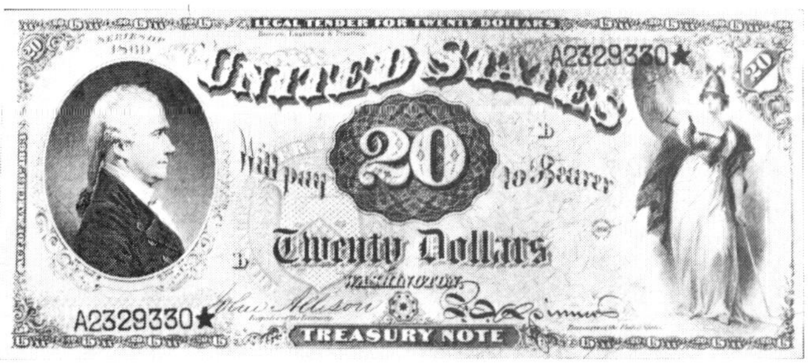

KL#	Series	Signatures	Seal	Fine	XF	CU
		Blue serial numbers				
526	1869	Allison-Spinner	Large red	325.	900.	2800.
		Blue Serial numbers. “XX” twice on face of note.				
527	1875	Allison-New	Small red	175.	350.	850.

KL#	Series	Signatures	Seal	Fine	XF	CU
528	1878	Allison-Gilfillan	Small red	190.	450.	1150.
		Blue Serial numbers. "XX" removed.				
529	1880	Scofield-Gilfillan	Large brown	125.	400.	1000.
530	1880	Bruce-Gilfillan	Large brown	125.	400.	1100.
531	1880	Bruce-Wyman	Large brown	125.	400.	1100.
532	1880	Bruce-Wyman	Large red	120.	400.	1000.
533	1880	Rosecrans-Jordan	Large red	120.	400.	1100.
534	1880	Rosecrans-Hyatt	Large red	120.	400.	1100.
535	1880	Rosecrans-Hyatt	Red spikes	120.	400.	1000.
536	1880	Rosecrans-Huston	Red spikes	120.	400.	1100.
537	1880	Rosecrans-Huston	Large brown	125.	400.	1100.
538	1880	Rosecrans-Nebeker	Large brown	125.	400.	1100.
539	1880	Rosecrans-Nebeker	Small red	100.	380.	750.
540	1880	Tillman-Morgan	Small red	100.	380.	800.
541	1880	Bruce-Roberts	Small red	100.	380.	800.
542	1880	Lyons-Roberts	Small red	100.	380.	800.
543	1880	Vernon-Treat	Small red	100.	380.	800.
544	1880	Vernon-Mc Clung	Small red	100.	380.	800.
		Red Serial numbers.				
545	1880	Teehee-Burke	Small red	100.	285.	700.
546	1880	Elliott-Burke	Small red	100.	285.	750.

Compound Interest Treasury Notes

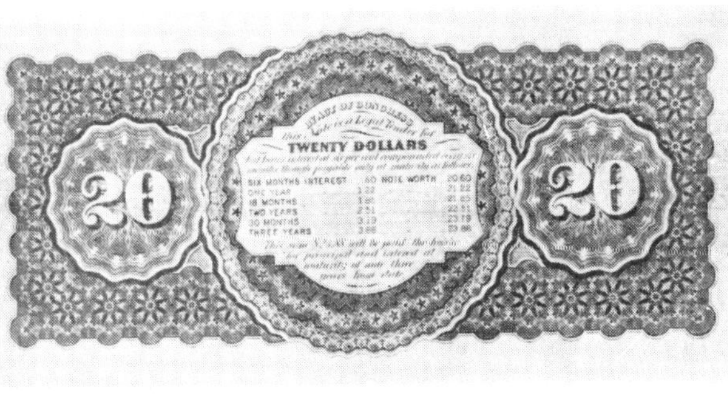

KL#	Act	Overprint Date	Signatures	Fine	XF	CU
547	1864	July 14, 1864	Chittenden-Spinner	—	—	—
548	1864	Aug. 15, 1864-Oct.16,1865	Colby-Spinner	—	—	—

Interest Bearing Notes

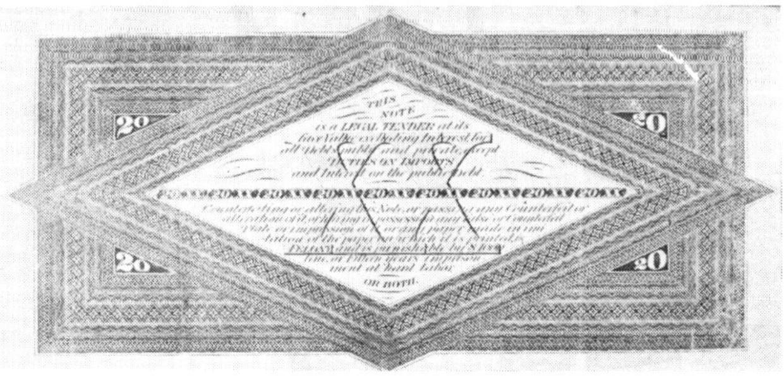

KL#	Act	Signatures	Fine	XF	CU
549	1863	Chittenden-Spinner	3500.	8500.	—

Gold Certificates

KL#	Issue/Act/Series	Signatures	Fine	XF	CU
550	First/1863	Colby-Spinner		(Two known)	

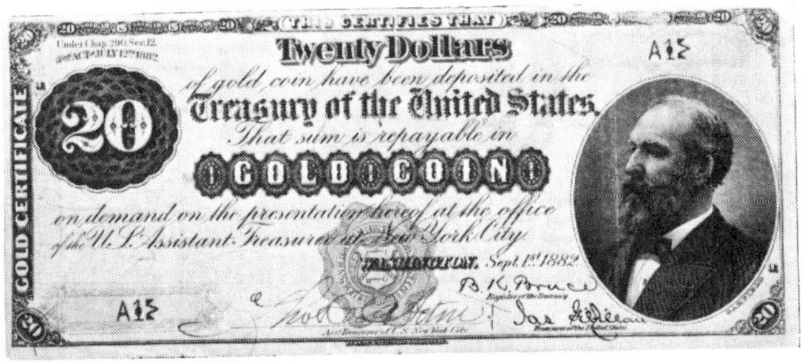

KL#	Series	Signatures	Seal	Fine	XF	CU
551	1882	Bruce Gilfillan-(countersigned by Asst. Treas. of the U.S. Thos. C. Acton)	Brown	—	—	—
552	1882	Bruce-Gilfillan	Brown	2000.	4000.	—
553	1882	Bruce-Wyman	Brown	1000.	2000.	—
554	1882	Rosecrans-Huston	Large brown	750.	3000.	—
555	1882	Lyons-Roberts	Small red	150.	325.	1100.

KL#	Series	Signatures	Seal	Fine	XF	CU
556	1905	Lyons-Roberts	Small red	550.	1250.	7500.
557	1905	Lyons-Treat	Small red	500.	1000.	6500.
558	1906	Vernon-Treat	Small red	75.00	135.	500.
559	1906	Vernon-McClung	Small red	60.00	125.	600.
560	1906	Napier-McClung	Small red	60.00	125.	600.
561	1906	Napier-Thompson	Small red	140.	290.	900.
562	1906	Parker-Burke	Small red	60.00	125.	600.
563	1906	Teehee-Burke	Small red	60.00	125.	600.
564	1922	Speelman-White	Small red	60.00	100.	325.

National Gold Bank Notes

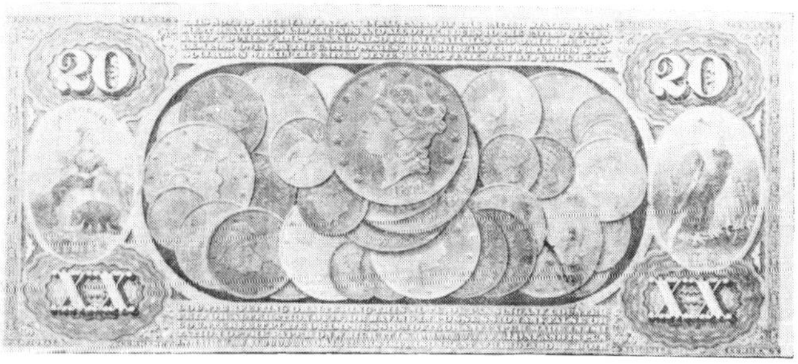

KL#	Series	Issuing Bank	Location	Good	Fine
566	Orig.	First Nat'l Gold Bank	San Francisco	1000.	2500.
567	Orig.	Nat'l Gold Bank of D.O. Mills	Sacramento	1000.	2500.
568	Orig.	First Nat'l Gold Bank	Stockton	1500.	3000.
569	Orig.	First Nat'l Gold Bank	Santa Barbara	1500.	3000.
570	Orig.	Farmers Nat'l Gold Bank	San Jose	1500.	3000.
571	1875	Farmers' Nat'l Gold Bank	San Francisco	1200.	2750.
572	1875	First Nat'l Gold Bank	Petaluma	1200.	2750.
573	1875	First Nat'l Gold Bank	Oakland	1200.	2750.
574	1875	Union Nat'l Gold Bank	Oakland	1200.	2750.

Silver Certificates

The Countersigned Series
Scofield-Gilfillan signatures. Blue serial numbers.
Types 1, 4 and 5: Place of deposit, New York.
Type 3: Place of deposit, Washington, D.C.

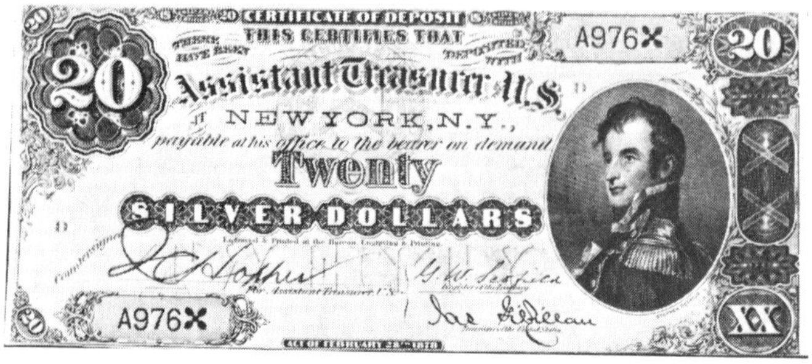

KL#	Series	Countersigned by:	Type	VG	VF
575	1878	J.C. Hopper, Asst. U.S. Treas.	1	2200.	3900.
576	1878	A.V. Wyman, Asst. Treas.	3	2500.	4100.
577	1878	T. Hillhouse, Asst. U.S. Treas.	4	2200.	3900.
578	1880	T. Hillhouse, Asst. U.S. Treas.	5	2000.	3750.

KL#	Series	Signatures	Seal	Fine	XF	CU
579	1880	Scofield-Gilfillan	Large brown	675.	1200.	5000.
580	1880	Bruce-Gilfillan	Large brown	500.	975.	5000.
581	1880	Bruce-Wyman	Large brown	500.	975.	5000.
		Large "XX" removed.				
582	1880	Bruce-Wyman	Small red	1850.	3000.	5800.

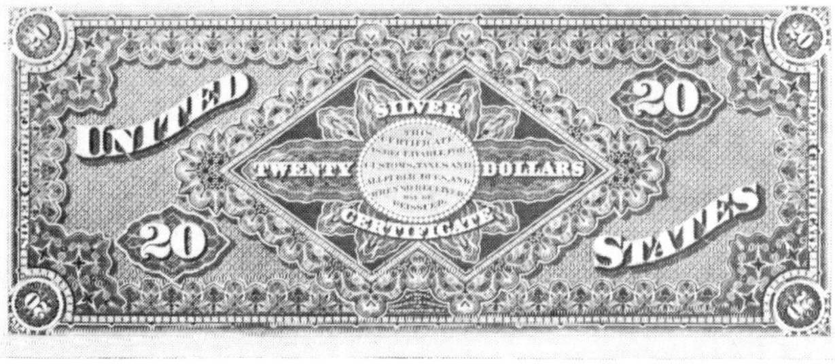

KL#	Series	Signatures	Seal	Fine	XF	CU
583	1886	Rosecrans-Hyatt	Large red	450.	1100.	6250.
584	1886	Rosecrans-Huston	Large brown	450.	1100.	6250.
585	1886	Rosecrans-Nebeker	Large brown	450.	1100.	6250.
586	1886	Rosecrans-Nebeker	Small red	750.	1500.	6500.
		"Series 1891" upper right and lower left.				
587	1891	Rosecrans-Nebeker	Small red	125.	350.	1800.
588	1891	Tillman-Morgan	Small red	125.	350.	2000.
589	1891	Bruce-Roberts	Small red	125.	350.	2000.
590	1891	Lyons-Roberts	Small red	125.	350.	2000.
		Large blue "XX" at left.				
591	1891	Parker-Burke	Small blue	125.	350.	1800.
592	1891	Teehee-Burke	Small blue	125.	350.	2000.

Treasury or Coin Notes

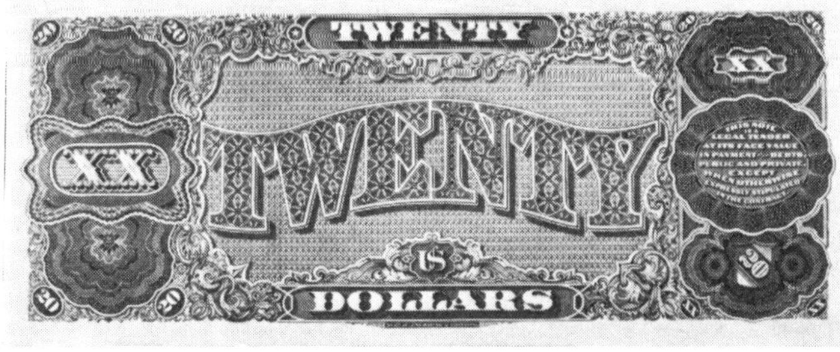

KL#	Series	Signatures	Seal	Fine	XF	CU
593	1890	Rosecrans-Huston	Large brown	600.	1900.	6500.
594	1890	Rosecrans-Nebeker	Large brown	600.	1900.	6500.
595	1890	Rosecrans-Nebeker	Small red	600.	1900.	6500.

KL#	Series	Signatures	Seal	Fine	XF	CU
596	1891	Tillman-Morgan	Small red	1200.	2600.	9000.
597	1891	Bruce-Roberts	Small red	1200.	2600.	9000.

Federal Reserve Notes

Series 1914

KL#	Bank	Signatures	Fine	XF	CU
		Red Seals			
598	Boston	Burke-Mc Adoo	75.00	175.	525.
599	New York	Burke-Mc Adoo	65.00	150.	475.
600	Philadelphia	Burke-Mc Adoo	65.00	150.	475.
601	Cleveland	Burke-Mc Adoo	65.00	150.	475.
602	Richmond	Burke-Mc Adoo	65.00	150.	475.
603	Atlanta	Burke-Mc Adoo	65.00	150.	475.
604	Chicago	Burke-Mc Adoo	65.00	150.	475.
605	St. Louis	Burke-Mc Adoo	65.00	150.	475.
606	Minneapolis	Burke-Mc Adoo	65.00	150.	475.
607	Kansas City	Burke-Mc Adoo	65.00	150.	475.
608	Dallas	Burke-Mc Adoo	65.00	150.	475.
609	San Francisco	Burke-Mc Adoo	65.00	150.	475.
		Blue Seals			
610	Boston	Burke-Mc Adoo	30.00	50.00	150.
611	Boston	Burke-Glass	30.00	50.00	150.
612	Boston	Burke-Houston	30.00	50.00	150.
613	Boston	White-Mellon	30.00	50.00	150.
614	New York	Burke-Mc Adoo	30.00	50.00	150.
615	New York	Burke-Glass	30.00	50.00	150.
616	New York	Burke-Houston	30.00	50.00	150.
617	New York	White-Mellon	30.00	50.00	150.
618	Philadelphia	Burke-Mc Adoo	30.00	50.00	150.
619	Philadelphia	Burke-Glass	30.00	50.00	150.
620	Philadelphia	Burke-Houston	30.00	50.00	150.
621	Philadelphia	White Mellon	30.00	50.00	150.
622	Cleveland	Burke-Mc Adoo	30.00	50.00	150.
623	Cleveland	Burke-Glass	30.00	50.00	150.
624	Cleveland	Burke-Houston	30.00	50.00	150.
625	Cleveland	White-Mellon	30.00	50.00	150.
626	Richmond	Burke-Mc Adoo	30.00	50.00	150.
627	Richmond	Burke-Glass	35.00	60.00	150.
628	Richmond	Burke-Houston	30.00	50.00	150.
629	Richmond	White-Mellon	30.00	50.00	150.
630	Atlanta	Burke-Mc Adoo	30.00	50.00	150.
631	Atlanta	Burke-Glass	30.00	50.00	150.
632	Atlanta	Burke-Houston	30.00	50.00	150.
633	Atlanta	White-Mellon	30.00	50.00	150.
634	Chicago	Burke-Mc Adoo	30.00	50.00	150.
635	Chicago	Burke-Glass	35.00	60.00	150.
636	Chicago	Burke-Houston	30.00	50.00	150.
637	Chicago	White-Mellon	30.00	50.00	150.
638	St. Louis	Burke-Mc Adoo	30.00	50.00	150.
639	St. Louis	Burke-Glass	35.00	60.00	190.
640	St. Louis	Burke-Houston	30.00	50.00	150.
641	St. Louis	White-Mellon	30.00	50.00	150.
642	Minneapolis	Burke-Mc Adoo	30.00	50.00	150.
643	Minneapolis	Burke-Glass	30.00	50.00	150.
644	Minneapolis	Burke-Houston	30.00	50.00	150.
645	Minneapolis	White-Mellon	30.00	50.00	150.
646	Kansas City	Burke-Mc Adoo	30.00	50.00	150.
647	Kansas City	Burke-Glass	30.00	50.00	150.
648	Kansas City	Burke-Houston	30.00	50.00	150.
649	Kansas City	White-Mellon	30.00	50.00	150.
650	Dallas	Burke-Mc Adoo	30.00	50.00	150.
651	Dallas	Burke-Glass	35.00	60.00	190.
652	Dallas	Burke-Houston	30.00	50.00	150.
653	Dallas	White-Mellon	30.00	50.00	150.
654	San Francisco	Burke-Mc Adoo	30.00	50.00	150.
655	San Francisco	Burke-Glass	30.00	60.00	190.
656	San Francisco	Burke-Houston	30.00	50.00	150.
657	San Francisco	White-Mellon	30.00	50.00	150.

Federal Reserve Bank Notes

Series 1915

KL#	Bank	Federal Sigs.	Bank Sigs.	Fine	XF	CU
658	Atlanta	Teehee-Burke	Bell-Wellborn	300.	450.	1650.
659	Atlanta	Teehee-Burke	Pike-Mc Cord	600.	950.	4000.
660	Chicago	Teehee-Burke	Mc Lallen-Mc Dougal	300.	450.	1650.
661	Kansas City	Teehee-Burke	Anderson-Miller	300.	450.	1650.
662	Kansas City	Teehee-Burke	Cross-Miller	300.	450.	1650.
663	Dallas	Teehee-Burke	Hoopes-Van Zandt	300.	450.	3500.
664	Dallas	Teehee-Burke	Gilbert-Van Zandt	550.	800.	1650.
665	Dallas	Teehee-Burke	Talley-Van Zandt	300.	450.	1650.

Series 1918

KL#	Bank	Federal Sigs.	Bank Sigs.	Fine	XF	CU
666	Atlanta	Elliott-Burke	Bell-Wellborn	350.	500.	1750.
667	St. Louis	Teehee-Burke	Attebery-Wells	550.	800.	4000.

Fifty Dollars

United States Notes

KL#	Series	Signatures	Seal	Fine	XF	CU
		First Obligation inscription on back. Red Serial numbers.				
668	1862	Chittenden-Spinner	Small red	1800.	7800.	—
		American Bank Note Co.				
		Second Obligation inscription on back. Red Serial numbers.				
669	1862	Chittenden-Spinner	Small red	1800.	7800.	—
		National Bank Note Co.				
		Second Obligation inscription on back. Red Serial numbers.				
670	1863	Chittenden-Spinner	Small red	1800.	7800.	—

KL#	Series	Signatures	Seal	Fine	XF	CU
		Blue Serial numbers. Ornate "L" twice on face.				
671	1869	Allison-Spinner	Large red	3200.	7800.	—

KL#	Series	Signatures	Seal	Fine	XF	CU
672	1874	Allison-Spinner	Small red	700.	2000.	4000.
673	1875	Allison-Spinner	Small red	800.	2100.	4200.
674	1878	Allison-Gilfillan	Small red	850.	2400.	4000.

KL#	Series	Signatures	Seal	Fine	XF	CU
		Blue Serial numbers in center, unlike any other series.				
675	1880	Bruce-Gilfillan	Large brown	450.	900.	2850.
676	1880	Bruce-Wyman	Large brown	450.	900.	2850.
677	1880	Rosecrans-Jordan	Large red	450.	850.	2250.
678	1880	Rosecrans-Hyatt	Large red	450.	850.	2250.
679	1880	Rosecrans-Hyatt	Red spikes	450.	850.	2250.
680	1880	Rosecrans-Huston	Red spikes	450.	850.	2250.
681	1880	Rosecrans-Huston	Large brown	450.	850.	2850.
682	1880	Tillman-Morgan	Small red	400.	750.	2000.
683	1880	Bruce-Roberts	Small red	400.	750.	2000.
684	1880	Lyons-Roberts	Small red	400.	750.	2000.

Compound Interest Treasury Notes

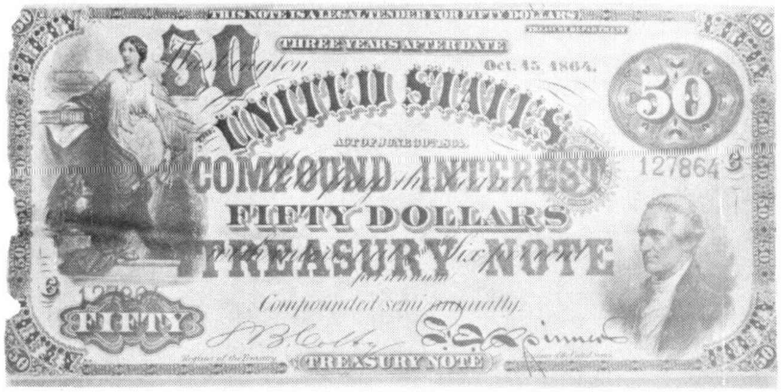

KL#	Act	Overprint Date	Signatures	Fine	XF	CU
685	1863	June 10, 1864	Chittenden-Spinner			(Unique)
686	1864	July 15, 1864	Chittenden-Spinner			(Unknown)
687	1864	Aug. 15, 1864-Sept. 1, 1865	Private Sale Aug. 1984, AU $12,500. Colby-Spinner			(Two known)

Interest Bearing Notes

KL#	Act	Term	Signatures	Fine	XF	CU
688	1863	One year	Chittenden-Spinner			(3 known)
688A	1861	Two years	Chittenden-Spinner			(Unique)
689	1863	Two years	Chittenden-Spinner			(Extremely rare)

KL#	Act	Term	Signatures	Fine	XF	CU
690	1861	Three years	Chittenden-Spinner			(Unknown)
691	1864	Three years	Colby-Spinner			(Unknown)
692	1865	Three years	Colby-Spinner			(Extremely rare)

Gold Certificates

KL#	Series	Signatures	Seal	Fine	XF	CU
693	1882	Bruce-Gilfillan (Countersigned)	Brown	—	—	—
694	1882	Bruce-Gilfillan	Brown	—	4500.	—
695	1882	Bruce-Wyman	Brown	—	4000.	—
696	1882	Rosecrans-Hyatt	Large red	1000.	3500.	—
697	1882	Rosecrans-Huston	Large brown	1000.	3500.	—
698	1882	Lyons-Roberts	Small red	450.	900.	3900.
699	1882	Lyons-Treat	Small red	450.	900.	3900.
700	1882	Vernon-Treat	Small red	450.	900.	3900.
701	1882	Vernon-McClung	Small red	450.	900.	3900.
702	1882	Napier-McClung	Small red	450.	900.	3900.

KL#	Series	Signatures	Seal	Fine	XF	CU
703	1913	Parker-Burke	Small red	250.	500.	3200.
704	1913	Teehee-Burke	Small red	250.	500.	3200.
705	1922	Speelman-White	Small red	135.	300.	1000.

National Gold Bank Notes

KL#	Series	Issuing Bank	Location	Good	Fine
706	Orig.	First Nat'l Gold Bank	San Francisco	3000.	(Rare)
707	Orig.	Nat'l Gold Bank	San Jose	3000.	(Rare)

Silver Certificates

The Countersigned Series
Scofield-Gilfillan signatures. Blue serial numbers.
Type 3 payable at Washington D.C.
Type 4 payable in New York.
Type 6 payable at San Francisco

KL#	Series	Countersigned by:	Type	Fine	XF	CU
		Large "FIFTY" below center seal.				
708	1878	A.V. Wyman, Asst. U.S. Treasurer	3		(Very Rare)	—
709	1878	T. Hillhouse, Asst. U.S. Treasurer	4		(Very Rare)	—
710	1878	R.M. Anthony, Asst. U.S. Treasurer	6	Possibly exists		—

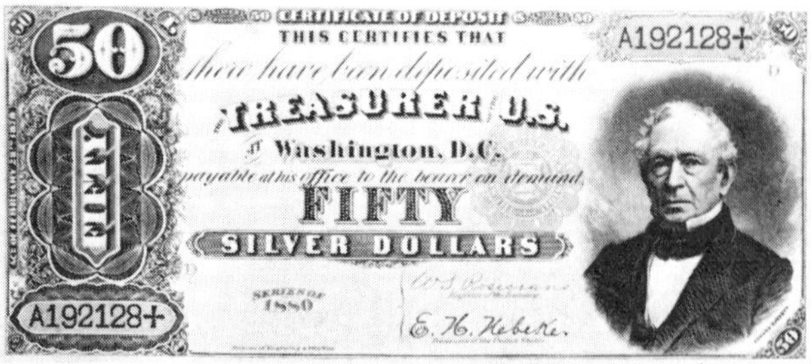

KL#	Series	Signatures	Seal	Fine	XF	CU
		Large "FIFTY" in center.				
711	1880	Scofield-Gilfillan	Large brown	2000.	6000.	10,000.
712	1880	Bruce-Gilfillan	Large brown	2000.	6000.	10,000.
713	1880	Bruce-Wyman	Large brown	2000.	6000.	10,000.
714	1880	Rosecrans-Huston	Large brown	2000.	6000.	10,000.
715	1880	Rosecrans-Nebeker	Small red	2000.	6000.	10,000.
716	1891	Rosecrans-Nebeker	Small red	325.	800.	4000.
717	1891	Tillman-Morgan	Small red	325.	800.	4000.
718	1891	Bruce-Roberts	Small red	325.	800.	4000.
719	1891	Lyons-Roberts	Small red	325.	800.	4000.
720	1891	Vernon-Treat	Small red	325.	800.	4000.

KL#	Series	Signatures	Seal	Fine	XF	CU
721	1891	Parker-Burke	Blue	325.	800.	4000.

Treasury or Coin Notes

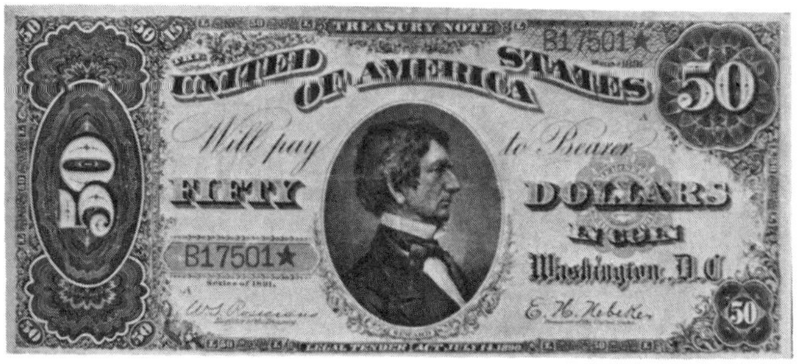

KL#	Series	Signatures	Seal	Fine	XF	CU
722	1891	Rosecrans-Nebeker	Small red	5000.	10,000.	—

Federal Reserve Notes
Series 1914

KL#	Bank	Signatures	Fine	XF	CU
		Red Seals			
723	Boston	Burke-Mc Adoo	150.	250.	900.
724	New York	Burke-Mc Adoo	150.	250.	900.
725	Philadelphia	Burke-Mc Adoo	150.	250.	900.
726	Cleveland	Burke-Mc Adoo	150.	250.	900.
727	Richmond	Burke-Mc Adoo	150.	250.	900.
728	Atlanta	Burke-Mc Adoo	150.	250.	900.
729	Chicago	Burke-Mc Adoo	150.	250.	900.
730	St. Louis	Burke-Mc Adoo	150.	250.	900.
731	Minneapolis	Burke-Mc Adoo	150.	250.	900.
732	Kansas City	Burke-Mc Adoo	150.	250.	900.
733	Dallas	Burke-Mc Adoo	150.	250.	900.
734	San Francisco	Burke-Mc Adoo	150.	250.	900.
		Blue Seals			
735	Boston	Burke-Mc Adoo	80.00	150.	450.
736	Boston	Burke-Glass	80.00	150.	450.
737	Boston	Burke-Houston	80.00	150.	450.
738	Boston	White-Mellon	80.00	150.	450.
739	New York	Burke-Mc Adoo	80.00	150.	450.
740	New York	Burke-Glass	80.00	150.	450.
741	New York	Burke-Houston	80.00	150.	450.
742	New York	White-Mellon	80.00	150.	450.
743	Philadelphia	Burke-Mc Adoo	80.00	150.	450.
744	Philadelphia	Burke-Glass	80.00	150.	450.
745	Philadelphia	Burke-Houston	80.00	150.	450.
746	Philadelphia	White-Mellon	80.00	150.	450.
747	Cleveland	Burke-Mc Adoo	80.00	150.	450.
748	Cleveland	Burke-Glass	80.00	150.	450.
749	Cleveland	Burke-Houston	80.00	150.	450.
750	Cleveland	White-Mellon	80.00	150.	450.
751	Richmond	Burke-Mc Adoo	80.00	150.	450.
752	Richmond	Burke-Glass	80.00	150.	450.
753	Richmond	Burke-Houston	80.00	150.	450.
754	Richmond	White-Mellon	80.00	150.	450.
755	Atlanta	Burke-Mc Adoo	80.00	150.	450.
756	Atlanta	Burke-Glass	80.00	150.	450.
757	Atlanta	Burke-Houston	80.00	150.	450.
758	Atlanta	White-Mellon	80.00	150.	450.
759	Chicago	Burke-Mc Adoo	80.00	150.	450.
760	Chicago	Burke-Glass	80.00	150.	450.
761	Chicago	Burke-Houston	80.00	150.	450.
762	Chicago	White-Mellon	80.00	150.	450.
763	St. Louis	Burke-Mc Adoo	80.00	150.	450.
764	St. Louis	Burke-Glass	80.00	150.	450.
765	St. Louis	Burke-Houston	80.00	150.	450.
766	St. Louis	White-Mellon	80.00	150.	450.
767	Minneapolis	Burke-Mc Adoo	80.00	150.	450.
768	Minneapolis	Burke-Glass	80.00	150.	450.
769	Minneapolis	Burke-Houston	80.00	150.	450.
770	Minneapolis	White-Mellon	80.00	150.	450.
771	Kansas City	Burke-Mc Adoo	80.00	150.	450.
772	Kansas City	Burke-Glass	80.00	150.	450.
773	Kansas City	Burke-Houston	80.00	150.	450.
774	Kansas City	White-Mellon	80.00	150.	450.
775	Dallas	Burke-Mc Adoo	80.00	150.	450.
776	Dallas	Burke-Glass	80.00	150.	450.
777	Dallas	Burke-Houston	80.00	150.	450.
778	Dallas	White-Mellon	80.00	150.	450.
779	San Francisco	Burke-Mc Adoo	80.00	150.	450.
780	San Francisco	Burke-Glass	80.00	150.	450.
781	San Francisco	Burke-Houston	80.00	150.	450.
782	San Francisco	White-Mellon	80.00	150.	450.

Federal Reserve Bank Notes
Series 1918

KL#	Bank	Federal Sigs.	Bank Sigs.	Fine	XF	CU
783	St. Louis	Teehee-Burke	Attebery-Wells	—	4000.	9200.

One Hundred Dollars
United States Notes

KL#	Series	Signatures	Seal	Fine	XF	CU
		First Obligation inscription on back. Red serial numbers.				
784	1862	Chittenden-Spinner	Small red	2500.	8500.	11,000.
		American Bank Note Co. or National Bank Note Co.				
		Second Obligation inscription on back. Red Serial numbers.				
785	1862	Chittenden-Spinner	Small red	2700.	8500.	11,000.
		Second Obligation on back. Red Serial numbers.				
786	1863	Chittenden-Spinner	Small red	2700.	9000.	11,000.

KL#	Series	Signatures	Seal	Fine	XF	CU
		Blue serial numbers				
787	1869	Allison-Spinner	Large red	3000.	9000.	16,500.
788	1875 Series A	Allison-New	Small red	3200.	9200.	10,000.
789	1875	Allison-Wyman	Small red	3200.	9200.	10,000.
790	1878	Allison-Gilfillan	Small red	3400.	9500.	10,000.
791	1880	Bruce-Gilfillan	Large brown	850.	2300.	5500.
792	1880	Bruce-Wyman	Large brown	850.	2300.	5500.
793	1880	Rosecrans-Jordan	Large red	850.	2300.	5500.
794	1880	Rosecrans-Hyatt	Large red	850.	2300.	5500.
795	1880	Rosecrans-Hyatt	Red spikes	850.	2500.	6000.
796	1880	Rosecrans-Huston	Red spikes	850.	2300.	5500.
797	1880	Rosecrans-Huston	Large brown	850.	2300.	5500.
798	1880	Tillman-Morgan	Small red	850.	2300.	5000.
799	1880	Bruce-Roberts	Small red	850.	2300.	5000.
800	1880	Lyons-Roberts	Small red	850.	2300.	5000.
801	1880	Napier-Mc Clung	Small red	850.	2300.	5000.

Compound Interest Treasury Notes

KL#	Act	Overprint Date	Signatures	Fine	XF	CU
802	1863	June 10, 1864	Chittenden-Spinner			(Extremely rare)
803	1864	July 15, 1864	Chittenden-Spinner			(Unknown)
804	1864	Aug. 15, 1864- Sept. 1, 1865	Colby-Spinner			(Extremely rare)

Interest Bearing Notes

KL#	Act	Term	Signatures	Fine	XF	CU
805	1863	One year	Chittenden-Spinner			(Two known)
805A	1861	Two years	Chittenden-Spinner			(Unknown)
806	1863	Two years	Chittenden-Spinner			(One known)
807	1861	Three years	Chittenden-Spinner			(Extremely rare)

808	1864	Three years	Colby Spinner			(Extremely rare)
809	1865	Three years	Colby-Spinner			(Two known)

Gold Certificates

KL#	Issue/Act/Series	Signatures	Fine	XF	CU
810	First/1863	Colby-Spinner			(Extremely rare)
811	Second/1863	Allison-Spinner			(Unknown)
812	Third/1863/1875	Allison-New			(Extremely rare)

KL#	Series	Signatures	Seal	Fine	XF	CU
813	1882	Bruce-Gilfillan (countersigned)	Brown	—		—(Unique)
814	1882	Bruce-Gilfillan	Brown	1500.	6000.	—
815	1882	Bruce-Wyman	Brown	1000.	5500.	—
816	1882	Rosecrans-Hyatt	Large red	1000.	5500.	—
817	1882	Rosecrans-Huston	Large brown	1000.	5500.	—
818	1882	Lyons-Roberts	Small red	400.	800.	4500.

KL#	Series	Signatures	Seal	Fine	XF	CU
819	1882	Lyons-Treat	Small red	400.	800.	4500.
820	1882	Vernon-Treat	Small red	400.	800.	4500.
821	1882	Vernon-McClung	Small red	400.	800.	4500.
822	1882	Napier-McClung	Small red	400.	800.	4500.
823	1882	Napier-Thompson	Small red	475.	950.	6000.
824	1882	Napier-Burke	Small red	400.	800.	4500.
825	1882	Parker-Burke	Small red	400.	800.	4500.
826	1882	Teehee-Burke	Small red	400.	800.	4500.
827	1922	Speelman-White	Small red	150.	375.	1400.

National Gold Bank Notes

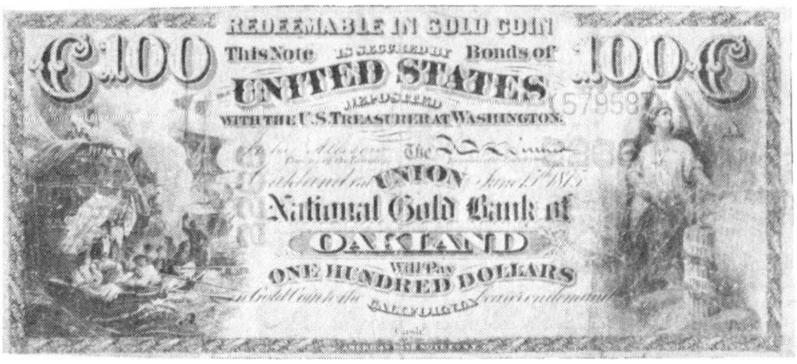

KL#	Series	Issuing Bank	Location	Good	Fine
828	Orig.	First Nat'l Gold Bank	San Francisco	4000.	Rare
829	1875	First Nat'l Gold Bank	San Francisco	4000.	Rare
830	Orig.	First Nat'l Gold Bank	Santa Barbara	4000.	Rare
831	Orig.	First Nat'l Gold Bank	Petaluma	4000.	Rare
832	1875	Union Nat'l Gold Bank	Oakland	4000.	Rare

Silver Certificates

The Countersigned Series:
Scofield-Gilfillan signatures. Blue serial numbers.
Type 3: Place of deposit, Washington, D.C.
Type 6: Place of deposit, San Francisco
Type 7: Place of deposit, New York.

KL#	Series	Countersigned by:	Type	Fine	XF	CU
833	1878	A. V. Wyman, Asst. U.S. Treas.	3		Very Rare	—
834	1878	R.M. Anthony, Asst. U.S. Treas.	6		Extremely Rare	—
835	1878	W.G. White, Asst. U.S. Treas.	7		Possibly exists	—

All have large red "100" below center seal.

KL#	Series	Signatures	Seal	Fine	XF	CU
		With large "C" below center seal.				
836	1880	Scofield-Gilfillan	Large brown	3500.	7500.	13,000.
837	1880	Bruce-Gilfillan	Large brown	3500.	7500.	13,000.
838	1880	Bruce-Wyman	Large brown	3500.	7500.	13,000.

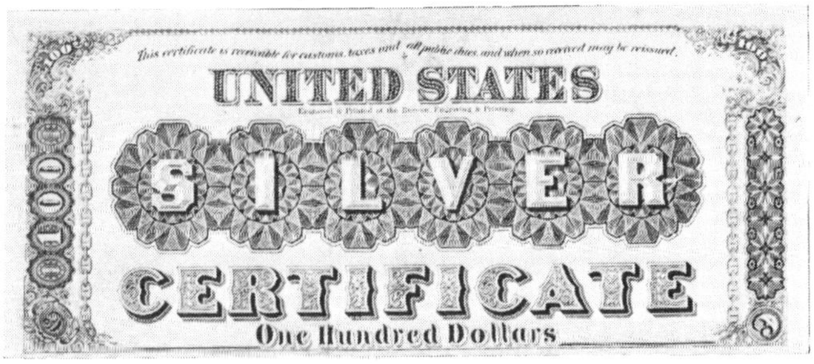

KL#	Series	Signatures	Seal	Fine	XF	CU
		No "C" below center seal.				
839	1880	Rosecrans-Huston	Large brown	2800.	6900.	12,000.
840	1880	Rosecrans-Nebeker	Small red	2800.	6900.	12,000.

KL#	Series	Signatures	Seal	Fine	XF	CU
841	1891	Rosecrans-Nebeker	Small red	850.	2600.	8500.
842	1891	Tillman-Morgan	Small red	850.	2600.	8500.

Treasury or Coin Notes

KL#	Series	Signatures	Seal	Fine	XF	CU
843	1890	Rosecrans-Huston	Large brown	7500.	15,000.	—

KL#	Series	Signatures	Seal	Fine	XF	CU
844	1891	Rosecrans-Nebeker	Small red	6000.	13,000.	—

Federal Reserve Notes
Series 1914

KL#	Bank	Signatures	Fine	XF	CU
		Red Seals			
845	Boston	Burke-Mc Adoo	175.	350.	1200.
846	New York	Burke-Mc Adoo	175.	350.	1200.
847	Philadelphia	Burke-Mc Adoo	175.	350.	1200.
848	Cleveland	Burke-Mc Adoo	175.	350.	1200.
849	Richmond	Burke-Mc Adoo	175.	350.	1200.
850	Atlanta	Burke-Mc Adoo	175.	350.	1200.
851	Chicago	Burke-Mc Adoo	175.	350.	1200.
852	St. Louis	Burke-Mc Adoo	175.	350.	1200.
853	Minneapolis	Burke-Mc Adoo	175.	350.	1200.
854	Kansas City	Burke-Mc Adoo	175.	350.	1200.
855	Dallas	Burke-Mc Adoo	175.	350.	1200.
856	San Francisco	Burke-Mc Adoo	175.	350.	1200.
		Blue Seals			
857	Boston	Burke-Mc Adoo	140.	190.	350.
858	Boston	Burke-Glass	140.	190.	350.
859	Boston	Burke-Houston	140.	190.	350.
860	Boston	White-Mellon	140.	190.	350.
861	New York	Burke-Mc Adoo	140.	190.	350.
862	New York	Burke-Glass	140.	190.	350.
863	New York	Burke-Houston	140.	190.	350.
864	New York	White-Mellon	140.	190.	350.
865	Philadelphia	Burke-Mc Adoo	140.	190.	350.
866	Philadelphia	Burke-Glass	140.	190.	350.
867	Philadelphia	Burke-Houston	140.	190.	350.
868	Philadelphia	White-Mellon	140.	190.	350.
869	Cleveland	Burke-Mc Adoo	140.	190.	350.
870	Cleveland	Burke-Glass	140.	190.	350.
871	Cleveland	Burke-Huston	140.	190.	350.
872	Cleveland	White-Mellon	140.	190.	350.
873	Richmond	Burke-Mc Adoo	140.	190.	350.
874	Richmond	Burke-Glass	140.	190.	350.
875	Richmond	Burke-Houston	140.	190.	350.
876	Richmond	White-Mellon	140.	190.	350.
877	Atlanta	Burke-Mc Adoo	140.	190.	350.
878	Atlanta	Burke-Glass	140.	190.	350.
879	Atlanta	Burke-Houston	140.	190.	350.
880	Atlanta	White-Mellon	140.	190.	350.
881	Chicago	Burke-Mc Adoo	140.	190.	350.
882	Chicago	Burke-Glass	140.	190.	350.
883	Chicago	Burke-Houston	140.	190.	350.
884	Chicago	White-Mellon	140.	190.	350.
885	St. Louis	Burke-Mc Adoo	140.	190.	350.
886	St. Louis	Burke-Glass	140.	190.	350.
887	St. Louis	Burke-Houston	140.	190.	350.
888	St. Louis	White-Mellon	140.	190.	350.
889	Minneapolis	Burke-Mc Adoo	140.	190.	350.
890	Minneapolis	Burke-Glass	140.	190.	350.
891	Minneapolis	Burke-Houston	140.	190.	350.
892	Minneapolis	White-Mellon	140.	190.	350.
893	Kansas City	Burke-Mc Adoo	140.	190.	350.
894	Kansas City	Burke-Glass	140.	190.	350.
895	Kansas City	Burke-Houston	140.	190.	350.
896	Kansas City	White-Mellon	140.	190.	350.
897	Dallas	Burke-Mc Adoo	140.	190.	350.
898	Dallas	Burke-Glass	140.	190.	350.
899	Dallas	Burke-Houston	140.	190.	350.
900	Dallas	White-Mellon	140.	190.	350.
901	San Francisco	Burke-Mc Adoo	140.	190.	350.
902	San Francisco	Burke-Glass	140.	190.	350.
903	San Francisco	Burke-Houston	140.	190.	350.
904	San Francisco	White-Mellon	140.	190.	350.

Five Hundred Dollars

United States Notes

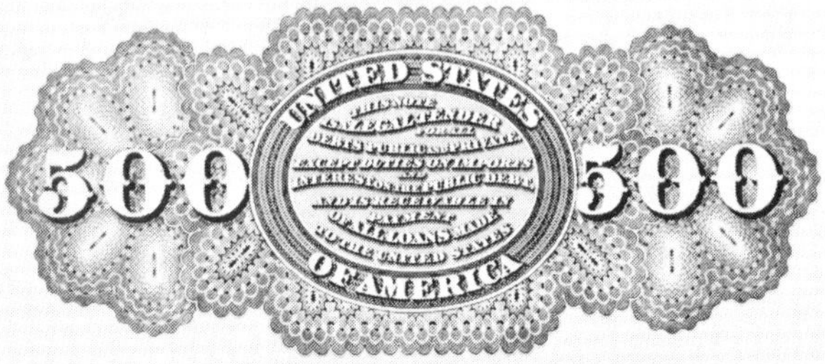

KL#	Series	Signatures	Seal	Fine	XF	CU
		First Obligation inscription on back. Red serial numbers.				
904A	1862	Chittenden-Spinner	Small red			(Extremely rare)
		Second Obligation inscription on back. Red serial numbers.				
905	1862	Chittenden-Spinner	Small red			(Extremely rare)
906	1863	Chittenden-Spinner	Small red			(Extremely rare)
		Blue serial numbers.				
907	1869	Allison-Spinner	Large red			(Extremely rare)
908	1874	Allison-Spinner	Small red			(Two known)
909	1875	Allison-New	Small red			(Extremely rare)
910	1875	Allison-Wyman	Small red			(Extremely rare)

KL#	Series	Signatures	Seal	Fine	XF	CU
911	1878	Allison-Gilfillan	Small red			(Three known)
912	1880	Scofield-Gilfillan	Large brown			(Extremely rare)
913	1880	Bruce-Wyman	Large brown			(Extremely rare)
914	1880	Rosecrans-Jordan	Large red			(Extremely rare)
915	1880	Rosecrans-Hyatt	Large red			(Extremely rare)
916	1880	Rosecrans-Huston	Large red			(Extremely rare)
917	1880	Rosecrans-Nebeker	Large brown			(Extremely rare)
918	1880	Tillman-Morgan	Small red			(Extremely rare)
919	1880	Bruce-Roberts	Small red			(Extremely rare)
920	1880	Lyons-Roberts	Small red			(Extremely rare)
921	1880	Napier-Mc Clung	Small red			(Extremely rare)

Compound Interest Treasury Notes

KL#	Act	Overprint Date	Signatures	Fine	XF	CU
922	1863	June 10, 1864	Chittenden-Spinner			(Unknown)
923	1864	July 15, 1864	Chittenden-Spinner			(Unknown)
924	1864	Aug. 15, 1864-Oct. 1, 1865	Colby-Spinner			(Unknown)

Interest Bearing Notes

KL#	Act	Term	Signatures	Fine	XF	CU
925	1863	One year	Chittenden-Spinner			(Unknown)
925A	1861	Two years	Chittenden-Spinner			(Unknown)
926	1863	Two years	Chittenden-Spinner			(Unknown)
927	1861	Three years	Chittenden-Spinner			(Unknown)
928	1864	Three years	Colby-Spinner			(Extremely rare)
929	1865	Three years	Colby-Spinner			(Unknown)

Gold Certificates

KL#	Issue/Act/Series	Signatures	Fine	XF	CU
930	First/1863	Colby-Spinner			(Unknown)
931	Second/1863	Allison-Spinner			(Unknown)
932	Third/1863/1875	Allison-New			(Unknown)

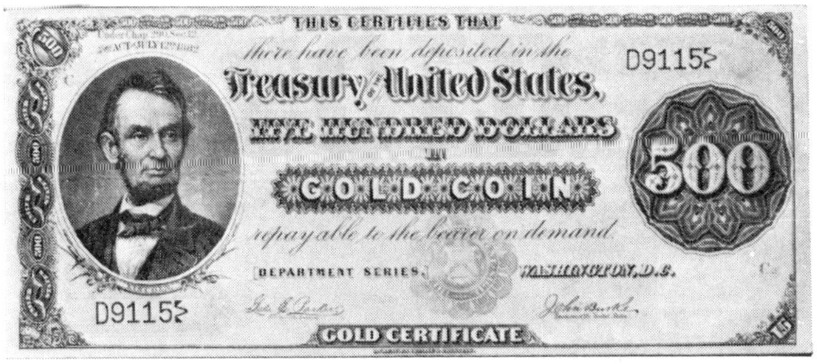

KL#	Issue/Act/Series	Signatures	Fine	XF	CU
933	1882	Bruce-Gilfillan (countersigned)			(Rare)
934	1882	Bruce-Gilfillan			(Rare)
935	1882	Bruce-Wyman			(Rare)
936	1882	Rosecrans-Hyatt			(Rare)
937	1882	Lyons-Roberts			(Rare)
938	1882	Parker-Burke			(Rare)
939	1882	Teehee-Burke			(Rare)
940	1922	Speelman-White			(Rare)

National Gold Bank Notes

KL#	Series	Issuing Bank	Location	Good	Fine
941	1875	First National Gold Bank	San Francisco		
942	Orig.	National Gold Bank and Trust Company	San Francisco		
943	Orig.	National Gold Bank of D.O. Mills and Company	Sacramento		

(Four of the above remain unredeemed, none are known)

Silver Certificates

The Countersigned Series
Scofield-Gilfillan signatures. Blue serial numbers.
Type 3: Place of deposit, Washington, D.C.
Type 6: Place of deposit, San Francisco
Type 7: Place of deposit, New York

KL#	Series	Countersigned by:	Type	Fine	XF	CU
944	1878	W.G. White, Asst. Treas.	7			(Unknown)
945	1878	J.C. Hopper, Asst. Treas.	7			(Unknown)
946	1878	T. Hillhouse, Asst. Treas.	7			(Unknown)
947	1878	R.M. Anthony, Asst. Treas.	6			(Unknown)
948	1878	A.U. Wyman, Asst. Treas.	3			(Unknown)

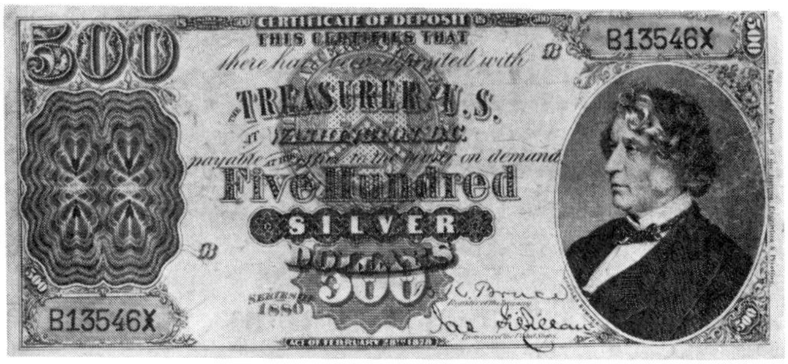

KL#	Series	Signatures	Seal	Fine	XF	CU
949	1880	Scofield-Gilfillan	Brown			(Unknown)
950	1880	Bruce-Gilfillan	Brown			(3 known)
951	1880	Bruce-Wyman	Brown			(1 known)

Federal Reserve Notes
Series 1918

KL#	Bank	Signatures	Fine	XF	CU
952	Boston	Burke-Glass			(Rare)
953	New York	Burke-Glass			(Rare)
954	New York	White-Mellon			(2 known)
955	Philadelphia	Burke-Glass			(Rare)
956	Cleveland	Burke-Glass			(Rare)
957	Richmond				(Unknown)
958	Atlanta	Burke-Glass			(Rare)
959	Chicago	Burke-McAdoo			(Rare)
960	Chicago	Burke-Glass			(Rare)
961	St. Louis				(Unknown)
962	Minneapolis				(Unknown)
963	Kansas City	Burke-Glass			(Rare)
964	Dallas	Burke-Glass			(Rare)
965	San Francisco	Burke-Glass			(Rare)

One Thousand Dollars
United States Notes

KL#	Series	Signatures	Seal	Fine	XF	CU
		First Obligation inscription on back. Red serial numbers.				
966	1862	Chittenden-Spinner	Small red			(Extremely rare)
		Second Obligation inscription on back. Red serial numbers.				
967	1862	Chittenden-Spinner	Small red			(Extremely rare)
968	1863	Chittenden-Spinner	Small red			(Extremely rare)
		Blue serial numbers				

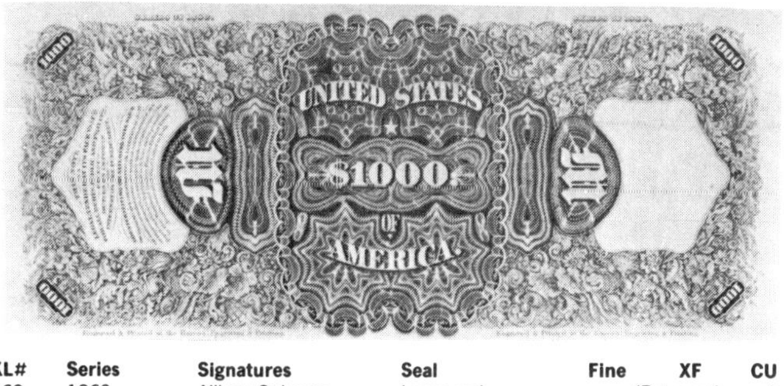

KL#	Series	Signatures	Seal	Fine	XF	CU
969	1869	Allison-Spinner	Large red			(Extremely rare)
970	1878	Allison-Gilfillan	Small red			(Extremely rare)
971	1880	Bruce-Wyman	Large brown			(Extremely rare)
972	1880	Rosecrans-Jordan	Large red			(Extremely rare)
973	1880	Rosecrans-Hyatt	Large red			(Extremely rare)
974	1880	Rosecrans-Huston	Large red			(Extremely rare)
975	1880	Rosecrans-Nebeker	Large brown			(Extremely rare)
976	1880	Tillman-Morgan	Small red			(Extremely rare)
977	1880	Tillman-Roberts	Small red			(Extremely rare)
978	1880	Bruce-Roberts	Small red			(Extremely rare)
979	1880	Lyons-Roberts	Small red			(Extremely rare)
980	1880	Vernon-Treat	Small red			(Extremely rare)
981	1880	Napier-McClung	Small red			(Extremely rare)

Compound Interest Treasury Notes

KL#	Act	Overprint Date	Signatures	Fine	XF	CU
982	1864	July 15, 1864	Chittenden-Spinner			(Unknown)
983	1864	Aug. 15, 1864-Sept. 15, 1865	Colby-Spinner			(Unknown)

Interest Bearing Notes

KL#	Act	Signatures	Fine	XF	CU
984	1863	Chittenden-Spinner			(Unknown)
984A	1861	Chittenden-Spinner			(Unknown)
985	1863	Chittenden-Spinner			(Unknown)
986	1861	Chittenden-Spinner			(Unknown)
987	1864	Colby-Spinner			(Unknown)
988	1865	Colby-Spinner			(1 known)

Gold Certificates

KL#	Issue/Act/Series	Signatures	Fine	XF	CU
989	First/1863	Colby-Spinner			(Unknown)
990	Second/1863	Allison-Spinner			(Unknown)
991	Third/1863/1875	Allison-New			(Unknown)

KL#	Series	Signatures	Seal	Fine	XF	CU
992	1882	Bruce-Gilfillan (countersigned)	Large brown			(Rare)
993	1882	Bruce-Gilfillan	Large brown			(Rare)
994	1882	Bruce-Wyman	Large brown			(Rare)
995	1882	Rosecrans-Hyatt	Large red			(Rare)
996	1882	Rosecrans-Huston	Large brown			(Rare)
997	1882	Rosecrans-Nebeker	Small red			(Rare)

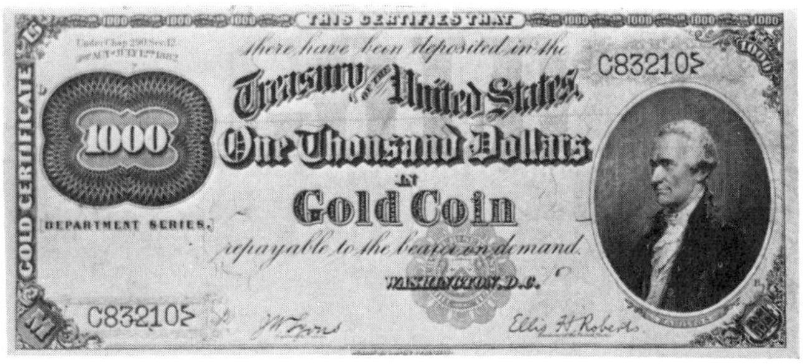

KL#	Series	Signatures	Seal	Fine	XF	CU
998	1882	Lyons-Roberts	Small red			(Rare)
999	1882	Lyons-Treat	Small red			(Rare)

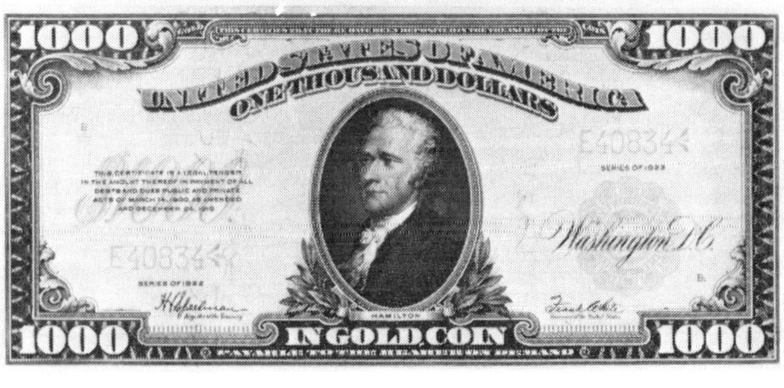

KL#	Series	Signatures	Seal	Fine	XF	CU
1000	1907	Vernon-Treat	Small red			(Rare)
1001	1907	Vernon-McClung	Small red			(Rare)
1002	1907	Napier-McClung	Small red			(Rare)
1003	1907	Parker-Burke	Small red			(Rare)
1004	1907	Teehee-Burke	Small red			(Rare)
1005	1907	Napier-Burke	Small red			(Rare)
1006	1907	Speelman-White	Small red			(Rare)

Silver Certificates

The Countersigned Series
Scofield-Gilfillan signatures. Blue serial numbers.
Type 3: Place of deposit, Washington, D.C.
Type 6: Place of deposit, San Francisco
Type 7: Place of deposit, New York

KL#	Series	Countersigned by:	Type	Fine	XF	CU
1007	1878	A.U. Wyman, Asst. Treas.	3			(Unknown)
1008	1878	R.M. Anthony, Asst. Treas.	6			(Unknown)
1009	1878	Unknown signers	7			(Unknown)

KL#	Series	Signatures	Seal	Fine	XF	CU
1010	1880	Scofield-Gilfillan	Large brown			(Unknown)
1011	1880	Bruce-Gilfillan	Large brown			(Unknown)
1012	1880	Bruce-Wyman	Large brown			(3 known)
1013	1891	Tillman-Morgan	Small red			(1 known)

Treasury or Coin Notes

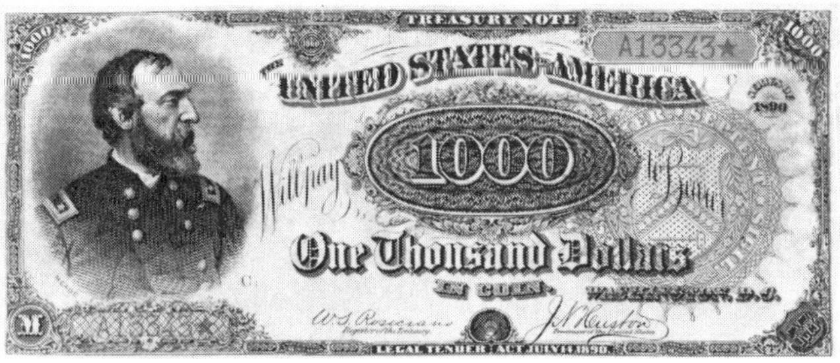

KL#	Series	Signatures	Seal	Fine	XF	CU
1014	1890	Rosecrans-Huston	Large brown			(3 known)
1015	1890	Rosecrans-Nebeker	Small red			(1 known)
1016	1891	Rosecrans-Nebeker	Small red			(1 known)
1017	1891	Tillman-Morgan	Small red			(1 known)

Federal Reserve Notes
Series 1918

KL#	Bank	Signatures	Fine	XF	CU
1018	Boston	Burke-Glass	—		(Rare)
1019	New York	Burke-Glass	—		(Rare)
1020	New York	Burke-Houston	—		(Rare)
1021	New York	White-Mellon	—		(Rare)
1022	Philadelphia	Burke-Glass	—		(Rare)
1023	Cleveland	Burke-Glass	—		(Rare)
1024	Richmond	Burke-Glass	—		(Rare)
1025	Atlanta	Burke-Glass	—		(Rare)
1026	Atlanta	White-Mellon	—		(3 known)
1027	Chicago	Burke-Glass	—		(Rare)
1028	St. Louis	Burke-Glass	—		(Rare)
1029	Minneapolis	Burke-Glass	—		(Rare)
1030	Kansas City	Burke-Glass	—		(Rare)
1031	Dallas	Burke-Glass	—		(Rare)
1032	San Francisco	Burke-Glass	—		(Rare)

Five Thousand Dollars
Interest Bearing Notes

KL#	Act	Term	Signatures	Fine	XF	CU
1044	1863	One year	Chittenden-Spinner			(Unknown)
1045	1861	Three years	Chittenden-Spinner			(Unknown)
1045A	1865	Three years	Colby-Spinner			(Unknown)

Gold Certificates

KL#	Issue/Act/Series	Signatures	Fine	XF	CU
1046	First/1863	Colby-Spinner			(Unknown)
1047	Second/1863	Allison-Spinner			(Unknown)
1048	Third/1863/1875	Allison-New			(Unknown)

KL#	Series	Signatures	Seal	Fine	XF	CU
1049	1882	Bruce-Gilfillan (countersigned)	Large brown		(Extremely rare)	
1050	1882	Bruce-Gilfillan	Large brown		(Extremely rare)	
1051	1882	Bruce-Wyman	Large brown		(Extremely rare)	
1052	1882	Rosecrans-Hyatt	Large red		(Extremely rare)	
1053	1882	Rosecrans-Nebeker	Small red		(Extremely rare)	
1054	1882	Lyons-Roberts	Small red		(Extremely rare)	
1055	1882	Vernon-Treat	Small red		(Extremely rare)	
1056	1882	Vernon-McClung	Small red		(Extremely rare)	
1057	1882	Napier-McClung	Small red		(Extremely rare)	
1058	1882	Parker-Burke	Small red		(Extremely rare)	
1059	1882	Teehee-Burke	Small red		(Extremely rare)	
1059A	1888	Rosecrans-Hyatt	Large red		(Extremely rare)	
1059B	1888	Rosecrans-Nebeker	Small red		(Extremely rare)	
1059C	1888	Lyons-Roberts	Small red		(Extremely rare)	

Federal Reserve Notes
Series 1918

KL#	Bank	Signatures	Fine	XF	CU
1060	Boston	Burke-Glass			(Unknown)
1061	New York	Burke-Glass			(Unknown)
1062	Cleveland	Burke-Glass			(Unknown)
1063	Richmond	Burke-Glass			(Unknown)
1064	Atlanta	Burke-Glass			(Unknown)
1065	Chicago	Burke-Glass			(1 known)
1066	St. Louis	Burke-Glass			(Unknown)
1067	San Francisco	Burke-Glass			(Unknown)

Ten Thousand Dollars
Gold Certificates

KL#	Issue/Act/Series	Signatures	Fine	XF	CU
1068	First/1863	Colby-Spinner			(Unknown)
1069	Second/1863	Allison-Spinner			(Unknown)
1070	Third/1863/1875	Allison-New			(Unknown)

KL#	Series	Signatures	Seal	Fine	XF	CU
1071	1882	Bruce-Gilfillan (countersigned)	Large brown		(Extremely rare)	
1072	1882	Bruce-Gilfillan	Large brown		(Extremely rare)	
1073	1882	Bruce-Wyman	Large brown		(Extremely rare)	
1074	1882	Rosecrans-Hyatt	Large red		(Extremely rare)	
1075	1882	Rosecrans-Nebeker	Small red		(Extremely rare)	
1076	1882	Lyons-Roberts	Small red		(Extremely rare)	
1077	1882	Vernon-Treat	Small red		(Extremely rare)	
1078	1882	Teehee-Burke	Small red		(Extremely rare)	
1078A	1888	Rosecrans-Hyatt	Large red		(Extremely rare)	
1078B	1888	Rosecrans-Nebeker	Small red		(Extremely rare)	
1078C	1888	Lyons Roberts	Small red		(Extremely rare)	
1079	1900	Teehee-Burke	Small red		*	

*All outstanding 1900 $10,000 Gold Certificates are the result of a 1935 fire in a Treasury storage area in Washington, D.C. While fighting the fire, a quantity of these redeemed and cancelled notes was thrown out into the street, where the notes were picked up by passers-by. They have no redemption value, though they sometimes sell in the paper money hobby in the $400-$750 price range.

Federal Reserve Notes
Series 1918

KL#	Bank	Signatures	Fine	XF	CU
1080	Boston	Burke-Glass			(Unknown)
1081	New York	Burke-Glass			(1 known)
1082	Cleveland	Burke-Glass			(Unknown)
1083	Richmond	Burke-Glass			(Unknown)
1084	St. Louis	Burke-Glass			(Unknown)
1085	San Francisco	Burke-Glass			(Unknown)

National Bank Notes

In the 72 years of their issue by more than 14,000 "home town" banks across the United States, the $17,000,000,000 ($17 billion) worth of National Bank Notes issued between December, 1863, and May, 1935, represent the most popularly collected series of United States paper money in the hobby today.

Their long and historically, as well as financially, interesting life began with the National Currency Act being signed into law by President Abraham Lincoln on Feb. 25, 1863. The dual aim of the legislation was to provide a ready and steady market for the sale of United States bonds issued to finance Federal involvement in the Civil War, and to create a sound bank currency to replace the generally insecure issues of the state banks then in circulation.

While National Bank Notes were only one of seven different types of U.S. paper money in circulation virtually simultaneously during and after the Civil War, they represent more interesting variations and types than any other. For more than half a century, from the implementation of the National Currency Act in 1863 until the creation of the Federal Reserve System in 1914, the National Bank Notes were an important part of the paper money in circulation.

The composition of these notes and the individual histories behind each of the issuing banks and its officers present unlimited fascination for the modern hobbyist.

The National Currency era came to end in May, 1935, when the Comptroller of the Currency shipped the last National Bank Notes to the issuing bank. The United States bonds which the banks had purchased to secure the value of their Nationals in circulation were called in for payment, ending nearly three-quarters of a century of an important era of "Main Street Banking."

Six distinct series make up the National Bank Note issue; four in large size, two in small size. Large size Nationals are comprised of 1) The Original Series, 2) Series of 1875, 3) Series of 1882 and 4) Series of 1902. In small size, there are the Series of 1929, Type 1 and Type 2. Within each of the large size series, there are several varieties and subtypes.

Alternatively, the Nationals are sometimes grouped according to Charter Period, thus: First Charter, Original Series and Series of 1875; Second Charter, Series of 1882; Third Charter, Series of 1902, and Small Size.

The terms Charter Period and Charter Number are particularly important to National Bank Notes and refer to the issuing authority of each particular bank.

The original National Currency Act of 1863 provided that banks organized under its provisions be chartered as National Banks for a period of 20 years.

In anticipation of the expiration of those first charters in February, 1883, an act was passed on July 12, 1882, extending the banks' existence for another 20 years. A similar extension was granted with an Act of Congress on April 12, 1902, and just before the 1922 expiration date, the National Currency Act was amended to provide 99-year lives for all National banks. This, in turn, was amended five years later, on Feb. 25, 1927, with the endowment of perpetual succession of their corporate identity on National banks.

A better understanding of National Bank Notes as a whole can be gained by a study of the several unique component parts of the National Currency issues.

Charter Number. Upon the approval of its organization as a National Bank, the Comptroller would issue each bank a unique charter number, designating its place on the roster of all such banks. Charter No. 1 was issued to The First National Bank of Philadelphia in June, 1863. Charter No. 14320, the highest to appear on a National Bank Note, was issued in early 1935 to The Liberty National Bank & Trust Company, Louisville, Ky.

The very earliest Original Series National Bank Notes were not required to have their charter number imprinted. However, when it was discovered that notes being presented at the Treasury for redemption could not be quickly sorted, an Act of June 20, 1874, was passed, requiring the charter number be overprinted twice on the face of each note. In the 1882 revision of the National Currency Act, the printing of the charter number as part of the engraved border design in six different places on the face of the note was required; this to facilitate the redemption of partial notes. The 1882 act also required the surcharge of the number on the face, and its printing in the center of the back, giving rise to the popular Series 1882 Brown Back type notes. The

Aldrich-Vreeland Act of May 30, 1908, provided for dropping the charter number from the back of the note, thus creating the 1882 Date Back and Value Back series.

The Series of 1902 notes, authorized by the Act of April 12, 1902, again provided for the engraving of the charter number six times on the face border, and overprinting of the number twice on the face.

The small size National Bank Notes which debuted in 1929 were no longer printed from plates specially engraved for each bank. Rather, for the Type 1 notes, the charter number was overprinted twice in black on the face, along with the bank, city and state names, and the officers' signatures. On the Type 2 small size Nationals, the charter number was printed an extra two times on the face, in brown ink, matching the Treasury seal and serial numbers.

Bank Title. Each National bank's title, once approved by the Comptroller of the Currency, was engraved on the face of all currency printing plates for that bank. On large size Nationals, the title, along with city and state of the bank's location, is printed in a variety of bold and interesting type faces in the center of the note. On small size Nationals, the title is printed to the left of the portrait. Prior to May 1, 1886, it took an act of Congress to change the title of a National Bank. Legislation on that date, though, gave the banks authority to change their name upon a vote of the stockholders and with the approval of the Comptroller of the Currency.

Date. While the engraved date near the title on the face of all large size National Bank Notes remains something of an enigma, it is generally believed to have been chosen by the Comptroller of the Currency to represent the approximate date of issue for the note. This is not an absolute indicator of issue, though, and thus has little significance to the collector.

Treasury Serial Number. From the first issues of National Bank Notes of Dec. 21, 1863, to Aug. 22, 1925, all National Bank Notes carried a U.S. Treasury serial number on the face of the note. On all notes except the $1 and $2, the Treasury serial number appears somewhere in the upper right of the note. On the First Charter $1 and $2 notes, the Treasury number runs vertically at the left end of the note. After Aug. 22, 1925, the Treasury number was replaced by a second impression of the issuing bank's serial number.

Bank Serial Number. Found on all National Bank Notes, except for the small size Type 2 notes, it indicates how many impressions of a particular plate configuration had been printed for a bank. For the Type 2 small size notes, the bank serial number is an indicator of how many notes of a particular denomination had been issued by a bank.

Treasury Signatures. On all National Bank Notes, the engraved signatures of the Register of the Treasury and the Treasurer of the U.S. appear on the face, usually just above center, the Register's to the left of the bank title, and the Treasurer's to the right; though there are exceptions to this placement. The particular combination of these signatures can pinpoint the period in which a plate was engraved for a given bank.

Bank Officers' Signatures. The original National Currency Act of 1863 required that each National Bank Note be signed by the Cashier and the bank's President or Vice President. These signatures, whether pen autographed, rubber stamped, or engraved, always appear at the bottom of the face of the note, the Cashier to the left, the President (or VP) to the right. The signatures gave a local stamp of approval to this type of currency, probably an important consideration when it was first issued and at a time when paper money was often distrusted. The thousands of persons whose signatures appear on National Bank Notes help give each individual note a unique history not found in other forms of U.S. currency.

Treasury Seal. Found on the face of all National Bank Notes, the overprinted Treasury seal was the final Federal authentication of the note, giving each note its validity as circulating currency. Generally found on the right side of the note's face, it varies in color (red, brown, blue), size and embellishment (8 or 12 scallops, 34 or 40 rays).

Geographic Letters. From 1902-1924, large block letters were overprinted with and near the bank's charter number on each National Bank Note to facilitate sorting at central redemption points. Each letter stood for a particular geographic area of the country where the issuing bank was located: N for New England, E for Eastern, S for Southern, M for Midwest, W for Western and P for Pacific.

Plate Position Letters. On all large size National Bank Notes, a letter from A through D appears twice on the face of the note to indicate from which position (top, 2nd, 3rd or bottom) on a printing plate the note had been produced. Because the great variety of plate configurations used, there is little significance attached by collectors to plate letters, except perhaps in the case of bank serial number 1 notes, in which case the A-position notes might be of greater value.

Among small size Nationals, the plate position letter is part of the serial number. On Series 1929 Nationals, the prefix letter of the serial number is the plate position. Since 1929s were printed six-up in a sheet, the plate positions letters (prefix) run from A through F.

Denominations. National Bank Notes were authorized, over the course of their history, in denominations of $1, $2, $3, $5, $10, $20, $50, $100, $500, $1,000, and $10,000. No notes of the $3 or $10,000 denomination were printed. No surviving $1,000 Nationals are known, although the Treasury still reports 21 outstanding. Only three, of a reported-outstanding 173, $500 Nationals are known in collections.

It should also be noted that not all banks issued all denominations in all series.

Circulation. While the original National Banking Act of Feb. 25, 1863, authorized state, as well as National, banks to issue circulating currency upon deposit of U.S. bonds with the Treasury as security, no state banks took advantage of this privilege before it was withdrawn from them by the Act of June 3, 1864, leaving the National banks in a monopoly position as far as bank-issued currency.

The 1863 legislation allowed National banks to issue notes to the total of 90% of the market value of specified series of United States bonds which they had deposited with the Treasurer of the United States. The revision of June 3, 1864, limited the total amount of National Bank Notes in circulation to $300 million; while a provision to apportion that total was added in March 3, 1865, legislation. That act — which also imposed a 10% tax on state bank notes in circulation, effectively killing them off — specified that half of the circulation be apportioned on the basis of population, and half on the basis of banking capital.

In 1870, additional circulation of $54 million was added to the total, and measures taken to more equitably distribute it, while a $500,000 circulation per bank limit was imposed. In 1875, the restrictions on a per bank basis, as well as total circulation, were taken off. In 1900, banks were allowed to issue notes to the full 100% market value of their bond deposits, instead of the 90%.

The circulation privilege was effectively withdrawn in favor of the Federal Reserve Bank System in July, 1935, when the last of the U.S. bonds carrying that privilege were called in. No new bonds of the type have been issued since.

Closing. A National bank could wind up its affairs in one of three manners, as specified by law.

A bank which violated provisions of the current legislation or charter, or which refused to redeem its notes, could be placed in charge of a receiver by order of the Comptroller of the Currency. It may have been allowed to reopen if it could be proved to be sound. If not, the receiver liquidated the bank's assets so as to provide for meeting the greatest amount of the bank's liabilities.

A bank could also go into voluntary liquidation on a two-thirds vote of the stockholders. Such might be done to allow the bank to be absorbed by or to absorb and consolidate with another bank, either National or state.

After Nov. 18, 1918, a National Bank could also close its corporate doors by consolidating with another bank, but not liquidating its assets.

National Bank Note Chronology

Act of Feb. 25, 1863. The original National Currency Act allowed banks with more than $50,000 capital to organize as National banks. Before starting business as such, the bank was required to deposit with the Treasurer of the United States, specified U.S. bonds to the amount of not less than one-third of its capital stock. With that deposit, the Comptroller of the Currency would issue the bank its "Certificate of Authority to Commence Business," its charter. Banks organized under this act were given a corporate life of 20 years from the date of the act.

Act of June 3, 1864. This act provided that any National bank now organized would have a 20-year charter from the date of organization. It also required that bonds deposited against note-issue be registered, interest bearing U.S. bonds.

Act of March 3, 1865. Besides provision mentioned in the earlier text, this allowed state banks with branches to convert to National status. At that time, National banks were not allowed to establish branch banks.

Act of July 12, 1870. This act provided for the organization of National Gold Banks. Subject to greater restrictions than other National Banks, the National Gold Banks could issue currency only to the total of 80% of their deposited bonds, and had to maintain in their vaults gold and silver equal to 25% of their circulation.

Act of Feb. 14, 1880. The act permitted the conversion of National Gold Banks to regular National banks, and allowed them to keep their original date of organization.

Act of July 12, 1882. This act created the Second Charter Period, allowing National banks to extend their charters for another 20 years.

Act of March 14, 1900. This act greatly increased the number of

National banks by allowing the organization of banks with a minimum of $25,000 capital in localities of fewer than 3,000 population.

Act of April 12, 1902. This act created the Third Charter Period by extending the charters of banks chartered or re-chartered under the 1882 act for another 20 years.

Act of May 30, 1908. A response to the financial panic of 1907, this act, known as the Aldrich-Vreeland Act, allowed the formation of voluntary National Currency Associations. To form such an association required at least 10 National banks with a total of at least $50 million in capital and a surplus of at least 2. After formation, such associations could deposit "other securities" against which they could circulate notes to the extent of 75% of their value. These other securities were usually short-term notes, payable within six months. Due to expire on June 30, 1914, the act was extended by the Federal Reserve Act of Dec. 23, 1913, to June 30, 1915, when it did expire.

Act of July 1, 1922. The act provided that all National banks then in existence would have a corporate life of 99 years from the date of the legislation. All National banks organized after this date would have a corporate existence of 99 years from the date of organization.

Act of Feb. 25, 1927. This act provided perpetual corporate life for all National banks then in existence or to be organized in the future. It also allowed National banks to establish branch banks and for the assumption of state banks by National banks.

First Charter Notes

Although the First Charter Period ran from Feb. 25, 1863, through July 11, 1882, notes of the First Charter type were issued until 1902, a 40-year period. This was due to the authorizing legislation which granted a National bank a charter good for 20 years from the date of reorganization, not the date of the National Bank Act (Feb. 25, 1863). Once a bank was chartered in this period, it issued the same type of notes for 20 years, despite the fact that the Second Charter Period may have come into effect (July 12, 1902) during the course of that time. When the bank's original 20-year charter expired, and it was re-chartered under the Second (or even Third) Period, it would begin issue of Second (or Third) Period notes, as appropriate to the date of its charter extension.

During the First Charter period, two different series of notes were issued, Original Series and Series of 1875.

Notes of the Original Series appeared in denominations from $1 through $1,000, and are distinguishable principally by their lack of overprinted charter numbers, although some banks did issue Original Series notes with charter numbers surcharged. The nearly identical Series 1875 notes all have red (or in rare cases, black) charter numbers imprinted, along with the notation at the left of the bank title "Series 1875."

Serial numbers of First Charter notes appear in either red or blue, with the blue variety being the scarcer.

Obligation of the face of the note reads: "This note is secured by bonds of the United States deposited with the U.S. Treasurer in Washington ... The (name and location of bank) will pay the bearer on demand — dollars." On back, there is the inscription: "This note is receivable at par in all parts of the United States, in payment of all taxes and excises and other dues to the United States, except duties on imports, and also for all salaries and other debts and demands owing by the United States to individuals, corporations and associations within the United States, except interest on the public debt."

Second Charter Notes

Three distinct note issues make up the National Currency of the Second Charter Period, July 12, 1882, through April 11, 1902. These types differ principally in their back designs for which collectors have evolved the nicknames Brown Back, Date Back and Value Back.

Like the notes of the First Charter Period, the Second Charter Period currency was issued for a span of 40 years, until 1922, when all charters had to be renewed.

The Brown Backs of Series 1882 were placed in circulation that year, and were issued until 1908. The Brown Backs take their name from the large charter number printed on the back in the center of two cartouches of geometric design in brown ink. All other printing on back was also in the brown shades which matched the predominant color of the note's face.

Called Date Backs because of the large 1882-1908 dates on their green-printed backs, the second issue of Series 1882 Nationals was a result of the previously described Aldrich-Vreeland Act. Denominations from $5-$100 were in circulation from June, 1908, to July, 1916, and the $50s and $100s continued current in this type until 1922. Date Back 1882 Nationals were issued only by banks which had issued Brown Backs, and the charters of which were still in force. Those banks whose charter expired in the 1908-1916 period were re-chartered and issued notes of the Third Charter Period.

The expiration of the Aldrich-Vreeland Act in 1915 gave rise to the third type of Series 1882 Nationals, the rare Value Backs (sometimes called Denomination Backs). As implied, the name comes from the large spelled-out indication of value in the center of the back design. As a type, they are the rarest of National Bank Notes, having been issued in the period 1916-1922 by banks which had issued the Date Back type and for which the charter was still in effect. Naturally, this number dwindled each successive year as banks were re-chartered and their note issues switched to the Third Period types.

The Date Back and Value Back notes of Series 1882 were something of emergency issues, produced at a time when it was felt an increase in the supply of currency in circulation was needed to combat hard times. Accordingly, for their issue, the Treasury accepted certain securities other than U.S. bonds on deposit against circulation. This addition is stated on the obligations of these notes.

Third Charter Notes

Passed to extend the life of those National banks whose charters were coming to expiration beginning in 1902, the Currency Act of April 12, 1902, created the Third Charter Period and the three distinct types of National Currency issued thereunder.

In 1922, Congress did away with the need for continual renewing of charters every 20 years by granting Nationals banks perpetual charters to operate.

Issued from 1902 until they were replaced by the small size National Currency in 1929, the Third Charter Nationals represented a change in design to distinguish them from the notes of the Second Charter Period.

The first issue of the Third Charter Period was the popular and often-rare Red Seals. Issued only from 1902-1908, due to the intervention of the Aldrich-Vreeland Emergency Money Act, the Red Seals were issued for a shorter period and by fewer banks than the other two Third Charter types. Their rarity, and the fact that they were issued by every U.S. state and Territory except Hawaii, make them a challenge among collectors who seek to build a state set of this type.

The latter two issues of the Third Charter Period both feature blue Treasury seals, and are principally distinguished by their backs.

The Series 1902 Date Back carries the dates 1902 and 1908 in the white space on the upper back. Like the Second Charter Date Backs, they are something of an emergency issue, having been released during the term of the Aldrich-Vreeland Act, 1908-1915, with the $50s and $100, as in Series 1882, being issued later, until 1926.

Upon expiration of that emergency currency measure, the issues of the Third Charter Period continued with the 1902 Plain Backs, named thus for their lack of the 1902-1908 dates on back. The most plentiful of all National Bank Notes, they were issued from 1915 to 1929, when they were superceded by the small size issue.

Small Size Nationals

When the rest of the currency classes were "down-sized" in July, 1929, the National Bank Notes were included. At the same time, their designs were standardized to fit in with the other types of notes in the same denominations.

Two separate types of small size Nationals were issued. Type 1, current from July, 1929-May, 1933, is distinguished chiefly by the appearance of the bank charter number only twice on the face of the note, in heavy black numerals. Serial numbers of the Type 1 notes consisted of a prefix letter A through F (corresponding to the note's position on the printing plate), six digits and the suffix A (or B, in the case of Ch. No. 2379, The Chase N.B., New York City, the only bank to issue more than six million small size notes in any denomination). The Type 2 Series 1929 Nationals had the same two charter imprints as Type 1, but had an extra pair in brown ink alongside the serial numbers. Serial numbering of the Type 2 notes was also different, being made up of a prefix letter A (B only in the case of The Bank of America National Trust and Savings Association of San Francisco) along with six digits.

The obligation was changed on the Series 1929 Nationals, to read as follows: "National Currency secured by United States bonds deposited with the Treasurer of the United Starts of America ... The (bank name and city/state) will pay to the bearer on demand — dollars." At right, across the brown Treasury seal, was the obligation: "Redeemable in lawful money of the United States at United States Treasury or at the bank of issue."

The calling in of the bonds which secured the National Currency issue ended this Golden Era for U.S. paper money in May, 1935.

Surviving National Bank Notes

Of the approximately $17 billion worth of National Currency issued between 1863-1935, it is estimated that some $50 million worth remain outstanding today, with most knowlegeable observers are in agreement that the surviving amount is about equally divided between large and small size issues, representing about 3/10s of 1% of the total issue.

National Bank Notes for Type Collectors

While it is not the most popular method of collecting National Currency, there is some demand for National Bank Notes by type and signature variety. Generally, only the highest grade notes from the most common banks are collected in this manner.

The listing below provides indication of which signature combinations were issued, and relative values for those notes on the most common banks of issue.

KL#	Type	Denom.	Signatures	VG	VF	CU
1086	Orig	$1	Colby Spinner	85.00	160.	800.
1087	Orig	$1	Jeffries-Spinner	600.	1100.	2500.
1088	Orig	$1	Allison-Spinner	85.00	160.	800.
1089	1875	$1	Allison-New	85.00	160.	650.
1090	1875	$1	Allison-Wyman	85.00	160.	650.
1091	1875	$1	Allison-Gilfillan	85.00	160.	650.
1092	1875	$1	Scofield-Gilfillan	85.00	160.	650.
1093	Orig	$2	Colby-Spinner	245.	450.	2000.
1094	Orig	$2	Jeffries-Spinner	1100.	1650.	4000.
1095	Orig	$2	Allison-Spinner	245.	450.	2000.
1096	1875	$2	Allison-New	225.	425.	1850.
1097	1875	$2	Allison-Wyman	225.	425.	1850.
1098	1875	$2	Allison-Gilfillan	225.	425.	1850.
1099	1875	$2	Scofield-Gilfillan	225.	425.	1850.
1100	Orig	$5	Chittenden-Spinner	90.00	300.	1250.
1101	Orig	$5	Colby-Spinner	90.00	300.	1250.
1102	Orig	$5	Jeffries-Spinner	600.	1500.	3500.
1103	Orig	$5	Allison-Spinner	90.00	300.	1250.
1104	1875	$5	Allison-New (Black Ch)	—	—	—
1105	1875	$5	Allison-New (Red Ch)	80.00	250.	1000.
1106	1875	$5	Allison-Wyman	80.00	250.	1000.
1107	1875	$5	Allison-Gilfillan	80.00	250.	1000.
1108	1875	$5	Scofield-Gilfillan	80.00	250.	1000.
1109	1875	$5	Bruce-Gilfillan	80.00	250.	1000.
1110	1875	$5	Bruce-Wyman	80.00	250.	1000.
1111	1875	$5	Bruce-Jordan	600.	1500.	3200.
1112	1875	$5	Rosecrans-Huston	80.00	250.	1000.
1113	1875	$5	Rosecrans-Jordan	80.00	250.	1000.
1114	'82BB	$5	Bruce-Gilfillan	75.00	125.	300.
1115	'82BB	$5	Bruce-Wyman	75.00	125.	300.
1116	'82BB	$5	Bruce-Jordan	75.00	125.	300.
1117	'82BB	$5	Rosecrans-Jordan	75.00	125.	300.
1118	'82BB	$5	Rosecrans-Hyatt	75.00	125.	300.
1119	'82BB	$5	Rosecrans-Houston	75.00	125.	300.
1120	'82BB	$5	Rosecrans-Nebeker	75.00	125.	300.
1121	'82BB	$5	Rosecrans-Morgan	200.	400.	1000.
1122	'82BB	$5	Tillman-Morgan	75.00	125.	300.
1123	'82BB	$5	Tillman-Roberts	75.00	125.	300.
1124	'82BB	$5	Bruce-Roberts	75.00	125.	300.
1125	'82BB	$5	Lyons-Roberts	75.00	125.	300.
1126	'82BB	$5	Vernon-Treat	75.00	125.	300.
1127	'82BB	$5	Rosecrans-Huston	55.00	100.	400.
1128	'82DB	$5	Rosecrans-Nebeker	55.00	100.	400.
1129	'82DB	$5	Rosecrans-Morgan	300.	750.	1800.
1130	'82DB	$5	Tillman-Morgan	55.00	100.	400.
1131	'82DB	$5	Tillman-Roberts	55.00	100.	400.
1132	'82DB	$5	Bruce-Roberts	55.00	100.	400.
1133	'82DB	$5	Lyons-Roberts	55.00	100.	400.
1134	'82DB	$5	Vernon-Treat	55.00	100	400.
1135	'82DB	$5	Napier-McClung	75.00	150.	800.
1136	'82VB	$5	Tillman-Morgan	85.00	220.	650.
1137	'82VB	$5	Tillman-Roberts	85.00	220.	650.
1138	'82VB	$5	Lyons-Roberts	85.00	220.	650.
1139	'82VB	$5	Bruce-Roberts	85.00	220.	650.
1140	'82VB	$5	Vernon-Treat	85.00	220.	650.
1141	'82VB	$5	Napier-McClung	85.00	220.	650.
1142	'82VB	$5	Teehee-Burke	125.	300.	2500.
1143	'02RS	$5	Lyons-Roberts	65.00	150.	300.
1144	'02RS	$5	Lyons-Treat	65.00	150.	300.
1145	'02RS	$5	Vernon-Treat	65.00	150.	300.
1146	'02DB	$5	Lyons-Roberts	20.00	45.00	150.
1147	'02DB	$5	Lyons-Treat	20.00	45.00	150.
1148	'02DB	$5	Vernon-Treat	20.00	45.00	150.
1149	'02DB	$5	Vernon-McClung	20.00	45.00	150.
1150	'02DB	$5	Napier-McClung	20.00	45.00	150.
1151	'02DB	$5	Napier-Thompson	30.00	70.00	400.
1152	'02DB	$5	Napier-Burke	20.00	45.00	150.
1153	'02DB	$5	Parker-Burke	20.00	45.00	150.
1154	'02DB	$5	Teehee-Burke	40.00	100.	300.
1155	'02PB	$5	Lyons-Roberts	20.00	45.00	125.
1156	'02PB	$5	Lyons-Treat	20.00	45.00	125.
1157	'02PB	$5	Vernon-McClung	20.00	45.00	125.
1158	'02PB	$5	Vernon-Treat	20.00	45.00	125.
1159	'02PB	$5	Napier-McClung	20.00	45.00	125.
1160	'02PB	$5	Napier-Thompson	25.00	55.00	140.
1161	'02PB	$5	Napier-Burke	20.00	45.00	125.
1162	'02PB	$5	Parker-Burke	20.00	45.00	125.
1163	'02PB	$5	Teehee-Burke	20.00	45.00	125.
1164	'02PB	$5	Elliott-Burke	20.00	45.00	125.
1165	'02PB	$5	Elliott-White	20.00	45.00	125.
1166	'02PB	$5	Speelman-White	20.00	45.00	125.
1167	'02PB	$5	Woods-White	20.00	45.00	125.
1168	'02PB	$5	Woods-Tate	20.00	45.00	125.
1169	'02PB	$5	Jones-Woods	100.	175.	400.
1170	'29TI	$5	Jones-Woods	10.00	15.00	40.00
1171	'29T2	$5	Jones Woods	12.00	20.00	55.00
1172	Orig	$10	Chittenden-Spinner	125.	225.	1800.
1173	Orig	$10	Colby-Spinner	125.	225.	1800.
1174	Orig	$10	Jeffries-Spinner	550.	1000.	2250.
1175	Orig	$10	Allison-Spinner	125.	225.	1800.
1176	1875	$10	Allison-New	125.	225.	1450.
1177	1875	$10	Allison-Wyman	125.	225.	1450.
1178	1875	$10	Allison-Gilfillan	125.	225.	1450.
1179	1875	$10	Scofield-Gilfillan	125.	225.	1450.
1180	1875	$10	Bruce-Gilfillan	125.	225.	1450.
1181	1875	$10	Bruce-Wyman	125.	225.	1450.
1182	1875	$10	Rosecrans-Huston	125.	225.	1450.
1183	1875	$10	Rosecrans-Nebeker	125.	225.	1450.
1184	1875	$10	Tillman-Morgan	(Reported, not confirmed)		
1185	'82BB	$10	Bruce-Gilfillan	95.00	150.	425.
1186	'82BB	$10	Bruce-Wyman	95.00	150.	425.
1187	'82BB	$10	Bruce-Jordan	95.00	150.	425.
1188	'82BB	$10	Rosecrans-Jordan	95.00	150.	425.
1189	'82BB	$10	Rosecrans-Hyatt	95.00	150.	425.
1190	'82BB	$10	Rosecrans-Huston	95.00	150.	425.
1191	'82BB	$10	Rosecrans-Nebeker	95.00	150.	425.
1192	'82BB	$10	Rosecrans-Morgan	300.	700.	1000.
1193	'82BB	$10	Tillman-Morgan	95.00	150.	425.
1194	'82BB	$10	Tillman-Roberts	95.00	150.	425.
1195	'82BB	$10	Bruce-Roberts	95.00	150.	425.
1196	'82BB	$10	Lyons-Roberts	95.00	150.	425.
1197	'82BB	$10	Lyons-Treat	95.00	150.	425.
1198	'82BB	$10	Vernon-Treat	95.00	150.	425.
1199	'82DB	$10	Rosecrans-Huston	65.00	125.	475.
1200	'82DB	$10	Rosecrans-Nebeker	65.00	125.	475.
1201	'82DB	$10	Rosecrans-Morgan	225.	600.	1100.
1202	'82DB	$10	Tillman-Morgan	65.00	125.	475.
1203	'82DB	$10	Tillman-Roberts	65.00	125.	475.
1204	'82DB	$10	Bruce-Roberts	65.00	125.	475.
1205	'82DB	$10	Lyons-Roberts	65.00	125.	475.
1206	'82DB	$10	Vernon-Treat	65.00	125.	475.
1207	'82DB	$10	Vernon-McClung	65.00	125.	475.
1208	'82DB	$10	Napier-McClung	65.00	125.	475.
1209	'82VB	$10	Tillman-Morgan	200.	350.	1500.
1210	'82VB	$10	Tillman-Roberts	150.	250.	2100.
1211	'82VB	$10	Bruce-Roberts	200.	350.	2500.
1212	'82VB	$10	Lyons-Roberts	150.	250.	2100.
1213	'82VB	$10	Vernon-Treat	175.	325.	2100.
1214	'82VB	$10	Napier-McClung	150.	250.	1500.
1215	'82VB	$10	Teehee-Burke	200.	350.	1500.
1216	'02RS	$10	Lyons-Roberts	65.00	150.	325.
1217	'02RS	$10	Lyons-Treat	65.00	150.	325.
1218	'02RS	$10	Vernon-Treat	85.00	225.	850.
1219	'02DB	$10	Lyons-Roberts	32.50	45.00	150.
1220	'02DB	$10	Lyons-Treat	32.50	45.00	150.
1221	'02DB	$10	Vernon-Treat	32.50	45.00	150.
1222	'02DB	$10	Vernon-McClung	32.50	45.00	150.
1223	'02DB	$10	Napier-McClung	32.50	45.00	150.
1224	'02DB	$10	Napier-Thompson	35.00	75.00	600.
1225	'02DB	$10	Napier-Burke	32.50	45.00	150
1226	'02DB	$10	Parker-Burke	32.50	45.00	150.
1227	'02DB	$10	Teehee-Burke	40.00	80.00	225.
1228	'02PB	$10	Lyons-Roberts	27.50	40.00	125.
1229	'02PB	$10	Lyons-Treat	27.50	40.00	125.
1230	'02PB	$10	Vernon-Treat	27.50	40.00	125.
1231	'02PB	$10	Vernon-McClung	27.50	40.00	125.
1232	'02PB	$10	Napier-McClung	27.50	40.00	125.
1233	'02PB	$10	Napier-Thompson	30.00	60.00	475.
1234	'02PB	$10	Napier-Burke	27.50	40.00	125.
1235	'02PB	$10	Parker-Burke	27.50	40.00	125.
1236	'02PB	$10	Teehee-Burke	27.50	40.00	125.
1237	'02PB	$10	Elliot-Burke	27.50	40.00	125.
1238	'02PB	$10	Elliot-White	27.50	40.00	125.
1239	'02PB	$10	Speelman-White	27.50	40.00	125.
1240	'02PB	$10	Woods-White	27.50	40.00	125.
1241	'02PB	$10	Woods-Tate	27.50	40.00	125.
1242	'02PB	$10	Jones-Woods	100.	250.	1000.
1243	'29T1	$10	Jones-Woods	12.50	17.50	50.00
1244	'29T2	$10	Jones-Woods	14.00	20.00	60.00
1245	Orig	$20	Chittenden-Spinner	300.	650.	3100.
1246	Orig	$20	Colby-Spinner	250.	550.	2950.
1247	Orig	$20	Jeffries-Spinner	1250.	2000.	4500.
1248	Orig	$20	Allison-Spinner	250.	550.	2950.
1249	1875	$20	Allison-New	200.	500.	2750.
1250	1875	$20	Allison-Wyman	200.	500.	2750.
1251	1875	$20	Allison-Gilfillan	200.	500.	2750.
1252	1875	$20	Scofield-Gilfillan	200.	500.	2750.
1253	1875	$20	Bruce-Gilfillan	200.	500.	2750.
1254	1875	$20	Bruce-Wyman	250.	650.	3800.
1255	1875	$20	Rosecrans-Huston	200.	500.	2750.
1256	1875	$20	Rosecrans-Nebeker	285.	750.	4250.
1257	1875	$20	Tillman-Morgan	300.	800.	4300.
1258	'82BB	$20	Bruce-Gilfillan	95.00	150.	425.
1259	'82BB	$20	Bruce-Wyman	95.00	150.	425.
1260	'82BB	$20	Bruce-Jordan	95.00	150.	425.
1261	'82BB	$20	Rosecrans-Jordan	95.00	150.	425.
1262	'82BB	$20	Rosecrans-Hyatt	95.00	150.	425.

KL#	Type	Denom.	Signatures	VG	VF	CU
1263	'82BB	$20	Rosecrans-Huston	95.00	150.	425.
1264	'82BB	$20	Rosecrans-Nebeker	95.00	150.	425.
1265	'82BB	$20	Rosecrans-Morgan	350.	850.	2000.
1266	'82BB	$20	Tillman-Morgan	95.00	150.	425.
1267	'82BB	$20	Tillman-Roberts	95.00	150.	425.
1268	'82BB	$20	Bruce-Roberts	95.00	150.	425.
1269	'82BB	$20	Lyons-Roberts	95.00	150.	425.
1270	'82BB	$20	Lyons-Treat	100.	175.	425.
1271	'82BB	$20	Vernon-Treat	100.	175.	425.
1272	'82DB	$20	Rosecrans-Huston	85.00	135.	625.
1273	'82DB	$20	Rosecrans-Nebeker	85.00	135.	625.
1274	'82DB	$20	Rosecrans-Morgan	400.	850.	1500.
1275	'82DB	$20	Tillman-Morgan	85.00	135.	625.
1276	'82DB	$20	Tillman-Roberts	85.00	135.	625.
1277	'82DB	$20	Bruce-Roberts	85.00	135.	625.
1278	'82DB	$20	Lyons-Roberts	85.00	135.	625.
1279	'82DB	$20	Vernon-Treat	85.00	135.	625.
1280	'82DB	$20	Napier-McClung	100.	200.	625.
1281	'82VB	$20	Tillman-Morgan	150.	375.	1250.
1282	'82VB	$20	Tillman-Roberts	250.	600.	1800.
1283	'82VB	$20	Bruce-Roberts	250.	600.	1800.
1284	'82VB	$20	Lyons-Roberts	150.	375.	1250.
1285	'82VB	$20	Lyons-Treat	150.	375.	1250.
1286	'82VB	$20	Vernon-Treat	150.	375.	1250.
1287	'82VB	$20	Napier-McClung	150.	375.	1250.
1288	'82VB	$20	Parker-Burke	—	(Rare)	—
1289	'82VB	$20	Teehee-Burke	175.	400.	2000.
1290	'02RS	$20	Lyons-Roberts	75.00	150.	450.
1291	'02RS	$20	Lyons-Treat	75.00	150.	450.
1292	'02RS	$20	Vernon-Treat	100.	200.	1600.
1293	'02DB	$20	Lyons-Roberts	30.00	45.00	200.
1294	'02DB	$20	Lyons-Treat	30.00	45.00	200.
1295	'02DB	$20	Vernon-Treat	30.00	45.00	200.
1296	'02DB	$20	Vernon-McClung	30.00	45.00	200.
1297	'02DB	$20	Napier-McClung	30.00	45.00	200.
1298	'02DB	$20	Napier-Thompson	40.00	85.00	500.
1299	'02DB	$20	Napier-Burke	30.00	45.00	200.
1300	'02DB	$20	Parker-Burke	30.00	45.00	200.
1301	'02DB	$20	Teehee-Burke	50.00	100.	200.
1302	'02PB	$20	Lyons-Roberts	27.50	45.00	150.
1303	'02PB	$20	Lyons-Treat	27.50	45.00	150.
1304	'02PB	$20	Vernon-Treat	27.50	45.00	150.
1305	'02PB	$20	Vernon-McClung	27.50	45.00	150.
1306	'02PB	$20	Napier-McClung	27.50	45.00	150.
1307	'02PB	$20	Napier-Thompson	40.00	80.00	500.
1308	'02PB	$20	Napier-Burke	27.50	45.00	150.
1309	'02PB	$20	Parker-Burke	27.50	45.00	150.
1310	'02PB	$20	Teehee-Burke	27.50	45.00	150.
1311	'02PB	$20	Elliott-Burke	27.50	45.00	150.
1312	'02PB	$20	Elliott-White	27.50	45.00	150.
1313	'02PB	$20	Speelman-White	27.50	45.00	150.
1314	'02PB	$20	Woods-White	35.00	100.	150.
1315	'02PB	$20	Woods-Tate	50.00	175.	450.
1316	'02PB	$20	Jones-Woods	500.	1000.	5000.
1317	'29T1	$20	Jones-Woods	23.50	27.50	60.00
1318	'29T2	$20	Jones-Woods	25.00	35.00	80.00
1319	Orig	$50	Chittenden-Spinner	1500.	3000.	—
1320	Orig	$50	Colby-Spinner	1500.	3000.	—
1321	Orig	$50	Allison-Spinner	1500.	3000.	—
1322	1875	$50	Allison-New	1400.	2800.	—
1323	1875	$50	Allison-Wyman	1500.	3000.	—
1324	1875	$50	Allison-Gilfillan	1400.	2800.	—
1325	1875	$50	Scofield-Gilfillan	1400.	2800.	—
1326	1875	$50	Bruce-Gilfillan	1400.	2800.	—
1327	1875	$50	Bruce-Wyman	1400.	2800.	—
1328	1875	$50	Rosecrans-Houston	1400.	2800.	—
1329	1875	$50	Rosecrans-Nebeker	1450.	2900.	—
1330	1875	$50	Tillman-Morgan	1400.	2800.	—
1331	'82BB	$50	Bruce-Gilfillan	275.	500.	2000.
1332	'82BB	$50	Bruce-Wyman	275.	500.	2000.
1333	'82BB	$50	Bruce-Jordan	275.	500.	2000.
1334	'82BB	$50	Rosecrans-Jordan	275.	500.	2000.
1335	'82BB	$50	Rosecrans-Hyatt	275.	500.	2000.
1336	'82BB	$50	Rosecrans-Huston	275.	500.	2000.
1337	'82BB	$50	Rosecrans-Nebeker	275.	500.	2000.
1338	'82BB	$50	Rosecrans-Morgan	600.	1100.	2500.
1339	'82BB	$50	Tillman-Morgan	275.	500.	2000.
1340	'82BB	$50	Tillman-Roberts	275.	500.	2000.
1341	'82BB	$50	Bruce-Roberts	275.	500.	2000.
1342	'82BB	$50	Lyons-Roberts	275.	500.	2000.
1343	'82BB	$50	Vernon-Treat	650.	1200.	2400.
1344	'82DB	$50	Rosecrans-Huston	350.	900.	2500.
1345	'82DB	$50	Rosecrans Nebeker	350.	900.	2500.
1346	'82DB	$50	Tillman-Morgan	350.	900.	2500.
1347	'82DB	$50	Tillman-Roberts	350.	900.	2500.
1348	'82DB	$50	Bruce-Roberts	350.	900.	2500.
1349	'82DB	$50	Lyons-Roberts	350.	900.	2500.
1350	'82DB	$50	Vernon-Treat	350.	900.	2500.
1351	'82DB	$50	Napier-McClung	350.	900.	2500.
1352	'82VB	$50	Lyons-Roberts	—	(Four known)	
1353	'02RS	$50	Lyons-Roberts	450.	1700.	4500.
1354	'02RS	$50	Lyons-Treat	450.	1700.	4500.
1355	'02RS	$50	Vernon-Treat	450.	1700.	4500.
1356	'02DB	$50	Lyons-Roberts	75.00	125.	500.
1357	'02DB	$50	Lyons-Roberts	75.00	125.	500.
1358	'02DB	$50	Vernon-Treat	75.00	125.	500.
1359	'02DB	$50	Vernon-McClung	75.00	125.	500.
1360	'02DB	$50	Napier-McClung	75.00	125.	500.
1361	'02DB	$50	Napier-Thompson	85.00	185.	750.
1362	'02DB	$50	Napier-Burke	75.00	130.	500.
1363	'02DB	$50	Parker-Burke	75.00	130.	500.
1364	'02DB	$50	Teehee-Burke	125.	275.	500.
1365	'02PB	$50	Lyons-Roberts	75.00	110.	400.
1366	'02PB	$50	Lyons-Treat	75.00	110.	400.
1367	'02PB	$50	Vernon-Treat	75.00	110.	400.
1368	'02PB	$50	Vernon-McClung	75.00	110.	400.
1369	'02PB	$50	Napier-McClung	75.00	110.	400.
1370	'02PB	$50	Napier-Thompson	85.00	160.	400.
1371	'02PB	$50	Napier-Burke	75.00	110.	400.
1372	'02PB	$50	Parker-Burke	75.00	110.	400.
1373	'02PB	$50	Teehee-Burke	75.00	110.	400.
1374	'02PB	$50	Elliott-Burke	75.00	110.	400.
1375	'02PB	$50	Elliott-White	75.00	110.	400.
1376	'02PB	$50	Speelman-White	75.00	110.	400.
1377	'02PB	$50	Woods-White	100.	250.	550.
1378	'29T1	$50	Jones-Woods	55.00	75.00	100.
1379	'29T2	$50	Jones-Woods	60.00	85.00	500.
1380	Orig	$100	Chittenden-Spinner	1675.	3500.	—
1381	Orig	$100	Colby-Spinner	1675.	3500.	—
1382	Orig	$100	Allison-Spinner	1675.	3500.	—
1383	1875	$100	Allison-New	1675.	3250.	—
1384	1875	$100	Allison-Wyman	1675.	3250.	—
1385	1875	$100	Allison-Gilfillan	1675.	3250.	—
1386	1875	$100	Scofield-Gilfillan	1675.	3250.	—
1387	1875	$100	Bruce-Gilfillan	1675.	3250.	—
1388	1875	$100	Bruce-Wyman	1675.	3250.	—
1389	1875	$100	Rosecrans-Huston	1675.	3250.	—
1390	1875	$100	Rosecrans-Nebeker	1675.	3250.	—
1391	1875	$100	Tillman-Morgan	1675.	3250.	—
1392	'82BB	$100	Bruce-Gilfillan	325.	600.	2750.
1393	'82BB	$100	Bruce-Wyman	325.	600.	2750.
1394	'82BB	$100	Bruce-Jordan	325.	600.	2750.
1395	'82BB	$100	Rosecrans-Jordan	325.	600.	2750.
1396	'82BB	$100	Rosecrans-Hyatt	325.	600.	2750.
1397	'82BB	$100	Rosecrans-Huston	325.	600.	2750.
1398	'82BB	$100	Rosecrans-Nebeker	325.	600.	2750.
1399	'82BB	$100	Rosecrans-Morgan	500.	1200.	2750.
1400	'82BB	$100	Tillman-Morgan	325.	600.	2750.
1401	'82BB	$100	Tillman-Roberts	325.	600.	2750.
1401A	'88BB	$100	Bruce-Roberts	325.	600.	2750.
1402	'82BB	$100	Lyons-Roberts	325.	600.	2750.
1403	'82BB	$100	Vernon-Treat	500.	1200.	2750.
1404	'82DB	$100	Rosecrans-Huston	350.	675.	3250.
1405	'82DB	$100	Rosecrans-Nebeker	350.	675.	3250.
1406	'82DB	$100	Tillman-Morgan	350.	675.	3250.
1407	'82DB	$100	Tillman-Roberts	350.	675.	3250.
1408	'82DB	$100	Bruce-Roberts	350.	675.	3250.
1409	'82DB	$100	Lyons-Roberts	350.	675.	3250.
1410	'82DB	$100	Vernon-Treat	350.	675.	3250.
1411	'82DB	$100	Napier-McClung	350.	675.	3250.
1412	'82VB	$100	Lyons-Roberts	—	(One known)	
1413	'02RS	$100	Lyons-Roberts	500.	1000.	5500.
1414	'02RS	$100	Lyons-Roberts	500.	1000.	5500.
1415	'02RS	$100	Vernon-Treat	500.	1000.	5500.
1416	'02DB	$100	Lyons-Roberts	160.	300.	600.
1417	'02DB	$100	Lyons-Treat	160.	300.	600.
1418	'02DB	$100	Vernon-Treat	160.	300.	600.
1419	'02DB	$100	Vernon-McClung	160.	300.	600.
1420	'02DB	$100	Napier-McClung	160.	300.	600.
1421	'02DB	$100	Napier-Thompson	200.	400.	950.
1422	'02DB	$100	Napier-Burke	160.	300.	600.
1423	'02DB	$100	Parker-Burke	160.	300.	600.
1424	'02DB	$100	Teehee-Burke	200.	300.	750.
1425	'02PB	$100	Lyons-Roberts	150.	275.	550.
1426	'02PB	$100	Lyons-Treat	150.	275.	550.
1427	'02PB	$100	Vernon-Treat	150.	275.	550.
1428	'02PB	$100	Vernon-McClung	150.	275.	550.
1429	'02PB	$100	Napier-McClung	150.	275.	550.
1430	'02PB	$100	Napier-Thompson	200.	350.	925.
1431	'02PB	$100	Parker-Burke	150.	275.	550.
1432	'02PB	$100	Teehee-Burke	150.	275.	550.
1433	'02PB	$100	Elliott-Burke	150.	275.	550.
1434	'02PB	$100	Elliott-White	150.	275.	550.
1435	'02PB	$100	Speelman-White	150.	275.	550.
1436	'02PB	$100	Woods-White	—	(Two known)	
1437	'29T1	$100	Jones-Woods	115.	140.	175.
1438	'29T2	$100	Jones-Woods	120.	140.	600.
1439	Orig	$500	Colby-Spinner	—	(One known)	
1440	1875	$500	Colby-Spinner	—	(One known)	
1441	1875	$500	Allison-New	—	(One known)	
1442	Orig	$1,000	Chittenden-Spinner	—	(Unknown)	
1443	1875	$1,000	Allison-Wyman	—	(Unknown)	

National Bank Note Valuations By State

Original Series $1 (KL #1086-1088)

	VG	VF	AU
Alabama	185.	420.	860.
Arkansas	250.	1650.	2800.
Colorado Territory	350.	750.	1500.
Connecticut	200.	445.	925.
Dakota Territory	350.	750.	1500.
Delaware	350.	750.	1500.
District of Columbia	250.	550.	1100.
Georgia	185.	420.	860.
Idaho Territory	—	—	—
Illinois	140.	300.	625.
Indiana	185.	420.	860.
Iowa	140.	300.	625.
Kansas	160.	350.	725.
Kentucky	200.	445.	925.
Louisiana	250.	550.	1100.
Maine	250.	550.	1100.
Maryland	185.	420.	860.
Massachusetts	145.	315.	650.
Michigan	160.	350.	725.
Minnesota	145.	315.	650.
Missouri	145.	315.	650.
Montana Territory	350.	750.	1500.
Nebraska	160.	350.	725.
Nebraska Territory	—	—	—
New Hampshire	220.	480.	1000.
New Jersey	145.	315.	650.
New Mexico Territory	350.	750.	1500.
New York	100.	175.	450.
North Carolina	200.	445.	925.
Ohio	145.	315.	650.
Pennsylvania	100.	175.	450.
Rhode Island	220.	480.	1000.
South Carolina	220.	480.	1000.
Tennessee	200.	445.	925.
Texas	140.	300.	625.
Utah Territory	350.	750.	1500.
Vermont	250.	550.	1100.
Virginia	200.	445.	925.
West Virginia	220.	480.	1000.
Wisconsin	145.	315.	650.
Wyoming Territory	—	—	—

Series 1875 $1 (KL# 1089-1092)

	VG	VF	AU
Colorado Territory	380.	800.	1550.
Connecticut	235.	500.	1000.
Delaware	380.	800.	1550.
Georgia	215.	460.	920.
Idaho Territory	—	—	—
Illinois	155.	325.	650.
Indiana	215.	460.	920.
Iowa	155.	325.	650.
Kansas	185.	380.	750.
Kentucky	235.	500.	1150.

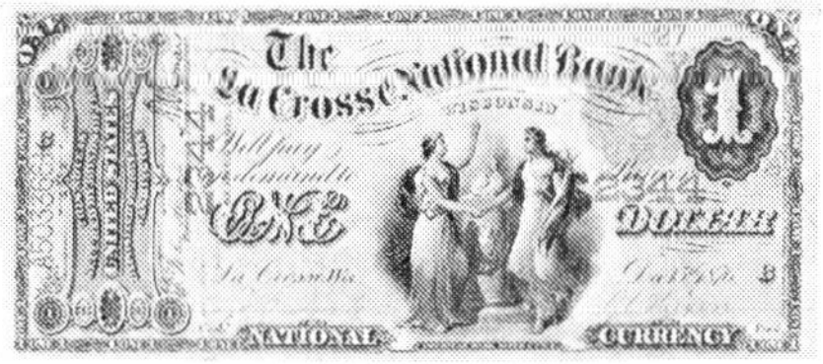

	VG	VF	AU
Maine	275.	575.	1150.
Massachusetts	165.	340.	675.
Michigan	185.	380.	750.
Minnesota	165.	340.	675.
Missouri	165.	340.	675.
Nebraska	185.	380.	750.
Nebraska Territory	—	—	—
New Hampshire	250.	530.	1050.
New Jersey	165.	340.	675.
New Mexico Territory	380.	800.	1550.
New York	100.	175.	450.
North Carolina	235.	500.	1000.
Ohio	165.	340.	675.
Pennsylvania	100.	175.	450.
Rhode Island	250.	530.	1050.
South Carolina	250.	530.	1050.
Tennessee	235.	500.	1000.
Texas	155.	325.	650.
Vermont	275.	575.	1150.
Wisconsin	165.	340.	675.

Original Series $2 (KL# 1093-1095)

	VG	VF	AU
Alabama	235.	425.	1000.
Arkansas	400.	1650.	2800.
Colorado Territory	550.	2200.	4000.
Connecticut	340.	1480.	2450.
Dakota Territory	550.	2200.	4000.
Delaware	550.	2200.	4000.
District of Columbia	400.	1650.	2800.
Georgia	310.	1360.	2250.
Idaho Territory	—	—	—
Illinois	240.	750.	1200.
Indiana	310.	1360.	2250.
Iowa	240.	750.	1200.
Kansas	260.	1125.	1885.
Kentucky	340.	1480.	2450.
Louisiana	400.	1650.	2800.
Maine	400.	1650.	2800.

	VG	VF	AU
Maryland	310.	1360.	2250.
Massachusetts	235.	1000.	1675.
Michigan	260.	1125.	1885.
Minnesota	250.	775.	1200.
Missouri	250.	775.	1200.
Montana Territory	550.	2200.	4000.
Nebraska	260.	1125.	1885.
Nebraska Territory	—	—	—
New Hampshire	360.	1575.	2600.
New Jersey	230.	1000.	1675.
New Mexico Territory	550.	2200.	4000.
New York	235.	425.	1000.
North Carolina	340.	1480.	2450.
Ohio	235.	1000.	1675.
Pennsylvania	235.	425.	1000.
Rhode Island	360.	1575.	2600.
South Carolina	360.	1575.	2600.
Tennessee	340.	1480.	2450.
Texas	—	—	—
Utah Territory	550.	2200.	4000.
Vermont	400.	1650.	2800.
Virginia	340.	1480.	2450.
West Virginia	—	—	—
Wisconsin	235.	1000.	1675.
Wyoming Territory	—	—	—

VG	VF	AU
225.	425.	—

Series 1875 $2 (KL# 1096-1099)

	VG	VF	AU
Colorado Territory	600.	2250.	4150.
Connecticut	375.	1450.	2500.
Delaware	600.	2250.	4150.
Georgia	340.	1350.	2250.
Idaho Territory	—	—	—
Illinois	245.	1000.	1650.
Indiana	340.	1350.	2250.
Iowa	245.	1000.	1650.
Kansas	290.	1150.	1900.
Kentucky	375.	1450.	2500.
Maine	450.	1700.	2900.
Massachusetts	260.	1050.	1725.
Michigan	290.	1150.	1900.
Minnesota	260.	1050.	1725.
Missouri	260.	1050.	1725.
Montana Territory	600.	2250.	4150.
Nebraska	290.	1150.	1900.
Nebraska Territory	—	—	—
New Hampshire	400.	1525.	2650.
New Jersey	260.	1050.	1725.
New Mexico Territory	600.	2250.	4150.
New York	235.	425.	1000.
North Carolina	375.	1450.	2500.
Ohio	260.	1050.	1725.
Pennsylvania	235.	425.	1000.
Rhode Island	400.	1525.	2650.
South Carolina	400.	1525.	2650.
Tennessee	375.	1450.	2500.
Texas	—	—	—
Vermont	450.	1700.	2900.
Wisconsin	260.	600.	1200.

Original Series $5
(KL# 1100-1103)

	VG	VF	AU
Alabama	125.	465.	900.
Arkansas	160.	575.	1150.
Colorado Territory	225.	750.	1500.
Connecticut	135.	500.	1000.
Dakota Territory	225.	750.	1500.
Delaware	225.	750.	1500.
District of Columbia	160.	575.	1150.
Florida	145.	540.	1080.
Georgia	125.	465.	900.
Idaho Territory	—	—	—
Illinois	110.	330.	660.
Indiana	125.	465.	900.
Iowa	110.	330.	660.
Kansas	105.	390.	780.
Kentucky	135.	500.	1000.
Louisiana	160.	575.	1150.
Maine	160.	575.	1150.
Maryland	125.	465.	900.
Massachusetts	115.	345.	700.
Michigan	105.	390.	780.
Minnesota	115.	345.	700.
Mississippi	160.	575.	1150.
Missouri	115.	345.	700.
Montana Territory	225.	750.	1500.
Montana	145.	540.	1080.
Nebraska	105.	390.	780.
Nebraska Territory	—	—	—
Nevada	225.	750.	1500.
New Hampshire	145.	540.	1080.
New Jersey	95.00	345.	700.
New Mexico Territory	225.	750.	1500.
New York	100.	300.	600.
North Carolina	135.	500.	1000.
Ohio	95.00	345.	700.
Oregon	160.	575.	1150.
Pennsylvania	80.00	300.	600.
Rhode Island	145.	540.	1080.
South Carolina	145	540	1080
Tennessee	135.	500.	1000.
Texas	110.	330.	660.
Utah Territory	225.	750.	1500.
Vermont	160.	575.	1150.
Virginia	135.	500.	1000.
West Virginia	145.	540.	1080.
Wisconsin	115.	345.	700.
Wyoming Territory	—	—	—

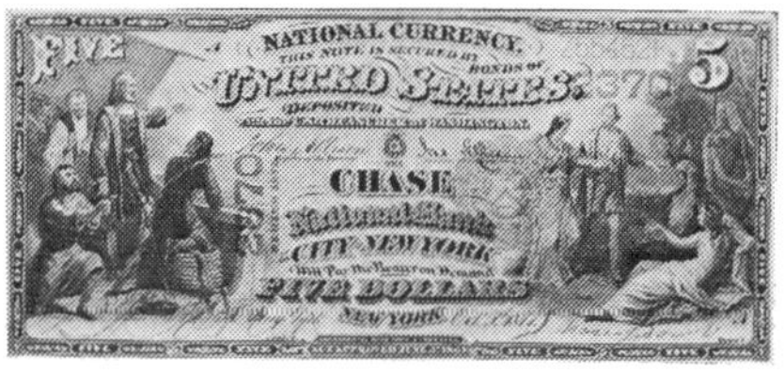

Series 1875 $5
(KL# 1104-1113)

	VG	VF	AU
Alabama	120.	425.	875.
Arizona Territory	225.	700.	1400.
Arkansas	160.	550.	1100.
California	90.00	300.	625.
Colorado Territory	225.	700.	1400.
Colorado	135.	450.	925.
Connecticut	135.	450.	925.
Dakota Territory	225.	700.	1400.
Delaware	225.	700.	1400.
District of Columbia	160.	550.	1100.
Florida	145.	475.	1000.
Georgia	120.	425.	875.
Idaho Territory	—	—	—
Illinois	110.	325.	625.
Indiana	120.	425.	875.
Iowa	110.	325.	625.
Kansas	105.	360.	740.
Kentucky	135.	450.	925.
Louisiana	160.	550.	1100.
Maine	160.	550.	1100.
Maryland	135.	450.	925.
Massachusetts	115.	325.	650.
Michigan	105.	360.	740.
Minnesota	115.	325.	650.
Missouri	115.	325.	650.
Montana Territory	225.	700.	1400.
Nebraska	100.	360.	740.
Nebraska Territory	—	—	—
New Hampshire	145.	475.	1000.
New Jersey	115.	325.	650.
New Mexico Territory	160.	550.	1100.
New York	100.	300.	575.
North Carolina	135.	450.	925.
North Dakota	145.	475.	1100.
Ohio	95.00	295.	660.
Pennsylvania	100.	300.	575.
Rhode Island	145.	475.	1000.
South Carolina	145.	475.	1000.
South Dakota	145.	475.	1000.
Tennessee	135.	450.	925.
Texas	110.	325.	625.
Utah Territory	225.	700.	1400.
Vermont	160.	550.	1100.
Virginia	135.	450.	925.
Washington	160.	550.	1100.
West Virginia	145.	475.	1000.
Wisconsin	115.	325.	650.
Wyoming Territory	—	—	—
Wyoming	160.	550.	1100.

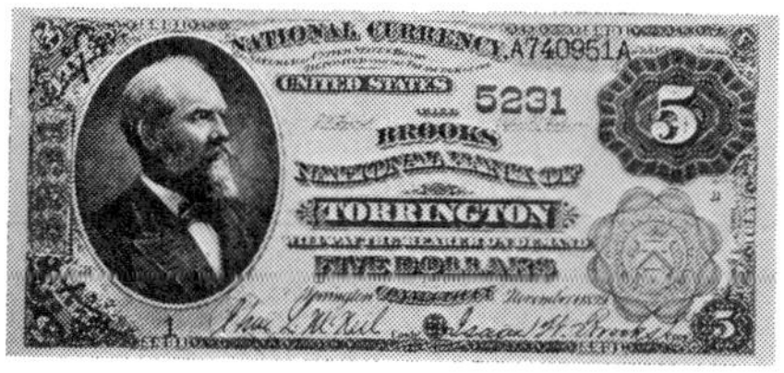

1882 Brown Back $5
(KL# 1114-1126)

	VG	VF	AU
Alabama	100.	275.	475.
Arizona Territory	175.	500.	800.
Arkansas	125.	350.	600.
California	70.00	200.	325.
Colorado	110.	300.	500.
Connecticut	110.	300.	500.
Dakota Territory	175.	500.	800.
Delaware	175.	500.	800.
District of Columbia	125.	350.	600.
Florida	115.	320.	540.
Georgia	100.	275.	475.
Hawaii	175.	500.	800.
Idaho Territory	—	—	—
Idaho	125.	350.	600.
Illinois	70.00	200.	325.
Indian Territory	175.	500.	800.
Indiana	100.	275.	475.
Iowa	70.00	200.	325.
Kansas	85.00	235.	385.
Kentucky	110.	300.	500.
Louisiana	125.	350.	600.
Maine	125.	350.	600.
Maryland	100.	275.	475.
Massachusetts	75.00	210.	340.
Michigan	85.00	235.	385.
Minnesota	75.00	210.	340.
Mississippi	125.	350.	600.
Missouri	75.00	210.	340.
Montana Territory	175.	500.	800.
Montana	115.	320.	540.
Nebraska	85.00	235.	385.
Nevada	175.	500.	800.
New Hampshire	115.	320.	540.
New Jersey	75.00	210.	340.
New Mexico Territory	175.	500.	800.
New York	65.00	125.	250.
North Carolina	110.	300.	500.
North Dakota	115.	320.	540.
Ohio	75.00	210.	325.
Oklahoma Territory	175.	500.	800.
Oklahoma	100.	275.	475.
Oregon	125.	350.	600.
Pennsylvania	65.00	125.	250.
Rhode Island	115.	320.	540.
South Carolina	115.	320.	540.
South Dakota	115.	320.	540.
Tennessee	110.	300.	500.
Texas	70.00	200.	325.
Utah Territory	175.	500.	800.
Utah	125.	350.	600.
Vermont	125.	350.	600.
Virginia	110.	300.	500.
Washington Territory	—	—	—
Washington	125.	350.	600.
West Virginia	115.	320.	540.
Wisconsin	75.00	210.	340.
Wyoming Territory	—	—	—
Wyoming	125.	350.	600.

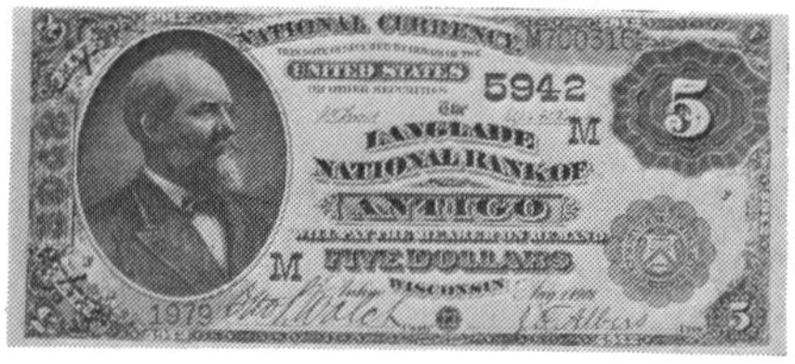

1882 Date Back $5
(KL# 1127-1135)

	VG	VF	AU
Alabama	75.00	190.	380.
Arizona Territory	140.	325.	675.
Arizona	100.	240.	480.
California	60.00	135.	275.
Colorado	85.00	200.	415.
Connecticut	85.00	200.	415.
Delaware	140.	325.	675.
District of Columbia	100.	240.	480.
Florida	90.00	215.	440.
Georgia	75.00	190.	380.
Hawaii	140.	325.	675.
Idaho	100.	240.	480.
Illinois	60.00	135.	275.
Indian Territory	140.	325.	675.
Indiana	75.00	190.	380.
Iowa	55.00	135.	275.
Kansas	65.00	160.	325.
Kentucky	85.00	200.	415.
Louisiana	100.	240.	480.
Maine	100.	240.	480.
Maryland	75.00	190.	380.
Massachusetts	60.00	140.	290.
Michigan	65.00	160.	325.
Minnesota	60.00	140.	290.
Mississippi	100.	240.	480.
Missouri	60.00	140.	290.
Montana	90.00	215.	440.
Nebraska	65.00	160.	325.
New Hampshire	90.00	215.	440.
New Jersey	60.00	140.	290.
New Mexico Territory	140.	325.	675.
New Mexico	100.	240.	480.
New York	60.00	115.	250.
North Carolina	85.00	200.	415.
North Dakota	90.00	215.	440.
Ohio	60.00	140.	290.
Oklahoma	75.00	190.	380.
Oregon	100.	240.	480.
Pennsylvania	60.00	115.	250.
Rhode Island	90.00	215.	440.
South Carolina	90.00	215.	440.
South Dakota	90.00	215.	440.
Tennessee	85.00	200.	415.
Texas	60.00	140.	275.
Utah	100.	240.	480.
Vermont	100.	240.	480.
Virginia	85.00	200.	415.
Washington	100.	240.	480.
West Virginia	90.00	215.	440.
Wisconsin	60.00	140.	290.
Wyoming	100.	240.	480.

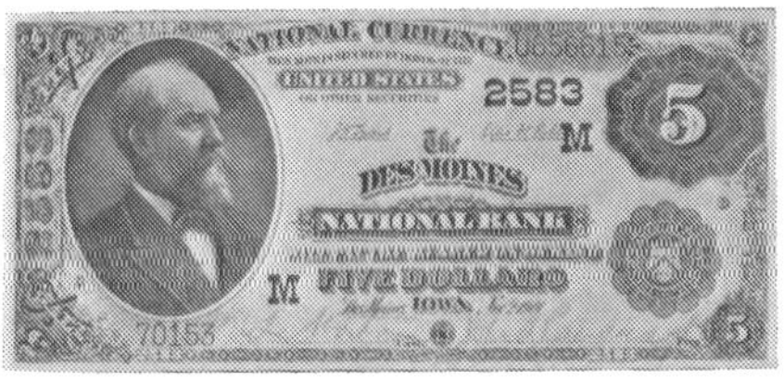

1882 Value Back $5
(KL# 1136-1142)

	VG	VF	AU
Alabama	155.	525.	1150.
California	110.	375.	820.
Colorado	115.	390.	850.
Connecticut	115.	390.	850.
Delaware	275.	900.	2000.
District of Columbia	200.	650.	1450.
Florida	180.	600.	1350.
Georgia	155.	525.	1150.
Hawaii	275.	900.	2000.
Idaho	200.	650.	1450.
Illinois	110.	375.	820.
Indian Territory	275.	900.	2000.
Indiana	155.	525.	1150.
Iowa	110.	375.	820.
Kansas	130.	435.	950.
Kentucky	170.	560.	1250.
Maine	200.	650.	1450.
Maryland	155.	525.	1150.
Massachusetts	170.	560.	1250.
Michigan	130.	435.	950.
Minnesota	115.	390.	850.
Mississippi	200.	650.	1450.
Missouri	115.	390.	850.
Nebraska	130.	435.	950.
Nevada	275.	900.	2000.
New Hampshire	180.	600.	1350.
New Jersey	115.	390.	850.
New Mexico	200.	650.	1450.
New York	85.00	220.	600.
North Carolina	170.	560.	1250.
North Dakota	180.	600.	1350.
Ohio	115.	390.	850.
Oklahoma	155.	525.	1150.
Oregon	200.	650.	1450.
Pennsylvania	85.00	220.	600.
Rhode Island	180.	600.	1350.
South Carolina	180.	600.	1350.
South Dakota	180.	600.	1350.
Tennessee	170.	560.	1250.
Texas	110.	375.	820.
Utah	200.	650.	1450.
Vermont	200.	650.	1450.
Virginia	170.	560.	1250.
Washington	200.	650.	1450.
West Virginia	180.	600.	1350.
Wisconsin	110.	375.	820.
Wyoming	200.	650.	1450.

1902 Red Seal $5
(KL# 1143-1145)

	VG	VF	AU
Alabama	115.	420.	850.
Alaska	220.	800.	1450.
Arizona Territory	220.	800.	1450.
Arkansas	150.	550.	1050.
California	80.00	290.	600.
Colorado	125.	450.	900.
Connecticut	125.	450.	900.
Delaware		—	—
District of Columbia	150.	550.	1050.
Florida	135.	475.	960.
Georgia	115.	420.	850.
Idaho	150.	550.	1050.
Illinois	80.00	290.	600.
Indian Territory	220.	800.	1450.
Indiana	115.	420.	850.
Iowa	80.00	290.	600.
Kansas	95.00	340.	700.
Kentucky	125.	450.	900.
Louisiana	150.	550.	1050.
Maine	150.	550.	1050.
Maryland	115.	420.	850.
Massachusetts	85.00	300.	625.
Michigan	95.00	340.	700.
Minnesota	85.00	300.	625.
Mississippi	150.	550.	1050.
Missouri	85.00	300.	625.
Montana	135.	475.	960.
Nebraska	95.00	340.	700.
Nevada	220.	800.	1450.
New Hampshire	135.	475.	960.
New Jersey	85.00	300.	625.
New Mexico Territory	220.	800.	1450.
New York	65.00	150.	350.
North Carolina	125.	450.	900.
North Dakota	135.	475.	960.
Ohio	85.00	300.	625.
Oklahoma Territory	220.	800.	1450.
Oklahoma	115.	420.	850.
Oregon	150.	550.	1050.
Pennsylvania	65.00	150.	350.
Rhode Island	135.	475.	960.
South Carolina	135.	475.	960.
South Dakota	135.	475.	960.
Tennessee	125.	450.	900.
Texas	80.00	290.	600.
Utah	150.	550.	1050.
Vermont	150.	550.	1050.
Virginia	125.	450.	900.
Washington	150.	550.	1050.
West Virginia	135.	475.	960.
Wisconsin	85.00	300.	625.
Wyoming	150.	550.	1050.

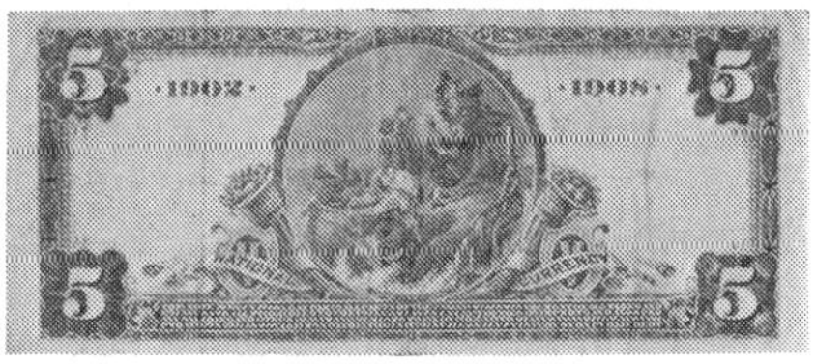

1902 Date Back $5
(KL# 1146-1154)

	VG	VF	AU
Alabama	25.00	55.00	160.
Alaska	150.	300.	600.
Arizona Territory	150.	300.	600.
Arizona	50.00	95.00	235.
Arkansas	50.00	95.00	235.
California	23.00	40.00	110.
Colorado	27.00	60.00	170.
Connecticut	27.00	60.00	170.
Delaware	150.	300.	600.
District of Columbia	50.00	95.00	235.
Florida	40.00	80.00	190.
Georgia	25.00	55.00	160.
Hawaii	150.	300.	600.
Idaho	50.00	95.00	235.
Illinois	23.00	40.00	110.
Indiana	25.00	55.00	160.
Iowa	23.00	40.00	110.
Kansas	26.00	45.00	130.
Kentucky	27.00	60.00	170.
Louisiana	50.00	95.00	235.
Maine	50.00	95.00	235.
Maryland	25.00	55.00	160.
Massachusetts	25.00	45.00	115.
Michigan	30.00	50.00	130.
Minnesota	25.00	45.00	115.
Mississippi	50.00	95.00	235.
Missouri	25.00	45.00	115.
Montana	40.00	80.00	190.
Nebraska	30.00	60.00	130.
Nevada	150.	300.	600.
New Hampshire	40.00	80.00	190.
New Jersey	25.00	45.00	115.
New Mexico Territory	150.	300.	600.
New Mexico	50.00	95.00	235.
New York	22.50	40.00	100.
North Carolina	27.00	60.00	170.
North Dakota	40.00	80.00	190.
Ohio	25.00	45.00	115.
Oklahoma	25.00	55.00	160.
Oregon	50.00	95.00	235.
Pennsylvania	22.50	40.00	100.
Rhode Island	40.00	80.00	190.
South Carolina	40.00	80.00	190.
South Dakota	40.00	80.00	190.
Tennessee	27.00	60.00	170.
Texas	23.00	40.00	110.
Utah	50.00	95.00	235.
Vermont	50.00	95.00	235.
Virginia	27.00	60.00	170.
Washington	50.00	95.00	235.
West Virginia	40.00	80.00	190.
Wisconsin	25.00	40.00	115.
Wyoming	50.00	95.00	235.

1902 Plain Back $5
(KL# 1155-1169)

	VG	VF	AU
Alabama	20.00	45.00	140.
Alaska	140.	290.	575.
Arizona	45.00	90.00	220.
Arkansas	45.00	90.00	220.
California	21.00	38.00	95.00
Colorado	25.00	50.00	150.
Connecticut	25.00	50.00	150.
Delaware	140.	290.	575.
District of Columbia	45.00	90.00	220.
Florida	35.00	75.00	185.
Georgia	20.00	45.00	140.
Hawaii	140.	290.	575.
Idaho	45.00	90.00	220.
Illinois	21.00	38.00	95.00
Indiana	20.00	45.00	140.
Iowa	21.00	38.00	95.00
Kansas	25.00	40.00	115.
Kentucky	25.00	50.00	150.
Louisiana	45.00	90.00	220.
Maine	45.00	90.00	220.
Maryland	20.00	45.00	140.
Massachusetts	22.00	39.00	100.
Michigan	25.00	40.00	115.
Minnesota	22.00	39.00	100.
Mississippi	45.00	90.00	220.
Missouri	22.00	39.00	100.
Montana	35.00	75.00	185.
Nebraska	20.00	38.00	115.
Nevada	140.	290.	575.
New Hampshire	35.00	75.00	185.
New Jersey	22.00	39.00	100.
New Mexico	45.00	90.00	220.
New York	20.00	37.50	90.00
North Carolina	25.00	50.00	150.
North Dakota	35.00	75.00	185.
Ohio	20.00	33.00	100.
Oklahoma	20.00	45.00	140.
Oregon	45.00	90.00	220.
Pennsylvania	20.00	37.50	90.00
Rhode Island	35.00	75.00	185.
South Carolina	35.00	75.00	185.
South Dakota	35.00	75.00	185.
Tennessee	25.00	50.00	150.
Texas	21.00	38.00	95.00
Utah	45.00	90.00	220.
Vermont	45.00	90.00	220.
Virginia	24.00	50.00	150.

	VG	VF	AU
Washington	45.00	90.00	220.
West Virginia	35.00	75.00	185.
Wisconsin	22.00	39.00	100.
Wyoming	45.00	90.00	220.

1929 Type 1 $5
(KL# 1170)

	VG	VF	AU
Alabama	16.00	30.00	45.00
Alaska	40.00	60.00	90.00
Arizona	25.00	50.00	70.00
Arkansas	25.00	50.00	70.00
California	11.00	22.00	30.00
Colorado	17.00	34.00	48.00
Connecticut	17.00	34.00	48.00
Delaware	40.00	60.00	90.00
District of Columbia	25.00	50.00	70.00
Florida	20.00	40.00	55.00
Georgia	16.00	30.00	45.00
Hawaii	40.00	60.00	90.00
Idaho	25.00	50.00	70.00
Illinois	11.00	22.00	30.00
Indiana	16.00	30.00	45.00
Iowa	11.00	22.00	30.00
Kansas	13.00	25.00	36.00
Kentucky	17.00	34.00	48.00
Louisiana	25.00	50.00	70.00
Maine	25.00	50.00	70.00
Maryland	16.00	30.00	45.00
Massachusetts	11.00	22.00	30.00
Michigan	13.00	25.00	36.00
Minnesota	12.00	23.00	32.00
Mississippi	25.00	50.00	70.00
Missouri	12.00	23.00	32.00
Montana	20.00	40.00	55.00
Nebraska	13.00	25.00	36.00
Nevada	40.00	60.00	90.00
New Hampshire	20.00	40.00	55.00
New Jersey	12.00	23.00	32.00
New Mexico	25.00	50.00	70.00
New York	10.00	15.00	28.00
North Carolina	17.00	34.00	48.00
North Dakota	20.00	40.00	55.00
Ohio	12.00	23.00	32.00
Oklahoma	16.00	30.00	45.00
Oregon	25.00	50.00	70.00
Pennsylvania	10.00	15.00	28.00
Rhode Island	20.00	40.00	55.00
South Carolina	20.00	40.00	55.00
South Dakota	20.00	40.00	55.00
Tennessee	17.00	34.00	48.00
Texas	11.00	22.00	30.00
Utah	25.00	50.00	70.00
Vermont	25.00	50.00	70.00
Virginia	17.00	34.00	48.00
Washington	25.00	50.00	70.00
West Virginia	20.00	40.00	55.00
Wisconsin	12.00	23.00	32.00
Wyoming	25.00	50.00	70.00

1929 Type 2 $5
(KL# 1171)

	VG	VF	AU
Alabama	19.00	36.00	50.00
Alaska	45.00	65.00	110.
Arizona	28.00	55.00	75.00
Arkansas	28.00	55.00	75.00
California	13.00	26.00	35.00
Colorado	20.00	40.00	55.00
Connecticut	20.00	40.00	55.00
Delaware	45.00	65.00	110.
District of Columbia	28.00	55.00	75.00
Florida	23.00	45.00	60.00
Georgia	19.00	36.00	50.00
Hawaii	45.00	65.00	100.
Idaho	28.00	55.00	75.00
Illinois	13.00	26.00	35.00
Indiana	19.00	36.00	50.00
Iowa	13.00	26.00	35.00
Kansas	16.00	30.00	40.00
Kentucky	20.00	40.00	55.00
Louisiana	28.00	55.00	75.00
Maine	28.00	55.00	75.00
Maryland	19.00	36.00	50.00
Massachusetts	13.00	26.00	35.00
Michigan	16.00	30.00	40.00
Minnesota	14.00	27.00	36.00
Mississippi	28.00	55.00	75.00
Missouri	14.00	27.00	36.00
Montana	23.00	45.00	60.00
Nebraska	16.00	30.00	40.00
Nevada	45.00	65.00	110.
New Hampshire	23.00	45.00	60.00
New Jersey	14.00	27.00	36.00
New Mexico	28.00	55.00	75.00
New York	12.00	20.00	32.00
North Carolina	20.00	40.00	55.00
North Dakota	23.00	45.00	60.00
Ohio	14.00	27.00	36.00
Oklahoma	19.00	36.00	50.00
Oregon	28.00	55.00	75.00
Pennsylvania	12.00	20.00	32.00
Rhode Island	23.00	45.00	60.00
South Carolina	23.00	45.00	60.00
South Dakota	23.00	45.00	60.00
Tennessee	20.00	40.00	55.00
Texas	13.00	26.00	35.00
Utah	28.00	55.00	75.00
Vermont	28.00	55.00	75.00
Virginia	20.00	40.00	55.00
Washington	28.00	55.00	75.00
West Virginia	23.00	45.00	60.00
Wisconsin	14.00	27.00	36.00
Wyoming	28.00	55.00	75.00

Original Series $10
(KL# 1172-1175)

	VG	VF	AU
Alabama	185.	620.	1800.
Arkansas	240.	750.	2250.
California	135.	440.	1300.
Colorado Territory	325.	1100.	3000.
Connecticut	200.	675.	2000.
Delaware	325.	1100.	3000.
District of Columbia	240.	750.	2250.
Florida	210.	710.	2100.
Georgia	185.	620.	1800.
Idaho Territory	—	—	—
Illinois	135.	440.	1300.
Indiana	185.	620.	1800.
Iowa	135.	440.	1300.
Kansas	155.	520.	1500.
Kentucky	200.	675.	2000.
Louisiana	240.	750.	2250.
Maine	240.	750.	2250.
Maryland	185.	620.	1800.
Massachusetts	140.	460.	1350.
Michigan	155.	520.	1500.
Minnesota	140.	460.	1350.
Mississippi	240.	750.	2250.
Missouri	140.	460.	1350.
Montana Territory	325.	1100.	3000.
Montana	210.	710.	2100.
Nebraska	155.	520.	1500.
Nebraska Territory	—	—	—
Nevada	325.	1100.	3000.
New Hampshire	210.	710.	2100.
New Jersey	140.	460.	1350.
New Mexico Territory	325.	1100.	3000.
New York	125.	225.	1200.
North Carolina	200.	675.	2000.
Ohio	140.	460.	1350.
Pennsylvania	125.	225.	1200.
Rhode Island	210.	710.	2100.
South Carolina	210.	710.	2100.
Tennessee	200.	675.	2000.
Texas	135.	440.	1300.
Utah Territory	325.	1100.	3000.
Vermont	240.	750.	2250.
Virginia	200.	675.	2000.
West Virginia	210.	710.	2100.
Wisconsin	140.	460.	1350.
Wyoming Territory	—	—	—

Series 1875 $10
(KL# 1176-1184)

	VG	VF	AU
Alabama	185.	550.	1800.
Arkansas	240.	657.	2250.
California	135.	400.	1300.
Colorado Territory	325.	950.	3000.
Colorado	200.	600.	2000.
Connecticut	200.	600.	2000.
Dakota Territory	325.	950.	3000.
Delaware	325.	950.	3000.
District of Columbia	240.	675.	2250.
Florida	210.	635.	2100.
Georgia	185.	550.	1800.
Idaho Territory	—	—	—
Illinois	135.	400.	1300.
Indiana	185.	550.	1800.
Iowa	135.	400.	1300.
Kansas	155.	460.	1500.
Kentucky	200.	600.	2000.
Louisiana	240.	675.	2250.
Maine	240.	675.	2250.
Maryland	185.	550.	1800.
Massachusetts	140.	420.	1350.
Michigan	155.	460.	1500.
Minnesota	140.	420.	1350.
Missouri	140.	420.	1350.
Montana Territory	325.	950.	3000.
Montana	210.	635.	2100.
Nebraska	155.	460.	1500.
Nebraska Territory	—	—	—
New Hampshire	210.	635.	2100.
New Jersey	140.	420.	1350.
New Mexico Territory	325.	950.	3000.
New York	125.	225.	800.
North Carolina	200.	600.	2000.
North Dakota	210.	635.	2100.
Ohio	140.	420.	1350.
Oregon	240.	675.	2250.
Pennsylvania	125.	225.	800.
Rhode Island	210.	635.	2100.
South Carolina	210.	635.	2100.
South Dakota	210.	635.	2100.
Tennessee	200.	600.	2000.
Texas	135.	400.	1300.
Utah Territory	325.	950.	3000.
Utah	240.	675.	2250.
Vermont	240.	675.	2250.
Virginia	200.	600.	2000.
West Virginia	210.	635.	2100.
Wisconsin	140.	420.	1100.
Wyoming Territory		—	—
Wyoming	240.	675.	2250.

1882 Brown Back $10
(KL# 1185-1198)

	VG	VF	AU
Alabama	110.	270.	500.
Arizona Territory	200.	500.	825.
Arkansas	140.	350.	600.
California	80.00	200.	345.

	VG	VF	AU
Colorado	120.	300.	525.
Connecticut	120.	300.	525.
Dakota Territory	200.	500.	825.
Delaware	200.	500.	825.
District of Columbia	140.	350.	600.
Florida	125.	320.	560.
Georgia	110.	270.	500.
Hawaii	200.	500.	825.
Idaho Territory	—	—	—
Idaho	140.	350.	600.
Illinois	80.00	200.	345.
Indian Territory	200.	500.	825.
Indiana	110.	270.	500.
Iowa	80.00	200.	345.
Kansas	95.00	230.	400.
Kentucky	120.	300.	525.
Louisiana	140.	350.	600.
Maine	140.	350.	600.
Maryland	110.	270.	500.
Massachusetts	85.00	210.	360.
Michigan	95.00	230.	400.
Minnesota	85.00	210.	360.
Mississippi	140.	350	600.
Missouri	85.00	210	360
Montana Territory	200.	500.	825.
Montana	125.	320.	560.
Nebraska	95.00	230.	400.
Nevada	200.	500.	825.
New Hampshire	125.	320.	560.
New Jersey	85.00	210.	360.
New Mexico Territory	200.	500.	825.
New York	75.00	150.	320.
North Carolina	120.	300.	525.
North Dakota	125.	320.	560.
Ohio	85.00	210.	360.
Oklahoma Territory	200.	500.	825.
Oklahoma	110.	270.	500.
Oregon	140.	350.	600.
Pennsylvania	75.00	150.	320.
Rhode Island	125.	320.	560.
South Carolina	125.	320.	560.
South Dakota	125.	320.	560.
Tennessee	120.	300.	525.
Texas	80.00	200.	345.
Utah Territory	200.	500.	825.
Utah	140.	350.	600.
Vermont	140.	350.	600.
Virginia	120.	300.	525.
Washington Territory	—	—	—
Washington	140.	350.	600.
West Virginia	125.	320.	560.
Wisconsin	85.00	210.	360.
Wyoming Territory	—	—	—
Wyoming	140.	350.	600.

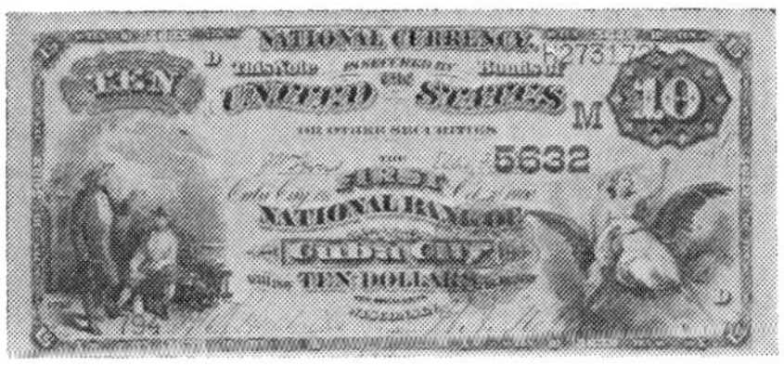

1882 Date Back $10 (KL# 1199-1208)

	VG	VF	AU
Alabama	90.00	215.	420.
Arizona Territory	170.	375.	725.
Arizona	120.	275.	525.
Arkansas	120.	275.	525.
California	65.00	150.	300.
Colorado	100.	230.	460.
Connecticut	100.	230.	460.
Delaware	170.	375.	725.
District of Columbia	120.	275.	525.
Florida	110.	245.	480.
Georgia	90.00	215.	420.
Hawaii	170.	375.	725.
Idaho	120.	275.	525.
Illinois	65.00	150.	300.
Indiana	90.00	215.	420.
Iowa	65.00	150.	300.
Kansas	80.00	180.	360.
Kentucky	100.	230.	460.
Louisiana	120.	275.	525.
Maine	120.	275.	525.
Maryland	90.00	215.	420.
Massachusetts	70.00	160.	315.
Michigan	80.00	180.	360.
Minnesota	70.00	160.	315.
Mississippi	120.	275.	525.
Missouri	70.00	160.	315.
Montana	110.	245.	480.
Nebraska	80.00	180.	360.
New Hampshire	110.	245.	480.
New Jersey	70.00	160.	315.
New Mexico Territory	170.	375.	725.
New Mexico	120.	275.	525.
New York	65.00	125.	250.
North Carolina	100.	230.	460.
North Dakota	110.	245.	480.
Ohio	70.00	160.	315.
Oklahoma	90.00	215.	420.
Oregon	120.	275.	525.
Pennsylvania	65.00	125.	250.
Rhode Island	110.	245.	480.
South Carolina	110.	245.	480.
South Dakota	110.	245.	480.
Tennessee	100.	230.	460.
Texas	65.00	150.	300.
Utah	120.	275	525.
Vermont	120.	275.	525.
Virginia	100.	230.	460.
Washington	120.	275.	525.
West Virginia	110.	245.	480.
Wisconsin	65.00	150.	300.
Wyoming	120.	275.	525.

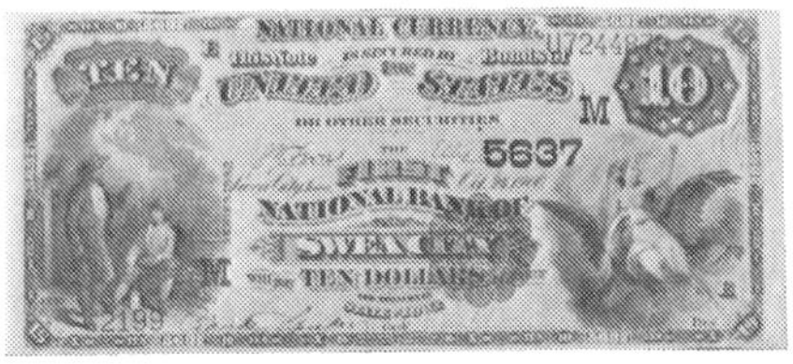

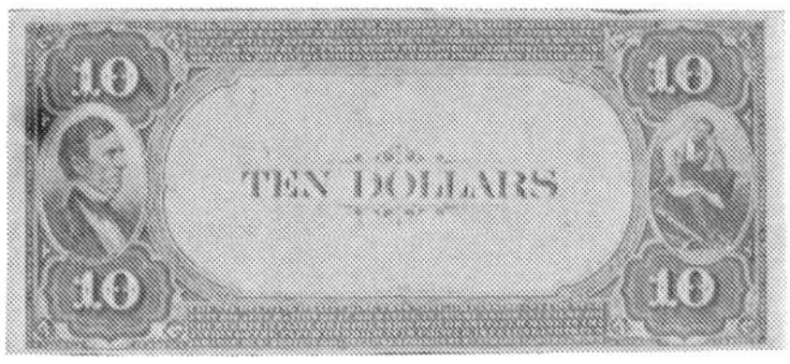

1882 Value Back $10 (KL# 1209-1215)

	VG	VF	AU
Alabama	155.	460.	950.
Arizona	200.	575.	1150.
Arkansas	200.	575.	1150.
California	135.	325.	650.
Colorado	170.	500.	1000.
Connecticut	170.	500.	1000.
Delaware	275.	800.	1700.
Florida	180.	530.	1050.
Georgia	155.	460.	950
Hawaii	275.	800.	1700.
Idaho	200.	575.	1150.
Illinois	150.	325.	650.
Indiana	155.	460.	950.
Iowa	150.	325.	650.
Kansas	165.	380.	775.
Kentucky	170.	500.	1000.
Louisiana	200.	575.	1150.
Maine	200.	575.	1150.
Maryland	155.	460.	950.
Massachusetts	160.	340.	675.
Michigan	165.	380.	775.
Minnesota	160.	340.	675.
Mississippi	200.	575.	1150.
Missouri	160.	340.	675.
Montana	180.	530.	1050.
Nebraska	155.	380.	775.
Nevada	275.	800.	1700.
New Hampshire	180.	530.	1050.
New Jersey	160.	340.	675.
New Mexico	200.	575.	1150.
New York	150.	250.	600.
North Carolina	170.	500.	1000.
North Dakota	180.	530.	1050.
Ohio	160.	340.	675.
Oklahoma	155.	460.	950.
Oregon	200.	575.	1150.
Pennsylvania	150.	250.	600.
Rhode Island	180.	530.	1050.
South Carolina	180.	530.	1050.
South Dakota	180.	530.	1050.
Tennessee	170.	500.	1000.
Texas	150.	325.	650.
Utah	200.	575.	1150.
Vermont	200.	575.	1150.
Virginia	170.	500.	1000.
Washington	200.	575.	1150.
West Virginia	180.	530.	1050.
Wisconsin	150.	340.	675.
Wyoming	200.	575.	1150.

1902 Red Seal $10 (KL# 1216-1218)

	VG	VF	AU
Alabama	120.	430.	925.
Alaska	220.	800.	1650.
Arizona Territory	220.	800.	1650.
Arkansas	150.	550.	1175.
California	85.00	300.	650.
Colorado	130.	460.	1000.
Connecticut	130.	460.	1000.
Delaware	220.	800.	1650.
District of Columbia	150.	550.	1175.
Florida	140.	500.	1075.
Georgia	120.	430.	925.
Idaho	150.	550.	1175.
Illinois	85.00	300.	650.
Indian Territory	220.	800.	1650.
Indiana	120.	430.	925.
Iowa	85.00	300.	650.
Kansas	90.00	310.	675.
Kentucky	130.	460.	1000.
Louisiana	150.	550.	1175.
Maine	150.	550.	1175.
Maryland	120.	430.	925.
Massachusetts	90.00	310.	675.
Michigan	100.	350.	750.
Minnesota	90.00	310.	675.
Mississippi	150.	550.	1175.
Missouri	90.00	310.	675.
Montana	140.00	500.	1075.
Nebraska	100.	350.	750.
Nevada	220.	800.	1650.
New Hampshire	140.	500.	1075.
New Jersey	90.00	310.	675.
New Mexico Territory	220.	800.	1650.
New York	65.00	150.	500.
North Carolina	130.	460.	1000.
North Dakota	140.	500.	1075.
Ohio	90.00	310.	675.
Oklahoma Territory	220.	800.	1650.
Oklahoma	120.	430.	925.
Oregon	150.	550.	1175.
Pennsylvania	65.00	150.	500.
Puerto Rico	—	—	—
Rhode Island	140.	500.	1075.
South Carolina	140.	500.	1075.
South Dakota	140.	500.	1075.
Tennessee	130.	460.	1000
Texas	85.00	300.	650.
Utah	150.	550.	1175.
Vermont	150.	550.	1175
Virginia	130.	460.	1000.
Washington	150.	550.	1175.
West Virginia	140.	500.	1075.
Wisconsin	90.00	310.	675.
Wyoming	150.	550.	1175.

1902 Date Back $10 (KL# 1219-1227)

	VG	VF	AU
Alabama	39.00	70.00	170.
Alaska	150.	300.	600.
Arizona Territory	150.	300.	600.
Arizona	55.00	100.	245.
Arkansas	55.00	100.	245.
California	29.00	49.00	120.
Colorado	40.00	72.00	185.
Connecticut	40.00	72.00	185.
Delaware	150.	300.	600.
District of Columbia	55.00	100.	245.

	VG	VF	AU
Florida	45.00	85.00	200.
Georgia	39.00	70.00	170.
Hawaii	150.	300.	600.
Idaho	55.00	100.	245.
Illinois	29.00	49.00	120.
Indiana	39.00	70.00	170.
Iowa	29.00	49.00	120.
Kansas	32.00	57.00	140.
Kentucky	34.00	68.00	185.
Louisiana	55.00	100.	245.
Maine	55.00	100.	245.
Maryland	39.00	70.00	170.
Massachusetts	30.00	51.00	125.
Michigan	32.00	57.00	140.
Minnesota	30.00	51.00	125.
Mississippi	55.00	100.	245.
Missouri	30.00	51.00	125.
Montana	45.00	85.00	200.
Nebraska	32.00	57.00	140.
Nevada	150.	300.	600.
New Hampshire	45.00	85.00	200.
New Jersey	30.00	51.00	125.
New Mexico Territory	150.	300.	600.
New Mexico	55.00	100.	245.
New York	27.50	45.00	110.
North Carolina	40.00	72.00	185.
North Dakota	45.00	85.00	200.
Ohio	30.00	46.00	125.
Oklahoma	39.00	70.00	170.
Oregon	55.00	100.	245.
Pennsylvania	27.50	45.00	110.
Puerto Rico	—	—	—
Rhode Island	45.00	85.00	200.
South Carolina	45.00	85.00	200.
South Dakota	45.00	85.00	200.
Tennessee	40.00	72.00	185.
Texas	29.00	49.00	120.
Utah	55.00	100.	245.
Vermont	55.00	100.	245.
Virginia	40.00	72.00	185.
Washington	55.00	100.	245.
West Virginia	45.00	85.00	200.
Wisconsin	30.00	51.00	125.
Wyoming	55.00	100.	245.

1902 Plain Back $10
(KL# 1228-1242)

	VG	VF	AU
Alabama	38.00	50.00	140.
Alaska	150.	290.	575.
Arizona	40.00	90.00	220.
Arkansas	40.00	90.00	220.
California	30.00	40.00	95.00
Colorado	40.00	60.00	150.
Connecticut	40.00	60.00	150.
Delaware	150.	290.	575.
District of Columbia	50.00	90.00	220.
Florida	40.00	75.00	185.
Georgia	38.00	50.00	140.
Hawaii	150.	290.	575.
Idaho	40.00	90.00	220.
Illinois	30.00	40.00	95.00
Indiana	38.00	50.00	140.
Iowa	30.00	40.00	95.00
Kansas	34.00	45.00	115.
Kentucky	30.00	50.00	150.
Louisiana	50.00	90.00	220.
Maine	40.00	90.00	220.
Maryland	38.00	50.00	140.
Massachusetts	31.00	42.00	100.
Michigan	34.00	45.00	115.
Minnesota	31.00	42.00	100.
Mississippi	40.00	90.00	220.
Missouri	31.00	42.00	100.
Montana	40.00	75.00	185.
Nebraska	34.00	45.00	115.
Nevada	150.	290.	575.
New Hampshire	40.00	75.00	185.
New Jersey	31.00	42.00	100.
New Mexico	40.00	90.00	220.
New York	27.50	40.00	90.00
North Carolina	30.00	50.00	150.

	VG	VF	AU
North Dakota	40.00	75.00	185.
Ohio	31.00	42.00	100.
Oklahoma	38.00	52.00	140.
Oregon	40.00	90.00	220.
Pennsylvania	27.50	40.00	90.00
Rhode Island	40.00	75.00	185.
South Carolina	40.00	75.00	185.
South Dakota	40.00	75.00	185.
Tennessee	30.00	50.00	150.
Texas	30.00	42.00	95.00
Utah	40.00	90.00	220.
Vermont	40.00	90.00	220.
Virginia	30.00	50.00	150.
Washington	40.00	90.00	220.
West Virginia	40.00	75.00	185.
Wisconsin	31.00	42.00	100.
Wyoming	40.00	90.00	220.

1929 Type 1 $10
(KL# 1243)

	VG	VF	AU
Alabama	18.00	28.00	40.00
Alaska	—	—	—
Arizona	35.00	50.00	75.00
Arkansas	28.00	40.00	60.00
California	14.00	22.00	32.00
Colorado	18.00	28.00	40.00
Connecticut	28.00	40.00	60.00
Delaware	35.00	50.00	75.00
District of Columbia	28.00	40.00	60.00
Florida	18.00	28.00	40.00
Georgia	22.00	34.00	50.00
Hawaii	50.00	65.00	95.00
Idaho	50.00	65.00	95.00
Illinois	15.00	24.00	35.00
Indiana	16.00	25.00	37.00
Iowa	15.00	24.00	35.00
Kansas	15.00	24.00	35.00
Kentucky	18.00	28.00	40.00
Louisiana	24.00	37.00	55.00
Maine	35.00	50.00	75.00
Maryland	22.00	34.00	50.00
Massachusetts	14.00	22.00	32.00
Michigan	16.00	25.00	37.00
Minnesota	16.00	25.00	37.00
Mississippi	24.00	37.00	55.00
Missouri	18.00	28.00	40.00
Montana	22.00	34.00	50.00
Nebraska	16.00	25.00	37.00
Nevada	35.00	50.00	75.00
New Hampshire	28.00	40.00	60.00
New Jersey	15.00	24.00	35.00
New Mexico	35.00	50.00	75.00
New York	12.50	17.50	32.00
North Carolina	24.00	37.00	55.00
North Dakota	24.00	37.00	55.00
Ohio	15.00	24.00	35.00
Oklahoma	18.00	28.00	40.00
Oregon	24.00	37.00	55.00
Pennsylvania	12.50	17.50	32.00
Rhode Island	50.00	65.00	95.00
South Carolina	28.00	40.00	60.00
South Dakota	28.00	40.00	60.00
Tennessee	22.00	34.00	50.00
Texas	15.00	24.00	35.00
Utah	24.00	37.00	55.00
Vermont	35.00	50.00	75.00
Virginia	22.00	34.00	50.00
Washington	24.00	37.00	55.00
West Virginia	24.00	37.00	55.00
Wisconsin	15.00	24.00	35.00
Wyoming	22.00	34.00	50.00

1929 Type 2 $10
(KL# 1244)

	VG	VF	AU
Alabama	21.00	35.00	45.00
Alaska	—	—	—
Arizona	36.00	60.00	80.00
Arkansas	25.00	50.00	65.00

	VG	VF	AU
California	—	—	—
Colorado	21.00	35.00	45.00
Connecticut	30.00	50.00	65.00
Delaware	36.00	60.00	80.00
District of Columbia	25.00	50.00	65.00
Florida	21.00	35.00	45.00
Georgia	24.00	40.00	55.00
Hawaii	55.00	70.00	100.
Idaho	65.00	90.00	120.
Illinois	17.00	30.00	38.00
Indiana	18.00	32.00	40.00
Iowa	17.00	30.00	38.00
Kansas	17.00	30.00	38.00
Kentucky	21.00	35.00	45.00
Louisiana	25.00	45.00	60.00
Maine	36.00	60.00	80.00
Maryland	24.00	40.00	55.00
Massachusetts	16.00	28.00	35.00
Michigan	18.00	32.00	40.00
Minnesota	18.00	32.00	40.00
Mississippi	25.00	45.00	60.00
Missouri	21.00	35.00	45.00
Montana	24.00	40.00	55.00
Nebraska	17.00	32.00	40.00
Nevada	36.00	60.00	80.00
New Hampshire	25.00	50.00	65.00
New Jersey	17.00	30.00	38.00
New Mexico	36.00	60.00	80.00
New York	14.00	20.00	35.00
North Carolina	25.00	45.00	60.00
North Dakota	25.00	45.00	60.00
Ohio	17.00	30.00	38.00
Oklahoma	21.00	35.00	45.00
Oregon	25.00	45.00	60.00
Pennsylvania	14.00	20.00	35.00
Rhode Island	65.00	90.00	120.
South Carolina	25.00	50.00	65.00
South Dakota	25.00	50.00	65.00
Tennessee	24.00	40.00	50.00
Texas	17.00	30.00	38.00
Utah	25.00	45.00	60.00
Vermont	36.00	60.00	80.00
Virginia	24.00	40.00	55.00
Washington	25.00	45.00	60.00
West Virginia	25.00	45.00	60.00
Wisconsin	17.00	30.00	38.00
Wyoming	24.00	40.00	55.00

Original Series $20
(KL# 1245-1248)

	VG	VF	AU
Alabama	340.	620.	1800.
Arkansas	400.	750.	2250.
California	275.	600.	1300.
Colorado Territory	540.	1150.	3000.
Connecticut	340.	675.	2000.
Delaware	540.	1150.	3000.
District of Columbia	400.	750.	2250.
Georgia	340.	620.	1800.
Idaho Territory	—	—	—
Illinois	275.	600.	1300.
Indiana	300.	620.	1800.
Iowa	275.	600.	1300.
Kansas	325.	650.	1500.
Kentucky	340.	675.	2000.
Louisiana	400.	750.	2250.
Maine	400.	750.	2250.
Maryland	340.	620.	1800.
Massachusetts	310.	460.	1350.
Michigan	325.	650.	1500.
Minnesota	310.	625.	1350.
Mississippi	400.	750.	2250.
Missouri	310.	625.	1350.
Montana Territory	540.	1150.	3000.
Montana	360.	710.	2100.
Nebraska	325.	625.	1500.
Nebraska Territory	—	—	—
Nevada	540.	1150.	3000.
New Hampshire	360.	710.	2100.
New Jersey	310.	625.	1350.
New Mexico Territory	540.	1150.	3000.

	VG	VF	AU
New York	295.	625.	1200.
North Carolina	340.	675.	2000.
Ohio	310.	460.	1350.
Pennsylvania	295.	625.	1200.
Rhode Island	360.	710.	2100.
South Carolina	360.	710.	2100.
Tennessee	340.	675.	2000.
Texas	275.	600.	1300.
Utah Territory	540.	1150.	3000.
Utah	400.	750.	2250.
Vermont	400.	750.	2250.
Virginia	340.	675.	2000.
West Virginia	360.	710.	2100.
Wisconsin	310.	625.	1350.
Wyoming Territory	—	—	—

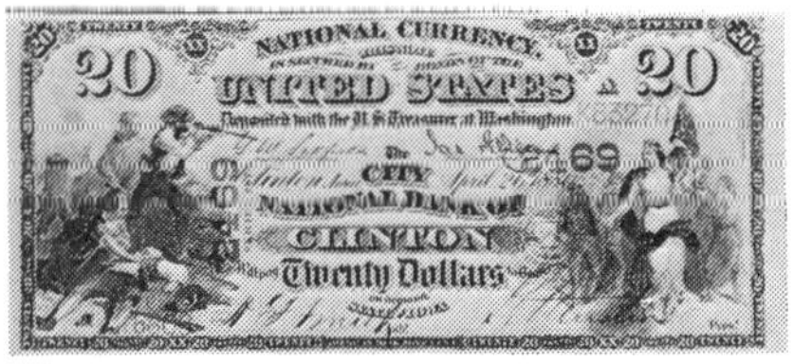

Series 1875 $20
(KL# 1249-1257)

	VG	VF	AU
Alabama	300.	680.	1800.
Arkansas	400.	850.	2250.
California	295.	650.	1300.
Colorado Territory	540.	1200.	3000.
Colorado	340.	750.	2000.
Connecticut	340.	750.	2000.
Dakota Territory	540.	1200.	3000.
Delaware	540.	1200.	3000.
District of Columbia	400.	850.	2250.
Georgia	300.	680.	1800.
Hawaii	540.	1200.	3000.
Idaho Territory	—	—	—
Illinois	295.	650.	1300.
Indiana	300.	680.	1800.
Iowa	295.	650.	1300.
Kansas	325.	675.	1500.
Kentucky	340.	750.	2000.
Louisiana	400.	850.	2250.
Maine	400.	850.	2250.
Maryland	300.	680.	1800.
Massachusetts	300.	650.	1350.
Michigan	325.	675.	1500.
Minnesota	300.	650.	1350.
Missouri	300.	650.	1350.
Montana Territory	540.	1200.	3000.
Montana	360.	800.	2100.
Nebraska	325.	675.	1500.
Nebraska Territory	—	—	—
Nevada	540.	1200.	3000.
New Hampshire	360.	800.	2100.
New Jersey	300.	650.	1350.
New Mexico Territory	540.	1200.	3000.
New York	275.	600.	1200.
North Carolina	340.	750.	2000.
North Dakota	360.	800.	2100.
Ohio	230.	500.	1350.
Oregon	400.	850.	2250.
Pennsylvania	275.	600.	1200.
Rhode Island	360.	800.	2100.
South Carolina	360.	800.	2100.
South Dakota	360.	800.	2100.
Tennessee	340.	750.	2000.
Texas	295.	640.	1300.
Utah Territory	540.	1200.	3000.
Utah	400.	850.	2250.
Vermont	400.	850.	2250.
Virginia	340.	750.	2000.
West Virginia	360.	800.	2100.
Wisconsin	300.	650.	1350.
Wyoming Territory	—	—	—
Wyoming	400.	850.	2250.

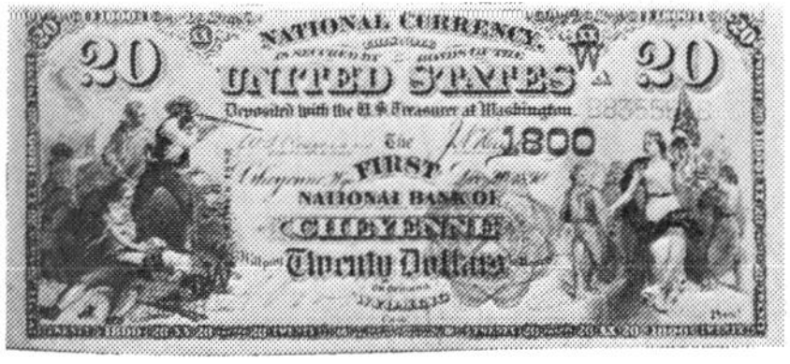

1882 Brown Back $20
(KL# 1258-1270)

	VG	VF	AU
Alabama	110.	300.	550.
Arizona Territory	220.	550.	900.
Arkansas	150.	400.	675.
California	80.00	160.	345.
Colorado	125.	340.	580.
Connecticut	125.	340.	580.
Dakota Territory	220.	550.	900.
Delaware	220.	550.	900.
District of Columbia	135.	360.	615.
Florida	135.	360.	615.
Georgia	110.	300.	550.
Hawaii	220.	550.	900.
Idaho Territory	—	—	—
Idaho	150.	400.	675.
Illinois	80.00	160.	345.
Indian Territory	220.	550.	900.
Indiana	110.	300.	500.
Iowa	80.00	160.	345.
Kansas	100.	250.	440.
Kentucky	125.	340.	580.
Louisiana	150.	400.	675.
Maine	150.	400.	675.
Maryland	110.	300.	550.
Massachusetts	90.00	175.	390.
Michigan	100.	250.	440.
Minnesota	90.00	175.	390.
Mississippi	150.	400.	675.
Missouri	90.00	175.	390.
Montana Territory	220.	550.	900.
Montana	135.	360.	615.
Nebraska	100.	250.	440.
Nevada	220.	550.	900.
New Hampshire	135.	360.	615.
New Jersey	90.00	175.	390.
New Mexico Territory	220.	550.	900.
New York	75.00	150.	350.
North Carolina	125.	340.	580.
North Dakota	135.	360.	615.
Ohio	90.00	230.	390.
Oklahoma Territory	220.	550.	900.
Oklahoma	120.	300.	550.
Oregon	150.	400.	675.
Pennsylvania	75.00	150.	350.
Rhode Island	135.	360.	615.
South Carolina	135.	360.	615.
South Dakota	135.	360.	615.
Tennessee	125.	340.	580.
Texas	80.00	160.	345.
Utah Territory	220.	550.	900.
Utah	150.	400.	675.
Vermont	150.	400.	675.
Virginia	125.	340.	580.
Washington Territory	—	—	—
Washington	140.	400.	675.
West Virginia	135.	360.	615.
Wisconsin	90.00	230.	390.
Wyoming Territory	—	—	—
Wyoming	150.	400.	675.

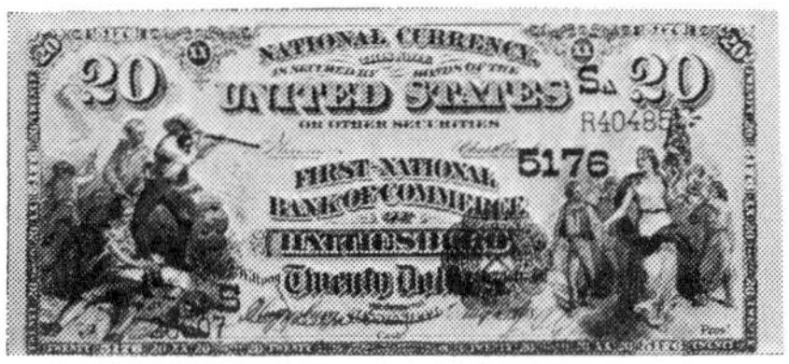

1882 Date Back $20
(KL# 1272-1280)

	VG	VF	AU
Alabama	105.	240.	460.
Alaska	200.	425.	800.
Arizona Territory	200.	425.	800.
Arizona	140.	300.	580.
Arkansas	140.	300.	580.
California	90.00	185.	325.
Colorado	115.	260.	500.
Connecticut	115.	260.	500.
Delaware	200.	425.	800.
District of Columbia	140.	300.	580.
Florida	125.	275.	525.
Georgia	105.	240.	460.
Hawaii	200.	425.	800.
Idaho	140.	300.	580.
Illinois	90.00	185.	325.
Indiana	105.	240.	460.
Iowa	90.00	185.	325.
Kansas	100.	210.	385.
Kentucky	115.	260.	500.
Louisiana	140.	300.	580.
Maine	140.	300.	580.
Maryland	105.	240.	460.
Massachusetts	95.00	195.	340.
Michigan	100.	210.	385.
Minnesota	95.00	195.	340.
Mississippi	140.	300.	580.
Missouri	95.00	195.	340.
Montana	125.	275.	525.
Nebraska	100.	210.	385.
New Hampshire	125.	275.	525.
New Jersey	95.00	195.	340.
New Mexico Territory	200.	425.	800.
New Mexico	140.	300.	580.
New York	85.00	135.	300.
North Carolina	115.	260.	500.
North Dakota	125.	275.	525.
Ohio	95.00	195.	340.
Oklahoma	105.	240.	460.
Oregon	140.	300.	580.
Pennsylvania	85.00	135.	300.
Rhode Island	125.	275.	525.
South Carolina	125.	275.	525.
South Dakota	125.	275.	525.
Tennessee	115.	260.	500.
Texas	90.00	175.	325.
Utah	140.	300.	580.
Vermont	140.	300.	580.
Virginia	115.	260.	500.
Washington	140.	300.	580.
West Virginia	125.	275.	525.
Wisconsin	95.00	195.	340.
Wyoming	140.	300.	580.

1882 Value Back $20
(KL# 1281-1289)

	VG	VF	AU
Alabama	185.	620.	1300.
Arizona	235.	775.	1650.
Arkansas	235.	775.	1650.
California	160.	410.	925.
Colorado	200.	680.	1400.
Connecticut	200.	680.	1400.
Delaware	325.	1100.	2250.
Florida	210.	720.	1500.
Georgia	185.	620.	1300.
Hawaii	325.	1100.	2250.
Idaho	235.	775.	1650.
Illinois	160.	410.	925.
Indiana	185.	620.	1300.
Iowa	160.	410.	925.
Kansas	185.	475.	1050.
Kentucky	200.	680.	1400.
Louisiana	235.	775.	1650.
Maine	235.	775.	1650.
Maryland	220.	600.	1300.
Massachusetts	170.	425.	965.
Michigan	185.	475.	1050.
Minnesota	170.	425.	965.
Mississippi	235.	775.	1650.
Missouri	170.	425.	965.

	VG	VF	AU
Montana	210.	720.	1500.
Nebraska	185.	475.	1050.
Nevada	325.	1100.	2250.
New Hampshire	210.	720.	1500.
New Jersey	170.	425.	965.
New Mexico	235.	775.	1650.
New York	150.	375.	850.
North Carolina	200.	680.	1400.
North Dakota	210.	720.	1500.
Ohio	170.	425.	965.
Oklahoma	185.	620.	1300.
Oregon	235.	775.	1650.
Pennsylvania	150.	375.	850.
Rhode Island	210.	720.	1500.
South Carolina	210.	720.	1500.
South Dakota	210.	720.	1500.
Tennessee	200.	680.	1400.
Texas	160.	410.	925.
Utah	235.	775.	1650.
Vermont	235.	775.	1650.
Virginia	200.	680.	1400.
Washington	235.	775.	1650.
West Virginia	210.	720.	1500.
Wisconsin	170.	425.	965.
Wyoming	235.	775.	1650.

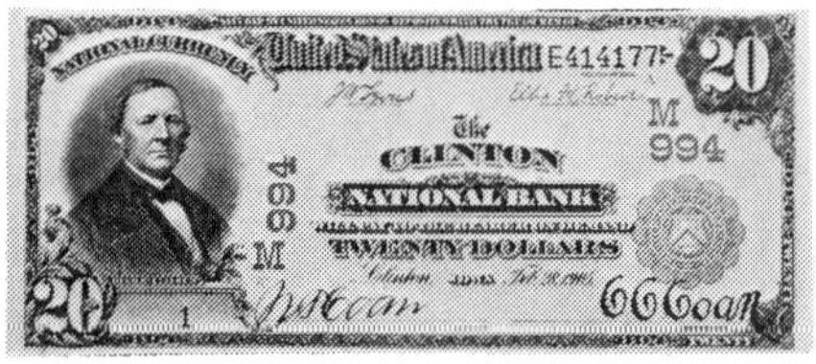

1902 Red Seal $20
(KL# 1290-1292)

	VG	VF	AU
Alabama	150.	475.	1150.
Arizona Territory	275.	875.	2100.
Arkansas	200.	600.	1500.
California	105.	325.	800.
Colorado	160.	500.	1250.
Connecticut	160.	500.	1250.
Delaware	275.	875.	2100.
District of Columbia	200.	600.	1500.
Florida	170.	540.	1350.
Georgia	150.	475.	1150.
Idaho	200.	600.	1500.
Illinois	105.	325.	800.
Indian Territory	275.	875.	2100.
Indiana	150.	475.	1150.
Iowa	105.	325.	800.
Kansas	125.	380.	950.
Kentucky	160.	500.	1250.
Louisiana	200.	600.	1500.
Maine	200.	600.	1500.
Maryland	150.	475.	1150.
Massachusetts	110.	340.	840.
Michigan	125.	380.	950.
Minnesota	110.	340.	840.
Mississippi	200.	600.	1500.
Missouri	110.	340.	840.
Montana	170.	540.	1350.
Nebraska	125.	380.	950.
Nevada	275.	875.	2100.
New Hampshire	170.	540.	1350.
New Jersey	110.	340.	840.
New Mexico Territory	275.	875.	2100.
New York	75.00	150.	450.
North Carolina	160.	500.	1250.
North Dakota	170.	540.	1350.
Ohio	110.	340.	840.
Oklahoma Territory	275.	875.	2100.
Oklahoma	150.	475.	1150.
Oregon	200.	600.	1500.
Pennsylvania	75.00	150.	450.
Puerto Rico	—	—	—
Rhode Island	170.	540.	1350.
South Carolina	170.	540.	1350.
South Dakota	170.	540.	1350.
Tennessee	160.	500.	1250.
Texas	105.	325.	800.
Utah	200.	600.	1500.
Vermont	200.	600.	1500.
Virginia	160.	500.	1250.
Washington	200.	600.	1500.
West Virginia	170.	540.	1350.
Wisconsin	110.	340.	840.
Wyoming	200.	600.	1500.

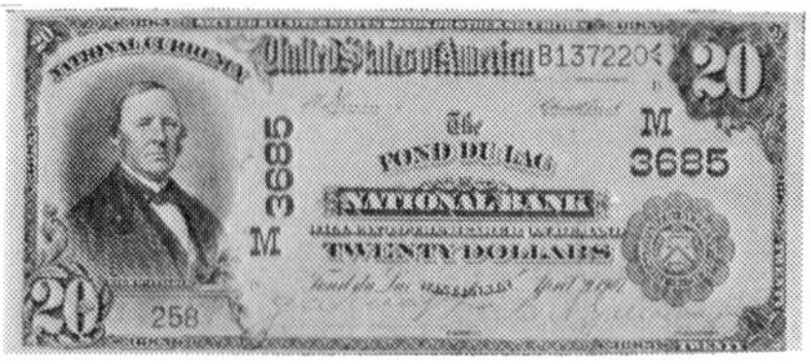

1902 Date Back $20
(KL# 1293-1301)

	VG	VF	AU
Alabama	105.	240.	460.
Alaska	200.	425.	800.
Arizona Territory	200.	425.	800.
Arizona	140.	300.	580.
Arkansas	140.	300.	580.
California	35.00	70.00	160.
Colorado	115.	260.	500.
Connecticut	115.	260.	500.
Delaware	200.	425.	800.
District of Columbia	140.	300.	580.
Florida	125.	275.	525.
Georgia	105.	240.	460.
Hawaii	200.	425.	800.
Idaho	140.	300.	580.
Illinois	35.00	70.00	160.
Indiana	105.	240.	460.
Iowa	35.00	70.00	160.
Kansas	50.00	100.	195.
Kentucky	115.	260.	500.
Louisiana	140.	300.	580.
Maine	140.	300.	580.
Maryland	105.	240.	460.
Massachusetts	40.00	80.00	170.
Michigan	50.00	100.	195.
Minnesota	40.00	80.00	170.
Mississippi	140.	300.	580.
Missouri	40.00	80.00	170.
Montana	125.	275.	525.
Nebraska	50.00	100.	195.
Nevada	200.	425.	800.
New Hampshire	125.	275.	525.
New Jersey	40.00	80.00	170.
New Mexico Territory	200.	425.	800.
New Mexico	140.	300.	580.
New York	30.00	45.00	150.
North Carolina	115.	260.	500.
North Dakota	125.	275.	525.
Ohio	40.00	80.00	170.
Oklahoma	105.	240.	460.
Oregon	140.	300.	580.
Pennsylvania	30.00	45.00	150.
Puerto Rico	—	—	—
Rhode Island	125.	275.	525.
South Carolina	125.	275.	525.
South Dakota	125.	275.	525.
Tennessee	115.	260.	500.
Texas	35.00	70.00	160.
Utah	140.	300.	580.
Vermont	140.	300.	580.
Virginia	115.	260.	500.
Washington	140.	300.	580.
West Virginia	125.	275.	525.
Wisconsin	40.00	80.00	170.
Wyoming	140.	300.	580.

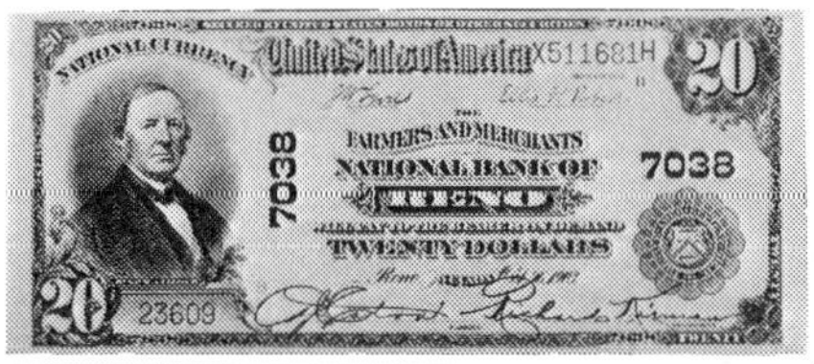

1902 Plain Back $20
(KL# 1302-1316)

	VG	VF	AU
Alabama	40.00	75.00	170.
Alaska	160.	325.	600.
Arizona	70.00	120.	250.
Arkansas	70.00	120.	250.
California	30.00	55.00	120.
Colorado	45.00	85.00	185.
Connecticut	45.00	85.00	185.
Delaware	160.	325.	600.
District of Columbia	70.00	120.	250.
Florida	55.00	90.00	220.
Georgia	40.00	75.00	170.
Hawaii	160.	325.	600.
Idaho	70.00	120.	250.
Illinois	30.00	55.00	120.
Indiana	40.00	75.00	170.
Iowa	30.00	55.00	120.
Kansas	35.00	65.00	140.
Kentucky	45.00	85.00	185.
Louisiana	70.00	120.	250.
Maine	70.00	120.	125.
Maryland	40.00	75.00	170.
Massachusetts	32.00	57.00	125.
Michigan	35.00	65.00	140.
Minnesota	32.00	57.00	125.
Mississippi	70.00	120.	250.
Missouri	32.00	57.00	125.
Montana	55.00	90.00	220.
Nebraska	35.00	65.00	140.
Nevada	160.	325.	600.
New Hampshire	55.00	90.00	220.
New Jersey	32.00	57.00	125.
New Mexico	70.00	120.	250.
New York	27.50	45.00	110.
North Carolina	45.00	85.00	185.
North Dakota	55.00	90.00	220.
Ohio	32.00	57.00	125.
Oklahoma	40.00	75.00	170.
Oregon	70.00	120.	250.
Pennsylvania	27.50	45.00	110.
Rhode Island	55.00	90.00	220.
South Carolina	55.00	90.00	220.
South Dakota	55.00	90.00	220.
Tennessee	45.00	85.00	185.
Texas	30.00	55.00	120.
Utah	70.00	120.	250.
Vermont	70.00	120.	250.
Virginia	45.00	85.00	185.
Washington	70.00	120.	250.
West Virginia	55.00	90.00	220.
Wisconsin	32.00	57.00	125.
Wyoming	70.00	120.	250.

1929 Type 1 $20
(KL# 1317)

	VG	VF	AU
Alabama	29.00	36.00	50.00
Alaska	—	—	—
Arizona	43.00	60.00	80.00
Arkansas	37.00	50.00	70.00
California	24.00	28.00	40.00
Colorado	29.00	36.00	50.00
Connecticut	37.00	50.00	70.00
Delaware	43.00	60.00	80.00
District of Columbia	37.00	50.00	70.00
Florida	29.00	36.00	50.00
Georgia	32.00	40.00	60.00
Idaho	60.00	85.00	115.
Illinois	25.00	30.00	43.00
Indiana	26.00	32.00	45.00
Iowa	25.00	30.00	43.00
Kansas	25.00	30.00	43.00
Kentucky	29.00	36.00	50.00
Louisiana	34.00	45.00	65.00
Maine	43.00	60.00	80.00
Maryland	32.00	40.00	60.00
Massachusetts	24.00	28.00	40.00
Michigan	26.00	32.00	45.00
Minnesota	26.00	32.00	45.00
Mississippi	34.00	45.00	65.00
Missouri	29.00	36.00	50.00
Montana	32.00	40.00	60.00
Nebraska	26.00	32.00	45.00
Nevada	43.00	60.00	80.00
New Hampshire	37.00	50.00	70.00
New Jersey	25.00	30.00	43.00
New Mexico	43.00	60.00	80.00
New York	23.50	27.50	40.00
North Carolina	34.00	45.00	65.00
North Dakota	34.00	45.00	65.00
Ohio	25.00	30.00	43.00
Oklahoma	29.00	36.00	50.00
Oregon	34.00	45.00	65.00
Pennsylvania	23.50	27.50	40.00

	VG	VF	AU
Rhode Island	60.00	85.00	115.
South Carolina	37.00	50.00	70.00
South Dakota	37.00	50.00	70.00
Tennessee	32.00	40.00	60.00
Texas	25.00	30.00	43.00
Utah	34.00	45.00	65.00
Vermont	43.00	60.00	80.00
Virginia	32.00	40.00	60.00
Washington	34.00	45.00	65.00
West Virginia	34.00	45.00	65.00
Wisconsin	25.00	30.00	43.00
Wyoming	32.00	40.00	60.00

1929 Type 2 $20
(KL# 1318)

	VG	VF	AU
Alabama	30.00	38.00	55.00
Alaska	—	—	—
Arizona	45.00	65.00	75.00
Arkansas	40.00	55.00	75.00
California	25.00	35.00	45.00
Colorado	30.00	40.00	55.00
Connecticut	40.00	55.00	75.00
Delaware	45.00	65.00	85.00
District of Columbia	40.00	55.00	75.00
Florida	30.00	40.00	55.00
Georgia	34.00	45.00	65.00
Idaho	65.00	90.00	120.
Illinois	26.00	38.00	48.00
Indiana	27.00	40.00	50.00
Iowa	26.00	38.00	48.00
Kansas	26.00	38.00	48.00
Kentucky	30.00	40.00	55.00
Louisiana	36.00	50.00	70.00
Maine	45.00	65.00	85.00
Maryland	34.00	45.00	65.00
Massachusetts	26.00	43.00	48.00
Michigan	—	—	—
Minnesota	27.00	40.00	50.00
Mississippi	36.00	50.00	70.00
Missouri	30.00	40.00	55.00
Montana	34.00	45.00	65.00
Nebraska	27.00	40.00	50.00
Nevada	45.00	65.00	75.00
New Hampshire	40.00	55.00	75.00
New Jersey	26.00	38.00	48.00
New Mexico	45.00	65.00	75.00
New York	25.00	35.00	45.00
North Carolina	36.00	50.00	70.00
North Dakota	36.00	50.00	70.00
Ohio	26.00	38.00	48.00
Oklahoma	30.00	43.00	55.00
Oregon	36.00	50.00	70.00
Pennsylvania	25.00	35.00	45.00
Rhode Island	65.00	90.00	120.
South CArolina	40.00	55.00	75.00
South Dakota	40.00	55.00	75.00
Tennessee	34.00	45.00	65.00
Texas	26.00	38.00	48.00
Utah	36.00	50.00	70.00
Vermont	45.00	65.00	85.00
Virginia	34.00	45.00	65.00
Washington	36.00	50.00	70.00
West Virginia	36.00	50.00	70.00
Wisconsin	26.00	38.00	48.00
Wyoming	34.00	45.00	65.00

Original Series $50
(KL# 1319-1321)

	VG	VF	AU
Alabama	2300.	4650.	8600.
Colorado Territory	3750.	7500.	15,000.
Connecticut	2500.	5000.	9400.
Delaware	3750.	7500.	15,000.
District of Columbia	2900.	5700.	10,500.
Georgia	2300.	4650.	8600.
Illinois	1650.	3300.	6250.
Indiana	2300.	4650.	8600.
Iowa	1650.	3300.	6250.
Kentucky	2500.	5000.	9400.
Louisiana	2900.	5700.	10,500.
Maine	2900.	5700.	10,500.
Maryland	2300.	4650.	8600.
Massachusetts	1725.	3450.	6500.
Michigan	1900.	3750.	7000.
Minnesota	1725.	3450	6500.
Missouri	1725.	3450.	6500.
Montana Territory	3750.	7500.	15,000.
Nebraska	1900.	3750	7000.
New Hampshire	2650.	5300.	9850.
New Jersey	1725.	3450.	6500.
New Mexico Territory	3750.	7500.	15,000.
New York	1500.	3000.	5750.
North Carolina	2500.	5000.	9400.
Ohio	1725.	3450.	6500.
Pennsylvania	1500.	3000.	5750.
Rhode Island	2650.	5300.	9850.
South Carolina	2650.	5300.	9850.
Tennessee	2500.	5000.	9400.
Texas	1650.	3300.	6250.
Utah Territory	3750.	7500.	15,000.
Utah	2900.	5700.	10,500.
Vermont	2900.	5700.	10,500.
Virginia	2500.	5000.	9400.

Series 1875 $50
(KL# 1322-1330)

	VG	VF	AU
Alabama	2100.	4200.	8000.
Arkansas	2700.	5250.	10,000.
California	1500.	3100.	6000.
Colorado Territory	3500.	7200.	14,000.
Colorado	2300.	4600.	8750.
Connecticut	2300.	4600.	8750.
Delaware	3500.	7200.	14,000.
District of Columbia	2700.	5250.	10,000.
Georgia	2100.	4200.	8000.
Illinois	1500.	3100.	6000.
Indiana	2100.	4200.	8000.
Iowa	1500.	3100.	6000.
Kansas	1750.	3500.	6800.
Kentucky	2300.	4600.	8750.
Louisiana	2700.	5250.	10,000.
Maine	2700.	5250.	10,000.
Maryland	2100.	4200.	8000.
Massachusetts	1575.	3250.	6250.
Michigan	1750.	3500.	6800.
Minnesota	1575.	3250.	6250.
Mississippi	2700.	5250.	10,000.
Missouri	1575.	3250.	6250.
Montana Territory	3500.	7200.	14,000.
Nebraska	1750.	3500.	6800.
New Hampshire	2450.	4900.	9400.
New Jersey	1575.	3250.	6250.
New Mexico Territory	3500.	7200.	14,000.
New York	1400.	2800.	5500.
Ohio	1575.	3250.	6250.
Pennsylvania	1400.	2800.	5500.
Rhode Island	2450.	4900.	9400.
South Carolina	2450.	4900.	9400.
Tennessee	2300.	4600.	8750.
Texas	1575.	3250.	6250.
Utah Territory	3500.	7200.	14,000.
Vermont	2700.	5250.	10,000.
Virginia	2300.	4600.	8750.
Wisconsin	1575.	3250.	6250.

1882 Brown Back $50
(KL# 1331-1343)

	VG	VF	AU
Alabama	575.	1550.	2600.
Arizona Territory	1000.	2750.	4500.
Arkansas	750.	1950.	3400.
California	420.	1100.	1900.
Colorado	625.	1700.	2900.
Connecticut	625.	1700.	2900.
Dakota Territory	1000.	2750.	4500.
Delaware	1000.	2750.	4500.
District of Columbia	750.	1950.	3400.
Florida	675.	1800.	3100.
Georgia	575.	1550.	2600.
Hawaii	1000.	2750.	4500.
Idaho	750.	1950.	3400.
Illinois	420.	1100.	1900.
Indian Territory	1000.	2750.	4500.
Indiana	575.	1550.	2600.
Iowa	420.	1100.	1900.
Kansas	485.	1250.	2200.
Kentucky	625.	1700.	2900.
Louisiana	750.	1950.	3400.
Maine	750.	1950.	3400.
Maryland	575.	1550.	2600.
Massachusetts	440.	1150.	2000.
Michigan	485.	1250.	2200.
Minnesota	440.	1150.	2000.
Mississippi	750.	1950.	3400.
Missouri	440.	1150.	2000.
Montana Territory	1000.	2750.	4500.
Montana	675.	1800.	3100.
Nebraska	485.	1250.	2200.
New Hampshire	675.	1800.	3100.
New Jersey	440.	1150.	2000.
New Mexico Territory	1000.	2750.	4500.
New York	275.	400.	1000.
North Carolina	625.	1700.	2900.
North Dakota	675.	1800.	3100.
Ohio	440.	1150.	2000.
Oklahoma Territory	1000.	2750.	4500.
Oklahoma	575.	1550.	2600.
Oregon	750.	1950.	3400
Pennsylvania	275.	400.	1000.
Rhode Island	675.	1800.	3100.
South Carolina	675.	1800.	3100.
South Dakota	675.	1800.	3100.
Tennessee	625.	1700.	2900.
Texas	420.	1100.	1900.
Utah Territory	1000.	2750.	4500.
Utah	750.	1950.	3400.
Vermont	750.	1950.	3400.
Virginia	625.	1700.	2950.
Washington	750.	1950.	3400.
West Virginia	675.	1800.	3100.
Wisconsin	440.	1150.	2000.

1882 Date Back $50
(KL# 1344-1351)

	VG	VF	AU
Alabama	525.	1350.	2450.
Arizona Territory	—	—	—
Arkansas	700.	1750.	3100.

	VG	VF	AU
California	380.	1000.	1750.
Colorado	580.	1500.	2700.
Connecticut	580.	1500.	2700.
Delaware	950.	2500.	4200.
District of Columbia	700.	1750.	3100.
Florida	620.	1600.	2850.
Georgia	525.	1350.	2450.
Idaho	700.	1750.	3100.
Illinois	380.	1000.	1750.
Indiana	525.	1350.	2450.
Iowa	380.	1000.	1750.
Kansas	450.	1150.	2100.
Kentucky	580.	1500.	2700.
Maryland	525.	1350.	2450.
Massachusetts	400.	1050.	1850.
Michigan	450.	1150.	2100.
Minnesota	400.	1050.	1850.
Missouri	400.	1050.	1850.
Montana	620.	1600.	2850.
Nebraska	450.	1150.	2100.
New Hampshire	620.	1600.	2850.
New Jersey	400.	1050.	1850.
New Mexico Territory	950.	2500.	4200.
New Mexico	700.	1750.	3100.
New York	350.	900.	1600.
North Carolina	580.	1500.	2700.
North Dakota	620.	1600.	2850.
Ohio	400.	1050.	1850.
Oklahoma	525.	1350.	2450.
Pennsylvania	350.	900.	1600.
South Carolina	620.	1600.	2850.
Tennessee	580.	1500.	2700.
Texas	380.	1000.	1750.
Utah	700.	1750.	3100.
Vermont	700.	1750.	3100.
Virginia	580.	1500.	2700.
Washington	700.	1750.	3100
West Virginia	620.	1600.	2850.

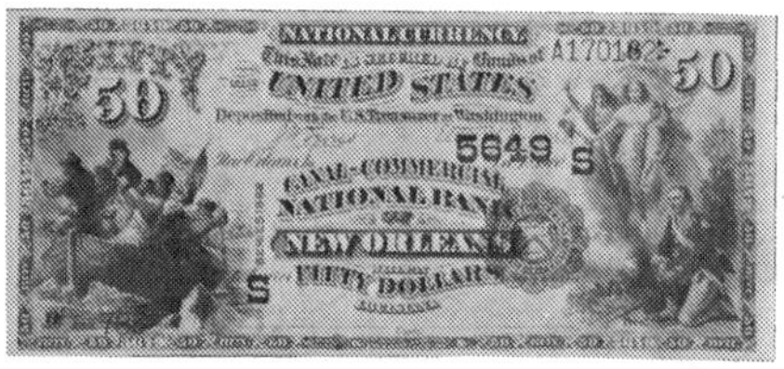

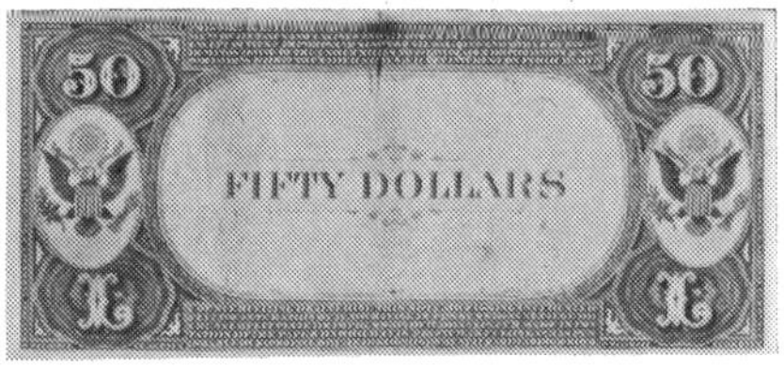

1882 Value Back $50
(KL# 1352)

	VG	VF	AU
Louisiana			(Three Known)
Ohio			(One Known)

1902 Red Seal $50
(KL# 1353-1355)

	VG	VF	AU
Arkansas	900.	4700.	7800.
California	500.	2700.	4600.
Colorado	750.	4000.	6800.
Connecticut	750.	4000.	6800.
Delaware	1250.	7000.	12,000.
Florida	800.	4200.	7250.
Idaho	900.	4700.	7800.
Illinois	500.	2700.	4600.
Indian Territory	1250.	7000.	12,000.
Indiana	700.	3750.	6400.
Iowa	500.	2700.	4600.
Kansas	575.	3100.	5300.
Kentucky	750.	4000.	6800.
Louisiana	900.	4700.	7800.
Maine	900.	4700.	7800.
Maryland	700.	3750.	6400.
Massachusetts	525.	2800.	4750.
Michigan	575.	3100.	5300.
Minnesota	525.	2800.	4750.
Mississippi	900.	4700.	7800.
Missouri	525.	2800.	4750.
Montana	800.	4200.	7250.
Nebraska	575.	3100.	5300.
Nevada	1250.	7000.	12,000.
New Hampshire	800.	4200.	7250.
New Jersey	525.	2800.	4750.
New York	450.	2500.	3500.
North Carolina	750.	4000.	6800.
North Dakota	800.	4200.	7250.
Ohio	525.	2800.	4750.
Oklahoma	700.	3750.	6400.
Oregon	900.	4700.	7800.
Pennsylvania	450.	2500.	3500.
Puerto Rico	—	—	—
Rhode Island	800.	4200.	7250.
South Dakota	800.	4200.	7250.
Tennessee	750.	4000.	6800.
Texas	500.	2700.	4600.
Vermont	900.	4700.	7800.
Virginia	750.	4000.	6800.
Washington	900.	4700.	7800.
West Virginia	800.	4200.	7250.
Wisconsin	525.	2800.	4750.

1902 Date Back $50
(KL# 1356-1364)

	VG	VF	AU
Alabama	125.	460.	800.
Arizona Territory	325.	1000.	1600.
Arkansas	220.	650.	1100.
California	85.00	320.	550.
Colorado	135.	500.	875.
Connecticut	135.	500.	875.
Delaware	325.	1000.	1600.
Florida	175.	575.	975.
Georgia	125.	460.	800.
Idaho	220.	650.	1100.
Illinois	85.00	320.	550.
Indiana	125.	460.	800.
Iowa	85.00	320.	550.
Kansas	105.	370.	650
Kentucky	135.	500.	875.
Louisiana	220.	650.	1100.
Maryland	125.	460.	800.
Massachusetts	90.00	335.	575.
Michigan	105.	370.	650.
Minnesota	90.00	335.	575.
Mississippi	220.	650.	1100.
Missouri	90.00	335.	575.
Montana	175.	575.	975.
Nebraska	105.	370.	650.
Nevada	325.	1000.	1600.
New Hampshire	175.	575.	975.
New Jersey	90.00	335.	575.
New York	75.00	125.	350.
North Carolina	135.	500.	875.
North Dakota	175.	575.	975.
Ohio	90.00	335.	575.
Oklahoma	125.	460.	800.
Oregon	220.	650.	1100.
Pennsylvania	75.00	125.	350.
Rhode Island	175.	575.	975.
South Dakota	175.	575.	975.
Tennessee	135.	500	875.
Texas	85.00	320.	550.
Utah	220.	650.	1100.
Vermont	220.	650.	1100.
Virginia	135.	500.	875.
Washington	220.	650.	1100.
West Virginia	175.	575.	975.
Wisconsin	90.00	335.	575.

1902 Plain Back $50
(KL# 1365-1377)

	VG	VF	AU
California	80.00	245.	400.
Colorado	125.	385.	625.
Connecticut	125.	385.	625.
Delaware	300.	700.	1200.
District of Columbia	200.	520.	840.
Florida	160.	440.	725.
Idaho	200.	520.	840.
Illinois	80.00	245.	400.
Indian Territory	300.	700.	1200.
Indiana	115.	350.	575.
Iowa	80.00	245.	400.
Kansas	95.00	290.	475.
Kentucky	125.	385.	625.
Louisiana	200.	520.	840.
Maryland	115.	350.	575.
Massachusetts	85.00	260.	420.
Michigan	95.00	290.	475.
Minnesota	85.00	260.	420.
Mississippi	200.	520.	840.
Missouri	85.00	260.	420.
Montana	160.	440.	725.
Nebraska	95.00	290.	475.
Nevada	300.	700.	1200.
New Hampshire	160.	440.	725.
New Jersey	85.00	260.	420.
New York	75.00	110.	350.
North Carolina	125.	385.	625.
North Dakota	160.	440.	725.
Ohio	85.00	260.	420.
Oklahoma	115.	350.	575.
Oregon	200.	520.	840.
Pennsylvania	75.00	110.	350.
Rhode Island	160.	440.	725.
South Dakota	160.	440.	725.
Tennessee	125.	385.	625.
Texas	80.00	245.	400.
Utah	200.	520.	840.
Vermont	200.	520.	840.
Washington	200.	520.	840.
West Virginia	160.	440.	725.
Wisconsin	85.00	260.	420.

1929 Type 1 $50
(KL# 1378)

	VG	VF	AU
California	55.00	75.00	95.00
Colorado	75.00	100.	155.
Connecticut	100.	140.	215.
Delaware	120.	165.	250.
Florida	75.00	100.	155.
Hawaii	150.	200.	350.
Idaho	150.	200.	350.
Illinois	62.00	85.00	130.
Indiana	65.00	90.00	135.
Iowa	62.00	85.00	130.
Kansas	62.00	85.00	130.
Kentucky	75.00	100.	155.
Louisiana	95.00	130.	200.
Maryland	90.00	120.	85.00
Massachusetts	125.	190.	650.
Michigan	65.00	90.00	135.
Minnesota	65.00	90.00	135.
Mississippi	95.00	130.	200.
Missouri	75.00	100.	155.
Montana	90.00	120.	185.
Nebraska	65.00	90.00	135.
Nevada	120.	165.	250.
New Hampshire	100.	140.	215.
New Jersey	62.00	85.00	130.
New York	55.00	75.00	95.00
North Carolina	95.00	130.	200.
North Dakota	95.00	130.	200.
Ohio	62.00	85.00	130.
Oklahoma	75.00	100.	155.
Oregon	95.00	130.	200.
Pennsylvania	55.00	75.00	95.00
Rhode Island	150.	200.	350.

	VG	VF	AU
South Dakota	100.	140.	215.
Tennessee	90.00	120.	185.
Texas	55.00	75.00	100.
Utah	95.00	130.	200.
Vermont	120.	165.	250.
Washington	95.00	130.	200.
West Virginia	95.00	130.	200.
Wisconsin	62.00	85.00	130.
Wyoming	90.00	120.	185.

1929 Type 2 $50

(KL# 1379)

	VG	VF	AU
Arkansas	—	—	—
California	115.	175.	600.
Colorado	150.	225.	700.
Hawaii	225.	375.	1200.
Illinois	125.	190.	650.
Indiana	135.	200.	675.
Kansas	125.	190.	650.
Kentucky	155.	225.	700.
Louisiana	190.	300.	900.
Maryland	175.	270.	850.
Michigan	135.	200.	675.
Minnesota	135.	200.	675.
Missouri	155.	225.	700.
Nebraska	135.	200.	675.
New Jersey	125.	190.	650.
New York	57.50	85.00	300.
Ohio	125.	190.	650.
Oklahoma	155.	225.	700.
Pennsylvania	57.50	85.00	400.
Rhode Island	250.	375.	1200.
Tennessee	175.	270.	850.
Texas	125.	190.	650.
Virginia	175.	270.	850.
Wisconsin	125.	190.	650.

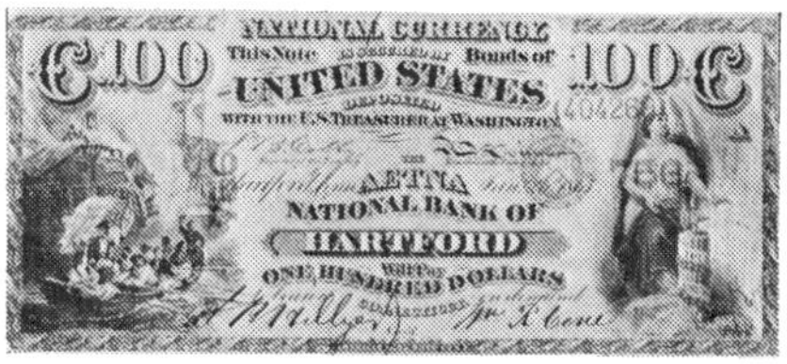

Original Series $100

(KL# 1380-1382)

	VG	VF	AU
Alabama	2200.	5300.	9800.
Colorado Territory	3600.	8500.	17,500.
Connecticut	2400.	5700.	10,600.
Delaware	3600.	8500.	17,500.
District of Columbia	2800.	6500.	12,000.
Georgia	2200.	5300.	9800.
Illinois	1550.	3800.	7100.
Indiana	2200.	5300.	9800.
Iowa	1550.	3800.	7100.
Kentucky	2400.	5700.	10,600.
Louisiana	2800.	6500.	12,000.
Maine	2800.	6500.	12,000.
Maryland	2200.	5300.	9800.
Massachusetts	1625.	4000.	7400.
Michigan	1800.	4350.	8000.
Minnesota	1625.	4000.	7400.
Missouri	1625.	4000.	7400.
Montana Territory	3600.	8500.	17,500.
New Hampshire	2550.	6000.	11,200.
New Jersey	1625.	4000.	7400.
New York	1400.	3500.	6500.
North Carolina	2400.	5700.	10,600.
Ohio	1625.	4000.	7400.
Pennsylvania	1400.	3500.	6500.
Rhode Island	2550.	6000.	11,200.
South Carolina	2550.	6000.	11,200.
Tennessee	2400.	5700.	10,600.
Texas	1550.	3800.	7100.
Utah Territory	3600.	8500.	17,500.

	VG	VF	AU
Vermont	2800.	6500.	12,000.
Virginia	2400.	5700.	10,600.
Wisconsin	1605.	4000.	7400.

Series 1875 $100

(KL# 1383-1391)

	VG	VF	AU
Alabama	—	—	—
Arkansas	—	—	—
California	1550.	3500.	6500.
Colorado Territory	3600.	8000.	15,750.
Colorado	2350.	5200.	9600.
Connecticut	2350.	5200.	9600.
Delaware	3600.	8000.	15,750.
District of Columbia	2750.	6000.	11,000.
Georgia	2150.	4750.	8800.
Illinois	1550.	3500.	6500.
Indiana	2150.	4750.	8800.
Iowa	1550.	3500.	6500.
Kansas	1800.	4000.	7450.
Kentucky	2350.	5200.	9600.
Louisiana	2750.	6000.	11,000.
Maine	2750.	6000.	11,000.
Maryland	2150.	4750.	8800.
Massachusetts	1625.	3700.	6800.
Michigan	1800.	4000.	7450.
Minnesota	1625.	3700.	6800.
Mississippi	2750.	6000.	11,000.
Missouri	1625.	3700.	6800.
Montana Territory	3600.	8000.	15,750.
Nebraska	1800.	4000.	7450.
New Hampshire	2500.	5500.	10,300.
New Jersey	1625.	3700.	6800.
New York	1400.	3250.	6000.
Ohio	1625.	3700.	6800.
Pennsylvania	1400.	3250.	6000.
Rhode Island	2500.	5500.	10,300.
South Carolina	2500.	5500.	10,300.
Tennessee	2350.	5200.	9600.
Texas	1550.	3500.	6500.
Utah Territory	3600.	8000.	15,750.
Vermont	2750.	6000.	11,000.
Virginia	2350.	5200.	9600.
Wisconsin	1625.	3700.	6800.

1882 Brown Back $100

(KL# 1392-1403)

	VG	VF	AU
Alabama	575.	1550.	2600.
Alaska	1000.	2750.	4500.
Arizona Territory	1000.	2750.	4500.
Arkansas	750.	1950.	3400.
California	420.	1100.	1900.
Colorado	625.	1700.	2900.
Connecticut	625.	1700.	2900.
Dakota Territory	1000.	2750.	4500.
Delaware	1000.	2750.	4500.
District of Columbia	750.	1950.	3400.
Florida	675.	1800.	3100.
Georgia	575.	1550.	2600.
Hawaii	1000.	2750.	4500.
Idaho	750.	1950.	3400.
Illinois	420.	1100.	1900.
Indian Territory	1000.	2750.	4500.
Indiana	575.	1550.	2100.
Iowa	420.	1100.	1900.
Kansas	485.	1250.	2200.
Kentucky	625.	1700.	2900.
Louisiana	750.	1950.	3400.
Maine	750.	1950.	3400.
Maryland	575.	1550.	2600.

	VG	VF	AU
Massachusetts	440.	1150.	2000.
Michigan	485.	1250.	2200.
Minnesota	440.	1150.	2000.
Mississippi	750.	1950.	3400.
Missouri	440.	1150.	2000.
Montana Territory	1000.	2750.	4500.
Montana	675.	1800.	3100.
Nebraska	485.	1250.	2200.
Nebraska Territory	—	—	—
New Hampshire	675.	1800.	3100.
New Jersey	440.	1150.	2000.
New Mexico Territory	1000.	2750.	4500.
New York	325.	600.	1750.
North Carolina	625.	1700.	2900.
North Dakota	575.	1800.	3100.
Ohio	440.	1150.	2000.
Oklahoma Territory	1000.	2750.	4500.
Oklahoma	575.	1550.	2600.
Oregon	750.	1950.	3400.
Pennsylvania	325.	600.	1750.
Rhode Island	675.	1800	3100.
South Carolina	675.	1800	3100
South Dakota	675.	1800.	3100.
Tennessee	625.	1700.	2900.
Texas	420.	1100.	1900.
Utah Territory	1000.	2750.	4500.
Utah	750.	1950.	3400.
Vermont	750.	1950.	3400.
Virginia	625.	1700.	2900.
Washington	750.	1950.	3400.
West Virginia	675.	1800.	3100.
Wisconsin	440.	1150.	2000.

1882 Date Back $100

(KL# 1404-1411)

	VG	VF	AU
Alabama	640.	1800.	2600.
Alaska	1150.	3250.	4500.
Arizona Territory	1150.	3250.	4500.
Arkansas	850.	2350.	3400.
California	460.	1300.	1875.
Colorado	725.	2000.	2900.
Connecticut	725.	2000.	2900.
Delaware	1150	3250.	4500.
District of Columbia	850.	2350.	3400.
Florida	765.	2150.	3050.
Georgia	640.	1800.	2600.
Hawaii	1150.	3250.	4500.
Idaho	850.	2350.	3400.
Illinois	460.	1300.	1875.
Indiana	640.	1800.	2600.
Iowa	460.	1300.	1875.
Kansas	550.	1550.	2200.
Kentucky	725.	2000.	2900.
Maryland	640.	1800.	2600.
Massachusetts	490.	1425.	2000.
Michigan	550.	1550.	2200.
Minnesota	490.	1425.	2000.
Missouri	490.	1425.	2000.
Montana	1150.	3250.	4500.
Nebraska	550.	1550.	2200.
New Hampshire	765.	2150.	3050.
New Jersey	490.	1425.	2000.
New Mexico Territory	1150.	3250.	4500.
New Mexico	850.	2350.	3400.
New York	350.	675.	1700.
North Carolina	725.	2000.	2900.
North Dakota	765.	2150.	3050.
Ohio	490.	1425.	2000.
Oklahoma	640.	1800.	2600.
Pennsylvania	350.	675.	1700.
South Carolina	765.	2150.	3050.
Tennessee	725.	2000.	2900.
Texas	460.	1300.	1875.
Utah	850.	2350.	3400.
Vermont	850.	2350.	3400.
Virginia	725.	2000.	2900.
Washington	850.	2350.	3400.
West Virginia	765.	2150.	3050.

1882 Value Back $100
(KL# 1412)

	VG	VF	AU
Louisiana		(One Known)	
Ohio		(One Known)	

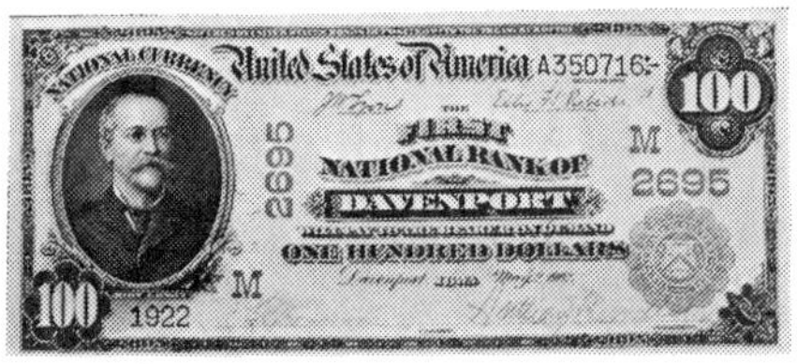

1902 Red Seal $100
(KL# 1413-1415)

	VG	VF	AU
Arkansas	900.	5000.	8400.
California	500.	2850.	4800.
Colorado	750.	4250.	7200.
Connecticut	750.	4250.	7200.
Delaware	1250.	7250.	13,000.
Florida	800.	4500.	7750.
Idaho	900.	5000.	8400.
Illinois	500.	2850.	4800.
Indian Territory	1250.	7250.	13,000.
Indiana	700.	3900.	6700.
Iowa	500.	2850.	4800.
Kansas	575.	3200.	5500.
Kentucky	750.	4250.	7200.
Louisiana	900.	5000.	8400.
Maine	900.	5000.	8400.
Maryland	700.	3900.	6700.
Massachusetts	525.	2950.	4950.
Michigan	575.	3200.	5500.
Minnesota	525.	2950.	4950.
Mississippi	800.	5000.	8400.
Missouri	525.	2950.	4950.
Montana	800.	4500.	7750.
Nebraska	575.	3200.	5500.
Nevada	1250.	7250.	13,000.
New Hampshire	800.	4500.	7750.
New Jersey	525.	2950.	4950.
New York	500.	1000.	4500.
North Carolina	750.	4250.	7200.
North Dakota	800.	4500.	7750.
Ohio	525.	2950.	4950.
Oklahoma Territory	1250.	7250.	13,000.
Oklahoma	700.	3900.	6700.
Oregon	800.	5000.	8400.
Pennsylvania	500.	1000.	4500.
Puerto Rico	—	—	—
Rhode Island	800.	4500.	7750.
South Dakota	800.	4500.	7750.
Tennessee	750.	4250.	7200.
Texas	500.	2850.	4800.
Vermont	900.	5000.	8400.
Virginia	750.	4250.	7200.
Washington	900.	5000.	8400.
West Virginia	800.	4500.	7750.
Wisconsin	525.	2950.	4950.

1902 Date Back $100
(KL# 1416-1424)

	VG	VF	AU
Alabama	215.	500.	900.
Arizona	450.	1100.	1700.
Arkansas	325.	700.	1200.
California	175.	350.	600.
Colorado	280.	525.	950.
Connecticut	230.	525.	950.
Delaware	450.	1100.	1700.
Florida	270.	625.	1050.
Georgia	215.	500.	900.
Idaho	325.	700.	1200.
Illinois	175.	350.	600.
Indiana	215.	500.	900.
Iowa	175.	350.	600.
Kansas	180.	400.	700.
Kentucky	280.	525.	950.
Louisiana	325.	700.	1200.
Maryland	215.	500.	900.
Massachusetts	165.	365.	625.
Michigan	180.	400.	700.
Minnesota	165.	365.	625.
Mississippi	325.	700.	1200.
Missouri	165.	365.	625.
Montana	270.	625.	1050.
Nebraska	180.	400.	700.
Nevada	400.	1100.	1700.
New Hampshire	270.	625.	1050.
New Jersey	165.	365.	625.
New York	160.	300.	575.
North Carolina	230.	525.	950.
North Dakota	270.	625.	1050.
Ohio	165.	305.	625.
Oklahoma	215.	500.	900.
Oregon	325.	700.	1200.
Pennsylvania	160.	300.	575.
Puerto Rico	—	—	—
Rhode Island	270.	625.	1050.
South Dakota	270.	625.	1050.
Tennessee	230.	525.	950.
Texas	175.	350.	1000.
Utah	325.	700.	1200.
Vermont	325.	700.	1200.
Virginia	230.	525.	950.
Washington	325.	700.	1200.
West Virginia	270.	625.	1050.
Wisconsin	165.	365.	625.

1902 Plain Back $100
(KL# 1425-1436)

	VG	VF	AU
California	150.	275.	425.
Colorado	220.	420.	675.
Connecticut	220.	420.	675.
Delaware	250.	350.	450.
Florida	250.	480.	800.
Idaho	300.	600.	950.
Illinois	150.	275.	425.
Indian Territory	250.	350.	450.
Indiana	200.	375.	600.
Iowa	150.	275.	425.
Kansas	170.	320.	500.
Kentucky	220.	420.	675.
Louisiana	300.	600.	950.
Maryland	200.	375.	600.
Massachusetts	150.	285.	440.
Michigan	170.	320.	500.
Minnesota	150.	285.	440.
Mississippi	300.	600.	950.
Missouri	150.	285.	440.
Montana	250.	480.	800.
Nebraska	170.	320.	500.
Nevada	250.	350.	450.
New Hampshire	250.	480.	800.
New Jersey	150.	285.	440.
New York	150.	275.	400.
North Carolina	220.	420.	675.
North Dakota	250.	480.	800.
Ohio	150.	285.	440.
Oklahoma	200.	375.	600.
Oregon	300.	600.	950.
Pennsylvania	150.	275.	400.
Rhode Island	250.	480.	800.
South Dakota	250.	480.	800.
Tennessee	220.	420.	675.
Texas	150.	275.	425.
Utah	300.	600.	950.
Vermont	300.	600.	950.
Washington	300.	600.	950.
Wisconsin	150.	285.	440

1929 Type 1 $100
(KL# 1437)

	VG	VF	AU
California	115.	140.	175.
Colorado	135.	165.	220.
Connecticut	180.	225.	300.
Delaware	200.	260.	350.
Florida	135.	165.	220.
Hawaii	250.	350.	450.
Idaho	250.	350.	450.
Illinois	125.	145.	180.
Indiana	125.	150.	190.
Iowa	120.	145.	180.
Kansas	120.	145.	180.
Kentucky	135.	165.	220.
Louisiana	165.	210.	270.
Maryland	155.	190.	250.
Massachusetts	120.	145.	180.
Michigan	125.	150.	190.
Minnesota	125.	150.	190.
Mississippi	165.	210.	270.
Missouri	135.	165.	220.
Montana	155.	190.	250.
Nebraska	125.	150.	190.
Nevada	200.	260.	350.
New Hampshire	180.	225.	300.
New Jersey	120.	145.	180.
New York	115.	140.	180.
North Carolina	165.	210.	160.
North Dakota	165.	210.	270.
Ohio	120.	145.	180.
Oklahoma	135.	165.	220.
Oregon	165.	210.	270.
Pennsylvania	115.	140.	160.
Rhode Island	200.	250.	450.
South Dakota	180.	225.	300.
Tennessee	150.	190.	250.
Texas	120.	145.	180.
Vermont	200.	260.	350.
Washington	165.	210.	270.
West Virginia	165.	210.	270
Wisconsin	120.	145.	180.
Wyoming	155.	190.	250.

1929 Type 2 $100
(KL# 1438)

	VG	VF	AU
Arkansas	—	—	—
California	155.	225.	600.
Colorado	200.	275.	750.
Hawaii	350.	550.	1500.
Illinois	165.	240.	650.
Indiana	175.	250.	675.
Kentucky	200.	275.	750.
Louisiana	260.	380.	1000.
Maryland	240.	350.	950.
Michigan	175.	250.	675.
Minnesota	175.	250.	675.
New Jersey	165.	240.	650.
New York	120.	140.	400.
Pennsylvania	120.	140.	400.
Rhode Island	350.	550.	1500.
Tennessee	240.	350.	950.
Texas	165.	240.	650.
Virginia	240.	350.	950.

Note-Issuing National Banks
State-City Alphabetical Listing with Bank Rarity Rating

The following pages present a complete listing of note-issuing National Banks arranged alphabetically by city within state. Only those banks which actually issued currency in the 1863-1935 period are listed.

The numerals shown after the charter number of a bank indicate the relative scarcity of known surviving notes in both Large (L) and Small (S) size issues. A dash in one of the columns indicates the bank did not issue notes in that size.

These bank and state rarity figures are derived from the *Standard Catalog of National Bank Notes*, by John Hickman and Dean Oakes, the standard reference to this popularly-collected currency series.

Bank Rarity Rating/Number of Known Notes

R6 Very Rare — 0-2 notes known
R5 Rare — 3-5 notes known
R4 Very Scarce — 6-11 notes known
R3 Scarce — 12-25 notes known
R2 Common — 25-50 notes known
R1 Very Common — 50+ notes known

State/Bank Rarity Valuation Tables

The following tables provide approximate base figures for the value of any National Bank Note with a particular state/bank rarity combination. These tables may be used in conjunction with the bank rarity listings which follow to help determine a ballpark value.

While other factors, such as popularity of bank or city name, changing collector demand or the note's type/variety/denomination combination will affect value, the figures given in these tables can generally be regarded as a base value.

All valuations are for notes in Very Fine condition. Except in cases of the highest bank/state rarity combinations, notes in lesser grade will command a lower price. Notes in higher grade will command a higher price.

State Rarity Ranking — Large Size Nationals

Rarity 1
Pennsylvania
New York
Indiana
Kansas
Kentucky
Maryland

Rarity 2
Iowa
Illinois
California
Texas

Rarity 3
Wisconsin
New Jersey
Missouri
Massachusetts
Minnesota
Ohio

Rarity 4
Michigan
Nebraska

Rarity 5
South Dakota
Virginia
Tennessee
Georgia
Oklahoma
North Carolina
Alabama
Louisiana
Connecticut
Florida

Rarity 6
Rhode Island
West Virginia
Colorado
South Carolina
Maine
Nevada
New Mexico Terr.

Rarity 7
North Dakota
Montana
New Hampshire
Delaware
Vermont
Wyoming
Dist. Columbia
Oregon
Arkansas
Utah
New Mexico
Mississippi

Rarity 8
Idaho
Arizona

Rarity 9
Indian Terr.
Hawaii
Alaska
Oklahoma Terr.
Colorado Terr.
Montana Terr.
Arizona Terr.
Utah Terr.
Dakota Terr.

Rarity 10
Porto Rico
Wyoming Terr.
Washington Terr.
Idaho Terr.
Nebraska Terr.

Bank Rarity	1	2	3	4	5	6
State Rarity 1	40	50	60	85	150	300
State Rarity 2	45	55	70	95	165	330
State Rarity 3	45	60	70	100	175	345
State Rarity 4	50	65	80	110	195	390
State Rarity 5	65	80	95	135	240	540
State Rarity 6	70	90	110	155	270	610
State Rarity 7	85	110	135	190	330	770
State Rarity 8	—	250	575	660	740	1,300
State Rarity 9	—	—	3,500	3,750	4,300	4,500
State Rarity 10	—	—	—	8,000	8,750	9,500

State Rarity Ranking — Small Size Nationals

Rarity 1
Pennsylvania
New York
California
Massachusetts
Illinois

Rarity 2
Wisconsin
Iowa
Kansas
New Jersey
Texas
Ohio

Rarity 3
Nebraska
Indiana
Minnesota
Michigan

Rarity 4
Alabama
Maryland
Colorado
Kentucky
Florida
Oklahoma
Tennessee
North Carolina
Missouri

Rarity 5
Virginia
West Virginia
Georgia
Washington
Mississippi
South Dakota
South Carolina
Wyoming
Connecticut
New Hampshire

Rarity 6
Louisiana
Oregon
Utah
North Dakota
Dist. Columbia

Rarity 7
Maine
Arkansas
Rhode Island

Rarity 8
New Mexico
Vermont

Rarity 9
Delaware
Idaho
Hawaii
Arizona
Montana
Nevada

Rarity 10
Alaska

Bank Rarity	1	2	3	4	5	6
State Rarity 1	20	25	30	35	60	175
State Rarity 2	20	25	30	35	65	195
State Rarity 3	25	30	35	40	70	200
State Rarity 4	25	30	35	40	80	230
State Rarity 5	30	35	40	50	95	280
State Rarity 6	35	40	45	55	110	315
State Rarity 7	35	40	45	55	125	350
State Rarity 8	40	50	65	75	150	440
State Rarity 9	125	165	175	200	330	960
State Rarity 10	—	—	4,000	4,000	—	—

National Banks, Year of Organization

Many collectors find it desirable to learn the year in which a particular National Bank was organized. The charter number which appears on the notes can yield that information when matched with the following list.

Ch. #s	Year
1 to 179	1863
180 to 682	1864
683 to 1626	1865
1627 to 1665	1866
1666 to 1675	1867
1676 to 1688	1868
1689 to 1696	1869
1697 to 1759	1870
1760 to 1912	1871
1913 to 2073	1872
2074 to 2131	1873
2132 to 2214	1874
2215 to 2315	1875
2316 to 2344	1876
2345 to 2375	1877
2376 to 2405	1878
2406 to 2445	1879
2446 to 2498	1880
2499 to 2606	1881
2607 to 2849	1882
2850 to 3101	1883
3102 to 3281	1884
3282 to 3427	1885
3428 to 3612	1886
3613 to 3832	1887
3833 to 3954	1888
3955 to 4190	1889
4191 to 4494	1890
4495 to 4673	1891
4674 to 4832	1892
4833 to 4934	1893
4935 to 4983	1894
4984 to 5029	1895
5030 to 5054	1896
5055 to 5108	1897
5109 to 5165	1898
5166 to 5240	1899
5241 to 5662	1900
5663 to 6074	1901
6075 to 6566	1902
6567 to 7081	1903
7082 to 7541	1904
7542 to 8027	1905
8028 to 8489	1906
8490 to 8979	1907
8980 to 9302	1908
9303 to 9622	1909
9623 to 9913	1910
9914 to 10119	1911
10120 to 10305	1912
10306 to 10472	1913
10473 to 10672	1914
10673 to 10810	1915
10811 to 10932	1916
10933 to 11126	1917
11127 to 11282	1918
11283 to 11570	1919
11571 to 11903	1920
11904 to 12082	1921
12083 to 12287	1922
12288 to 12481	1923
12482 to 12615	1924
12616 to 12866	1925
12867 to 13022	1926
13023 to 13159	1927
13160 to 13269	1928
13270 to 13412	1929
13413 to 13516	1930
13517 to 13586	1931
13587 to 13654	1932
13655 to 13920	1933
13921 to 14317	1934
14318 to 14348	1935

ALABAMA

City, Bank	Ch. No.	L	S
Abbeville			
The First National Bank Of Abbeville	5987	5	–
The Henry National Bank Of Abbeville	10959	5	–
Albany			
The Central National Bank Of Albany	10423	4	–
The Morgan County National Bank Of Albany	6380	4	–
Albertville			
The Albertville National Bank	11820	6	5
The First National Bank Of Albertville	11819	–	4
Alexander City			
The First National Bank Of Alexander City	7417	6	4
Andalusia			
The Andalusia National Bank	11955	4	3
The First National Bank Of Andalusia	5970	5	6
Anniston			
The Anniston City National Bank	4250	6	–
The Anniston National Bank	4250	3	–
The Anniston National Bank	4250	3	4
The City National Bank Of Anniston	6021	6	–
The Commercial National Bank Of Anniston	11753	4	4
The First National Bank Of Anniston	3041	5	3
Ashford			
The First National Bank Of Ashford	10102	6	6
Ashland			
The First National Bank Of Ashland	9580	6	4
Athens			
The First National Bank Of Athens	6146	6	–
Atmore			
The First National Bank Of Atmore	10697	6	5
Attalla			
The First National Bank Of Attalla	7951	6	–
Auburn			
The First National Bank Of Auburn	12455	4	6
Bessemer			
First National Bank In Bessemer	6961	6	4
The Bessemer National Bank	6961	6	–
The City National Bank Of Bessemer	11905	5	6
The First National Bank At Bessemer	13789	–	6
The First National Bank Of Bessemer	4220	6	–
Birmingham			
American-Traders National Bank Of Birmingham	7020	2	3
The Alabama National Bank Of Birmingham	3587	6	–
The American National Bank Of Birmingham	3734	6	–
The Berney National Bank Of Birmingham	3442	6	–
The Birmingham National Bank	3679	6	–
The City National Bank Of Birmingham	3993	6	–
The Ensley National Bank Of Birmingham	12906	4	4
The First National Bank Of Birmingham	3185	1	1
The National Bank Of Birmingham	2065	6	–
The Traders National Bank Of Birmingham	7020	4	–
The Woodlawn-American National Bank Of Birmingham	13358	–	2
Boaz			
The First National Bank Of Boaz	10441	6	–
The National Bank Of Boaz	11870	6	5
Brantley			
The First National Bank Of Brantley	7991	6	6
Bridgeport			
The American National Bank Of Bridgeport	11168	6	6
The First National Bank Of Bridgeport	4591	6	–
Brundidge			
The First National Bank Of Brundidge	7429	6	5
Camden			
The Camden National Bank	8217	6	6
Childersburg			
The First National Bank Of Childersburg	10066	6	–
Citronelle			
The First National Bank Of Citronelle	6835	6	–
Clanton			
The First National Bank Of Clanton	11515	6	5
Coffee Springs			
The First National Bank Of Coffee Springs	11259	6	6
Collinsville			
The First National Bank Of Collinsville	11337	5	4
Columbia			
The First National Bank Of Columbia	8095	6	–
Cullman			
The First National Bank Of Cullman	7097	6	–
The Leeth National Bank Of Cullman	9614	4	3
Decatur			
First National Bank In Decatur	10336	–	3
The Central National Bank Of Decatur	10423	6	5
The City National Bank Of Decatur	10336	4	5
The First National Bank Of Decatur	3699	6	–
The Morgan County National Bank Of Decatur	6380	6	5
Demopolis			
The Commercial National Bank Of Demopolis	10035	5	4
The First National Bank Of Demopolis	4394	6	–
Dothan			
The Dothan National Bank	5909	3	–
The First National Bank Of Dothan	5249	3	3
The Houston National Bank Of Dothan	7932	4	6
The Third National Bank Of Dothan	7938	6	–
Dozier			
The First National Bank Of Dozier	9681	6	5
Elba			
The First National Bank Of Elba	6897	6	4
Ensley			
The First National Bank Of Ensley	5962	6	–
Enterprise			
The Farmers And Merchants National Bank Of Enterprise	10421	5	5
Enterprise			
The First National Bank Of Enterprise	6319	5	6
Eufaula			
The Commercial National Bank Of Eufaula	5024	4	6
The East Alabama National Bank Of Eufaula	3622	5	–
The Eufaula National Bank	2309	6	–
Eutaw			
The First National Bank Of Eutaw	3931	4	5
Evergreen			
The First National Bank Of Evergreen	7687	5	6
Fairfield			
The Fairfield American National Bank, Fairfield	11766	–	4
Fayette			
The First National Bank Of Fayette	10377	6	5
Florala			
The First National Bank Of Florala	8910	5	6
Florence			
The First National Bank Of Florence	3981	4	3
The Florence National Bank	4135	6	–
Fort Payne			
The First National Bank In Fort Payne	11451	5	4
The First National Bank Of Fort Payne	4064	6	–
Gadsden			
The American National Bank Of Gadsden	13412	–	3
The First National Bank In Gadsden	13728	–	6
The First National Bank Of Gadsden	3663	4	3
The Gadsden National Bank	8560	4	5
Gainesville			
The Gainesville National Bank	1822	6	–
Geneva			
The Farmers National Bank Of Geneva	10307	6	6
The First National Bank Of Geneva	5714	6	–
Goodwater			
The First National Bank Of Goodwater	12960	6	5
Greensboro			
The First National Bank Of Greensboro	5693	4	5
Greenville			
The First National Bank Of Greenville	5572	5	3
Guntersville			
The First National Bank Of Guntersville	10990	6	3
Hartford			
The First National Bank Of Hartford	7592	6	5
Hartselle			
The First National Bank Of Hartselle	8067	4	6
Haynesville			
The First National Bank Of Haynesville	7975	6	–
Headland			
The Farmers And Merchants National Bank Of Headland	11445	6	–
The First National Bank Of Headland	7424	5	4
The Headland National Bank	13752	–	6
Huntsville			
The Farmers And Merchants National Bank Of Huntsville	4689	6	–
The First National Bank Of Huntsville	4067	6	4
The Henderson National Bank Of Huntsville	8765	5	4
The National Bank Of Huntsville	1560	6	–
Jackson			
The First National Bank Of Jackson	5983	6	–
Jacksonville			
The First National Bank Of Jacksonville	4319	6	6
The Tredegar National Bank Of Jacksonville	4319	5	–
Jasper			
The First National Bank Of Jasper	7746	4	4
Leeds			
The Leeds-American National Bank	13359	–	5
Lincoln			
The First National Bank Of Lincoln	10131	6	6
Linden			
The First National Bank Of Linden	7148	6	5
Lineville			
The Citizens National Bank Of Lineville	8856	6	–
The First National Bank Of Lineville	7516	6	–
The Lineville National Bank	7551	6	5
Luverne			
The First National Bank Of Luverne	7992	6	6
Midland City			
The First National Bank Of Midland City	8458	6	5
Mobile			
Merchants National Bank Of Mobile	13097	4	–
The Alabama National Bank Of Mobile	1817	6	–
The American National Bank & Trust Company Of Mobile	13414	–	3
The Bank Of Mobile, National Banking Assoc Of Mobile	7062	6	–
The City National Bank Of Mobile	5219	6	–
The First National Bank Of Mobile	1595	3	1
The Merchants National Bank Of Mobile	13097	–	1
The Mobile National Bank	13195	4	5
The National Commercial Bank Of Mobile	1817	6	–
Monroeville			
The First National Bank Of Monroeville	12642	6	4
Montgomery			
The Alabama National Bank Of Montgomery	12993	4	4
The American National Bank Of Montgomery	7141	6	–
The Capital National Bank Of Montgomery	8460	6	–
The Exchange National Bank Of Montgomery	8284	3	–
The Farley National Bank Of Montgomery	4180	6	–
The First National Bank Of Montgomery	1814	3	2
The Fourth National Bank Of Montgomery	5877	3	–
The Merchants & Planters Farley Natl. Bank Of Montgomery	4180	6	–
The Merchants And Planters National Bank Of Montgomery	2029	6	–
Montgomery			
The New Farley National Bank Of Montgomery	8460	6	–
New Brockton			
The First National Bank Of New Brockton	10457	6	–
New Decatur			
The Central National Bank Of New Decatur	10423	6	–
The Morgan County National Bank Of New Decatur	6380	6	–
Newville			
The First National Bank Of Newville	9927	6	6
Oneonta			
The First National Bank Of Oneonta	12006	6	5
Opelika			
The Farmers National Bank Of Opelika	9550	5	2
The First National Bank Of Opelika	3452	4	4
The National Bank Of Opelika	11635	3	3
Opp			
The First National Bank Of Opp	7985	4	3
Oxford			
The First National Bank Of Oxford	7073	3	6
The Oxford National Bank	9925	6	–
Ozark			
The First National Bank Of Ozark	7629	6	–
Pell City			
The First National Bank Of Pell City	9506	6	–
Piedmont			
The First National Bank Of Piedmont	7464	6	5
Prattville			
The First National Bank Of Prattville	9055	6	6
Reform			
The First National Bank Of Reform	11233	6	–
Russellville			
The First National Bank Of Russellville	11846	6	4
Samson			
The First National Bank Of Samson	8028	6	6
Scottsboro			
The First National Bank Of Scottsboro	8963	6	5
Selma			
The City National Bank Of Selma	1736	1	3
The First National Bank Of Selma	1537	6	–
The Selma National Bank	7084	4	4
Sheffield			
The First National Bank Of Sheffield	3617	6	–
The Sheffield National Bank	6759	5	5
Slocomb			
The First National Bank Of Slocomb	7871	6	–
The Slocomb National Bank	7940	6	3
Stevenson			
The First National Bank Of Stevenson	9855	6	5
Sylacauga			
The City National Bank Of Sylacauga	10879	6	4
The First National Bank Of Sylacauga	7451	6	6
The Merchants And Planters National Bank Of Sylacauga	7484	4	4
Talladega			
The First National Bank Of Talladega	3899	6	–
The Isbell National Bank Of Talladega	4838	4	5
The Talladega National Bank	7558	5	4
Tallassee			
The First National Bank Of Tallassee	10766	6	6
Thomasville			
The Citizens National Bank Of Thomasville	7371	6	–
The First National Bank Of Thomasville	5664	6	–
Troy			
First Farmers & Merchants National Bank Of Troy	5593	–	2
The Farmers And Merchants National Bank Of Troy	7044	4	6
The First National Bank Of Troy	5593	5	6
Tuscaloosa			
The City National Bank Of Tuscaloosa	6173	4	3
The First National Bank Of Tuskaloosa	1853	5	4
The Merchants National Bank Of Tuscaloosa	3678	6	–
Tuscumbia			
The First National Bank Of Tuscumbia	11281	5	5
Union Springs			
The American National Bank Of Union Springs	12962	6	4
The First National Bank Of Union Springs	7467	5	6
Wetumpka			
The First National Bank Of Wetumpka	7568	6	6

ALASKA

City, Bank	Ch. No.	L	S
Fairbanks			
First National Bank Of Fairbanks	7718	1	4
Juneau			
The First National Bank Of Juneau	5117	4	3
Ketchikan			
The First National Bank Of Ketchikan	12578	–	3

ARIZONA TERRITORY

City, Bank	Ch. No.	L	S
Bisbee			
The First National Bank Of Bisbee	7182	6	–
Clifton			
The First National Bank Of Clifton	5821	6	–
Douglas			
The First National Bank Of Douglas	6633	6	–
Globe			
The First National Bank Of Globe	6579	6	–
The Globe National Bank	8193	6	–
Nogales			
The First National Bank Of Nogales	6591	6	–
The Sandoval National Bank Of Nogales	6591	6	–
Phoenix			
The First National Bank Of Phoenix	3054	6	–
The National Bank Of Arizona At Phoenix	3728	6	–
The Phoenix National Bank	4729	6	–

City, Bank	Ch. No.	L	S
Prescott			
The First National Bank Of Prescott	3122	6	–
The Prescott National Bank	4851	5	–
Tempe			
The Tempe National Bank	5720	6	–
Tombstone			
The First National Bank Of Tombstone	6439	6	–
Tucson			
The Arizona National Bank Of Tucson	4440	6	–
The Consolidated National Bank Of Tucson	4287	6	–
The First National Bank Of Tucson	2639	5	–
Yuma			
The First National Bank Of Yuma	7591	6	–
The Yuma National Bank	9608	6	–

ARIZONA

City, Bank	Ch. No.	L	S
Clifton			
The First National Bank Of Clifton	5821	4	–
Douglas			
The First National Bank Of Douglas	6633	4	–
Flagstaff			
The First National Bank Of Flagstaff	11120	5	6
Florence			
The First National Bank Of Florence	10008	5	
Globe			
The First National Bank Of Globe	6579	4	–
Holbrook			
The First National Bank Of Holbrook	12198	4	6
Mesa			
The First National Bank Of Mesa	11130	6	4
Nogales			
The First National Bank Of Nogales	6591	6	3
The Nogales National Bank	11012	5	5
Phoenix			
First National Bank Of Arizona At Phoenix	3728	6	3
The Commercial National Bank Of Phoenix	11559	4	–
The National Bank Of Arizona At Phoenix	3728	4	–
The Phoenix National Bank	4729	4	3
Prescott			
First National Bank In Prescott	13262	–	3
The Prescott National Bank	4851	6	–
Tempe			
The Tempe National Bank	5720	6	5
Tombstone			
The First National Bank Of Tombstone	6439	5	–
Tucson			
The Arizona National Bank Of Tucson	4440	4	–
The Consolidated National Bank Of Tucson	4287	2	1
The Tucson National Bank	11159	6	–
Winslow			
The First National Bank Of Winslow	12581	4	4
Yuma			
The First National Bank Of Yuma	7591	5	–
The Yuma National Bank	9608	4	–

ARKANSAS

City, Bank	Ch. No.	L	S
Arkadelphia			
The Citizens National Bank Of Arkadelphia	10087	6	6
Ashdown			
The First National Bank In Ashdown	13534	–	5
The First National Bank Of Ashdown	10486	6	6
Batesville			
The First National Bank Of Batesville	7556	3	6
The Maxfield National Bank Of Batesville	8864	6	–
The National Bank Of Batesville	8864	6	–
Benton			
The First National Bank Of Benton	9494	6	–
Bentonville			
The Benton County National Bank Of Bentonville	8135	5	6
The First National Bank Of Bentonville	7523	5	5
Berryville			
The First National Bank Of Berryville	10406	5	3
Camden			
The Camden National Bank	4066	6	–
The Citizens National Bank Of Camden	14096	–	6
The First National Bank Of Camden	1631	6	–
The First National Bank Of Camden	4066	5	5
Clarksville			
The Farmers National Bank Of Clarksville	11580	5	5
The First National Bank Of Clarksville	9633	6	6
Conway			
The First National Bank Of Conway	13719	–	6
Corning			
The First National Bank Of Corning	7311	6	–
Cotton Plant			
The First National Bank Of Cotton Plant	10723	6	–
Dardanelle			
The First National Bank Of Dardanelle	11276	6	–
De Witt			
The First National Bank Of De Witt	10178	6	6
Dequeen			
The First National Bank Of Dequeen	5929	5	6
Earle			
The First National Bank Of Earle	9324	6	–
El Dorado			
The Citizens National Bank Of El Dorado	7323	6	–
The First National Bank Of El Dorado	7046	6	3
Eudora			
The First National Bank Of Eudora	12813	–	6
Eureka Springs			
The First National Bank Of Eureka Springs	8495	6	6
Fayetteville			
The Arkansas National Bank Of Fayetteville	8786	5	5
Fayetteville			
The First National Bank Of Fayetteville	7346	4	3
The National Bank Of Fayetteville	7952	6	–
Fordyce			
The First National Bank Of Fordyce	9501	6	4
Forrest City			
The First National Bank Of Forrest City	10550	5	–
The National Bank Of Eastern Arkansas Of Forrest City	13637	–	6
Fort Smith			
The American National Bank Of Fort Smith	3634	5	–
The City National Bank Of Fort Smith	10609	4	4
The First National Bank Of Fort Smith	1631	6	–
The First National Bank Of Fort Smith	1950	3	3
The Fort Smith National Bank	4995	6	–
The Merchants National Bank Of Fort Smith	7240	3	3
The National Bank Of Western Arkansas At Fort Smith	1950	6	–
Gentry			
The First National Bank Of Gentry	12340	6	6
Gravette			
The First National Bank Of Gravette	8237	6	5
Green Forest			
The First National Bank Of Green Forest	10422	6	6
Greenwood			
First National Bank In Greenwood	10983	6	6
The Citizens National Bank Of Greenwood	10983	6	–
The First National Bank Of Greenwood	6786	6	–
Gurdon			
The First National Bank Of Gurdon	13210	6	4
Harrison			
First National Bank In Harrison	10801	6	6
The Citizens National Bank Of Harrison	12291	6	–
The First National Bank Of Harrison	5890	6	–
The Peoples National Bank Of Harrison	10801	6	–
Hartford			
First National Bank In Hartford	11830	6	6
New First National Bank Of Hartford	11830	6	–
The Farmers And Miners National Bank Of Hartford	11830	6	–
The First National Bank Of Hartford	11748	6	–
Heber Springs			
The First National Bank Of Heber Springs	11180	6	–
Helena			
Phillips National Bank Of Helena	13520	–	4
The First National Bank Of Helena	3662	4	–
Holly Grove			
The First National Bank Of Holly Grove	12296	6	6
Hope			
The Citizens National Bank Of Hope	10579	6	4
The First National Bank Of Hope	12533	–	4
The Hope National Bank	8594	6	–
Horatio			
The First National Bank Of Horatio	10447	6	–
Hot Springs			
The Arkansas National Bank Of Hot Springs	2832	6	5
The Citizens National Bank Of Hot Springs	7531	6	–
The Hot Springs National Bank	2887	6	–
Huntsville			
The First National Bank Of Huntsville	8952	6	6
Huttig			
The First National Bank Of Huttig	10060	6	6
Jonesboro			
The First National Bank Of Jonesboro	8086	6	–
Judsonia			
The First National Bank Of Judsonia	10439	6	–
Lake Village			
The First National Bank In Lake Village	13632	–	4
The First National Bank Of Lake Village	11262	6	5
Lamar			
The First National Bank Of Lamar	12238	6	6
Leslie			
The First National Bank Of Leslie	10138	6	–
Lewisville			
The First National Bank Of Lewisville	9354	6	6
Lincoln			
The First National Bank Of Lincoln	11825	6	–
Little Rock			
The Commercial National Bank Of Little Rock	14000	–	3
The England National Bank Of Little Rock	9037	5	–
The Exchange National Bank Of Little Rock	3300	4	–
The First National Bank Of Little Rock	1648	6	–
The German National Bank Of Little Rock	3318	6	–
The Merchants National Bank Of Little Rock	1648	5	–
The State National Bank Of Little Rock	6902	5	–
Malvern			
The First National Bank Of Malvern	7634	6	6
Mansfield			
The First National Bank Of Mansfield	11195	6	6
The National Bank Of Mansfield	11196	6	5
Marked Tree			
The First National Bank Of Marked Tree	11122	5	–
Marshall			
The Arkansas National Bank Of Marshall	10795	6	–
The First National Bank Of Marshall	10794	6	–
Mcgehee			
The First National Bank Of Mcgehee	13280	5	5
Mena			
The First National Bank Of Mena	7163	6	–
Mena			
The National Bank Of Mena	7829	6	–
The Planters National Bank Of Mena	13693	–	5
Mineral Springs			
The First National Bank Of Nashville	11113	6	6
Morrilton			
The First National Bank Of Morrilton	10434	6	–
Newark			
The First National Bank Of Newark	9022	5	3
Newport			
The First National Bank Of Newport	6758	3	5
Paragould			
National Bank Of Commerce Of Paragould	10004	6	4
The First National Bank Of Paragould	6846	6	–
The New First National Bank Of Paragould	13155	6	5
Paris			
The First National Bank Of Paris	11592	6	5
Perry			
The First National Bank Of Perry	6706	6	–
Pine Bluff			
National Bank Of Commerce Of Pine Bluff	14056	–	5
The First National Bank Of Pine Bluff	2776	6	–
The Simmons National Bank Of Pine Bluff	6680	5	4
Pinebluff			
The National Bank Of Arkansas At Pine Bluff	10768	6	6
Prairie Grove			
The First National Bank Of Prairie Grove	8030	5	–
Rector			
The First National Bank Of Rector	10853	6	6
Rogers			
The American National Bank Of Rogers	10750	5	5
The First National Bank Of Rogers	7789	6	6
Russellville			
The First National Bank Of Russellville	4582	6	–
Siloam Springs			
The Farmers National Bank Of Siloam Springs	9871	6	–
The First National Bank In Siloam Springs	13274	3	6
The First National Bank Of Siloam Springs	9871	5	–
Springdale			
The First National Bank Of Springdale	8763	5	6
Stuttgart			
The First National Bank Of Stuttgart	10459	5	6
Texarkana			
The Gate City National Bank Of Texarkana	4401	6	–
The State National Bank Of Texarkana	7138	4	3
Van Buren			
The First National Bank Of Van Buren	7361	5	6
Waldron			
The First National Bank Of Waldron	5849	6	6
Walnut Ridge			
The First National Bank Of Lawrence County At Walnut Ridge	11312	–	6
The First National Bank Of Walnut Ridge	9332	6	–
The Planters National Bank Of Walnut Ridge	12083	6	6
Willisville			
The First National Bank Of Ava	10911	–	5
Wynne			
The First National Bank Of Wynne	10807	–	6

CALIFORNIA GOLD

City, Bank	Ch. No.	L	S
Oakland			
The First National Gold Bank Of Oakland	2248	4	–
The Union National Gold Bank Of Oakland	2266	5	–
Petaluma			
The First National Gold Bank Of Petaluma	2193	3	–
Sacramento			
The National Gold Bank Of D. O. Mills & Co., Sacramento	2014	3	–
San Francisco			
The First National Gold Bank Of San Francisco	1741	1	–
The National Gold Bank & Trust Company	1994	3	–
San Jose			
The Farmers National Gold Bank Of San Jose	2158	2	–
Santa Barbara			
The First National Gold Bank Of Santa Barbara	2104	4	–

CALIFORNIA

City, Bank	Ch. No.	L	S
Alameda			
The Alameda National Bank	9220	5	–
The Citizens National Bank Of Alameda	10150	4	–
The Commercial National Bank Of Alameda	11942	4	4
The First National Bank Of Alameda	2431	6	–
Alhambra			
The Alhambra National Bank, Alhambra	9966	6	–
The First National Bank Of Alhambra	8490	5	5
The National Bank Of Alhambra	9966	6	–
Alturas			
The First National Bank Of Alturas	7219	5	–
Anaheim			
Anaheim First National Bank, Anaheim	10228	–	3
The Anaheim National Bank	10228	4	5
The First National Bank Of Anaheim	6481	5	6
The Golden State National Bank Of Anaheim	11823	6	–
Antioch			
The First National Bank Of Antioch	9892	5	3

City, Bank	Ch. No.	L	S
Arcata			
The First National Bank Of Arcata	10372	6	–
Artesia			
The First National Bank Of Artesia	8063	5	6
Auburn			
The First National Bank Of Auburn	9227	6	–
Azusa			
The First National Bank Of Azusa	8065	5	3
The United States National Bank Of Azusa	8074	6	–
Bakersfield			
First National Bank In Bakersfield	10357	6	2
First National Bank Of Bakersfield	11327	6	–
The First National Bank Of Bakersfield	6044	5	–
The National Bank Of Bakersfield	10357	5	–
Banning			
The First National Bank Of Banning	9459	4	4
Bellflower			
The Commercial National Bank Of Bellflower	12754	–	5
The First National Bank Of Bellflower	12328	5	6
Berkeley			
Berkeley National Bank	7849	6	–
First National Bank In Berkeley	12320	4	–
The College National Bank Of Berkeley	11495	4	–
The First National Bank Of Berkeley	5380	4	–
Beverly Hills			
The First National Bank Of Beverly Hills	11461	4	4
The Liberty National Bank Of Beverly Hills	12909	6	–
Biola			
The First National Bank Of Biola	11769	6	–
Brawley			
The First National Bank Of Brawley	9673	6	–
Brea			
Oilfields National Bank In Brea	13877	–	3
The Oilfields National Bank Of Brea	13001	6	5
Burbank			
The First National Bank Of Burbank	10099	6	–
Calexico			
The Calexico National Bank	9705	6	–
The First National Bank Of Calexico	9686	5	–
Calipatria			
The First National Bank Of Calipatria	10687	6	–
Calistoga			
The Calistoga National Bank	9551	6	5
The First National Bank Of Calistoga	7388	6	–
Campbell			
The Growers National Bank Of Campbell	11572	5	–
Caruthers			
The First National Bank Of Caruthers	11330	6	6
Centerville			
The First National Bank Of Centerville	11743	5	–
Chico			
First National Bank Of Chico	13711	–	4
First National Trust & Savings Of Chico	8798	6	4
The Butte County National Bank Of Chico	9294	6	–
The First National Bank Of Chico	8798	5	–
Chino			
The First National Bank Of Chino	10271	6	–
Chowchilla			
The Chowchilla National Bank	11151	6	–
Claremont			
The Claremont National Bank	10208	6	–
The First National Bank Of Claremont	9467	5	4
Cloverdale			
The First National Bank Of Cloverdale	11282	5	6
Clovis			
The First National Bank Of Clovis	10213	6	–
Coachella			
The First National Bank Of Coachella	10292	6	6
Coalinga			
The First National Bank Of Coalinga	9323	6	–
Colton			
The Citizens National Bank Of Colton	13356	–	6
The Colton National Bank	8608	5	–
The First National Bank Of Colton	3573	4	–
Colusa			
The First National Bank Of Colusa	10072	6	–
Compton			
The First National Bank Of Compton	8085	6	–
Concord			
The First National Bank Of Concord	9945	6	–
Corcoran			
First National Bank In Corcoran	14230	–	6
The First National Bank Of Corcoran	9546	6	5
Corona			
The Corona National Bank	8436	6	–
The First National Bank Of Corona	7867	4	2
Covina			
The Covina National Bank	8222	6	3
The First National Bank Of Covina	5830	3	5
Crescent Heights			
West Hollywood National Bank Of Crescent Heights	11880	6	–
Crockett			
The First National Bank Of Crockett	11326	5	5
Crows Landing			
The First National Bank Of Crows Landing	9765	6	5
Cucamonga			
The First National Bank Of Cucamonga	7152	6	6
Culver City			
The First National Bank Of Culver City	11732	–	5
Del Rey			
The First National Bank Of Del Rey	11041	4	6
Delano			
First National Bank In Delano	10387	–	6
The First National Bank Of Delano	9195	6	–
Dinuba			
The First National Bank Of Dinuba	9158	6	–
The United States National Bank Of Dinuba	9156	6	–
Dixon			
The First National Bank Of Dixon	10120	6	5
Downey			
The First National Bank Of Downey	11701	6	5
Ducor			
The First National Bank Of Ducor	10301	6	6
El Centro			
The El Centro National Bank	9349	6	–
The First National Bank Of El Centro	9350	6	–
El Monte			
The First National Bank Of El Monte	6993	5	4
Elsinore			
The First National Bank Of Elsinore	11922	6	5
Emeryville			
The First National Bank Of Emeryville	9410	6	–
Escondido			
The Escondido National Bank	8040	6	–
The First National Bank In Escondido	13029	6	–
The First National Bank Of Escondido	7801	5	–
Eureka			
The First National Bank Of Eureka	5986	2	4
The Humboldt National Bank Of Eureka	10528	5	–
Exeter			
The First National Bank Of Exeter	9370	6	–
Fairfield			
The First National Bank Of Fairfield	10984	–	4
Florence			
The Florence National Bank	12624	6	6
Fontana			
The First National Bank Of Fontana	12976	–	4
Fort Bragg			
Coast National Bank In Fort Bragg	13787	–	5
The Coast National Bank Of Fort Bragg	9626	6	5
The First National Bank Of Fort Bragg	9626	6	–
Fowler			
The First National Bank Of Fowler	7390	6	–
The Fowler National Bank	10312	6	–
Fresno			
First National Bank In Fresno	11473	4	4
The Farmers National Bank Of Fresno	5162	4	–
The First National Bank Of Fresno	3321	5	–
The Fresno National Bank	3870	6	–
The Growers National Bank Of Fresno	11473	4	–
The Union National Bank Of Fresno	8718	5	–
Fullerton			
First National Trust & Savings Bank Of Fullerton	12764	6	4
The Farmers And Merchants National Bank Of Fullerton	9538	6	–
The First National Bank Of Fullerton	5654	4	–
Garden Grove			
The First National Bank Of Garden Grove	11251	5	5
Gardena			
The First National Bank Of Gardena	10453	4	–
Geyserville			
The First National Bank Of Geyserville	11678	6	–
Gilroy			
The First National Bank Of Gilroy	10166	6	–
Glendale			
First National Bank In Glendale	10412	6	6
The First National Bank Of Glendale	7987	5	–
The Glendale National Bank, Glendale	10412	6	–
Glendora			
The First National Bank Of Glendora	8652	6	3
Graham			
The Graham National Bank	12673	6	6
Grass Valley			
First National Bank In Grass Valley	12433	4	5
The First National Bank Of Grass Valley	3648	6	–
Gridley			
The First National Bank Of Gridley	11164	6	–
Hanford			
The Farmers And Merchants National Bank Of Hanford	7658	6	–
The First National Bank Of Hanford	5863	5	4
The Hanford National Bank	6873	6	–
Hardwick			
The First National Bank Of Hardwick	10364	6	6
Hayward			
The First National Bank Of Hayward	10018	6	–
Healdsburg			
The First National Bank Of Healdsburg	10184	4	6
The Healdsburg National Bank	10204	5	–
Hemet			
The First National Bank Of Hemet	10764	6	4
Hermosa Beach			
The First National Bank Of Hermosa Beach	12209	4	5
The National Bank Of Hermosa Beach	12271	5	6
Hollister			
The First National Bank Of Hollister	9378	5	–
The Hollister National Bank	13510	–	5
Hollywood			
The First National Bank Of Hollywood	7543	5	–
The Hollywood National Bank	7803	6	–
Holtville			
The First National Bank Of Holtville	9770	6	5
Huntington Beach			
The First National Bank Of Huntington Beach	7868	6	–
Huntington Park			
The National Bank Of Huntington Park	11925	6	–
Hynes			
The First National Bank Of Hynes	9919	5	5
Imperial			
The First National Bank Of Imperial	6027	5	–
Inglewood			
The First National Bank Of Inglewood	9093	6	–
Jamestown			
The Jamestown National Bank	10362	6	–
The Union National Bank Of Jamestown	10284	6	–
Kerman			
The First National Bank Of Kerman	9234	6	–
Kingsburg			
The First National Bank Of Kingsburg	8409	6	–
La Habra			
The First National Bank Of La Habra	11827	6	–
La Verne			
The First National Bank Of La Verne	9599	5	5
Laton			
The First National Bank Of Laton	9818	6	–
Lemoore			
The First National Bank Of Lemoore	7779	5	4
Lindsay			
The First National Bank Of Lindsay	7965	6	–
The Lindsay National Bank	9710	6	–
Livermore			
The Farmers And Merchants National Bank Of Livermore	9914	6	–
The First National Bank Of Livermore	8002	5	–
Lodi			
The Citizens National Bank Of Lodi	12112	5	–
The First National Bank Of Lodi	7719	3	–
The Lodi National Bank	11126	4	–
Loma Linda			
The First National Bank Of Loma Linda	13332	–	4
Long Beach			
California First National Bank Of Long Beach	11873	–	3
The American National Bank Of Long Beach	6749	6	–
The California National Bank Of Long Beach	11873	4	–
The City National Bank Of Long Beach	8870	5	–
The Exchange National Bank Of Long Beach	8510	5	–
The First National Bank Of Long Beach	5456	4	–
The Long Beach National Bank, Long Beach	8510	6	–
The National Bank Of Long Beach	6730	4	–
The Seaside National Bank Of Long Beach	12819	6	5
Lordsburg			
The First National Bank Of Lordsburg	9599	6	–
Los Altos			
The First National Bank Of Los Altos	11522	5	6
Los Angeles			
Central National Bank In Los Angeles	13187	–	6
Citizens National Trust And Savings Bank Of Los Angeles	5927	4	2
Los Angeles-First Natl. Trust & Savings Bank, Los Angeles	2491	3	–
Merchants National Trust & Savings Bank Of Los Angeles	3538	4	–
Security-First National Bank Of Los Angeles	2491	–	1
The American National Bank Of Los Angeles	6545	4	–
The Central National Bank Of Los Angeles	8827	6	–
The Citizens National Bank Of Los Angeles	5927	6	–
The Commercial National Bank Of Los Angeles	6864	3	–
The Commercial National Trust & Sav. Bank Of Los Angeles	6864	4	–
The Farmers And Merchants National Bank Of Los Angeles	6617	1	1
The First National Bank Of Los Angeles	2491	1	–
The First National Bank Of Wilmington	9515	4	–
The Los Angeles National Bank	2938	5	–
The Merchants National Bank Of Los Angeles	3538	3	–
The National Bank Of California Of Los Angeles	4096	3	–
The National Bank Of Commerce Of Los Angeles	8117	6	–
The National Bank Of Commerce Of Los Angeles	12755	5	5
The National City Bank Of Los Angeles	12410	4	–
The Pacific National Bank Of Los Angeles	12454	2	6
The Peoples National Bank Of Los Angeles	12755	5	–
The Seaboard National Bank Of Los Angeles	12545	–	1
The Security National Bank Of Los Angeles	8827	6	–
The Southern California National Bank Of Los Angeles	3538	6	–
The Southwestern National Bank Of Los Angeles	5993	6	–
The United States National Bank Of Los Angeles	7632	3	–
The Western National Bank In Los Angeles	13187	–	5
Los Angelos			
The Hollywood National Bank Of Los Angelos	12804	–	4
Los Banos			
The First National Bank Of Los Banos	9933	4	–
Los Gatos			
The First National Bank Of Los Gatos	10091	5	4
Madera			
The Commercial National Bank Of Madera	10197	6	–
The First National Bank Of Madera	7336	6	–
Maricopa			
The First National Bank Of Maricopa	9957	6	–
Martinez			
The First Natl. Bank Of Contra Costa County At Martinez	8692	4	–
The National Bank Of Martinez	12511	5	–
Marysville			
The First National Bank Of Marysville	11123	6	6
Mc Cloud			
The Mc Cloud National Bank	9479	6	3
Mc Farland			
The First National Bank Of Mc Farland	10387	6	4
Merced			
First National Bank In Merced	13028	–	4
The Farmers And Merchants National Bank Of Merced	10352	5	–
The First National Bank Of Merced	3733	6	–
The First National Bank Of Merced	9437	6	–
Modesto			
California National Bank Of Modesto	10988	6	–
The First National Bank Of Modesto	3136	5	–

City, Bank	Ch. No.	L	S
Monrovia			
First National Bank In Monrovia	7705	6	–
The American National Bank Of Monrovia	7705	6	–
The First National Bank Of Monrovia	3743	5	–
The Natioanl Bank Of Monrovia	7705	6	–
Monterey			
The First National Bank Of Monterey	7058	6	3
Monterey Park			
The First National Bank Of Monterey Park	12061	–	6
Mountain View			
The Farmers And Merchants National Bank Of Mountain View	11532	6	–
The First National Bank Of Mountain View	10324	5	4
Napa			
The First National Bank Of Napa	7176	5	2
National City			
The Peoples National Bank Of National City	9512	6	–
Needles			
The Needles National Bank	4873	6	–
Newman			
The First National Bank Of Newman	9760	6	–
Oakdale			
The First National Bank Of Oakdale	7502	4	4
Oakland			
Central National Bank Of Oakland	9502	2	2
First National Bank In Oakland	12665	3	3
The First National Bank Of Oakland	2248	3	–
The New First National Bank Of Oakland	12665	6	–
The Union National Bank Of Oakland	2266	5	–
Ocean Park			
The First National Bank Of Ocean Park	7690	5	–
Oceanside			
The First National Bank Of Oceanside	8069	6	–
Olive			
The First National Bank Of Olive	10891	5	5
Ontario			
The Citizens National Bank Of Ontario	13092	6	4
The First National Bank Of Ontario	6268	4	3
The Ontario National Bank	9935	4	–
Orange			
The First National Bank Of Orange	8181	5	3
The National Bank Of Orange	9878	4	–
Orange Cove			
The First National Bank Of Orange Cove	11616	6	4
Orland			
The First National Bank Of Orland	10378	5	6
Orosi			
The First National Bank Of Orosi	9167	6	–
The National Bank Of Orosi	10328	6	6
Oroville			
Rideout Smith National Bank Of Oroville	10282	6	–
The First National Bank Of Oroville	6919	6	5
Oxnard			
The First National Bank Of Oxnard	9481	6	–
Pacific Grove			
The First National Bank Of Pacific Grove	13375	–	2
Palo Alto			
Palo Alto National Bank	13212	–	2
The First National Bank Of Palo Alto	7069	6	–
Parlier			
The First National Bank Of Parlier	10124	5	–
Pasadena			
National Bank And Trust Company Of Pasadena	11425	6	–
Pasadena National Bank	12385	4	4
Pasadena-First National Bank, Pasadena	12385	–	6
The Crown City National Bank Of Pasadena	9366	6	–
The First National Bank Of Pasadena	3499	4	5
The National Bank Of Commerce Of Pasadena	10082	6	–
The National Bank Of Pasadena	10082	4	–
The Pasadena National Bank	3568	4	–
The Security National Bank Of Pasadena	10167	3	2
The Union National Bank Of Pasadena	9121	5	–
Paso Robles			
First National Bank In Paso Robles	12172	5	5
The First National Bank Of Paso Robles	9844	6	–
The Paso Robles National Bank	12172	6	–
Petaluma			
The First National Bank Of Petaluma	2193	6	–
The Petaluma National Bank	6904	4	–
The Sonoma County National Bank Of Petaluma	9918	4	–
Pittsburg			
The First National Bank Of Pittsburg	11359	6	–
Placentia			
The Placentia National Bank	10092	5	–
Placerville			
The Placerville National Bank	12056	5	5
Pleasanton			
The First National Bank Of Pleasanton	9897	5	3
Pomona			
The American National Bank Of Pomona	4663	4	–
The First National Bank Of Pomona	3518	3	2
The National Bank Of Pomona	4663	6	–
Port Chicago			
The First National Bank Of Bay Point	11561	6	–
Porterville			
The First National Bank Of Porterville	6808	5	6
Puente			
The First National Bank Of Puente	9894	4	4
Red Bluff			
The First National Bnak Of Red Bluff	10114	6	–
The Red Bluff National Bank	10114	5	–
Redding			
The Northern California National Bank Of Redding	10100	5	3
The Redding National Bank	10070	4	–
Redlands			
First National Bank In Redlands	12316	5	–
The Citizens National Bank Of Redlands	8073	5	–
The First National Bank Of Redlands	3892	4	–
The Redlands National Bank	7259	6	–
Redondo Beach			
The Farmers And Merchants National Bank Of Redondo	7895	5	–
The First National Bank Of Redondo	8143	4	4
Redwood City			
The First Natl. Bank Of San Mateo County At Redwood City	7279	3	2
Reedley			
The First National Bank Of Reedley	8857	6	–
The Reedley National Bank	9688	6	–
Rialto			
The Citizens National Bank Of Rialto	11867	6	6
The First National Bank Of Rialto	8768	5	5
Richmond			
First National Bank In Richmond	12341	4	4
The First National Bank Of Richmond	9735	5	–
Riverbank			
The First National Bank Of Riverbank	10427	6	–
Riverdale			
The First National Bank Of Riverdale	10200	6	6
Riverside			
First National Bank In Riverside	8377	5	2
The Citizens National Bank Of Riverside	8907	4	–
The Citizens National Trust & Savings Bank Of Riverside	8907	5	2
The First National Bank Of Riverside	3348	4	–
The National Bank Of Riverside	8377	5	–
The Orange Growers National Bank Of Riverside	6833	6	–
The Riverside National Bank	4757	6	–
Rodeo			
The First National Bank Of Rodeo	11201	6	–
Roseville			
The First National Bank Of Roseville	11961	6	–
The Railroad National Bank Of Roseville	11992	6	–
The Roseville National Bank	11961	6	–
Sacramento			
The California National Bank Of Sacramento	8504	2	1
The Capital National Bank Of Sacramento	10107	2	2
The Fort Sutter National Bank Of Sacramento	7776	5	–
The Merchants National Bank Of Sacramento	11875	4	4
The National Bank Of D. O. Mills & Co., Sacramento	2014	2	–
Saint Helena			
The Carver National Bank Of Saint Helena	3757	6	–
The First National Bank Of Saint Helena	3757	6	–
Salida			
The First National Bank Of Salida	11601	5	6
Salinas			
The First National Bank Of Salinas	5074	6	–
The Salinas National Bank	13380	–	3
San Bernardino			
American National Bank Of San Bernardino	10931	4	2
The Farmers Exchange National Bank Of San Bernardino	8618	5	–
The First National Bank Of San Bernardino	3527	6	–
The San Bernardino National Bank	3818	4	4
San Diego			
The American National Bank Of San Diego	7418	6	–
The California National Bank Of San Diego	3828	6	–
The Consolidated National Bank Of San Diego	3056	6	–
The First National Bank Of San Diego	3050	3	–
The First National Trust & Savings Bank Of San Diego	3050	–	2
The Marine National Bank Of San Diego	9483	6	–
The Merchants National Bank Of San Diego	4886	4	–
The National Bank Of Commerce Of San Diego	6869	6	–
The San Diego National Bank	3780	6	–
The Union National Bank Of San Diego	10435	5	–
The United States National Bank Of San Diego	10391	4	4
San Dimas			
The First National Bank Of San Dimas	10068	6	3
San Fernando			
The First National Bank Of San Fernando	9575	5	–
The San Fernando National Bank	10273	6	–
San Francisco			
Bank Of America Natl. Trust & Savings Assoc., San Francisco	13044	–	1
Bank Of Italy Natl. Trust & Savings Assoc., San Francisco	13044	1	1
Brotherhood National Bank Of San Francisco	13016	4	–
City National Bank Of San Francisco	13016	–	3
Crocker First National Bank Of San Francisco	1741	1	1
Mercantile National Bank Of San Francisco	9683	2	–
Merchants National Bank Of San Francisco	9882	3	–
Pacific National Bank Of San Francisco	12579	2	2
The American National Bank Of San Francisco	6426	2	–
The Anglo & London Paris National Bank Of San Francisco	9174	1	1
The Anglo California National Bank Of San Francisco	9174	–	1
The Bank Of California National Association, San Francisco	9655	1	1
San Francisco			
The California National Bank Of San Francisco	3592	6	–
The Citizens National Bank Of San Francisco	7713	6	–
The Crocker National Bank Of San Francisco	3555	1	–
The Crocker-Woolworth National Bank Of San Francisco	3555	4	–
The First National Bank Of San Francisco	1741	1	–
The Germania National Bank Of San Francisco	6592	6	–
The London Paris National Bank Of San Francisco	9174	4	–
The Merchants National Bank Of San Francisco	8487	5	–
The National Bank Of The Pacific, San Francisco	7894	5	–
The Nevada National Bank Of San Francisco	5105	2	–
The San Francisco National Bank	5096	1	–
The Seaboard National Bank Of San Francisco	9141	3	–
The United States National Bank Of San Francisco	7691	5	–
The Wells-Fargo Nevada National Bank Of San Francisco	5105	1	–
The Western Metropolis National Bank Of San Francisco	9882	5	–
The Western National Bank Of San Francisco	5688	3	–
Wells-Fargo Nevada National Bank Of San Francisco	5105	1	–
San Jacinto			
The First National Bank Of San Jacinto	7997	5	4
San Joaquin			
The First National Bank Of San Joaquin	11484	5	–
San Jose			
San Jose National Bank	13338	–	2
The First National Bank Of San Jose	2158	3	2
The Garden City National Bank Of San Jose	3715	6	–
San Leandro			
First National Bank In San Leandro	13217	–	3
The First National Bank Of San Leandro	9800	6	–
The San Leandro National Bank	12802	6	–
San Luis Obispo			
The First National Bank Of San Luis Obispo	3826	6	–
The Union National Bank Of San Luis Obispo	7877	4	–
San Marino			
The San Marino National Bank, San Marino	13335	–	3
San Mateo			
The National Bank Of San Mateo	9424	5	4
San Pedro			
The First National Bank Of San Pedro	7057	4	–
San Rafael			
First National Bank In San Rafael	12640	–	5
The Marin County National Bank Of San Rafael	10177	4	–
Sanger			
The First National Bank Of Sanger	9308	6	–
Santa Ana			
The American National Bank Of Santa Ana	11869	5	–
The California National Bank Of Santa Ana	9904	4	–
The Commercial National Bank Of Santa Ana	13200	6	4
The Farmers And Merchants National Bank Of Santa Ana	7980	5	–
The First National Bank Of Santa Ana	3520	2	2
Santa Barbara			
County National Bank & Trust Company Of Santa Barbara	2456	4	4
First National Trust & Savings Bank Of Santa Barbara	2104	5	3
The First National Bank Of Santa Barbara	2104	3	–
The Santa Barbara County National Bank	2456	4	–
Santa Cruz			
County First National Bank Of Santa Cruz	9745	4	3
Santa Cruz County National Bank	9745	5	–
The Farmers And Merchants National Bank Of Santa Cruz	10571	–	4
The First National Bank Of Santa Cruz	8403	5	–
Santa Maria			
The First National Bank Of Santa Maria	7480	5	–
Santa Monica			
The American National Bank Of Santa Monica	12787	6	4
The First National Bank In Santa Monica	6945	6	–
The First National Bank Of Santa Monica	3845	6	–
The Merchants National Bank Of Santa Monica	6945	6	–
Santa Paula			
The First National Bank & Trust Company Of Santa Paula	4120	6	–
The First National Bank Of Santa Paula	4120	5	–
Santa Rosa			
The First National Bank Of Santa Rosa	12201	5	–
The Santa Rosa National Bank	3558	5	–
Sausalito			
The First National Bank Of Sausalito	12453	6	–
Scotia			
The First National Bank Of Scotia	9787	5	4
Sebastopol			
The First National Bank Of Sebastopol	9648	6	6
The Sebastopol National Bank	11161	5	4

City, Bank	Ch. No.	L	S
Seeley			
The First National Bank Of Seeley	10462	6	–
Selma			
The First National Bank Of Selma	5395	5	–
The Selma National Bank	10293	6	–
Sierra Madre			
The First National Bank Of Sierra Madre	8707	6	–
Sonoma			
The First National Bank Of Sonoma	10259	6	–
Sonora			
The First National Bank Of Sonora	7202	4	4
The Sonora National Bank	10461	6	–
South Pasadena			
First National Bank In South Pasadena	12797	5	–
The First National Bank Of South Pasadena	8544	6	–
South San Francisco			
The Citizens National Bank Of South San Francisco	12364	6	–
Stockton			
The First National Bank Of Stockton	2412	4	5
The San Joaquin Valley National Bank Of Stockton	10817	5	–
The Stockton National Bank	2794	6	–
Suisun			
Bank Of Suisun National Association, Suisun City	11684	–	5
The First National Bank Of Suisun	10149	6	–
Taft			
The First National Bank Of Taft	10088	6	–
Terra Bella			
The First National Bank Of Terra Bella	9889	6	5
Torrance			
The First National Bank Of Torrance	10396	5	4
Torrance National Bank	14202	–	6
Tranquility			
The First National Bank Of Tranquility	11433	6	6
Tropico			
The First National Bank Of Tropico	10412	6	–
Tulare			
The First National Bank Of Tulare	8626	4	–
The National Bank Of Tulare	10201	6	–
Turlock			
The First National Bank In Turlock	7738	6	–
Tustin			
The First National Bank Of Tustin	10134	5	2
Ukiah			
The First National Bank Of Ukiah	10977	5	6
Upland			
The Commercial National Bank Of Upland	9570	5	–
The First National Bank Of Upland	8266	5	4
Vacaville			
The First National Bank Of Vacaville	9795	5	5
Vallejo			
Mechanics And Merchants National Bank Of Vallejo	13368	–	3
The First National Bank Of Vallejo	9573	5	–
The Vallejo Commercial National Bank	11206	5	–
Van Nuys			
The First National Bank Of Van Nuys	10168	6	–
Venice			
The First National Bank Of Venice	10233	6	6
Ventura			
National Bank Of Ventura	9685	4	–
The First National Bank Of Ventura	7210	4	6
The Union National Bank Of Ventura	12996	6	3
Victorville			
The First National Bank Of Victorville	11005	6	5
Visalia			
National Bank Of Visalia	9173	4	–
The First National Bank Of Visalia	7063	6	–
The New First National Bank Of Visalia	12678	6	–
Walnut Creek			
The First National Bank Of Walnut Creek	10281	6	–
Walnut Park			
The Walnut Park National Bank	12572	–	6
Watsonville			
The Pajaro Valley National Bank Of Watsonville	9621	5	4
Weed			
The First National Bank Of Weed	9873	5	3
Whittier			
First National Trust & Savings Bank Of Whittier	5588	6	–
The First National Bank Of Whittier	5588	4	–
The Whittier National Bank	7999	4	4
The Whittier National Trust & Savings Bank, Whittier	7999	–	3
Willits			
The First National Bank Of Willits	11566	6	6
Willows			
The First National Bank Of Willows	9713	4	5
Winter			
The Winters National Bank, Winters	13312	–	2
Winters			
The First National Bank Of Winters	10133	5	–
Woodlake			
The First National Bank Of Woodlake	10309	5	6
Woodland			
Bank Of Woodland National Association	10878	–	3
The First National Bank Of Woodland	9493	5	–
Yreka			
First National Bank In Yreka	13340	–	3
The First National Bank Of Yreka	10731	5	–
Yuba City			
The First National Bank Of Yuba City	10299	6	–

COLORADO TERRITORY

City, Bank	Ch. No.	L	S
Central City			
The First National Bank Of Central City	2129	3	–
The Rocky Mountain Natl Bank Of Central City	1652	6	–
Colorado Springs			
The First National Bank Of Colorado Springs	2179	6	–
Denver			
The City National Bank Of Denver	1955	6	–
The Colorado National Bank Of Denver	1651	3	–
The First National Bank Of Denver	1016	4	–
Georgetown			
The First National Bank Of Georgetown	1991	6	–
The Miners National Bank Of Georgetown	2199	6	–
Golden			
The First National Bank Of Golden	2140	6	–
Pueblo			
The First National Bank Of Pueblo	1833	4	–
The Peoples National Bank Of Pueblo	2134	6	–
The Stock Growers National Bank Of Pueblo	2310	6	–
Trinidad			
The First National Bank Of Trinidad	2300	6	–

COLORADO

City, Bank	Ch. No.	L	S
Akron			
The Citizens National Bank Of Akron	10901	5	5
The First National Bank Of Akron	8548	6	–
Alamosa			
The Alamosa National Bank	8541	6	6
The American National Bank Of Alamosa	7904	6	5
The First National Bank Of Alamosa	3114	6	–
Arvada			
The First National Bank Of Arvada	7501	6	6
Aspen			
The Aspen National Bank	4733	6	–
The First National Bank Of Aspen	3485	5	–
The Peoples National Bank Of Aspen	8815	6	–
Ault			
The Farmers National Bank Of Ault	8167	5	5
The First National Bank Of Ault	8088	6	–
Berthoud			
The Berthoud National Bank	7995	5	4
The First National Bank Of Berthoud	8033	6	–
Boulder			
First National Bank In Boulder	14021	–	6
The Boulder National Bank	3246	6	–
The First National Bank Of Boulder	2352	4	4
The National State Bank Of Boulder	2355	5	5
Brighton			
The First National Bank Of Brighton	7577	6	6
Brush			
The First National Bank Of Brush	6437	5	4
The Stockman's National Bank Of Brush	8520	6	–
Buena Vista			
The First National Bank Of Buena Vista	8735	6	6
Canon City			
The First National Bank Of Canon City	3879	5	–
The Fremont County National Bank Of Canon City	8433	5	–
Carbondale			
The First National Bank Of Carbondale	9009	6	4
Castle Rock			
The First National Bank Of Douglas County At Castle Rock	6556	5	6
Cedaredge			
The First National Bank Of Cedaredge	10272	6	4
Center			
The First National Bank Of Center	9743	6	–
Central City			
The First National Bank Of Central City	2129	5	6
The Rocky Mountain National Bank Of Central City	1652	6	–
Clifton			
The First National Bank Of Clifton	9875	6	–
Colorado City			
The City National Bank Of Colorado Springs	6238	5	4
The First National Bank Of Colorado City	6238	6	–
Colorado Springs			
The Colorado Springs National Bank	8572	4	4
The El Paso National Bank Of Colorado Springs	5283	5	–
The Exchange National Bank Of Colorado Springs	3913	5	2
The First National Bank Of Colorado Springs	2179	3	2
Cortez			
The Cortez National Bank	8967	6	–
The First National Bank Of Cortez	8967	6	–
The Montezuma Valley National Bank Of Cortez	9100	6	4
Craig			
The First National Bank Of Craig	10558	6	6
Creede			
The First National Bank Of Creede	4716	6	–
Cripple Creek			
The First National Bank Of Cripple Creek	4845	5	–
Del Norte			
The First National Bank Of Del Norte	4264	6	–
Delta			
The Delta National Bank	8675	5	–
The First National Bank Of Delta	5467	5	–
Denver			
The American National Bank Of Denver	4159	6	–
The American National Bank Of Denver	12517	3	2
The Capitol National Bank Of Denver	6355	6	–
The Central National Bank Of Denver	8774	6	–
The Colorado National Bank Of Denver	1651	6	2
The Commercial National Bank Of Denver	4113	6	–
The Continental National Bank Of Denver	6355	6	–
The Denver National Bank	3269	2	1
The Drovers National Bank Of Denver	11564	5	–
The Federal National Bank Of Denver	10064	5	–
The First National Bank Of Denver	1016	2	1
The German National Bank Of Denver	2351	5	–
The Hamilton National Bank Of Denver	9887	5	–
The Merchants National Bank Of Denver	2523	6	–
The National Bank Of Commerce, Denver	4358	6	–
The National City Bank Of Denver	13098	–	3
The Peoples National Bank Of Denver	4084	6	–
The State National Bank Of Denver	2694	6	–
The Union National Bank Of Denver	4382	6	–
The United States National Bank Of Denver	7408	2	1
Dolores			
The First National Bank Of Dolores	10770	6	–
Durango			
The Burns National Bank Of Durango	9797	5	4
The Durango National Bank	4126	6	–
The First National Bank Of Durango	2637	5	4
The Smelter National Bank Of Durango	4776	6	–
Eads			
The First National Bank In Eads	14213	–	6
The First National Bank Of Eads	8412	6	4
Eagle			
The First National Bank Of Eagle County, Eagle	9013	6	–
Eaton			
The Eaton National Bank	8658	6	–
The First National Bank Of Eaton	6057	5	–
Elizabeth			
The First National Bank Of Elizabeth	8271	6	–
Englewood			
The First National Bank Of Englewood	9907	4	4
Fleming			
The First National Bank Of Fleming	11571	5	5
Florence			
The First National Bank Of Florence	5381	6	5
Fort Collins			
The First National Bank In Fort Collins	14146	–	6
The First National Bank Of Fort Collins	2622	3	3
The Fort Collins National Bank	5503	3	4
The Poudre Valley National Bank Of Fort Collins	7837	4	3
Fort Morgan			
The First National Bank Of Fort Morgan	7004	4	3
The Morgan County National Bank Of Fort Morgan	7832	6	–
Fountain			
The First National Bank Of Fountain	6772	6	6
Fowler			
The First National Bank Of Fowler	7637	6	6
Fruita			
The First National Bank Of Fruita	8840	6	6
Georgetown			
The Merchants National Bank Of Georgetown	2394	6	–
Gill			
The First National Bank Of Gill	9697	6	–
Glenwood Springs			
The Citizens National Bank Of Glenwood Springs	6957	5	–
The First National Bank Of Glenwood Springs	3661	5	–
The Glenwood National Bank Of Glenwood Springs	3722	6	–
Golden			
The Rubey National Bank Of Golden	6497	6	6
The Woods-Rubey National Bank Of Golden	6497	6	–
Granada			
The First National Bank Of Granada	7809	6	–
Grand Junction			
First National Bank In Grand Junction	13902	–	6
The First National Bank Of Grand Junction	3860	6	–
The Grand Valley National Bank Of Grand Junction	6137	5	–
The Mesa County National Bank Of Grand Junction	7766	6	–
Greeley			
The City National Bank Of Greeley	10038	6	–
The First National Bank Of Greeley	3178	4	4
The Greeley National Bank	4437	4	–
The Greeley National Bank	13928	–	5
The Greeley Union National Bank, Greeley	4437	4	1
The Union National Bank Of Greeley	7604	6	–
Gunnison			
The First National Bank Of Gunnison	2686	5	6
The Iron National Bank Of Gunnison	2975	6	–
Haxtun			
The First National Bank Of Haxtun	11099	5	5
Holly			
The First National Bank Of Holly	7704	6	6
Holyoke			
The First National Bank Of Holyoke	9278	6	6
Hotchkiss			
The First National Bank Of Hotchkiss	5976	6	6
Hugo			
The First National Bank Of Hugo	8489	5	6
The Hugo National Bank	10786	6	–
Idaho Springs			
The First National Bank Of Idaho Springs	2962	5	–
The Merchants And Miners National Bank Of Idaho Springs	5989	6	–
Johnstown			
The First National Bank Of Johnstown	8636	6	4
Julesburg			
The Citizens National Bank Of Julesburg	9603	6	–
The First National Bank Of Julesburg	8205	6	4
La Jara			
The First National Bank Of La Jara	9840	5	6
La Junta			
The First National Bank Of La Junta	4507	5	5
Lafayette			
The First National Bank Of Lafayette	8909	6	5
Lake City			
The First National Bank Of Lake City	2354	6	–

City, Bank	Ch. No.	L	S
Lamar			
The First National Bank Of Lamar	3749	6	6
The Lamar National Bank	9036	6	3
Las Animas			
The First National Bank Of Las Animas	6030	6	5
Leadville			
The American National Bank Of Leadville	3949	5	–
The Carbonate National Bank Of Leadville	3746	4	–
The First National Bank Of Leadville	2420	5	–
Limon			
The First National Bank Of Limon	11504	6	5
Littleton			
The First National Bank Of Littleton	7533	6	6
The Littleton National Bank	11949	6	6
Longmont			
The American National Bank Of Longmont	11253	6	–
The Farmers National Bank Of Longmont	4653	6	–
The First National Bank Of Longmont	3354	6	–
The First National Bank Of Longmont	11253	–	3
The Longmont National Bank	7839	6	3
Loveland			
First National Bank In Loveland	13624	–	4
The First National Bank Of Loveland	7648	5	5
The Loveland National Bank	8116	5	–
Mancos			
The First National Bank Of Mancos	9674	6	5
Meeker			
The First National Bank Of Meeker	7435	6	–
Monte Vista			
The First National Bank Of Monte Vista	7228	5	6
Montrose			
The First National Bank Of Montrose	4007	4	6
The Montrose National Bank	7288	6	6
Olathe			
The First National Bank Of Olathe	9719	6	6
Ordway			
The First National Bank Of Ordway	8695	6	6
Otis			
The First National Bank Of Otis	10852	6	5
Ouray			
The First National Bank Of Ouray	4109	6	–
Palisades			
The Palisades National Bank	8004	5	4
Paonia			
The First National Bank Of Paonia	6671	6	6
Platteville			
The First National Bank Of Platteville	8755	6	–
The Platteville National Bank	9451	6	–
Pueblo			
The American National Bank Of Pueblo	4108	6	–
The Central National Bank Of Pueblo	2541	6	–
The First National Bank Of Pueblo	1833	4	2
The Mercantile National Bank Of Pueblo	4108	5	–
The Pueblo National Bank	4498	6	–
The Stock Growers National Bank Of Pueblo	2310	6	–
The Western National Bank Of Pueblo	2546	4	3
Rico			
The First National Bank Of Rico	4334	6	–
Rifle			
The First National Bank Of Rifle	6178	6	–
Rocky Ford			
The First National Bank Of Rocky Ford	7082	6	–
The Rocky Ford National Bank	9117	6	4
Saguache			
Saguache County National Bank Of Saguache	9997	6	3
The First National Bank Of Saguache	9997	6	–
Salida			
The Commercial National Bank Of Salida	7888	6	6
The First National Bank Of Salida	4172	6	4
The Merchants National Bank Of Salida	8951	6	–
Sedgwick			
The First National Bank Of Sedgwick	9045	6	5
Silverton			
The First National Bank Of Silverton	2930	6	6
The Silverton National Bank	7784	6	–
South Pueblo			
The South Pueblo National Bank	2541	6	–
The Western National Bank Of South Pueblo	2546	6	–
Steamboat Springs			
The First National Bank Of Steamboat Springs	6454	6	6
Sterling			
The Farmers National Bank Of Sterling	9454	6	–
The First National Bank Of Sterling	5624	4	–
The Logan County National Bank Of Sterling	7973	6	–
Sugar City			
The Citizens National Bank Of Sugar City	6472	6	–
Telluride			
The First National Bank Of Telluride	4417	5	–
Trinidad			
The First National Bank Of Trinidad	2300	4	4
The Trinidad National Bank	3450	3	5
Victor			
The First National Bank Of Victor	5586	6	–
Walsenburg			
The First National Bank Of Walsenburg	7022	6	–
Wellington			
The First National Bank Of Wellington	7793	5	5
Windsor			
The Farmers National Bank Of Windsor	9120	6	–
The First National Bank Of Windsor	8296	6	–
Wray			
The First National Bank Of Wray	8752	6	3
The National Bank Of Wray	9676	6	5
Yuma			
The First National Bank Of Yuma	10093	6	6

CONNECTICUT

City, Bank	Ch. No.	L	S
Ansonia			
The Ansonia National Bank	1093	6	6
Bethel			
The Bethel National Bank	10289	6	6
The First National Bank Of Bethel	1141	6	–
Birmingham			
The Birmingham National Bank, Birmingham	1098	4	–
The Birmingham National Bank, Derby	1098	3	4
Bridgeport			
The Bridgeport National Bank	910	6	–
The City National Bank Of Bridgeport	921	5	–
The Connecticut National Bank Of Bridgeport	927	4	–
The First National Bank & Trust Company Of Bridgeport	335	–	2
The First National Bank Of Bridgeport	335	4	3
The First National Bank Of Bridgeport	335	4	5
The First-Bridgeport National Bank, Bridgeport	335	4	–
The Pequonnock National Bank Of Bridgeport	928	5	–
Bristol			
The Bristol National Bank	2250	4	–
Brooklyn			
The Windham County National Bank Of Brooklyn	1360	5	–
Canaan			
The Canaan National Bank	8511	6	5
Clinton			
The Clinton National Bank	1314	4	5
Danbury			
City National Bank & Trust Company Of Danbury	1132	6	5
The City National Bank Of Danbury	1132	5	–
The Danbury National Bank	943	4	4
The National Pahquioque Bank Of Danbury	1132	6	–
Danielson			
The Windham County National Bank Of Danielson	1360	6	5
Danielsonville			
The Windham County National Bank Of Danielsonville	1360	6	–
Deep River			
The Deep River National Bank	1139	4	5
East Haddam			
The National Bank Of New England Of East Haddam	7812	6	–
The National Bank Of New England, East Haddam	1480	6	–
East Port Chester			
The Byram National Bank Of East Port Chester	12973	6	5
Essex			
The Essex National Bank	8936	6	5
The Saybrook National Bank Of Essex	1084	6	–
Falls Village			
The National Iron Bank Of Falls Village	1214	6	6
Greenwich			
The Greenwich National Bank	8243	6	–
Guilford			
The Guilford National Bank	5358	6	–
Hartford			
Hartford National Bank & Trust Company	1338	5	3
The Aetna National Bank Of Hartford	756	5	–
The American National Bank Of Hartford	1165	6	–
The Capitol National Bank & Trust Company Of Hartford	13038	–	2
The Capitol National Bank Of Hartford	13038	4	–
The Charter Oak National Bank Of Hartford	486	4	–
The City National Bank Of Hartford	1377	5	–
The Colonial National Bank Of Hartford	10796	5	–
The Farmers And Mechanics National Bank Of Hartford	1321	4	–
The First National Bank Of Hartford	121	3	2
The Hartford National Bank	1338	3	–
The Hartford-Aetna National Bank	1338	2	–
The Mercantile National Bank Of Hartford	1300	6	–
The National Exchange Bank Of Hartford	361	3	–
The Phoenix National Bank Of Hartford	670	3	–
Jewett City			
The Jewett City National Bank	1478	6	–
Killingly			
The First National Bank Of Killingly At West Killingly	450	4	–
Litchfield			
The First National Bank Of Litchfield	709	4	3
Meridan			
The First National Bank Of Meridan	250	4	5
Meriden			
The Home National Bank Of Meriden	720	4	3
The Meriden National Bank	1382	4	3
Middletown			
The Central National Bank Of Middletown	1340	4	4
The First National Bank Of Middletown	397	6	6
The Middlesex County National Bank Of Middletown	845	6	–
The Middletown National Bank	1216	3	–
The Middletown National Bank, Middletown	1216	–	4
Moosup			
The Plainfield National Bank Of Moosup	10145	–	6
Mystic			
The Mystic National Bank	1268	6	–
Mystic Bridge			
The First National Bank Of Mystic Bridge	251	6	–

City, Bank	Ch. No.	L	S
Mystic River			
The Mystic River National Bank	645	5	5
Naugatuck			
The Naugatuck National Bank	3020	5	6
New Britain			
The City National Bank Of New Britain	12846	6	6
The Mechanics National Bank Of New Britain	3668	6	–
The New Britain National Bank	1184	5	6
New Canaan			
The First National Bank & Trust Of New Canaan	1249	–	5
The First National Bank Of New Canaan	1249	5	–
New Haven			
The First National Bank And Trust Company Of New Haven	2682	5	–
The First National Bank Of New Haven	2	6	–
The First National Bank Of New Haven	2682	3	1
The Merchants National Bank Of New Haven	1128	5	3
The National New Haven Bank	1243	5	–
The National Tradesmen's Bank & Trust Company, New Haven	1202	6	3
The National Tradesmen's Bank Of New Haven	1202	4	–
The New Haven Bank National Banking Association, New Haven	1243	4	5
The New Haven County National Bank, New Haven	1245	5	–
The Second National Bank Of New Haven	227	4	–
The Tradesmen's National Bank Of New Haven	13704	–	4
The Yale National Bank Of New Haven	796	4	–
New London			
The First National Bank Of New London	196	6	–
The National Bank Of Commerce Of New London	666	4	4
The National Union Bank Of New London	1175	6	–
The National Whaling Bank Of New London	978	6	5
The New London City National Bank	1037	3	4
New Milford			
The First National Bank Of New Milford	1193	5	4
Norwalk			
The Central National Bank Of Norwalk	2342	6	–
The Fairfield County National Bank Of Norwalk	754	4	–
The National Bank Of Norwalk	942	4	4
Norwich			
The First National Bank Of Norwich	65	5	–
The First National Bank Of Norwich	458	5	–
The Merchants National Bank Of Norwich	1481	6	–
The Norwich National Bank	1358	6	–
The Second National Bank Of Norwich	224	6	–
The Shetucket National Bank Of Norwich	1379	6	–
The Thames National Bank Of Norwich	657	3	–
The Uncas National Bank Of Norwich	1187	5	–
Pawcatuck			
The Pawcatuck National Bank	919	6	–
Plainfield			
The First National Bank Of Plainfield	10145	6	6
Plainville			
The First National Bank Of Plainville	9313	6	–
Plantsville			
The Plantsville National Bank	12637	6	5
Portland			
The First National Bank Of Portland	1013	5	–
Putnam			
The First National Bank Of Putnam	448	6	–
The Thompson National Bank Of Putnam	1477	6	–
Ridgefield			
The First National Bank & Trust Company Of Ridgefield	5309	6	5
The First National Bank Of Ridgefield	5309	6	–
Rockville			
The First National Bank Of Rockville	186	5	6
The Rockville National Bank	509	6	5
Seymour			
The Valley National Bank Of Seymour	5499	6	–
South Norwalk			
The City National Bank Of South Norwalk	2643	4	5
The First National Bank Of South Norwalk	502	5	–
Southington			
The Southington National Bank	2814	6	–
Southport			
The Southport National Bank	660	6	–
Stafford Springs			
The First National Bank Of Stafford Springs	3914	5	–
The Stafford National Bank Of Stafford Springs	686	6	–
Stamford			
The First National Bank Of Stamford	4	4	–
The First-Stamford National Bank & Trust Co. Of Stamford	4	–	2
The First-Stamford National Bank, Stamford	4	3	5
The Peoples National Bank Of Stamford	12400	6	6
The Stamford National Bank	1038	5	–
Stonington			
The First National Bank Of Stonington	735	4	5
Suffield			
The First National Bank Of Suffield	497	5	4
Thomaston			
The Thomaston National Bank	3964	6	6
Thompson			
The Thompson National Bank	1477	6	–
Tolland			
The Tolland County National Bank Of Tolland	1385	6	–
Torrington			
The Brooks National Bank Of Torrington	5231	6	–
The Torrington National Bank	5235	4	4
The Torrington National Bank And Trust Company	5235	–	4

City, Bank	Ch. No.	L	S
Wallingford			
The First National Bank Of Wallingford	2599	5	4
Waterbury			
The Citizens & Manufacturers National Bank Of Waterbury	2494	–	4
The Citizens National Bank Of Waterbury	791	5	–
The Fourth National Bank Of Waterbury	3768	6	–
The Manufacturers National Bank Of Waterbury	2494	6	–
The Waterbury National Bank	780	5	4
West Meriden			
The First National Bank Of West Meriden	250	5	–
Westport			
The First National Bank Of Westport	394	5	–
Willimantic			
The First National Bank Of Willimantic	2388	6	–
Windham			
The Windham National Bank, Willmantic	1614	6	6
The Windham National Bank, Windham	1614	6	–
Winsted			
The First National Bank Of Winsted	2414	6	6
The Hurlbut National Bank Of Winsted	1494	5	4
The Winsted National Bank	2419	6	–

DELAWARE

City, Bank	Ch. No.	L	S
Dagsboro			
The First National Bank Of Dagsboro	8972	5	4
Delaware City			
The Delaware City National Bank	1332	5	6
Delmar			
The First National Bank Of Delmar	7211	6	5
Dover			
The First National Bank Of Dover	1567	4	2
Felton			
The First National Bank Of Felton	9132	6	–
Frankford			
The First National Bank Of Frankford	8918	6	5
Frederica			
The First National Bank Of Frederica	5421	6	–
Georgetown			
The First National Bank Of Georgetown	5930	6	–
Harrington			
The First National Bank Of Harrington	3883	6	6
Laurel			
The Peoples National Bank Of Laurel	6726	6	5
Lewes			
The Lewes National Bank	5148	5	–
Middletown			
The Citizens National Bank Of Middletown	1181	5	–
The Peoples National Bank Of Middletown	3019	6	–
Milford			
The First National Bank And Trust Company Of Milford	2340	6	3
The First National Bank Of Milford	2340	4	–
Newark			
The National Bank Of Newark	1536	6	–
Newport			
The Newport National Bank	997	4	–
Odessa			
The New Castle County National Bank Of Odessa	1281	4	4
Seaford			
The First National Bank Of Seaford	795	6	4
The Sussex National Bank Of Seaford	3693	6	–
Selbyville			
The Selbyville National Bank	6718	6	–
Smyrna			
The Fruit Growers National Bank & Trust Company Of Smyrna	2336	6	4
The Fruit Growers National Bank Of Smyrna	2336	6	–
The National Bank Of Smyrna	2381	5	4
Wilmington			
The Central National Bank Of Wilmington	3395	3	3
The First National Bank Of Wilmington	473	6	
The National Bank Of Delaware	1420	5	6
The National Bank Of Wilmington And Brandywine	1190	5	–
The Union National Bank Of Wilmington	1390	4	4
Wyoming			
The First National Bank Of Wyoming	9428	6	6

DISTRICT OF COLUMBIA

City, Bank	Ch. No.	L	S
Georgetown			
The Farmers And Mechanics National Bank Of Georgetown	1928	3	–
The National Bank Of Commerce Of Georgetown	682	6	–
Hagertown, Md			
The Citizens National Bank Of Washington City, Dc	1893	5	–
Washington			
American National Bank Of Washington	6716	3	–
District National Bank Of Washington	9545	–	3
Federal National Bank Of Washington	10316	4	–
Federal-American National Bank Of Washington	10316	5	6
Hamilton National Bank Of Washington	13782	–	2
National Metropolitan Citizens Bank Of Washington	1069	6	–
The Central National Bank Of Washington City	2382	3	–
The Citizens National Bank Of Hagerstown, Md	1893	5	–
The Columbia National Bank Of Washington	3625	3	3
The Commercial National Bank Of Washington	7446	2	3
The District National Bank Of Washington	9545	3	–
Washington			
The Dupont National Bank Of Washington	10825	5	–
The Farmers & Mechanics National Bank Of Washington	1928	4	–
The First National Bank Of Washington	26	5	–
The Franklin National Bank Of Washington	10504	3	3
The German-American National Bank Of Washington	2358	6	–
The Lincoln National Bank Of Washington	4247	5	4
The Merchants National Bank Of Washington	627	6	–
The National Bank Of The Metropolis Of Washington	526	6	–
The National Bank Of The Republic Of Washington	875	5	–
The National Bank Of Washington	3425	3	2
The National Capital Bank Of Washington	4107	5	–
The National City Bank Of Washington	7936	6	–
The National Metropolitan Bank Of Washington	1069	6	–
The National Metropolitan Bank Of Washington	1069	2	3
The Ohio National Bank Of Washington	4522	6	–
The Riggs National Bank Of Washington	5046	2	1
The Second National Bank Of Washington	2038	3	4
The Traders National Bank Of Washington	4244	5	–
The West End National Bank Of Washington	4195	6	–

FLORIDA

City, Bank	Ch. No.	L	S
Alachua			
The First National Bank Of Alachua	8980	6	6
Apalachicola			
The First National Bank Of Apalachicola	6274	6	–
Arcadia			
The De Soto National Bank Of Arcadia	8728	5	3
The First National Bank Of Arcadia	5534	5	5
Avon Park			
The First National Bank Of Avon Park	10826	6	–
Bartow			
The Florida National Bank At Bartow	13389	–	4
The Polk County National Bank Of Bartow	4627	6	–
Bradenton			
The First National Bank Of Bradenton	10245	–	5
The First National Bank Of Bradentown	10245	5	–
Brooksville			
The First National Bank In Brooksville	13320	–	4
The First National Bank Of Brooksville	9891	4	–
Chipley			
The First National Bank Of Chipley	7778	5	6
Clearwater			
The First National Bank Of Clearwater	12905	6	3
Clermont			
The First National Bank Of Clermont	11921	6	–
Coral Gables			
The Coral Gables First National Bank	13008	–	4
Daytona			
The First National Bank Of Daytona	10545	6	–
De Funiak Springs			
The First National Bank Of De Funiak Springs	7404	5	4
Deland			
The Barnett National Bank Of Deland	13388	–	4
The First National Bank Of Deland	9657	5	–
Fernandina			
The Citizens National Bank Of Fernandina	10024	6	–
The First National Bank Of Fernandina	4558	5	4
Fort Lauderdale			
The First National Bank Of Fort Lauderdale	12020	6	–
Fort Meade			
The First National Bank Of Fort Meade	10386	6	–
Fort Myers			
The First National Bank In Fort Myers	14195	–	6
The First National Bank Of Fort Myers	9035	6	4
Gainesville			
The First National Bank Of Gainesville	3894	4	4
The Florida National Bank Of Gainesville	10310	5	–
The Gainesville National Bank	8802	5	–
Graceville			
The First National Bank Of Graceville	7423	4	6
Homestead			
The First National Bank Of Homestead	13641	–	2
Jacksonville			
The Atlantic National Bank Of Jacksonville	6888	2	1
The Barnett National Bank Of Jacksonville	9049	3	2
The First National Bank Of Florida, Jacksonville	2174	6	–
The Florida National Bank Of Jacksonville	8321	2	2
The Fourth National Bank Of Jacksonville	9628	6	–
The Heard National Bank Of Jacksonville	10136	5	–
The Merchants National Bank Of Jacksonville	4332	6	–
The National Bank Of Jacksonville	3869	6	–
The National Bank Of The State Of Florida, Jacksonville	3327	6	–
Jasper			
The First National Bank Of Jasper	7757	6	6
Key West			
The First National Bank Of Key West	4672	3	3
The Island City National Bank Of Key West	7942	6	–
Lake City			
The First National Bank Of Lake City	7540	6	4
Lake Hamilton			
The First National Bank Of Lake Hamilton	11703	6	–
Lake Worth			
The First National Bank Of Lake Worth	11716	6	–
Lakeland			
The First National Bank Of Lakeland	9811	5	–
The Florida National Bank At Lakeland	13370	–	2
Leesburg			
The First National Bank Of Leesburg	11038	4	6
Live Oak			
The First National Bank Of Live Oak	6055	5	4
Madison			
The First National Bank Of Madison	7190	5	–
Marianna			
The First National Bank Of Marianna	6110	5	4
Miami			
The First National Bank Of Miami	6370	5	1
The Florida National Bank And Trust Company At Miami	13570	–	3
The Fort Dallas National Bank Of Miami	6774	6	–
Miami Beach			
Mercantile National Bank Of Miami Beach	13828	–	6
The Miami Beach First National Bank	12047	–	3
Milton			
First National Bank In Milton	13968	–	6
The First National Bank Of Milton	7034	6	6
Ocala			
The Central National Bank Of Ocala	6825	6	–
The First National Bank Of Ocala	3470	6	–
The Merchants National Bank Of Ocala	3815	6	–
The Munroe And Chambliss National Bank Of Ocala	10578	6	4
The Ocala National Bank	9926	4	4
Orlando			
First National Bank & Trust Company In Orlando	10069	6	5
The Citizens National Bank Of Orlando	3802	6	–
The First National Bank In Orlando	10069	6	–
The First National Bank Of Orlando	3469	5	–
The Peoples National Bank Of Orlando	10069	6	–
Palatka			
The First National Bank Of Palatka	3223	6	–
The Palatka Atlantic National Bank	13214	–	3
The Palatka National Bank	3266	6	–
The Putnam National Bank Of Palatka	4813	6	6
Palm Beach			
The First National Bank Of Palm Beach	12275	6	–
Panama City			
The First National Bank Of Panama City	10346	4	6
Pensacola			
The American National Bank Of Pensacola	5603	2	1
The Citizens & Peoples Bank Of Pensacola	9007	3	2
The Citizens National Bank Of Pensacola	4837	6	–
The First National Bank Of Pensacola	2490	3	–
The National Bank Of Commerce Of Pensacola	10535	4	–
The Peoples National Bank Of Pensacola	9007	6	–
Perry			
The First National Bank Of Perry	7865	5	6
Plant City			
The First National Bank Of Plant City	10236	6	–
Punta Gorda			
The First National Bank Of Punta Gorda	10512	5	–
Quincy			
The First National Bank Of Quincy	7253	4	–
Saint Augustine			
The First National Bank Of St. Augustine	3462	3	–
The St. Augustine National Bank	11420	5	5
Saint Cloud			
The First National Bank Of St. Cloud	9707	6	–
Saint Petersburg			
The Alexander National Bank Of St. Petersburg	12623	5	–
The Central National Bank & Trust Co Of St. Petersburg	7796	6	–
The Central National Bank Of St. Petersburg	7796	5	–
The First National Bank Of St. Petersburg	7730	4	–
The National Bank Of St. Petersburg	7796	6	–
Sanford			
The First National Bank Of Sanford	3798	5	–
The Sanford Atlantic National Bank	13157	–	4
Sarasota			
The American National Bank Of Sarasota	12751	6	–
The First National Bank Of Sarasota	10414	6	–
The Palmer National Bank And Trust Company Of Sarasota	13352	–	1
Seabreeze			
The First National Bank Of Seabreeze	12546	–	–
Tallahassee			
The First National Bank Of Tallahassee	4132	5	–
Tampa			
The American National Bank Of Tampa	7153	5	–
The Exchange National Bank Of Tampa	4949	3	3
The First National Bank Of Tampa	3497	3	1
The Gulf National Bank Of Tampa	4478	6	–
The National City Bank Of Tampa	10958	3	–
The Tampa National Bank	4539	6	–
Tarpon Springs			
The First National Bank Of Tarpon Springs	12274	6	–
Vero			
The First National Bank Of Vero	11156	6	–
West Palm Beach			
The American National Bank Of West Palm Beach	12057	6	–

City, Bank	Ch. No.	L	S
West Palm Beach			
The First National Bank Of West Palm Beach	11073	6	–
The West Palm Beach Atlantic National Bank	13300	–	6
Winter Garden			
The First National Bank Of Winter Garden	11389	5	6
Winter Haven			
Exchange National Bank Of Winter Haven	13437	–	3
The American National Bank In Winter Haven	13383	–	3
The American National Bank Of Winter Haven	12100	6	6
The National Bank Of Winter Haven	12100	6	–
The Snell National Bank Of Winter Haven	10379	6	6

GEORGIA

City, Bank	Ch. No.	L	S
Adel			
The First National Bank Of Adel	9777	6	–
Albany			
Albany Exchange National Bank	5512	5	4
New Georgia National Bank Of Albany	12863	5	–
The Albany National Bank	5512	6	–
The Citizens First National Bank Of Albany	3872	6	–
The Citizens National Bank Of Albany	7777	6	–
The City National Bank Of Albany	13223	4	3
The First National Bank Of Albany	3872	6	–
The Georgia National Bank Of Albany	9729	5	–
The Third National Bank Of Albany	6336	6	–
Americus			
The Americus National Bank	8305	6	–
The First National Bank Of Americus	2009	6	–
The Peoples National Bank Of Americus	2839	6	–
Arlington			
The First National Bank Of Arlington	8314	5	6
Athens			
The Georgia National Bank Of Athens	6525	3	–
The National Bank Of Athens	1639	3	4
Atlanta			
The American National Bank Of Atlanta	9105	3	–
The Atlanta & Lowry National Bank	1559	2	4
The Atlanta National Bank	1559	2	–
The Capital City National Bank Of Atlanta	5490	6	–
The First National Bank Of Atlanta	1559	–	1
The Fourth National Bank Of Atlanta	5045	2	5
The Fulton National Bank Of Atlanta	9617	3	4
The Gate City National Bank Of Atlanta	2424	6	–
The Georgia National Bank Of Atlanta	1605	6	–
The Lowry National Bank Of Atlanta	5318	2	–
The State National Bank Of Atlanta	2064	6	–
The Third National Bank Of Atlanta	5030	3	–
Augusta			
The Merchants And Planters National Bank Of Augusta	1703	6	–
The National Bank Of Augusta	1613	4	–
The National Exchange Bank Of Augusta	1860	2	3
Ava			
The First National Bank Of Ava	10911	–	5
Bainbridge			
First National Bank Of Bainbridge	6004	4	4
The First National Bank Of Bainbridge	6004	4	–
Barnesville			
The Citizens National Bank Of Barnesville	12404	6	6
The First National Bank Of Barnesville	6243	4	6
Blakely			
The First National Bank Of Blakely	7018	5	5
Blue Ridge			
The North Georgia National Bank Of Blue Ridge	6079	5	–
Brunswick			
The National Bank Of Brunswick	4944	2	4
The Oglethorpe National Bank Of Brunswick	3753	6	–
Buena Vista			
First National Bank Of Buena Vista	7963	6	–
Byromville			
The Byrom National Bank Of Byromville	9607	6	–
Calhoun			
The Calhoun National Bank	7549	6	5
Carrollton			
The First National Bank Of Carrollton	5264	4	6
Cartersville			
The Cartersville National Bank	12635	4	–
The First National Bank Of Cartersville	4012	5	4
Cedartown			
The First National Bank Of Cedartown	4075	6	–
The Liberty National Bank Of Cedartown	11833	6	4
Claxton			
The First National Bank Of Claxton	10333	6	6
Cochran			
The First National Bank Of Cochran	7567	6	–
Colquitt			
The Colquitt National Bank, Colquitt	9254	6	–
The First National Bank Of Colquitt	6498	6	–
Columbus			
The Chattahoochee National Bank Of Columbus	1630	6	–
The First National Bank Of Columbus	2338	4	4
The Fourth National Bank Of Columbus	4691	4	4
The National Bank Of Columbus	2338	3	–
The Third National Bank Of Columbus	3937	4	–
Commerce			
The First National Bank Of Commerce	7431	5	6
Conyers			
The First National Bank Of Conyers	11255	6	–
Cordele			
The American National Bank Of Cordele	9074	6	–
The Cordele National Bank	5975	4	–
The First National Bank In Cordele	14257	–	6
Cordele			
The First National Bank Of Cordele	4554	6	–
Cornelia			
The First National Bank Of Cornelia	9613	5	5
Covington			
The First National Bank Of Covington	8945	6	–
Cuthbert			
The First National Bank Of Cuthbert	10279	6	–
Dalton			
The First National Bank Of Dalton	3907	5	5
Dawson			
The City National Bank Of Dawson	6496	4	5
The Dawson National Bank	4115	4	4
Dublin			
The City National Bank Of Dublin	8128	6	
The First National Bank Of Dublin	6374	4	–
Eastman			
The First National Bank Of Eastman	9593	6	–
Elberton			
The First National Bank In Elberton	14061	–	6
The First National Bank Of Elberton	9252	3	3
Fitzgerald			
The Exchange National Bank Of Fitzgerald	8250	5	6
The First National Bank Of Fitzgerald	6082	3	6
The National Bank Of Fitzgerald	13550	–	6
The Third National Bank Of Fitzgerald	8966	6	–
Forsyth			
The First National Bank Of Forsyth	5644	6	–
Fort Gaines			
The First National Bank Of Fort Gaines	6002	6	6
Fort Valley			
The First National Bank Of Fort Valley	7459	6	–
Gainesville			
The First National Bank Of Gainesville	3983	5	4
The Gainesville National Bank	7616	5	6
Greensboro			
Greensboro National Bank	6967	4	–
The Copelan National Bank Of Greensboro	8452	5	–
Griffin			
The City National Bank Of Griffin	2075	5	–
The First National Bank Of Griffin	2075	6	6
The Second National Bank Of Griffin	11597	5	–
Hampton			
The First National Bank Of Hampton	10089	6	–
Hartwell			
The First National Bank Of Hartwell	11695	4	5
Hawkinsville			
The First National Bank Of Hawkinsville	7580	5	–
Jackson			
Jackson National Bank	13897	–	3
The First National Bank Of Jackson	5709	6	–
The Jackson National Bank	9186	4	5
Jefferson			
The First National Bank Of Jefferson	9039	3	4
La Fayette			
The First National Bank Of La Fayette	7247	6	–
La Grange			
The First National Bank Of La Grange	3093	6	–
The La Grange National Bank	7762	4	3
Lavonia			
The First National Bank Of Lavonia	8470	4	3
The Vickery National Bank Of Lavonia	8470	6	–
Lawrenceville			
First National Bank Of Lawrenceville	11936	–	5
Louisville			
The First National Bank Of Louisville	6207	5	6
Lyons			
First National Bank Of Lyons	7979	6	6
Macon			
The American National Bank Of Macon	4547	4	–
The Bibb National Bank Of Macon	10945	5	–
The Citizens National Bank Of Macon	8990	5	–
The Commercial National Bank Of Macon	9212	5	–
The First National Bank & Trust Company In Macon	10270	–	3
The First National Bank Of Macon	1617	5	–
The Fourth National Bank Of Macon	8365	4	–
The Macon National Bank	10270	4	5
The Merchants National Bank Of Macon	3740	6	–
Madison			
The First National Bank Of Madison	7300	4	3
Marietta			
The First National Bank Of Marietta	3830	5	6
Maysville			
The Atkins National Bank Of Maysville	7986	6	–
Mcdonough			
The First National Bank Of Mcdonough	7969	4	5
Milledgeville			
The First National Bank Of Milledgeville	9672	3	4
Millen			
The First National Bank Of Millen	9088	6	6
Montezuma			
The First National Bank Of Montezuma	6576	6	–
Monticello			
The Farmers National Bank Of Monticello	9329	4	5
The First National Bank Of Monticello	9346	4	4
Moultrie			
Moultrie National Bank, Moultrie	13161	–	4
The First National Bank Of Moultrie	7565	6	–
Nashville			
The First National Bank Of Nashville	9106	6	–
New Brunswick			
The First National Bank Of New Brunswick	3116	6	–
Newnan			
The Coweta National Bank Of Newnan	6047	6	–
The First National Bank Of Newnan	1861	3	4
The Manufacturers National Bank Of Newnan	8477	6	6
The Newnan National Bank	3382	6	–
Ocilla			
The First National Bank Of Ocilla	8580	6	4
Pelham			
The First National Bank Of Pelham	9870	6	5
Pembroke			
The Pembroke National Bank	8680	4	6
Quitman			
Peoples-First National Bank Of Quitman	7994	–	5
The First National Bank Of Quitman	7994	4	5
The Peoples National Bank Of Quitman	11290	6	6
Reynolds			
The First National Bank Of Reynolds	9615	6	6
Rockmart			
The Citizens National Bank Of Rockmart	8628	6	–
Rome			
The Cherokee National Bank Of Rome	9636	6	–
The Exchange National Bank Of Rome	10303	4	–
The First National Bank Of Rome	2368	4	5
The Merchants National Bank Of Rome	3670	6	–
The National City Bank Of Rome	10302	5	3
The Rome National Bank	4369	6	–
Sandersville			
The Cohen National Bank Of Sandersville	9641	6	–
The First National Bank Of Sandersville	7934	4	–
The George D Warthen National Bank Of Sandersville	13725	–	6
Savannah			
The Citizens And Southern National Bank Of Savannah	13068	–	1
The Liberty National Bank And Trust Company Of Savannah	13472	–	4
The Merchants National Bank Of Savannah	1640	4	–
The National Bank Of Savannah	3406	4	–
The Savannah National Bank	1255	6	–
Senoia			
The First National Bank Of Senoia	8527	6	–
Shellman			
The First National Bank Of Shellman	8417	6	6
Sparta			
The First National Bank Of Sparta	7067	6	–
The Hancock National Bank Of Sparta	12317	4	6
Statesboro			
The First National Bank Of Statesboro	7468	5	6
Sylvania			
The National Bank Of Sylvania	10829	6	6
Sylvester			
The First National Bank Of Sylvester	6180	6	–
Tallapoosa			
The First National Bank Of Tallapoosa	7220	6	–
Thomasville			
The First National Bank Of Thomasville	3767	6	6
The Thomasville National Bank	3767	6	–
Thomson			
The First National Bank Of Thomson	9302	6	6
Tifton			
The First National Bank Of Tifton	6542	6	–
The National Bank Of Tifton	8350	4	4
Toccoa			
The First National Bank Of Toccoa	6687	6	–
Union Point			
The National Bank Of Union Point	7330	6	–
Valdosta			
The First National Bank Of Valdosta	4429	4	4
Vidalia			
The First National Bank Of Vidalia	9879	5	6
Vienna			
The First National Bank Of Vienna	9618	6	–
Washington			
The Citizens National Bank Of Washington	8894	5	–
The National Bank Of Wilkes At Washington	8848	4	6
Waycross			
The First National Bank Of Waycross	4963	5	5
Waynesboro			
The First National Bank Of Waynesboro	7899	6	4
West Point			
The First National Bank Of West Point	8046	5	–
Winder			
The First National Bank Of Winder	9051	6	–
Winder National Bank	10805	4	4
Wrightsville			
The First National Bank Of Wrightsville	8023	6	–

HAWAII

City, Bank	Ch. No.	L	S
Honolulu			
Bishop First National Bank Of Honolulu	5550	–	1
Bishop National Bank Of Hawaii At Honolulu	5550	–	2
The First National Bank Of Hawaii	5550	1	–
Kahului			
The Baldwin National Bank Of Kahului	8207	5	–
Lahaina			
The Lahaina National Bank	8101	6	–
Paia			
The First National Bank Of Paia	10451	6	–
Wailuku			
The First National Bank Of Wailuku	5994	6	–

IDAHO TERRITORY

City, Bank	Ch. No.	L	S
Boise City			
The Boise City National Bank	3471	6	–
The First National Bank Of Idaho, Boise City	1668	6	–
Hailey			
The First National Bank Of Hailey	3895	6	–
Ketchum			
The First National Bank Of Ketchum	3142	6	–
Lewiston			
The First National Bank Of Lewiston	2972	6	–
The Lewiston National Bank	3023	6	–

City, Bank	Ch. No.	L	S
Moscow			
The First National Bank Of Moscow	3408	6	–
Pocatello			
The First National Bank Of Pacatello	4023	6	–

IDAHO

City, Bank	Ch. No.	L	S
American Falls			
The First National Bank Of American Falls	8869	6	–
Ashton			
The First National Bank Of Ashton	10269	6	–
Blackfoot			
The First National Bank Of Blackfoot	7419	4	5
Boise			
The Idaho National Bank Of Boise	8346	4	–
The Overland National Bank Of Boise	10751	5	–
The Pacific National Bank Of Boise	10083	3	–
Boise City			
The Boise City National Bank	3471	3	5
The First National Bank Of Idaho, Boise City	1668	4	3
Bonners Ferry			
The First National Bank Of Bonners Ferry	10727	6	6
Buhl			
The First National Bank Of Buhl	11065	6	–
Burley			
The Cassia National Bank Of Burley	12256	–	6
The First National Bank Of Burley	10341	6	–
Caldwell			
The American National Bank Of Caldwell	9333	6	–
The First National Bank Of Caldwell	4690	4	6
The Western National Bank Of Caldwell	8225	4	–
Challis			
The First National Bank Of Challis	9477	6	–
Coeur D' Alene			
First National Bank In Coeur D' Alene	13288	–	3
The First National Bank Of Coeur D' Alene	6793	6	–
Coeur D'Alene			
The Exchange National Bank Of Coeur D' Alene	7120	6	–
The First Exchange National Bank Of Coeur D'Alene	7120	5	–
Cottonwood			
The First National Bank Of Cottonwood	7923	6	6
Driggs			
The First National Bank Of Driggs	10278	6	–
Dubois			
The First National Bank Of Dubois	11508	6	–
Emmett			
The First National Bank Of Emmett	6145	6	–
Fairfield			
The First National Bank Of Fairfield	10162	6	–
Firth			
The First National Bank Of Firth	11198	6	–
Genessee			
The First National Bank Of Genessee	4808	6	–
Gooding			
The First National Bank Of Gooding	9371	5	–
Grangeville			
The First National Bank Of Grangeville	6927	5	6
Hagerman			
The First National Bank Of Hagerman	10294	6	–
Hailey			
The Blaine County National Bank Of Hailey	11053	6	–
The First National Bank Of Hailey	3895	6	–
The Hailey National Bank	9145	6	6
Idaho Falls			
American National Bank Of Idaho Falls	6982	6	3
The First National Bank Of Idaho Falls	5820	6	–
The Idaho Falls National Bank	11278	5	–
Jerome			
The First National Bank Of Jerome	9680	5	–
Kellogg			
The First National Bank Of Kellogg	9566	6	6
Kendrick			
The First National Bank Of Kendrick	4790	6	–
Lewiston			
Lewiston National Bank	13819	–	6
The American National Bank Of Lewiston	11745	6	–
The Empire National Bank Of Lewiston	10212	5	–
The First National Bank Of Lewiston	2972	4	5
The Idaho National Bank Of Lewiston	5600	6	–
The Lewiston National Bank	3023	5	6
Malad City			
The First National Bank Of Malad City	8822	6	5
Meridian			
The First National Bank Of Meridian	10221	6	–
Montpelier			
The First National Bank Of Montpelier	7381	6	–
Moscow			
The First National Bank Of Moscow	3408	6	6
The Moscow National Bank	4584	6	–
Mountain Home			
The First National Bank Of Mountain Home	6521	5	–
Mullan			
The First National Bank Of Mullan	8906	6	6
Nampa			
The Citizens National Bank Of Nampa	10693	6	–
The Farmers And Merchants National Bank Of Nampa	10916	6	–
The First National Bank Of Nampa	8370	5	–
Newdale			
The First National Bank Of Newdale	10975	6	–
Nezperce			
The First National Bank Of Nezperce	6697	6	–
Parma			
The First National Bank Of Parma	11496	5	6
Payette			
The First National Bank Of Payette	5906	5	–
The Payette National Bank	8075	5	–
Pocatello			
The Bannock National Bank Of Pocatello	6347	6	–
The First National Bank Of Pocatello	4023	6	–
The Idaho National Bank Of Pocatello	4827	6	–
Preston			
The First National Bank Of Preston	7526	6	6
Rexburg			
The First National Bank Of Rexburg	7133	5	–
Rigby			
The Jefferson County National Bank Of Rigby	11458	6	–
Ririe			
The First National Bank Of Ririe	10920	6	–
Rupert			
The First National Bank Of Rupert	10429	6	–
The Rupert National Bank	10517	6	–
Saint Anthony			
The Commercial National Bank Of Saint Anthony	7230	6	5
The First National Bank Of Saint Anthony	5764	5	–
Saint Maries			
The First National Bank Of Saint Maries	10771	6	6
Salmon			
The Citizens National Bank Of Salmon	9432	5	5
The First National Bank Of Salmon	8080	6	–
Sandpoint			
The Bonner County National Bank Of Sandpoint	9263	6	5
The First National Bank Of Sandpoint	8341	6	5
Shelley			
The First National Bank Of Shelley	11434	6	–
Shoshone			
The First National Bank Of Shoshone	6577	6	–
The Lincoln County National Bank Of Shoshone	9272	6	6
Soldier			
The First National Bank Of Soldier	10162	6	–
Twin Falls			
The First National Bank Of Twin Falls	7608	6	–
The Twin Falls National Bank	11274	6	6
Wallace			
The First National Bank Of Wallace	4773	5	4
The Wallace National Bank	9134	6	–
Weiser			
The First National Bank Of Weiser	6754	4	–
The Weiser National Bank	8139	6	–
Wendell			
The First National Bank Of Wendell	9491	6	–

ILLINOIS

City, Bank	Ch. No.	L	S
Abingdon			
The First National Bank Of Abingdon	3377	5	–
Albany			
The First National Bank Of Albany	6089	6	–
Albion			
The Albion National Bank	9025	6	6
The First National Bank Of Albion	8429	4	6
Aledo			
The Farmers National Bank Of Aledo	9649	6	5
The First National Bank Of Aledo	7145	5	–
Alexis			
The First National Bank Of Alexis	4967	6	6
Allendale			
The Farmers National Bank Of Allendale	10318	6	–
The First National Bank Of Allendale	8293	5	4
Altamont			
The First National Bank In Altamont	13993	–	6
The First National Bank Of Altamont	8733	6	6
Alton			
The Alton National Bank	1428	2	6
The Citizens National Bank Of Alton	5188	3	6
The First National Bank Of Alton	1445	6	–
Altona			
The Altona National Bank	13625	–	6
The First National Bank Of Altona	11331	6	5
Amboy			
The First National Bank Of Amboy	5223	4	6
Anna			
The Anna National Bank	5525	6	6
The First National Bank Of Anna	4449	4	6
Annapolis			
The First National Bank Of Annapolis	10257	5	5
Arcola			
The First National Bank Of Arcola	2204	6	6
Arenzville			
The First National Bank Of Arenzville	9183	4	3
Arthur			
The First National Bank Of Arthur	5233	5	6
Assumption			
The First National Bank Of Assumption	5316	5	5
Atlanta			
The Atlanta National Bank	3711	5	4
The First National Bank Of Atlanta	2283	5	–
Atwood			
The First National Bank Of Atwood	6359	6	6
Augusta			
The First National Bank Of Augusta	6751	6	6
Aurora			
The American National Bank Of Aurora	4469	4	5
The Aurora National Bank	2945	5	4
The First National Bank In Aurora	13565	–	6
The First National Bank Of Aurora	38	4	4
The German American National Bank Of Aurora	4469	6	–
The Merchants National Bank Of Aurora	3854	3	3
The Old Second National Bank Of Aurora	4596	2	2
The Second National Bank Of Aurora	1909	5	–
The Union National Bank Of Aurora	1792	6	–
Austin			
The Austin National Bank, Austin	10337	6	–
Barrington			
The First National Bank Of Barrington	11283	5	6
Barry			
The First National Bank Of Barry	5771	3	5
Batavia			
The Batavia National Bank	9500	5	4
The First National Bank Of Batavia	339	6	–
The First National Bank Of Batavia	4646	4	5
Beardstown			
The First National Bank Of Beardstown	3640	4	3
Beecher			
The First National Bank Of Beecher	7726	6	–
Belleville			
The Belleville National Bank	13236	–	3
The First National Bank Of Belleville	2154	4	6
The St. Clair National Bank Of Belleville	11478	6	4
Belvidere			
The First National Bank Of Belvidere	1097	5	5
The Second National Bank Of Belvidere	3190	6	4
Bement			
The First National Bank Of Bement	4829	6	–
Benld			
The First National Bank Of Benld	7728	6	5
The National Bank Of Benld	7728	6	–
Benton			
The Coal Belt National Bank Of Benton	8234	6	–
The First National Bank Of Benton	6136	4	5
Berwyn			
The First American National Bank & Trust Co. Of Berwyn	12426	–	6
The First National Bank Of Berwyn	12426	6	5
Biggsville			
The First National Bank Of Biggsville	3003	5	–
Blandinsville			
The First National Bank In Blandinsville	13597	–	6
The First National Bank Of Blandinsville	8908	6	6
Bloomington			
The First National Bank Of Bloomington	819	5	6
The National Bank Of Bloomington	819	6	–
The National State Bank Of Bloomington	2386	6	–
The State National Bank Of Bloomington	5119	6	–
The Third National Bank Of Bloomington	2676	6	–
Blue Mound			
The First National Bank Of Blue Mound	9530	6	–
Bowmanville			
The Bowmanville National Bank, Bowmanville	10237	6	–
Braidwood			
The First National Bank In Braidwood	11895	6	–
The Miners National Bank Of Braidwood	1964	6	–
Breese			
The First National Bank Of Breese	9893	6	4
Bridgeport			
The First National Bank Of Bridgeport	8347	6	3
Brighton			
The First National Bank Of Brighton	9397	4	4
Brookport			
The Brookport National Bank	6713	6	5
Brownstown			
The First National Bank Of Brownstown	10397	6	6
Bushnell			
The Farmers National Bank Of Bushnell	1791	6	–
The First National Bank Of Bushnell	4709	3	4
Cairo			
The Alexander County National Bank Of Cairo	3735	6	–
The Cairo National Bank	6815	4	–
The City National Bank Of Cairo	785	6	–
The First National Bank Of Cairo	33	6	–
The Security National Bank Of Cairo	13804	–	5
Caledonia			
The Caledonia National Bank	10567	6	6
Cambridge			
The Farmers National Bank Of Cambridge	2572	4	6
The First National Bank Of Cambridge	2540	5	6
Canton			
The Canton National Bank	3593	6	5
The First National Bank Of Canton	415	5	6
Carbondale			
First National Bank In Carbondale	12596	6	5
The Carbondale National Bank	7598	6	5
The First National Bank Of Carbondale	4904	5	–
Carlinville			
The Carlinville National Bank	4299	6	6
The First National Bank Of Carlinville	2042	6	–
Carlyle			
The First National Bank Of Carlisle	5548	5	4
Carmi			
The First National Bank Of Carmi	4934	3	3
The National Bank Of Carmi	5357	5	4
Carrier Mills			
The First National Bank Of Carrier Mills	8015	5	5
Carrollton			
The Greene County National Bank Of Carrollton	2390	2	–
Carterville			
The First National Bank Of Carterville	7889	5	5
Carthage			
The Hancock County National Bank Of Carthage	1167	4	5
Casey			
The Casey National Bank	8043	6	6
The First National Bank In Casey	13673	–	6
The First National Bank Of Casey	6026	6	5
Catlin			
The First National Bank Of Catlin	7276	6	6
Centralia			
The Centralia National Bank	11904	6	–
The City National Bank Of Centralia	11923	6	4
The First National Bank Of Centralia	1001	6	–
The Old National Bank Of Centralia	3303	6	5
Chadwick			
The First National Bank Of Chadwick	5619	5	6

City, Bank	Ch. No.	L	S
Champaign			
The Champaign National Bank	2829	6	6
The First National Bank Of Champaign	913	6	5
Charleston			
The Charleston National Bank	14024	–	5
The First National Bank Of Charleston	763	4	6
The National Trust Bank Of Charleston	11358	5	4
The Second National Bank Of Charleston	1851	5	–
Chatsworth			
The Commercial National Bank Of Chatsworth	5519	5	6
Chester			
The First National Bank Of Chester	4187	6	–
Chicago			
Addison National Bank Of Chicago	13119	5	–
Albany Park National Bank & Trust Company Of Chicago	11737	6	4
Alliance National Bank Of Chicago	12001	4	6
American National Bank & Trust Company Of Chicago	13216	–	4
Columbia National Bank Of Chicago	3677	6	–
Inland-Irving National Bank Of Chicago	10179	–	6
Jackson Park National Bank Of Chicago	12391	5	6
Liberty National Bank Of Chicago	14246	–	4
National Builders Bank Of Chicago	13146	3	4
Straus National Bank And Trust Company Of Chicago	13216	–	5
The Albany Park National Bank Of Chicago	11737	5	–
The American Exchange National Bank Of Chicago	3500	6	–
The American National Bank Of Chicago	5111	6	–
The Atlas Exchange National Bank Of Chicago	10763	5	–
The Atlas National Bank Of Chicago	3503	5	–
The Austin National Bank Of Chicago	10337	3	6
The Bankers National Bank Of Chicago	4787	4	–
The Bowmanville National Bank Of Chicago	10237	6	4
The Calumet National Bank Of Chicago	3102	4	5
The Central National Bank Of Chicago	2047	6	–
The Chemical National Bank Of Chicago	4666	6	–
The Chicago National Bank	2601	6	–
The City National Bank Of Chicago	818	6	–
The Commercial National Bank Of Chicago	713	3	–
The Continental And Commercial National Bank Of Chicago	2894	2	–
The Continental National Bank Of Chicago	2894	3	–
The Cook County National Bank Of Chicago	1845	6	–
The Corn Exchange National Bank Of Chicago	1709	6	–
The Corn Exchange National Bank Of Chicago	5106	2	–
The District National Bank Of Chicago	14110	–	6
The Douglass National Bank Of Chicago	12227	3	4
The Drovers Deposit National Bank Of Chicago	6535	5	–
The Drovers National Bank Of Chicago	6535	6	3
The Federal National Bank Of Chicago	7926	5	–
The Fifth National Bank Of Chicago	320	5	–
The First National Bank Of Chicago	8	6	–
The First National Bank Of Chicago	2670	2	–
The First National Bank Of Englewood	4073	6	–
The Fort Dearborn National Bank Of Chicago	3698	3	–
The Fourth National Bank Of Chicago	276	5	–
The German National Bank Of Chicago	1734	6	–
The Globe National Bank Of Chicago	4489	6	–
The Halsted Exchange National Bank Of Chicago	12945	–	5
The Hamilton National Bank Of Chicago	6723	5	–
The Hide And Leather National Bank Of Chicago	2450	6	–
The Home National Bank Of Chicago	2048	5	–
The Kenwood National Bank Of Chicago	11999	5	–
The La Salle Street National Bank Of Chicago	9750	5	–
The Lawndale National Bank Of Chicago	10247	4	3
The Lawrence Avenue National Bank Of Chicago	12873	5	6
The Lincoln National Bank Of Chicago	3647	6	–
The Live Stock Exchange National Bank Of Chicago	9010	4	–
The Live Stock National Bank Of Chicago	13674	–	3
The Manufacturers National Bank Of Chicago	724	6	–
The Mechanics National Bank Of Chicago	466	6	–
The Merchants National Bank Of Chicago	642	6	–
The Metropolitan National Bank Of Chicago	3179	6	–
The Mid-City National Bank Of Chicago	13684	–	5
The Milwaukee Avenue National Bank Of Chicago	14245	–	5
The Monroe National Bank Of Chicago	8121	6	–
The Mutual National Bank Of Chicago	11092	3	4
The National Bank Of America, Chicago	2826	6	–
The National Bank Of Commerce In Chicago	8842	5	–
The National Bank Of Commerce Of Chicago	1693	6	–
The National Bank Of Illinois, Chicago	1867	6	–
The National Bank Of North American, Chicago	6290	5	–
The National Bank Of The Republic Of Chicago	4605	1	1
The National City Bank Of Chicago	8532	4	–
The National Live Stock Bank Of Chicago	3847	6	–
The National Produce Bank Of Chicago	8842	5	–
The Northwestern National Bank Of Chicago	508	5	–
The Oakland National Bank Of Chicago	3916	6	–
Chicago			
The Park National Bank Of Chicago	3502	6	–
The Portage Park National Bank Of Chicago	12285	5	5
The Prairie National Bank Of Chicago	7358	5	–
The Prairie State National Bank Of Chicago	3882	6	–
The Rogers Park National Bank, Rogers Park	10305	6	6
The Roseland National Bank Of Chicago	12605	5	5
The Scandinavian National Bank Of Chicago	1978	6	–
The Second National Bank Of Chicago	225	6	–
The Third National Bank Of Chicago	236	5	–
The Traders National Bank Of Chicago	966	6	–
The Union National Bank Of Chicago	698	6	–
The Union National Bank Of Chicago	3278	6	–
The Union Stock Yards National Bank Of Chicago	1678	6	–
The United States National Bank Of Chicago	3677	6	–
The Washington Park National Bank Of Chicago	3916	4	4
The West Englewood National Bank Of Chicago	12004	6	–
The West Side National Bank Of Chicago	11009	4	5
The West Side-Atlas National Bank Of Chicago	11009	–	5
Chicago Heights			
The Citizens National Bank Of Chicago Heights	13373	–	6
The First National Bank & Trust Company Of Chicago Heights	5876	6	5
The First National Bank Of Chicago Heights	5876	5	–
Chillicothe			
The First National Bank Of Chillicothe	5584	6	5
Chrisman			
The First National Bank Of Chrisman	7111	6	6
Christopher			
The First National Bank Of Christopher	8260	6	4
Cicero			
First National Bank Of Cicero	11662	4	5
Clifton			
The First National Bank Of Clifton	6318	6	5
Clinton			
The Dewitt County National Bank Of Clinton	1926	4	5
Coal City			
The First National Bank Of Coal City	10132	6	6
Cobden			
The First National Bank Of Cobden	5630	6	5
Coffeen			
The Coffeen National Bank	7579	6	6
Colchester			
The National Bank Of Colchester	8485	6	6
Collinsville			
The First National Bank Of Collinsville	6125	5	4
Columbia			
The First National Bank In Columbia	13805	–	4
The First National Bank Of Columbia	7717	6	5
Compton			
The First National Bank Of Compton	7031	6	6
Coulterville			
The First National Bank Of Coulterville	12000	5	5
Cowden			
The First National Bank Of Cowden	9700	6	–
Crescent City			
The First National Bank Of Crescent City	6598	5	6
Crossville			
The First National Bank Of Crossville	8801	6	4
Cuba			
The First National Bank Of Cuba	11144	6	6
Cullom			
The First National Bank Of Cullom	8684	6	5
Dahlgren			
The First National Bank Of Dahlgren	7750	6	–
Dallas City			
The First National Bank Of Dallas City	5609	4	5
Danvers			
The First National Bank Of Danvers	6740	6	6
Danville			
The Danville National Bank	5812	5	–
The First National Bank Of Danville	113	5	4
The Palmer National Bank Of Danville	4731	5	4
The Palmer-American National Bank Of Danville	4731	–	6
The Second National Bank Of Danville	2584	4	4
De Kalb			
First National Bank In De Kalb	14008	–	6
The De Kalb National Bank	2702	6	–
The First National Bank Of De Kalb	2702	6	5
Decatur			
The Citizens National Bank Of Decatur	4576	4	4
The Decatur National Bank	2124	6	–
The First National Bank Of Decatur	477	6	–
The Millikin National Bank Of Decatur	5089	–	2
The National Bank Of Decatur	4920	3	4
Deland			
The First National Bank Of Deland	5699	5	4
Delavan			
The Tazewell County National Bank Of Delavan	3781	4	5
Des Plaines			
The First National Bank Of Des Plaines	10319	5	5
Dieterich			
The First National Bank Of Dieterich	9582	5	4
Divernon			
The First National Bank Of Divernon	10296	6	–
Dixon			
The City National Bank In Dixon	13856	–	6
The City National Bank Of Dixon	3294	6	5
The Dixon National Bank	1881	4	5
Dixon			
The Lee County National Bank Of Dixon	902	6	–
Dolton			
The First National Bank Of Dolton	8679	5	4
Dongola			
The First National Bank Of Dongola	10086	6	–
Downers Grove			
The First National Bank Of Downers Grove	9725	5	6
Dundee			
The First National Bank Of Dundee	5638	5	5
Duquoin			
The First National Bank Of Duquoin	4737	6	4
Dwight			
The First National Bank Of Dwight	8044	6	4
Earlville			
The Earlville National Bank	7555	5	–
The First National Bank Of Earlville	3323	5	5
East Peoria			
The First National Bank In East Peoria	14010	–	6
The First National Bank Of East Peoria	6724	5	5
East Saint Louis			
First National Bank In East St. Louis	11596	5	4
The City National Bank Of East St. Louis	8932	6	–
The Drovers National Bank Of East St. Louis	10399	5	–
The First National Bank Of East St. Louis	4328	5	–
The Security National Bank Of East St. Louis	12178	5	–
The Southern Illinois National Bank Of East St. Louis	5070	3	4
Edwardsville			
The Edwardsville National Bank	11039	4	–
The Edwardsville National Bank & Trust Company	11039	–	2
The First National Bank Of Edwardsville	5062	4	–
Effingham			
The First National Bank Of Effingham	4233	4	6
El Paso			
The First National Bank Of El Paso	2997	5	–
The National Bank Of El Paso	2997	6	–
The Woodford County National Bank Of El Paso	5510	5	–
Eldorado			
The First National Bank Of Eldorado	7539	5	–
Elgin			
The Elgin National Bank	4735	5	6
The First National Bank Of Elgin	1365	4	5
The Home National Bank Of Elgin	2016	3	6
The Union National Bank Of Elgin	7236	4	4
Elmhurst			
The First National Bank Of Elmhurst	9836	5	5
Enfield			
The First National Bank Of Enfield	7948	4	4
Equality			
The First National Bank Of Equality	6978	5	–
Erie			
The First National Bank Of Erie	6951	4	5
Evanston			
City National Bank & Trust Company Of Evanston	5279	6	4
First National Bank And Trust Company Of Evanston	13709	–	6
The City National Bank Of Evanston	5279	5	–
The Evanston National Bank	4767	6	–
Fairbury			
The First National Bank Of Fairbury	1987	6	–
Fairfield			
The Fairfield National Bank	6609	4	4
The First National Bank Of Fairfield	5009	5	6
Fairmount			
The First National Bank Of Fairmount	11443	6	5
Farmer City			
The First National Bank Of Farmer City	2156	5	–
The John Weedman National Bank Of Farmer City	3407	5	5
The Old First National Bank Of Farmer City	4958	5	6
Farmersville			
The First National Bank Of Farmersville	10057	6	–
Findlay			
The Findlay National Bank, Findlay	8212	6	–
The First National Bank Of Findlay	6861	6	–
Flora			
The First National Bank Of Flora	1961	4	3
The Flora National Bank	11509	6	6
Forrest			
The First National Bank Of Forrest	7680	6	–
Freeburg			
The First National Bank Of Freeburg	7941	5	5
Freeport			
First National Bank Of Freeport	13695	–	4
The First National Bank Of Freeport	319	6	–
The First National Bank Of Freeport	2875	4	3
The Freeport National Bank	2875	6	–
The Second National Bank Of Freeport	385	5	6
Galena			
The Galena National Bank	3279	6	6
The Merchants National Bank Of Galena	979	3	6
The National Bank Of Galena	831	5	–
Galesburg			
First Galesburg National Bank & Trust Company	241	5	3
The First National Bank Of Galesburg	241	4	–
The Galesburg National Bank	3138	4	–
The Second National Bank Of Galesburg	491	6	–
Galva			
The Farmers And Merchants National Bank Of Galva	2793	6	–
The First National Bank Of Galva	827	6	–
The Galva First National Bank, Galva	2793	5	5
Gardner			
The First National Bank Of Gardner	9406	6	6

City, Bank	Ch. No.	L	S
Garrett			
The First National Bank Of Garrett	6192	6	–
Geneseo			
The Farmers National Bank Of Geneseo	2332	5	5
Genesso			
The First National Bank Of Genesseo	534	4	4
Geneva			
The First National Bank Of Geneva	8740	5	5
Georgetown			
The First National Bank In Georgetown	13448	–	6
The First National Bank Of Georgetown	5285	6	6
The Georgetown National Bank	7365	6	–
Gibson City			
The First National Bank Of Gibson	8174	5	4
Gillespie			
The American National Bank Of Gillespie	12314	6	6
The Gillespie National Bank	7903	6	4
Gilman			
The First National Bank Of Gilman	5856	6	5
Golconda			
First National Bank In Golconda	14173	–	6
The First National Bank Of Golconda	7385	6	6
Goreville			
The First National Bank Of Goreville	7606	6	6
Gorham			
The First National Bank Of Gorham	10690	–	5
Grand Ridge			
The First National Bank Of Grand Ridge	6684	6	6
Grand Tower			
The First National Bank Of Grand Tower	7712	6	4
Granite City			
First Granite City National Bank	6564	–	2
The First National Bank Of Granite City	5433	4	4
The Granite City National Bank	6564	5	5
Grant Park			
The First National Bank Of Grant Park	11952	6	4
The Grant Park National Bank	5124	6	–
Granville			
The First National Bank Of Granville	10458	6	–
The Granville National Bank	14035	–	5
Grayville			
The Farmers National Bank Of Grayville	6460	6	5
The First National Bank Of Grayville	4999	5	4
Greenfield			
The First National Bank Of Greenfield	8473	6	5
Greenup			
The First National Bank Of Greenup	6191	6	–
The Greenup National Bank	8115	5	4
Greenville			
The Bradford National Bank Of Greenville	9734	4	4
The First National Bank Of Greenville	1841	6	–
Gridley			
The First National Bank Of Gridley	11208	5	–
Griggsville			
The Griggsville National Bank	2116	6	6
Hamilton			
The First National Bank Of Hamilton	9883	5	5
Harrisburg			
The City National Bank Of Harrisburg	5153	5	3
The First National Bank Of Harrisburg	4003	4	4
Harvey			
The First National Bank Of Harvey	8667	6	6
Havana			
The Havana National Bank	2242	5	4
Hegewisch			
The Inter State National Bank Of Hegewisch	8605	4	–
Henry			
The First National Bank Of Henry	1482	5	–
The Henry National Bank	7049	5	6
Herrin			
The City National Bank Of Herrin	8670	6	6
The First National Bank Of Herrin	5303	4	6
Highland			
The First National Bank Of Highland	6653	4	4
Hillsboro			
The Hillsboro National Bank Of Hillsboro	2789	5	4
The Peoples National Bank Of Hillsboro	8006	6	5
Hindsboro			
The First National Bank Of Hindsboro	5538	5	6
Hinsdale			
The First National Bank Of Hinsdale	11308	–	4
Homer			
The First National Bank In Homer	11882	6	6
The First National Bank Of Homer	2965	6	–
Hoopeston			
Hoopeston National Bank	9425	4	6
The City National Bank Of Hoopeston	13744	–	3
The First National Bank Of Hoopeston	2808	6	5
Hopedale			
The Hopedale National Bank	9398	6	6
Humboldt			
The First National Bank Of Humboldt	7168	6	6
Hume			
The First National Bank Of Hume	11108	6	6
Irving			
The Irving National Bank	8647	6	6
Irving Park			
The Irving Park National Bank, Irving Park	10179	5	5
Ivesdale			
First National Bank Of Ivesdale	6133	6	5
Jacksonville			
The Ayers National Bank Of Jacksonville	5763	3	2
The First National Bank Of Jacksonville	511	3	–
The Jacksonville National Bank	1719	4	–
Jefferson Park			
The Jefferson Park National Bank Of Chicago	10108	6	5
The Jefferson Park National Bank, Jefferson Park	10108	6	–
Jerseyville			
The First National Bank Of Jerseyville	2328	6	–
The National Bank Of Jerseyville	4952	2	–
Johnston City			
The First National Bank Of Johnston City	7458	6	–
Joliet			
The Citizens National Bank Of Joliet	6423	6	–
The First National Bank Of Joliet	512	3	–
The Joliet National Bank, Joliet	4520	3	4
The Will County National Bank Of Joliet	1882	4	4
Jonesboro			
The First National Bank Of Jonesboro	12373	6	6
Kankakee			
The City National Bank Of Kankakee	4342	4	1
The First National Bank Of Kankakee	1793	6	–
Kansas			
The Farmers National Bank Of Kansas	9293	6	–
The First National Bank Of Kansas	2011	3	–
The Kansas National Bank	9293	6	6
Keithsburg			
The Farmers National Bank Of Keithsburg	1805	6	–
Kewanee			
The First National Bank Of Kewanee	1785	4	3
The Kewanee National Bank	4854	6	–
The Union National Bank Of Kewanee	2501	6	–
Kinmundy			
The First National Bank Of Kinmundy	6143	5	3
Kirkwood			
The First National Bank Of Kirkwood	2313	5	5
Knoxville			
The Farmers National Bank Of Knoxville	3287	5	5
The First National Bank Of Knoxville	759	6	–
La Harpe			
The First National Bank Of La Harpe	8468	6	6
La Salle			
La Salle National Bank & Trust Company	2503	–	4
The City National Bank Of La Salle	2804	6	–
The First National Bank Of La Salle	114	6	–
The La Salle National Bank	2503	1	5
Lacon			
The First National Bank Of Lacon	347	6	6
Lake			
The Drovers National Bank Of Union Stock Yards, Lake	2858	5	–
Lake Forest			
The First National Bank Of Lake Forest	8937	5	4
Lanark			
The First National Bank Of Lanark	1755	4	4
The National Bank Of Lanark	14297	–	6
Lawrenceville			
The First National Bank Of Lawrenceville	5385	5	4
Le Roy			
The First National Bank Of Le Roy	6586	6	6
Leland			
The First National Bank Of Leland	7864	5	–
Lerna			
The First National Bank Of Lerna	8224	6	6
Lewiston			
The First National Bank Of Lewiston	1808	6	–
Lewistown			
The Lewistown National Bank	4941	5	5
Lexington			
The First National Bank Of Lexington	2824	6	–
Libertyville			
The First Lake County National Bank Of Libertyville	6514	–	6
The First National Bank Of Libertyville	6514	6	6
The Lake County National Bank Of Libertyville	6670	6	5
Lincoln			
First National Bank In Lincoln	14118	–	5
The American National Bank Of Lincoln	3613	5	5
The First National Bank Of Lincoln	2126	2	–
The German-American National Bank Of Lincoln	3613	5	–
The Lincoln National Bank	3369	4	3
Litchfield			
The First National Bank Of Litchfield	3962	4	4
The Litchfield National Bank	10079	5	5
Little York			
The First National Bank Of Little York	6065	6	–
Livingston			
The First National Bank Of Livingston	11845	6	5
Lockport			
The First National Bank Of Lockport	8933	5	4
Lovington			
The First National Bank Of Lovington	5494	6	–
The Shepherd National Bank Of Lovington	5494	6	–
Mackinaw			
The First National Bank Of Mackinaw	8732	5	5
Macomb			
The First National Bank Of Macomb	967	5	–
The Macomb National Bank	9169	5	4
The Union National Bank Of Macomb	1872	4	4
Madison			
The First National Bank Of Madison	8457	5	6
Malta			
The First National Bank Of Malta	5815	6	5
Manhattan			
The First National Bank Of Manhattan	8713	6	6
Manlius			
The First National Bank Of Manlius	8648	5	6
Mansfield			
The First National Bank Of Mansfield	6096	5	–
Maquon			
The First National Bank Of Maquon	8482	5	–
Marengo			
The First National Bank Of Marengo	1870	6	6
Marine			
The First National Bank Of Marine	10582	–	4
Marion			
The First National Bank Of Marion	4502	4	5
Marissa			
The First National Bank Of Marissa	6691	5	4
The First National Bank Of Marissa	13735	–	3
Marseilles			
The First National Bank Of Marseilles	1852	5	–
Marshall			
The Dulaney National Bank Of Marshall	4759	5	5
Martinsville			
The First National Bank Of Martinsville	6721	5	6
Mascoutah			
The First National Bank In Mascoutah	13795	–	5
The First National Bank Of Mascoutah	9736	5	5
Mason City			
The First National Bank Of Mason City	1850	6	–
Mattoon			
The First National Bank Of Mattoon	1024	6	–
The Mattoon National Bank	2147	6	–
The National Bank Of Mattoon	10045	6	6
The State National Bank Of Mattoon	10144	6	–
Mazon			
The First National Bank Of Mazon	10186	4	5
Mcleansboro			
The First National Bank Of Mcleansboro	6649	6	6
The Peoples National Bank Of Mcleansboro	9408	6	5
Mendota			
The First National Bank Of Mendota	1177	6	5
The Mendota National Bank	5086	6	6
The National Bank Of Mendota	13611	–	6
Metcalf			
The First National Bank Of Metcalf	7954	6	6
Metropolis			
The City National Bank Of Metropolis	8745	6	6
The First National Bank Of Metropolis	3156	6	5
The National State Bank Of Metropolis	5254	5	5
Middletown			
The First National Bank Of Middletown	7791	6	–
Milford			
The First National Bank Of Milford	5149	4	6
Millstadt			
The First National Bank Of Millstadt	8425	5	4
Minonk			
The First National Bank Of Minonk	9601	6	–
Minooka			
The Farmers First National Bank Of Minooka	9208	6	5
Moline			
The First National Bank Of Moline	160	6	–
The Moline National Bank	1941	6	–
Momence			
The First National Bank Of Momence	7079	6	6
Monmouth			
The First National Bank Of Monmouth	85	6	–
The First National Bank Of Monmouth	2751	6	–
The Monmouth National Bank	1706	6	–
The National Bank Of Monmouth	4400	3	4
The Peoples National Bank Of Monmouth	4313	6	5
The Second National Bank Of Monmouth	2205	5	5
Monticello			
The First National Bank Of Monticello	4826	4	4
The National Bank Of Monticello	13865	–	6
Morris			
The Farmers And Merchants National Bank Of Morris	8163	4	6
The First National Bank Of Morris	1773	3	6
The Grundy County National Bank Of Morris	531	3	5
Morrison			
The First National Bank Of Morrison	1033	4	5
Morrisonville			
The First National Bank Of Morrisonville	6745	6	5
Mound City			
The First National Bank Of Mound City	7443	6	6
Mounds			
The First National Bank Of Mounds	10445	6	6
Mount Auburn			
The First National Bank Of Mt. Auburn	9922	6	5
Mount Carmel			
American-First National Bank Of Mount Carmel	5782	–	5
The American National Bank Of Mt. Carmel	5782	5	4
The First National Bank Of Mount Carmel	4480	5	5
Mount Carroll			
The First National Bank Of Mount Carroll	409	5	–
Mount Olive			
The First National Bank In Mount Olive	13452	–	6
The First National Bank Of Mount Olive	7350	5	6
The Mount Olive National Bank	14285	–	6
Mount Prospect			
The Mount Prospect National Bank	10048	5	–
Mount Pulaski			
The First National Bank Of Mt. Pulaski	3839	3	5
Mount Sterling			
The First National Bank Of Mount Sterling	2402	4	–
Mount Vernon			
The Ham National Bank Of Mount Vernon	5057	4	5
The Mount Vernon National Bank	1996	6	–
The Third National Bank Of Mt. Vernon	5689	5	3
Moweaqua			
The First National Bank Of Moweaqua	7739	5	–
Mulberry Grove			
The First National Bank Of Mulberry Grove	7379	4	4
Murphysboro			
The City National Bank Of Murphysboro	4804	4	4
The First National Bank Of Murphysboro	4019	6	5
Naperville			
The First National Bank Of Naperville	4551	6	–

City, Bank	Ch. No.	L	S
Nashville			
The Farmers And Merchants National Bank Of Nashville	8221	6	4
The First National Bank Of Nashville	6524	4	4
National City			
The National Stock Yards National Bank Of National City	12991	–	2
The National Stock Yards National Bank, National Stock Yards	9118	5	–
Nauvoo			
The First National Bank Of Nauvoo	8898	6	–
Nebo			
The First National Bank Of Nebo	10492	5	5
Neoga			
The Cumberland County National Bank Of Neoga	5426	5	6
The Cumberland County National Bank Of Neoga	13892	–	6
The Neoga National Bank	7841	6	–
New Douglas			
The Prange National Bank Of New Douglas	13696	–	6
New Haven			
The First National Bank Of New Haven	8053	6	–
Newman			
The Newman National Bank	7575	6	6
Newton			
The First National Bank Of Newton	5869	5	5
Noble			
The First National Bank Of Noble	9527	6	6
Nokomis			
The Farmers National Bank Of Nokomis	7547	5	–
The Nokomis National Bank	1934	6	6
Normal			
The First National Bank Of Normal	4930	6	6
Norris City			
The First National Bank Of Norris City	7971	5	5
O'Fallon			
The First National Bank Of O'Fallon	6924	4	3
Oak Park			
The First National Bank Of Oak Park	11507	5	–
Oakford			
The First National Bank Of Oakford	8256	5	5
Oakland			
The Oakland National Bank	2212	5	5
Oblong			
The First National Bank Of Oblong	8607	5	3
The Oil Belt National Bank Of Oblong	8696	6	5
Odell			
The Farmers National Bank Of Odell	9624	6	–
Odin			
The First National Bank Of Odin	9525	6	5
Ogden			
The First National Bank Of Ogden	5304	6	6
Okawville			
The First National Bank Of Okawville	11754	5	4
The Old Exchange National Bank Of Okawville	11780	5	4
Olney			
The First National Bank Of Olney	1641	5	4
The Olney National Bank	2629	6	–
Omaha			
The First National Bank Of Omaha	10291	6	–
Oneida			
The First National Bank Of Oneida	10752	6	6
Oquawka			
The First National Bank Of Oquawka	6086	6	–
Oregon			
The First National Bank Of Oregon	1969	6	–
Ottawa			
The First National Bank Of Ottawa	1154	4	4
The National City Bank Of Ottawa	1465	5	
Palatine			
The First National Bank Of Palatine	11934	6	6
Palestine			
The First National Bank Of Palestine	8892	6	6
Pana			
The First National Bank Of Pana	4038	6	–
The Pana National Bank	6734	4	6
Paris			
First National Bank & Trust Company Of Paris	3376	6	6
The Citizens National Bank Of Paris	6451	5	5
The Edgar County National Bank Of Paris	2100	4	5
The First National Bank Of Paris	1555	3	–
The First National Bank Of Paris	3376	5	–
Pawnee			
The National Bank Of Pawnee	7440	6	–
Pawpaw			
The First National Bank Of Pawpaw	6228	6	–
Paxton			
The First National Bank Of Paxton	1876	6	–
The First National Bank Of Paxton	2926	6	6
Pekin			
The American National Bank Of Pekin	3770	5	4
The Farmers National Bank Of Pekin	2287	4	6
The First National Bank Of Pekin	1637	6	–
The German-American National Bank Of Pekin	3770	5	–
The Herget National Bank Of Pekin	9788	4	3
Peoria			
Commercial Merchants National Bank & Trust Co Of Peoria	3296	–	4
Merchants And Illinois National Bank Of Peoria	3254	4	5
The Central National Bank & Trust Company Of Peoria	3214	4	2
The Central National Bank Of Peoria	3214	4	–
The Commercial German National Bank Of Peoria	3296	4	–
The Commercial National Bank Of Peoria	3296	6	–
The Commercial National Bank Of Peoria	3296	4	6
The First National Bank Of Peoria	176	2	3
The German-American National Bank Of Peoria	3070	5	–
The Illinois National Bank Of Peoria	5361	6	–
The Mechanics National Bank Of Peoria	1117	6	–
Peoria			
The Merchants National Bank Of Peoria	3254	6	–
The Peoria National Bank	2878	6	–
The Second National Bank Of Peoria	207	6	–
Percy			
The First National Bank Of Percy	7627	6	5
Peru			
State-National Bank Of Peru	13577	–	4
The First National Bank Of Peru	441	6	–
The Peru National Bank	2951	5	5
The State-National Bank Of Peru	13577	–	4
Petersburg			
The First National Bank Of Petersburg	3043	3	–
The State National Bank Of Petersburg	3043	–	5
Philo			
The First National Bank Of Philo	6211	6	–
Pinckneyville			
The First National Bank Of Pinckneyville	6025	4	4
Piper City			
The First National Bank Of Piper City	5322	4	5
Pittsfield			
The First National Bank Of Pittsfield	1042	5	3
Plymouth			
The First National Bank Of Plymouth	12658	6	6
Polo			
The Exchange National Bank Of Polo	1806	4	6
Pontiac			
The Livingston County National Bank Of Pontiac	1837	5	6
The National Bank Of Pontiac	2141	5	6
Potomac			
The Potomac National Bank	6824	6	–
Prairie City			
The First National Bank Of Prairie City	2254	6	–
Princeton			
Citizens First National Bank Of Princeton	2413	–	5
The Citizens National Bank Of Princeton	2413	4	5
The Farmers National Bank Of Princeton	2165	4	6
The First National Bank Of Princeton	903	4	6
Prophetstown			
The Farmers National Bank Of Prophetstown	6375	5	3
The First National Bank Of Prophetstown	1968	6	–
Quincy			
The First National Bank Of Quincy	424	6	–
The Merchants And Farmers National Bank Of Quincy	703	6	–
The Quincy National Bank	3752	5	–
The Quincy-Ricker National Bank & Trust Company	3752	4	4
The Ricker National Bank Of Quincy	2519	2	–
Ramsey			
The Ramsey National Bank	9895	5	4
Ransom			
The First National Bank Of Ransom	8289	6	6
Rantoul			
The First National Bank Of Rantoul	5193	6	5
Ravenswood			
The Ravenswood National Bank	10215	6	–
Raymond			
The First National Bank Of Raymond	6910	6	6
Ridge Farm			
The City National Bank Of Ridge Farm	8630	6	6
The First National Bank Of Ridge Farm	5313	6	6
Ridgway			
The First National Bank Of Ridgway	9439	6	6
Riverside			
The First National Bank Of Riverside	12386	6	6
Robinson			
The First National Bank Of Robinson	5049	6	6
The Second National Bank Of Robinson	13605	–	4
Rochelle			
The First National Bank Of Rochelle	1922	6	–
The Rochelle National Bank	1907	4	6
Rock Falls			
The First National Bank Of Rock Falls	6998	4	4
Rock Island			
The First National Bank Of Rock Island	108	6	–
The Peoples National Bank Of Rock Island	2155	3	–
The Rock Island National Bank	1889	5	–
Rockford			
The Commercial National Bank Of Rockford	11679	6	5
The First National Bank Of Rockford	429	6	–
The Forest City National Bank Of Rockford	4325	4	4
The Illinois National Bank And Trust Company Of Rockford	13652	–	4
The Manufacturers National Bank & Trust Co. Of Rockford	3952	6	4
The Manufacturers National Bank Of Rockford	3952	4	–
The Rockford National Bank	1816	3	3
The Second National Bank Of Rockford	482	6	–
The Security National Bank Of Rockford	11731	5	5
The Swedish-American National Bank Of Rockford	9823	5	4
The Third National Bank Of Rockford	479	5	4
The Winnebago National Bank Of Rockford	883	5	–
Roodhouse			
The First National Bank Of Roodhouse	8637	5	5
Roseville			
The First National Bank Of Roseville	5883	6	–
Rossville			
The Farmers National Bank Of Rossville	9877	6	–
The First National Bank Of Rossville	5398	6	5
Rushville			
The First National Bank Of Rushville	1453	6	–
Saint Anne			
The First National Bank Of Saint Anne	5470	6	–
Saint Charles			
The Kane County National Bank Of Saint Charles	2021	6	–
The St. Charles National Bank, St. Charles	6219	4	4
Saint Francisville			
The First National Bank Of St. Francisville	8846	6	–
The Peoples National Bank Of St. Francisville	8846	6	4
Saint Peter			
The First National Bank Of Saint Peter	9896	6	5
Salem			
The Salem National Bank	1715	5	4
Sandoval			
The First National Bank Of Sandoval	9786	6	5
Savanna			
The First National Bank Of Savanna	8540	4	4
The National Bank Of Savanna	13886	–	5
Secor			
The First National Bank Of Secor	6007	6	6
Seneca			
The First National Bank Of Seneca	1773	6	–
Sesser			
The First National Bank Of Sesser	8758	6	6
Shawneetown			
The City National Bank Of Shawneetown	9435	5	6
The First National Bank Of Shawneetown	915	6	–
The Gallatin National Bank Of Shawneetown	1775	5	–
The National Bank Of Shawneetown	7752	5	6
Shelbyville			
The Citizens National Bank Of Shelbyville	7396	5	–
The First National Bank Of Shelbyville	2128	3	6
Sidell			
The First National Bank Of Sidell	8374	6	6
Smithton			
The First National Bank Of Smithton	13525	–	4
South Chicago			
The Calumet National Bank Of South Chicago	3102	6	–
Sparta			
The First National Bank Of Sparta	7015	4	5
Spring Valley			
The Spring Valley National Bank	3465	6	–
Springfield			
The Farmers National Bank Of Springfield	2688	6	–
The First National Bank Of Springfield	205	3	3
The Illinois National Bank Of Springfield	3548	3	3
The Ridgely National Bank Of Springfield	1662	3	–
The State National Bank Of Springfield	1733	3	–
St Elmo			
The First National Bank Of St Elmo	9388	6	4
Staunton			
The First National Bank Of Staunton	10173	6	4
The Staunton National Bank	10777	4	5
Sterling			
First Sterling National Bank	1717	–	5
The First National Bank Of Sterling	1717	5	6
The Sterling National Bank	2709	4	6
Steward			
The First National Bank Of Steward	6543	6	6
Stewardson			
The First National Bank Of Stewardson	9438	6	–
Stockton			
The First National Bank Of Stockton	13666	–	6
Stonington			
The First National Bank Of Stonington	5291	5	6
Strawn			
The Farmers National Bank Of Strawn	7151	6	6
Streator			
The City National Bank Of Streator	4476	6	
The First National Bank Of Streator	2170	6	–
The Streator National Bank	2681	5	5
The Union National Bank Of Streator	2176	6	6
Stronghurst			
The First National Bank Of Stronghurst	5813	5	–
Sullivan			
The First National Bank Of Sullivan	7692	5	5
Sumner			
The First National Bank Of Sumner	6907	6	4
Sycamore			
The Citizens National Bank Of Sycamore	9572	6	–
The First National Bank Of Sycamore	1896	5	4
The Sycamore National Bank	1896	5	–
Tamaroa			
The First National Bank Of Tamaroa	8629	6	6
Tampico			
The First National Bank Of Tampico	9230	5	3
Taylorville			
Farmers National Bank Of Taylorville	5410	4	5
The Farmers National Bank Of Taylorville	5410	4	–
The First National Bank Of Taylorville	3579	5	6
The Taylorville National Bank	8940	2	6
Thomasboro			
The First National Bank Of Thomasboro	8155	6	6
Toledo			
The First National Bank In Toledo	13682	–	5
The First National Bank Of Toledo	5273	4	5
Toluca			
The Citizens National Bank Of Toluca	11333	6	6
The First National Bank Of Toluca	4871	6	–
Tremont			
The First National Bank Of Tremont	6421	6	6
The Tremont National Bank	9325	6	–
Trenton			
The First National Bank Of Trenton	10125	6	6

City, Bank	Ch. No.	L	S
Triumph			
The First National Bank Of Triumph	7660	6	5
Tuscola			
The First National Bank Of Tuscola	1723	6	6
Ullin			
The First National Bank Of Ullin	8180	6	6
Urbana			
The First National Bank Of Urbana	2915	6	6
Vandalia			
The Farmers And Merchants National Bank Of Vandalia	1779	6	–
The First National Bank Of Vandalia	4994	5	4
The National Bank Of Vandalia	1517	6	–
Vermilion			
The First National Bank Of Vermilion	10365	6	6
Vienna			
The First National Bank Of Vienna	4433	4	5
Villa Grove			
The First National Bank Of Villa Grove	7088	5	4
Virginia			
The Centennial National Bank Of Virginia	2330	4	5
The Farmers National Bank Of Virginia	1471	5	–
Waddams Grove			
The First National Bank Of Waddams Grove	11675	6	–
Walnut			
The First National Bank Of Walnut	2684	6	–
Waltonville			
The First National Bank Of Waltonville	11516	6	–
Warren			
The Farmers National Bank Of Warren	849	6	–
The First National Bank In Warren	9096	6	–
The National Farmers Bank Of Warren	9096	6	–
Warsaw			
The Farmers National Bank Of Warsaw	9929	6	–
The First National Bank Of Warsaw	495	6	–
Waterloo			
The First National Bank Of Waterloo	10180	6	3
Watseka			
The First National Bank Of Watseka	1721	5	6
Waukegan			
The First National Bank Of Waukegan	945	6	4
The Waukegan National Bank	10355	4	4
Waverly			
The First National Bank Of Waverly	6116	3	4
Wayne City			
The First National Bank Of Wayne City	10460	5	4
Wenona			
The First National Bank Of Wenona	3620	6	–
West Frankfort			
The First National Bank Of West Frankfort	7673	6	6
West Salem			
The First National Bank Of West Salem	9338	6	6
Westervelt			
The Farmers National Bank Of Westervelt	10641	6	6
Westfield			
The First National Bank Of Westfield	8216	4	6
Westville			
The First National Bank Of Westville	7500	6	6
Wheaton			
The First National Bank Of Wheaton	9368	6	6
White Hall			
Peoples-First National Bank Of White Hall	7121	5	6
The First National Bank Of White Hall	7121	5	–
The White Hall National Bank, White Hall	7077	4	4
Wilmette			
The First National Bank Of Wilmette	10828	–	4
Wilmington			
The Commercial National Bank Of Wilmington	1964	6	6
The First National Bank Of Wilmington	177	5	–
Wilsonville			
The First National Bank Of Wilsonville	12630	6	6
Winchester			
The First National Bank Of Winchester	1484	6	–
The Peoples National Bank Of Winchester	1821	4	–
Windsor			
The First National Bank Of Windsor	7339	6	–
Witt			
The First National Bank Of Witt	7538	6	–
The National Bank Of Witt	13144	6	5
The Oland National Bank Of Witt	7538	6	–
The Security National Bank Of Witt	13650	–	4
The Witt National Bank	10264	6	–
Wood River			
The First National Bank Of Wood River	11876	5	4
Woodhull			
The First National Bank In Woodhull	12525	6	–
The First National Bank Of Woodhull	10716	6	–
Woodlawn			
The First National Bank Of Woodlawn	11774	6	4
Woodstock			
First National Bank Of Woodstock	14137	–	6
The American National Bank Of Woodstock	6811	6	6
The First National Bank Of Woodstock	372	6	–
The First National Bank Of Woodstock	2675	6	–
Worden			
The First National Bank Of Worden	10669	6	6
The Wall National Bank Of Worden	10669	6	–
Wyanet			
The First National Bank Of Wyanet	9277	6	5
Wyoming			
The First National Bank Of Wyoming	2815	6	–
The National Bank Of Wyoming	6629	5	6
Xenia			
The First National Bank Of Xenia	12096	6	6
Yorkville			
The Yorkville National Bank	6239	6	5
Zeigler			
The First National Bank Of Zeigler	12097	5	4

INDIANA

City, Bank	Ch. No.	L	S
Albion			
The Albion National Bank	8912	6	6
Alexandria			
The Alexandria National Bank	4835	6	–
Ambia			
The First National Bank Of Ambia	9510	6	–
Amo			
The First National Bank Of Amo	8154	6	6
Anderson			
The First National Bank Of Anderson	44	6	–
The Madison County National Bank Of Anderson	2346	6	–
The National Exchange Bank Of Anderson	4685	6	6
The Peoples State National Bank Of Anderson	10290	6	–
Angola			
The First National Bank Of Angola	7023	6	6
Arcadia			
The First National Bank Of Arcadia	9488	6	–
Argos			
The First National Bank Of Argos	9726	6	–
Attica			
The Central National Bank And Trust Company Of Attica	3755	–	4
The Central National Bank Of Attica	3755	5	–
The Citizens National Bank Of Attica	3755	6	–
The First National Bank Of Attica	577	6	–
Auburn			
The City National Bank Of Auburn	6509	6	5
The First National Bank Of Auburn	2238	6	–
Aurora			
The Aurora National Bank	2963	6	–
The First National Bank Of Aurora	699	3	5
Batesville			
The First National Bank Of Batesville	7824	6	5
Bedford			
The Bedford National Bank	1892	6	–
The Bedford National Bank	5187	4	5
The Citizens National Bank Of Bedford	5173	5	5
The Indiana National Bank Of Bedford	3013	6	–
The Stone City National Bank Of Bedford	13788	–	6
Bicknell			
The First National Bank Of Bicknell	7155	6	6
Birdseye			
The Birdseye National Bank	8835	6	6
Bloomington			
The Bloomington National Bank	8415	6	5
The First National Bank Of Bloomington	1888	4	5
Bluffton			
Old-First National Bank In Bluffton	13305	–	5
The First National Bank Of Bluffton	58	6	–
The Old National Bank Of Bluffton	13305	–	3
Blufton			
First National Bank In Blufton	13317	–	3
Boonville			
First National Bank Of Boonville	10613	6	6
The Boonville National Bank	2207	6	–
The City National Bank Of Boonville	10613	6	–
The Farmers And Merchants National Bank Of Boonville	9266	5	–
Boswell			
The First National Bank Of Boswell	5476	6	6
Brazil			
The Citizens National Bank Of Brazil	8620	5	5
The First National Bank Of Brazil	3583	6	5
The Riddell National Bank Of Brazil	5267	4	3
Brookville			
The Brookville National Bank	1619	6	–
The Franklin County National Bank Of Brookville	5629	5	5
The National Brookville Bank Of Brookville	7805	5	4
Brownstown			
The First National Bank Of Brownstown	9143	6	5
Butler			
The First National Bank Of Butler	9286	6	6
Cambridge City			
The First National Bank & Trust Company Of Cambridge City	2734	6	6
The First National Bank Of Cambridge City	70	6	–
The First National Bank Of Cambridge City	2734	6	–
The Wayne National Bank Of Cambridge City	8871	6	–
Cannelton			
Cannelton National Bank	9682	6	5
First Cannelton National Bank	9682	–	5
The First National Bank Of Cannelton	9401	6	6
Carlisle			
The First National Bank Of Carlisle	8805	6	–
Cayuga			
The First National Bank Of Cayuga	9189	6	5
Center Point			
The First National Bank Of Center Point	9250	5	5
Centerville			
The First National Bank Of Centerville	2696	6	–
The First National Bank Of Centreville	37	4	–
Charlestown			
The First National Bank Of Charlestown	6952	6	6
Cicero			
The Citizens National Bank Of Cicero	10720	5	6
Clay City			
The First National Bank Of Clay City	9540	5	5
Clinton			
The First National Bank Of Clinton	6480	5	6
Cloverdale			
The First National Bank Of Cloverdale	10465	6	6
Coatesville			
The First National Bank Of Coatesville	8447	6	6
Columbia City			
The Columbia City National Bank, Columbia City	7175	6	–
The First National Bank Of Columbia City	7132	5	–
Columbus			
The First National Bank Of Columbus	1066	6	6
Connersville			
The Fayette National Bank Of Connersville	6265	6	–
The First National Bank Of Connersville	1034	4	5
Converse			
The First National Bank Of Converse	11671	–	6
Corydon			
The Corydon National Bank	7760	6	–
The First National Bank Of Corydon	6625	6	–
Covington			
The First National Bank Of Covington	9860	6	–
Crawfordsville			
The Citizens National Bank Of Crawfordsville	2533	5	5
The Elston National Bank Of Crawfordsville	7773	5	–
The First National Bank Of Crawfordsville	571	5	4
Crown Point			
The First National Bank Of Crown Point	2183	5	5
Dana			
The First National Bank Of Dana	5997	6	6
Danville			
The First National Bank Of Danville	152	5	5
Decatur			
The Decatur National Bank	3028	6	–
The First National Bank Of Decatur	3028	6	6
Delphi			
The Citizens National Bank Of Delphi	6986	6	6
The First National Bank Of Delphi	1949	6	–
Dillsboro			
The First National Bank Of Dillsboro	6882	5	6
Dublin			
The First National Bank Of Dublin	8804	6	6
Dunkirk			
The First National Bank Of Dunkirk	4888	6	–
Dyer			
The First National Bank Of Dyer	6909	5	6
East Chicago			
The First National Bank And Trust Company Of East Chicago	7601	5	5
The First National Bank In East Chicago	13531	–	4
The First National Bank Of East Chicago	7601	5	–
The Indiana Harbor National Bank Of East Chicago	10171	6	–
The Union National Bank Of Indiana Harbor At East Chicago	13532		3
The United States National Bank Of Indiana Harbor	12058	5	4
Edinburg			
The Farmers National Bank Of Edinburg	6905	5	6
Elkhart			
The Elkhart National Bank	2502	6	–
The First National Bank Of Elkhart	206	6	5
The Indiana National Bank Of Elkhart	4841	6	–
Elwood			
The First National Bank Of Elwood	4675	5	6
Evansville			
Old National Bank In Evansville	12444	4	4
The Bankers National Bank Of Evansville	8832	6	–
The Citizens National Bank Of Evansville	2188	3	1
The City National Bank Of Evansville	6200	5	–
The Evansville National Bank	730	6	–
The First National Bank Of Evansville	28	6	–
The First National Bankof Evansville	2692	6	–
The German National Bank Of Evansville	1772	6	–
The Mercantile National Bank Of Evansville	8492	6	–
The Merchants National Bank Of Evansville	989	5	–
The National City Bank Of Evansville	12132	5	3
The Old National Bank Of Evansville	3281	6	–
The Old State National Bank Of Evansville	7478	5	–
Fairland			
The Fairland National Bank	8337	5	5
Farmersburg			
The First National Bank Of Farmersburg	11035	6	–
Farmland			
The First National Bank Of Farmland	6504	6	–
Ferdinand			
The Ferdinand National Bank	7830	6	–
Fishers			
The Fishers National Bank	10419	6	6
Flora			
The Bright National Bank Of Flora	8014	6	6
The First National Bank Of Flora	7802	6	–
Fort Branch			
The Farmers And Merchants National Bank Of Fort Branch	9077	6	6
The First National Bank Of Fort Branch	9073	6	6
Fort Wayne			
First & Tri State National Bank & Trust Co Of Fort Wayne	2701	–	3
First National Bank Of Fort Wayne	2701	4	4
Fort Wayne National Bank	13818	–	5
Lincoln National Bank & Trust Company Of Fort Wayne	7725	6	2
Old-First National Bank And Trust Company Of Fort Wayne	3285	–	3
The First And Hamilton National Bank Of Fort Wayne	2701	4	–
The First National Bank Of Fort Wayne	11	6	–
The First National Bank Of Fort Wayne	2701	3	–
The Fort Wayne National Bank	865	6	–

City, Bank	Ch. No.	L	S
Fort Wayne			
The German-American National Bank Of Fort Wayne	7725	6	–
The Hamilton National Bank Of Fort Wayne	2439	4	–
The Lincoln National Bank Of Fort Wayne	7725	5	–
The Merchants National Bank Of Fort Wayne	1100	6	–
The Old National Bank Of Fort Wayne	3285	4	4
The White National Bank Of Fort Wayne	4725	6	–
Fortville			
The First National Bank Of Fortville	9299	5	5
Fowler			
The First National Bank Of Fowler	5430	4	6
Frankfort			
The American National Bank Of Frankfort	6217	4	–
The First National Bank Of Frankfort	1854	4	4
Franklin			
Franklin National Bank	13378	–	5
The Citizens National Bank Of Franklin	3967	6	5
The First National Bank Of Franklin	50	6	–
The Franklin National Bank	3338	5	6
The Johnson County National Bank Of Franklin	14075	–	6
The National Bank Of Franklin	2769	6	–
The Second National Bank Of Franklin	78	6	–
Freeland Park			
The First National Bank Of Freeland Park	7437	6	–
Fremont			
The First National Bank Of Fremont	10718	6	5
Gary			
The First National Bank Of Gary	8426	5	5
The National Bank Of America At Gary	11094	5	5
Gas City			
The First National Bank Of Gas City	4825	6	–
Goodland			
The First National Bank Of Goodland	7863	5	5
Goshen			
First National Bank Of Goshen	14113	–	6
The City National Bank Of Goshen	2067	4	6
The First National Bank Of Goshen	146	6	–
Greencastle			
The Central National Bank Of Greencastle	2896	4	3
The Citizens National Bank Of Greencastle	10409	6	–
The First National Bank Of Greencastle	219	4	5
Greens Fork			
The First National Bank Of Greens Fork	7124	5	6
Greensburg			
Citizens Third National Bank & Trust Company Of Greensbrg	2844	–	6
The Citizens National Bank Of Greensburg	1890	4	4
The First National Bank Of Greensburg	356	6	–
The Greensburg National Bank	5435	5	5
The Third National Bank And Trust Company Of Greensburg	2844	6	6
Third National Bank Of Greensburg	2844	5	–
Greenwood			
The Citizens National Bank Of Greenwood	8461	6	6
The First National Bank Of Greenwood	8422	6	6
Hagerstown			
The First National Bank Of Hagerstown	7902	6	–
Hammond			
Citizens National Bank Of Hammond	8199	5	–
The Citizens German National Bank Of Hammond	8199	6	–
The First National Bank Of Hammond	3478	4	–
The Hammond National Bank And Trust Company, Hammond	8199	6	4
Hartford City			
The First National Bank Of Hartford City	6959	6	6
Hartsville			
The First National Bank Of Hartsville	7354	6	6
Holland			
The Holland National Bank	9090	5	6
Hope			
The Citizens National Bank Of Hope	5726	6	–
Huntingburg			
The First National Bank Of Huntingburg	8929	6	5
Huntington			
The First National Bank Of Huntington	145	6	–
The First National Bank Of Huntington	2508	5	6
Indianapolis			
American National Bank Of Indianapolis	13759	–	3
National City Bank Of Indianapolis	10121	3	–
The American National Bank Of Indianapolis	5672	4	–
The Capital National Bank Of Indianapolis	4158	5	–
The Citizens National Bank Of Indianapolis	617	6	–
The Columbia National Bank Of Indianapolis	5845	6	–
The Commercial National Bank Of Indianapolis	10671	6	–
The Continental National Bank Of Indianapolis	9537	5	6
The First National Bank Of Indianapolis	55	4	–
The First National Bank Of Indianapolis	2556	6	–
The Fletcher American National Bank Of Indianapolis	9829	2	2
The Fletcher National Bank Of Indianapolis	5116	5	–
The Fourth National Bank Of Indianapolis	783	6	–
The Indiana National Bank Of Indianapolis	984	3	1
Indianapolis			
The Indianapolis National Bank	581	6	–
The Merchants National Bank Of Indianapolis	869	2	3
The Meridian National Bank Of Indianapolis	1878	6	–
The Union National Bank Of Indianapolis	6513	6	–
Jasonville			
The First National Bank Of Jasonville	7342	6	6
Jeffersonville			
The Citizens National Bank Of Jeffersonville	1466	6	–
The First National Bank Of Jeffersonville	956	5	4
Kendallville			
The Citizens National Bank Of Kendallville	12532	6	6
The First National Bank Of Kendallville	41	6	–
The First National Bank Of Kendallville	2687	6	–
Kewanna			
The American National Bank Of Kewanna	10616	6	6
The First National Bank Of Kewanna	8192	6	–
Kirklin			
The First National Bank Of Kirklin	9115	6	–
Knightstown			
The Citizens National Bank Of Knightstown	9152	5	5
The First National Bank Of Knightstown	872	5	4
Knox			
The First National Bank Of Knox	5919	6	–
Kokomo			
The Citizens National Bank Of Kokomo	4121	5	6
The First National Bank Of Kokomo	894	6	–
The Howard National Bank Of Kokomo	2375	4	6
The Kokomo National Bank	6261	6	–
La Fayette			
The American National Bank Of La Fayette	7415	6	–
The City National Bank Of La Fayette	5940	4	–
The First National Bank Of La Fayette	23	6	–
The First National Bank Of La Fayette	2717	5	–
The First-Merchants National Bank Of La Fayette	11148	5	4
The Fowler National Bank Of La Fayette	3280	6	–
The Indiana National Bank Of La Fayette	1967	6	–
The La Fayette National Bank	2213	5	–
The Merchants National Bank Of La Fayette	4468	4	–
The National Fowler Bank Of La Fayette	5889	5	5
The National State Bank Of La Fayette	930	4	–
The Perrin National Bank Of La Fayette	4656	6	–
The Second National Bank Of La Fayette	417	6	–
The Union National Bank Of La Fayette	882	6	–
La Grange			
The First National Bank Of La Grange	2184	6	–
The National Bank Of La Grange	4972	5	–
La Porte			
The First National Bank & Trust Company Of La Porte	377	6	5
The First National Bank Of La Porte	377	5	–
Lawrenceburg			
The Citizens National Bank Of Lawrenceburg	4281	6	–
The City National Bank Of Lawrenceburg	2889	6	–
The Dearborn National Bank Of Lawrenceburg	7909	5	6
The First National Bank Of Lawrenceburg	82	6	–
The Lawrenceburg National Bank	1418	6	–
Lawrenceburgh			
The Peoples National Bank Of Lawrenceburgh	2612	3	5
Lebanon			
The First National Bank Of Lebanon	2057	2	5
The Lebanon National Bank	2660	6	–
Lewisville			
The First National Bank Of Lewisville	5526	6	6
Liberty			
The First National Bank Of Liberty	1925	6	–
The Union County National Bank Of Liberty	2007	6	5
Lima			
The National State Bank Of Lima	1234	6	–
Linton			
Citizens National Bank Of Linton	14258	–	4
The First National Bank Of Linton	7411	5	5
Logansport			
The City And State National Bank & Trust Co Of Logansport	5076	–	6
The City National Bank Of Logansport	5076	4	4
The First National Bank Of Logansport	3084	5	3
The Logansport National Bank	1031	6	–
The National Bank Of Logansport	13580	–	3
The State National Bank Of Logansport	2596	6	–
Loogootee			
The First National Bank Of Loogootee	7241	6	–
Lowell			
First National Bank In Lowell	5931	5	6
The First National Bank Of Lowell	5369	6	–
The Lowell National Bank	6765	6	6
The State National Bank Of Lowell	5931	6	–
Lynnville			
The Lynnville National Bank	8868	6	6
Madison			
The First National Bank Of Madison	111	4	5
The National Branch Bank Of Madison	1457	4	5
Marion			
First National Bank In Marion	13717	–	4
The First National Bank Of Marion	4189	4	3
The Marion National Bank	7758	4	4
Martinsville			
The Citizens National Bank Of Martinsville	4964	5	–
The First National Bank Of Martinsville	794	4	5
The National Bank Of Martinsville	13643	–	5
Matthews			
The First National Bank Of Matthews	5998	6	–
Mays			
The First National Bank Of Mays	8700	6	6
Medaryville			
The First National Bank Of Medaryville	8537	6	–
Mentone			
The First National Bank Of Mentone	8368	6	–
Michigan City			
The First National Bank Of Michigan City	2101	6	–
The First National Bank Of Michigan City	2747	6	6
The Merchants National Bank Of Michigan City	9381	5	4
Milltown			
The First National Bank Of Milltown	8650	6	6
Milroy			
The First National Bank Of Milroy	11782	5	5
Mishawaka			
The First National Bank Of Mishawaka	5167	5	5
Mitchell			
The First National Bank Of Mitchell	6433	6	6
Monrovia			
The First National Bank Of Monrovia	6354	6	6
Monterey			
The First National Bank Of Monterey	9784	6	5
Montezuma			
The First National Bank Of Montezuma	7463	6	6
Montgomery			
The First National Bank Of Montgomery	5734	6	–
Monticello			
The First National Bank Of Monticello	2208	6	–
The Monticello National Bank	6172	6	–
Montpelier			
The First National Bank Of Montpelier	5278	6	6
Mooresville			
The First National Bank Of Mooresville	6876	6	–
Morgantown			
The First National Bank Of Morgantown	7652	5	–
Mount Vernon			
The First National Bank Of Mount Vernon	366	4	–
The Mount Vernon National Bank	7786	6	–
The Mount Vernon National Bank And Trust Company	12780	6	6
The Old First National Bank Of Mount Vernon	12466	6	6
Mulberry			
The Citizens National Bank Of Mulberry	10234	6	5
The Farmers National Bank Of Mulberry	4801	6	–
Muncie			
The Citizens National Bank Of Muncie	2234	6	–
The Delaware County National Bank Of Muncie	4809	5	4
The Farmers National Bank Of Muncie	4674	6	–
The Merchants National Bank Of Muncie	2234	4	3
The Merchants National Bank Of Muncie	4852	5	–
The Muncie National Bank	793	6	–
The Peoples National Bank Of Muncie	7454	6	–
The Union National Bank Of Muncie	2234	5	–
Nappanee			
The First National Bank Of Nappanee	8785	6	6
New Albany			
The First National Bank Of New Albany	701	6	–
The Merchants National Bank Of New Albany	965	6	–
The New Albany National Bank	775	5	5
The Second National Bank Of New Albany	2166	4	4
New Carlisle			
The First National Bank Of New Carlisle	5639	6	6
New Castle			
The Bundy National Bank Of New Castle	2202	6	–
The Farmers And First National Bank Of New Castle	9852	5	5
The Farmers National Bank Of New Castle	9852	6	–
The First National Bank Of New Castle	804	4	–
New Harmony			
New Harmony National Bank	13542	–	5
The First National Bank Of New Harmony	6699	6	6
New Point			
The First National Bank Of New Point	8408	6	–
Newport			
The First National Bank Of Newport	1897	6	–
Noblesville			
The American National Bank Of Noblesville	9756	6	6
The First National Bank Of Noblesville	4882	5	–
North Manchester			
The First National Bank Of North Manchester	2903	6	–
The Lawrence National Bank Of North Manchester	3474	5	–
North Vernon			
The First National Bank Of North Vernon	4678	5	6
The North Vernon National Bank	9122	5	6
Oakland City			
The First National Bank Of Oakland City	9562	6	6
Odon			
The First National Bank Of Odon	7260	6	6
Orleans			
The National Bank Of Orleans	5558	6	6
Owensville			
The First National Bank Of Owensville	5432	6	–

City, Bank	Ch. No.	L	S
Patoka			
The Patoka National Bank	9352	6	6
Peru			
The Citizens National Bank Of Peru	1879	5	5
The First National Bank Of Peru	363	6	5
Petersburg			
The First National Bank Of Petersburg	5300	6	6
Plainfield			
The First National Bank And Trust Company Of Plainfield	7011	6	6
The First National Bank Of Plainfield	7011	6	–
Plymouth			
The First National Bank Of Marshall County At Plymouth	2119	3	5
Portland			
The First National Bank Of Portland	7180	5	4
Poseyville			
The Bozeman Waters First National Bank Of Poseyville	13503	–	4
The Bozeman Waters National Bank Of Poseyville	8149	5	4
The First National Bank Of Poseyville	7036	6	6
Princeton			
The American National Bank Of Princeton	8166	6	–
The Farmers National Bank Of Princeton	9463	5	4
The Gibson County National Bank Of Princeton	2066	6	–
The Peoples National Bank Of Princeton	2180	5	–
The Peoples-American National Bank Of Princeton	10551	6	5
Redkey			
The Farmers And Merchants National Bank Of Redkey	9670	6	–
Remington			
The Farmers National Bank Of Remington	11355	6	5
The First National Bank Of Remington	8060	6	–
Rensselaer			
The First National Bank Of Rensselaer	6651	6	–
Richmond			
The First National Bank Of Richmond	17	6	–
The First National Bank Of Richmond	2680	4	3
The Richmond National Bank	1102	6	–
The Richmond National Bank	2090	5	–
The Second National Bank Of Richmond	1988	4	4
The Union National Bank Of Richmond	3413	5	–
Ridgeville			
The First National Bank Of Ridgeville	8351	6	6
Rising Sun			
The National Bank Of Rising Sun	1959	4	6
Rochester			
The First National Bank Of Rochester	1952	6	–
The First National Bank Of Rochester	7655	5	6
Rockport			
The First National Bank Of Rockport	6194	6	6
Rockville			
The First National Bank Of Rockville	63	6	–
The National Bank Of Rockville	2361	6	–
The Rockville National Bank	5067	4	6
Rosedale			
The Harrison National Bank Of Rosedale	9006	6	–
The Rosedale National Bank	9006	6	6
Rushville			
The American National Bank Of Rushville	12420	6	4
The Peoples National Bank Of Rushville	7374	6	–
The Rush County National Bank Of Rushville	1869	5	6
The Rushville National Bank	1456	6	5
Russiaville			
The First National Bank Of Russiaville	5524	6	6
Salem			
The National Bank Of Salem	2173	6	–
Seymour			
The First National Bank Of Seymour	1032	6	4
The Seymour National Bank	4652	6	4
Shelburn			
The First National Bank Of Shelburn	7513	6	–
Shelbyville			
The Farmers National Bank Of Shelbyville	4800	5	5
The First National Bank Of Shelbyville	1263	4	6
The Shelby National Bank Of Shelbyville	7946	6	5
Sheridan			
The Farmers National Bank Of Sheridan	6070	6	–
The First National Bank Of Sheridan	5296	6	–
The First National State Bank Of Sheridan	5296	6	–
Shirley			
The First National Bank Of Shirley	9209	6	–
South Bend			
The Citizens National Bank Of South Bend	4764	5	4
The First National Bank Of South Bend	126	4	2
The Merchants National Bank Of South Bend	6334	5	3
The South Bend National Bank	1739	6	–
Spencer			
The First National Bank Of Spencer	2178	6	–
The Spencer National Bank	9715	4	6
Spurgeon			
The First National Bank Of Spurgeon	12028	6	6
Sullivan			
Peoples National Bank And Trust Company Of Sullivan	5392	6	5
The Farmers National Bank Of Sullivan	2369	6	–
The First National Bank Of Sullivan	1932	6	–
The National Bank Of Sullivan	5392	4	–
Sunman			
The Farmers National Bank Of Sunman	8878	6	6
Swayzee			
The First National Bank At Swayzee	13862	–	6
The First National Bank Of Swayzee	8820	6	5

City, Bank	Ch. No.	L	S
Tell City			
The Citizens National Bank Of Tell City	7375	5	5
The First National Bank Of Tell City	2201	6	–
The Tell City National Bank	5756	5	5
Tennyson			
The Tennyson National Bank	8956	6	5
Terre Haute			
First-Mckeen National Bank & Trust Company Of Terre Haute	47	6	3
Terre Haute First National Bank	2742	–	6
Terre Haute National Bank & Trust Co. , Terre Haute	7562	5	3
The First National Bank Of Terre Haute	47	6	–
The First National Bank Of Terre Haute	2742	3	–
The Mckeen National Bank Of Terre Haute	7922	2	–
The Merchants National Bank Of Terre Haute	13938	–	4
The National State Bank Of Terre Haute	1103	5	–
The Terre Haute National Bank	7562	5	–
The Vigo County National Bank Of Terre Haute	3929	6	–
Thorntown			
The First National Bank Of Thorntown	1046	6	–
The Home National Bank Of Thorntown	5842	6	6
Tipton			
The Citizens National Bank Of Tipton	7496	6	5
The First National Bank Of Tipton	6251	5	–
Trafalgar			
The Farmers National Bank Of Trafalgar	7491	6	6
Union City			
The Commercial National Bank Of Union City	5094	6	–
The First National Bank Of Union City	815	6	–
Valparaiso			
The Farmers National Bank Of Valparaiso	2403	6	–
The First National Bank Of Porter County, Valparaiso	2704	5	–
The First National Bank Of Valparaiso	105	6	–
The Valparaiso National Bank	6215	3	6
Veedersburg			
The First National Bank Of Veedersburg	11044	6	6
Vernon			
The First National Bank Of Vernon	4688	6	6
Vevay			
The First National Bank Of Vevay	346	5	6
Vincennes			
The American National Bank Of Vincennes	3864	6	–
The First National Bank Of Vincennes	1873	2	6
The German National Bank Of Vincennes	3864	6	–
The Second National Bank Of Vincennes	4901	6	–
The Vincennes National Bank	1454	6	–
Wabash			
The Farmers And Merchants National Bank Of Wabash	6309	5	–
The Farmers And Wabash National Bank Of Wabash	6309	6	4
The First National Bank Of Wabash	129	6	–
The Wabash National Bank	3935	5	–
Wadesville			
The Farmers National Bank Of Wadesville	8927	6	6
Wakarusa			
The First National Bank Of Wakarusa	11043	6	5
Warren			
The First National Bank Of Warren	7930	6	–
Warsaw			
The First National Bank Of Warsaw	88	6	–
Washington			
The Peoples National Bank & Trust Company Of Washington	3842	6	6
The Peoples National Bank Of Washington	3842	5	–
The Washington National Bank	2043	5	6
West Baden			
The West Baden National Bank	6388	6	6
Westport			
The First National Bank Of Westport	9175	6	–
Whiteland			
The Whiteland National Bank	9492	6	–
Whiting			
The First National Bank Of Whiting	6526	4	–
Wilkinson			
The Farmers National Bank Of Wilkinson	9279	6	6
Williamsburg			
The First National Bank Of Williamsburg	8625	6	6
Winamac			
The Citizens National Bank Of Winamac	8747	6	–
The First National Bank Of Winamac	7761	6	5
Winchester			
The First National Bank Of Winchester	889	6	–
Winslow			
The First National Bank Of Winslow	9159	6	5

IOWA

City, Bank	Ch. No.	L	S
Ackley			
The First National Bank Of Ackley	8762	3	5
Adair			
The First National Bank Of Adair	8699	6	–
Adel			
The First National Bank Of Adel	8981	3	–
Afton			
The First National Bank Of Afton	2326	6	–
Akron			
The First National Bank Of Akron	7322	4	5
Albia			
The Albia National Bank	3012	6	–
The First National Bank Of Albia	1799	4	6
The Peoples National Bank Of Albia	8603	4	4
Algona			
The First National Bank Of Algona	3197	4	–
Allerton			
The Farmers National Bank Of Allerton	9231	5	–
The First National Bank Of Allerton	2191	6	–
Alta			
The First National Bank Of Alta	7126	5	–
Ames			
The Ames National Bank	10408	4	4
The Union National Bank Of Ames	3017	4	5
Anamosa			
The Anamosa National Bank	4696	3	4
The First National Bank Of Anamosa	1813	6	–
Arlington			
The American National Bank Of Arlington	9664	4	4
The German-American National Bank Of Arlington	9664	5	–
Armstrong			
The First National Bank Of Armstrong	5442	5	–
Atlantic			
The Atlantic National Bank	2762	3	4
The First National Bank Of Atlantic	1836	6	–
Audubon			
The First National Bank Of Audubon	4891	4	5
Aurelia			
The Farmers National Bank Of Aurelia	9724	5	5
The First National Bank Of Aurelia	7108	5	5
Ayrshire			
The First National Bank Of Ayrshire	5479	5	6
Bagley			
The First National Bank Of Bagley	6995	4	4
Bancroft			
The First National Bank Of Bancroft	5643	4	–
Bedford			
The Bedford National Bank	5165	3	4
The First National Bank Of Bedford	2298	6	–
Belle Plaine			
The Citizens National Bank Of Belle Plaine	4754	3	4
The First National Bank Of Belle Plaine	2012	4	–
Belmond			
The First National Bank Of Belmond	8478	6	–
Blanchard			
The First National Bank Of Blanchard	4902	6	–
Blockton			
The First National Bank Of Blockton	8211	6	5
Bloomfield			
The First National Bank Of Bloomfield	1299	6	–
The National Bank Of Bloomfield	9303	4	5
Bode			
The First National Bank Of Bode	10371	5	5
Boone			
The Boone National Bank	6838	4	–
The Citizens National Bank Of Boone	13817	–	4
The First National Bank Of Boone	2051	6	–
The First National Bank Of Boone	3273	4	3
The National Bank Of Boone	3273	5	–
Brighton			
The Brighton National Bank	2033	6	–
The National Bank Of Brighton	5554	6	–
Britt			
The First National Bank Of Britt	5020	5	–
Brooklyn			
The First National Bank Of Brooklyn	3284	6	–
Buffalo Center			
The First National Bank Of Buffalo Center	5154	4	3
Burlington			
First National Bank Of Burlington	351	6	–
The First National Bank Of Burlington	351	4	–
The Merchants National Bank Of Burlington	1744	2	6
The National State Bank Of Burlington	751	4	–
Burt			
The Burt National Bank	5703	5	–
The First National Bank Of Burt	5685	3	6
Cambridge			
The First National Bank Of Cambridge	9014	4	–
Carroll			
The First National Bank Of Carroll	3969	5	–
Casey			
The Abram Rutt National Bank Of Casey	8099	4	6
Cedar Falls			
The Cedar Falls National Bank	3871	3	5
The Citizens National Bank Of Cedar Falls	5507	6	–
The First National Bank Of Cedar Falls	2177	6	–
Cedar Rapids			
The Cedar Rapids National Bank	3643	1	2
The Citizens National Bank Of Cedar Rapids	5113	6	–
The City National Bank Of Cedar Rapids	483	5	–
The Commercial National Bank Of Cedar Rapids	9168	5	–
The First National Bank Of Cedar Rapids	500	6	–
The Merchants National Bank Of Cedar Rapids	2511	2	2
Centerville			
The Centerville National Bank	2841	4	5
The Farmers National Bank Of Centerville	2197	6	–
The First National Bank Of Centreville, Centerville	337	5	4
Chariton			
National Bank And Trust Company Of Chariton	13458	–	3
The Chariton And Lucas County National Bank Of Chariton	9024	2	5
The Chariton National Bank	6014	4	–
The First National Bank Of Chariton	1724	5	–
The Lucas County National Bank Of Chariton	9024	4	–
Charles City			
The Charles City National Bank	2579	6	–
The Citizens National Bank Of Charles City	4677	4	3

City, Bank	Ch. No.	L	S
Charles City			
The Commercial National Bank Of Charles City	5979	3	3
The First National Bank Of Charles City	1810	2	–
Charter Oak			
The First National Bank Of Charter Oak	4376	4	5
Chelsea			
The First National Bank Of Chelsea	5412	4	4
Cherokee			
The First National Bank Of Cherokee	3049	5	4
The Security National Bank Of Cherokee	10711	4	5
Churdan			
The First National Bank Of Churdan	6737	5	4
Clarence			
The First National Bank Of Clarence	7682	4	6
Clarinda			
The Clarinda National Bank	3112	5	–
The First National Bank Of Clarinda	2028	5	–
Clarion			
The First National Bank Of Clarion	3796	5	5
The Wright County National Bank Of Clarion	3788	6	–
Clear Lake			
The First National Bank Of Clear Lake	7869	5	3
Clearfield			
The First National Bank Of Clearfield	9549	5	6
Clinton			
First National Bank Of Lyons At Clinton	2733	6	–
The City National Bank Of Clinton	2469	2	2
The Clinton National Bank	994	3	3
The Merchants National Bank Of Clinton	3736	3	4
Clutier			
The First National Bank Of Clutier	5366	6	–
Coin			
The First National Bank Of Coin	7309	6	6
Colfax			
The First National Bank In Colfax	13686	–	5
The First National Bank Of Colfax	7114	5	5
College Springs			
The First National Bank Of College Springs	11295	6	–
Columbus Junction			
The Louisa County National Bank Of Columbus Junction	2032	4	4
Conrad			
The First National Bank Of Conrad	9447	5	6
Coon Rapids			
The Coon Rapids National Bank	6080	6	–
The First National Bank Of Coon Rapids	5514	4	5
Corning			
The Farmers National Bank Of Corning	8100	5	–
The First National Bank Of Corning	2936	6	–
The National Bank Of Corning	4268	6	–
The Okey - Vernon National Bank Of Corning	8725	4	1
Corwith			
The First National Bank Of Corwith	5775	6	–
Corydon			
The First National Bank Of Corydon	10146	4	–
Council Bluffs			
First National Bank In Council Bluffs	14028	–	5
The City National Bank Of Council Bluffs	9306	3	3
The Commercial National Bank Of Council Bluffs	5838	3	–
The Council Bluffs National Bank	3427	6	–
The First National Bank Of Council Bluffs	1479	2	3
The Pacific National Bank Of Council Bluffs	1684	5	–
Cresco			
The First National Bank Of Cresco	4897	5	4
Creston			
The Creston National Bank	2833	4	6
The First National Bank In Creston	12636	–	2
The First National Bank Of Creston	2586	6	–
Crystal Lake			
The Farmers National Bank Of Crystal Lake	9853	5	6
The First National Bank Of Crystal Lake	5305	6	–
Cumberland			
The First National Bank Of Cumberland	7326	6	–
Davenport			
The Citizens National Bank Of Davenport	1671	4	–
The Davenport National Bank	848	6	–
The First National Bank Of Davenport	15	6	–
The First National Bank Of Davenport	2695	1	1
The Iowa National Bank Of Davenport	4022	3	–
Dayton			
The First National Bank Of Dayton	5302	4	4
De Witt			
The First National Bank Of De Witt	3182	2	3
Decorah			
The First National Bank Of Decorah	493	6	–
The National Bank Of Decorah	5081	4	5
Deep River			
The First National Bank Of Deep River	6705	6	–
Denison			
The First National Bank Of Denison	4784	3	3
Des Moines			
Central National Bank & Trust Company Of Des Moines	13321	–	1
Iowa-Des Moines National Bank & Trust Company, Des Moines	2307	–	1
The Citizens National Bank Of Des Moines	1970	4	–
The Des Moines National Bank	2583	2	–
The First National Bank Of Des Moines	389	6	–
The Iowa National Bank Of Des Moines	2307	2	–
The Merchants National Bank Of Des Moines	2631	6	–
The National State Bank Of Des Moines	950	6	–
The Second National Bank Of Des Moines	485	6	–
Des Moines			
The Valley National Bank Of Des Moines	2886	1	3
Dexter			
The First National Bank Of Dexter	10030	5	–
Diagonal			
The First National Bank Of Diagonal	9125	4	4
Dike			
The First National Bank Of Dike	5372	6	–
Doon			
The First National Bank Of Doon	6764	4	5
Dougherty			
The First National Bank Of Dougherty	5576	6	5
Dubuque			
The Commercial National Bank Of Dubuque	1801	6	–
The Consolidated National Bank Of Dubuque	2327	3	5
The Dubuque National Bank	3140	4	–
The First National Bank Of Dubuque	317	2	3
The Merchants National Bank Of Dubuque	846	6	–
The National State Bank Of Dubuque	1540	6	–
The Second National Bank Of Dubuque	2327	4	–
Dunkerton			
The First National Bank Of Dunkerton	6722	4	4
Dunlap			
The First National Bank Of Dunlap	4139	5	–
Dyersville			
The First National Bank Of Dyersville	9555	5	6
Dysart			
The First National Bank Of Dysart	5934	4	–
Eagle Grove			
First National Bank In Eagle Grove	4694	6	–
The First National Bank Of Eagle Grove	3439	6	–
The Merchants National Bank Of Eagle Grove	4694	6	–
Eldon			
The First National Bank Of Eldon	5342	4	5
Eldora			
The First National Bank Of Eldora	5140	4	5
The Hardin County National Bank Of Eldora	9233	4	4
Elkader			
The First National Bank Of Elkader	1815	4	5
Elliott			
The First National Bank Of Elliott	6857	5	5
Emmetsburg			
The Emmetsburg National Bank	8035	6	–
The First National Bank Of Emmetsburg	3337	4	–
Essex			
The Commercial National Bank Of Essex	5803	4	5
The First National Bank Of Essex	5738	4	4
Estherville			
The First National Bank Of Estherville	4700	6	–
Everly			
The First National Bank Of Everly	7828	4	5
Exira			
The First National Bank Of Exira	6870	5	6
Fairfield			
The Fairfield National Bank	8986	6	–
The First National Bank Of Fairfield	1475	3	3
Farmington			
The First National Bank Of Farmington	5579	5	–
Farnhamville			
The First National Bank Of Farnhamville	11907	5	5
Farragut			
The First National Bank Of Farragut	6700	6	6
Fayette			
The First National Bank Of Fayette	9592	6	–
Floyd			
The First National Bank Of Floyd	9821	6	6
Fonda			
The First National Bank Of Fonda	6550	5	3
Fontanelle			
The First National Bank Of Fontanelle	7061	4	6
Forest City			
The First National Bank Of Forest City	4889	4	–
The Forest City National Bank	5011	4	4
Fort Dodge			
The Commercial National Bank Of Fort Dodge	4566	2	5
The First National Bank Of Fort Dodge	1661	2	4
The Fort Dodge National Bank	2763	3	3
The Merchants National Bank Of Fort Dodge	1947	6	–
The Webster County National Bank Of Fort Dodge	11304	6	–
Fort Madison			
The First National Bank Of Fort Madison	3974	6	–
The Fort Madison National Bank	1611	6	–
Fredericksburg			
The First National Bank Of Fredericksburg	10541	3	6
Galva			
The First National Bank Of Galva	10501	4	–
Garden Grove			
The First National Bank Of Garden Grove	5464	6	–
Garner			
The Farmers National Bank Of Garner	8367	6	6
The First National Bank Of Garner	4810	4	–
George			
The First National Bank Of George	9910	4	5
Gilmore City			
The First National Bank Of Gilmore	6611	6	–
Gladbrook			
The First National Bank Of Gladbrook	5461	4	4
Glenwood			
The Mills County National Bank Of Glenwood	1862	4	6
Glidden			
The First National Bank Of Glidden	4814	4	4
Goldfield			
The First National Bank Of Goldfield	5373	6	–
Gowrie			
The First National Bank Of Gowrie	5707	4	5
Graettinger			
The First National Bank Of Graettinger	5571	5	5
Grafton			
The First National Bank Of Grafton	6610	6	–
Grand River			
The First National Bank Of Grand River	9737	5	5
Greene			
The First National Bank Of Greene	3071	6	–
The Merchants National Bank Of Greene	6880	5	–
Greenfield			
The First National Bank Of Greenfield	5334	3	–
Grinnel			
The Poweshiek County National Bank Of Grinnell	13473	–	2
Grinnell			
The Citizens National Bank Of Grinnell	7439	5	6
The First National Bank Of Grinnell	1629	6	–
The Merchants National Bank Of Grinnell	2953	5	–
Griswold			
The First National Bank Of Griswold	3048	6	–
The Griswold National Bank	8915	4	6
Grundy Center			
The First National Bank Of Grundy Center	3225	5	–
The Grundy County National Bank Of Grundy Center	3396	4	5
Guthrie			
The Citizens National Bank Of Guthrie Center	7736	6	–
Guthrie Center			
The First National Bank Of Guthrie Center	5424	3	5
Hamburg			
The Farmers National Bank Of Hamburg	6017	6	–
The First National Bank Of Hamburg	2364	6	–
Hampton			
First National Bank Of Hampton	13842	–	3
The Citizens National Bank Of Hampton	7843	3	3
The First National Bank Of Hampton	2573	6	–
Harlan			
The First National Bank Of Harlan	5207	6	–
The Harlan National Bank	10354	4	–
Harris			
The First National Bank Of Harris	6949	6	–
Hartley			
The First National Bank Of Hartley	4881	4	–
Harvey			
The First National Bank Of Harvey	6936	4	4
Havelock			
The First National Bank Of Havelock	7294	4	–
Hawarden			
First National Bank In Hawarden	13939	–	4
The First National Bank Of Hawarden	4594	5	4
Hawkeye			
The First National Bank Of Hawkeye	8900	5	5
Hedrick			
The First National Bank Of Hedrick	5540	5	–
The Hedrick National Bank	12656	5	6
Henderson			
The Farmers National Bank Of Henderson	7382	5	5
Holstein			
The First National Bank Of Holstein	4553	6	–
Hubbard			
The First National Bank Of Hubbard	8970	4	6
Hudson			
The First National Bank Of Hudson	5659	6	–
Hull			
The First National Bank Of Hull	6953	4	5
Humboldt			
The First National Bank In Humboldt	13766	–	5
The First National Bank Of Humboldt	8277	5	4
Ida Grove			
The First National Bank Of Ida Grove	3930	6	–
Imogene			
The First National Bank Of Imogene	8295	6	5
Independence			
The First National Bank Of Independence	1581	6	–
The First National Bank Of Independence	3263	2	–
The First National Bank Of The City Of Independence	3263	6	–
The Peoples National Bank Of Independence	2187	2	–
Indianola			
The First National Bank Of Indianola	1811	4	–
Inwood			
The Farmers National Bank Of Inwood	8257	4	6
The First National Bank Of Inwood	7304	5	–
Iowa City			
The First National Bank Of Iowa City	18	6	–
The First National Bank Of Iowa City	2738	3	3
The Iowa City National Bank	977	6	–
The Iowa City National Bank	2821	6	–
Iowa Falls			
The First National Bank Of Iowa Falls	3252	4	5
The State National Bank Of Iowa Falls	7521	4	5
Irston			
The First National Bank Of Ireston	4794	6	–
Jefferson			
The Farmers And Merchants National Bank Of Jefferson	10123	6	–
The First National Bank Of Jefferson	8262	5	–
Jesup			
The First National Bank Of Jesup	2856	6	–
Jewell			
The First National Bank Of Jewell Junction	5743	5	5
Kanawha			
The First National Bank Of Kanawha	9018	5	4
Keokuk			
Keokuk National Bank	14309	–	6
The First National Bank Of Keokuk	80	6	–
The Keokuk National Bank	1992	3	4

City, Bank	Ch. No.	L	S
Keokuk			
The State National Bank Of Keokuk	1441	6	–
Kimballton			
The Landmands National Bank Of Kimballton	9619	5	5
Kingsley			
The Farmers National Bank Of Kingsley	9116	6	4
Klemme			
The First National Bank Of Klemme	6659	5	4
Knoxville			
Knoxville-Citizens National Bank & Trust Co Of Knoxville	12849	–	6
The Citizens National Bank Of Knoxville	4633	4	3
The Community National Bank And Trust Company	13707	–	4
The Knoxville National Bank	1871	3	–
The Marion County National Bank Of Knoxville	1986	4	–
La Porte City			
The First National Bank Of La Porte City	4114	4	–
Lake City			
The First National Bank Of Lake City	4966	5	5
Lake Mills			
The First National Bank Of Lake Mills	5123	5	–
Lansing			
The First National Bank Of Lansing	405	6	–
Laurens			
The First National Bank Of Laurens	4795	4	6
Lawler			
The First National Bank Of Lawler	10599	3	–
Lehigh			
The First National Bank Of Lehigh	5868	5	5
Lemars			
The First National Bank Of Lemars	2728	3	4
The Lemars National Bank	2818	6	–
Lenox			
First National Bank In Lenox	14040	–	6
The First National Bank Of Lenox	5517	4	4
Leon			
The Exchange National Bank Of Leon	5489	3	–
The First National Bank Of Leon	1696	6	–
Lime Springs			
The First National Bank Of Lime Springs	6750	6	4
Lineville			
The First National Bank Of Lineville	7261	6	–
Linn Grove			
The First National Bank Of Linn Grove	7137	6	5
Lisbon			
The First National Bank Of Lisbon	2182	6	–
Little Rock			
The First National Bank Of Little Rock	8119	5	6
Logan			
The First National Bank Of Logan	6771	4	4
Lorimor			
The First National Bank Of Lorimor	12248	5	4
Lost Nation			
The First National Bank Of Lost Nation	5402	5	5
Lyons			
The Citizens National Bank Of Lyons	4536	6	–
The First National Bank Of Lyons	66	6	–
The First National Bank Of Lyons	2733	4	–
Macksburg			
The Macksburg National Bank	6852	6	6
Malvern			
The Farmers National Bank Of Malvern	4834	6	–
The First National Bank Of Malvern	2247	5	–
The Malvern National Bank	8057	6	6
Manchester			
The First National Bank Of Manchester	4221	4	–
Manilla			
The First National Bank Of Manilla	5873	4	5
The Manilla National Bank	6041	5	–
Manning			
The First National Bank Of Manning	3455	4	3
Maquoketa			
The First National Bank Of Maquoketa	999	5	5
Marathon			
The First National Bank Of Marathon	4789	6	5
Marcus			
The First National Bank Of Marcus	9819	6	–
Marengo			
The First National Bank Of Marengo	2484	3	–
Marion			
The First National Bank Of Marion	117	6	–
The First National Bank Of Marion	2753	4	4
Marshalltown			
The City National Bank Of Marshalltown	4359	6	–
The Commercial National Bank Of Marshalltown	2971	6	–
The Farmers National Bank Of Marshalltown	2115	6	–
The First National Bank Of Marshalltown	411	5	–
Mason City			
The City National Bank Of Mason City	4587	5	–
The First National Bank Of Mason City	2574	2	2
The Security National Bank Of Mason City	10428	4	–
Mcgregor			
The First National Bank Of Mcgregor	323	4	5
Melvin			
The First National Bank Of Melvin	5616	5	–
Milford			
The First National Bank Of Milford	5539	5	–
The Milford National Bank	9298	6	–
The Security National Bank Of Milford	9298	6	5
Milton			
The National Bank Of Milton	10243	6	6
Missouri Valley			
The First National Bank Of Missouri Valley	3189	5	4
Monroe			
The First National Bank Of Monroe	2215	6	–
The Monroe National Bank	7357	6	6
Montezuma			
The First National Bank Of Montezuma	2961	5	6
Monticello			
The Monticello National Bank	2080	6	–
Montour			
The First National Bank Of Montour	7469	5	3
Moulton			
The First National Bank Of Moulton	5319	5	–
Mount Pleasant			
The First National Bank Of Mt. Pleasant	299	3	4
The National State Bank Of Mt. Pleasant	922	4	–
Muscatine			
The First National Bank Of Muscatine	1577	4	2
The Merchants Exchange National Bank Of Muscatine	1577	6	–
The Muscatine National Bank	692	6	–
Nashua			
The First National Bank Of Nashua	2411	6	–
Nevada			
Nevada National Bank	14065	–	6
The First National Bank Of Nevada	2555	3	–
New Hampton			
The First National Bank Of New Hampton	2588	4	–
The Second National Bank Of New Hampton	7607	3	4
New London			
The First National Bank Of New London	5420	6	–
The New London National Bank	8352	5	6
New Sharon			
The First National Bank Of New Sharon	8950	5	–
Newell			
The First National Bank Of Newell	10191	5	4
Newton			
The First National Bank Of Newton	650	6	–
The First National Bank Of Newton	2644	4	5
The Newton National Bank	13609	–	3
Nora Springs			
The First National Bank Of Nora Springs	4761	5	5
Northboro			
The First National Bank Of Northboro	9015	4	6
Northwood			
The First National Bank Of Northwood	8373	5	4
Norway			
The First National Bank Of Norway	7287	5	–
Odebolt			
The Farmers National Bank Of Odebolt	5817	6	–
The First National Bank Of Odebolt	4511	3	3
Oelwein			
The First National Bank On Oelwein	5778	2	4
Olin			
The First National Bank Of Olin	7585	5	–
Orange City			
The First National Bank Of Orange City	6132	6	–
Osage			
Osage Farmers National Bank, Osage	4885	–	4
The Farmers National Bank Of Osage	4885	5	–
The Osage National Bank	1618	4	–
Osceola			
The First National Bank Of Osceola	1776	6	–
The Osceola National Bank	6033	5	–
Oskaloosa			
The Farmers And Traders National Bank Of Oskaloosa	2895	6	–
The Farmers National Bank Of Oskaloosa	8076	4	–
The First National Bank Of Oskaloosa	147	6	–
The National State Bank Of Oskaloosa	1101	6	–
The Oskaloosa National Bank	2417	4	–
Ottumwa			
The First National Bank Of Ottumwa	107	4	4
The Iowa National Bank Of Ottumwa	1726	5	6
The Ottumwa National Bank	2621	3	5
Panora			
The Guthrie County National Bank Of Panora	3226	4	–
Parkersburg			
The First National Bank Of Parkersburg	9846	5	–
Pella			
The Citizens National Bank Of Pella	8047	5	–
The First National Bank Of Pella	1891	6	–
The Pella National Bank	2063	3	4
Perry			
The First National Bank Of Perry	3026	4	–
The Peoples National Bank Of Perry	10130	5	–
The Perry National Bank, Perry	10130	3	–
Peterson			
The First National Bank Of Peterson	4601	5	4
Pleasantville			
The First National Bank Of Pleasantville	5564	5	–
Pocahontas			
The First National Bank In Pocahontas	12544	6	–
The First National Bank Of Pocahontas	6303	5	–
Pomeroy			
The First National Bank Of Pomeroy	6063	4	6
Prairie City			
The First National Bank Of Prairie City	6755	5	5
Prescott			
The First National Bank Of Prescott	5912	4	4
Preston			
The First National Bank Of Preston	8273	5	5
Primghar			
The Farmers National Bank Of Primghar	6650	6	–
The First National Bank Of Primghar	4155	5	4
Radcliffe			
The First National Bank Of Radcliffe	6435	5	4
Rake			
The Farmers First National Bank Of Rake	11735	–	3
Randolph			
The First National Bank Of Randolph	7833	5	5
Red Oak			
The Farmers National Bank Of Red Oak	6056	4	6
The First National Bank Of Red Oak	2130	4	3
The Red Oak National Bank	3055	4	4
The Valley National Bank Of Red Oak	2230	6	–
Remsen			
The First National Bank Of Remsen	6975	4	4
Renwick			
The First National Bank Of Renwick	7988	6	–
Riceville			
The First National Bank Of Riceville	8442	5	4
Richland			
The First National Bank Of Richland	5611	6	–
Rippey			
The First National Bank Of Rippey	7609	5	4
Rock Rapids			
The First National Bank Of Rock Rapids	3153	3	5
The Lyon County National Bank Of Rock Rapids	7089	4	5
Rock Valley			
The First National Bank Of Rock Valley	5200	4	4
Rockford			
The First National Bank Of Rockford	3053	5	–
Rockwell			
The First National Bank Of Rockwell	10217	5	6
Rockwell City			
The First National Bank Of Rockwell City	5185	4	–
The Rockwell City National Bank	11582	6	5
Roland			
The First National Bank Of Roland	11249	5	2
Rolfe			
The First National Bank Of Rolfe	4954	5	–
Royal			
The Citizens National Bank Of Royal	10395	5	–
Ruthven			
The First National Bank Of Ruthven	5541	5	–
Sac City			
The First National Bank Of Sac City	4450	4	–
Saint Ansgar			
The First National Bank Of Saint Ansgar	10684	5	4
Sanborn			
The First National Bank Of Sanborn	4824	6	–
Seymour			
The First National Bank Of Seymour	8247	5	6
The Seymour National Bank	11210	6	–
Shannon City			
The First National Bank Of Shannon City	9723	4	5
Sheffield			
The First National Bank Of Sheffield	12430	6	5
Sheldon			
The First National Bank Of Sheldon	3848	3	–
The Sheldon National Bank	7880	4	3
Shenandoah			
Shenandoah National Bank	12950	6	3
The Commercial National Bank Of Shenandoah	8971	6	–
The Farmers National Bank Of Shenandoah	11588	6	–
The First National Bank Of Shenandoah	2363	6	–
The Shenandoah National Bank	2679	5	–
Sibley			
The First National Bank Of Sibley	3320	6	4
Sidney			
The National Bank Of Sidney	5145	4	4
Sigourney			
The First National Bank Of Sigourney	1786	3	6
Sioux Center			
The First National Bank Of Sioux Center	7369	6	5
Sioux City			
Sioux National Bank In Sioux City	4510	4	4
The American National Bank Of Sioux City	3940	6	–
The Citizens National Bank Of Sioux City	1976	6	–
The City National Bank Of Sioux City	7401	6	–
The Commercial National Bank Of Sioux City	4630	6	–
The Corn Exchange National Bank Of Sioux City	4235	6	–
The First National Bank Of Sioux City	1757	2	3
The Iowa State National Bank Of Sioux City	3968	4	–
The Live Stock National Bank Of Sioux City	5022	2	1
The Merchants National Bank Of Sioux City	4209	6	–
The National Bank Of Commerce Of Sioux City	10139	5	–
The National Bank Of Sioux City	4431	6	–
The Northwestern National Bank Of Sioux City	4510	4	–
The Security National Bank Of Sioux City	3124	3	3
The Sioux National Bank Of Sioux City	2535	5	–
The Toy National Bank Of Sioux City	10139	3	2
Sioux Rapids			
First National Bank, Sioux Rapids	7189	6	–
The First National Bank In Sioux Rapids	13400	–	5
The First National Bank Of Sioux Rapids	9585	4	–
Spencer			
The Citizens National Bank Of Spencer	6941	4	–
The First National Bank Of Spencer	3898	6	–
Spirit Lake			
First National Bank In Spirit Lake	13020	5	3
The First National Bank Of Spirit Lake	4758	4	–
The Spirit Lake National Bank	8032	5	–
Stanton			
The First National Bank Of Stanton	6434	6	6
State Center			
The First National Bank Of State Centre	8931	6	4
Storm Lake			
The Citizens First National Bank Of Storm Lake	10034	5	5

City, Bank	Ch. No.	L	S
Storm Lake			
The Citizens National Bank Of Storm Lake	10034	5	–
The Commercial National Bank Of Storm Lake	10223	6	–
The First National Bank Of Storm Lake	2595	5	–
Story City			
The First National Bank Of Story City	9017	4	3
The Story City National Bank	10222	5	–
Strawberry Point			
The First National Bank Of Strawberry Point	9069	5	–
Stuart			
The First National Bank Of Stuart	2721	4	5
Sumner			
The First National Bank Of Sumner	8198	3	2
Sutherland			
The First National Bank Of Sutherland	3610	6	
Swea City			
The First National Bank Of Swea City	5637	5	–
Tabor			
The First National Bank Of Tabor	4609	5	–
Tama City			
The First National Bank Of Tama	1880	4	–
The First National Bank Of Tama City	1880	5	–
Terril			
The First National Bank Of Terril	10238	4	–
Thompson			
The First National Bank Of Thompson	5054	5	4
Thornton			
The First National Bank Of Thornton	8340	6	3
Tipton			
The City National Bank Of Tipton	6760	3	–
The First National Bank Of Tipton	2983	5	–
Tipton National Bank	13232	–	4
Titonka			
The First National Bank Of Titonka	5597	5	6
Toledo			
The First National Bank Of Toledo	6432	4	–
The National Bank Of Toledo	13073	–	3
Traer			
The First National Bank Of Traer	5135	4	3
Valley Junction			
The First National Bank Of Valley Junction	5891	6	4
Villisca			
The First National Bank Of Villisca	2766	3	6
The Nodaway Valley National Bank Of Villisca	14041	–	3
The Villisca National Bank	7506	5	4
Vinton			
The Farmers National Bank Of Vinton	5088	4	–
The First National Bank Of Vinton	1593	6	–
Washington			
The Citizens National Bank Of Washington	6122	6	–
The First National Bank Of Washington	398	6	–
The First National Bank Of Washington	2656	6	–
The Washington National Bank	1762	4	4
Waterloo			
The Black Hawk National Bank Of Waterloo	6854	3	–
The Commercial National Bank Of Waterloo	2910	3	–
The First National Bank Of Waterloo	792	5	–
The Leavitt And Johnson National Bank Of Waterloo	5120	2	–
The National Bank Of Waterloo	13702	–	4
The Pioneer National Bank Of Waterloo	5120	4	3
The Waterloo National Bank	5700	5	–
Waukon			
The First National Bank Of Waukon	4021	3	
The Peoples National Bank Of Waukon	10207	3	–
Waverly			
The First National Bank Of Waverly	3105	3	3
Webster City			
The Farmers National Bank Of Webster City	3420	5	4
The First National Bank Of Webster City	1874	3	4
The Hamilton County National Bank Of Webster City	2984	6	–
Wesley			
The First National Bank Of Wesley	5457	6	–
West Union			
The Fayette County National Bank Of West Union	2015	2	5
What Cheer			
The First National Bank Of What Cheer	3192	4	3
Whiting			
First National Bank Of Whiting	10861	5	5
Williams			
The First National Bank Of Williams	5585	5	6
Winfield			
The Farmers National Bank Of Winfield	10640	4	5
Winterset			
The Citizens National Bank Of Winterset	2002	4	3
The First National Bank Of Winterset	1403	5	6
The National Bank Of Winterset	1403	6	–
Woodbine			
The First National Bank Of Woodbine	4745	4	4
Wyoming			
The First National Bank Of Wyoming	1943	4	6

KANSAS

City, Bank	Ch. No.	L	S
Abilene			
The Abilene National Bank	3777	4	4
The Farmers National Bank Of Abilene	8379	5	4
The First National Bank Of Abilene	2427	6	–
Alma			
First National Bank In Alma	13601	–	4
The Alma National Bank	5104	5	5
The Commercial National Bank Of Alma	8357	6	–
The Farmers National Bank Of Alma	10195	6	6
The First National Bank Of Alma	3769	6	–
Almena			
The First National Bank Of Almena	8255	4	4
Americus			
The Farmers National Bank Of Americus	10902	6	–
Anthony			
The Anthony National Bank	3394	6	–
The Citizens National Bank Of Anthony	6752	5	4
The First National Bank Of Anthony	3385	5	4
The Harper County National Bank Of Anthony	3384	6	–
Arkansas City			
The American National Bank Of Arkansas City	3992	6	–
The Farmers National Bank Of Arkansas City	4640	6	–
The First National Bank Of Arkansas City	3360	6	
The Home National Bank Of Arkansas City	4487	5	4
The Security National Bank Of Arkansas City	10746	5	4
Ashland			
The First National Bank Of Ashland	3710	6	–
The Stockgrowers National Bank Of Ashland	5386	6	6
Atchison			
The Atchison National Bank	2082	5	–
The City National Bank Of Atchison	11405	5	4
The Exchange National Bank Of Atchison	2758	4	–
The First National Bank Of Atchison	1672	3	–
The United States National Bank Of Atchison	3612	6	–
Attica			
The First National Bank Of Attica	10359	6	6
Atwood			
The Farmers National Bank Of Atwood	10644	–	5
Augusta			
The First National Bank Of Augusta	6643	6	5
Barnard			
The First National Bank Of Barnard	8396	6	5
Baxter Springs			
The American National Bank Of Baxter Springs	11056	6	4
The Baxter National Bank Of Baxter Springs	5952	5	5
The First National Bank Of Baxter Springs	1838	6	–
Beaver			
The Farmers National Bank Of Beaver	11177	–	5
Belleville			
The First National Bank Of Belleville	3386	6	–
The Peoples National Bank Of Belleville	9559	6	5
Beloit			
The First National Bank Of Beloit	3231	4	4
The German National Bank Of Northern Kansas At Beloit	6701	6	–
The Union National Bank Of Beloit	6701	6	–
Bonner Springs			
The First National Bank Of Bonner Springs	9197	5	6
Burlingame			
The Burlingame National Bank	9157	6	–
The First National Bank Of Burlingame	4040	6	5
Burlington			
The Burlington National Bank	1979	5	–
The Farmers National Bank Of Burlington	6955	5	–
The Peoples National Bank Of Burlington	3170	5	5
Burr Oak			
The First National Bank Of Burr Oak	3880	6	–
The Jewell County National Bank Of Burr Oak	7302	5	5
Caldwell			
The Caldwell National Bank	6333	6	–
The First National Bank Of Caldwell	3658	6	–
Caney			
The Caney Valley National Bank Of Caney	5349	5	4
The Home National Bank Of Caney	5516	5	6
Cawker City			
The Farmers And Merchants National Bank Of Cawker City	4618	6	–
The First National Bank Of Cawker City	2640	6	–
Cedar Vale			
The Cedar Vale National Bank	5608	6	6
The Citizens National Bank Of Cedar Vale	6530	6	4
The Dosbaugh National Bank Of Cedar Vale	6530	6	–
Centralia			
The First National Bank Of Centralia	3824	5	5
Chanute			
The Chanute National Bank	4036	6	–
The First National Bank Of Chanute	3819	5	2
The National Bank Of Chanute	6072	6	–
Cherokee			
The First National Bank Of Cherokee	5447	6	5
Cherryvale			
The Cherryvale National Bank	4288	6	–
The First National Bank Of Cherryvale	3277	6	–
The Montgomery County National Bank Of Cherryvale	4749	5	5
The Peoples National Bank Of Cherryvale	7383	6	–
Chetopa			
The First National Bank Of Chetopa	1902	6	–
The National Bank Of Chetopa	11374	6	6
Cimarron			
The First National Bank In Cimarron	13329	–	5
The First National Bank Of Cimarron	3751	6	–
Clay Center			
The First National Bank Of Clay Center	3072	5	5
The Peoples National Bank Of Clay Center	3345	5	4
Clifton			
The First National Bank Of Clifton	7178	3	5
Clyde			
The Exchange National Bank Of Clyde	11775	–	5
The First National Bank Of Clyde	3115	6	–
Coffeyville			
The Condon National Bank Of Coffeyville	6797	4	3
The First National Bank Of Coffeyville	3324	5	3
Colby			
The Citizens National Bank Of Colby	11047	6	–
The First National Bank Of Colby	3512	6	–
The Thomas County National Bank Of Colby	13076	3	3
Coldwater			
The Coldwater National Bank	6767	5	5
The First National Bank Of Coldwater	3703	6	–
Collyer			
The First National Bank Of Collyer	11855	–	5
Colony			
The First National Bank Of Colony	11631	6	6
Columbus			
The First National Bank Of Columbus	6103	6	5
Concordia			
The Citizens National Bank Of Concordia	3748	6	–
The Concordia National Bank	3090	6	–
The First National Bank Of Concordia	3066	6	–
Conway Springs			
The First National Bank Of Conway Springs	8467	5	5
Cottonwood Falls			
The Chase County National Bank Of Cottonwood Falls	2764	6	–
The Exchange National Bank Of Cottonwood Falls	6590	4	4
Council Grove			
The Council Grove National Bank	5757	4	5
The First National Bank Of Council Grove	2001	6	–
Delphos			
The First National Bank Of Delphos	7532	5	6
Dexter			
The First National Bank Of Dexter	9225	3	–
Dighton			
The First National Bank Of Dighton	3888	6	–
The First National Bank Of Dighton	9773	6	3
Dodge City			
First National Bank In Dodge City	7285	6	5
The First National Bank Of Dodge City	3596	6	–
The National Bank Of Commerce Of Dodge City	7285	6	–
Downs			
The Downs National Bank	11318	6	5
The Exchange National Bank Of Downs	3563	6	–
The First National Bank Of Downs	3569	6	–
Edmond			
The First National Bank Of Edmond	9160	6	–
Edna			
The First National Bank Of Edna	7590	6	5
El Dorado			
The El Dorado National Bank	6494	5	4
The Exchange National Bank Of El Dorado	3213	6	–
The Farmers And Merchants National Bank Of El Dorado	4981	5	5
The First National Bank Of El Dorado	1957	6	–
The Merchants National Bank Of El Dorado	3833	6	–
The National Bank Of El Dorado	3035	6	–
Elk City			
The First National Bank Of Elk City	8145	6	5
The Peoples National Bank Of Elk City	8708	6	–
Ellsworth			
The Central National Bank Of Ellsworth	3447	6	6
The First National Bank Of Ellsworth	3249	6	–
Emporia			
The Citizens National Bank Of Emporia	5498	4	4
The Commercial National Bank And Trust Company Of Emporia	11781	5	4
The Emporia National Bank	1983	3	–
The First National Bank Of Emporia	1915	2	–
Englewood			
The First National Bank Of Englewood	9097	6	–
Erie			
The First National Bank Of Erie	3963	4	–
Eureka			
The Citizens National Bank Of Eureka	5655	6	5
The First National Bank Of Eureka	3148	6	–
The Home National Bank Of Eureka	7303	6	6
Formoso			
The First National Bank Of Formoso	8596	5	5
Fort Leavenworth			
The Army National Bank Of Fort Leavenworth	8796	4	3
Fort Scott			
The Citizens National Bank Of Fort Scott	3175	4	4
The First National Bank Of Fort Scott	1763	6	–
The Merchants National Bank Of Fort Scott	1927	6	–
Fowler			
The First National Bank Of Fowler	9595	6	5
Frankfort			
The First National Bank Of Frankfort	2809	6	–
Fredonia			
The First National Bank Of Fredonia	3835	6	–
The Fredonia National Bank	7218	6	–
Galena			
The Galena National Bank	4798	5	5
Garden City			
The Finney County National Bank Of Garden City	3900	6	–
The First National Bank Of Garden City	3448	6	4
The Garden City National Bank	7646	6	4
Garnett			
The Anderson County National Bank Of Garnett	4032	6	–
The First National Bank Of Garnett	2973	6	–
The National Bank Of Commerce Of Garnett	5292	5	6

City, Bank	Ch. No.	L	S
Gaylord			
The First National Bank Of Gaylord	6970	6	5
Girard			
The First National Bank Of Girard	3216	5	5
Glasco			
The First National Bank Of Glasco	7683	4	5
Goff			
The First National Bank Of Goff	7416	6	5
Goodland			
The Farmers National Bank Of Goodland	7882	6	–
The First National Bank In Goodland	14163	–	6
The First National Bank Of Goodland	6039	6	6
Great Bend			
The Citizens National Bank Of Great Bend	5705	4	5
The Farmers National Bank Of Great Bend	11707	4	4
The First National Bank Of Great Bend	3363	4	4
Greenleaf			
The First National Bank Of Greenleaf	3567	6	–
Greensburg			
The Farmers National Bank Of Greensburg	10557	6	6
The First National Bank In Greensburg	10557	–	6
The First National Bank Of Greensburg	3667	6	–
Gypsum			
The Gypsum Valley National Bank Of Gypsum	9695	5	4
Halstead			
The Halstead National Bank	3443	6	–
Hamilton			
The First National Bank Of Hamilton	6932	6	5
Harper			
First National Bank In Harper	8307	6	5
The First National Bank Of Harper	3265	6	–
The Harper National Bank	3431	6	–
The National Bank Of Harper	8307	6	–
The Security National Bank Of Harper	8308	6	–
Hartford			
The Hartford National Bank	8197	6	6
Havensville			
The First National Bank Of Havensville	5506	6	5
Hays City			
The First National Bank Of Hays City	3885	6	–
Herington			
The First National Bank Of Herington	4058	6	5
Hiawatha			
The First National Bank Of Hiawatha	2589	4	5
Highland			
The First National Bank Of Highland	9136	6	6
Hill City			
The First National Bank Of Hill City	3758	6	–
Hillsboro			
The First National Bank Of Hillsboro	6120	6	4
Hoisington			
The First National Bank Of Hoisington	9232	5	5
The Hoisington National Bank	12694	–	5
Holton			
The First National Bank Of Holton	3061	6	–
The National Bank Of Holton	5041	6	–
Horton			
The First National Bank Of Horton	3810	5	5
Howard			
The First National Bank Of Howard	3242	4	5
The Howard National Bank	3794	5	5
Hoxie			
The First National Bank Of Hoxie	5687	5	5
Hugoton			
The First National Bank Of Hugoton	11300	–	5
Humboldt			
The Humboldt First National Bank, Humboldt	3807	6	–
The Humboldt National Bank	6963	6	5
Hutchinson			
The American National Bank Of Hutchinson	10765	6	4
The Commercial National Bank Of Hutchinson	8430	4	–
The Exchange National Bank Of Hutchinson	13106	–	5
The Farmers National Bank Of Hutchinson	10765	6	
The First National Bank Of Hutchinson	3180	3	–
The Hutchinson National Bank	3199	6	–
The National Bank Of Commerce Of Hutchinson	3861	6	–
Independence			
Citizens-First National Bank Of Independence	4592	5	4
First National Bank In Independence	4592	–	5
The Citizens National Bank Of Independence	4592	5	–
The Commercial National Bank Of Independence	4499	4	5
The First National Bank Of Independence	3021	6	–
The Security National Bank Of Independence	13492	–	4
Iola			
First National Bank Of Iola	5287	5	–
The Northrup National Bank Of Iola	5287	5	–
Jetmore			
The First National Bank Of Jetmore	3805	6	–
Jewell City			
The First National Bank Of Jewell City	3591	6	5
Junction City			
The Central National Bank Of Junction City	4284	4	5
The First National Bank Of Junction City	1977	6	–
The First National Bank Of Junction City	3543	4	5
Kanorado			
The First National Bank Of Kanorado	11860	–	5
Kansas City			
Security National Bank Of Kansas City	13801	–	1
The Bankers National Bank Of Kansas City	8602	6	–
The Commercial National Bank Of Kansas City	6311	2	2
Kansas City			
The First National Bank Of Kansas City	3706	6	–
The Inter-State National Bank Of Kansas City, Kansas	4381	4	–
The Peoples National Bank Of Kansas City	9309	4	3
The Wyandotte National Bank Of Kansas City	3726	6	–
Kensington			
The First National Bank Of Kensington	7493	6	5
Kingman			
The Citizens National Bank Of Kingman	3737	6	–
The Farmers National Bank Of Kingman	7412	6	–
The First National Bank Of Kingman	3509	6	–
The Kingman National Bank	3559	6	–
Kinsley			
The First National Bank Of Kinsley	3759	6	–
The National Bank Of Kinsley	5810	6	–
Kiowa			
The First National Bank Of Kiowa	8220	6	5
Kirwin			
The First National Bank Of Kirwin	3454	6	–
La Harpe			
The First National Bank Of La Harpe	7226	5	5
Lacrosse			
The First National Bank Of Lacrosse	3970	6	–
Larned			
First National Bank In Larned	7125	5	4
The First National Bank Of Larned	2666	6	–
The Moffet Brothers National Bank Of Larned	7125	5	–
Lawrence			
The Douglas County National Bank Of Lawrence	3849	6	–
The First National Bank Of Lawrence	3584	–	3
The Lawrence National Bank	3849	4	3
The Merchants National Bank Of Lawrence	3584	3	4
The National Bank Of Lawrence	1590	6	–
The Second National Bank Of Lawrence	1732	6	–
The Watkins National Bank Of Lawrence	3881	4	–
Leavenworth			
The First National Bank Of Leavenworth	182	4	4
The Leavenworth National Bank	3033	4	4
The Manufacturers National Bank Of Leavenworth	3908	5	–
The Metropolitan National Bank Of Leavenworth	3194	6	–
The Second National Bank Of Leavenworth	1448	6	–
Lebanon			
The First National Bank Of Lebanon	5799	6	5
Leoti City			
The First National Bank Of Leoti City	3844	6	–
Leroy			
The First National Bank Of Leroy	6149	6	5
Lewis			
The First National Bank Of Lewis	10863	6	–
Liberal			
The First National Bank Of Liberal	6720	6	6
The Peoples National Bank Of Liberal	13406	–	4
Lincoln			
The Farmers National Bank Of Lincoln	6672	6	4
The First National Bank Of Lincoln	3464	6	–
Lindsborg			
The First National Bank Of Lindsborg	3589	6	5
Logan			
The First National Bank Of Logan	6841	5	5
Longton			
The First National Bank Of Longton	8525	6	–
The Home National Bank Of Longton	9911	6	5
Louisburg			
The First National Bank Of Louisburg	11798	6	5
Lucas			
The First National Bank Of Lucas	7561	6	5
Luray			
The First National Bank Of Luray	10065	6	5
Lyndon			
The First National Bank Of Lyndon	7222	5	5
Lyons			
The Chandler National Bank Of Lyons	14048	–	3
The First National Bank Of Lyons	3577	6	–
The Lyons National Bank	5353	5	5
Madison			
The First National Bank Of Madison	5529	6	5
Manhattan			
The First National Bank Of Manhattan	2094	5	–
The First National Bank Of Manhattan	3782	4	4
The Union National Bank Of Manhattan	4008	4	4
Mankato			
First National Bank In Mankato	6817	6	3
The First National Bank Of Mankato	3745	6	–
The Jewell County National Bank Of Mankato	3812	6	–
The Mankato National Bank	6817	6	–
Marion			
The Cottonwood Valley National Bank Of Marion	3928	6	–
The Farmers And Drovers National Bank Of Marion	10980	–	5
The First National Bank Of Marion	3018	6	–
The Marion National Bank	7911	6	5
Marysville			
The First National Bank Of Marysville	2791	5	–
Mayetta			
The First National Bank Of Mayetta	9934	6	5
Mc Cune			
The First National Bank Of Mc Cune	12191	5	5
Mcpherson			
The First National Bank Of Mcpherson	3521	6	–
The Mcpherson National Bank	3803	6	–
The Second National Bank Of Mcpherson	3791	6	–
Meade			
The First National Bank Of Meade	7192	6	5
Meade Center			
The First National Bank Of Meade Center	3695	6	–
The Meade County National Bank Of Meade Center	3853	6	–
Medicine Lodge			
The Citizens National Bank Of Medicine Lodge	3594	6	–
The First National Bank Of Medicine Lodge	3253	6	–
Millbrook			
The First National Bank Of Millbrook	3758	6	–
Minneapolis			
The Citizens National Bank Of Minneapolis	4931	5	5
The First National Bank Of Minneapolis	3353	6	–
The Minneapolis National Bank	3731	5	–
Moline			
The First National Bank Of Moline	7318	6	6
The Moline National Bank	8369	6	–
Mound Valley			
The First National Bank Of Mound Valley	8107	6	–
Mount Hope			
The First National Bank Of Mt. Hope	5559	6	6
Natoma			
The First National Bank Of Natoma	9384	5	5
Neodesha			
The First National Bank Of Neodesha	6914	6	5
The Neodesha National Bank	6895	6	5
Ness City			
First National Bank In Ness City	8142	–	6
The Citizens National Bank Of Ness City	8081	5	–
The First National Bank Of Ness City	3542	6	–
The National Bank Of Ness City	8142	6	6
Newton			
The First National Bank Of Newton	2777	6	5
The German National Bank Of Newton	3473	6	–
The Midland National Bank Of Newton	4860	6	5
The Newton National Bank	3297	6	–
Norcatur			
Decatur County National Bank Of Oberlin	8290	–	6
The First National Bank Of Norcatur	8290	6	6
Norton			
The First National Bank Of Norton	3687	5	4
The National Bank Of Norton	8339	6	–
Nortonville			
The First National Bank Of Nortonville	5359	6	6
Oakley			
The First National Bank Of Oakley	10041	6	4
Oberlin			
The Farmers National Bank Of Oberlin	7298	6	5
The First National Bank Of Oberlin	3511	6	–
The Oberlin National Bank	4642	5	4
Olathe			
The First National Bank Of Olathe	1828	6	–
The First National Bank Of Olathe	3720	5	4
Onaga			
The First National Bank Of Onaga	12353	6	5
Osage City			
The First National Bank Of Osage City	3813	6	–
Osborne			
The Exchange National Bank Of Osborne	3472	5	4
The Farmers National Bank Of Osborne	5834	6	5
The First National Bank Of Osborne	3319	5	–
Oswego			
First National Bank At Oswego	11576	6	5
The First National Bank Of Oswego	3038	5	–
Ottawa			
The First National Bank Of Ottawa	1718	4	4
The Peoples National Bank Of Ottawa	1910	4	4
Overbrook			
The First National Bank Of Overbrook	7195	5	5
Paola			
The First National Bank Of Paola	1864	5	–
The Miami County National Bank Of Paola	3350	4	3
The National Bank Of Paola	3795	6	–
The Peoples National Bank Of Paola	3991	6	–
Parsons			
The Farmers National Bank Of Parsons	11537	5	–
The First National Bank Of Parsons	1951	3	5
Peabody			
The First National Bank Of Peabody	3134	6	6
Phillipsburg			
The First National Bank Of Phillipsburg	3601	4	5
Pittsburg			
American Exchange National Bank Of Commerce In Pittsburg	8418	6	–
The First National Bank Of Pittsburg	3463	3	4
The Manufacturers National Bank Of Pittsburg	4136	6	–
The National Bank Of Commerce In Pittsburg	8418	6	–
The National Bank Of Pittsburg	3475	5	4
Plainville			
The First National Bank Of Plainville	7313	6	–
Pleasanton			
The First National Bank Of Pleasanton	8803	6	6
Prairie View			
The First National Bank Of Prairie View	9373	5	5
Pratt			
First National Bank In Pratt	6229	6	5
The First National Bank Of Pratt	3649	6	–
The National Bank Of Pratt	6229	6	–
The Pratt County National Bank Of Pratt	3787	6	–
Randall			
The Randall National Bank	11887	6	–
Richmond			
The First National Bank Of Richmond	11728	6	–
The Peoples National Bank Of Richmond	11728	–	4
Russell			
The First National Bank Of Russell	3657	6	–
Russell Springs			
The First National Bank Of Russell Springs	3775	6	–
Sabetha			
The Citizens National Bank Of Sabetha	2990	6	–
The First National Bank Of Sabetha	2954	6	–

City, Bank	Ch. No.	L	S
Sabetha			
The National Bank Of Sabetha	4626	4	5
Saint John			
The First National Bank Of Saint John	3467	6	5
The St. John National Bank	7844	5	5
Saint Marys			
The First National Bank Of St. Marys	3374	3	5
The National Bank Of Saint Marys	4619	6	–
Salina			
The American National Bank Of Salina	4317	6	–
The Farmers National Bank Of Salina	4742	4	4
The First National Bank Of Salina	2538	6	–
The National Bank Of America At Salina	4945	4	4
The Salina National Bank	3531	6	–
Scandia			
First National Bank In Belleville	3779	5	4
The First National Bank Of Scandia	3779	6	–
The National Bank Of Belleville	3779	6	–
Scott City			
The First National Bank Of Scott City	8808	5	4
Sedan			
The First National Bank Of Sedan	3855	5	5
The Peoples National Bank Of Sedan	7535	6	–
The Sedan National Bank	4150	6	–
Seneca			
The First National Bank Of Seneca	2952	5	–
The National Bank Of Seneca	5101	5	4
Smith Center			
The Smith County National Bank Of Smith Center	3630	6	–
Smith Centre			
The First National Bank Of Smith Centre	3546	6	5
Solomon			
The Solomon National Bank	9794	5	6
Spearville			
The First National Bank Of Spearville	10161	6	5
Stafford			
The Farmers National Bank Of Stafford	8883	6	5
The First National Bank Of Stafford	3852	6	–
Sterling			
The First National Bank Of Sterling	3207	6	5
Stockton			
The First National Bank Of Stockton	3440	6	–
The National State Bank Of Stockton	8274	6	–
The Stockton National Bank	7815	6	5
Strong City			
The Strong City National Bank	3002	6	–
Syracuse			
The First National Bank Of Syracuse	8114	6	5
Thayer			
The First National Bank Of Thayer	9465	6	4
Topeka			
National Bank Of Topeka	12740	–	3
The Capital National Bank Of Topeka	7907	6	–
The Central National Bank Of Topeka	3078	2	2
The Farmers National Bank Of Topeka	10390	4	4
The First National Bank Of Topeka	1660	6	–
The First National Bank Of Topeka	2646	4	–
The Kansas National Bank Of Topeka	3790	6	–
The Kansas Valley National Bank	1660	6	–
The Kaw Valley National Bank Of Topeka	11398	3	5
The Merchants National Bank Of Topeka	3909	3	3
The State National Bank Of Topeka	2192	6	–
The Topeka National Bank	1945	6	–
Toronto			
The First National Bank Of Toronto	6819	6	4
Towanda			
The First National Bank Of Towanda	11154	6	–
The Towanda National Bank	12935	6	3
Troy			
The First National Bank Of Troy	8162	5	5
Union Stockyards			
The Union Stockyards National Bank, Union Stockyards	9758	6	4
Valley Falls			
The First National Bank Of Valley Falls	11816	6	6
Wakeney			
The First National Bank Of Wakeeney	3776	6	–
Wamego			
The First National Bank Of Wamego	3434	3	4
Washington			
The First National Bank Of Washington	2912	4	–
The Washington National Bank	3167	5	–
Waverly			
The First National Bank Of Waverly	6101	6	5
Wellington			
First National Bank In Wellington	3091	6	5
The First National Bank Of Wellington	2879	6	–
The National Bank Of Commerce Of Wellington	8399	5	5
The State National Bank Of Wellington	3564	6	–
The Sumner National Bank Of Wellington	3865	6	–
The Wellington National Bank	3091	6	–
West Moreland			
The First National Bank Of West Moreland	3304	6	–
Wetmore			
The First National Bank Of Wetmore	8974	6	6
White City			
The First National Bank Of White City	7970	5	5
Wichita			
First National Bank In Wichita	2782	–	1
The First National Bank Of Wichita	1913	6	–
The Fourth National Bank Of Wichita	3683	4	–
The Kansas National Bank Of Wichita	2782	6	–
The National Bank Of Commerce Of Wichita	5169	5	–
The National Bank Of Wichita	6392	6	–
The Southwest National Bank Of Wichita	12346	–	3
The State National Bank Of Wichita	3524	6	–
The Union National Bank Of Wichita	11010	–	5
The West Side National Bank Of Wichita	3756	6	–
The Wichita National Bank	2786	6	–
Winfield			
The Cowley County National Bank Of Winfield	4556	5	–
The First National Bank Of Winfield	3218	4	3
The Winfield National Bank	3351	5	5
Wyandotte			
The First National Bank Of Wyandotte	1840	6	–
Yates Center			
The Woodson National Bank Of Yates Center	3108	6	–
The Yates Center National Bank	6326	6	–

KENTUCKY

City, Bank	Ch. No.	L	S
Adairville			
The First National Bank Of Adairville	8814	6	6
Ashland			
The Ashland National Bank	2010	3	4
The Merchants National Bank Of Ashland	4559	6	–
The Second National Bank Of Ashland	3944	6	4
The Third National Bank Of Ashland	12293	6	4
Augusta			
The Farmers National Bank Of Augusta	4612	5	–
The First National Bank Of Augusta	4616	6	–
Barbourville			
The First National Bank Of Barbourville	6262	6	6
The National Bank Of John A Black Of Barbourville	7284	5	6
The Union National Bank Of Barbourville	13906	–	6
Bardwell			
The First National Bank Of Bardwell	8331	5	5
Beattyville			
The National Bank Of Beattyville	7751	6	–
Berea			
The Berea National Bank	8435	6	4
Bowling Green			
The American National Bank Of Bowling Green	9365	5	4
The Bowling Green National Bank	7804	5	–
The Citizens National Bank Of Bowling Green	5900	4	4
The Liberty National Bank Of Bowling Green	11589	6	–
The National Southern Kentucky Bank Of Bowling Green	2149	6	–
The Warren National Bank Of Bowling Green	10448	6	–
Brooksville			
The First National Bank Of Brooksville	8830	6	5
Buffalo			
The First National Bank Of Buffalo	11538	6	6
Burnside			
The First National Bank Of Burnside	8903	6	6
Campbellsville			
The Taylor National Bank Of Campbellsville	6342	6	5
Cannel City			
The Morgan County National Bank Of Cannel City	7891	5	5
Carlisle			
The First National Bank Of Carlisle	5959	4	–
Carrollton			
The Carrollton National Bank	3074	5	5
The First National Bank Of Carrollton	2592	4	4
Catlettsburg			
The Big Sandy National Bank Of Catlettsburg	4200	6	–
The Catlettsburg National Bank	2740	5	–
The Kentucky National Bank Of Catlettsburg	9602	4	6
Cave City			
The H. Y. Davis National Bank Of Cave City	7919	6	–
Caverna			
The Caverna National Bank	2206	6	–
Central City			
The First National Bank Of Central City	8229	6	5
Clay			
The Farmers National Bank Of Clay	8943	6	6
Clay City			
The Clay City National Bank	4217	6	5
Clinton			
The First National Bank Of Clinton	9098	5	5
Columbia			
The First National Bank And Trust Company Of Columbia	6769	6	5
The First National Bank Of Columbia	6769	6	–
Corbin			
The First National Bank Of Corbin	7544	6	5
The Whitley National Bank Of Corbin	9634	6	5
Covington			
The Citizens National Bank Of Covington	4260	4	5
The Commercial National Bank Of Covington	8564	5	–
The Covington City National Bank	1859	5	–
The Farmers And Traders National Bank Of Covington	2722	5	–
The First National Bank And Trust Company Of Covington	718	5	3
The First National Bank Of Covington	718	3	–
The German National Bank Of Covington	1847	3	–
The Liberty National Bank Of Covington	1847	5	–
The Merchants National Bank Of Covington	8110	6	–
Cynthiana			
The Farmers National Bank Of Cynthiana	2560	4	4
The National Bank Of Cynthiana	1900	5	5
Danville			
The Boyle National Bank Of Danville	3317	6	–
The Central National Bank Of Danville	1600	6	–
The Citizens National Bank Of Danville	3381	5	4
Danville			
The Farmers National Bank Of Danville	2409	4	5
The First National Bank Of Danville	1601	6	–
Dawson Springs			
The First National Bank Of Dawson Springs	11548	6	5
Dry Ridge			
The First National Bank Of Dry Ridge	7012	5	6
East Bernstadt			
The First National Bank Of East Bernstadt	10254	6	6
Eddyville			
The First National Bank Of Eddyville	7492	6	–
Elizabethtown			
The First National Bank Of Elizabethtown	3042	5	–
The First-Hardin National Bank Of Elizabethtown	6028	3	4
The Hardin National Bank Of Elizabethtown	6028	6	–
Falmouth			
The First National Bank Of Falmouth	11947	6	6
Fleming			
The First National Bank Of Fleming	11988	6	4
Flemingsburg			
The Fleming County National Bank Of Flemingsburg	2323	6	–
Frankfort			
The Frankfort National Bank	4091	6	–
The National Branch Bank Of Kentucky, Frankfort	5376	5	5
The State National Bank Of Frankfort	4090	3	4
Franklin			
The Farmers And Merchants National Bank Of Franklin	7402	6	–
The First National Bank Of Franklin	1760	6	–
Fulton			
The City National Bank Of Fulton	6167	6	4
The First National Bank Of Fulton	4563	6	6
Georgetown			
The First National Bank Of Georgetown	2927	6	5
The Georgetown National Bank	8579	5	5
Glasgow			
The Citizens National Bank Of Glasgow	8439	6	5
The Farmers National Bank Of Glasgow	9722	6	6
The First National Bank Of Glasgow	4819	6	6
The New Farmers National Bank Of Glasgow	13651	–	6
The Third National Bank Of Glasgow	6872	6	–
The Trigg National Bank Of Glasgow	5486	4	6
Grayson			
The First National Bank Of Grayson	12982	–	5
Greenup			
The First National Bank Of Greenup	7037	5	5
Greenville			
The First National Bank Of Greenville	4356	5	5
Harlan			
The Citizens National Bank Of Harlan	12243	5	5
The First National Bank Of Harlan	9791	6	–
The Harlan National Bank	12295	6	4
Harrodsburg			
First-Mercer National Bank Of Harrodsburg	2531	–	6
Mercer County National Bank Of Harrodsburg	13612	–	3
The First National Bank Of Harrodsburg	1807	6	–
The Mercer National Bank Of Harrodsburg	2531	4	6
Hartford			
The First National Bank Of Hartford	5792	6	–
Hazard			
The First National Bank Of Hazard	8258	5	–
Henderson			
Ohio Valley National Bank Of Henderson	13983	–	5
The First National Bank Of Henderson	13757	–	5
The Henderson National Bank	1615	4	–
The Planters National Bank Of Henderson	2931	6	–
Hickman			
The Farmers And Merchants National Bank Of Hickman	4465	6	–
Hodgenville			
Farmers National Bank Of Hodgenville	6894	6	6
The Farmers National Bank Of Hodgenville	6894	5	–
The La Rue National Bank Of Hodgenville	9843	6	–
The Lincoln National Bank Of Hodgenville	13479	–	5
Hopkinsville			
The First National Bank Of Hopkinsville	3856	5	6
Horse Cave			
The First National Bank Of Horse Cave	7602	6	6
Hustonville			
The National Bank Of Hustonville	2917	6	5
Jackson			
The First National Bank Of Jackson	9320	5	3
Jenkins			
The First National Bank Of Jenkins	10062	5	6
The Jenkins National Bank	10062	6	–
Lancaster			
The Citizens National Bank Of Lancaster	2888	5	5
The National Bank Of Lancaster	1493	5	6
Latonia			
The First National Bank Of Latonia	6248	6	6
Lawrenceburg			
The Anderson County National Bank Of Lawrenceburg	2190	6	–
The Anderson National Bank Of Lawrenceburg	8604	4	5
The Lawrenceburg National Bank	7497	5	4
The Witherspoon National Bank Of Lawrenceburg	8862	6	–
Lebanon			
The Citizens National Bank Of Lebanon	3988	4	4
The Farmers National Bank Of Lebanon	4271	5	4
The Marion National Bank Of Lebanon	2150	5	4

City, Bank	Ch. No.	L	S
Lebanon			
The National Bank Of Lebanon	1694	6	–
Lexington			
First National Bank & Trust Company Of Lexington	906	–	1
Phoenix National Bank And Trust Company Of Lexington	3052	3	–
The Fayette National Bank Of Lexington	1720	3	4
The First And City National Bank Of Lexington	906	3	–
The First National Bank Of Lexington	760	5	–
The Lexington City National Bank	906	5	–
The National Exchange Bank Of Lexington	2393	6	–
The Phoenix And Third National Bank Of Lexington	3052	3	–
The Phoenix National Bank Of Lexington	3942	5	–
The Second National Bank Of Lexington	2901	4	4
The Third National Bank Of Lexington	3052	6	–
Litchfield			
The Grayson County National Bank Of Litchfield	5314	6	–
London			
The First National Bank Of London	3943	6	–
The National Bank Of London	7890	6	6
Louisa			
The First National Bank Of Louisa	7110	5	5
The Louisa National Bank	7122	6	5
Louisville			
Liberty National Bank And Trust Company Of Louisville	14320	–	3
National Bank Of Commerce Of Louisville	9241	5	–
The American National Bank Of Louisville	4956	4	–
The American-Southern National Bank Of Louisville	4956	6	–
The Citizens National Bank Of Louisville	2164	3	–
The Citizens Union National Bank Of Louisville	2164	4	3
The Continental National Bank Of Louisville	7457	6	–
The First National Bank Of Louisville	109	3	2
The Fourth National Bank Of Louisville	2784	6	–
The German National Bank Of Louisville	2062	4	–
The Kentucky National Bank Of Louisville	1908	6	–
The Louisville City National Bank	788	6	–
The Louisville National Bank & Trust Company, Louisville	5161	6	–
The Louisville National Bank, Louisville	5161	6	–
The Louisville National Banking Company	5161	6	–
The Merchants National Bank Of Louisville	2161	6	–
The National Bank Of Kentucky Of Louisville	5312	1	3
The Planters National Bank Of Louisville	790	6	–
The Second National Bank Of Louisville	777	5	–
The Southern National Bank Of Louisville	5195	5	–
The Third National Bank Of Louisville	2171	4	–
The Union National Bank Of Louisville	4145	4	–
The Western National Bank Of Louisville	7457	6	–
Ludlow			
The First National Bank Of Ludlow	5323	6	5
Madisonville			
The Farmers National Bank Of Madisonville	8451	5	5
The Morton National Bank Of Madisonville	8386	6	–
Manchester			
The First National Bank Of Manchester	7605	4	6
Mayfield			
The City National Bank Of Mayfield	5033	5	–
The Farmers National Bank Of Mayfield	6834	6	–
The First National Bank Of Mayfield	2245	3	4
Maysville			
The Bank Of Maysville, National Banking Association	9561	6	–
The First National Bank Of Maysville	2467	4	–
The National Bank Of Maysville	1702	6	–
The State National Bank Of Maysville	2663	3	4
Middleborough			
The National Bank Of Middleborough	7086	6	4
Middlesborough			
The First National Bank Of Middlesborough	4201	6	–
Monticello			
The Citizens National Bank Of Monticello	6419	6	6
The National Bank Of Monticello	1931	6	–
Morehead			
The Lenora National Bank Of Morehead	7593	6	–
Morganfield			
The Morganfield National Bank	7490	5	4
The National Bank Of Union County, Morganfield	2209	5	–
Mount Sterling			
The Farmers National Bank Of Mount Sterling	2216	6	–
The Montgomery National Bank Of Mt. Sterling	6160	5	5
The Mt. Sterling National Bank	2185	4	4
The Traders National Bank Of Mt. Sterling	6129	5	4
Munfordville			
The National Bank Of Munfordville	11336	6	–
Murray			
The First National Bank Of Murray	10779	6	5
New Castle			
The National Bank Of New Castle	2196	6	–
Newport			
The American National Bank Of Newport	2726	6	4
The First National Bank Of Newport	2276	6	–
The German National Bank Of Newport	2726	5	–
The Newport National Bank	4765	5	4
Nicholasville			
The First National Bank Of Nicholasville	1831	5	4
Olive Hill			
The Olive Hill National Bank	7281	6	–
Owensboro			
First National Bank And Trust Company Of Owensboro	2576	6	6
The First National Bank Of Owensboro	2576	4	–
The National Deposit Bank Of Owensboro	4006	4	3
The Owensboro National Bank	4006	6	–
The United States National Bank Of Owensboro	9456	4	–
Owenton			
The Farmers National Bank Of Owenton	2968	6	4
The First National Bank In Owenton	14026	–	6
The First National Bank Of Owenton	2868	5	6
The National Bank Of Owen At Owneton	1963	6	–
Paducah			
The American German National Bank Of Paducah	2070	5	–
The City National Bank Of Paducah	2093	3	4
The First National Bank Of Paducah	1599	6	6
The Peoples National Bank Of Paducah	12961	6	4
Paintsville			
The Citizens National Bank Of Paintsville	7164	6	–
The First National Bank Of Paintsville	13763	–	6
The Paintsville National Bank	6100	4	4
The Second National Bank Of Paintsville	13023	–	5
Paris			
The First National Bank Of Paris	6323	4	4
The National Bank And Trust Company Of Paris	14076	–	6
Pikeville			
The Day And Night National Bank Of Pikeville	11944	6	6
The First National Bank Of Pikeville	6622	5	4
The Pikeville National Bank	7030	5	4
Pineville			
The Bell National Bank Of Pineville	7215	6	6
The First National Bank Of Pineville	4598	6	–
Prestonsburg			
The First National Bank Of Prestonsburg	7254	6	6
Princeton			
The Farmers National Bank Of Princeton	5257	5	4
The First National Bank Of Princeton	3064	4	4
Providence			
The Union National Bank Of Providence	9708	6	4
Richmond			
Madison-Southern National Bank & Trust Co. Of Richmond	1790	–	4
The Citizens National Bank Of Richmond	7653	5	6
The Farmers National Bank Of Richmond	1309	5	–
The First National Bank Of Richmond	1728	6	–
The Madison National Bank & Trust Company Of Richmond	1790	6	5
The Madison National Bank Of Richmond	1790	5	–
The Richmond National Bank	4430	6	–
The Second National Bank Of Richmond	2374	6	–
The Southern National Bank Of Richmond	9832	3	6
Russell			
The First National Bank Of Russell	8792	6	6
Russell Springs			
The First National Bank Of Russell Springs	11348	6	5
Russellville			
The Citizens National Bank Of Russellville	6546	5	6
The Logan County National Bank Of Russellville	2169	6	–
The National Deposit Bank Of Russellville	9842	6	–
Salyersville			
The Salyersville National Bank	8905	6	6
Scottsville			
The Allen County National Bank Of Scottsville	9356	6	–
The First National Bank Of Scottsville	8599	6	–
Sebree			
The First National Bank Of Sebree	7242	5	5
Somerset			
The Citizens National Bank Of Somerset	11544	6	4
The Farmers National Bank Of Somerset	5881	5	4
The First National Bank Of Somerset	3832	6	4
The National Bank Of Somerset	1748	6	–
Springfield			
The First National Bank Of Springfield	1767	5	6
Stanford			
First National Bank In Stanford	14039	–	6
The Farmers National Bank Of Stanford	1705	6	–
The First National Bank Of Stanford	2788	6	5
The Lincoln County National Bank Of Stanford	5132	5	4
The Lincoln National Bank Of Stanford	3954	6	–
The National Bank Of Stanford	1204	6	–
Stone			
The First National Bank Of Stone	11890	6	6
Sturgis			
The First National Bank Of Sturgis	6244	6	–
Uniontown			
The First National Bank Of Uniontown	8622	6	–
Versailles			
The Commercial National Bank Of Versailles	1835	6	–
Wallins Creek			
The Wallins National Bank Of Wallins Creek	12202	6	6
West Liberty			
The First National Bank Of West Liberty	7916	6	–
Whitesburg			
The First National Bank Of Whitesburg	10433	6	5
Wickliffe			
The First National Bank Of Wickliffe	5443	6	–
Williamsburg			
The First National Bank Of Williamsburg	7174	6	6
Wilmore			
The First National Bank Of Wilmore	9880	6	4
Winchester			
The Citizens National Bank Of Winchester	2148	5	6
The Clark County National Bank Of Winchester	995	4	4
The Winchester National Bank	3290	6	–

LOUISIANA

City, Bank	Ch. No.	L	S
Abbeville			
The First National Bank Of Abbeville	5807	6	5
Alexandria			
The First National Bank Of Alexandria	5021	5	–
Arcadia			
The First National Bank Of Arcadia	7476	5	5
Baton Rouge			
City National Bank Of Baton Rouge	13737	–	4
Louisiana National Bank Of Baton Rouge	9834	–	2
The First National Bank Of Baton Rouge	2633	5	–
The Louisiana National Bank Of Baton Rouge	9834	3	–
Bogalusa			
The First National Bank Of Bogalusa	8959	6	–
Crowley			
First National Bank Of Crowley	12523	4	5
The First National Bank Of Arcadia Parish At Crowley	10700	5	–
The First National Bank Of Crowley	5520	4	–
De Ridder			
First National Bank In De Ridder	14168	–	4
Delhi			
The First National Bank Of Delhi	14225	–	6
The Macon Ridge National Bank Of Delhi	10912	6	5
Deridder			
The First National Bank Of Deridder	9237	5	4
Eunice			
The First National Bank Of Eunice	8677	6	–
Franklin			
The First National Bank Of Franklin	4555	4	–
Gibsland			
The First National Bank Of Gibsland	10049	6	–
Gretna			
The First National Bank Of Jefferson Parrish At Gretna	13732	–	4
Hammond			
The Citizens National Bank Of Hammond	11977	4	4
Homer			
The Commercial National Bank Of Homer	11638	5	–
The Homer National Bank	4216	5	5
Jeanerette			
The First National Bank Of Jeanerette	7768	4	5
Jennings			
The First National Bank Of Jennings	5066	6	–
The Jennings National Bank	11450	5	–
The State National Bank Of Jennings	7765	6	–
Lafayette			
The Commercial National Bank Of Lafayette	13209	6	5
The First National Bank Of Lafayette	5023	4	4
Lake Arthur			
The First National Bank Of Lake Arthur	7047	6	–
Lake Charles			
Calcasieu National Bank In Lake Charles	13573	–	4
The Calcasieu N.B. Of Southwest Louisiana At Lake Charles	10836	4	6
The Calcasieu National Bank Of Lake Charles	5157	5	–
The Calcasieu National Bank Of Lake Charles	10836	–	6
The First National Bank Of Lake Charles	4154	4	4
The Lake Charles National Bank	6088	6	–
Lake Providence			
The First Natl Bank Of Lake Providence At Providence	6291	5	2
Leesville			
The First National Bank Of Leesville	6264	6	–
Mansfield			
The American National Bank Of Mansfield	11669	–	4
The First National Bank Of Mansfield	7232	6	–
Minden			
The First National Bank Of Minden	10544	5	6
Monroe			
The Citizens National Bank Of Monroe	11242	6	–
The Monroe National Bank	4082	6	–
The Quachita National Bank In Monroe	13655	–	3
The Quachita National Bank Of Monroe	3692	6	–
The Quachita National Bank Of Monroe	8654	5	5
The Union National Bank Of Monroe	10153	6	–
Morgan City			
The First National Bank Of Morgan City	6801	4	–
New Iberia			
The New Iberia National Bank	3671	6	4
The Peoples National Bank Of New Iberia	4524	4	5
The State National Bank Of New Iberia	6858	5	4
New Orleans			
Canal-Commercial National Bank Of New Orleans	5649	5	–

City, Bank	Ch. No.	L	S
New Orleans			
Hibernia National Bank Of New Orleans	8734	4	–
The American National Bank Of New Orleans	3978	6	–
The City National Bank Of New Orleans	1591	6	–
The Commercial National Bank Of New Orleans	5649	2	–
The Crescent City National Bank Of New Orleans	1937	6	–
The First National Bank Of New Orleans	162	6	–
The German-American National Bank Of New Orleans	7876	4	–
The Germania National Bank Of New Orleans	1591	5	–
The Hibernia National Bank In New Orleans	13688	–	2
The Hibernia National Bank Of New Orleans	2086	6	–
The Louisiana National Bank Of New Orleans	1626	3	–
The Merchants National Bank Of New Orleans	7498	6	–
The Mutual National Bank Of New Orleans	1898	6	–
The National Bank Of Commerce In New Orleans	13689	–	2
The New Hibernia National Bank Of New Orleans	8734	6	–
The New Orleans National Bank	1778	3	–
The New Orleans National Banking Association	1825	6	–
The Peoples National Bank Of New Orleans	7498	6	–
The Southern National Bank Of New Orleans	4337	6	–
The State National Bank Of New Orleans	1774	3	–
The Teutonia National Bank Of New Orleans	1747	6	–
The Union National Bank Of New Orleans	1796	4	–
The Whitney National Bank Of New Orleans	3069	6	–
The Whitney-Central National Bank, New Orleans	3069	1	–
Whitney National Bank Of New Orleans	3069	–	1
New Roads			
The First National Bank Of New Roads	7169	6	–
Norco			
The St. Charles National Bank Of Norco	13839	–	5
Opelousas			
The First National Bank Of Opelousas	4340	6	–
The Opelousas National Bank	6920	6	–
The Planters National Bank Of Opelousas	9872	6	–
Paterson			
The First National Bank Of Paterson	5843	6	–
Ruston			
The First National Bank Of Ruston	11795	6	6
Shreveport			
Commercial National Bank In Shreveport	13648	–	1
The American National Bank Of Shreveport	8440	4	6
The Citizens National Bank Of Shreveport	5752	6	–
The City National Bank Of Shreveport	10870	6	–
The Commercial National Bank Of Shreveport	3600	2	2
The Exchange National Bank Of Shreveport	11521	5	6
The First National Bank Of Shreveport	3595	2	2
The Shreveport National Bank	5844	6	–
Tallulah			
The Madison National Bank Of Tallulah	12923	5	5
Ville Platte			
The First National Bank Of Ville Platte	10588	6	5
Welsh			
The First National Bank Of Welsh	6360	6	–
The Welsh National Bank	6418	6	–

MAINE

City, Bank	Ch. No.	L	S
Auburn			
The First National Bank Of Auburn	154	6	–
The National Shoe And Leather Bank Of Auburn	2270	6	5
Augusta			
First National Granite Bank Of Augusta	498	4	1
The Augusta National Bank	3271	6	–
The First National Bank Of Augusta	367	4	–
The Freeman's National Bank Of Augusta	406	6	–
The Granite National Bank Of Augusta	498	5	–
Bangor			
The Farmers National Bank Of Bangor	1687	6	–
The First National Bank Of Bangor	112	4	–
The Kenduskeag National Bank Of Bangor	518	5	–
The Merchants National Bank Of Bangor	1437	4	5
The Second National Bank Of Bangor	306	6	–
The Traders National Bank Of Bangor	1095	6	–
The Veazie National Bank Of Bangor	2089	6	–
Bath			
The Bath National Bank	494	4	3
The First National Bank Of Bath	61	6	–
The First National Bank Of Bath	2743	3	3
The Lincoln National Bank Of Bath	761	4	–
The Marine National Bank Of Bath	782	5	–
The Sagadahock National Bank Of Bath	1041	6	–
Belfast			
The Belfast National Bank	840	3	–
The City National Bank Of Belfast	7586	5	4
The Peoples National Bank Of Belfast	4806	6	–
Bethel			
The Bethel National Bank	7613	6	6
Biddeford			
The Biddeford National Bank	1575	5	–
The First National Bank Of Biddeford	1089	5	4
Boothbay Harbor			
The First National Bank Of Boothbay Harbor	5598	6	–
Bowdoinham			
The National Village Bank Of Bowdoinham	944	6	–
Bridgton			
The Bridgton National Bank	9181	6	–
Brunswick			
The Brunswick National Bank, Brunswick	1315	–	6
The First National Bank Of Brunswick	192	5	4
The Pejepscot National Bank Of Brunswick	1315	5	6
The Union National Bank Of Brunswick	1118	5	6
Bucksport			
The Bucksport National Bank	1079	5	–
Calais			
The Calais National Bank	1425	5	5
Camden			
The Camden National Bank	2311	4	5
The Megunticook National Bank Of Camden	6231	6	–
Caribou			
The Caribou National Bank	6190	6	6
Damariscotta			
The First National Bank Of Damariscotta	446	6	5
The New Castle National Bank Of Damariscotta	953	6	6
Dexter			
The First National Bank Of Dexter	2259	6	–
Dover			
The Kineo National Bank Of Dover	3690	6	–
Eastport			
The Frontier National Bank Of Eastport	1495	6	5
Eden			
The First National Bank Of Bar Harbor	3941	6	4
Ellsworth			
The Burrill National Bank Of Ellsworth	3804	6	–
The First National Bank Of Ellsworth	3814	6	–
The Liberty National Bank Of Ellsworth	3804	5	4
Fairfield			
The First National Bank Of Fairfield	2175	6	–
The National Bank Of Fairfield	4973	6	–
Farmington			
The First National Bank Of Farmington	4459	5	5
The Peoples National Bank Of Farmington	5861	5	5
The Sandy River National Bank Of Farmington	901	6	–
Fort Fairfield			
The First National Bank Of Fort Fairfield	13843	–	6
The Fort Fairfield National Bank	4781	6	6
Fort Kent			
The First National Bank In Fort Kent	14224	–	6
The First National Bank Of Fort Kent	11403	6	4
Gardiner			
The Cobbossoe National Bank Of Gardiner	939	6	–
The Gardiner National Bank	1174	5	–
The Merchants National Bank Of Gardiner	3219	6	–
The National Bank Of Gardiner	9609	6	6
The Oakland National Bank Of Gardiner	740	6	–
Guilford			
The First National Bank Of Guilford	4780	6	–
Hallowell			
The American National Bank Of Hallowell	624	6	–
The First National Bank Of Hallowell	310	6	–
The Hallowell National Bank	3247	6	–
The Northern National Bank Of Hallowell	532	6	–
Houlton			
The Farmers National Bank Of Houlton	4252	6	5
The First National Bank Of Houlton	2749	5	4
Kennebunk			
The Ocean National Bank Of Kennebunk	1254	6	–
Kezar Falls			
The Kezar Falls National Bank	9826	6	5
Lewiston			
The First National Bank Of Lewiston	330	3	3
The Manufacturers National Bank Of Lewiston	2260	4	3
Limerick			
The Limerick National Bank	2785	4	5
Machias			
The Machias National Bank	11462	6	–
Madison			
The First National Bank Of Madison	4647	6	–
New Castle			
The New Castle National Bank	953	6	–
North Berwick			
The North Berwick National Bank	1523	5	4
Norway			
Norway National Bank	13750	–	5
The Norway National Bank	1956	5	6
Oakland			
The Messalonskee National Bank Of Oakland	2231	6	–
The West Waterville National Bank Of Oakland	2231	6	–
Orono			
The Orono National Bank	1134	6	–
Phillips			
The Phillips National Bank	4957	6	6
The Union National Bank Of Phillips	2267	6	–
Pittsfield			
The First National Bank Of Pittsfield	13777	–	5
The Pittsfield National Bank	4188	5	5
Portland			
First National Bank At Portland	13716	–	4
National Bank Of Commerce Of Portland	13710	–	5
Portland			
The Canal National Bank Of Portland	941	3	2
The Casco National Bank Of Portland	1060	5	–
The Chapman National Bank Of Portland	4868	3	–
The Cumberland National Bank Of Portland	1511	5	–
The First National Bank Of Portland	221	2	4
The Merchants National Bank Of Portland	1023	4	–
The National Traders Bank Of Portland	1451	5	–
The Portland National Bank	4128	4	3
The Second National Bank Of Portland	878	6	–
Presque Isle			
Northern National Bank Of Presque Isle	13768	–	5
The Presque Isle National Bank	3827	6	5
Richmond			
The First National Bank Of Richmond	662	6	–
The Richmond National Bank	909	6	–
Rockland			
The Lime Rock National Bank Of Rockland	2097	6	–
The North National Bank Of Rockland	2371	3	5
The Rockland National Bank	1446	3	5
Rumford			
The Rumford National Bank	6287	6	5
Saco			
The Saco National Bank	1535	5	–
The York National Bank Of Saco	1528	4	4
Sanford			
The Sanford National Bank	5050	5	–
Searsport			
The Searsport National Bank	2642	6	6
Skowhegan			
The First National Bank Of Skowhegan	239	4	4
The Second National Bank Of Skowhegan	298	6	–
South Berwick			
The South Berwick National Bank	959	4	–
Springvale			
The Springvale National Bank	7835	6	6
Thomaston			
The Georges National Bank Of Thomaston	1142	4	6
The Thomaston National Bank	890	4	5
The Thomaston National Bank, Thomaston	1142	–	4
Van Buren			
The First National Bank Of Van Buren	10628	6	6
Waldoboro			
The Medomak National Bank Of Waldoboro	1108	4	5
The Waldoboro National Bank	744	6	–
Waterville			
Peoples-Ticonic National Bank Of Waterville	880	–	4
The Merchants National Bank Of Waterville	2306	6	–
The Peoples National Bank Of Waterville	880	4	6
The Ticonic National Bank Of Waterville	762	4	5
The Waterville National Bank	798	6	–
Winthrop			
The National Bank Of Winthrop	553	6	–
Wiscasset			
The First National Bank Of Wiscasset	1549	4	–
York Village			
The York County National Bank Of York Village	4844	6	–

MARYLAND

City, Bank	Ch. No.	L	S
Aberdeen			
The First National Bank Of Aberdeen	4634	6	5
Annapolis			
The Farmers National Bank Of Annapolis	1244	4	–
The First National Bank Of Annapolis	826	6	–
The Traders National Bank Of Baltimore	826	5	–
Baltimore			
Baltimore National Bank	13745	–	3
Maryland National Bank Of Baltimore	5776	4	–
National Central Bank Of Baltimore	11207	–	2
The American National Bank Of Baltimore	4518	6	–
The Central National Bank Of Baltimore	1797	6	–
The Citizens National Bank Of Baltimore	1384	2	–
The Commercial And Farmers National Bank Of Baltimore	1303	4	–
The Continental National Bank Of Baltimore	4533	6	–
The Drovers And Mechanics National Bank Of Baltimore	2499	3	4
The Equitable National Bank Of Baltimore	4530	6	–
The Farmers And Merchants National Bank Of Baltimore	1337	3	3
The First National Bank Of Baltimore	204	3	–
The First National Bank Of Baltimore	1413	3	1
The Manufacturers National Bank Of Baltimore	2653	4	–
The Merchants National Bank Of Baltimore	1336	3	–
The Merchants National Bank Of Baltimore	1413	2	–
The Merchants-Mechanics Bank Of Baltimore	1413	3	–
The Merchants-Mechanics First National Bank Of Baltimore	1413	3	–
The National Bank Of Baltimore	1432	2	6
The National Bank Of Commerce Of Baltimore	4285	2	–
The National City Bank Of Baltimore	9639	6	–
The National Exchange Bank Of Baltimore	1109	2	–
The National Farmers And Planters Bank Of Baltimore	1252	4	–

City, Bank	Ch. No.	L	S
Baltimore			
The National Howard Bank Of Baltimore	4218	6	–
The National Marine Bank Of Baltimore	2453	3	3
The National Mechanics Bank Of Baltimore	1413	4	–
The National Union Bank Of Maryland Of Baltimore	1489	2	–
The Old Town National Bank Of Baltimore	5984	2	–
The Second National Bank Of Baltimore	414	2	–
The Third National Bank Of Baltimore	814	3	–
The Western National Bank Of Baltimore	1325	3	4
Barton			
The First National Bank Of Barton	6399	5	4
Bel Air			
The Farmers And Merchants National Bank Of Bel Air	9474	6	5
The First National Bank Of Bel Air	13680	–	4
The Harford National Bank Of Bel Air	2797	6	–
The Second National Bank Of Bel Air	3933	4	4
Berlin			
The First National Bank Of Berlin	8319	6	–
Brunswick			
Peoples National Bank Of Brunswick	8244	4	3
The Peoples National Bank In Brunswick	14044	–	2
Cambridge			
The Dorchester National Bank Of Cambridge	4085	5	–
The Farmers And Merchants National Bank Of Cambridge	5880	5	4
The National Bank Of Cambridge	2498	3	4
Canton			
The Canton National Bank	4799	4	5
Catonsville			
The First National Bank Of Catonsville	5093	4	–
Centreville			
The Centreville National Bank Of Maryland, Centreville	2341	4	4
The Queen Anne's National Bank Of Centreville	3205	6	6
Chesapeake City			
The National Bank Of Chesapeake City	6845	6	–
Chestertown			
The First National Bank Of Chestertown	13798	–	6
The Kent National Bank Of Chestertown	1500	6	–
The Second National Bank Of Chestertown	4327	6	–
The Third National Bank Of Chestertown	9744	6	6
Clear Spring			
The Clear Spring National Bank	9699	4	4
Cockeysville			
The National Bank Of Cockeysville	4496	5	4
Cumberland			
The Citizens National Bank Of Cumberland	5332	6	–
The First National Bank Of Cumberland	381	3	3
The Second National Bank Of Cumberland	1519	3	1
The Third National Bank Of Cumberland	2416	3	–
Denton			
The Denton National Bank	2547	3	3
The Peoples National Bank Of Denton	5122	5	–
Easton			
The Easton National Bank Of Maryland	1434	3	3
The Farmers And Merchants National Bank Of Easton	4046	6	–
Elkton			
The National Bank Of Elkton	1236	5	6
The Second National Bank Of Elkton	4162	6	–
Ellicott City			
Patapaco National Bank In Ellicott City	13773	–	4
The Patapsco National Bank Of Ellicott City	3585	4	3
Federalsburg			
The First National Bank Of Federalsburg	10210	5	4
Frederick			
Frederick County National Bank, Frederick	13747	–	6
The Central National Bank Of Frederick	1138	4	–
The Citizens National Bank Of Frederick	3476	3	3
The Farmers And Mechanics National Bank Of Frederick	1267	3	3
The First National Bank Of Frederick	1589	5	–
The Frederick County National Bank Of Frederick	1449	3	3
Friendsville			
The First National Bank Of Friendsville	6196	5	4
Frostburg			
Frostburg National Bank	13979	–	4
The Citizens National Bank Of Frostburg	4926	4	3
The First National Bank Of Frostburg	1412	6	–
The First National Bank Of Frostburg	4149	4	3
Gaithersburg			
The First National Bank Of Gaithersburg	4608	4	3
Grantsville			
The First National Bank Of Grantsville	5943	4	4
Hagerstown			
The Citizens National Bank Of Hagerstown	1893	6	–
The First National Bank Of Hagerstown	1431	3	4
The Nicodemus National Bank Of Hagerstown	12590	3	2
The Peoples National Bank Of Hagerstown	4856	4	–
The Second National Bank Of Hagerstown	4049	3	3
Hampstead			
The First National Bank Of Hampstead	9755	6	6

City, Bank	Ch. No.	L	S
Hancock			
The First National Bank Of Hancock	7859	6	4
The Peoples National Bank Of Hancock	13853	–	4
Havre De Grace			
The Citizens National Bank Of Havre De Grace	5445	3	2
The First National Bank Of Havre De Grace	3010	5	5
Hyattsville			
The First National Bank Of Hyattsville	7519	4	6
Kitzmillerville			
The First National Bank Of Kitzmillerville	8302	6	4
La Plata			
The Southern Maryland National Bank Of La Plata	8456	6	3
Laurel			
The Citizens National Bank Of Laurel	4364	6	6
Leonardtown			
The First National Bank Of Saint Mary's, Leonardtown	6606	4	1
Lonaconing			
The First National Bank Of Lonaconing	7732	6	4
Mechanicsville			
The National Bank Of Mechanicsville	9429	6	–
Midland			
The First National Bank Of Midland	5331	5	5
Monrovia			
The First National Bank Of Monrovia	9238	6	–
Mount Airy			
The First National Bank Of Mount Airy	7160	5	5
Mount Rainier			
The First National Bank Of Mount Rainier	12443	5	6
Mount Savage			
The First National Bank Of Mount Savage	6144	5	3
New Windsor			
The First National Bank Of New Windsor	747	5	6
North East			
The First National Bank Of North East	7064	6	5
Oakland			
The First National Bank Of Oakland	5623	4	3
The Garrett National Bank In Oakland	13776	–	4
The Garrett National Bank Of Oakland	6588	4	3
Parkton			
The First National Bank In Parkton	13776	–	4
The First National Bank Of Parkton	9444	6	4
Perryville			
The National Bank Of Perryville	11193	5	2
Pikesville			
The Pikesville National Bank	8867	6	6
Pocomoke City			
Citizens National Bank In Pocomoke City	14106	–	5
The Citizens National Bank Of Pocomoke City	6202	6	6
The Pocomoke City National Bank	4191	6	4
Poolesville			
The Poolesville National Bank	8860	6	6
Port Deposit			
The Cecil National Bank At Port Deposit	13840	–	4
The Cecil National Bank Of Port Deposit	1211	3	4
The National Bank Of Port Deposit	5610	6	–
Rising Sun			
The National Bank Of Rising Sun	2481	5	3
Rockville			
The Montgomery County National Bank Of Rockville	3187	3	4
Salisbury			
The Peoples National Bank Of Salisbury	6761	5	–
The Salisbury National Bank	3250	6	4
Sandy Spring			
The First National Bank Of Sandy Spring	5561	6	4
Silver Spring			
The Silver Spring National Bank	9830	5	5
Snow Hill			
The Commercial National Bank Of Snow Hill	6297	5	3
The First National Bank Of Snow Hill	3783	4	3
Sykesville			
The First National Bank Of Sykesville	8578	6	–
The Sykesville National Bank	8587	4	4
Thurmont			
The Thurmont National Bank	5829	6	–
Towson			
The Second National Bank Of Towson	8381	4	4
The Towson National Bank	3588	3	3
Union Bridge			
The First National Bank Of Union Bridge	9066	5	–
Upper Marlboro			
The First National Bank Of So. Maryland Of Upper Marlboro	5471	4	6
Westernport			
The Citizens National Bank Of Westernport	5831	5	3
Westminster			
The Farmers And Mechanics National Bank Of Westminster	1526	4	4
The First National Bank Of Westminster	742	3	3
The Union National Bank Of Westminster	1596	3	3
White Hall			
The White Hall National Bank	9469	6	–
Williamsport			
The Washington County National Bank Of Williamsport	1551	3	–
Woodbine			
The Woodbine National Bank	8799	6	6

MASSACHUSETTS

City, Bank	Ch. No.	L	S
Abington			
The Abington National Bank	1386	6	6
Adams			
The First National Bank Of Adams	462	5	6
The Greylock National Bank Of Adams	4562	4	6
Amesbury			
The Amesbury National Bank	2929	6	–
The Powow River National Bank Of Amesbury	1049	5	6
Amherst			
The First National Bank Of Amherst	393	5	5
Andover			
The Andover National Bank	1129	5	–
Arlington			
The Arlington National Bank	11868	6	6
The First National Bank Of Arlington	4664	6	–
Ashburnham			
The First National Bank Of Ashburnham	2113	6	–
Athol			
The Athol National Bank	2172	6	6
The First National Bank Of Athol	13733	–	5
The Millers River National Bank Of Athol	708	5	5
Attleboro			
The First National Bank Of Attleboro	2232	3	4
Ayer			
The First National Bank Of Ayer	3073	6	6
Barre			
The First National Bank Of Barre	96	6	–
The First National Bank Of Barre	2685	5	–
The Second National Bank Of Barre	10165	6	–
Beverly			
The Beverly National Bank	969	6	4
Blackstone			
The Worcester County National Bank Of Blackstone	1207	6	–
Boston			
Boston-Continental National Bank, Boston	11903	–	5
Continental National Bank Of Boston	12540	–	6
Engineers National Bank Of Boston	12540	6	5
Federal National Bank Of Boston	12336	2	4
The American National Bank Of Boston	5840	6	–
The Atlantic National Bank Of Boston	643	3	–
The Atlantic National Bank Of Boston	643	6	3
The Atlas National Bank Of Boston	654	6	–
The Blackstone National Bank Of Boston	514	4	–
The Blue Hill National Bank Of Dorchester, Boston	684	6	–
The Boston National Bank	408	4	–
The Boston National Bank	11903	5	4
The Boylston National Bank Of Boston	545	4	–
The Broadway National Bank Of Boston	551	4	–
The Brotherhood Of Locomotive Engineers N.B. Of Boston	12540	5	–
The Central National Bank Of Boston	2103	5	–
The Citizens National Bank Of Boston	11339	4	–
The Colonial National Bank Of Boston	5163	6	–
The Columbian National Bank Of Boston	1029	3	–
The Commercial National Bank Of Boston	3923	5	–
The Commercial Security National Bank Of Boston	3923	6	–
The Commonwealth-Atlantic National Bank Of Boston	643	5	–
The Continental National Bank Of Boston	524	3	–
The Eleventh Ward National Bank Of Boston	1993	6	–
The Eliot National Bank Of Boston	536	5	–
The Everett National Bank Of Boston	1469	6	–
The Faneuil Hall National Bank Of Boston	847	4	–
The First National Bank Of Boston	200	3	2
The First Ward National Bank Of Boston	2112	5	–
The Fourth National Bank Of Boston	2277	4	–
The Fourth-Atlantic National Bank Of Boston	643	4	–
The Freeman's National Bank Of Boston	665	6	–
The Globe National Bank Of Boston	936	5	–
The Hamilton National Bank Of Boston	778	6	–
The Howard National Bank Of Boston	578	4	–
The Kidder National Gold Bank Of Boston	1699	6	–
The Lincoln National Bank Of Boston	2846	5	–
The Manufacturers National Bank Of Boston	2111	5	–
The Market National Bank Of Boston	505	4	–
The Massachusetts National Bank Of Boston	974	5	–
The Mattapan National Bank Of Boston	11137	6	–
The Maverick National Bank Of Boston	677	5	–
The Mechanics National Bank Of Boston	932	5	–
The Merchandise National Bank Of Boston	2304	5	–
The Merchants National Bank Of Boston	475	3	–
The Metropolitan National Bank Of Boston	2289	6	–
The Monument National Bank Of Boston	1005	6	–
The Mount Vernon National Bank Of Boston	716	6	–
The Mutual National Bank Of Boston	9579	6	–
The National Bank Of Brighton, Boston	1099	6	–
The National Bank Of Commerce, Boston	554	4	–
The National Bank Of North America, Boston	672	3	–
The National Bank Of Redemption Of Boston	515	4	–
The National Bank Of The Commonwealth, Boston	1827	6	–
The National Bank Of The Republic, Boston	379	5	–
The National City Bank Of Boston	609	4	–
The National Eagle Bank Of Boston	993	4	–
The National Exchange Bank Of Boston	529	6	–

City, Bank	Ch. No.	L	S
Boston			
The National Hamilton Bank Of Boston	5158	6	–
The National Hide And Leather Bank Of Boston	460	3	–
The National Market Bank Of Brighton, Boston	806	5	–
The National Revere Bank Of Boston	1295	5	–
The National Rockland Bank Of Roxbury At Boston	615	4	–
The National Rockland Bank Of Roxbury, Boston	615	6	–
The National Security Bank Of Boston	1675	5	–
The National Shawmut Bank Of Boston	5155	2	–
The National Suffolk Bank Of Boston	6104	6	–
The National Union Bank Of Boston	985	3	–
The National Webster Bank Of Boston	1527	5	–
The New England National Bank Of Boston	603	5	–
The North National Bank Of Boston	525	4	–
The Old Boston National Bank Of Boston	1015	6	–
The Pacific National Bank Of Boston	2373	5	–
The Peoples National Bank Of Roxbury At Boston	595	5	–
The Second National Bank Of Boston	322	4	–
The Shawmut National Bank Of Boston	582	5	–
The Shoe And Leather National Bank Of Boston	646	3	–
The South End National Bank Of Boston	4202	6	–
The State National Bank Of Boston	1028	4	–
The Suffolk National Bank Of Boston	629	5	–
The Third National Bank Of Boston	359	4	–
The Traders National Bank Of Boston	1442	6	–
The Tremont National Bank Of Boston	625	4	–
The Washington National Bank Of Boston	601	4	–
The Winthrop National Bank Of Boston	2304	4	–
Webster And Atlas National Bank Of Boston	1527	4	3
Braintree			
The Braintree National Bank	11347	6	5
Brockton			
The Brockton National Bank	2504	6	–
The Home National Bank Of Brockton	2152	6	–
Brookline			
The Brookline National Bank	3553	6	–
Buzzards Bay			
The Buzzards Bay National Bank	13222	–	4
Cambridge			
The Cambridgeport National Bank Of Cambridge	1228	6	–
The Charles River National Bank Of Cambridge	731	6	–
The First National Bank Of Cambridge	433	6	–
The Lechmere National Bank Of Cambridge	614	–	6
The Manufacturers National Bank Of Cambridge	11152	6	–
The National City Bank Of Cambridge	770	6	–
Canton			
The Neponset National Bank Of Canton	663	5	–
Charlestown			
The Bunker Hill National Bank Of Charlestown	635	6	–
The Monument National Bank Of Charlestown	1005	5	–
Chelsea			
The Broadway National Bank Of Chelsea	9651	5	5
The First National Bank Of Chelsea	533	6	–
The Lincoln National Bank Of Chelsea	14087	–	6
The National City Bank Of Chelsea	11270	6	6
The Winnissimet National Bank Of Chelsea	4074	6	–
Chicopee			
The First National Bank Of Chicopee	1056	5	–
Clinton			
The First National Bank Of Clinton	440	4	–
Concord			
The Concord National Bank	833	5	5
Conway			
The Conway National Bank	895	6	4
Danvers			
The Danvers National Bank	7452	4	6
The First National Bank Of Danvers	594	6	–
Dedham			
The Dedham National Bank	669	4	–
The Dedham National Bank	12567	6	5
Dorchester			
The First National Bank Of Dorchester	156	6	–
East Cambridge			
The Cambridge National Bank, East Cambridge	449	6	–
The Lechmere National Bank Of East Cambridge	614	5	5
Easthampton			
The First National Bank Of Easthampton	428	5	1
Edgartown			
The Edgartown National Bank	7957	6	6
The Marthas Vineyard National Bank Of Edgartown	1274	5	–
Fairhaven			
The National Bank Of Fairhaven	490	4	3
Fall River			
The Fall River National Bank	590	4	4
The First National Bank Of Fall River	256	3	–
The Massasoit National Bank Of Fall River	612	6	–
The Massasoit-Pocasset National Bank Of Fall River	6821	6	–
The Metacomet National Bank Of Fall River	924	4	–
The National Union Bank Of Fall River	1288	6	–
The Pocasset National Bank Of Fall River	679	5	–
The Second National Bank Of Fall River	439	5	–
Falmouth			
The Falmouth National Bank	1320	5	5
Fitchburg			
The Fitchburg National Bank	1077	5	–
Fitchburg			
The Rollstone National Bank Of Fitchburg	702	6	–
The Safety Fund National Bank Of Fitchburg	2153	3	4
The Wachusett National Bank Of Fitchburg	2265	5	–
Foxboro			
The Foxboro National Bank Of Foxborough	9426	6	5
Framingham			
The Framingham National Bank	528	5	3
Franklin			
The Franklin National Bank, Franklin	1207	4	4
Gardner			
The First National Bank Of Gardner	884	4	4
Georgetown			
The Georgetown National Bank	2297	6	–
Gloucester			
Gloucester National Bank Of Gloucester	13604	–	6
The Cape Ann National Bank Of Gloucester	899	3	5
The City National Bank Of Gloucester	2292	4	–
The First National Bank Of Gloucester	549	5	–
The Gloucester National Bank	1162	6	6
Grafton			
The First National Bank Of Grafton	188	6	–
The Grafton National Bank	824	5	–
Great Barrington			
The National Mahaiwe Bank Of Great Barrington	1203	4	6
Greenfield			
First National Bank And Trust Company Of Greenfield	474	–	5
The First National Bank Of Greenfield	474	4	6
The Franklin County National Bank Of Greenfield	920	6	–
The Packard National Bank Of Greenfield	2264	6	–
Harwich			
The Cape Cod National Bank Of Harwich	712	4	–
Haverhill			
Merrimack National Bank Of Haverhill	14266	–	6
The Essex National Bank Of Haverhill	589	5	6
The First National Bank Of Haverhill	481	5	6
The Haverhill National Bank	484	3	5
The Merchants National Bank Of Haverhill	4833	6	–
The Merrimack National Bank Of Haverhill	633	5	4
The Second National Bank Of Haverhill	3510	6	–
Hingham			
The Hingham National Bank	1119	6	–
Holliston			
The Holliston National Bank	802	6	–
Holyoke			
Holyoke National Bank	1939	4	4
The City National Bank Of Holyoke	2430	4	–
The Hadley Falls National Bank Of Holyoke	1246	5	–
The Home National Bank Of Holyoke	3128	5	–
The Park National Bank Of Holyoke	4703	6	5
Hopkinton			
The Hopkinton National Bank	626	4	6
Hudson			
The Hudson National Bank	2618	4	5
Hyannis			
The Barnstable County National Bank Of Hyannis	13395	–	6
The First National Bank Of Hyannis	1107	4	–
Hyde Park			
The Hyde Park National Bank	7920	6	–
Ipswich			
The First National Bank Of Ipswich	4774	6	6
Lancaster			
The Lancaster National Bank	583	6	–
The Lancaster National Bank Of Clinton	583	6	–
Lawrence			
Bay State Merchants National Bank Of Lawrence	1014	–	6
The Arlington National Bank Of Lawrence	4300	6	–
The Bay State National Bank Of Lawrence	1014	4	3
The Lawrence National Bank	1962	6	–
The Merchants National Bank Of Lawrence	3977	5	–
The National Pemberton Bank Of Lawrence	1048	6	–
The Pacific National Bank Of Lawrence	2347	5	–
Lee			
The Lee National Bank	885	4	6
Leicester			
The Leicester National Bank	918	6	–
Lenox			
The Lenox National Bank	4013	4	6
Leominster			
The First National Bank Of Leominster	513	6	–
The Leominster National Bank	3204	6	5
The Merchants National Bank Of Leominster	10059	5	1
Lowell			
The Appleton National Bank Of Lowell	986	4	4
The First National Bank Of Lowell	331	5	–
The Merchants National Bank Of Lowell	506	6	–
The Middlesex National Bank Of Lowell	12343	–	6
The Old Lowell National Bank Of Lowell	1329	5	6
The Prescott National Bank Of Lowell	960	5	–
The Railraod National Bank Of Lowell	753	5	–
The Traders National Bank Of Lowell	4753	6	–
The Union National Bank Of Lowell	6077	3	6
The Wamesit National Bank Of Lowell	781	5	–
Union Old Lowell National Bank, Lowell	6077	–	5
Lynn			
The Central National Bank Of Lynn	1201	5	6
The First National Bank Of Lynn	638	4	–
The Lynn National Bank	3429	6	–
Lynn			
The Manufacturers National Bank Of Lynn	4580	6	6
The National City Bank Of Lynn	697	5	5
The National Security Bank Of Lynn	2563	6	–
The State National Bank In Lynn	12362	6	–
The State National Bank Of Lynn	11169	6	–
Malden			
The First National Bank Of Malden	588	4	4
The Second National Bank Of Malden	11014	–	5
Mansfield			
The First National Bank Of Mansfield	5944	5	5
Marblehead			
The Marblehead National Bank	767	6	–
The National Grand Bank Of Marblehead	676	5	5
Marlboro			
The First National Bank Of Marlboro	158	6	–
The First National Bank Of Marlboro	2770	6	6
Marlborough			
The Peoples National Bank Of Marlborough	2404	4	5
Medford			
First National Bank In Medford	12979	6	5
The Medford National Bank	5247	6	–
Melrose			
The Melrose National Bank	4769	6	–
Merrimac			
The First National Bank Of Amesbury	268	6	–
The First National Merrimac Bank	268	6	6
Methuen			
The Methuen National Bank	12800	4	4
The National Bank Of Methuen	1485	5	–
Middleborough			
The Middleborough National Bank	3994	5	–
Milford			
The Home National Bank Of Milford	2275	2	6
The Milford National Bank	866	5	–
The Milford National Bank & Trust Company	866	6	6
Millbury			
Millbury National Bank	13835	–	6
The Millbury National Bank	572	5	6
Milton			
The Blue Hill National Bank Of Milton	684	4	6
Monson			
The Monson National Bank	503	5	6
Nantucket			
The Pacific National Bank Of Nantucket	714	3	6
Natick			
The Natick National Bank	2107	6	–
New Bedford			
The Citizens National Bank Of New Bedford	2262	6	–
The First National Bank Of New Bedford	261	2	3
The Mechanics National Bank Of New Bedford	743	4	–
The Merchants National Bank Of New Bedford	799	3	3
The National Bank Of Commerce, New Bedford	690	4	–
The Safe Deposit National Bank Of New Bedford	12405	4	4
Newburyport			
First And Ocean National Bank Of Newburyport	1011	6	5
The First National Bank Of Newburyport	279	5	–
The Mechanicks National Bank Of Newburyport	584	6	–
The Merchants National Bank Of Newburyport	1047	5	5
The Ocean National Bank Of Newburyport	1011	5	–
Newton			
Newton National Bank	13252	3	4
The First National Bank Of Newton	3598	–	6
The Newton National Bank	789	6	–
Newtonville			
The First National Bank Of Newton, Newtonville	488	6	–
North Adams			
North Adams National Bank, North Adams	1210	–	4
The Adams National Bank Of North Adams	1210	6	–
The Berkshire National Bank Of North Adams	2396	6	–
The North Adams National Bank, North Adams	1210	4	–
North Attleborough			
The Attleborough National Bank Of North Attleborough	1604	6	–
The Jewelers National Bank Of North Attleborough	7675	6	–
The Manufacturers National Bank Of North Attleborough	9086	6	6
The North Attleborough National Bank	3365	6	–
North Easton			
The First National Bank Of Easton	416	5	5
Northampton			
Northampton National Bank And Trust Company	1018	–	5
The First National Bank Of Northampton	383	4	6
The Hampshire County National Bank Of Northampton	418	5	–
The Northampton National Bank Of Northampton	1018	4	6
Northborough			
The Northborough National Bank	1279	5	6
Norwood			
The Norwood National Bank	8474	6	–
Orange			
The Orange National Bank	2255	5	5
Oxford			
The Oxford National Bank	764	5	–
Palmer			
The Palmer National Bank	2324	4	5

City, Bank	Ch. No.	L	S
Peabody			
The South Danvers National Bank Of Peabody	958	5	–
The Warren National Bank Of Peabody	616	5	5
Pepperell			
The First National Bank Of Pepperell	5964	6	6
Pittsfield			
The Agricultural National Bank Of Pittsfield	1082	3	–
The Pittsfield National Bank	1260	4	–
The Pittsfield-Third National Bank & Trust Co, Pittsfield	1260	–	5
The Third National Bank Of Pittsfield	2525	5	–
Plymouth			
The Old Colony National Bank Of Plymouth	996	4	5
The Plymouth National Bank	779	5	5
Provincetown			
The First National Bank Of Provincetown	736	5	5
Quincy			
The National Granite Bank Of Quincy	832	6	–
The National Mount Wollaston Bank Of Quincy	517	4	5
Randolph			
The Randolph National Bank	558	5	–
Reading			
The First National Bank In Reading	13558	–	6
The First National Bank Of Reading	4488	6	6
Rockland			
The First National Bank Of Rockland	3868	6	–
Rockport			
The Rockport National Bank	1194	6	–
Roxbury			
The Peoples National Bank Of Roxbury	595	5	–
Salem			
The Asiatic National Bank Of Salem	634	5	–
The First National Bank Of Salem	407	5	–
The Mercantile National Bank Of Salem	691	5	–
The Merchants National Bank Of Salem	726	5	–
The National Exchange Bank Of Salem	817	6	–
The Naumkeag National Bank Of Salem	647	5	–
The Salem National Bank	704	6	–
Salisbury			
The Powow River National Bank Of Salisbury	1049	6	–
Shelburne Falls			
The Shelburne Falls National Bank	1144	3	3
Somerville			
The Somerville National Bank	4771	4	5
South Danvers			
The Warren National Bank Of South Danvers	616	6	–
South Deerfield			
The Produce National Bank Of South Deerfield	8150	5	6
South Framingham			
The South Framingham National Bank	2485	6	–
South Weymouth			
The First National Bank Of South Weymouth	618	5	–
Southbridge			
The Peoples National Bank Of Southbridge	11388	5	6
The Southbridge National Bank	934	4	6
Spencer			
Spencer National Bank	13394	–	4
The Spencer National Bank	2288	5	6
Springfield			
Springfield National Bank, Springfield	4907	–	4
The Agawam National Bank Of Springfield	1055	4	–
The Chapin National Bank Of Springfield	2435	3	4
The Chicopee National Bank Of Springfield	988	4	–
The City National Bank Of Springfield	2433	6	–
The First National Bank Of Springfield	14	6	–
The John Hancock National Bank Of Springfield	982	6	–
The Pynchon National Bank Of Springfield	987	6	–
The Second National Bank Of Springfield	181	4	–
The Springfield Chapin Natl Bank & Trust Co, Springfield	4907	–	4
The Springfield National Bank	4907	3	–
The Third National Bank & Trust Company Of Springfield	308	–	4
The Third National Bank Of Springfield	308	3	–
Stockbridge			
The Housatonic National Bank Of Stockbridge	1170	4	5
Stoneham			
The Stoneham National Bank	4240	6	–
Taunton			
The Bristol County National Bank Of Taunton	766	5	–
The Machinists National Bank Of Taunton	947	4	4
The Taunton National Bank	957	5	–
Tisbury			
The Marthas Vineyard National Bank Of Tisbury	1274	4	5
Townsend			
The Townsend National Bank	805	4	5
Turners Falls			
The Crocker National Bank Of Turners Falls	2058	4	5
Uxbridge			
The Blackstone National Bank Of Uxbridge	1022	5	5
Wakefield			
The National Bank Of South Reading, Wakefield	1455	6	–
The Wakefield National Bank, Wakefield	1455	6	–
Waltham			
The Waltham National Bank	688	5	5
Ware			
The Ware National Bank	628	5	–
Warsham			
The National Bank Of Wareham	1440	6	5
Watertown			
The Union Market National Bank Of Watertown	2108	4	4
Webster			
The First National Bank Of Webster	2312	4	6
The First National Bank Of Webster	13411	–	5
The Webster National Bank	11236	5	6
Webster National Bank	13780	–	6
Wellesley			
The Wellesley National Bank	7297	5	5
West Newton			
The First National Bank Of West Newton	3598	6	–
Westboro			
The First National Bank Of Westboro	421	5	4
Westfield			
Hampden National Bank And Trust Company Of Westfield	1367	–	6
The First National Bank Of Westfield	190	3	5
The Hampden National Bank Of Westfield	1367	5	6
Westminster			
The Westminster National Bank	2284	6	–
The Westminster National Bank Of Gardner	2284	6	–
Weymouth			
The Union National Bank Of Weymouth	510	6	–
Whitinsville			
The Whitinsville National Bank	769	5	5
Whitman			
The Whitman National Bank	4660	6	6
Williamstown			
The Williamstown National Bank	3092	5	5
Winchendon			
The First National Bank Of Winchendon	327	5	5
Winchester			
The Middlesex County National Bank Of Winchester	5071	6	–
The Winchester National Bank	11103	5	5
Woburn			
Tanners National Bank In Woburn	14033	–	6
The First National Bank Of Woburn	746	6	–
The Tanners National Bank Of Woburn	11067	6	6
The Woburn National Bank	7550	6	6
Worcester			
The Central National Bank Of Worcester	455	6	–
The Citizens National Bank Of Worcester	765	6	–
The City National Bank Of Worcester	476	6	–
The First National Bank Of Worcester	79	4	–
The Mechanics National Bank Of Worcester	1135	5	5
The Merchants National Bank Of Worcester	7595	3	–
The Quinsigamond National Bank Of Worcester	1073	6	–
The Security National Bank Of Worcester	2273	6	–
The Worcester National Bank	442	5	–
Worcester County National Bank Of Worcester	7595	4	3
Worchester			
The First National Bank Of Worchester	2699	6	–
Wrentham			
The National Bank Of Wrentham	1085	5	6
Yarmouth			
The First National Bank Of Yarmouth	516	4	5

MICHIGAN

City, Bank	Ch. No.	L	S
Adrian			
The First National Bank Of Adrian	1973	5	–
The National Bank Of Commerce Of Adrian	9421	5	5
Albion			
The Albion National Bank	7552	6	–
The First National Bank Of Albion	3316	6	–
The National Exchange Bank Of Albion	1544	6	–
Algonac			
The First National Bank Of Algonac	12944	6	6
Allegan			
The First National Bank Of Allegan	1829	5	–
Almont			
The First National Bank Of Almont	12793	–	6
Alpena			
The Alpena National Bank	2847	6	5
Alpha			
The First National Bank Of Alpha	10601	6	6
Ann Arbor			
The First National Bank And Trust Company Of Ann Arbor	2714	–	3
The First National Bank Of Ann Arbor	22	5	–
The First National Bank Of Ann Arbor	2714	4	–
Battle Creek			
Central National Bank & Trust Company Of Battle Creek	7013	–	5
Central National Bank Of Battle Creek	7013	3	3
Old Merchants National Bank & Trust Company Of Battle Creek	7589	–	2
The Central National Bank At Battle Creek	13858	–	6
The City National Bank & Trust Company Of Battle Creek	11852	6	3
The City National Bank Of Battle Creek	11852	4	–
The First National Bank Of The City Of Battle Creek	1205	6	–
The Merchants National Bank Of Battle Creek	3896	6	–
The National Bank Of Battle Creek	3314	6	–
The Old National Bank & Trust Company Of Battle Creek	7589	6	–
The Old National Bank Of Battle Creek	7589	5	–
Bay City			
The Bay National Bank Of Bay City	2853	6	–
The First National Bank Of Bay City	410	6	–
The First National Bank Of Bay City	2853	5	4
The National Bank Of Bay City	13622	–	4
The Old Second National Bank Of Bay City	4953	6	–
The Second National Bank Of Bay City	2145	4	–
Benton Harbor			
Farmers & Merchants Natl Bank & Trust Co Of Benton Harbr	10529	5	4
The American National Bank Of Benton Harbor	10143	5	–
The American Natl Bank & Trust Company Of Benton Harbor	10143	6	4
The Farmers And Merchants National Bank Of Benton Harbor	10529	5	–
The First National Bank Of Benton Harbor	4261	6	–
Bessemer			
The Bessemer National Bank	13607	–	4
The First National Bank Of Bessemer	3947	6	–
Big Rapids			
The Big Rapids National Bank	2944	6	–
The Northern National Bank Of Big Rapids	1832	6	–
Birmingham			
The Birmingham National Bank	13703	–	6
The First National Bank Of Birmingham	9874	6	6
Blissfield			
The First National Bank Of Blissfield	11813	6	6
Boyne City			
The First National Bank Of Boyne City	9020	4	6
Bronson			
The Peoples National Bank Of Bronson	9704	6	6
Buchanan			
The First National Bank Of Buchanan	2046	6	–
The First National Bank Of Buchanan	3925	6	6
Burr Oak			
The First National Bank Of Burr Oak	9497	6	5
Calumet			
The First National Bank Of Calumet	3457	4	4
Capac			
The First National Bank Of Capac	10631	5	6
Caspian			
The Caspian National Bank	11802	6	5
Cassopolis			
The First National Bank Of Cassopolis	1812	4	1
Centreville			
The First National Bank Of Centreville	2095	5	–
Charlotte			
The First National Bank Of Charlotte	1758	5	6
The Merchants National Bank Of Charlotte	3034	6	–
Cheboygan			
The First National Bank Of Cheboygan	3235	5	6
Chesaning			
The First National Bank Of Chesaning	11454	6	–
Coldwater			
The Coldwater National Bank	1235	6	4
The Southern Michigan National Bank Of Coldwater	1924	3	3
Concord			
The First National Bank Of Concord	3251	6	–
Constantine			
The Farmers National Bank Of Constantine	2211	6	–
The First National Bank Of Constantine	813	6	–
Corunna			
The First National Bank Of Corunna	1256	6	–
Croswell			
The First National Bank Of Croswell	9792	6	–
Crystal Falls			
The Crystal Falls National Bank	11547	4	2
The Iron County National Bank Of Crystal Falls	7525	4	5
Dearborn			
The First National Bank Of Dearborn	12989	–	3
Decatur			
The First National Bank Of Decatur	1722	4	–
Detroit			
First And Old National Bank Of Detroit	10527	3	–
First National Bank In Detroit	10527	2	1
First National Bank, Detriot	10527	–	2
First Wayne National Bank Of Detriot	10527	–	1
Guardian National Bank Of Commerce Of Detroit	8703	–	2
Old Detroit National Bank	6492	6	–
The American Exchange National Bank Of Detroit	3357	5	–
The American National Bank Of Detroit	1542	5	–
The Commercial National Bank Of Detroit	2591	3	–
The Detroit National Bank	2870	6	–
The First National Bank Of Detroit	97	5	–
The First National Bank Of Detroit	2707	4	–
The Griswold National Bank Of Detroit	12847	4	–
The Merchants And Manufacturers National Bank Of Detroit	2365	5	–
The Merchants National Bank Of Detroit	10600	3	–
The National Bank Of Commerce Of Detroit	8703	4	–
The National Insurance Bank Of Detroit	1433	6	–
The Preston National Bank Of Detroit	3730	5	–
The Second National Bank Of Detroit	116	4	–
The Third National Bank Of Detroit	3514	6	–
The Union National Bank Of Detroit	3487	6	–
Dowagiac			
The Dowagiac National Bank	10073	6	5
The First National Bank Of Dowagiac	1625	6	–
Durand			
The First National Bank Of Durand	5415	6	–
East Saginaw			
The East Saginaw National Bank	3123	6	–
The First National Bank Of East Saginaw	637	6	–

City, Bank	Ch. No.	L	S
East Saginaw			
The Home National Bank Of East Saginaw	2761	6	–
The Merchants National Bank Of East Saginaw	1550	5	–
The Second National Bank Of East Saginaw	1918	6	–
Eaton Rapids			
The First National Bank Of Eaton Rapids	2367	5	6
Escanaba			
The Escanaba National Bank	8496	4	4
The First National Bank Of Escanaba	3761	4	4
Evart			
The First National Bank Of Evart	12561	–	3
Fenton			
The First National Bank Of Fenton	81	6	–
Flint			
First National Bank & Trust Company At Flint	10997	–	4
First National Bank At Flint	10997	6	5
The Citizens National Bank Of Flint	1780	6	–
The First National Bank Of Flint	1588	5	–
The First National Bank Of Flint	3361	4	–
The Flint National Bank	3361	6	–
The National Bank Of Flint	7664	6	–
Flushing			
The First National Bank Of Flushing	2708	6	–
Gladstone			
First National Bank In Gladstone	14111	–	6
The First National Bank Of Gladstone	10886	5	4
Grand Haven			
The First National Bank Of Grand Haven	1849	6	–
The National Bank Of Grand Haven	4578	6	–
Grand Rapids			
Grand Rapids National Bank	3293	4	3
Grand Rapids National City Bank	3293	5	–
Peoples National Bank Of Grand Rapids	13799	–	4
The American National Bank Of Grand Rapids	13328	–	3
The City National Bank Of Grand Rapids	812	6	–
The Fifth National Bank Of Grand Rapids	3488	5	–
The First National Bank Of Grand Rapids	294	6	–
The Fourth National Bank Of Grand Rapids	2611	2	–
The Grand Rapids National Bank	2460	2	–
The National Bank Of Grand Rapids	13758	–	3
The National City Bank Of Grand Rapids	3293	4	–
The Old National Bank Of Grand Rapids	2890	2	–
Greenville			
The City National Bank Of Greenville	3243	6	–
The First National Bank Of Greenville	2054	6	–
The Greenville National Bank	11843	6	6
Hamtramck			
The Peoples National Bank Of Hamtramck	11082	6	–
Hancock			
The First National Bank Of Hancock	2143	4	5
The National Metals Bank Of Hancock	14249	–	5
The Superior National Bank Of Hancock	9087	4	4
Hart			
The First National Bank Of Hart	6727	3	5
Hartford			
The Olney National Bank Of Hartford	9854	6	5
Hastings			
National Bank Of Hastings	13857	–	6
The Hastings National Bank	1745	5	6
Hermansville			
The First National Bank Of Hermansville	11954	6	5
Hillsdale			
The First National Bank Of Hillsdale	168	4	5
The Hillsdale County National Bank Of Hillsdale	14062	–	6
The Second National Bank Of Hillsdale	1470	6	–
Holly			
The First National Bank Of Holly	1752	5	–
The Merchants National Bank Of Holly	1965	6	–
Houghton			
The Citizens National Bank Of Houghton	5896	4	4
The First National Bank Of Houghton	1247	6	–
The Houghton National Bank	7676	4	4
The National Bank Of Houghton	3334	5	–
Howell			
First National Bank In Howell	14144	–	6
The First National Bank Of Howell	11586	6	4
Hubbell			
The First National Bank At Hubbell	13824	–	6
The First National Bank Of Hubbell	9359	6	6
Ionia			
The First National Bank Of Ionia	275	5	–
The Ionia County National Bank Of Ionia	14187	–	6
The National Bank Of Ionia	5789	4	4
The Second National Bank Of Ionia	2008	6	–
Iron Mountain			
The First National Bank Of Iron Mountain	3806	5	4
The National Bank Of Iron Mountain	11929	5	–
The United States National Bank Of Iron Mountain	11929	5	2
Iron River			
The First National Bank Of Iron River	8545	4	4
The Iron River National Bank	14102	–	5
Ironwood			
The First National Bank Of Ironwood	3971	6	–
The Gogebic National Bank Of Ironwood	9517	5	4
The Iron National Bank Of Ironwood	11469	4	5
The Merchants And Miners National Bank Of Ironwood	12387	5	3
Ishpeming			
The First National Bank Of Ishpeming	2084	6	–
The Ishpeming National Bank	3095	6	–
The Miners First National Bank Of Ishpeming	13931	–	4

City, Bank	Ch. No.	L	S
Ishpeming			
The Miners National Bank Of Ishpeming	5668	3	4
Ithaca			
The Commercial National Bank Of Ithaca	9654	4	5
The First National Bank Of Ithaca	3217	6	–
The Ithaca National Bank	6485	6	6
Jackson			
National Union Bank & Trust Company Of Jackson	11289	5	5
The First National Bank Of Jackson	1065	6	–
The National Bank Of Jackson	13741	–	4
The National Union Bank Of Jackson	11289	4	–
The Peoples National Bank Of Jackson	1533	4	5
Union & Peoples National Bank Of Jackson	1533	–	3
Kalamazoo			
Kalamazoo National Bank & Trust Company, Kalamazoo	3211	6	6
The City National Bank Of Kalamazoo	3210	5	–
The First National Bank And Trust Company Of Kalamazoo	191	6	3
The First National Bank Of Kalamazoo	191	4	–
The Kalamazoo National Bank	3211	4	–
The Michigan National Bank Of Kalamazoo	1359	5	
L'Anse			
The Baraga County National Bank Of L'Anse	9509	6	6
L'Anse Creuse			
The First National Bank Of L'Anse Creuse	12661	6	–
Lake Linden			
The First National Bank Of Lake Linden	3948	4	5
Lansing			
Lansing National Bank	14032	–	5
The Capital National Bank Of Lansing	8148	4	3
The City National Bank Of Lansing	3513	4	4
The Lansing National Bank	1953	6	–
The Second National Bank Of Lansing	264	6	–
Lapeer			
The First National Bank Of Lapeer	1731	4	5
Laurium			
The First National Bank Of Laurium	8598	4	4
Lawton			
The First National Bank Of Lawton	12084	6	6
Leslie			
The First National Bank Of Leslie	2162	6	–
Lincoln Park			
The Lincoln Park National Bank	12999	–	5
Lowell			
The Lowell National Bank	1280	6	–
Ludington			
The First National Bank & Trust Company Of Ludington	2773	6	5
The First National Bank Of Ludington	2773	6	–
Lyons			
The National Bank Of Lyons	2008	6	–
Manistee			
The First National Bank Of Manistee	2539	4	5
The Manistee National Bank	2606	6	–
Manistique			
The First National Bank In Manistique	13513	–	6
The First National Bank Of Manistique	5348	5	5
Marine City			
The Liberty National Bank Of Marine City	11260	5	6
Marquette			
The First National Bank & Trust Company Of Marquette	390	4	4
The First National Bank Of Marquette	390	2	–
The Marquette National Bank	6003	5	–
The Union National Bank Of Marquette	12027	4	4
Marshall			
The First National Bank Of Marshall	1515	4	5
The National Bank Of Michigan Of Marshall	1518	6	–
The National City Bank Of Marshall	2023	6	–
Mason			
The Dart National Bank Of Mason	12697	6	6
The First National Bank Of Mason	1764	6	–
Menominee			
The First National Bank Of Menominee	3256	3	3
The Lumbermen's National Bank Of Menominee	4454	4	4
Milford			
The First National Bank Of Milford	2379	6	–
Monroe			
The First National Bank Of Monroe	1587	5	5
Morenci			
The First National Bank Of Morenci	5669	6	–
Mount Clemens			
First National Bank In Mount Clemens	12971	3	5
The First National Bank Of Mount Clemens	2214	6	–
Mount Pleasant			
The First National Bank Of Mount Pleasant	3215	6	–
Muir			
The First National Bank Of Muir	2017	6	–
Munising			
The First National Bank Of Alger County At Munising	9000	4	6
Muskegon			
The Hackley National Bank Of Muskegon	4398	5	–
The Hackley Union National Bank Of Muskegon	4398	–	4
The Lumbermans National Bank Of Muskegon	2081	6	–
The Merchants National Bank Of Muskegon	3088	6	–
The Muskegon National Bank	1730	5	–
The National Lumbermans Bank Of Muskegon	4840	5	5
The Union National Bank Of Muskegon	4125	4	–
Negaunee			
The First National Bank Of Negaunee	2085	6	–
The First National Bank Of Negaunee	3717	5	4
The Negaunee National Bank	9556	4	4

City, Bank	Ch. No.	L	S
Niles			
The Citizens National Bank Of Niles	1886	6	–
The City National Bank & Trust Company Of Niles	13307	6	4
The First National Bank Of Niles	1761	6	–
Norway			
The First National Bank Of Norway	6863	4	2
Ontonagon			
The First National Bank In Ontonagon	13929	–	6
The First National Bank Of Ontonagon	6820	6	5
Ovid			
The First National Bank Of Ovid	3264	6	–
Owosso			
The First National Bank Of Owosso	1573	5	–
The Second National Bank Of Owosso	3410	6	–
Paw Paw			
The First National Bank Of Paw Paw	1521	5	6
Petoskey			
The First National Bank Of Petoskey	5607	4	4
Plymouth			
First National Bank In Plymouth	12953	5	5
The First National Bank Of Plymouth	1916	6	–
The First National Exchange Bank Of Plymouth	4649	3	–
The Plymouth National Bank	3109	6	–
Pontiac			
Community National Bank Of Pontiac	13739	–	5
First National Bank & Trust Company In Pontiac	12288	5	4
First National Bank In Pontiac	12288	4	–
The American National Bank Of Pontiac	12288	6	–
The First National Bank At Pontiac	13600	–	5
The First National Bank Of Pontiac	434	6	–
The First National Bank Of Pontiac	2607	6	–
The National Bank Of Pontiac	11549	6	–
The Pontiac National Bank	3388	6	–
The Second National Bank Of Pontiac	1574	6	–
Port Huron			
First National Bank & Trust Company Of Port Huron	4446	5	5
First National Bank In Port Huron	4446	6	–
First National Trust & Savings Bank Of Port Huron	4446	–	5
The First National Bank Of Port Huron	1857	6	–
The First National Exchange Bank Of Port Huron	4446	6	–
Quincy			
The First National Bank Of Quincy	2550	6	6
Reed City			
The First National Bank Of Reed City	4413	6	6
Richland			
The Farmers National Bank Of Richland	9099	6	–
Richmond			
The First National Bank Of Richmond	10742	6	6
Rochester			
The First National Bank Of Rochester	9218	6	6
The Rochester National Bank	13841	–	6
Rockland			
The First National Bank Of Rockland	5199	6	6
The Ontonagon County National Bank Of Rockland	5199	6	–
Romeo			
The Citizens National Bank Of Romeo	2186	5	2
The First National Bank Of Romeo	354	6	–
Royal Oak			
The First National Bank Of Royal Oak	12657	6	6
Saginaw			
Second National Bank & Trust Company Of Saginaw	1918	–	3
The Citizens National Bank Of Saginaw	2492	6	–
The Commercial National Bank Of Saginaw	3911	5	–
The First National Bank Of Saginaw	1768	6	–
The Second National Bank Of Saginaw	1918	3	4
Saint Clair			
The First National Bank Of St. Clair	1789	5	–
Saint Clair Heights			
The Michigan National Bank Of Saint Clair Heights	10632	6	–
Saint Clair Shores			
The First National Bank Of Saint Clair Shores	12661	6	6
Saint Ignace			
The First National Bank Of St. Ignace	3886	5	4
Saint Johns			
The First National Bank Of Saint Johns	1539	6	–
The St. Johns National Bank	3378	3	6
Saint Joseph			
The Commercial National Bank & Trust Co Of St. Joseph	5594	6	5
The Commercial National Bank Of St. Joseph	5594	5	–
The First National Bank Of St. Joseph	1866	5	–
Saint Louis			
The First National Bank Of Saint Louis	3239	6	–
Sault Ste Marie			
The First National Bank Of Sault Ste Marie	3547	4	4
The Sault Ste Marie National Bank	3747	6	–
Schoolcraft			
The First National Bank Of Schoolcraft	1725	6	–
South Haven			
The First National Bank Of South Haven	1823	6	–
Stanton			
The First National Bank Of Stanton	2914	6	–
Sturgis			
The First National Bank Of Sturgis	825	6	–
The National Bank Of Sturgis	3276	6	–
The Sturgis National Bank	3276	5	4
Tecumseh			
The National Bank Of Tecumseh	1063	6	–
Three Rivers			
The First National Bank Of Three Rivers	600	6	4
The Manufacturers National Bank Of Three Rivers	1919	6	–
The Three Rivers National Bank	3133	6	–

City, Bank	Ch. No.	L	S
Traverse City			
The First National Bank Of Traverse City	3325	6	5
Union City			
The Farmers National Bank Of Union City	2372	5	–
The Union City National Bank	1826	5	5
Utica			
The First National Bank Of Utica	12826	–	6
Vassar			
Millington National Bank, Millington	8723	5	6
The First National Bank Of Vassar	2987	6	–
The Vassar National Bank	8723	6	–
Wakefield			
The First National Bank Of Wakefield	11305	6	5
Watervliet			
The First National Bank Of Watervliet	10498	6	5
White Pigeon			
The First National Bank Of White Pigeon	4527	6	–
Whitehall			
The First National Bank Of Whitehall	2429	6	–
Wyandotte			
The First National Bank Of Wyandotte	12616	–	5
Yale			
The First National Bank Of Yale	5482	5	5
Ypsilanti			
The First National Bank Of Ypsilanti	155	5	4

MINNESOTA

City, Bank	Ch. No.	L	S
Ada			
The Ada National Bank	10665	6	6
The First National Bank Of Ada	5433	6	–
Adams			
The First National Bank Of Adams	8059	6	4
Adrian			
The First National Bank Of Adrian	7960	6	–
The National Bank Of Adrian	9033	5	6
Aitkin			
The Farmers National Bank Of Aitkin	10783	–	6
The First National Bank Of Aitkin	6803	5	5
Albert Lea			
The Albert Lea National Bank	4702	6	–
The Citizens National Bank Of Albert Lea	6128	5	–
The First National Bank Of Albert Lea	3560	4	5
The Security National Bank Of Albert Lea	6431	6	–
Alden			
The First National Bank Of Alden	6631	6	5
Alexandria			
The Farmers National Bank Of Alexandria	5859	3	–
The First National Bank Of Alexandria	2995	5	–
Amboy			
The First National Bank Of Amboy	9775	5	–
Anoka			
First National Bank In Anoka	13547	–	6
The Anoka National Bank	3000	6	6
The First National Bank Of Anoka	2800	6	–
Appleton			
The First National Bank Of Appleton	4831	6	–
The First National Bank Of Appleton	8813	6	4
Argyle			
The First National Bank Of Argyle	5907	5	–
Atwater			
The First National Bank Of Atwater	10570	6	–
Aurora			
The First National Bank Of Aurora	11345	6	–
Austin			
The Austin National Bank	4131	4	5
The Citizens National Bank Of Austin	4847	6	–
The First National Bank Of Austin	1690	4	3
Avoca			
The First National Bank Of Avoca	11224	6	–
Bagley			
The First National Bank Of Bagley	6813	5	5
Balaton			
The First National Bank Of Balaton	6840	5	–
Barnesville			
The Barnesville National Bank	6098	6	–
The First National Bank Of Barnesville	4959	4	4
Barnum			
The First National Bank Of Barnum	11761	6	6
Battle Lake			
The First National Bank Of Battle Lake	8756	5	5
Baudette			
The First National Bank Of Baudette	10710	6	5
Beardsley			
The First National Bank Of Beardsley	7438	6	–
Beaver Creek			
The First National Bank Of Beaver Creek	9321	6	–
Belle Plaine			
The First National Bank Of Belle Plaine	7273	6	5
Bemidji			
The First National Bank Of Bemidji	5582	5	5
The Lumbermens National Bank Of Bemidji	8241	6	–
The Northern Bank Of Bemidji	8241	4	5
Benson			
The First National Bank Of Benson	6154	4	–
Bertha			
The First National Bank Of Bertha	7373	5	5
Big Lake			
The First National Bank Of Big Lake	11611	6	–
Biwabik			
The First National Bank Of Biwabik	8697	5	–
Blackduck			
The First National Bank Of Blackduck	9147	5	–
Blooming Prairie			
The First National Bank Of Blooming Prairie	6775	5	3
Blue Earth			
First & Farmers National Bank Of Blue Earth	5393	–	4
Blue Earth			
The Farmers National Bank Of Blue Earth	7641	4	6
The First National Bank Of Blue Earth	5393	6	6
Bovey			
The First National Bank Of Bovey	11054	6	5
Boyd			
The Boyd National Bank	6571	6	–
Braham			
The First National Bank Of Braham	7387	5	5
Brainerd			
The First National Bank Of Brainerd	2590	5	4
Brandon			
The First National Bank Of Brandon	10862	6	–
Breckenridge			
The Breckenridge National Bank	6335	5	–
The First National Bank Of Breckenridge	4644	6	5
Brewster			
The First National Bank Of Brewster	10946	6	5
Bricelyn			
The First National Bank Of Bricelyn	6478	5	–
Browerville			
The First National Bank Of Browerville	7227	5	6
Browns Valley			
The First National Bank Of Browns Valley	7341	6	–
Buffalo			
The Buffalo National Bank	12959	–	6
The First National Bank Of Buffalo	11023	5	–
Caledonia			
The First National Bank Of Caledonia	7508	6	5
Camb			
The First National Bank Of Cambridge	7428	5	5
Campbell			
The First National Bank Of Campbell	6259	6	–
Canby			
The First National Bank Of Canby	6366	5	6
The National Citizens Bank Of Canby	7427	5	5
Cannon Falls			
The Farmers And Merchants National Bank Of Cannon Falls	6704	5	–
The First National Bank In Cannon Falls	13713	–	6
The First National Bank Of Cannon Falls	2387	6	–
Carlton			
The First National Bank Of Carlton	6973	6	5
Cass Lake			
The First National Bank Of Cass Lake	6352	6	5
Ceylon			
The First National Bank Of Ceylon	6029	4	5
Chaska			
The First National Bank Of Chaska	8378	5	6
Chatfield			
The First National Bank Of Chatfield	6608	5	5
Chisholm			
The First National Bank Of Chisholm	7647	5	5
Chokio			
The First National Bank Of Chokio	5969	6	–
Clarkfield			
The First National Bank Of Clarkfield	6448	6	–
Clearbrook			
The First National Bank Of Clearbrook	11392	6	–
Clinton			
The First National Bank Of Clinton	7161	6	–
Cloquet			
The First National Bank Of Cloquet	5405	4	4
Cokato			
The First National Bank Of Cokato	12395	6	5
Cold Spring			
The First National Bank Of Cold Spring	8051	6	6
Coleraine			
The First National Bank Of Coleraine	8322	6	6
Cottonwood			
The First National Bank Of Cottonwood	6584	5	6
Crookston			
The First National Bank Of Crookston	2567	4	4
The Merchants National Bank Of Crookston	3262	4	–
Crosby			
The First National Bank Of Crosby	9838	5	5
Dawson			
The First National Bank Of Dawson	6321	5	5
The Northwestern National Bank Of Dawson	13564	–	5
Deer Creek			
First National Bank In Deer Creek	13303	–	5
The First National Bank Of Deer Creek	7268	5	–
Deer River			
The First National Bank Of Deer River	9131	6	6
Deerwood			
The First National Bank Of Deerwood	9703	4	5
Delano			
The First National Bank Of Delano	9903	6	–
Detroit			
The First National Bank Of Detroit	3426	4	–
The Merchants National Bank Of Detroit	8122	5	–
Detroit Lakes			
Becker County National Bank Of Detroit Lakes	13075	–	5
Dodge Center			
The Farmers National Bank Of Dodge Center	6623	6	–
The First National Bank Of Dodge Center	6682	6	–
Duluth			
American Exchange National Bank Of Duluth	9374	3	–
Duluth National Bank	12140	4	4
First & American National Bank Of Duluth	3626	–	1
The City National Bank Of Duluth	6520	3	2
The Duluth National Bank	2768	6	–
The Duluth Union National Bank, Duluth	3626	6	–
The First National Bank Of Duluth	1954	6	–
The First National Bank Of Duluth	3626	3	–
Duluth			
The Marine National Bank Of Duluth	4421	6	–
The Merchants National Bank Of Duluth	3453	6	–
The Minnesota National Bank Of Duluth	11810	4	3
The National Bank Of Commerce Of Duluth	4001	6	–
The Northern National Bank Of Duluth	9327	3	3
The Pioneer National Bank Of Duluth	13078	5	4
The Union National Bank Of Duluth	3626	6	–
Western National Bank Of Duluth	13116	5	4
Dunnell			
The First National Bank Of Dunnell	6738	5	5
Eagle Bend			
The First National Bank Of Eagle Bend	6266	5	4
East Grand Forks			
The First National Bank Of East Grand Forks	4638	5	–
Elbow Lake			
The First National Bank Of Elbow Lake	4617	5	5
Elgin			
The First National Bank Of Elgin	7184	6	–
Elk River			
The First National Bank Of Elk River	8757	5	5
Ellsworth			
The First National Bank Of Ellsworth	5570	5	–
Elmore			
The First National Bank Of Elmore	5377	5	5
Ely			
The First National Bank Of Ely	8592	5	5
Emmons			
The First National Bank Of Emmons	6784	5	4
Erskine			
The First National Bank Of Erskine	11173	5	–
Eveleth			
The First National Bank Of Eveleth	5553	5	5
The Miners National Bank Of Eveleth	6991	5	4
Eyota			
The First National Bank Of Eyota	5374	5	–
Fairfax			
The First National Bank Of Fairfax	9771	5	6
Fairmont			
The Fairmont National Bank	8551	5	5
The First National Bank Of Fairmont	4936	5	5
The Martin County National Bank Of Fairmont	5423	3	4
Faribault			
The Citizens National Bank Of Faribault	1863	4	–
The First National Bank Of Faribault	1686	5	–
The Security National Bank & Trust Company Of Faribault	11668	–	5
The Security National Bank Of Faribault	11668	5	–
Farmington			
The First National Bank Of Farmington	11687	–	4
Fergus Falls			
Fergus Falls Natl Bank & Trust Company, Fergus Falls	2648	–	4
The Citizens National Bank Of Fergus Falls	2934	6	–
The Fergus Falls National Bank	2648	4	5
The First National Bank Of Fergus Falls	2030	4	4
Fertile			
The Citizens National Bank Of Fertile	6693	6	–
The First National Bank Of Fertile	5988	6	–
Foley			
The First National Bank Of Foley	7933	5	4
Forest Lake			
The First National Bank Of Forest Lake	11652	5	6
Fosston			
The First National Bank Of Fosston	6889	5	5
Frazee			
The First National Bank Of Frazee	7024	5	5
Fulda			
The First National Bank Of Fulda	6054	6	–
Gilbert			
The First National Bank Of Gilbert	9262	5	4
Glencoe			
The First National Bank Of Glencoe	2571	4	5
Glenwood			
The First National Bank Of Glenwood	7742	5	–
Gonvick			
The First National Bank Of Gonvick	10830	5	–
Good Thunder			
The First National Bank Of Good Thunder	11552	6	4
Goodhue			
The First National Bank Of Goodhue	7603	5	–
Graceville			
The First National Bank Of Graceville	7213	5	5
Grand Meadow			
The First National Bank Of Grand Meadow	6933	6	6
Grand Rapids			
The First National Bank Of Grand Rapids	6563	5	5
Granite Falls			
The First National Bank Of Granite Falls	8416	5	
Grey Eagle			
The First National Bank Of Grey Eagle	8729	5	–
The National Bank Of Grey Eagle	12607	5	5
Hallock			
The First National Bank Of Hallock	6934	5	–
Halstad			
The First National Bank Of Halstad	7196	6	5
Hancock			
The First National Bank Of Hancock	6996	3	5
The Hancock National Bank	7033	3	5
Hanley Falls			
The First National Bank Of Hanley Falls	6285	6	–
Hanska			
The First National Bank Of Hanska	11288	5	–
Harmony			
The First National Bank Of Harmony	8683	6	5
Hastings			
The First National Bank Of Hastings	496	5	5
The Hastings National Bank	11212	–	5

City, Bank	Ch. No.	L	S
Hastings			
The Merchants National Bank Of Hastings	1538	6	–
Hawley			
The First National Bank Of Hawley	7772	6	6
Hendricks			
The Farmers National Bank Of Hendricks	9457	4	6
The First National Bank Of Hendricks	6468	6	6
Henning			
The First National Bank Of Henning	6906	5	5
Herman			
The First National Bank Of Herman	8049	4	6
Heron Lake			
The First National Bank Of Heron Lake	5383	5	4
Hibbing			
The First National Bank Of Hibbing	5745	5	4
The Hibbing National Bank	12568	6	–
Hills			
The First National Bank Of Hills	6199	6	–
Hutchinson			
The Farmers National Bank Of Hutchinson	10147	5	6
International Falls			
The First National Bank Of International Falls	7380	4	4
Iona			
The First National Bank Of Iona	7128	6	–
Ironton			
The First National Bank Of Ironton	10382	5	5
Isanti			
The First National Bank Of Isanti	1554	6	6
Ivanhoe			
The Farmers And Merchants National Bank Of Ivanhoe	11627	5	6
The First National Bank Of Ivanhoe	6467	5	6
The Ivanhoe National Bank	6637	6	–
Jackson			
The Brown National Bank Of Jackson	7797	5	5
The First National Bank Of Jackson	5852	4	–
The Jackson National Bank	6992	5	–
Jasper			
The First National Bank Of Jasper	6523	5	–
Jordan			
The First National Bank Of Jordan	11218	5	5
Kasson			
National Farmers Bank Of Kasson	11042	6	5
The First National Bank Of Kasson	2159	6	–
The National Bank Of Dodge County At Kasson	10580	5	4
The National Bank Of Kasson	4969	6	–
Keewatin			
The First National Bank Of Keewatin	10903	6	5
Kerkhoven			
The First National Bank Of Kerkhoven	11365	5	6
Kiester			
The First National Bank Of Kiester	10603	6	4
Lake Benton			
The First National Bank Of Lake Benton	4509	6	–
The National Citizens Bank Of Lake Benton	6696	5	6
Lake City			
The First National Bank Of Lake City	1740	6	–
Lake Crystal			
The American National Bank Of Lake Crystal	11401	5	6
The First National Bank Of Lake Crystal	6918	5	5
Lake Park			
The First National Bank Of Lake Park	7143	6	–
Lake Wilson			
The First National Bank Of Lake Wilson	11293	6	6
Lakefield			
The First National Bank Of Lakefield	6537	5	–
Lamberton			
The First National Bank Of Lamberton	7221	5	–
Lancaster			
The First National Bank Of Lancaster	11356	6	–
Lanesboro			
The First National Bank Of Lanesboro	10507	5	6
Le Roy			
The First National Bank Of Le Roy	7109	6	4
Le Sueur			
The First National Bank Of Le Sueur	7199	6	6
Le Sueur Center			
The First National Bank Of Le Sueur Center	6921	6	5
Litchfield			
The First National Bank Of Litchfield	6118	4	–
The Northwestern National Bank Of Litchfield	13486	–	3
Little Falls			
The American National Bank In Little Falls	13353	–	3
The American National Bank Of Little Falls	4655	5	–
The First National Bank Of Little Falls	4034	4	4
The German American National Bank Of Little Falls	4655	5	–
Littlefork			
The First National Bank Of Littlefork	11863	6	–
Long Prairie			
The First National Bank Of Long Prairie	6208	6	–
The Peoples National Bank Of Long Prairie	7080	5	4
Luverne			
First And Farmers National Bank In Luverne	12634	5	6
The Farmers National Bank Of Luverne	7770	6	–
The First National Bank Of Luverne	3428	5	–
The National Bank Of Luverne	8977	6	–
Lyle			
The First National Bank Of Lyle	5706	5	4
Mabel			
The First National Bank Of Mabel	9031	5	4
Madelia			
The Citizens National Bank Of Madelia	13784	–	5
Madelia			
The First National Bank Of Madelia	7100	5	–
Madison			
The First National Bank Of Madison	6795	5	6
The Klein National Bank Of Madison	13561	–	5
Mahnomen			
First National Bank In Mahnomen	12941	–	5
The First National Bank Of Mahnomen	8726	6	–
Mankato			
First National Bank & Trust Company Of Mankato	1683	–	5
First National Bank Of Mankato	1683	–	6
National Bank Of Commerce In Mankato	14220	–	6
The Citizens National Bank Of Mankato	2005	6	–
The First National Bank Of Mankato	1683	4	5
The Mankato National Bank	3562	6	–
The National Bank Of Commerce Of Mankato	6519	4	6
The National Citizens Bank Of Mankato	4727	3	3
Mapleton			
The First National Bank Of Mapleton	6787	5	5
Marble			
The First National Bank Of Marble	11608	5	4
Marshall			
The First National Bank Of Marshall	4614	5	4
The Lyon County National Bank Of Marshall	4595	5	–
Mc Intosh			
The First National Bank Of Mc Intosh	6488	5	5
Melrose			
The First National Bank Of Melrose	7566	6	–
Menahga			
The First National Bank Of Menahga	11740	6	5
Milaca			
The First National Bank Of Milaca	9050	5	5
Minneapolis			
Bloomington-Lake National Bank Of Minneapolis	12972	4	4
First National Bank & Trust Company Of Minneapolis	710	–	2
First National Bank In Minneapolis	710	1	1
Midland National Bank & Trust Company Of Minneapolis	9409	4	2
Minnehaha National Bank Of Minneapolis	13096	6	5
The Central National Bank Of Minneapolis	13108	6	3
The Clarke National Bank Of Minneapolis	6449	6	–
The Columbia National Bank Of Minneapolis	4739	6	–
The Commercial National Bank Of Minneapolis	10261	6	–
The First & Security National Bank Of Minneapolis	710	3	–
The First National Bank Of Minneapolis	710	3	–
The Flour City National Bank Of Minneapolis	3784	6	–
The Lincoln National Bank Of Minneapolis	11178	6	–
The Manufacturers National Bank Of Minneapolis	3098	6	–
The Marquette National Bank Of Minneapolis	11861	4	5
The Merchants National Bank Of Minneapolis	1830	6	–
The Metropolitan National Bank Of Minneapolis	9442	2	5
The Midland National Bank Of Minneapolis	9409	4	–
The Minneapolis National Bank	11778	6	–
The Minnesota National Bank Of Minneapolis	6449	6	–
The National Bank Of Commerce Of Minneapolis	3206	6	–
The National City Bank Of Minneapolis	10261	6	–
The National Exchange Bank Of Minneapolis	719	6	–
The Nicollet National Bank Of Minneapolis	3145	6	–
The Northwestern National Bank Of Minneapolis	2006	1	1
The Richfield National Bank Of Minneapolis	12115	6	6
The Scandinavian-American National Bank Of Minneapolis	9409	5	–
The Security National Bank Of Minneapolis	8720	3	–
The State National Bank Of Minneapolis	1623	5	–
The Swedish-American National Bank Of Minneapolis	4951	5	–
The Transportation Brotherhoods National Bank Of Minneapo	12282	5	–
The Union National Bank Of Minneapolis	2795	6	–
Minneota			
The Farmers And Merchants National Bank Of Minneota	6917	4	5
The First National Bank Of Minneota	6413	6	5
Minnesota Lake			
The Farmers National Bank Of Minnesota Lake	6532	5	6
The First National Bank Of Minnesota Lake	6204	6	–
Montevideo			
The First National Bank Of Montevideo	6860	5	–
Montgomery			
The First National Bank Of Montgomery	11215	6	5
Moorhead			
First National Bank In Moorhead	13297	–	4
The First & Moorhead National Bank, Moorhead	2569	6	–
The First National Bank Of Moorhead	2569	4	–
The Moorhead National Bank	4713	5	–
Moose Lake			
The First National Bank Of Moose Lake	12947	6	5
Mora			
The First National Bank Of Mora	7292	5	5
Morris			
The First National Bank Of Morris	2933	6	–
The Morris National Bank	6310	3	5
Motley			
The First National Bank Of Motley	7764	6	5
Motordale			
The First National Bank Of Motordale	11550	6	–
Mountain Lake			
The First National Bank Of Mountain Lake	9267	5	4
Nashwauk			
The American National Bank Of Nashwauk	11579	5	4
The First National Bank Of Nashwauk	10736	5	4
New Brighton			
The Twin City National Bank Of New Brighton	4302	6	–
New Duluth			
The New Duluth National Bank	4750	6	–
New Germany			
First National Bank Of New Germany	11550	5	–
New Prague			
The First National Bank Of New Prague	7092	5	3
New Ulm			
The Citizens National Bank Of New Ulm	2318	6	–
The First National Bank Of New Ulm	631	6	–
Northfield			
Northfield National Bank And Trust Company	13350	–	4
The First National Bank Of Northfield	2073	4	4
The Northfield National Bank	5895	4	–
Olivia			
The Citizens National Bank Of Olivia	13081	–	3
The Peoples First National Bank Of Olivia	9063	6	–
Ortonville			
The Citizens National Bank Of Ortonville	6747	6	–
The First National Bank Of Ortonville	6459	4	5
Osakis			
The First National Bank Of Osakis	6837	5	5
Owatonna			
The Farmers National Bank Of Owatonna	2122	4	–
The First National Bank Of Owatonna	1911	4	4
The National Farmers Bank Of Owatonna	4928	4	–
Park Rapids			
The Citizens National Bank Of Park Rapids	13692	–	5
The First National Bank Of Park Rapids	5542	4	5
Parkers Prairie			
The First National Bank Of Parkers Prairie	6661	4	5
Paynesville			
The First National Bank Of Paynesville	11332	4	–
Pelican Rapids			
The First National Bank Of Pelican Rapids	6349	5	–
Pequot			
The First National Bank Of Pequot	11267	6	–
Perham			
The First National Bank Of Perham	6276	5	–
Pine City			
The First National Bank Of Pine City	11581	6	6
Pipestone			
Pipestone National Bank	10936	5	6
The First National Bank Of Pipestone	3982	4	5
Plainview			
The First National Bank Of Plainview	6293	4	4
Preston			
National Bank Of Preston	9059	6	–
The First National Bank Of Preston	6279	4	5
Princeton			
The First National Bank Of Princeton	4807	6	–
The First National Bank Of Princeton	7708	5	5
Proctor			
The First National Bank Of Proctor	11125	5	5
The Peoples National Bank Of Proctor	11974	6	–
Raymond			
The First National Bank Of Raymond	8050	4	
Red Lake Falls			
The Farmers National Bank Of Red Lake Falls	9837	6	–
The First National Bank Of Red Lake Falls	3659	6	–
Red Wing			
The First National Bank Of Red Wing	1487	4	3
The Goodhue County National Bank Of Red Wing	7307	4	4
The Red Wing National Bank And Trust Company, Red Wing	13396	–	3
Redwood Falls			
The First National Bank Of Redwood Falls	5826	5	–
Renville			
The First National Bank Of Renville	6583	5	–
Richfield			
The Richfield National Bank	12115	6	–
Rochester			
The First National Bank Of Rochester	579	4	3
The Rochester National Bank	2316	5	–
The Union National Bank Of Rochester	2088	4	5
Roseau			
The First National Bank Of Roseau	6783	5	5
The Roseau County National Bank Of Roseau	11848	6	6
Rosemount			
The First National Bank Of Rosemount	11776	6	–
Royalton			
The First National Bank Of Royalton	6731	6	–
Rush City			
The First National Bank Of Rush City	6954	5	–
Rushford			
The First National Bank Of Rushford	6436	5	5
Rushmore			
The First National Bank Of Rushmore	6862	6	–
Ruthton			
The First National Bank Of Ruthton	5892	6	–
Saint Anthony			
The First National Bank Of Saint Anthony	1830	6	–

City, Bank	Ch. No.	L	S
Saint Charles			
The First National Bank Of Saint Charles	6237	6	–
Saint Cloud			
The American National Bank Of Saint Cloud	11818	5	4
The First National Bank Of Saint Cloud	2790	4	–
The German-American National Bank Of Saint Cloud	3009	6	–
The Merchants National Bank Of St. Cloud	4797	3	–
Saint James			
The Citizens & Security National Bank Of St. James	7021	6	5
The Citizens National Bank Of St. James	7021	6	–
The First National Bank Of Saint James	4859	5	–
Saint Paul			
National Exchange Bank Of St. Paul	10940	5	–
The American National Bank Of Saint Paul	6828	5	3
The Capital National Bank Of Saint Paul	8108	2	–
The Commercial National Bank Of Saint Paul	3689	6	–
The Empire National Bank & Trust Company Of St. Paul	12922	–	3
The First National Bank Of Saint Paul	203	3	1
The Merchants National Bank Of Saint Paul	2020	2	–
The Midway National Bank Of St. Paul	13131	5	4
The National Bank Of Commerce In St Paul	10475	6	–
The National German-American Bank Of Saint Paul	2943	5	–
The National Marine Bank Of Saint Paul	1258	6	–
The Second National Bank Of Saint Paul	725	4	–
The St. Paul National Bank	2959	4	–
The Third National Bank Of Saint Paul	3233	6	–
The Twin Cities National Bank Of St. Paul	11741	3	4
Saint Peter			
The First National Bank Of Saint Peter	1794	4	5
Sandstone			
The First National Bank Of Sandstone	9464	5	5
Sauk Centre			
The First National Bank Of Sauk Centre	3155	6	6
The Merchants National Bank Of Sauk Centre	6417	5	5
Shakopee			
The First National Bank Of Shakopee	1597	6	–
The First National Bank Of Shakopee	3039	6	4
The Merchants And Farmers National Bank Of Shakopee	3127	6	–
Sherburn			
The Sherburn National Bank	6348	5	5
Slayton			
The First National Bank Of Slayton	5256	5	–
Sleepy Eye			
The First National Bank Of Sleepy Eye	6387	4	4
The First National Bank Of Sleepy Eye Lake	6387	6	–
South Saint Paul			
Stockyards National Bank Of South Saint Paul	6732	4	4
Spring Valley			
The First National Bank Of Spring Valley	6316	4	5
Springfield			
The First National Bank Of Springfield	8269	6	–
Staples			
The City National Bank Of Staples	8523	5	5
The First National Bank Of Staples	5568	4	5
Starbuck			
The First National Bank Of Starbuck	9596	1	4
Stephen			
The First National Bank Of Stephen	9064	5	5
Stewartville			
The First National Bank Of Stewartville	5330	6	6
The Stewartville National Bank	13615	–	5
Stillwater			
The First National Bank Of Stillwater	1514	6	–
The First National Bank Of Stillwater	2674	4	3
The Lumbermans National Bank Of Stillwater	1783	5	–
Swanville			
The First National Bank Of Swanville	10824	6	5
Thief River Falls			
The First National Bank Of Thief River Falls	5894	4	5
Tower			
The First National Bank Of Tower	3924	6	–
Tracy			
The First National Bank Of Tracy	4992	6	–
Truman			
The Truman National Bank	6364	5	5
Twin Valley			
The First National Bank Of Twin Valley	6401	5	5
Two Harbors			
First National Bank In Two Harbors	12357	5	4
The First National Bank Of Two Harbors	6304	6	–
Tyler			
The First National Bank Of Tyler	6203	5	6
Ulen			
The First National Bank Of Ulen	7081	6	–
Verndale			
The First National Bank Of Verndale	6022	4	6
Virginia			
The First National Bank Of Virginia	6527	5	4
Wabasha			
The First National Bank Of Wabasha	3100	5	3

City, Bank	Ch. No.	L	S
Waconia			
The First National Bank Of Waconia	11410	5	4
Wadena			
The First National Bank In Wadena	12507	6	4
The First National Bank Of Wadena	4821	4	–
The Merchants National Bank Of Wadena	4916	4	5
The National Bank Of Wadena	12507	6	–
Walker			
The First National Bank Of Walker	8476	5	5
Warren			
The First National Bank Of Warren	5866	5	–
The Warren National Bank	11286	5	–
Waseca			
The Farmers National Bank Of Waseca	9253	5	4
The First National Bank Of Waseca	6544	4	4
Waterville			
The First National Bank Of Waterville	7283	5	6
Welcome			
The Welcome National Bank	6331	5	4
Wells			
The First National Bank Of Wells	4669	5	–
The Wells National Bank	6788	5	–
Wendell			
The First National Bank Of Wendell	10898	5	6
West Concord			
First National Bank In West Concord	14167	–	6
The First National Bank Of West Concord	5362	4	5
West Minneapolis			
First National Bank Of Hopkins	7958	–	4
Security National Bank Of Hopkins	12518	–	4
The First National Bank Of West Minneapolis	7958	6	–
The Security National Bank Of West Minneapolis	12518	6	–
Westbrook			
The First National Bank Of Westbrook	6412	5	5
Wheaton			
The First National Bank Of Wheaton	6035	5	5
The National Bank Of Wheaton	8993	5	–
Willmar			
The First National Bank Of Willmar	6151	3	–
Wilmont			
The First National Bank Of Wilmont	5301	6	–
Windom			
The First National Bank Of Windom	5063	5	4
The Windom National Bank	6396	6	6
Winnebago			
The Blue Earth Valley National Bank Of Winnebago	10393	5	5
The First National Bank Of Winnebago City	5406	5	–
Winona			
The First National Bank Of Winona	550	5	–
The First National Bank Of Winona	3224	2	2
The Merchants National Bank Of Winona	2268	3	–
The National Bank Of Winona	3224	6	–
The Second National Bank Of Winona	1842	5	–
The United National Bank Of Winona	1643	6	–
The Winona Deposit National Bank	1782	6	–
The Winona National And Savings Bank, Winona	10865	–	3
Winthrop			
First National Bank In Winthrop	14042	–	6
The First National Bank Of Winthrop	7014	5	5
Woodstock			
The First National Bank Of Woodstock	7625	5	5
Worthington			
The Citizens National Bank Of Worthington	5910	5	–
The First National Bank Of Worthington	3550	6	–
The Worthington National Bank	8989	5	4

MISSISSIPPI

City, Bank	Ch. No.	L	S
Aberdeen			
The First National Bank Of Aberdeen	3656	4	4
Ackerman			
The First National Bank Of Ackerman	9251	6	–
Biloxi			
The First National Bank Of Biloxi	10576	5	4
Brookhaven			
The First National Bank Of Brookhaven	10494	5	5
Canton			
The First National Bank Of Canton	6847	6	4
Clarksdale			
The First National Bank Of Clarksdale	6595	6	–
The Planters National Bank Of Clarksdale	12222	6	5
Collins			
The First National Bank Of Collins	9728	6	–
Columbia			
The Citizens National Bank Of Columbia	10326	6	–
Columbus			
First-Columbus National Bank, Columbus	10738	–	2
The Columbus National Bank	10738	6	6
The First National Bank Of Columbus	2638	6	–
The National Bank Of Commerce Of Columbus	10361	5	3
Corinth			
The Citizens National Bank Of Corinth	9751	5	–
The First National Bank Of Corinth	9094	3	5
Greenville			
The First National Bank Of Greenville	3765	5	5
Greenwood			
The First National Bank Of Greenwood	7216	3	3
Gulfport			
First National Bank In Gulfport	13553	–	6
The First National Bank Of Gulfport	6188	3	4
Hattiesburg			
First National Bank Of Commerce Of Hattiesburg	5176	5	–
First National Bank Of Hattiesburg	5176	4	4
The Commercial National Bank Of Hattiesburg	12478	5	5
The First National Bank Of Hattiesburg	5177	6	–

City, Bank	Ch. No.	L	S
Hattiesburg			
The National Bank Of Commerce Of Hattiesburg	5176	6	–
Itta Bena			
The First National Bank Of Itta Bena	10688	5	5
Iuka			
The First National Bank Of Iuka	10154	6	–
Jackson			
Capital National Bank In Jackson	13708	–	5
The Capital National Bank Of Jackson	6646	4	4
The First National Bank Of Jackson	1610	6	–
The First National Bank Of Jackson	3332	4	6
The Jackson-State National Bank	10523	6	–
The State National Bank Of Jackson	10463	6	–
Laurel			
The Commercial National Bank And Trust Company Of Laurel	11898	5	5
The First National Bank Of Laurel	6681	4	2
The Laurel National Bank	6923	6	–
Lumberton			
The First National Bank Of Lumberton	5613	5	5
Mc Comb City			
The First National Bank Of Mc Comb City	7461	5	5
Meridian			
First National Bank In Meridian	13551	–	4
The Citizens National Bank Of Meridian	7266	3	3
The First National Bank Of Meridian	2957	4	6
The Meridian National Bank	3176	6	–
Moss Point			
The Pascagoula National Bank Of Moss Point	8593	5	3
Natchez			
Britton And Koontz National Bank In Natchez	13722	–	5
The Britton And Koontz National Bank Of Natchez	12537	6	4
The First National Bank Of Natchez	3701	6	–
The National Bank Of Commerce Of Natchez	6305	6	–
New Albany			
The First National Bank Of New Albany	8514	5	–
Okolona			
The First National Bank Of Okolona	9196	6	–
Oxford			
The First National Bank Of Oxford	9865	4	5
Philadelphia			
The First National Bank Of Philadelphia	9041	5	–
Pontotoc			
The First National Bank Of Pontotoc	9040	4	4
Poplarville			
The National Bank Of Poplarville	8719	6	–
Port Gibson			
The Mississippi National Bank Of Port Gibson	5715	6	–
Ripley			
The First National Bank Of Ripley	9204	6	–
Rosedale			
The First National Bank Of Rosedale	10745	6	–
The Rosedale National Bank	12073	6	–
Shaw			
The First National Bank Of Shaw	7200	6	–
Starkville			
The First National Bank Of Starkville	3688	6	–
Summit			
The National Bank Of Summit	9753	6	–
The Progressive National Bank Of Summit	10338	6	–
Tupelo			
The First National Bank Of Tupelo	4521	6	–
Vicksburg			
Citizens National Bank Of Vicksburg	7507	6	–
The American National Bank Of Vicksburg	6121	6	–
The First National Bank And Trust Company Of Vicksburg	3258	–	3
The First National Bank Of Vicksburg	3258	3	6
The Merchants National Bank & Trust Company Of Vicksburg	3430	–	3
The Merchants National Bank Of Vicksburg	3430	6	–
The National Bank Of Vicksburg	803	6	–
West Point			
The First National Bank Of West Point	2891	5	3
Yazoo City			
The Delta National Bank Of Yazoo City	12587	6	1
The First National Bank Of Yazoo City	3566	6	–

MISSOURI

City, Bank	Ch. No.	L	S
Adrian			
The First National Bank Of Adrian	10375	6	–
Albany			
The First National Bank Of Albany	7205	6	5
Appleton City			
The First National Bank Of Appleton City	2636	4	6
Aurora			
The First National Bank Of Aurora	4409	6	–
Bethany			
The First National Bank Of Bethany	8009	5	6
Bolivar			
The First National Bank Of Bolivar	7271	6	6
Boonville			
The Boonville National Bank	10915	5	4
The Central National Bank Of Boonville	1584	3	–
Bosworth			
The First National Bank Of Bosworth	7573	4	5
Braymer			
The First National Bank Of Braymer	7351	5	3
Brookfield			
The First National Bank Of Brookfield	12820	6	6
Brunswick			
The First National Bank Of Brunswick	4083	6	6
Burlington Junction			
The First National Bank Of Burlington Junction	6242	6	6

City, Bank	Ch. No.	L	S
Butler			
The Bates County National Bank Of Butler	1843	5	–
The Bates National Bank Of Butler	6405	6	–
The Butler National Bank	2561	6	–
Cabool			
The Cabool National Bank	8877	6	–
The First National Bank Of Cabool	8877	5	–
Cainesville			
The First National Bank Of Cainesville	8407	5	6
Calfornia			
The Moniteau National Bank Of Calfornia	1712	1	4
Cameron			
The First National Bank Of Cameron	4259	4	5
Campbell			
The First National Bank Of Campbell	6885	6	6
Canton			
The First National Bank Of Canton	7729	6	–
Cape Girardeau			
The First National Bank Of Cape Girardeau	4611	5	3
Carondelet			
The First National Bank Of Carondelet	454	6	–
Carrollton			
The First National Bank Of Carrollton	4079	4	5
Carthage			
The Carthage National Bank	4815	6	–
The Central National Bank Of Carthage	4441	4	5
The First National Bank Of Carthage	2013	6	–
The First National Bank Of Carthage	3005	4	5
Caruthersville			
The First National Bank Of Caruthersville	10784	6	6
The National Bank Of Caruthersville	14092	–	4
Cassville			
The First National Bank Of Cassville	8979	5	6
Centralia			
The First National Bank Of Centralia	6875	6	5
Chaffee			
The First National Bank Of Chaffee	9928	6	5
Chillicothe			
The Citizens National Bank Of Chillicothe	4111	4	5
The First National Bank Of Chillicothe	3686	4	5
Clayton			
Clayton National Bank	13481	–	5
The Clayton National Bank	12329	6	5
The First National Bank Of Clayton	12333	5	4
Clinton			
The Clinton National Bank	7806	4	6
The First National Bank Of Clinton	1940	6	–
The Peoples National Bank Of Clinton	8509	4	4
Columbia			
The Boone County National Bank Of Columbia	1770	4	4
The Exchange National Bank Of Columbia	1467	3	4
The First National Bank Of Columbia	67	6	–
Cowgill			
The First National Bank Of Cowgill	6926	5	6
Dexter			
The First National Bank Of Dexter	11320	5	6
Edina			
The First National Bank Of Edina	9490	6	–
Eldorado Springs			
The First National Bank Of Eldorado Springs	10055	5	–
Excelsior Springs			
The First National Bank Of Excelsior Springs	7741	6	–
Fairview			
The First National Bank Of Fairview	8916	5	6
Fulton			
The Farmers First National Bank Of Fulton	8358	6	–
The First National Bank Of Fulton	8358	5	–
Gallatin			
The First National Bank Of Gallatin	5827	4	4
Golden City			
The Citizens National Bank Of Golden City	10633	6	–
The First National Bank Of Golden City	7684	5	6
Grant City			
The First National Bank Of Grant City	3380	6	–
Green City			
American National Bank Of Green City	8570	5	–
The City National Bank Of Green City	9029	6	–
Hamilton			
The First National Bank Of Hamilton	4151	4	6
Hannibal			
The First National Bank Of Hannibal	1571	6	–
The First National Bank Of Hannibal	4010	6	–
The Hannibal National Bank	6635	3	4
Harrisonville			
The Citizens National Bank Of Harrisonville	6343	6	6
The First National Bank Of Harrisonville	3754	6	–
Holden			
The First National Bank Of Holden	10384	5	6
Hopkins			
The First National Bank Of Hopkins	4174	6	–
Independence			
The First National Bank Of Independence	1529	6	–
The First National Bank Of Independence	4157	4	4
Jackson			
The Peoples National Bank Of Jackson	7494	6	–
Jamesport			
The First National Bank Of Jamesport	7460	6	–
Jasper			
The First National Bank Of Jasper	6369	6	5
Jefferson City			
The Exchange National Bank Of Jefferson City	13142	5	4
The First National Bank Of Jefferson City	1809	3	4
Jefferson City			
The National Exchange Bank Of Jefferson City	2055	6	–
Joplin			
Conqueror First National Bank Of Joplin	13162	5	3
The Cunningham National Bank Of Joplin	8947	5	–
The First National Bank Of Joplin	3841	5	–
The Joplin National Bank	4425	4	–
The Joplin National Bank & Trust Company, Joplin	4425	6	6
Kansas City			
Drovers National Bank In Kansas City	12794	–	4
Fidelity National Bank & Trust Company Of Kansas City	11344	3	2
National Bank Of Commerce Of Kansas City	10231	4	–
The Aetna National Bank Of Kansas City	4251	6	–
The American National Bank Of Kansas City	3544	4	–
The Central Exchange National Bank Of Kansas City	11491	6	–
The Central National Bank Of Kansas City	8660	6	–
The Citizens National Bank Of Kansas City	2613	6	–
The City National Bank Of Kansas City	5250	6	–
The Columbia National Bank Of Kansas City	11472	–	4
The Commercial National Bank Of Kansas City	1995	6	–
The Commonwealth National Bank Of Kansas City	10039	5	–
The Continental National Bank & Trust Company Of Kansas City	12260	6	–
The Continental National Bank Of Kansas City	4786	6	–
The Continental Natl Bank Of Jackson County At Kansas City	11377	6	–
The Drovers National Bank Of Kansas City	9560	5	–
The First National Bank Of Kansas City	1612	6	–
The First National Bank Of Kansas City	3456	3	4
The Gate City National Bank Of Kansas City	9404	4	–
The German American National Bank Of Kansas City	3793	6	–
The Inter-State National Bank Of Kansas City, Missouri	4381	4	5
The Kansas City National Bank	1901	6	–
The Liberty National Bank Of Kansas City	10039	4	5
The Merchants National Bank Of Kansas City	2440	6	–
The Metropolitan National Bank Of Kansas City	4464	6	–
The Midland National Bank Of Kansas City	3904	6	–
The Midwest National Bank & Trust Company Of Kansas City	10892	6	–
The Midwest National Bank Of Kansas City	10892	6	–
The Missouri National Bank Of Kansas City	4494	6	–
The National Bank Of Commerce Of Kansas City, Missouri	3760	2	–
The National Bank Of Kansas City	3489	6	–
The National Bank Of The Republic Of Kansas City	8738	4	–
The National City Bank Of Kansas City	11037	4	–
The National Exchange Bank Of Kansas City	3863	6	–
The National Reserve Bank Of Kansas City	9677	4	–
The New England National Bank Of Kansas City	5138	2	–
The Park National Bank Of Kansas City	9383	6	5
The Security National Bank Of Kansas City	9172	5	
The Southwest National Bank Of Commerce Of Kansas City	10231	3	–
The Southwest National Bank Of Kansas City	9311	6	–
The Stock Yards National Bank Of Kansas City	10413	5	4
The Union National Bank Of Kansas City	3637	5	–
Traders National Bank Of Kansas City	9236	4	–
King City			
The Citizens National Bank Of King City	6383	3	3
The First National Bank & Trust Company Of King City	4373	5	–
The First National Bank Of King City	4373	2	–
Kirksville			
The Baird National Bank Of Kirksville	5871	6	–
The Citizens National Bank Of Kirksville	8276	5	3
The First National Bank Of Kirksville	2713	6	–
The National Bank Of Kirksville	5107	6	5
Knob Noster			
The First National Bank Of Knob Noster	1877	6	–
La Grange			
The First National Bank Of La Grange	1839	6	–
Lamar			
The First National Bank Of Lamar	4057	4	6
Lancaster			
The First National Bank Of Lancaster	2218	6	–
Lathrop			
The First National Bank Of Lathrop	5544	6	–
Leeds			
The Leeds National Bank	9383	6	–
Liberal			
The First National Bank Of Liberal	7094	6	–
Liberty			
The First National Bank Of Liberty	3712	6	5
Linn Creek			
The First National Bank Of Linn Creek	7853	6	6
Louisiana			
The Exchange National Bank Of Louisiana	3103	6	–
The Mercantile National Bank Of Louisiana	3111	6	–
Ludlow			
The Farmers National Bank Of Ludlow	8657	6	–
The First National Bank Of Ludlow	7900	6	6
The Ludlow National Bank	13293	–	5
Luxemburg			
Lafayette National Bank And Trust Company Of Luxemburg	13514	–	3
Macon			
The First National Bank Of Macon	2862	6	–
Manchester			
The First National Bank Of Manchester	7643	6	–
Maplewood			
The Citizens National Bank Of Maplewood	12955	5	3
Marceline			
The First National Bank Of Marceline	7066	6	6
Marshall			
The First National Bank Of Marshall	2884	6	–
Marshfield			
The First National Bank Of Marshfield	10009	6	–
Maryville			
The First National Bank Of Maryville	3268	3	6
The Maryville National Bank	4243	6	–
Memphis			
The Scotland County National Bank Of Memphis	2432	6	6
Mexico			
The First National Bank Of Mexico	2881	6	5
Milan			
The First National Bank Of Milan	3110	6	–
Moberly			
The First National Bank Of Moberly	4000	6	–
Monett			
The First National Bank Of Monett	5973	4	3
Mount Vernon			
The First National Bank Of Mount Vernon	13504	–	6
Mountain Grove			
The First National Bank Of Mountain Grove	7282	5	5
Neosho			
The First National Bank Of Neosho	6382	5	5
Nevada			
The First National Bank Of Nevada, Missouri	3959	4	4
The Thornton National Bank Of Nevada	9382	4	3
North Kansas City			
The National Bank & Trust Company Of North Kansas City	10367	–	6
The National Bank In North Kansas City	13690	–	6
The National Bank Of North Kansas City	10367	6	6
Odessa			
The National Bank Of Odessa	4141	6	–
Palmyra			
The First National Bank Of Palmyra	1735	6	–
The First National Bank Of Palmyra	2979	6	–
Paris			
The First National Bank Of Paris	1803	6	–
The National Bank Of Paris	3322	6	–
The Paris National Bank	5794	2	5
Peirce City			
The First National Bank Of Peirce City	4225	4	2
The Peirce City National Bank	4225	6	–
Perryville			
The First National Bank Of Perryville	11402	–	6
Platte City			
The Farmers National Bank Of Platte City	2356	6	–
The First National Bank Of Platte City	4329	6	–
Plattsburg			
The First National Bank Of Plattsburg	4215	3	4
Pleasant Hill			
The Farmers National Bank Of Pleasant Hill	7154	6	–
The First National Bank Of Pleasant Hill	1751	6	–
Polo			
The First National Bank Of Polo	7884	5	–
Purdy			
The First National Bank Of Purdy	10122	6	5
Ridgeway			
The First National Bank Of Ridgeway	6549	4	–
Rolla			
The National Bank Of Rolla	1865	5	6
Saint Charles			
The First National Bank Of Saint Charles	260	4	3
Saint Joseph			
The American National Bank Of St. Joseph	9042	3	4
The Burnes National Bank Of St. Joseph	8021	3	4
The First National Bank Of Buchanan County, St Joseph	4939	3	–
The First National Bank Of Saint Joseph	1580	5	–
The First National Bank Of St. Joseph	4939	3	6
The German American National Bank Of St. Joseph	9042	4	–
The National Bank Of St. Joseph	2970	5	–
The Saxton National Bank Of Saint Joseph	2898	6	–
The Schuster-Hax National Bank Of St. Joseph	4053	6	–
The State National Bank Of Saint Joseph	1667	6	–
The State National Bank Of Saint Joseph	4228	6	–
The Tootle-Lacy National Bank Of Saint Joseph	6272	4	–

City, Bank	Ch. No.	L	S
Saint Joseph			
The Tootle-Lemon National Bank Of St. Joseph	6272	3	–
Saint Louis			
Mercantile Commerce National Bank In St. Louis	4178	–	3
South Side National Bank Of St. Louis	13264	6	4
The American Exchange National Bank In St. Louis	13726	–	4
The American Exchange National Bank Of Saint Louis	7570	6	–
The American Exchange National Bank Of St. Louis	12506	5	–
The Bankers Worlds Fair National Bank Of St. Louis	7179	6	–
The Boatmen's National Bank Of St. Louis	12916	–	1
The Broadway National Bank Of St. Louis	9460	6	–
The Central National Bank Of St. Louis	8455	3	–
The Chemical National Bank Of St. Louis	4575	6	–
The City National Bank Of St. Louis	7808	5	–
The Continental National Bank Of St. Louis	4048	3	–
The Fifth National Bank Of St. Louis	2835	6	–
The First National Bank Of St. Louis	89	6	–
The Fourth National Bank Of St. Louis	283	4	–
The Grand Ave. National Bank Of St. Louis	12220	4	–
The Grand National Bank Of St. Louis	12220	4	2
The Laclede National Bank Of St. Louis	4262	6	–
The Mechanics National Bank Of Saint Louis	5788	4	–
The Mechanics-American National Bank Of St. Louis	7715	2	–
The Mercantile National Bank Of St. Louis	9297	4	–
The Merchants National Bank Of St. Louis	1501	6	–
The Merchants-Laclede National Bank Of Saint Louis	5002	2	–
The Missouri National Bank Of St. Louis	12220	5	–
The National Bank Of Commerce In St. Louis	4178	1	–
The National Bank Of The Republic Of St. Louis	4232	6	–
The National Bank Of The State Of Missouri, Saint Louis	1665	5	–
The National City Bank Of St. Louis	11989	3	5
The Republic National Bank Of St. Louis	11973	5	–
The Second National Bank Of Saint Louis	139	6	–
The Security Natl Bank Savings & Trust Co Of St Louis	12066	5	3
The State National Bank Of St. Louis	5172	1	–
The Telegraphers National Bank Of St. Louis	12389	4	2
The Third National Bank Of Saint Louis	170	2	–
The Twelfth Street National Bank Of St. Louis	12491	5	4
The Union National Bank Of St. Louis	1381	6	–
The Valley National Bank Of St. Louis	1858	6	–
The Washington National Bank Of St. Louis	6773	4	–
Salem			
The First National Bank Of Salem	7921	6	3
Salisbury			
The Farmers And Merchants National Bank Of Salisbury	8359	6	–
Sarcoxie			
The First National Bank Of Sarcoxie	5515	6	4
Savannah			
The First National Bank Of Savannah	5780	4	–
Sedalia			
The Citizens National Bank Of Sedalia	1971	3	5
The First National Bank Of Sedalia	1627	6	–
The Sedalia National Bank	4392	4	5
The Third National Bank Of Sedalia	2919	4	3
Seneca			
The First National Bank Of Seneca	7656	6	–
Seymour			
The Peoples National Bank Of Seymour	9932	5	6
Shelbina			
The First National Bank Of Shelbina	1711	6	–
The Shelbina National Bank	9137	6	–
Springfield			
The American National Bank Of Springfield	4360	6	–
The Central National Bank Of Springfield	3718	6	–
The First National Bank Of Springfield	1701	6	–
The Greene County National Bank Of Springfield	1677	5	–
The Mcdaniel National Bank Of Springfield	10074	5	5
The Merchants National Bank Of Springfield	9315	6	–
The National Bank Of Springfield	1701	6	–
The National Exchange Bank Of Springfield	5082	5	–
The Union National Bank Of Springfield	5209	4	4
St Louis			
First National Bank In St. Louis	170	3	2
St. Louis National Bank	12216	5	5
The St. Louis National Bank	1112	4	–
St. Louis			
The American Exchange National Bank Of Saint Louis	12506	–	5
Steele			
The First National Bank Of Steele	12452	6	5
Steelville			
The First National Bank Of Steelville	8914	6	6
Stewartsville			
The First National Bank Of Stewartsville	4160	4	5
Sweet Springs			
The First National Bank Of Sweet Springs	11372	6	–
Tarkio			
The First National Bank Of Tarkio	3079	4	5
Trenton			
The First National Bank Of Trenton	1966	6	–
The First National Bank Of Trenton	3957	6	–
The Grundy County National Bank Of Trenton	3946	6	–
The Trenton National Bank	4933	4	4
Unionville			
National Bank Of Unionville	13268	6	6
The Marshall National Bank Of Unionville	3068	4	5
The National Bank Of Unionville	3137	5	–
Versailles			
The First National Bank In Versailles	13367	–	5
The First National Bank Of Versailles	7256	5	–
Warrensburg			
The First National Bank Of Warrensburg	1856	6	–
The Peoples National Bank Of Warrensburg	5156	4	5
Washington			
The First National Bank Of Washington	5388	6	–
Webb City			
The First National Bank Of Carterville	4475	4	–
The First National Bank Of Webb City	4475	6	–
The National Bank Of Webb City	8016	4	–
Wellston			
The First National Bank Of Wellston	8011	5	4
West Plains			
The First National Bank Of West Plains	5036	4	6
Windsor			
The First National Bank Of Windsor	9519	5	4

MONTANA TERRITORY

City, Bank	Ch. No.	L	S
Anaconda			
The First National Bank Of Anaconda	3965	6	–
Billings			
The First National Bank Of Billings	3097	5	–
Bozeman			
The Bozeman National Bank	2803	6	–
The First National Bank Of Bozeman	2027	6	–
The Gallatin Valley National Bank Of Bozeman	3075	6	–
Butte			
The First National Bank Of Butte	2566	6	–
Deer Lodge			
The First National Bank Of Deer Lodge	1975	6	–
Dillon			
The Dillon National Bank	3173	6	–
The First National Bank Of Dillon	3120	6	–
Fort Benton			
The First National Bank Of Fort Benton	2476	5	–
Great Falls			
The First National Bank Of Great Falls	3525	6	–
Helena			
The First National Bank Of Helena	1649	4	–
The Merchants National Bank Of Helena	2732	6	–
The Montana National Bank Of Helena	1960	6	–
The Montana National Bank Of Helena	2813	6	–
The Peoples National Bank Of Helena	2105	6	–
The Second National Bank Of Helena	2757	6	–
Livingston			
The First National Bank Of Livingston	3006	6	–
The Livington National Bank	4117	6	–
The National Park Bank Of Livingston	3605	6	–
Miles City			
The First National Bank Of Miles City	2752	4	–
The Stock Growers National Bank Of Miles City	3276	6	–
Missoula			
The First National Bank Of Missoula	2106	6	–
The Missoula National Bank	2106	4	–
The Western Montana National Bank Of Missoula	3995	6	–
Sulphur Springs			
The First National Bank Of White Sulphur Springs	3375	6	–

MONTANA

City, Bank	Ch. No.	L	S
Anaconda			
The Anaconda National Bank	9583	6	–
The First National Bank Of Anaconda	3965	6	–
The National Bank Of Anaconda	12542	5	3
Antelope			
The First National Bank Of Antelope	11350	6	–
Baker			
The First National Bank Of Baker	10443	6	–
Benton			
The Northwestern National Bank Of Great Falls	2476	6	–
Big Timber			
The Big Timber National Bank	4932	6	–
Big Timer			
The First National Bank Of Big Timber	4590	6	–
Billings			
The First National Bank Of Billings	3097	6	–
The Merchants National Bank Of Billings	9355	5	–
The Midland National Bank Of Billings	12407	4	2
The Yellowstone National Bank Of Billings	4593	5	–
The Yellowstone-Merchants National Bank Of Billings	4593	6	–
Boulder Valley			
The First National Bank Of Boulder Valley	4323	6	–
Bozeman			
The Bozeman National Bank	2803	6	–
The Commercial National Bank Of Bozeman	4968	4	3
The Gallatin Valley National Bank Of Bozeman	3075	6	–
The National Bank Of Gallatin Valley At Bozeman	7441	6	–
Butte			
The Silver Bow National Bank Of Butte	4283	4	–
Butte City			
The First National Bank Of Butte	2566	3	4
Carter			
The First National Bank Of Carter	10995	6	–
Castle			
The First National Bank Of Castle	4572	6	–
Chester			
The First National Bank Of Chester	11105	6	–
Chinook			
The Farmers National Bank In Chinook	13837	–	5
The Farmers National Bank Of Chinook	10053	6	5
The First National Bank Of Chinook	6097	5	6
Circle			
The First National Bank Of Circle	11101	–	4
Columbus			
The First National Bank Of Columbus	9396	5	5
Conrad			
The First National Bank Of Conrad	9759	5	3
Culbertson			
The First National Bank Of Culbertson	8168	6	–
Cut Bank			
The First National Bank Of Cut Bank	9574	6	–
Deer Lodge			
The United States National Bank Of Deer Lodge	9899	6	5
Denton			
The First National Bank Of Denton	10819	5	–
Dillon			
The Dillon National Bank	3173	6	–
The First National Bank Of Dillon	3120	4	4
Fairfield			
The First National Bank Of Fairfield	11307	6	–
Fairview			
The First National Bank Of Fairview	12015	6	–
Forsyth			
The First National Bank Of Forsyth	7320	6	–
Fort Benton			
The First National Bank Of Fort Benton	2476	6	–
The Stockmens National Bank Of Fort Benton	4194	4	–
Fresno			
The First National Bank Of Fresno	11096	6	–
Geraldine			
The First National Bank Of Geraldine	10803	5	4
Geyser			
The First National Bank Of Geyser	10952	3	–
Glasgow			
The First National Bank Of Glasgow	7990	4	3
The Glasgow National Bank	8655	5	–
Glendive			
The First National Bank Of Glendive	7101	6	4
The Merchants National Bank Of Glendive	8055	6	–
Grass Range			
The First National Bank Of Grass Range	10939	4	6
Great Falls			
The Commercial National Bank Of Great Falls	10530	6	–
The First National Bank Of Great Falls	3525	3	2
The Great Falls National Bank	4541	4	3
The Merchants National Bank Of Great Falls	4434	6	–
Hamilton			
The First National Bank Of Hamilton	9486	5	4
Hardin			
The First National Bank Of Hardin	9215	6	5
Harlem			
The First National Bank Of Harlem	7644	6	6
Harlowton			
The Farmers National Bank Of Harlowton	11085	5	6
The First National Bank Of Harlowton	9270	6	6
The Musselshell Valley National Bank Of Harlowton	9270	6	–
Havre			
The Citizens National Bank Of Havre	9440	6	–
The First National Bank Of Havre	5676	6	–
The Havre National Bank	9782	6	–
Helena			
First National Bank And Trust Company Of Helena	4396	–	2
The American National Bank Of Helena	4396	3	3
The First National Bank Of Helena	1649	6	–
The Helena National Bank	4406	6	–
The Merchants National Bank Of Helena	2732	6	–
The Montana National Bank Of Helena	2813	6	–
The National Bank Of Montana, Helena	5671	3	4
The Second National Bank Of Helena	2757	6	–
Highwood			
The First National Bank Of Highwood	11131	6	–
Hobson			
The First National Bank Of Hobson	10715	4	6
Ismay			
The First National Bank Of Ismay	9103	6	5
Kalispell			
The Conrad National Bank Of Kalispell	4803	3	1
The First National Bank Of Kalispell	4586	3	3
The Globe National Bank Of Kalispell	4651	6	–
The Kalispell National Bank	8635	6	–
Laurel			
The Citizens National Bank Of Laurel	8716	6	–
The First National Bank Of Laurel	8669	6	–
Lewistown			
The First National Bank Of Fergus County In Lewiston	7274	6	–
The First National Bank Of Lewistown	7274	3	–
The National Bank Of Lewistown	12608	–	3

City, Bank	Ch. No.	L	S
Libby			
The First National Bank Of Libby	9594	5	–
Lima			
The First National Bank Of Lima	11492	3	3
The Security National Bank Of Lima	11492	5	–
Livingston			
The Livingston National Bank	4117	6	–
The National Park Bank Of Livingston	3605	4	6
Malta			
The First National Bank Of Malta	9738	6	–
Miles City			
The Commercial National Bank Of Miles City	5015	5	–
The First National Bank In Miles City	12536	6	3
The First National Bank Of Miles City	2752	3	–
The State National Bank Of Miles City	5015	5	–
The Stock Growers National Bank Of Miles City	3275	6	–
Missoula			
The First National Bank Of Missoula	2106	3	1
The Western Montana National Bank Of Missoula	3995	4	2
Moore			
The First National Bank Of Moore	8539	6	–
Neihart			
The First National Bank Of Neihart	4600	6	–
Opheim			
The First National Bank Of Opheim	11097	6	–
Phillipsburg			
The First National Bank Of Phillipsburg	4658	6	–
The Merchants And Miners National Bank Of Phillipsburg	4843	6	–
Plains			
The First National Bank Of Plains	7172	4	3
Plentywood			
The First National Bank Of Plentywood	10438	6	–
Plevna			
Baker National Bank, Baker	11074	–	5
Polson			
The First National Bank Of Polson	9449	6	–
Raymond			
The First National Bank Of Raymond	11078	5	–
Red Lodge			
The United States National Bank Of Red Lodge	9841	6	3
Reserve			
The First National Bank Of Reserve	10986	6	4
Ronan			
The First National Bank Of Ronan	9864	6	–
Rosebud			
The First National Bank Of Rosebud	11437	6	–
Roundup			
The First National Bank Of Roundup	9165	6	–
Roy			
The First National Bank Of Roy	10991	5	–
Saco			
The First National Bank Of Saco	9789	6	–
Scobey			
The First National Bank Of Scobey	10838	5	5
The Merchants National Bank Of Scobey	11098	6	–
Sidney			
The Farmers National Bank Of Sidney	10552	6	–
The First National Bank Of Sidney	9004	5	–
Stevensville			
The First National Bank Of Stevensville	10709	6	–
Three Forks			
The First National Bank Of Three Forks	9337	6	–
Townsend			
The First National Bank Of Townsend	9982	6	–
Twin Bridges			
The First National Bank Of Twin Bridges	11008	5	–
Valier			
The First National Bank Of Valier	9520	6	5
White Sulphur Springs			
The First National Bank Of White Sulphur Springs	3375	5	3
Whitefish			
The First National Bank Of Whitefish	8589	6	2
Whitehall			
The First National Bank Of Whitehall	11024	5	–
Wibaux			
The First National Bank Of Wibaux	8259	6	4
Winifred			
The First National Bank Of Winifred	11006	6	–
Wolf Point			
The First National Bank Of Wolf Point	11036	–	4

NEBRASKA

City, Bank	Ch. No.	L	S
Adams			
The First National Bank Of Adams	9223	6	6
Ainsworth			
The First National Bank Of Ainsworth	4089	6	–
The National Bank Of Ainsworth	8992	5	4
Albion			
The Albion National Bank	4173	5	4
The First National Bank Of Albion	3960	4	4
Allen			
The First National Bank Of Allen	8372	6	–
Alliance			
The Alliance National Bank	5657	4	–
The First National Bank Of Alliance	4226	5	4
The Nebraska National Bank Of Alliance	13617	–	4
Alma			
The First National Bank Of Alma	3580	6	–
Amherst			
The First National Bank Of Amherst	9092	6	4
Anoka			
The Anoka National Bank	6464	6	–
Ansley			
The First National Bank Of Ansley	7393	6	–
Arapahoe			
The First National Bank Of Arapahoe	3302	6	–
Arlington			
The First National Bank Of Arlington	4583	5	6

City, Bank	Ch. No.	L	S
Ashland			
The Farmers And Merchants National Bank Of Ashland	13435	–	4
The First National Bank Of Ashland	2121	6	–
The National Bank Of Ashland	2921	4	4
Atkinson			
The Atkinson National Bank	7881	6	–
The First National Bank Of Atkinson	6489	5	5
Auburn			
The Farmers And Merchants National Bank Of Auburn	4588	6	–
The First National Bank Of Auburn	3343	4	5
Aurora			
The Aurora National Bank	9056	6	–
The Fidelity National Bank Of Aurora	8246	6	–
The First National Bank Of Aurora	2897	5	6
Bancroft			
The First National Bank Of Bancroft	8863	6	5
Bayard			
The First National Bank Of Bayard	9666	5	5
Bazile Mills			
The First National Bank Of Bazile Mills	8469	6	–
Beatrice			
The Beatrice National Bank	3081	4	4
The First National Bank Of Beatrice	2357	3	3
The German National Bank Of Beatrice	4148	6	–
The Nebraska National Bank Of Beatrice	4185	6	–
Beaver City			
The First National Bank Of Beaver City	3619	6	–
Beemer			
The First National Bank Of Beemer	6818	4	5
Belden			
The First National Bank Of Belden	10025	5	3
Benedict			
The First National Bank Of Benedict	8105	6	3
Bertrand			
The First National Bank Of Bertrand	8466	6	–
Blair			
The Blair National Bank	8027	6	–
The First National Bank Of Blair	2724	6	–
Bloomfield			
The First National Bank Of Bloomfield	6503	6	–
Blue Hill			
The First National Bank Of Blue Hill	3419	5	6
Bradshaw			
The First National Bank Of Bradshaw	8097	5	3
Bridgeport			
The First National Bank Of Bridgeport	9711	6	–
Bristow			
The First National Bank Of Bristow	9448	6	–
Broken Bow			
The Central Nebraska National Bank Of Broken Bow	3927	6	–
The Custer County National Bank Of Broken Bow	3445	6	–
The Custer National Bank Of Broken Bow	5995	5	–
The First National Bank Of Broken Bow	3449	6	–
Brownville			
The First National Bank Of Brownville	1846	5	–
Brunswick			
The First National Bank Of Brunswick	10033	6	–
Burwell			
The First National Bank Of Burwell	7340	6	–
Butte			
The First National Bank Of Butte	9623	4	4
Callaway			
The First National Bank Of Callaway	9258	6	–
Cambridge			
The First National Bank Of Cambridge	6506	5	4
Campbell			
The First National Bank Of Campbell	8975	6	–
Carroll			
The First National Bank Of Carroll	5957	5	–
Cedar Rapids			
The First National Bank Of Cedar Rapids	8282	6	–
Central City			
The Central City National Bank	8385	4	5
The First National Bank Of Central City	2871	6	–
Chadron			
The First National Bank Of Chadron	3823	5	4
Chappell			
The First National Bank Of Chappell	9790	6	–
Clarks			
The First National Bank Of Clarks	6939	6	–
Clay Center			
The First National Bank Of Clay Center	3574	6	–
Coleridge			
The Coleridge National Bank, Coleridge	10023	5	3
The First National Bank Of Coleridge	9796	5	–
Columbus			
The Central National Bank Of Columbus	8328	3	4
The Commercial National Bank Of Columbus	5180	4	5
The First National Bank Of Columbus	2807	4	5
The German National Bank Of Columbus	8328	6	–
Cozad			
First National Bank In Cozad	13426	–	4
The First National Bank Of Cozad	4165	6	–
Craig			
The First National Bank Of Craig	9591	5	6
Crawford			
The First National Bank Of Crawford	6900	6	–
Creighton			
The Creighton National Bank	8797	4	6
The First National Bank Of Creighton	4242	6	–
Crete			
The City National Bank Of Crete	9731	4	4
The Crete National Bank	4820	6	–
The First National Bank Of Crete	2706	5	–
Crofton			
The First National Bank Of Crofton	8186	4	2
Curtis			
The First National Bank Of Curtis	8812	6	–

City, Bank	Ch. No.	L	S
David City			
The Central Nebraska National Bank Of David City	3801	5	4
The City National Bank Of David City	3934	5	4
The First National Bank Of David City	2902	4	3
De Witt			
The First National Bank Of De Witt	4895	6	–
Decatur			
The First National Bank Of Decatur	8988	4	4
Diller			
The First National Bank Of Diller	7355	6	–
Dodge			
The First National Bank Of Dodge	7333	6	–
Dorchester			
The First National Bank Of Dorchester	3390	4	–
Elgin			
The First National Bank Of Elgin	5440	5	4
Elm Creek			
The First National Bank Of Elm Creek	3999	6	–
Elmwood			
The First National Bank Of Elmwood	5787	6	–
Elwood			
The First National Bank Of Elwood	7204	4	4
Emerson			
The First National Bank Of Emerson	7425	5	4
Exeter			
The Exeter National Bank	3117	6	–
The First National Bank Of Exeter	3121	6	–
Fairbury			
The Bonham National Bank Of Fairbury	8995	6	–
The Farmers And Merchants National Bank Of Fairbury	10340	5	–
The First National Bank Of Fairbury	2994	4	3
Fairfield			
The First National Bank Of Fairfield	3493	6	–
Fairmont			
The First National Bank Of Fairmont	3230	6	–
Falls City			
The First National Bank Of Falls City	2746	3	4
Franklin			
The First National Bank Of Franklin	3549	6	–
Fremont			
The Commercial National Bank Of Fremont	4504	4	–
The Farmers And Merchants National Bank Of Fremont	3188	6	–
The First National Bank Of Fremont	1974	4	–
The Fremont National Bank	2848	4	3
The Stephens National Bank Of Fremont	13408	–	3
The Union National Bank Of Fremont	3188	3	3
Friend			
The First National Bank Of Friend	2960	4	4
Fullerton			
The First National Bank Of Fullerton	2964	4	4
The Fullerton National Bank	5384	4	4
Geneva			
The First National Bank Of Geneva	4052	6	–
The Geneva National Bank	4484	6	–
Genoa			
The First National Bank Of Genoa	5189	4	5
The Genoa National Bank	6805	6	4
Gering			
The First National Bank Of Gering	8062	6	–
The Gering National Bank	9694	5	4
Gibbon			
The First National Bank Of Gibbon	3921	6	–
Gordon			
The First National Bank Of Gordon	8521	5	4
Gothenburg			
The Citizens National Bank Of Gothenburg	8113	6	–
The First National Bank Of Gothenburg	4890	6	–
The Gothenburg National Bank	6202	5	
Grand Island			
The Citizens National Bank Of Grand Island	3101	6	–
The First National Bank Of Grand Island	2779	3	2
The Grand Island National Bank	9395	3	2
The Security National Bank Of Grand Island	4357	6	–
Grant			
The First National Bank Of Grant	4170	6	–
Greeley			
The First National Bank Of Greeley	7622	6	6
Greenwood			
The First National Bank Of Greenwood	3403	6	–
Gresham			
The First National Bank Of Gresham	8172	6	4
Hampton			
The First National Bank Of Hampton	8285	6	5
Harrison			
The First National Bank Of Harrison	8888	6	–
The Sioux National Bank Of Harrison	12552	6	4
Hartington			
The First National Bank Of Hartington	4528	4	4
The Hartington National Bank	5400	4	–
Harvard			
The First National Bank Of Harvard	4129	6	–
Hastings			
The City National Bank Of Hastings	3099	6	–
The Exchange National Bank Of Hastings	3086	4	–
The First National Bank Of Hastings	2528	3	3
The German National Bank Of Hastings	3732	6	–
The Hastings National Bank	13515	–	3
The Nebraska National Bank Of Hastings	3732	4	3
Havelock			
The First National Bank Of Havelock	9772	6	3
The Havelock National Bank Of Lincoln	9772	–	–
Hay Springs			
The First National Bank Of Hay Springs	8760	6	5
Hayes Center			
The First National Bank Of Hayes Center	8031	5	4
Hebron			
The First National Bank Of Hebron	2756	5	–
Hemingford			
The First National Bank Of Hemingford	10242	6	–

City, Bank	Ch. No.	L	S
Henderson			
The First National Bank Of Henderson	8183	6	–
Holdrege			
The City National Bank Of Holdrege	4345	5	–
The First National Bank Of Holdrege	3208	4	4
The Holdrege National Bank	3875	6	–
The United States National Bank Of Holdrege	4345	6	–
Hooper			
The First National Bank Of Hooper	5297	4	5
Humboldt			
The First National Bank Of Humboldt	3238	6	–
The National Bank Of Humboldt	7065	5	–
Humphrey			
The First National Bank Of Humphrey	5337	6	6
Imperial			
The First National Bank Of Imperial	9762	5	5
Indianola			
The First National Bank Of Indianola	3483	6	–
Johnson			
The First National Bank Of Johnson	8161	5	4
The German National Bank Of Johnson	8383	6	–
Kearney			
The Buffalo County National Bank Of Kearney	3526	6	
The Central National Bank Of Kearney	6600	5	–
The City National Bank Of Kearney	3958	4	–
The Commercial National Bank Of Kearney	8651	6	–
The First National Bank Of Kearney	2806	6	–
The Kearney National Bank	3201	6	–
Kimball			
The American National Bank Of Kimball	13420	–	1
Laurel			
The First National Bank Of Laurel	9793	5	–
The Laurel National Bank	9979	5	–
Lawrence			
The First National Bank Of Lawrence	8851	6	–
Leigh			
The First National Bank Of Leigh	9831	5	3
Lexington			
The Dawson County National Bank Of Lexington	4161	5	–
Liberty			
The First National Bank Of Liberty	4080	6	–
Lincoln			
City National Bank In Lincoln	13017	5	–
National Bank Of Commerce Of Lincoln	7239	3	3
The American Exchange National Bank Of Lincoln	4606	6	–
The Capital National Bank Of Lincoln	2988	6	–
The Central National Bank Of Lincoln	8885	4	–
The City National Bank Of Lincoln	5213	2	–
The Columbia National Bank Of Lincoln	4435	6	–
The Continental National Bank Of Lincoln	13333	–	3
The First National Bank Of Lincoln	1798	2	1
The German National Bank Of Lincoln	3571	6	–
The Lincoln National Bank	2750	5	–
The Marsh National Bank Of Lincoln	2988	6	–
The State National Bank Of Lincoln	1899	6	–
Litchfield			
The First National Bank Of Litchfield	8093	5	6
Lodgepole			
The First National Bank Of Lodgepole	9741	6	–
Loomis			
The First National Bank Of Loomis	5419	5	6
Loup City			
First National Bank In Loup City	13620	–	4
The First National Bank Of Loup City	3373	6	–
The First National Bank Of Loup City	7277	6	6
Lynch			
The First National Bank Of Lynch	9785	6	–
Lyons			
The First National Bank Of Lyons	6221	6	5
Madison			
The Farmers National Bank Of Madison	8317	6	5
The First National Bank Of Madison	3773	4	4
The Madison National Bank	10021	6	–
Marquette			
The First National Bank Of Marquette	8400	5	6
Mc Cook			
The Citizens National Bank Of Mc Cook	9436	6	–
The First National Bank Of Mc Cook	3379	5	4
The Mc Cook National Bank	8823	5	2
Minatare			
The First National Bank Of Minatare	13316	–	6
Minden			
The First National Bank Of Minden	3057	5	6
The Minden Exchange National Bank	9400	6	5
Mitchell			
The First National Bank Of Mitchell	7026	6	–
Morrill			
The First National Bank Of Morrill	9653	6	–
Naper			
The First National Bank Of Naper	9665	6	6
Nebraska City			
The James Sweet National Bank Of Nebraska City	2536	6	–
The Merchants National Bank Of Nebraska City	2536	5	5
The Nebraska City National Bank	1855	3	2
The Otoe County National Bank Of Nebraska City	1417	2	4
Neligh			
The First National Bank Of Neligh	4110	6	–
The National Bank Of Neligh	13568	–	5
The Neligh National Bank	5690	5	–
Nelson			
The First National Bank Of Nelson	3495	6	–
Newman Grove			
The First National Bank Of Newman Grove	5282	5	4
Norfolk			
The Citizens National Bank Of Norfolk	3741	5	–
The First National Bank Of Norfolk	2774	6	–
The Nebraska National Bank Of Norfolk	7329	6	–
The Norfolk National Bank	3347	4	5
North Auburn			
The First National Bank Of Auburn, North Auburn	3343	6	–
North Bend			
The First National Bank Of North Bend	3059	4	5
The National Bank Of North Bend	7449	6	–
North Platte			
The First National Bank Of North Platte	3496	4	3
The North Platte National Bank	4024	6	–
O'Neill			
The First National Bank Of O'Neill	3424	4	5
The O'Neill National Bank	5770	3	4
Oakdale			
The First National Bank Of Oakdale	13339	–	3
Oakland			
The Farmers And Merchants National Bank Of Oakland	10022	5	4
The First National Bank Of Oakland	4610	4	4
Ogalalla			
The First National Bank Of Ogalalla	3652	6	–
Omaha			
Corn Exchange National Bank Of Omaha	9730	5	–
The American National Bank Of Omaha	4087	6	–
The City National Bank Of Omaha	9466	6	–
The Commercial National Bank Of Omaha	3163	6	–
The First National Bank Of Omaha	209	4	–
The Merchants National Bank Of Omaha	2775	4	–
The National Bank Of Commerce Of Omaha	4270	6	–
The Nebraska National Bank Of Omaha	2665	3	–
The Omaha National Bank	1633	1	2
The State National Bank Of Omaha	3603	6	–
The Union National Bank Of Omaha	3516	6	–
The United States National Bank Of Omaha	2978	3	1
Ord			
The First National Bank Of Ord	3339	3	3
The Ord National Bank	3481	6	–
Orleans			
The Citizens National Bank Of Orleans	8567	6	–
The First National Bank Of Orleans	3342	6	–
Osceola			
The First National Bank Of Osceola	6493	4	5
Oshkosh			
The First National Bank Of Oshkosh	10081	6	–
Overton			
The First National Bank Of Overton	7925	6	–
The Overton National Bank	13446	–	3
Oxford			
The First National Bank Of Oxford	7520	6	–
Pawnee City			
The Farmers National Bank Of Pawnee City	4078	4	–
The First National Bank Of Pawnee City	2825	6	–
The National Bank Of Pawnee City	6541	6	–
Pender			
The First National Bank Of Pender	4791	5	5
The Pender National Bank	5308	6	–
Pierce			
The First National Bank Of Pierce	4280	6	–
Pilger			
The Farmers National Bank In Pilger	13453	–	3
The Farmers National Bank Of Pilger	5941	3	–
The First National Bank Of Pilger	5937	4	–
Plainview			
The First National Bank Of Plainview	9504	5	–
Plattsmouth			
The First National Bank Of Plattsmouth	1914	4	–
Plum Creek			
The First National Bank Of Lexington	3292	6	–
The First National Bank Of Plum Creek	3292	6	–
Polk			
The First National Bank Of Polk	8533	6	–
Ponca			
The First National Bank Of Ponca	3627	6	–
Randolph			
The First National Bank Of Randolph	7421	4	4
The Security National Bank Of Randolph	7477	5	4
Ravenna			
The First National Bank Of Ravenna	4043	6	–
Red Cloud			
The First National Bank Of Red Cloud	2811	6	–
The Red Cloud National Bank	3181	6	–
Rulo			
The First National Bank Of Rulo	3674	6	–
Rushville			
The First National Bank Of Rushville	4176	6	–
The Stockmen's National Bank Of Rushville	9191	5	6
Saint Edward			
The First National Bank Of St. Edward	5346	6	–
The Smith National Bank Of Saint Edward	5793	5	5
Saint James			
The First National Bank Of St. James	8335	6	–
The First National Bank Of Wynot	8335	6	–
Saint Paul			
The Citizens National Bank Of St. Paul	3891	6	–
The First National Bank Of St. Paul	3126	6	–
The Saint Paul National Bank	3129	2	–
Sargent			
The First National Bank Of Sargent	7384	6	–
Schuyler			
The First National Bank Of Schuyler	2778	4	–
The Schuyler National Bank	3152	5	–
Scottsbluff			
The First National Bank Of Scottsbluff	6240	5	–
The Scottsbluff National Bank	9581	4	3
Scribner			
The First National Bank Of Scribner	6901	6	6
Seward			
The First National Bank Of Seward	2771	4	6
The Jones National Bank Of Seward	3060	4	4
Shelby			
The First National Bank Of Shelby	7949	5	3
Shelton			
The First National Bank Of Shelton	4042	6	–
The Shelton National Bank	9200	6	–
Sidney			
The American National Bank Of Sidney	13425	–	3
The First National Bank Of Sidney	6201	5	–
South Auburn			
The Carson National Bank Of Auburn	3628	4	2
The Carson National Bank Of South Auburn	3628	6	–
South Omaha			
Stock Yards National Bank Of South Omaha	9908	3	2
The Live Stock National Bank Of South Omaha	8949	4	2
The Packers National Bank Of South Omaha	4589	4	–
The South Omaha National Bank	3611	5	–
The Union Stock Yards National Bank Of South Omaha	4632	6	–
South Sioux City			
The First National Bank Of South Sioux City	4557	6	–
Spalding			
The First National Bank Of Spalding	7574	6	–
Spencer			
The First National Bank Of Spencer	7325	5	–
Stanton			
The First National Bank Of Stanton	3364	5	3
The Stanton National Bank	7836	5	3
Sterling			
The First National Bank Of Sterling	4163	6	–
Stromsburg			
The First National Bank Of Stromsburg	8286	4	3
Stuart			
The First National Bank Of Stuart	6947	5	4
Superior			
Security National Bank Of Superior	14083	–	4
The First National Bank Of Superior	3529	6	–
The Superior National Bank	5397	6	–
Sutton			
The First National Bank Of Sutton	3240	6	–
The Sutton National Bank	3653	5	–
Syracuse			
The First National Bank Of Syracuse	3083	3	4
Tecumseh			
The Citizens National Bank Of Tecumseh	6166	6	–
The First National Bank Of Tecumseh	2955	6	–
The Tecumseh National Bank	4276	6	–
Tekamah			
The First National Bank Of Tekamah	4324	3	3
Tilden			
The First National Bank Of Tilden	9217	5	3
The Tilden National Bank	10011	6	4
Tobias			
The First National Bank Of Tobias	3725	6	–
The Tobias National Bank	7578	6	–
Trenton			
The First National Bank Of Trenton	8218	6	–
University Place			
The First National Bank Of University Place	7737	6	–
Utica			
The First National Bank Of Utica	8811	4	4
Valentine			
The First National Bank Of Valentine	6378	5	4
Wahoo			
The First National Bank Of Wahoo	2780	3	1
The Saunders County National Bank Of Wahoo	3118	5	6
Wakefield			
The Farmers National Bank Of Wakefield	9904	4	–
The First National Bank Of Wakefield	5368	6	–
Walthill			
The First National Bank, Walthill	8685	5	4
The Walthill National Bank	9816	6	6
Wausa			
The Commercial National Bank Of Wausa	10017	6	–
The First National Bank Of Wausa	9994	4	–
Wayne			
The Citizens National Bank Of Wayne	9244	5	–
The First National Bank Of Wayne	3392	6	4
The Wayne National Bank	4354	6	–
Weeping Water			
The City National Bank Of Weeping Water	5281	5	–
The First National Bank Of Weeping Water	3523	3	3
West Point			
The First National Bank Of West Point	3370	6	4
The West Point National Bank	3340	4	5
Wilber			
The First National Bank Of Wilber	2991	6	–
The National Bank Of Wilber	6415	6	–
Wilcox			
The First National Bank Of Wilcox	7861	5	4
Winnebago			
The First National Bank Of Winnebago	9671	5	–
Wisner			
The Citizens National Bank Of Wisner	6866	5	3
The First National Bank Of Wisner	4029	4	4
Wolbach			
The First National Bank Of Wolbach	8413	6	–
Wood River			
The First National Bank Of Wood River	3939	4	6
Wymore			
The City National Bank Of Wymore	9138	6	–
The First National Bank Of Wymore	4210	4	3
The Wymore National Bank	14282	–	4
York			
Farmers National Bank Of York	7821	5	–
The City National Bank Of York	4935	4	3
The First National Bank Of York	2683	3	3
The Nebraska National Bank Of York	4245	6	–
The York National Bank	3162	6	–

NEVADA

City, Bank	Ch. No.	L	S
Austin			
The First National Bank Of Nevada, Austin	1331	6	–

City, Bank	Ch. No.	L	S
Carson City			
The First National Bank Of Carson City	9242	6	–
East Ely			
The Copper National Bank Of East Ely	9578	6	–
Elka			
The First National Bank Of Elko	7743	3	3
Ely			
The Ely National Bank	9310	6	3
The First National Bank Of Ely	8561	5	5
Eureka			
The Farmers And Merchants National Bank Of Eureka	11784	–	3
Goldfield			
The First National Bank Of Goldfield	9078	6	–
Lovelock			
The First National Bank Of Lovelock	7654	6	4
Mc Gill			
The Mc Gill National Bank	9452	5	4
Reno			
First National Bank In Reno	7038	–	1
The Farmers And Merchants National Bank Of Reno	7038	2	–
The First National Bank Of Reno	2478	6	–
The Nixon National Bank Of Reno	8424	4	–
The Reno National Bank, Reno	8424	2	2
Rhyolite			
The First National Bank Of Rhyolite	8686	6	–
Tonopah			
The Nevada First National Bank Of Tonopah	8530	6	5
Winnemucca			
The First National Bank Of Winnemucca	3575	4	3

NEW HAMPSHIRE

City, Bank	Ch. No.	L	S
Berlin			
Berlin City National Bank, Berlin	14100	–	4
The Berlin National Bank	4523	4	3
The City National Bank Of Berlin	5622	6	6
Bristol			
The First National Bank Of Bristol	5151	6	5
Charlestown			
The Connecticut River National Bank Of Charlestown	537	6	6
Claremont			
Claremont National Bank	13829	–	6
The Claremont National Bank	596	4	5
The Peoples National Bank Of Claremont	4793	5	4
Colebrook			
The Colebrook National Bank	4041	4	6
The Farmers And Traders National Bank Of Colebrook	5183	6	6
Concord			
The First National Bank Of Concord	318	3	5
The Mechanic's National Bank Of Concord	2447	2	4
The National State Capital Bank Of Concord	758	3	4
Conway			
The Conway National Bank	9476	6	–
Derry			
The Derry National Bank	499	5	6
Dover			
The Cochecho National Bank Of Dover	1087	6	–
The Dover National Bank	1043	6	–
The Merchants National Bank Of Dover	5274	6	4
The Strafford National Bank Of Dover	1353	5	–
East Jaffrey			
The Monadnock National Bank Of East Jaffrey	1242	4	4
Exeter			
The National Granite State Bank Of Exeter	1147	5	–
The Rockingham National Bank Of Exeter	12889	6	4
Farmington			
Farmington National Bank	13764	–	6
The Farmington National Bank	2022	4	6
Francestown			
The First National Bank Of Francestown	576	5	–
Franklin			
The Franklin National Bank	2443	4	5
Gonic			
The First National Bank Of Gonic	838	6	–
Gorham			
The White Mountain National Bank Of Gorham	9001	6	4
Groveton			
The Coos County National Bank Of Groveton	5317	6	6
The Gorham National Bank, Gorham	5258	6	–
The Groveton National Bank	5258	6	–
Hanover			
The Dartmouth National Bank Of Hanover	1145	6	5
Hillsborough			
The First National Bank Of Hillsborough	1688	4	6
Keene			
The Ashuelot National Bank Of Keene	946	4	–
The Ashuelot-Citizens National Bank Of Keene	946	4	4
The Cheshire National Bank Of Keene	559	4	4
The Citizens National Bank Of Keene	2299	4	–
The Keene National Bank	877	3	5
Laconia			
The Laconia National Bank	1645	5	4
The Peoples National Bank Of Laconia	4037	5	5
Lakeport			
The Lakeport National Bank Of Laconia	4740	6	5
The National Bank Of Lakeport	4740	5	–
Lancaster			
The Lancaster National Bank	2600	4	5
Lebanon			
The National Bank Of Lebanon	808	4	4
Littleton			
The Littleton National Bank	1885	6	5
Manchester			
The Amoskeag National Bank Of Manchester	574	4	5
The Amoskeag National Bank, Manchester	574	6	–
The City National Bank Of Manchester	1520	6	–
The First National Bank Of Manchester	1153	4	6
The Manchester National Bank	1059	4	5
The Merchants National Bank Of Manchester	1520	4	4
The National Bank Of The Commonwealth Of Manchester	4693	6	–
The Second National Bank Of Manchester	2362	6	–
Milford			
The Souhegan National Bank Of Milford	1070	4	3
Nashua			
The First National Bank Of Nashua	84	6	–
The First National Bank Of Nashua	2741	6	–
The Indian Head National Bank Of Nashua	1310	4	4
The Second National Bank Of Nashua	2240	3	2
New Market			
The New Market National Bank	1330	5	5
Newport			
The Citizens National Bank Of Newport	3404	4	6
The First National Bank Of Newport	888	2	4
Peterborough			
The First National Bank Of Peterborough	1179	5	5
Pittsfield			
The Pittsfield National Bank	1020	6	–
Plymouth			
The Pemigewasset National Bank Of Plymouth	2587	4	5
Portsmouth			
The First National Bank Of Portsmouth	19	4	3
The First National Bank Of Portsmouth	19	4	–
The National Mechanics And Traders Bank Of Portsmouth	401	4	5
The New Hampshire National Bank Of Portsmouth	1052	5	5
The Rockingham National Bank Of Portsmouth	1025	5	–
Rochester			
The New Public National Bank Of Rochester	13861	–	6
The Public National Bank Of Rochester	11893	6	5
The Rochester National Bank	2138	4	–
Sanbornton			
The Citizens National Bank Of Sanbornton	1333	6	–
The Citizens National Bank Of Tilton	1333	4	5
Sandwich			
The Carroll County National Bank Of Sandwich	1071	6	–
Somersworth			
The First National Bank Of Somersworth	1180	5	5
The Great Falls National Bank Of Somersworth	1180	6	–
The Somersworth National Bank Of Great Falls	1183	6	–
The Somersworth National Bank, Somersworth	1183	4	4
Warner			
The Kearsarge National Bank Of Warner	1674	6	–
West Derry			
The First National Bank Of West Derry	8038	6	5
Wilton			
The Wilton National Bank	13247	–	4
Winchester			
The Winchester National Bank	887	3	4
Wolfborough			
The Lake National Bank Of Wolfborough	1486	6	–
Wolfeboro			
The Wolfeboro National Bank	8147	6	6
Woodsville			
The Woodsville National Bank	5092	5	6

NEW JERSEY

City, Bank	Ch. No.	L	S
Absecon			
The First National Bank Of Absecon	10823	–	4
Allendale			
The First National Bank Of Allendale	12706	–	5
Allenhurst			
Allenhurst National Bank & Trust Company, Allenhurst	12891	–	4
Allentown			
The Farmers National Bank Of Allentown	3501	3	5
Alpha			
The Alpha National Bank	12823	6	5
Arlington			
The First National Bank & Trust Company Of Kearney	8627	5	5
The First National Bank Of Arlington	8627	5	–
Asbury Park			
The Asbury Park National Bank	3792	6	–
The Asbury Park National Bank And Trust Company	13363	–	3
The First National Bank Of Asbury Park	3451	6	–
The Seacoast National Bank Of Asbury Park	6673	6	–
Atlantic City			
Chelsea Second Natl Bank & Trust Co Of Atlantic City	5884	–	4
The Atlantic City National Bank	2527	4	4
The Boardwalk National Bank Of Atlantic City	8800	3	2
The Chelsea National Bank Of Atlantic City	5884	4	5
The Second National Bank Of Atlantic City	3621	3	5
The Union National Bank Of Atlantic City	4420	5	5
Atlantic Highlands			
The Atlantic Highlands National Bank	4119	6	6
Barnegat			
The First National Bank Of Barnegat	8497	6	5
Bayonne			
The First National Bank Of Bayonne	8454	5	–
Beach Haven			
Beach Haven National Bank & Trust Company	11658	–	2
Belleville			
Peoples National Bank & Trust Company Of Belleville	12019	5	5
The First National Bank Of Belleville	8382	6	3
Belmar			
The Belmar National Bank	13848	–	6
The First National Bank Of Belmar	5363	6	6
Belvidere			
The Belvidere National Bank	1096	3	–
The First National Bank Of Belvidere	13628	–	3
The Warren County National Bank Of Belvidere	4980	5	–
Bergenfield			
The Bergenfield National Bank	11368	4	–
The Bergenfield National Bank & Trust Co., Bergenfield	11368	6	5
Berlin			
The Berlin National Bank, Berlin	9779	6	2
Bernardsville			
The Bernardsville National Bank	6960	5	5
Beverly			
The First National Bank & Trust Company Of Beverly	8704	6	5
The First National Bank Of Beverly	8704	5	–
Blackwood			
The First National Bank & Trust Company Of Blackwood	9597	6	6
The First National Bank Of Blackwood	9597	6	–
Blairstown			
The First National Bank Of Blairstown	5621	6	5
The Peoples National Bank Of Blairstown	9833	5	5
Bloomfield			
The Bloomfield National Bank	4056	5	–
Bloomsbury			
The Bloomsbury National Bank	2271	5	–
The Citizens National Bank Of Bloomsbury	10712	4	5
Bogota			
The Bogota National Bank	11543	5	5
Boonton			
The Boonton National Bank	4274	6	6
Bordentown			
The First National Bank Of Bordentown	9268	6	5
Bound Brook			
The Bound Brook National Bank	8512	6	–
The First National Bank Of Bound Brook	3866	5	4
Bradley Beach			
The First National Bank Of Bradley Beach	10224	6	6
Branchville			
The Branchville National Bank	13855	–	4
The First National Bank Of Branchville	7364	6	6
Bridgeton			
The Bridgeton National Bank	2999	3	5
The Cumberland National Bank Of Bridgeton	1346	3	4
The Farmers And Merchants National Bank Of Bridgeton	9498	5	–
Burlington			
The Mechanics National Bank Of Burlington	1222	2	2
Butler			
The First National Bank Of Butler	6912	4	5
Caldwell			
The Caldwell National Bank	7131	6	4
The Citizens National Bank & Trust Company Of Caldwell	9612	6	5
The Citizens National Bank Of Caldwell	9612	5	–
Califon			
The Califon National Bank	9260	6	–
Camden			
First Camden National Bank & Trust Company, Camden	1209	3	2
The American National Bank Of Camden	13120	–	5
The Camden National Bank	3372	4	–
The First National Bank Of Camden	431	5	–
The First National State Bank Of Camden	1209	4	–
The National State Bank Of Camden	1209	5	–
The Third National Bank And Trust Company Of Camden	13203	–	4
Cape May			
The First National Bank Of Cape May	5839	6	–
The Merchants National Bank Of Cape May	9285	6	5
Cape May Court House			
The First National Bank Of Cape May Court House	7945	4	5
Carlstadt			
The Carlstadt National Bank	5416	5	1
Carteret			
First National Bank In Carteret	14153	–	6
Cedar Grove			
The First National Bank Of Cedar Grove	13136	–	5
Clayton			
The Clayton National Bank	10471	6	6
Clementon			
National Bank Of Clementon	14006	–	6
Cliffside Park			
The Cliffside Park National Bank	11618	5	6
The United National Bank Of Cliffside Park	14162	–	5
Clifton			
The Clifton National Bank	12690	–	5
The First National Bank Of Clifton	11983	4	5
Clinton			
The Clinton National Bank	1114	5	5
The First National Bank Of Clinton	2246	4	4

City, Bank	Ch. No.	L	S
Closter			
The Closter National Bank	8394	5	–
The Closter National Bank & Trust Company, Closter	8394	6	5
Collingswood			
The Citizens National Bank Of Collingswood	13969	–	5
The Collingswood National Bank	7983	6	4
Cranbury			
The First National Bank Of Cranbury	3168	5	5
Cranford			
The Cranford National Bank	7171	6	–
The First National Bank Of Cranford	12263	4	5
Deckertown			
The Farmers National Bank Of Deckertown	1221	6	–
The Farmers National Bank Of Sussex	1221	4	2
Dover			
The National Union Bank Of Dover	2076	3	5
The Peoples National Bank Of Dover	5136	6	–
Dumont			
The Dumont National Bank	11361	5	5
Dunellen			
The First National Bank Of Dunellen	8501	6	6
East Newark			
The First National Bank Of East Newark	9661	6	–
The Kearny National Bank, Kearny	9661	6	6
East Orange			
The East Orange National Bank	4766	5	–
Eatontown			
The First National Bank Of Eatontown	10110	6	3
Edgewater			
The Edgewater National Bank	13893	–	6
The First National Bank Of Edgewater	8401	5	5
Elizabeth			
The First National Bank Of Elizabeth	487	5	–
The National State Bank Of Elizabeth	1436	4	5
The Peoples National Bank Of Elizabeth	11744	4	5
Elmer			
The First National Bank Of Elmer	6707	5	4
Englewood			
The Citizens National Bank & Trust Company Of Englewood	4365	6	4
The Citizens National Bank Of Englewood	4365	6	–
Englishtown			
The First National Bank Of Englishtown	7223	5	6
Fairview			
The First National Bank Of Fairview	12465	4	4
Flemington			
The Flemington National Bank	2331	4	6
The Flemington National Bank & Trust Company, Flemington	2331	–	5
The Hunterdon County National Bank Of Flemington	892	3	3
Fords			
The Fords National Bank	11428	6	6
Fort Lee			
The First National Bank Of Fort Lee	8874	5	6
The Palisade National Bank Of Fort Lee	12497	6	6
Freehold			
The Central National Bank Of Freehold	4182	6	6
The First National Bank Of Freehold	452	4	6
The Freehold National Banking Company, Freehold	951	4	–
The National Freehold Banking Company	7436	6	–
Frenchtown			
The Union National Bank Of Frenchtown	1459	4	5
Garfield			
First National Bank In Garfield	13946	–	6
The First National Bank Of Garfield	8462	5	4
Glassboro			
The First National Bank Of Glassboro	3843	5	4
Glen Rock			
Glen Rock National Bank, Glen Rock	12609	–	3
Gloucester City			
The Gloucester City National Bank	3936	6	–
Guttenberg			
Liberty National Bank In Guttenberg	14014	–	5
The First National Bank Of Guttenberg	8390	4	
The Liberty National Bank Of Guttenberg	12806	5	5
Hackensack			
The Bergen County National Bank Of Hackensack	13364	–	5
The City National Bank & Trust Company Of Hackensack	12014	–	4
The City National Bank Of Hackensack	12014	4	–
The First National Bank Of Hackensack	1905	6	–
The Hackensack National Bank	5921	4	–
The Peoples National Bank Of Hackensack	7799	5	–
Hackettstown			
The Hackettstown National Bank	1259	3	5
The Peoples National Bank Of Hackettstown	8267	4	4
Haddon Heights			
The First National Bank Of Haddon Heights	13530	–	4
The Haddon Heights National Bank	9413	6	–
Haddonfield			
The Haddonfield National Bank	3996	5	–
Haledon			
The Haledon National Bank	12854	–	6
Hamburg			
The Hardyston National Bank Of Hamburg	8227	5	6
Hamilton Square			
The First National Bank Of Hamilton Square	12646	–	5
Harrison			
The Harrison National Bank	13034	6	4
Hawthorne			
The First National Bank Of Hawthorne	12663	–	4
High Bridge			
The First National Bank Of High Bridge	5333	4	5
Highland Park			
The First National Bank Of Highland Park	12598	5	4
Hightstown			
The Central National Bank Of Hightstown	1759	6	–
The First National Bank Of Hightstown	1737	4	4
Hillsdale			
The Hillsdale National Bank	12902	4	3
Hillside			
The Hillside National Bank	11727	5	6
Hoboken			
The First National Bank Of Hoboken	1444	3	3
The Second National Bank Of Hoboken	3744	3	–
Hope			
The First National Bank Of Hope	10118	5	5
Hopewell			
The Hopewell National Bank	4254	6	4
Irvington			
The Irvington National Bank	7981	4	5
Jamesburg			
The First National Bank Of Jamesburg	288	5	6
Jersey City			
Bergen National Bank Of Jersey City	12255	4	–
Hudson County National Bank, Jersey City	1182	4	3
Journal Square National Bank Of Jersey City	12255	3	3
The First National Bank Of Jersey City	374	1	2
The Franklin National Bank Of Jersey City	12397	3	4
The Hudson County National Bank Of Jersey City	1182	3	–
The Labor National Bank Of Jersey City	12939	5	6
The Merchants National Bank Of Jersey City	9229	4	–
The Second National Bank Of Jersey City	695	4	–
The Third National Bank Of Jersey City	3680	3	–
Union Trust & Hudson County National Bank, Jersey City	1182	3	–
Keansburg			
The Keansburg National Bank	10376	6	5
Kearny			
Kearny National Bank	13537	–	3
Keyport			
The First National Bank Of Keyport	3164	6	–
The Peoples National Bank Of Keyport	4147	6	5
Lakehurst			
The First National Bank Of Lakehurst	12571	–	5
Lakewood			
The First National Bank Of Lakewood	5232	6	–
The Peoples National Bank Of Lakewood	7291	6	4
Lambertville			
The Amwell National Bank Of Lambertville	2339	5	5
The Lambertville National Bank	1272	4	3
Laurel Springs			
The Laurel Springs National Bank	12022	–	6
Leonia			
The First National Bank Of Leonia	11950	5	–
Linden			
Linden National Bank	13540	–	6
The Linden National Bank	11545	5	–
The Linden National Bank & Trust Company, Linden	11545	5	5
Little Falls			
The Little Falls National Bank	8829	6	6
Little Ferry			
The Little Ferry National Bank	12378	6	5
Livingston			
Livingston National Bank	13129	–	5
Lodi			
The First National Bank Of Lodi	9420	4	–
Long Branch			
The Citizens National Bank Of Long Branch	6038	5	–
The First National Bank Of Long Branch	4138	6	–
Lyndhurst			
The First National Bank Of Lyndhurst	10417	6	5
Madison			
The First National Bank Of Madison	2551	3	4
Manasquan			
The First National Bank Of Manasquan	3040	6	–
The Manasquan National Bank	9213	6	4
Matawan			
The Farmers And Merchants National Bank Of Matawan	6440	5	4
Mays Landing			
The First National Bank Of Mays Landing	8582	6	6
Medford			
The Burlington County National Bank Of Medford	1191	4	4
Merchantville			
Merchantville National Bank & Trust Co, Merchantville	8323	–	6
The First National Bank & Trust Company Of Merchantville	8323	6	6
The First National Bank Of Merchantville	8323	6	–
Metuchen			
Metuchen National Bank	13916	–	6
The Metuchen National Bank	7754	4	4
Milford			
The First National Bank Of Milford	8779	5	5
Millburn			
The First National Bank Of Millburn	8661	6	6
Milltown			
The First National Bank Of Milltown	10935	–	4
Millville			
The Mechanics National Bank & Trust Company Of Millville	5208	–	6
The Mechanics National Bank Of Millville	5208	4	4
The Millville National Bank	1270	4	5
Minotola			
The First National Bank Of Minotola	10440	6	5
Montclair			
The Essex National Bank Of Montclair	9577	6	–
The First National Bank & Trust Company Of Montclair	9339	4	3
The First National Bank Of Montclair	9339	6	–
The Montclair National Bank	12268	6	3
The Peoples National Bank Of Montclair	12675	–	5
Moorestown			
The Moorestown National Bank	3387	5	–
Morristown			
The First National Bank Of Morristown	1188	4	2
The National Iron Bank Of Morristown	1113	4	–
Mount Holly			
The Farmers National Bank Of New Jersey At Mount Holly	1168	4	–
The Mount Holly National Bank	1356	4	4
The Union National Bank At Mount Holly	2343	6	–
The Union Natl Bank & Trust Co At Mount Holly	2343	6	3
Mullica Hill			
The Farmers National Bank Of Mullica Hill	6728	5	5
Netcong			
The Citizens National Bank Of Netcong	6692	5	5
New Brunswick			
The First National Bank Of New Brunswick	208	6	–
The National Bank Of New Jersey, New Brunswick	587	4	3
The Peoples National Bank Of New Brunswick	3697	5	5
New Egypt			
First National Bank In New Egypt	13910	–	5
The First National Bank Of New Egypt	8254	6	–
Newark			
Lincoln National Bank Of Newark	12570	3	3
New Jersey Natl Bank & Trust Company Of Newark	9912	5	3
The American National Bank Of Newark	9605	4	–
The Broad & Market National Bank & Trust Co. Of Newark	9912	5	–
The Broad And Market National Bank Of Newark	9912	4	–
The Essex County National Bank Of Newark	1217	3	–
The First National Bank Of Newark	52	4	–
The Forest Hill National Bank Of Newark	12604	6	–
The German National Bank Of Newark	2045	6	–
The Labor National Bank Of Newark	12771	6	–
The Manufacturers National Bank Of Newark	2040	3	–
The Mechanics National Bank Of Newark	1251	4	–
The Merchants & Manufacturers National Bank Of Newark	1818	3	–
The Merchants National Bank Of Newark	1818	3	–
The National Newark Banking Company	1316	4	–
The National State Bank Of Newark	1452	3	4
The Newark City National Bank	1220	4	–
The North Ward National Bank Of Newark	2083	3	5
The Second National Bank Of Newark	362	6	–
Union National Bank In Newark	12771	–	4
Union National Bank Of Newark	2045	3	–
Newton			
The Merchants National Bank Of Newton	876	3	–
The Sussex And Merchants National Bank Of Newton	925	5	4
The Sussex National Bank Of Newton	925	4	–
North Arlington			
The North Arlington National Bank	12033	6	6
North Bergen			
The First National Bank Of North Bergen	12732	5	4
North Hudson			
The National Bank Of North Hudson At Union City	9867	4	3
North Merchantville			
The Pennsauken Township National Bank Of North Merchantvi	12903	–	6
North Plainfield			
The Borough National Bank Of North Plainfield	9391	6	–
Nutley			
The First National Bank Of Nutley	11409	–	5
The Franklin National Bank Of Nutley	12750	–	4
Oaklyn			
The Oaklyn National Bank	12621	–	4
Ocean City			
The First National Bank Of Ocean City	6060	3	3
The Ocean City National Bank	12521	6	4
Ocean Grove			
The Ocean Grove National Bank	5403	5	6
Orange			
The Orange National Bank	1317	6	–
The Second National Bank Of Orange	4724	3	4
Palasades Park			
The Palasades Park National Bank & Trust Company	11909	–	4
Palisades Park			
The National Bank Of Palisades Park	14088	–	6
The Palisades Park National Bank	11909	4	–
Palmyra			
The Palmyra National Bank	11793	6	5
Passaic			
Passaic National Bank And Trust Company	12205	3	1
The American National Bank Of Passaic	12834	5	6
The Lincoln National Bank Of Passaic	13123	4	5
The Passaic National Bank	3572	5	–
Paterson			
Labor Co-Operative National Bank Of Paterson	12560	5	–
National Bank Of America In Paterson	12383	3	4
The Broadway National Bank Of Paterson	12726	5	–
The First National Bank Of Paterson	329	3	3

City, Bank	Ch. No.	L	S
Paterson			
The Passaic County National Bank Of Paterson	810	6	–
The Paterson National Bank	4072	3	3
The Second National Bank Of Paterson	810	5	5
Paulsboro			
The First National Bank & Trust Company Of Paulsboro	5981	6	5
The First National Bank Of Paulsboro	5981	4	–
Peapack-Gladstone			
The Peapack-Gladstone National Bank	12002	5	–
Pedricktown			
The First National Bank Of Pedricktown	8007	5	5
Pemberton			
The Peoples National Bank & Trust Company Of Pemberton	8129	6	6
The Peoples National Bank Of Pemberton	8129	6	–
Penn's Grove			
The Penn's Grove National Bank	5387	6	–
Pennington			
The First National Bank Of Pennington	5718	6	5
Penns Grove			
The Penns Grove National Bank & Trust Company	5387	6	5
Perth Amboy			
The City National Bank Of Perth Amboy	11351	6	–
The First National Bank Of Perth Amboy	5215	3	4
The Perth Amboy National Bank	12524	6	4
Phillipsburg			
The Phillipsburg National Bank	1239	3	–
The Phillipsburg National Bank & Trust Company	1239	5	3
The Second National Bank Of Phillipsburg	5556	3	4
Pitman			
Pitman National Bank	8500	6	–
Pitman National Bank & Trust Company, Pitman	8500	6	4
Plainfield			
The City National Bank Of Plainfield	2243	3	–
The First National Bank Of Plainfield	447	3	3
The First National Bank Of Plainfield	13629	–	4
The Plainfield National Bank	13174	–	4
Pleasantville			
The First National Bank Of Pleasantville	6508	6	3
The Pleasantville National Bank	12510	6	4
Point Pleasant			
The Ocean County National Bank Of Point Pleasant Beach	5712	4	5
Point Pleasent Beach			
Point Pleasent Beach National Bank & Trust Company	13215	–	5
Port Norris			
The First National Bank Of Port Norris	10036	5	6
Princeton			
The First National Bank Of Princeton	4872	3	3
The Princeton National Bank	1681	6	–
Prospect Park			
The Prospect Park National Bank	12861	6	5
Rahway			
The Citizens National Bank Of Rahway	12828	4	5
The National Bank Of Rahway	896	6	–
The Rahway National Bank	5260	4	4
The Union National Bank Of Rahway	881	6	–
Ramsey			
The First National Bank & Trust Company Of Ramsey	9367	–	4
The First National Bank Of Ramsey	9367	6	
Red Bank			
The Broad Street National Bank Of Red Bank	11553	5	–
The First National Bank Of Red Bank	445	4	–
The Navesink National Bank Of Red Bank	4535	6	–
The Second National Bank & Trust Company Of Red Bank	2257	5	5
The Second National Bank Of Red Bank	2257	3	–
Ridgefield Park			
The First National Bank Of Ridgefield Park	9780	6	–
Ridgewood			
Citizens National Bank & Trust Company Of Ridgewood	11759	6	5
First National Bank & Trust Company Of Ridgewood	5205	–	6
The Citizens National Bank Of Ridgewood	11759	6	–
The First National Bank Of Ridgewood	5205	4	–
Riverside			
The First National Bank Of Riverside	12984	–	3
The Riverside National Bank	6823	6	–
Riverton			
The Cinnaminson National Bank Of Riverton	8484	6	–
Rockaway			
The First National Bank Of Rockaway	8566	6	–
Roebling			
The First National Bank & Trust Company Of Roebling	11620	–	4
The First National Bank Of Roebling	11620	5	4
Roosevelt			
First National Bank Of Carteret	8437	6	6
The First National Bank Of Roosevelt	8437	6	–
Roselle			
The First National Bank Of Roselle	8483	6	5
Rutherford			
The Rutherford National Bank, Rutherford	5005	3	3
Salem			
The City National Bank & Trust Company Of Salem	3922	6	4
The City National Bank Of Salem	3922	5	–
The Salem National Bank & Trust Company, Salem	1326	6	5
The Salem National Banking Company	1326	5	–
Sea Bright			
The Sea Bright National Bank	14177	–	6
Sea Isle City			
The First National Bank Of Sea Isle City	12279	6	6
Seabright			
The First National Bank Of Seabright	5926	5	6
Secaucus			
The First National Bank Of Secaucus	9380	5	4
Somers Point			
The First National Bank Of Somers Point	12559	–	6
Somerville			
The First National Bank Of Somerville	395	3	–
The Second National Bank Of Somerville	4942	4	5
South Amboy			
The First National Bank Of South Amboy	3878	4	6
South Plainfield			
The First National Bank Of South Plainfield	11847	6	–
South River			
The First National Bank Of South River	6179	6	6
Spring Lake			
The First National Bank Of Spring Lake	5730	6	6
Summit			
The First National Bank & Trust Company Of Summit	5061	5	4
The First National Bank Of Summit	5061	5	–
Swedesboro			
The Swedesboro National Bank	2923	5	4
Tenafly			
The First National Bank Of Tenafly	8614	6	–
Toms River			
The First National Bank Of Toms River	2509	3	3
The Ocean County National Bank Of Toms River	1400	6	–
Town Of Union			
The First National Bank Of Town Of Union	9544	5	–
The First National Bank Of Union City	9544	4	3
Trenton			
The Broad Street National Bank Of Trenton	3709	4	4
The First National Bank Of Trenton	281	2	–
The First-Mechanics National Bank Of Trenton	1327	4	1
The Mechanics National Bank Of Trenton	1327	2	–
The Prospect National Bank Of Trenton	12949	–	5
The Security National Bank Of Trenton	13039	–	3
Tuckahoe			
The First National Bank Of Tuckahoe	14189	–	3
The Tuckahoe National Bank	8681	6	6
Ventnor City			
The Ventnor City National Bank	10248	6	4
Vincentown			
The First National Bank Of Vincentown	370	5	3
Vineland			
The Vineland National Bank	2399	5	–
The Vineland National Bank	2918	5	–
Washington			
The First National Bank Of Washington	860	3	4
The Washington National Bank	5121	5	–
Weehawken			
The Hamilton National Bank Of Weehawken	12829	5	6
West Englewood			
The West Englewood National Bank	12402	4	5
West Hoboken			
The National Bank Of North Hudson At West Hoboken	9867	4	–
West New York			
National Bank Of West New York	14305	–	6
The First National Bank Of West New York	12064	5	4
West Orange			
The First National Bank Of West Orange	9542	4	5
West Paterson			
The Westside National Bank Of West Paterson	12848	6	5
Westfield			
The First National Bank Of Westfield	4719	6	–
The National Bank Of Westfield	10142	5	5
The Peoples National Bank Of Westfield	8623	6	–
Westville			
The First National Bank Of Westville	10430	6	6
Westwood			
The First National Bank Of Westwood	8777	5	4
Wharton			
The First National Bank Of Wharton	13047	6	6
White House Station			
The First National Bank Of White House Station	9061	5	6
Wildwood			
The Marine National Bank Of Wildwood	6278	5	5
Williamstown			
The First National Bank Of Williamstown	7265	6	4
Woodbine			
The Woodbine National Bank	12977	–	1
Woodbridge			
The First National Bank & Trust Company Of Woodbridge	8299	–	4
The First National Bank Of Woodbridge	8299	3	6
Woodbury			
The Farmers And Mechanics National Bank Of Woodbury	3716	4	4
The First National Bank & Trust Company Of Woodbury	1199	5	4
The First National Bank Of Woodbury	1199	4	–
Woodstown			
The First National Bank Of Woodstown	399	4	5
The Woodstown National Bank	11734	6	–
The Woodstown National Bank & Trust Company, Woodstown	11734	6	5
Wyckoff			
The First National Bank Of Wyckoff	12272	–	5
Yardville			
The Yardville National Bank	12606	–	6

NEW MEXICO TERRITORY

City, Bank	Ch. No.	L	S
Alamogordo			
The Citizens National Bank Of Alamogordo	8315	6	–
The First National Bank Of Alamogordo	5244	6	–
Albuquerque			
The Albuquerque National Bank	3222	6	–
The First National Bank Of Albuquerque	2614	3	–
The State National Bank Of Albuquerque	7186	5	–
Artesia			
The First National Bank Of Artesia	7043	6	–
The State National Bank Of Artesia	9468	6	–
Belen			
The First National Bank Of Belen	6597	6	–
Carlsbad			
The First National Bank Of Carlsbad	5487	6	–
The National Bank Of Carlsbad	6884	6	–
Cimarron			
The First National Bank Of Cimarron	9292	6	–
Clayton			
The First National Bank Of Clayton	5713	5	–
Clovis			
The Clovis National Bank	8767	6	–
The First National Bank Of Clovis	8784	6	–
Deming			
The Deming National Bank	6974	6	–
The First National Bank Of Deming	3160	6	–
The National Bank Of Deming	4746	6	–
Eddy			
The First National Bank Of Eddy	4455	6	–
Elida			
The First National Bank Of Elida	8348	6	–
Engle			
The First National Bank Of Cutter	8662	6	–
Farmington			
The First National Bank Of Farmington	6183	6	–
The San Juan County National Bank Of Farmington	9151	6	–
Gallup			
The First National Bank Of Gallup	9988	6	–
Hagerman			
The First National Bank Of Hagerman	7503	6	–
The Hagerman National Bank	7503	6	–
Hope			
The First National Bank Of Hope	9441	6	–
Lake Arthur			
The First National Bank Of Lake Arthur	8584	5	–
Lakewood			
The Lakewood National Bank	8782	6	–
Las Cruces			
The First National Bank Of Las Cruces	7720	6	–
Las Vegas			
The First National Bank Of Las Vegas	2436	4	–
The San Miguel National Bank Of Las Vegas	2454	4	–
Lordsburg			
The First National Bank Of Lordsburg	8880	6	–
Melrose			
The First National Bank Of Melrose	8397	6	–
Nara Visa			
The First National Bank Of Nara Visa	8663	5	–
Portales			
The Citizens National Bank Of Portales	8304	6	–
The First National Bank Of Portales	6187	6	–
Raton			
The Citizens National Bank Of Raton	6363	6	–
The First National Bank Of Raton	4734	3	–
The National Bank Of New Mexico Of Raton	8098	6	–
The Raton National Bank	8120	5	–
Roswell			
The American National Bank Of Roswell	6714	6	–
The Citizens National Bank Of Roswell	6777	5	–
The First National Bank Of Roswell	5220	6	–
The Roswell National Bank	6714	6	–
Santa Fe			
The First National Bank Of Santa Fe	1750	3	–
The Second National Bank Of New Mexico	2024	4	–
Santa Rosa			
The First National Bank Of Santa Rosa	6081	6	–
Silver City			
The American National Bank Of Silver City	8132	6	–
The First National Bank Of Silver City	3554	6	–
The Silver City National Bank	3539	6	–
Socorro			
The First National Bank Of Socorro	2627	6	–
The New Mexico National Bank Of Socorro	4485	6	–
The Socorro National Bank	4574	6	–
Sunnyside			
The First National Bank Of Fort Sumner	8617	6	–
Texico			
The First National Bank Of Texico	8173	6	–
The Texico National Bank	8391	6	–
Tucumcari			
The First National Bank Of Tucumcari	6288	6	–

NEW MEXICO

City, Bank	Ch. No.	L	S
Alamogordo			
The First National Bank Of Alamogordo	5244	6	–
Albuquerque			
Albuquerque National Bank	12485	3	–
Albuquerque National Trust And Savings Bank	12485	4	2

City, Bank	Ch. No.	L	S
Albuquerque			
First National Bank In Albuquerque	13814	–	4
The Citizens National Bank Of Albuquerque	11442	5	–
The First National Bank Of Albuquerque	2614	2	2
The State National Bank Of Albuquerque	7186	4	–
Artesia			
The First National Bank Of Artesia	7043	4	4
The State National Bank Of Artesia	9468	6	–
Belen			
The First National Bank Of Belen	6597	5	2
Carlsbad			
The Carlsbad National Bank	12569	–	5
The First National Bank Of Carlsbad	5487	6	–
The National Bank Of Carlsbad	6884	6	–
Cimarron			
The First National Bank Of Cimarron	9292	6	–
Clayton			
The First National Bank Of Clayton	5713	5	–
Clovis			
The Clovis National Bank	8767	5	5
The First National Bank Of Clovis	8784	6	–
Deming			
The Deming National Bank	6974	6	–
The First National Bank In Deming	6974	6	–
Elida			
The First National Bank Of Elida	8348	6	5
Farmington			
The First National Bank Of Farmington	6183	6	5
The San Juan County National Bank Of Farmington	9151	6	–
Gallup			
The First National Bank In Gallup	11900	5	4
The First National Bank Of Gallup	9988	6	–
The National Bank Of Gallup	11900	6	–
Hagerman			
The First National Bank Of Hagerman	7503	5	4
Hope			
The First National Bank Of Hope	9441	5	–
Lake Arthur			
The First National Bank Of Lake Arthur	8584	6	–
Lakewood			
The Lakewood National Bank	8782	6	–
Las Cruces			
The First National Bank Of Las Cruces	7720	6	6
Las Vegas			
The First National Bank Of Las Vegas	2436	3	–
The San Miguel National Bank Of Las Vegas	2454	5	–
Lordsburg			
The First National Bank Of Lordsburg	8880	6	–
Magdalena			
The First National Bank Of Magdalena	10268	5	–
Melrose			
The First National Bank Of Melrose	8397	4	6
Nara Visa			
The First National Bank Of Nara Visa	8663	6	6
Portales			
The First National Bank Of Portales	6187	5	4
Raton			
First National Bank In Raton	12924	–	2
The First National Bank Of Raton	4734	4	–
The National Bank Of New Mexico Of Raton	8098	6	6
Roswell			
The American National Bank Of Roswell	6714	5	–
The Citizens National Bank Of Roswell	6777	5	–
The First National Bank Of Roswell	5220	4	3
Santa Fe			
The First National Bank Of Santa Fe	1750	3	2
Santa Rosa			
The First National Bank Of Santa Rosa	6081	4	5
Silver City			
The American National Bank Of Silver City	8132	3	3
The Silver City National Bank	3539	6	–
Sunnyside			
The First National Bank Of Fort Sumner	8617	6	–
Tucumcari			
The First National Bank Of Tucumcari	6288	5	6
The First-American National Bank Of Tucumcari	14081	–	6

NEW YORK

City, Bank	Ch. No.	L	S
Adams			
The Adams National Bank	2845	6	–
The Citizens National Bank Of Adams	4103	6	–
The Farmers National Bank Of Adams	4061	4	4
The First National Bank Of Adams	71	6	–
The Hungerford National Bank Of Adams	1531	5	–
Addison			
The First National Bank Of Addison	5178	4	5
Afton			
First National Bank Of Afton	11513	6	5
Akron			
The Wickware National Bank Of Akron	5631	5	–
Albany			
The Albany City National Bank, Albany	1291	6	–
The First National Bank Of Albany	267	3	–
The Merchants National Bank Of Albany	1045	6	–
The National Albany Exchange Bank	739	6	
The National Commercial Bank And Trust Company Of Albany	1301	3	2
The National Commercial Bank Of Albany	1301	3	–
The National Exchange Bank Of Albany	3282	5	–
The National Mechanics And Farmers Bank Of Albany	1289	6	–
The New York State National Bank Of Albany	1262	3	2
The Union National Bank Of Albany	1123	6	–
Albion			
The Citizens National Bank Of Albion	4998	3	6
The First National Bank Of Albion	166	5	–
The Orleans County National Bank Of Albion	1509	4	–
Alexandria Bay			
The First Natl. Bank Of The Thousand Islands, Alexandria Bay	5284	5	6
Allegany			
The First National Bank Of Allegany	7009	4	6
Altamont			
The First National Bank Of Altamont	9866	6	6
Amenia			
The First National Bank Of Amenia	706	3	4
Amityville			
First National Bank And Trust Company Of Amityville	8873	6	6
The First National Bank Of Amityville	8873	6	–
Amsterdam			
The Amsterdam City National Bank, Amsterdam	4211	4	3
The Farmers National Bank Of Amsterdam	1335	4	5
The First National Bank Of Amsterdam	1307	4	4
The Manufacturers National Bank Of Amsterdam	2239	6	–
The Merchants National Bank Of Amsterdam	2920	6	–
Andes			
The First National Bank Of Andes	302	6	–
The National Bank Of Andes	11243	6	5
Andover			
The Andover National Bank	13909	–	6
The Burrows National Bank Of Andover	8146	6	6
Angelica			
The First National Bank Of Angelica	564	6	–
Arcade			
The First National Bank Of Arcade	10410	6	4
Ardsley			
The First National Bank Of Ardsley	12992	–	6
Argyle			
The First National Bank Of Argyle	8343	6	6
The National Bank Of Argyle	13521	–	4
Athens			
The Athens National Bank	10856	5	5
Atlanta			
The Atlanta National Bank	12071	5	5
Attica			
The Attica National Bank	2437	6	–
The First National Bank Of Attica	199	6	–
Auburn			
The Auburn City National Bank	1285	6	–
The Auburn-Cayuga National Bank & Trust Company, Auburn	1345	–	4
The Cayuga County National Bank Of Auburn	1345	4	6
The First National Bank Of Auburn	231	6	–
The National Bank Of Auburn	1345	–	5
The National Bank Of Auburn	1350	4	5
The National Exchange Bank Of Auburn	1351	6	–
Aurora			
The First National Bank Of Aurora	412	5	5
Babylon			
The Babylon National Bank	4906	6	–
The Babylon National Bank	10358	6	–
The Babylon National Bank And Trust Company, Babylon	10358	–	4
Bainbridge			
The First National Bank Of Bainbridge	2543	4	5
Baldwin			
The Baldwin National Bank	11474	5	6
The Baldwin National Bank And Trust Company, Baldwin	11474	–	5
Baldwinsville			
The First National Bank & Trust Company Of Baldwinsville	292	–	6
The First National Bank Of Baldwinsville	292	6	6
Ballston Spa			
The Ballston Spa National Bank	1253	4	4
The First National Bank Of Ballston Spa	954	4	5
Barker			
The Somerset National Bank Of Barker	10126	6	5
Batavia			
The First National Bank Of Batavia	340	3	2
The Genesee County National Bank Of Batavia	2421	6	–
The National Bank Of Genesee, Batavia	1074	6	
Bath			
The Bath National Bank	10235	4	5
The First National Bank Of Bath	165	6	–
Bay Shore			
The First National Bank & Trust Company Of Bay Shore	10029	6	6
The First National Bank Of Bay Shore	10029	6	–
Bayside			
The Bayside National Bank	7939	6	–
Belfast			
The First National Bank Of Belfast	9644	6	5
Bellerose			
The First National Bank Of Bellerose	13234	–	3
Bellmore			
The First National Bank Of Bellmore	11072	6	4
Bellport			
The Bellport National Bank	12473	6	6
Binghamton			
The City National Bank Of Binghamton	1189	4	5
The First National Bank Of Binghamton	202	3	4
The Merchants National Bank Of Binghamton	2136	6	–
The National Broome County Bank Of Binghamton	1513	5	–
Bliss			
The Bliss National Bank	10754	5	5
Bolivar			
The First National Bank Of Bolivar	13246	–	6
Bolton Landing			
The Bolton National Bank Of Bolton Landing	13089	6	6
Boonville			
The First National Bank Of Boonville	2320	5	4
The National Exchange Bank Of Boonville	8022	6	5
Brasher Falls			
The Brasher Falls National Bank	10943	6	6
Brewster			
The First National Bank Of Brewsters	2225	4	5
Bridgehampton			
The Bridgehampton National Bank	9669	6	6
Brockport			
Brockport National Bank	13965	–	4
The First National Bank Of Brockport	382	4	4
Bronxville			
The Gramatan National Bank & Trust Company Of Bronxville	8240	6	4
The Gramatan National Bank Of Bronxville	8240	5	–
Brooklyn			
First National Bank Of Brooklyn	923	5	–
The Atlantic National Bank Of Brooklyn	1491	6	–
The Farmers And Citizens National Bank Of Brooklyn	1223	6	–
The First National Bank Of The City Of Brooklyn	923	3	–
The Greenpoint National Bank Of Brooklyn	10054	6	–
The Nassau National Bank Of Brooklyn	658	3	–
The National City Bank Of Brooklyn	1543	6	–
The Sprague National Bank Of Brooklyn	2976	4	–
The Sprague National Bank Of New York	2976	6	–
Brown Station			
The Ashokan National Bank Of Brown Station	9482	6	–
Brushton			
The First National Bank Of Brushton	9643	6	6
Buffalo			
Community-South Side National Bank Of Buffalo	11768	5	–
Lafayette National Bank Of Buffalo	11435	4	–
The Amherst National Bank Of Buffalo	11883	6	–
The Broadway National Bank Of Buffalo	11319	5	–
The Central National Bank Of Buffalo	7823	4	–
The City National Bank Of Buffalo	5174	5	–
The Columbia National Bank Of Buffalo	4741	2	–
The Community National Bank Of Buffalo	11768	6	–
The Community National Bank Of Buffalo	11768	3	–
The East Side National Bank Of Buffalo	13220	5	3
The Farmers And Mechanics National Bank Of Buffalo	453	4	–
The First National Bank Of Buffalo	235	6	–
The Genesee National Bank Of Buffalo	12337	4	4
The Lincoln National Bank Of Buffalo	13219	–	2
The Lincoln-East Side National Bank Of Buffalo	13952	–	6
The Manufacturers And Traders National Bank Of Buffalo	6186	2	–
The Marine National Bank Of Buffalo	6184	2	–
The Merchants National Bank Of Buffalo	11836	5	–
The Niagara National Bank Of Buffalo	13441	–	2
The Riverside National Bank Of Buffalo	12445	5	–
The South Side National Bank Of Buffalo	12313	5	–
The Third National Bank Of Buffalo	850	4	–
Caledonia			
The First National Bank Of Caledonia	5648	5	5
Callicoon			
First National Bank In Callicoon	13590	–	3
The Callicoon National Bank	9427	4	6
Cambridge			
The Cambridge Valley National Bank Of North White Creek	1275	5	–
The Cambridge Valley National Bank, Cambridge	1275	5	6
Camden			
The First National Bank And Trust Company Of Camden	2448	5	5
The First National Bank Of Camden	2448	3	–
Canajoharie			
National Spraker Bank In Canajoharie	13876	–	4
The Canajoharie National Bank	1122	5	5
The National Spraker Bank Of Canajoharie	1257	3	5
Canandaigua			
The Canandaigua National Bank	3817	4	–
The Canandaigua National Bank And Trust Company	3817	6	4
The County National Bank Of Canandaigua	10047	6	–
The First National Bank Of Canandaigua	259	6	–
The Ontario County National Bank Of Canandaigua	2765	6	–
Canastota			
The Canastota National Bank	1525	6	–
The First National Bank Of Canastota	4419	6	5
Candor			
The First National Bank Of Candor	353	6	3
Canton			
The First National Bank Of Canton	3696	4	4
The St. Lawrence County National Bank Of Canton	8531	4	6
Carmel			
The Putnam County National Bank Of Carmel	976	4	4
Carthage			
Carthage National Exchange Bank, Carthage	13584	–	4
The Carthage National Bank	3672	4	5
The First National Bank Of Carthage	2442	6	–
The National Exchange Bank & Trust Company Of Carthage	6094	–	5
The National Exchange Bank Of Carthage	6094	4	–
Castleton			
The National Bank Of Castleton	842	6	–
The National Exchange Bank Of Castleton	5816	5	–
The National Exchange Bank Of Castleton On Hudson	5816	6	5

City, Bank	Ch. No.	L	S
Cato			
The First National Bank Of Cato	9857	6	5
Catskill			
Catskill National Bank And Trust Company, Catskill	1294	–	5
The Catskill National Bank	1294	4	5
The Tanners National Bank Of Catskill	1198	3	4
Cazenovia			
The Cazenovia National Bank	5675	6	–
The National Bank Of Cazenovia	1271	5	–
Cedarhurst			
Peninsula National Bank Of Cedarhurst	11854	5	4
Central Park			
The Central Park National Bank	12951	–	6
Central Square			
The First National Bank Of Central Square	10109	6	6
Central Valley			
The Central Valley National Bank	9990	6	4
Champlain			
The First National Bank Of Champlain	316	4	3
Chappaqua			
The Chappaqua National Bank	12746	–	3
Chateaugay			
The First National Bank Of Chateaugay	8893	6	5
Cherry Creek			
Cherry Creek National Bank	14078	–	6
The Cherry Creek National Bank	10481	3	3
Cherry Valley			
Otsego County National Bank Of Cherry Valley	13748	–	6
The National Central Bank Of Cherry Valley	1136	4	5
Chester			
The Chester National Bank	1349	4	6
Chittenango			
The First National Bank Of Chittenango	179	6	–
Clayton			
The First National Bank Of Clayton	3797	4	6
The First National Exchange Bank Of Clayton	5108	–	5
The National Exchange Bank Of Clayton	5108	5	5
Clifton Springs			
The Ontario National Bank Of Clifton Springs	8717	6	6
Clinton			
The Hayes National Bank Of Clinton	10295	6	5
Clyde			
The Briggs National Bank Of Clyde	2468	4	–
The First National Bank Of Clyde	304	6	–
Cobleskill			
The First National Bank Of Cobleskill	461	3	2
Cohoes			
The National Bank Of Cohoes	1347	4	4
Cold Spring			
The National Bank Of Cold Spring On Hudson	4416	5	6
Conewango Valley			
The Conewango Valley National Bank	10930	6	6
Cooperstown			
The Cooperstown National Bank	7305	6	5
The First National Bank Of Cooperstown	280	3	1
The Second National Bank Of Cooperstown	223	3	2
The Worthington National Bank Of Cooperstown	420	6	–
Copenhagen			
The Copenhagen National Bank	10077	6	6
Corinth			
The Corinth National Bank	6479	6	6
Corning			
First National Bank & Trust Company Of Corning	2655	4	5
The First National Bank Of Corning	2655	4	–
Cornwall			
The Cornwall National Bank	10084	5	5
The First National Bank Of Cornwall	7344	6	–
Corona			
The First National Bank Of Corona	8853	6	–
Cortland			
Second National Bank And Trust Company Of Cortland	2827	6	4
The First National Bank Of Cortland	226	6	–
The National Bank Of Cortland	2272	4	4
The Second National Bank Of Cortland	2827	5	–
Coxsackie			
The National Bank Of Coxsackie	1398	4	–
Croghan			
The Croghan National Bank	10948	5	5
Croton On Hudson			
The First National Bank Of Croton On Hudson	9171	6	5
Cuba			
The Cuba National Bank	1143	4	4
The First National Bank Of Cuba	2451	3	5
Cutchogue			
The First National Bank Of Cutchogue	12551	5	6
Dansville			
The First National Bank Of Dansville	75	6	–
The Merchants And Farmers National Bank Of Dansville	4482	5	5
Delhi			
The Delaware National Bank Of Delhi	1323	3	4
The First National Bank Of Delhi	94	6	–
The First National Bank Of Port Jervis	94	3	4
Deposit			
The Deposit National Bank	472	5	–
The Farmers National Bank Of Deposit	9434	5	5
Dexter			
The First National Bank Of Dexter	8463	6	5
Dolgeville			
The First National Bank Of Dolgeville	6447	5	5
Dover Plains			
The Dover Plains National Bank	822	5	6
Downsville			
The First National Bank Of Downsville	7878	6	4
Dryden			
The First National Bank Of Dryden	6487	6	5
Dundee			
The Dundee National Bank	2463	6	6
Dunkirk			
The Lake Shore National Bank Of Dunkirk	2916	4	4
The Merchants National Bank Of Dunkirk	2619	2	3
Earlville			
The First National Bank Of Earlville	4493	5	5
East Aurora			
The First National Bank Of East Aurora	9950	6	–
East Hampton			
The East Hampton National Bank	7763	6	6
East Islip			
The First National Bank Of East Islip	9322	6	5
East Northport			
The Citizens National Bank Of East Northport	12593	6	6
East Rochester			
The First National Bank Of East Rochester	10141	6	3
East Rockaway			
East Rockaway National Bank & Trust Company, East Rockaway	12818	–	6
The East Rockaway National Bank	12818	6	6
East Setauket			
The Tinker National Bank Of East Setauket	11511	6	–
East Worcester			
The East Worcester National Bank	9060	6	–
Edmeston			
The First National Bank Of Edmeston	3681	5	6
Edwards			
The Edwards National Bank	10569	6	6
Ellenville			
The First National Bank Of Ellenville	45	4	–
The Home National Bank Of Ellenville	2117	5	6
Elmira			
First National Bank & Trust Company Of Elmira	149	–	2
The Chemung Canal National Bank Of Elmira	811	6	–
The Elmira National Bank	4105	6	–
The First National Bank Of Elmira	119	6	–
The Merchants National Bank Of Elmira	5137	4	–
The National Bank Of Chemung, Elmira	1391	6	–
The Second National Bank Of Elmira	149	4	6
Elmsford			
The First National Bank Of Elmsford	12956	5	5
Fairport			
Fairport National Bank And Trust Company, Fairport	10869	4	5
The Fairport National Bank	10869	6	–
Falconer			
The First National Bank Of Falconer	5407	4	4
Far Rockaway			
The National Bank Of Far Rockaway	9271	6	3
Farmingdale			
The First National Bank Of Farmingdale	8882	6	5
Fayetteville			
The National Bank Of Fayetteville	1110	6	–
Fishkill			
The Fishkill National Bank Of Beacon	35	5	5
The National Bank Of Fishkill	971	5	–
Fishkill Landing			
The First National Bank Of Fishkill Landing	35	4	–
Fleischmann			
The First National Bank Of Fleischmanns	8847	–	6
Fleischmanns			
The First National Bank Of Griffin Corners	8847	5	–
Floral Park			
The First National Bank And Trust Company Of Floral Park	12449	–	3
Florida			
The Florida National Bank	9956	6	6
The National Bank Of Florida	13825	–	6
Flushing			
The Flushing National Bank	9691	4	–
Fond			
The National Mohawk River Bank Of Fonda	1212	3	5
Forestville			
The First National Bank Of Forestville	10444	3	3
Fort Edward			
The Farmers National Bank Of Fort Edward	1348	6	–
The First National Bank Of Fort Edward	3330	6	–
The Fort Edward National Bank	7630	6	5
The National Bank Of Fort Edward	1218	6	–
The North Granville National Bank, North Granville	1348	6	–
Fort Plain			
The Fort Plain National Bank	2860	4	6
The National Fort Plain Bank	467	6	–
Frankfort			
Citizens First National Bank Of Frankfort	10351	5	4
The Citizens National Bank Of Frankfort	10351	6	–
The First National Bank Of Frankfort	3582	6	–
Franklin			
The First National Bank Of Franklin	282	4	5
Franklin Square			
The Franklin Square National Bank	12997	–	5
Franklinville			
The Farmers National Bank Of Franklinville	2755	6	–
The First National Bank Of Franklinville	2345	6	–
The Peoples National Bank Of Franklinville	8157	6	–
The Union National Bank Of Franklinville	2755	4	5
Fredonia			
The Fredonia National Bank	841	5	–
The National Bank Of Fredonia	9019	3	4
Freeport			
The Citizens National Bank Of Freeport	11518	6	–
The First National Bank And Trust Company Of Freeport	7703	6	3
The First National Bank Of Freeport	7703	4	–
Friendship			
The Citizens National Bank Of Friendship	2632	5	–
The First National Bank Of Friendship	265	6	–
The Union National Bank Of Friendship	11055	4	5
Fulton			
Citizens National Bank And Trust Company Of Fulton	1178	–	5
The Citizens National Bank Of Fulton	1178	4	–
The First National Bank Of Fulton	968	4	–
Fultonville			
The Fultonville National Bank	2869	6	6
Gainesville			
The Gainesville National Bank	5867	4	6
Gasport			
The First National Bank Of Gasport	10623	6	6
Geneseo			
Genesee Valley National Bank And Trust Company Of Geneseo	886	–	5
Genesso			
The Genessee Valley National Bank, Geneseo	886	3	3
Geneva			
The First National Bank Of Geneva	167	6	–
The Geneva National Bank	949	5	–
Genoa			
The First National Bank Of Genoa	9921	6	6
Germantown			
The Germantown National Bank	12242	5	6
Glen Head			
The First National Bank Of Glen Head	13126	–	3
Glens Falls			
Glens Falls National Bank And Trust Company	7699	–	6
The First National Bank Of Glens Falls	980	4	5
The Glens Falls National Bank	1293	6	–
The Merchants National Bank Of Glens Falls	4846	6	–
The National Bank Of Glens Falls	7699	4	5
Gloversville			
City National Bank And Trust Company Of Gloversville	9305	–	3
The City National Bank Of Gloversville	9305	4	–
The Fulton County National Bank Of Gloversville	3312	5	–
The Fulton County Natl Bank & Trust Co Of Gloversville	3312	–	3
The National Bank Of Gloversville	1938	6	–
The National Fulton County Bank Of Gloversville	1474	6	–
Goshen			
The Goshen National Bank	1408	4	5
The National Bank Of Orange County Of Goshen	1399	4	4
Gouverneur			
First National Bank In Gouverneur	13911	–	6
The First National Bank Of Gouverneur	2510	4	4
Grand Gorge			
The First National Bank Of Grand Gorge	7618	6	5
Granville			
The Farmers National Bank Of Granville	3154	5	5
The Granville National Bank	4985	4	6
The National Bank Of Granville	2294	6	–
The Washington County National Bank Of Granville	7255	5	4
Great Neck Station			
The First Natl. Bank Of Great Neck At Great Neck Station	12659	5	6
Greenport			
The First National Bank Of Greenport	334	6	5
The Peoples National Bank Of Greenport	3232	6	6
Greenwich			
The First National Bank Of Greenwich	2517	5	–
The Washington County National Bank Of Greenwich	1266	6	–
Greenwood			
The First National Bank Of Greenwood	8058	6	6
Groton			
The First National Bank Of Groton	1083	4	5
Hamden			
The First National Bank Of Hamden	12017	5	5
Hamilton			
The National Hamilton Bank, Hamilton	1334	4	4
Hammond			
The Citizens National Bank Of Hammond	10216	6	6
Hampton Bays			
The Hampton Bays National Bank	12987	4	4
Hancock			
The First National Bank Of Hancock	8613	5	5
Harrison			
The First National Bank Of Harrison	12601	6	4
Harrisville			
The First National Bank Of Harrisville	10767	6	4
Hartsdale			
The Hartsdale National Bank	12705	–	6
Hartwick			
The Hartwick National Bank	11657	6	5
Hastings Upon Hudson			
The First National Bank Of Hastings Upon Hudson	8586	6	6
Havana			
The First National Bank Of Havana	301	6	–
The Havana National Bank	343	6	–
The Second National Bank Of Havana	343	6	–
Haverstraw			
The National Bank Of Haverstraw	2229	4	–

City, Bank	Ch. No.	L	S
Haverstraw			
The National Bank Of Haverstraw And Trust Company	2229	5	6
Hempstead			
The First National Bank Of Hempstead	4880	4	5
The Second National Bank Of Hempstead	11375	5	–
Herkimer			
The First National Bank Of Herkimer	3183	4	4
The Herkimer National Bank	5141	4	4
Hermon			
The First National Bank Of Hermon	5605	6	–
Heuvelton			
The First National Bank Of Heuvelton	10446	5	5
Hicksville			
The Long Island National Bank Of Hicksville	11087	5	5
Highland			
The First National Bank Of Highland	5336	5	6
Highland Falls			
The Citizens National Bank Of Highland Falls	8838	6	–
The First National Bank & Trust Company Of Highland Falls	8850	–	6
The First National Bank Of Highland Falls	8850	6	6
Hobart			
The First National Bank Of Hobart	193	6	–
The National Bank Of Hobart	4497	5	4
Holcomb			
The Hamlin National Bank Of Holcomb	10046	6	5
Holland Patent			
The First National Bank Of Holland Patent	5299	4	6
Homer			
The First National Bank Of Homer	2398	5	–
The Homer National Bank	3186	6	5
Hoosick Falls			
The First National Bank Of Hoosick Falls	2471	3	5
The Peoples National Bank Of Hoosick Falls	5874	3	5
The Peoples-First National Bank Of Hoosick Falls	2471	–	3
Hornellsville			
Citizens National Bank And Trust Company Of Hornell	2522	6	6
The Citizens National Bank Of Hornell	2522	5	–
The Citizens National Bank Of Hornellsville	2522	6	–
The First National Bank Of Hornell	262	5	5
The First National Bank Of Hornellsville	262	5	–
Horseheads			
The First National Bank Of Horseheads	8301	5	4
Hudson			
The Farmers National Bank Of Hudson	990	5	5
The First National Bank And Trust Company Of Hudson	396	6	3
The First National Bank Of Hudson	396	3	–
The National Hudson River Bank Of Hudson	1091	5	–
Hunter			
The Greene County National Bank Of Hunter	7485	6	–
Huntington			
First National Bank And Trust Company Of Huntington	6587	–	5
The First National Bank Of Huntington	6587	5	–
Ilion			
Ilion National Bank And Trust Company, Ilion	1670	5	4
The Ilion National Bank	1670	4	–
The Manufacturers National Bank Of Ilion	9109	4	4
Interlaken			
The Wheeler National Bank Of Interlaken	13037	6	5
Inwood			
The First National Bank Of Inwood	12460	–	5
Irvington			
The Irvington National Bank	6371	6	5
The Irvington National Bank And Trust Company, Irvington	6371	–	5
Islip			
The First National Bank Of Islip	8794	6	3
Ithaca			
The First National Bank Of Ithaca	222	3	4
The Merchants And Farmers National Bank Of Ithaca	729	6	–
The Tompkins County National Bank Of Ithaca	1561	4	5
Jamaica			
The First National Bank Of Jamaica	8268	4	–
Jamestown			
American National Bank Of Jamestown	9748	3	2
Swedish American National Bank Of Jamestown	9748	6	–
The Chautauqua County National Bank Of Jamestown	1563	6	–
The City National Bank Of Jamestown	938	6	–
The First National Bank Of Jamestown	548	3	4
The Jamestown National Bank	3846	6	–
The Liberty National Bank Of Jamestown	11360	4	–
The National Chautauqua County Bank Of Jamestown	8453	4	4
The Second National Bank Of Jamestown	938	6	–
Jeffersonville			
The First National Bank Of Jeffersonville	10456	6	6
Johnstown			
The First National Bank Of Johnstown	2418	6	–
Jordan			
The Jordan National Bank	12375	5	5
Keeseville			
The Keeseville National Bank	1753	3	5
Kenmore			
The First National Bank Of Kenmore	12208	4	4
Kinderhook			
The National Bank Of Kinderhook	1026	5	–
The National Union Bank Of Kinderhook	929	3	3
Kings Park			
Kings Park National Bank	12489	6	6
The National Bank Of Kings Park	14019	–	5
Kingston			
National Ulster County Bank & Trust Company Of Kingston	1050	6	4
The First National Bank Of Kingston	451	6	–
The First National Bank Of Rondout	2493	3	–
The Kingston National Bank	1149	6	–
The National Ulster County Bank Of Kingston	1050	4	–
The National Ulster County Bank Of Kingston	13822	–	5
The State Of New York National Bank Of Kingston	955	4	5
La Fargeville			
The First National Bank Of La Fargeville	13365	–	6
Lacona			
The First National Bank Of Lacona	10175	6	5
Lake George			
First National Bank Of Lake George	8793	6	6
Lake Ronkonkoma			
The National Bank Of Lake Ronkonkoma	13130	–	6
Lancaster			
The Citizens National Bank Of Lancaster	11912	3	4
Lansingburgh			
The National Bank Of Lansingburgh	1426	6	–
The National Exchange Bank Of Lansingburgh	1534	6	–
Larchmont			
The Larchmont National Bank	6019	5	–
The Larchmont National Bank And Trust Company, Larchmont	6019	4	3
Le Roy			
The First National Bank Of Le Roy	937	6	–
The Le Roy National Bank	6087	5	6
The National Bank Of Le Roy	3283	6	–
Leonardsville			
The First National Bank Of Leonardsville	217	6	–
Lestershire			
The First National Bank Of Lestershire	7813	6	–
Liberty			
The National Bank Of Liberty	10037	4	4
The Sullivan County National Bank Of Liberty	4925	4	4
Lindenhurst			
The First National Bank Of Lindenhurst	8833	5	6
Lisbon			
The First National Bank Of Lisbon	12018	6	6
Lisle			
The First National Bank Of Lisle	10816	5	5
Little Falls			
The Herkimer County National Bank Of Little Falls	1344	5	–
The Little Falls National Bank	2406	3	4
The National Herkimer County Bank Of Little Falls	2400	3	–
Livingston Manor			
The Livingston Manor National Bank	10043	5	3
Livonia			
The Stewart National Bank And Trust Company Of Livonia	13006	–	6
The Stewart National Bank Of Livonia	13006	5	6
The Stewart National Bank Of Livonia	13006	–	6
Lockport			
Niagara County National Bank & Trust Company, Lockport	639	5	2
The First National Bank Of Lockport	211	5	–
The National Exchange Bank Of Lockport	1039	3	–
The Niagara County National Bank Of Lockport	639	3	–
Long Beach			
The National Bank Of Long Beach	11755	5	–
The National City Bank Of Long Beach	13074	4	6
Long Island City			
The Commercial National Bank Of Long Island City	10329	6	–
Lowville			
The Black River National Bank Of Lowville	2426	6	5
The First National Bank Of Lowville	348	5	–
Lynbrook			
The Lynbrook National Bank	8923	6	–
The Lynbrook National Bank And Trust Company	8923	–	1
The Peoples National Bank And Trust Company Of Lynbrook	11603	5	5
The Peoples National Bank Of Lynbrook	11603	6	–
Lyons			
The Gavitt National Bank Of Lyons	7479	4	–
The Lyons National Bank	1027	5	3
Lyons Falls			
The Lyons Falls National Bank	12836	5	4
Macedon			
The First National Bank Of Macedon	12494	5	6
Mahopac			
The Mahopac National Bank	13121	–	5
Malone			
The Citizens National Bank Of Malone	11897	–	4
The Farmers National Bank Of Malone	598	5	6
The National Bank Of Malone	914	6	–
The Peoples National Bank Of Malone	3307	6	–
The Third National Bank Of Malone	3366	6	–
Mamaroneck			
First National Bank In Mamaroneck	13592	–	3
The First National Bank And Trust Company Of Mamaroneck	5411	6	5
The First National Bank Of Mamaroneck	5411	4	–
Manhasset			
First National Bank And Trust Company Of Manhasset	11924	–	5
The First National Bank Of Manhasset	11924	5	–
Marathon			
The First National Bank Of Marathon	3193	4	6
Marcellus			
The First National Bank Of Marcellus	9869	5	4
Margaretville			
The Peoples National Bank Of Margaretville	5924	5	5
Mariner Harbor			
The Mariner Harbor National Bank	8194	6	6
Marion			
The First National Bank Of Marion	10546	6	6
Marlboro			
The First National Bank Of Marlboro	8834	6	5
Massena			
The First National Bank And Trust Company Of Massena	6694	6	6
The First National Bank Of Massena	6694	6	–
Matteawan			
The Matteawan National Bank	4914	6	–
The Matteawan National Bank Of Beacon	4914	4	4
Mattituck			
The Mattituck National Bank And Trust Company	13445	–	5
Maybrook			
The Maybrook National Bank	11927	5	5
Mechanicsville			
The First National Bank Of Mechanicsville	3171	6	6
Mechanicville			
The Manufacturers National Bank Of Mechanicville	5037	4	6
Medina			
The First National Bank Of Medina	229	6	–
The Medina National Bank	4986	6	–
Merrick			
The First National Bank Of Merrick	12503	6	5
Mexico			
The First National Bank Of Mexico	5293	6	5
Middleburgh			
The First National Bank Of Middleburgh	2487	4	6
Middleport			
The First National Bank Of Middleport	9206	5	6
Middleton			
The Merchants National Bank Of Middleton	3333	4	6
Middletown			
The First National Bank Of Middletown	523	5	–
The Merchants And Manufacturers National Bank Of Middletown	3333	6	–
The Middletown National Bank	1276	6	–
The National Bank Of Middletown	13956	–	5
The Wallkill National Bank Of Middletown	1473	6	–
Middleville			
The Middleville National Bank	11656	5	4
Milford			
The Milford National Bank	5210	5	5
Millerton			
The Millerton National Bank	2661	5	3
Mineola			
The Central National Bank Of Mineola	13404	–	5
The First National Bank Of Mineola	9187	5	4
Minoa			
First National Bank Of Minoa	13476	–	5
Mohawk			
The National Mohawk Valley Bank Of Mohawk	1130	3	4
Monroe			
The Monroe National Bank	7563	5	–
Montgomery			
First National Bank In Montgomery	13559	–	5
The National Bank Of Montgomery	7982	6	6
Monticello			
The National Union Bank Of Monticello	1503	3	4
Montour Falls			
Montour National Bank In Montour Falls	13583	–	3
Montour National Bank Of Montour Falls	10497	5	5
Moravia			
The First National Bank Of Moravia	99	3	4
The Moravia National Bank	2353	5	–
Morris			
The First National Bank Of Morris	4870	3	5
Morristown			
The Frontier National Bank Of Morristown	8371	5	6
Morrisville			
The First National Bank Of Morrisville	245	4	6
Mount Kisco			
The Mount Kisco National Bank	5026	4	–
The Mount Kisco Natl Bank & Trust Company, Mount Kisco	5026	5	5
Mount Morris			
Genesee River National Bank & Trust Co Of Mount Morris	1416	–	6
Genesee River National Bank Of Mount Morris	1416	–	6
The Genesee River National Bank Of Mount Morris	1416	4	5
Mount Vernon			
The East Chester National Bank Of Mount Vernon	1772	5	–
The First National Bank Of Mount Vernon	5271	4	4
The Mount Vernon National Bank	8516	6	–
Nanuet			
Nanuet National Bank	13314	–	6
Narrowsburg			
The First National Bank Of Narrowsburg	12496	–	5
New Berlin			
The First National Bank Of New Berlin	151	5	–
The National Bank Of New Berlin	10199	6	4
New Brighton			
The First National Bank Of Staten Island At New Brighton	3444	6	–
New Hartford			
The First National Bank Of New Hartford	11785	6	5

City, Bank	Ch. No.	L	S
New Paltz			
The Huguenot National Bank Of New Paltz	1186	3	4
New Rochelle			
The National City Bank Of New Rochelle	6427	3	–
New York			
Bowery And East River National Bank Of New York	1105	3	–
Chatham & Phenix Natl Bank & Trust Company, New York	10778	1	3
College Point National Bank Of New York	13105	–	3
Grace National Bank Of New York	12553	3	3
Irving National Bank Of New York	345	3	–
Irving National Exchange Bank Of New York	345	3	–
Lafayette National Bank Of Brooklyn In New York	12892	–	3
Liberty National Bank And Trust Company In New York	12352	4	3
Liberty National Bank In New York	12352	3	–
National Bank Of Commerce In New York	733	1	–
National Bank Of Yorkville In New York	12965	4	4
Seventh Avenue National Bank Of New York	11844	4	–
Seventh National Bank Of New York	11844	4	–
Sterling National Bank And Trust Company Of New York	13295	–	3
Straus National Bank And Trust Company Of New York	13254	–	4
The Aetna National Bank Of New York	7450	5	–
The American Exchange National Bank Of New York	1394	1	–
The American Exchange Pacific Natl Bank Of New York	1394	4	–
The American National Bank Of New York	750	6	–
The Astor National Bank Of New York	5112	4	–
The Atlantic National Bank Of New York	1388	6	–
The Atlantic National Bank Of The City Of New York	1080	6	–
The Audubon National Bank Of New York	9569	6	–
The Bank Of America National Association, New York	13193	3	3
The Bank Of New York National Banking Association	1393	2	–
The Battery Park National Bank Of New York	7447	4	–
The Bayside National Bank Of New York	13334	–	1
The Beaver National Bank Of New York	8634	6	–
The Bowery National Bank Of New York	1297	5	–
The Bronx National Bank Of The City Of New York	8926	4	–
The Brooklyn National Bank Of New York	13292	4	4
The Bushwick National Bank Of New York	12419	6	–
The Central National Bank Of The City Of New York	376	3	–
The Central National Bank Of The City Of New York	12874	4	6
The Chase National Bank Of The City Of New York	2370	1	1
The Chatham & Phenix National Bank Of New York	1375	5	–
The Chatham & Phenix Natl Bank Of The City Of New York	10778	3	–
The Chatham National Bank Of New York	1375	4	–
The Chemical National Bank Of New York	1499	3	–
The Citizens Central National Bank Of New York	1290	3	–
The Citizens National Bank Of New York	1290	6	–
The Claremont National Bank Of New York	13027	6	–
The Coal And Iron National Bank Of The City Of New York	7203	3	–
The Columbus National Bank Of New York	4512	6	–
The Commercial National Bank Of New York City	3359	6	–
The Consolidated National Bank Of New York	6425	5	–
The Continental National Bank Of New York	1389	2	–
The Croton National Bank Of New York	1556	6	–
The Domestic Exchange National Bank Of New York	5237	6	–
The Dunbar National Bank Of New York	13237	2	2
The East River National Bank Of The City Of New York	1105	4	–
The Eighth National Bank Of New York	384	6	–
The Elmhurst National Bank Of New York	13035	5	5
The Equitable National Bank Of New York	6284	5	–
The Fidelity National Bank In New York	13959	–	6
The Fifth National Bank Of The City Of New York	341	3	–
The First National Bank Of The City Of New York	29	1	1
The Flushing National Bank In New York	13296	–	4
The Fordham National Bank Of New York	12825	4	–
The Fort Greene National Bank In New York	13336	–	5
The Fourth National Bank Of The City Of New York	290	2	–
The Franklin National Bank Of New York	4855	6	–
The Fulton National Bank Of New York	1497	6	–
The Gallatin National Bank Of The City Of New York	1324	3	–
The Garfield National Bank Of The City Of New York	2598	3	–
The Gotham National Bank Of New York	9717	4	–
New York			
The Grocers National Bank Of New York	1371	6	–
The Hamilton National Bank Of New York	12300	3	–
The Hanover National Bank Of The City Of New York	1352	2	–
The Harriman National Bank Of The City Of New York	9955	4	–
The Hide And Leather National Bank Of New York	4567	5	–
The Importers And Traders National Bank Of New York	1231	3	–
The Inter-State National Bank Of New York	4152	6	–
The Irving National Bank Of New York	1357	3	–
The Jamaica National Bank, New York	12550	4	4
The Kingsboro National Bank Of Brooklyn In New York	13304	5	6
The Leather Manufacturers National Bank Of New York	1196	3	–
The Lebanon National Bank Of New York	12214	4	5
The Liberty National Bank Of New York	4645	2	–
The Lincoln National Bank Of The City Of New York	2608	2	–
The Long Island National Bank Of New York	12885	5	–
The Maiden Lane National Bank Of New York	7107	5	–
The Manufacturers National Bank Of Brooklyn	1443	4	–
The Manufacturers National Bank Of New York City	1443	6	–
The Marine National Bank Of The City Of New York	1215	4	–
The Market And Fulton National Bank Of New York	964	4	–
The Market National Bank Of New York	964	4	–
The Mechanics & Metals Natl Bank Of The City Of New York	1250	2	–
The Mechanics And Traders National Bank Of New York	1624	6	–
The Mechanics National Bank Of The City Of New York	1250	3	–
The Melrose National Bank Of New York	12900	5	6
The Mercantile National Bank Of The City Of New York	1067	2	–
The Merchants Exchange National Bank Of The City Of New York	1080	3	–
The Merchants National Bank Of The City Of New York	1370	2	–
The Metropolitan National Bank Of New York	1121	4	–
The National Bank Of Bay Ridge In New York	12344	6	–
The National Bank Of Bayside In New York	13334	–	5
The National Bank Of Commerce In New York	733	1	–
The National Bank Of Deposit, New York	3771	6	–
The National Bank Of North America In New York	4581	3	–
The National Bank Of North America Of New York	1373	6	–
The National Bank Of Queens County In New York	13296	–	4
The National Bank Of Ridgewood In New York	12897	4	–
The National Bank Of The Commonwealth, New York	1372	6	–
The National Bank Of The Republic Of New York	1000	2	–
The National Bank Of The State Of New York, New York	1476	5	–
The National Bank Of The United States In New York	4567	5	–
The National Broadway Bank Of New York	687	5	–
The National Bronx Bank Of New York	12900	–	4
The National Citizens Bank Of The City New York	1290	5	–
The National City Bank Of New York	1461	1	1
The National Commercial Bank Of New York	5237	6	–
The National Copper Bank Of New York	8665	5	–
The National Currency Bank Of New York	444	6	–
The National Mechanics Banking Association Of New York	1075	3	–
The National Nassau Bank Of New York	9939	6	–
The National Park Bank Of New York	891	1	3
The National Reserve Bank Of The City Of New York	6425	6	–
The National Safety Bank & Trust Company Of New York	13260	–	3
The National Shoe And Leather Bank Of The City Of New York	917	3	–
The National Union Bank Of New York	4898	4	–
The Natl. Butchers And Drovers Bank Of The City Of New York	1261	3	–
The New Amsterdam National Bank Of New York	5783	4	–
The New York County National Bank Of New York	1116	4	–
The New York National Exchange Bank Of New York	345	5	–
The Ninth National Bank Of The City Of New York	387	5	–
The Northern National Bank Of New York	6253	6	–
The Ocean National Bank Of The City Of New York	1232	6	–
The Ozone Park National Bank Of New York	12280	4	4
The Pacific National Bank Of New York City	1224	6	–
The Peoples National Bank Of Brooklyn In New York	9219	4	4
The Phenix National Bank Of The City Of New York	1374	3	–
The Progress National Bank Of New York	11844	6	–
New York			
The Public National Bank And Trust Company Of New York	11034	2	2
The Public National Bank Of New York	11034	2	–
The Queensboro National Bank Of The City Of New York	12398	5	6
The Richmond Hill National Bank Of New York	11655	5	–
The Richmond National Bank Of New York	11655	–	4
The Rockaway Beach National Bank Of New York	12252	6	–
The Saint Nicholas National Bank Of New York	972	3	–
The Seaboard National Bank Of The City Of New York	3415	4	–
The Seaboard National Bank Of The City Of New York	12123	4	–
The Second National Bank Of New York	62	6	–
The Second National Bank Of The City Of New York	2668	3	–
The Seventh National Bank Of New York	998	5	–
The Seventh Ward National Bank Of New York	998	3	–
The Seward National Bank & Trust Company Of New York	13045	3	4
The Seward National Bank Of New York	13045	5	–
The Sherman National Bank Of New York	8922	5	–
The Sixth National Bank Of New York City	254	4	–
The Southern National Bank Of New York	3359	6	–
The Springfield Gardens National Bank Of New York	13149	–	4
The Standard National Bank Of New York	5003	6	–
The Tenth National Bank Of New York	307	4	–
The Third National Bank Of New York	87	3	–
The Thirty-Fourth Street National Bank Of New York	6441	6	–
The Tradesmen's National Bank Of The City Of New York	905	2	–
The Union National Bank Of New York	1278	5	–
The Union Square National Bank Of New York	1691	6	–
The United National Bank Of New York City	5990	5	–
The United States National Bank Of New York	2507	6	–
The Washington National Bank Of The City Of New York	4335	6	–
The Washington Square National Bank Of New York	13360	–	6
The Western National Bank Of New York	3700	4	–
The Western National Bank Of The United States In New York	4567	5	–
Union Exchange National Bank Of New York	9360	4	–
United National Bank In New York	12406	6	–
Washington National Bank Of New York	13360	–	6
New York City			
The Harriman Natl. Bank & Trust Co. Of The City Of New York	9955	4	3
Newark			
Arcadia National Bank & Trust Company Of Newark	6802	5	–
Arcadia National Bank Of Newark	6802	4	–
The First National Bank Of Newark	349	3	3
Newark Valley			
The First National Bank Of Newark Valley	10111	6	6
Newburgh			
Highland-Quassaick National Bank & Trust Co Of Newburgh	1106	6	3
The Highland National Bank & Trust Company Of Newburgh	1106	6	–
The Highland National Bank Of Newburgh	1106	4	–
The National Bank Of Newburgh	468	3	4
The Quassaick National Bank Of Newburgh	1213	3	–
Newport			
The National Bank Of Newport	1655	5	4
Niagara Falls			
National Bank Of Niagara & Trust Co Of Niagara Falls	12284	4	–
The Cataract National Bank Of Niagara Falls	12284	4	–
The Falls National Bank Of Niagara Falls	11489	6	6
The First National Bank Of Niagara Falls	4899	6	–
Nichols			
The Nichols National Bank	9399	5	5
North Creek			
The North Creek National Bank	9716	5	5
North Rose			
The First National Bank Of North Rose	10016	5	6
North Tonawanda			
The State National Bank Of North Tonawanda	6809	3	–
Northport			
The First National Bank & Trust Company Of Northport	5936	6	6
The First National Bank Of Northport	5936	5	–
Norwich			
The Chenango County Natl Bank & Trust Company Of Norwich	3011	6	5
The Chenango National Bank Of Norwich	3011	4	–
The National Bank And Trust Company Of Norwich	1354	5	4
The National Bank Of Norwich	1354	3	–
Nunda			
The First National Bank Of Nunda	2224	5	–
Nyack			
The Nyack National Bank	2378	3	4
The Nyack National Bank And Trust Company	2378	–	4
The Rockland County National Bank Of Nyack	1286	6	–

City, Bank	Ch. No.	L	S
Odessa			
The First National Bank Of Odessa	13493	–	3
Ogdensburg			
The National Bank Of Ogdensburg	2446	3	–
Old Forge			
The First National Bank Of Old Forge	10964	4	6
Olean			
The Citizens National Bank Of Olean	7102	6	–
The Exchange National Bank Of Olean	2376	3	1
The First National Bank Of Olean	1887	3	3
The Olean National Bank	9822	5	–
Oneida			
The First National Bank Of Oneida	519	6	–
The National State Bank Of Oneida	2401	4	–
The Oneida Valley National Bank Of Oneida	1090	4	5
Oneonta			
The Citizens National Bank And Trust Company Of Oneonta	8920	5	4
The Citizens National Bank Of Oneonta	8920	5	–
The First National Bank Of Oneonta	420	6	–
The Wilber National Bank Of Oneonta	2151	4	4
Oriskany Falls			
The First National Bank Of Oriskany Falls	6630	6	–
Ossining			
The Ossining National Bank	6552	5	–
Oswego			
First & Second National Bank & Trust Company Of Oswego	255	–	3
Second National Bank And Trust Company Of Oswego	296	5	6
The First National Bank Of Oswego	255	3	5
The Lake Ontario National Bank Of Oswego	1355	6	–
The National Marine Bank Of Oswego	821	5	–
The Second National Bank Of Oswego	296	4	–
Ovid			
The First National Bank Of Ovid	7840	5	6
Owego			
The First National Bank Of Owego	1019	4	6
The National Union Bank Of Owego	1311	6	–
The Owego National Bank	2996	4	5
The Tioga National Bank Of Owego	862	5	–
Oxford			
The First National Bank Of Oxford	273	4	5
The National Bank Of Oxford	14025	–	4
Ozone Park			
The First National Bank Of Ozone Park	8865	6	–
Painted Post			
The Bronson National Bank Of Painted Post	3800	6	–
The First National Bank Of Painted Post	13664	–	4
The Painted Post National Bank	11956	6	6
Palmyra			
The First National Bank Of Palmyra	295	2	6
Patchogue			
The Citizens National Bank Of Patchogue	6785	6	–
The Peoples National Bank Of Patchogue	12788	–	5
Pawling			
The National Bank Of Pawling	1269	5	4
Pearl River			
First National Bank And Trust Company Of Pearl River	10526	6	6
The First National Bank Of Pearl River	10526	5	–
Peekskill			
The Peekskill National Bank	8398	5	6
The Peekskill National Bank And Trust Company, Peekskill	8398	–	5
The Westchester County National Bank Of Peekskill	1422	4	5
Pelham			
The Pelham National Bank	11951	6	–
Penn Yan			
The First National Bank Of Penn Yan	169	6	–
The Yates County National Bank Of Penn Yan	2405	6	–
Perry			
The First National Bank Of Perry	4519	4	4
Phelps			
The Phelps National Bank	9839	5	4
Philmont			
Philmont National Bank	13945	–	6
The First National Bank Of Philmont	7233	6	6
Pine Bush			
The National Bank Of Pine Bush	13960	–	6
The Pine Bush National Bank	9940	5	4
Pine Plains			
The Stissing National Bank Of Pine Plains	981	5	6
Plattsburg			
Merchants National Bank In Plattsburg	13548	–	5
Plattsburg National Bank And Trust Company, Plattsburg	5785	3	4
The City National Bank Of Plattsburg	6613	6	–
The Plattsburg National Bank	5785	4	–
Plattsburgh			
The First National Bank Of Plattsburgh	266	5	6
The Iron National Bank Of Plattsburgh	2534	5	–
The Merchants National Bank Of Plattsburgh	3174	4	5
The Second National Bank Of Plattsburgh	321	6	–
The Vilas National Bank Of Plattsburgh	321	6	–
Poland			
The Citizens National Bank Of Poland	9804	5	5
The National Bank Of Poland	4223	6	–
The Poland National Bank	2441	6	–
Port Chester			
The First National Bank & Trust Company Of Port Chester	402	6	4
The First National Bank Of Port Chester	402	3	–
Port Henry			
The Citizens National Bank Of Port Henry	4858	4	4
The First National Bank Of Port Henry	1697	4	–
Port Jefferson			
The First National Bank Of Port Jefferson	5068	5	5
Port Jervis			
The National Bank And Trust Company Of Port Jervis	1363	4	4
The National Bank Of Port Jervis	1363	3	–
Port Leyden			
The Port Leyden National Bank	11742	6	6
Port Richmond			
Staten Island Natl Bank & Trust Company Of New York	6198	5	4
The Port Richmond National Bank	6198	6	–
Potsdam			
The Citizens National Bank Of Potsdam	5228	4	5
The National Bank Of Potsdam	868	4	–
Poughkeepsie			
Merchants National Bank & Trust Company Of Poughkeepsie	1380	–	5
The City National Bank Of Poughkeepsie	1305	5	–
The Fallkill National Bank Of Poughkeepsie	659	3	–
The Farmers And Manufacturers National Bank Of Poughkeepsie	1312	3	4
The First National Bank Of Poughkeepsie	465	4	4
The Merchants National Bank Of Poughkeepsie	1380	4	–
The Poughkeepsie National Bank	1306	6	–
Pulaski			
The Pulaski National Bank	1496	5	–
Ravena			
The First National Bank Of Ravena	9529	6	5
Red Creek			
The Red Creek National Bank	10781	5	5
Red Hook			
The First National Bank Of Red Hook	752	3	4
Redwood			
The Redwood National Bank	10374	6	6
Remsen			
The First National Bank Of Remsen	6482	6	4
Rhinebeck			
The First National Bank Of Rhinebeck	1157	3	5
Richburg			
The First National Bank Of Richburg	2553	6	–
Richfield Springs			
The First National Bank Of Richfield Springs	2651	4	5
Ridgewood			
The Ridgewood National Bank	9414	6	–
Ripley			
The First National Bank Of Ripley	6386	5	6
Riverhead			
The Suffolk County National Bank Of Riverhead	4230	5	5
Rochester			
Lincoln National Bank Of Rochester	8026	3	–
The Clarke National Bank Of Rochester	1397	6	–
The Commercial National Bank Of Rochester	2383	6	–
The Farmers And Mechanics National Bank Of Rochester	1072	6	–
The First National Bank And Trust Company Of Rochester	13330	–	3
The First National Bank Of Rochester	527	6	–
The Flour City National Bank Of Rochester	1362	4	–
The National Bank Of Commerce Of Rochester	8111	3	–
The National Bank Of Rochester	8026	4	
The National Bank Of Rochester	12538	3	–
The National Union Bank Of Rochester	1282	6	–
The Traders National Bank Of Rochester	1104	2	–
Rockville Centre			
The First National Bank Of Rockville Centre	8872	6	6
Rome			
The Central National Bank Of Rome	1376	5	–
The Farmers National Bank And Trust Company Of Rome	2410	–	5
The Farmers National Bank Of Rome	2410	3	–
The First National Bank Of Rome	1414	5	–
The Fort Stanwix National Bank Of Rome	1410	4	–
Romulus			
The Romulus National Bank	11739	6	6
Rondout			
The First National Bank Of Rondout	34	5	–
The First National Bank Of Rondout, Kingston	2493	4	5
The National Bank Of Rondout	1120	6	–
The Rondout National Bank Of Kingston	1120	5	4
Roosevelt			
The First National Bank Of Roosevelt	11953	6	6
Roscoe			
The First National Bank & Trust Company Of Roscoe	8191	–	4
The First National Bank Of Roscoe	8191	5	–
Roslyn			
The Roslyn National Bank And Trust Company	13326	–	4
Rouses Point			
The First National Bank Of Rouses Point	11969	6	6
Roxbury			
The National Bank Of Roxbury	7678	6	5
Rye			
The Rye National Bank	5662	4	5
Saint Johnsville			
The First National Bank Of Saint Johnsville	375	6	4
Saint Regis Falls			
The St. Regis Falls National Bank	7733	6	5
Salamanca			
The First National Bank Of Salamanca	2472	3	5
The Salamanca National Bank	2610	5	–
Salem			
The First National Bank Of Salem	3309	6	–
The National Bank Of Salem	1127	6	–
The Peoples National Bank Of Salem	3245	5	6
The Salem National Bank	7588	5	6
Sandy Hill			
The Commercial National Bank Of Sandy Hill	8297	6	–
The First National Bank Of Sandy Hill	184	6	–
The Hudson Falls National Bank, Hudson Falls	8297	6	6
The National Bank Of Sandy Hill	2838	6	–
The Peoples National Bank Of Hudson Falls	3244	6	–
The Peoples National Bank Of Sandy Hill	3244	5	–
The Sandy Hill National Bank	6470	6	–
The Sandy Hill National Bank Of Hudson Falls	6470	5	3
Saranac Lake			
Adirondack National Bank & Trust Company Of Saranac Lake	5072	6	4
The Adirondack National Bank Of Saranac Lake	5072	6	–
The Saranac Lake National Bank	8935	6	5
Saratoga Springs			
Saratoga National Bank Of Saratoga Springs	893	6	5
The Citizens National Bank Of Saratoga Springs	2615	4	–
The Commercial National Bank Of Saratoga Springs	1227	6	–
The First National Bank Of Saratoga Springs	893	4	–
Saugerties			
The First National Bank & Trust Company Of Saugerties	1040	6	4
The First National Bank Of Saugerties	1040	4	–
The Saugerties National Bank	1208	4	–
Savona			
The Savona National Bank	11349	6	6
Sayville			
The Oystermen's National Bank Of Sayville	5186	4	5
Scarsdale			
Scarsdale National Bank And Trust Company, Scarsdale	11708	4	3
The Scarsdale National Bank	11708	6	–
Schenectady			
The Mohawk National Bank Of Schenectady	1226	4	4
The Union National Bank Of Schenectady	4711	4	4
Schenevus			
The Schenevus National Bank	4962	4	5
Schoharie			
The Schoharie County National Bank Of Schoharie	1510	6	–
Schuylerville			
The National Bank Of Schuylerville	1298	6	6
Seneca Falls			
The Exchange National Bank Of Seneca Falls	3329	3	–
The First National Bank Of Seneca Falls	102	6	–
The National Exchange Bank Of Seneca Falls	1240	6	–
Sharon Springs			
The First National Bank Of Sharon Springs	7512	6	3
Sherburne			
The Sherburne National Bank	1166	4	4
Sidney			
First National Bank In Sidney	13563	–	5
The Peoples National Bank Of Sidney	8513	5	–
The Sidney National Bank	3822	4	6
Silver Creek			
The First National Bank Of Silver Creek	10159	4	3
The Silver Creek National Bank	10258	4	4
Silver Springs			
The Silver Springs National Bank	6148	4	6
Sing Sing			
The First National Bank & Trust Company Of Ossining	471	4	4
The First National Bank Of Ossining	471	4	–
The First National Bank Of Sing Sing	471	6	–
Skaneateles			
National Bank And Trust Company Of Skaneateles	5360	6	4
The First National Bank Of Skaneateles	303	6	–
The National Bank Of Skaneateles	5360	3	–
Smithtown Branch			
The National Bank Of Smithtown Branch	9820	6	–
Sodus			
The First National Bank Of Sodus	9418	6	5
Somers			
The Farmers And Drovers National Bank Of Somers	1304	5	–
South East			
The Croton River National Bank Of South East	830	5	–
South Fallsburg			
The South Fallsburg National Bank	11809	4	5
South Glens Falls			
The First National Bank Of South Glens Falls	5851	6	6
South Otselic			
The Otselic Valley National Bank Of South Otselic	7774	5	3
South Worcester			
The First National Bank Of South Worcester	103	6	–
Southampton			
The First National Bank Of Southampton	10185	4	4
Spring Valley			
The First National Bank Of Spring Valley	5390	6	5

City, Bank	Ch. No.	L	S
Springville			
The Citizens National Bank Of Springville	6330	4	3
The First National Bank Of Springville	2892	6	–
Stamford			
The National Bank Of Stamford	2602	4	4
Stapleton			
The Richmond Borough National Bank Of Stapleton	7290	6	–
The Stapleton National Bank	6562	4	–
Suffern			
The Suffern National Bank	5846	4	–
The Suffern National Bank & Trust Company, Suffern	5846	–	4
Syracuse			
American Exchange National Bank Of Syracuse	5286	6	–
Commercial National Bank Of Syracuse	6965	5	–
Lincoln National Bank & Trust Company Of Syracuse	13393	–	3
The First National Bank Of Syracuse	6	4	–
The Fourth National Bank Of Syracuse	1569	6	–
The Liberty National Bank Of Syracuse	12122	6	–
The Mechanics National Bank Of Syracuse	1401	6	–
The Merchants National Bank & Trust Company Of Syracuse	1342	5	4
The Merchants National Bank Of Syracuse	1342	4	–
The National Bank Of Syracuse	5465	4	–
The Salt Springs National Bank Of Syracuse	1287	4	–
The Second National Bank Of Syracuse	140	6	–
The Syracuse National Bank	1341	6	–
The Third National Bank Of Syracuse	159	4	–
Tannersville			
The Mountains National Bank Of Tannersville	11057	4	5
Tarrytown			
The First National Bank Of Tarrytown	364	6	–
The Tarrytown National Bank	2626	4	–
Theresa			
The Farmers National Bank Of Theresa	8158	6	4
Ticonderoga			
The First National Bank Of Ticonderoga	4491	6	–
The Ticonderoga National Bank	9900	6	5
Tonawanda			
The First National Bank Of Tonawanda	4869	3	–
Tottenville			
The Tottenville National Bank	8334	6	6
Troy			
The Central National Bank Of Troy	1012	5	–
The First National Bank Of Troy	163	5	–
The Manufacturers National Bank Of Troy	721	3	3
The Merchants And Mechanics National Bank Of Troy	904	6	–
The Mutual National Bank Of Troy	992	3	–
The National Bank Of Troy	2873	6	–
The National City Bank Of Troy	7612	4	4
The National Exchange Bank Of Troy	621	6	–
The National State Bank Of Troy	991	3	–
The Troy City National Bank	640	4	–
The Union National Bank Of Troy	963	5	3
The United National Bank Of Troy	940	3	5
Trumansburg			
The First National Bank Of Trumansburg	7541	4	5
Tuckahoe			
The Crestwood National Bank In Tuckahoe	13889	–	6
The First National Bank & Trust Company Of Tuckahoe	10525	5	4
The First National Bank Of Tuckahoe	10525	5	–
Tully			
The First National Bank Of Tully	5746	5	6
Tupper Lake			
The Tupper Lake National Bank	8153	5	5
Tuxedo			
The Tuxedo National Bank	11404	5	6
Unadilla			
The National Unadilla Bank Of Unadilla	1463	6	–
The Unadilla National Bank	9516	4	4
Union			
The Farmers National Bank Of Union	9276	6	–
Union Springs			
The First National Bank Of Union Springs	342	6	–
Unionville			
The First National Bank Of Unionville	11448	6	5
Utica			
First National Bank And Trust Company Of Utica	1395	4	–
The First National Bank Of Utica	120	6	–
The First National Bank Of Utica	1395	2	–
The Oneida National Bank And Trust Company Of Utica	1392	–	3
The Oneida National Bank Of Utica	1392	2	–
The Second National Bank Of Utica	185	3	–
The Utica City National Bank Of Utica	1308	3	–
Utica National Bank And Trust Company, Utica	1308	4	5
Valley Stream			
The Valley Stream National Bank	11881	6	–
Valley Stream Natl Bank & Trust Company, Valley Stream	11881	6	6
Vernon			
The National Bank Of Vernon	1264	3	5
Walden			
The First National Bank & Trust Company Of Walden	10923	–	5
The National Bank Of Walden	5053	5	–
The Third National Bank Of Walden	10923	5	–
The Walden National Bank	2348	6	–
Wallkill			
The Wallkill National Bank	10155	6	4
Walton			
The First National Bank & Trust Company Of Walton	4495	–	4
The First National Bank Of Walton	4495	4	–
Wappingers Falls			
The National Bank Of Wappingers Falls	9326	6	6
Warrensburgh			
The Emerson National Bank Of Warrensburgh	9135	5	6
Warsaw			
The Wyoming County National Bank Of Warsaw	737	4	3
Warwick			
The First National Bank Of Warwick	314	5	4
Washingtonville			
The First National Bank Of Washingtonville	9065	6	6
Waterford			
The Saratoga County National Bank Of Waterford	1229	6	–
Waterloo			
The First National Bank Of Waterloo	368	5	4
Watertown			
The City National Bank Of Watertown	4296	6	–
The First National Bank Of Watertown	73	6	–
The Jefferson County National Bank Of Watertown	1490	4	3
The National Bank And Loan Company Of Watertown	1508	4	–
The National Union Bank Of Watertown	1507	4	–
The Second National Bank Of Watertown	671	6	–
The Watertown National Bank	2657	4	4
Waterville			
The National Bank Of Waterville	1361	5	4
Watkins			
Glen National Bank Of Watkins	9977	5	5
The First National Bank Of Penn Yan	358	6	–
The First National Bank Of Watkins	358	6	–
The First National Bank Of Watkins	3047	6	–
The Second National Bank Of Watkins	456	4	–
The Watkins National Bank, Watkins	456	6	–
Waverly			
The Citizens National Bank Of Waverly	12954	5	4
The First National Bank Of Waverly	297	5	4
The Waverly National Bank	1192	5	–
Wayland			
The First National Bank Of Wayland	5196	5	5
Webster			
Webster National Bank	13145	6	5
Weedsport			
The First National Bank Of Weedsport	11020	6	5
Wells			
The Hamilton County National Bank Of Wells	13289	–	6
Wellsville			
The Citizens National Bank Of Wellsville	4988	4	4
The First National Bank Of Wellsville	2850	5	–
West Hempstead			
The West Hempstead National Bank	13104	–	6
West Seneca			
Lackawanna National Bank, Lackawanna	6964	–	4
The Lackawanna National Bank Of West Seneca	6964	6	–
The Lackawanna National Bank, Lackawanna	6964	4	–
The Seneca National Bank Of West Seneca	12925	6	6
West Troy			
The National Bank Of Watervliet	1265	3	4
The National Bank Of West Troy	1265	6	–
West Winfield			
The First National Bank Of West Winfield	801	4	–
The West Winfield National Bank	7483	5	6
Westbury			
The Wheatley Hills National Bank Of Westbury	11730	6	6
Westfield			
The First National Bank Of Westfield	504	6	–
The Grape Belt National Bank Of Westfield	12476	4	6
The National Bank Of Westfield	3166	3	4
Westport			
The Lake Champlain National Bank Of Westport	9405	6	6
White Plains			
The First National Bank Of White Plains	6351	5	–
The Peoples National Bank & Trust Company Of White Plains	12574	5	5
The Peoples National Bank Of White Plains	12574	6	–
Whitehall			
The First National Bank Of Whitehall	285	6	–
The Merchants National Bank Of Whitehall	2233	4	4
The National Bank Of Whitehall	8388	5	6
The Old National Bank Of Whitehall	1160	6	–
Whitesboro			
The Whitestown National Bank Of Whitesboro	11284	5	–
Whitestone			
The First National Bank Of Whitestone	8957	5	–
Whitestown			
The National Bank Of Whitestown	1458	6	–
Whitesville			
The First National Bank Of Whitesville	7850	6	6
Whitney Point			
The First National Bank Of Whitney Point	7679	6	5
Willsboro			
The Essex County National Bank Of Willsboro	11971	6	6
Windham			
The First National Bank Of Windham	12164	–	4
The National Bank Of Windham	13962	–	2
Windsor			
The Windsor National Bank	9415	5	5
Winthrop			
The First National Bank Of Winthrop	10747	5	6
Wolcott			
The First National Bank Of Wolcott	5928	6	5
Woodmere			
The Hewlett-Woodmere National Bank Of Woodmere	12294	6	6
Woodridge			
The First National Bank Of Woodridge	11059	5	5
Wyoming			
The National Bank Of Wyoming	13229	–	6
Yonkers			
Central National Bank Of Yonkers	13319	–	4
The Citizens National Bank Of Yonkers	2074	5	–
The First National Bank & Trust Company Of Yonkers	653	–	4
The First National Bank Of Yonkers	653	3	6
The Yonkers National Bank	9825	5	–
The Yonkers National Bank And Trust Company, Yonkers	9825	5	4

NORTH CAROLINA

City, Bank	Ch. No.	L	S
Albemarle			
The First National Bank Of Albemarle	11091	6	2
Asheboro			
The First National Bank Of Asheboro	8953	6	5
Asheville			
First National Bank And Trust Company Of Asheville	12244	–	3
The American National Bank Of Asheville	8772	4	5
The Blue Ridge National Bank Of Asheville	5110	5	–
The First National Bank Of Asheville	3418	6	–
The National Bank Of Asheville	4094	6	–
The National Bank Of Commerce Of Asheville	12244	5	5
Ayden			
First National Bank In Ayden	13554	–	5
Benson			
The First National Bank Of Benson	12614	5	–
Burlington			
The First National Bank Of Burlington	8649	4	6
The National Bank Of Burlington	13613	–	3
Charlotte			
The Charlotte National Bank	5055	3	1
The Commercial National Bank Of Charlotte	2135	2	2
The First National Bank Of Charlotte	1547	3	4
The Merchants And Farmers National Bank Of Charlotte	1781	3	3
The Traders National Bank Of Charlotte	2314	6	–
The Union National Bank Of Charlotte	9164	4	3
Cherryville			
The First National Bank Of Cherryville	9548	4	–
Concord			
The Concord National Bank	3903	4	4
Creedmoor			
The First National Bank Of Creedmoor	8902	6	–
Dunn			
The First National Bank Of Dunn	7188	1	–
Durham			
The Citizens National Bank Of Durham	7698	4	4
The Depositors National Bank Of Durham	13657	–	3
The First National Bank Of Durham	3811	2	2
Elizabeth City			
The First And Citizens National Bank Of Elizabeth City	4628	3	3
The First National Bank Of Elizabeth City	4628	6	–
Elkin			
The Elkin National Bank	5673	5	6
Fayetteville			
Fourth National Bank Of Fayetteville	8682	6	–
The Fayetteville National Bank	1756	5	–
The National Bank Of Fayetteville	5677	4	–
The Peoples National Bank Of Fayetteville	2003	5	–
Forest City			
The First National Bank Of Forest City	9203	6	–
The National Bank Of Forest City	12461	5	–
Gastonia			
The Citizens National Bank Of Gastonia	7536	4	2
The First National Bank Of Gastonia	4377	3	2
The Third National Bank Of Gastonia	11477	6	–
Goldsboro			
The National Bank Of Goldsboro	5048	4	5
The Wayne National Bank Of Goldsboro	10614	3	4
Graham			
The National Bank Of Alamance Of Graham	8844	5	4
Greensboro			
American Exchange National Bank Of Greensboro	10112	3	–
American National Bank And Trust Company Of Greensboro	10112	6	–
Security National Bank Of Greensboro	13761	–	3
The American Exchange National Bank Of Greensboro	10112	4	–
The City National Bank Of Greensboro	5168	6	–
The Commercial National Bank Of Greensboro	9123	6	–
The Greensboro National Bank	5031	4	–
The National Bank Of Greensboro	2322	4	–
Greenville			
The National Bank Of Greenville	8160	6	6
Hamlet			
The First National Bank Of Hamlet	10851	6	–
Henderson			
First National Bank In Henderson	13636	–	3
The First National Bank Of Henderson	7564	3	4
Hendersonville			
The Citizens National Bank Of Hendersonville	10734	4	6
The First National Bank Of Hendersonville	8837	6	–

City, Bank	Ch. No.	L	S
Hendersonville			
The Peoples National Bank Of Hendersonville	9571	6	–
Hickory			
The First National Bank Of Hickory	4597	4	2
High Point			
The Commercial National Bank Of High Point	4568	3	3
The First National Bank Of High Point	3490	6	–
The National Bank Of High Point	3490	6	–
Jefferson			
The First National Bank Of Jefferson	8571	6	–
The First National Bank Of West Jefferson	8571	6	6
Kings Mountain			
The First National Bank Of Kings Mountain	5451	4	3
Kinston			
The First National Bank Of Kinston	9085	4	6
The National Bank Of Kinston	9044	5	6
Laurinburg			
The First National Bank Of Laurinburg	5651	6	6
Leaksville			
The First National Bank Of Leaksville	12259	6	6
Lenoir			
The First National Bank Of Lenoir	8445	5	6
The Union National Bank Of Lenoir	13523	–	6
Lexington			
The First National Bank Of Lexington	5698	6	–
The National Bank Of Lexington	5698	6	–
Lincolnton			
The County National Bank Of Lincolnton	8184	6	–
The First National Bank Of Lincolnton	6744	3	2
Louisburg			
The Farmers National Bank Of Louisburg	10260	5	–
The First National Bank Of Louisburg	7554	5	5
Lumberton			
The First National Bank Of Lumberton	7398	4	–
The National Bank Of Lumberton	10610	6	–
Marion			
The First National Bank Of Marion	6095	5	3
Mebane			
The First National Bank Of Mebane	11697	5	3
Monroe			
The First National Bank Of Monroe	8712	5	4
Mooresville			
The First National Bank Of Mooresville	9531	5	5
Morganton			
The First National Bank Of Morganton	5450	6	4
Mount Airy			
The First National Bank Of Mount Airy	4896	6	–
Mount Olive			
The First National Bank Of Mount Olive	10629	6	6
Murfreesboro			
The First National Bank Of Murfreesboro	11557	6	–
Murphy			
The First National Bank Of Murphy	9458	6	–
New Bern			
The First National Bank Of New Bern	13298	–	5
New Berne			
The National Bank Of New Berne	1632	4	–
Newton			
The Shuford National Bank Of Newton	6075	5	4
Oxford			
The First National Bank Of Oxford	5885	5	–
The National Bank Of Granville At Oxford	8996	6	–
Raleigh			
The Citizens National Bank Of Raleigh	1766	4	–
The Commercial National Bank Of Raleigh	9067	2	4
The Merchants National Bank Of Raleigh	9471	4	–
The National Bank Of Raleigh	3389	6	–
The Raleigh National Bank Of North Carolina	1557	5	–
The State National Bank Of Raleigh	1682	6	–
Reidsville			
First National Bank Of Reidsville	11229	6	4
Rocky Mount			
The First National Bank Of Rocky Mount	7362	6	–
The First National Bank Of Rocky Mount	10630	6	–
The National Bank Of Rocky Mount	10630	6	–
The Planters National Bank & Trust Company Of Rocky Mount	10608	–	6
The Planters National Bank Of Rocky Mount	10608	6	6
Salem			
The First National Bank Of Salem	1659	6	–
Salisbury			
The First National Bank Of Salisbury	2981	2	4
The Peoples National Bank Of Salisbury	9076	5	–
Sanford			
The First National Bank Of Sanford	6616	6	–
The National Bank Of Lillington	6616	6	–
The National Bank Of Sanford	13791	–	6
Selma			
The First National Bank Of Selma	10739	6	–
Shelby			
Shelby National Bank	7959	6	–
The First National Bank Of Shelby	6776	3	2
Smithfield			
The Citizens National Bank Of Smithfield	11440	6	–
The First & Citizens National Bank Of Smithfield	10502	5	–
The First National Bank Of Smithfield	10502	5	–
Snow Hill			
The First National Bank Of Snow Hill	10887	6	–
Statesville			
The Commercial National Bank Of Statesville	9335	5	–
The First National Bank Of Statesville	3682	5	5
Tarboro			
The First National Bank Of Tarboro	8356	5	–
Thomasville			
The First National Bank Of Thomasville	8788	4	2
Wadesboro			
The First National Bank Of Wadesboro	4947	4	3
Warsaw			
The First National Bank Of Warsaw	11767	6	–
Washington			
The First National Bank Of Washington	4997	5	4
Waynesville			
The First National Bank Of Waynesville	6554	6	5
Weldon			
The First National Bank Of Roanoke Rapids	5767	4	–
The First National Bank Of Weldon	5767	6	–
Wilmington			
The American National Bank Of Wilmington	9124	5	–
The Atlantic National Bank Of Wilmington	4726	6	–
The Commercial National Bank Of Wilmington	12176	6	–
The First National Bank Of Wilmington	1656	6	–
The Murchison National Bank Of Wilmington	5182	2	–
The National Bank Of Wilmington	4960	6	–
The Southern National Bank Of Wilmington	7913	6	–
Wilson			
National Bank Of Wilson	13626	–	5
The First National Bank Of Wilson	2321	4	6
Winston			
The First National Bank Of Winston	2319	6	–
The Merchants National Bank Of Winston	9916	6	–
The Peoples National Bank Of Winston	4292	3	5
The Wachovia National Bank Of Winston	2425	6	–
Winston-Salem			
The Farmers National Bank And Trust Company Of Winston-Salem	12278	4	2

NORTH DAKOTA

City, Bank	Ch. No.	L	S
Abercrombie			
The First National Bank Of Abercrombie	8419	6	–
Alexander			
The First National Bank Of Alexander	11297	6	–
Ambrose			
The First National Bank Of Ambrose	9386	6	6
Anamoose			
The Anamoose National Bank	9390	6	–
The First National Bank Of Anamoose	9412	6	–
Antler			
The First National Bank Of Antler	7855	6	–
Ashley			
The First National Bank Of Ashley	10864	5	6
Bathgate			
The Bathgate National Bank	11112	6	6
The First National Bank Of Bathgate	4537	6	–
Beach			
The First National Bank Of Beach	9484	6	–
Belfield			
The First National Bank Of Belfield	9539	5	6
Binford			
The First National Bank Of Binford	8265	6	6
Bisbee			
The First National Bank Of Bisbee	6733	6	–
Bismarck			
The Capital National Bank Of Bismarck	2986	6	–
The City National Bank Of Bismarck	9622	6	–
The Dakota National Bank And Trust Company Of Bismarck	13398	–	3
The First National Bank Of Bismarck	2434	4	4
Bottineau			
The Bottineau National Bank	7879	6	6
The First National Bank Of Bottineau	6085	5	–
Bowbells			
The First National Bank Of Bowbells	7116	6	6
Bowman			
The First National Bank Of Bowman	8976	6	6
Brinsmade			
The First National Bank Of Brinsmade	8502	6	–
Buffalo			
The First National Bank Of Buffalo	6559	5	6
Buxton			
The First National Bank Of Buxton	10814	6	5
Cando			
The Cando National Bank	7377	6	–
The First National Bank Of Cando	5798	6	6
Carpio			
The First National Bank Of Carpio	7315	5	6
Carrington			
The First National Bank Of Carrington	5551	6	–
Carson			
The First National Bank Of Carson	13454	–	4
Casselton			
The Cass County National Bank Of Casselton	7142	5	–
The First National Bank Of Casselton	2792	4	6
Cavalier			
The First National Bank Of Cavalier	10116	6	–
Churchs Ferry			
The First National Bank Of Churchs Ferry	6337	6	5
Cooperstown			
The First National Bank In Cooperstown	13362	–	3
The First National Bank Of Cooperstown	5375	5	–
Courtenay			
The First National Bank Of Courtenay	6210	6	6
Crary			
The First National Bank Of Crary	6407	6	6
Crosby			
The First National Bank Of Crosby	10596	5	6
Crystal			
The First National Bank Of Crystal	7918	6	–
Devil's Lake			
The First National Bank Of Devil's Lake	3397	4	4
The Merchants National Bank Of Devil's Lake	3714	6	–
The Ramsey County National Bank Of Devil's Lake	5886	6	5
Dickinson			
The Dakota National Bank Of Dickinson	7663	5	–
The First National Bank Of Dickinson	4384	6	4
The Liberty National Bank Of Dickinson	12401	6	6
The Merchants National Bank Of Dickinson	8201	6	–
Drake			
First National Bank In Drake	12393	6	5
The First National Bank Of Drake	9524	6	–
Drayton			
The First National Bank Of Drayton	6225	5	–
East Fairview			
The First National Bank Of East Fairview	10425	6	–
Edgeley			
The First National Bank Of Edgeley	7914	6	–
Edmore			
The First National Bank Of Edmore	6601	6	6
Egeland			
The First National Bank Of Egeland	7872	6	6
Ellendale			
The Ellendale National Bank	9631	6	–
The Farmers National Bank Of Ellendale	9521	6	–
The First National Bank Of Ellendale	6398	5	6
Enderlin			
The First National Bank Of Enderlin	6486	6	–
Fairmount			
The First National Bank Of Fairmount	6255	6	–
Fargo			
The Citizens National Bank Of Fargo	3602	6	–
The Dakota National Bank Of Fargo	12026	5	4
The Fargo National Bank	5087	5	4
The First National Bank & Trust Company Of Fargo	2377	–	3
The First National Bank Of Fargo	2377	4	–
The Merchants National Bank And Trust Company Of Fargo	13323	–	4
The Merchants National Bank Of Fargo	8170	4	–
The National Bank Of North Dakota, Fargo	4256	6	–
The Red River Valley National Bank Of Fargo	2514	5	–
The Security National Bank Of Fargo	11555	5	–
Fessenden			
The First National Bank Of Fessenden	5408	5	6
Fingal			
The First National Bank Of Fingal	7295	6	6
Finley			
The First National Bank Of Finley	7324	6	–
Forman			
The First National Bank Of Forman	6474	6	6
Garrison			
First National Bank In Garrison	13501	–	3
The First National Bank Of Garrison	9778	6	6
Glen Ullin			
First National Bank In Glen Ullin	13410	–	4
The First National Bank Of Glen Ullin	9016	6	–
Goodrich			
The First National Bank Of Goodrich	8077	6	5
Grafton			
The First National Bank Of Grafton	2840	5	–
The Grafton National Bank	3096	4	3
Grand Forks			
First National Bank In Grand Forks	13790	–	5
First National Bank Of Grand Forks	2570	–	1
The First National Bank Of Grand Forks	2570	3	–
The Grand Forks National Bank	3301	6	–
The Merchants National Bank Of Grand Forks	4812	6	–
The Northwestern National Bank Of Grand Forks	11142	3	–
The Second National Bank Of Grand Forks	3504	6	–
The Union National Bank Of Grand Forks	4372	6	–
Hampden			
The First National Bank Of Hampden	7650	6	6
Hankinson			
The Citizens National Bank Of Hankinson	8084	6	–
The First National Bank Of Hankinson	6218	6	6
Hannaford			
The First National Bank Of Hannaford	7727	6	–
Harvey			
The First National Bank Of Harvey	5488	4	6
Hatton			
The Farmers And Merchants National Bank Of Hatton	7905	6	5
The First National Bank Of Hatton	6743	6	6
Hebron			
The First National Bank Of Hebron	10741	6	5
Hettinger			
The First National Bank Of Hettinger	8991	6	5
The Livestock National Bank Of Hettinger	11677	6	–
Hillsboro			
First National Bank Of Hillsboro	3400	–	5
The First National Bank Of Hillsboro	3400	6	–
The Hillsboro National Bank	3411	5	–
Hope			
The First National Bank Of Hope	5893	5	–
The Hope National Bank	8395	4	–
Hunter			
The First National Bank Of Hunter	6985	6	6
Jamestown			
The Citizens National Bank Of Jamestown	7820	6	–
The James River National Bank Of Jamestown	2580	6	6

City, Bank	Ch. No.	L	S
Jamestown			
The James River Natl Bank & Trust Co. Of Jamestown	2580	–	6
The Lloyds National Bank Of Jamestown	4561	6	–
Kenmare			
First-Kenmare National Bank	6555	–	6
The First National Bank Of Kenmare	6064	6	6
The Kenmare National Bank	6555	6	6
Kensal			
The First National Bank Of Kensal	7943	6	–
Knox			
The First National Bank Of Knox	6898	6	–
Kramer			
The First National Bank Of Kramer	8029	6	6
Kulm			
First National Bank Of Kulm	11069	–	6
The First National Bank Of Kulm	11069	6	–
La Moure			
The Farmers National Bank Of La Moure	9714	5	–
The First National Bank Of La Moure	6690	6	6
Lakota			
The First National Bank Of Lakota	4143	6	–
The National Bank Of Lakota	5455	6	6
Langdon			
The Cavalier County National Bank Of Langdon	9075	6	–
The First National Bank Of Langdon	4802	5	–
Lansford			
The First National Bank Of Lansford	8187	6	–
Larimore			
The First National Bank Of Larimore	2854	6	–
The National Bank Of Larimore	6286	6	–
Leeds			
The First National Bank Of Leeds	6312	6	–
Lidgerwood			
Farmers National Bank Of Lidgerwood	8230	6	–
First National Bank In Lidgerwood	12776	6	5
The First National Bank Of Lidgerwood	5772	5	–
The Lidgerwood National Bank	8230	6	–
Linton			
The First National Bank Of Linton	9590	6	6
Lisbon			
The First National Bank Of Lisbon	3669	5	–
Litchville			
The First National Bank Of Litchville	8298	4	6
Maddock			
The First National Bank Of Maddock	8226	6	–
Makoti			
The First National Bank Of Makoti	11184	6	6
Mandan			
The First National Bank Of Mandan	2585	4	6
The Merchants National Bank Of Mandan	10604	5	–
Marion			
The First National Bank Of Marion	9161	6	–
Marmarth			
The First National Bank Of Marmarth	9082	6	5
Mayville			
The First National Bank Of Mayville	3673	6	–
Mcclusky			
The First National Bank Of Mcclusky	8881	6	6
Mccumber			
The First National Bank Of Mccumber	7846	6	–
Mchenry			
The First National Bank Of Mchenry	8124	6	–
Mcville			
The First National Bank Of Mcville	10721	6	6
Milnor			
The First National Bank Of Milnor	8280	6	6
The Milnor National Bank	8264	6	–
Milton			
The First National Bank Of Milton	6518	6	–
Minnewaukan			
The First National Bank Of Minnewaukan	5500	6	–
Minot			
First National Bank & Trust Company In Minot	6429	–	4
First National Bank In Minot	6429	6	6
First National Bank In Minot	6429	–	6
The First National Bank Of Minot	4009	6	–
The Minot National Bank	6315	6	–
The Second National Bank Of Minot	6429	5	–
The Union National Bank Of Minot	7689	5	6
Mohall			
First National Bank Of Mohall	7008	6	–
Mott			
The First National Bank Of Mott	9489	6	5
Munich			
The First National Bank Of Munich	7569	6	6
Mylo			
The First National Bank Of Mylo	7857	6	–
Napoleon			
The First National Bank Of Napoleon	11378	–	6
Neche			
The First National Bank Of Neche	11110	6	6
New England			
The First National Bank Of New England	9776	5	4
New Rockford			
The First National Bank Of New Rockford	6393	5	6
New Salem			
The First National Bank Of New Salem	6428	6	–
Nome			
The First National Bank Of Nome	9287	6	–
Northwood			
The Citizens National Bank Of Northwood	9754	5	6
The First National Bank Of Northwood	5980	6	6
Oakes			
The First National Bank Of Oakes	6457	6	5
The Oakes National Bank	6988	5	–
Omemee			
The First National Bank Of Omemee	6475	6	6
Osnabrock			
The First National Bank Of Osnabrock	7234	5	6
Overly			
The First National Bank Of Overly	8096	6	–
Page			
The First National Bank Of Page	6463	6	6
Park River			
The First National Bank Of Park River	3436	5	6
Parshall			
The First National Bank Of Parshall	11226	6	6
Pembina			
The First National Bank Of Pembina	3438	6	–
Petersburg			
The First National Bank Of Petersburg	11185	6	6
Plaza			
The First National Bank Of Plaza	9689	6	6
Portland			
First And Farmers National Bank Of Portland	13594	–	6
The First National Bank Of Portland	7693	6	6
Reeder			
The First National Bank Of Reeder	9681	6	6
Reynolds			
The First National Bank Of Reynolds	10496	5	5
Rock Lake			
The First National Bank Of Rock Lake	8019	6	6
Rolette			
The First National Bank Of Rolette	7866	6	–
Rolla			
The First National Bank Of Rolla	6157	6	6
Rugby			
The First National Bank Of Rugby	6341	6	–
Ryder			
The First National Bank Of Ryder	9214	6	6
Saint Thomas			
The First National Bank Of Saint Thomas	4550	6	6
Sanborn			
The First National Bank Of Sanborn	8448	5	–
Sarles			
The First National Bank Of Adams	7852	6	–
Scranton			
The First National Bank Of Scranton	10405	6	6
Sharon			
The First National Bank Of Sharon	9005	6	6
Sheldon			
The First National Bank Of Sheldon	6977	6	–
Sheyenne			
The First National Bank Of Sheyenne	8886	6	–
Stanley			
The First National Bank Of Stanley	9472	6	–
Starkweather			
The First National Bank Of Starkweather	6397	6	6
Steele			
The First National Bank Of Steele	8997	6	6
Streeter			
The First National Bank Of Streeter	10724	6	–
Taylor			
The Security National Bank Of Taylor	12502	–	6
Thompson			
The First National Bank Of Thompson	11599	–	4
Tolley			
The First National Bank Of Tolley	7810	6	–
Tower City			
The First National Bank Of Tower City	6557	6	6
Towner			
The First National Bank Of Towner	7955	6	–
Turtle Lake			
The First National Bank Of Turtle Lake	8821	6	–
Tuttle			
The First National Bank Of Tuttle	11338	6	–
Valley City			
First National Bank Of Valley City	13324	–	6
The American National Bank And Trust Company Of Valley City	13385	–	3
The American National Bank Of Valley City	5364	5	–
The American National Bank Of Valley City	13385	–	6
The First & Security National Bank Of Valley City	11417	6	–
The First National Bank Of Valley City	2548	6	–
The National Bank Of Valley City	13324	–	5
The Security National Bank Of Valley City	11417	5	–
Van Hook			
The First National Bank Of Van Hook	10966	4	6
Wahpeton			
The Citizens National Bank Of Wahpeton	4552	4	4
The German-American National Bank Of Wahpeton	7695	6	–
The National Bank In Wahpeton	12875	–	5
The National Bank Of Wahpeton	4106	4	–
Walhalla			
The First National Bank Of Walhalla	9133	5	4
Washburn			
The First National Bank Of Washburn	6327	6	6
Westhope			
The First National Bank Of Westhope	7162	6	–
Williston			
The Citizens National Bank Of Williston	8324	6	–
The First National Bank Of Williston	5567	6	6
Willow City			
The First National Bank Of Willow City	6766	6	–
The Merchants National Bank Of Willow City	7332	6	6
Wilton			
The First National Bank Of Wilton	11712	6	6
Wimbledon			
The First National Bank Of Wimbledon	6712	6	–
The Merchants National Bank Of Wimbledon	8917	6	–
Wyndmere			
The First National Bank Of Wyndmere	7166	6	–
Yates			
The First National Bank Of Yates	9698	6	–

OHIO

City, Bank	Ch. No.	L	S
Ada			
The First National Bank Of Ada	5425	5	6
Adena			
The Peoples National Bank Of Adena	6016	6	–
Akron			
The Citizens National Bank Of Akron	4961	6	–
The City National Bank Of Akron	2946	6	–
The First National Bank Of Akron	27	5	–
The First National Bank Of Akron	2698	6	–
The First-Second National Bank Of Akron	9953	6	–
The National City Bank Of Akron	6763	6	–
The Second National Bank Of Akron	40	6	–
The Second National Bank Of Akron	2716	5	–
Alliance			
Alliance First National Bank, Alliance	3421	5	5
The First National Bank Of Alliance	2041	6	–
The First National Bank Of Alliance	3721	6	–
Amesville			
The First National Bank Of Amesville	7235	6	5
Ansonia			
The First National Bank Of Ansonia	9194	6	6
Arcanum			
The Farmers National Bank Of Arcanum	9255	6	–
The First National Bank Of Arcanum	4839	5	–
The First-Farmers National Bank Of Arcanum	4839	6	5
Arnettsville			
The First National Bank Of Pitsburg	9563	6	6
Ashland			
The First National Bank Of Ashland	183	6	5
Ashtabula			
The Ashtabula National Bank	2031	5	–
The Farmers National Bank And Trust Company Of Ashtabula	975	–	5
The Farmers National Bank Of Ashtabula	975	6	6
The Marine National Bank Of Ashtabula	4506	6	4
The Marine National Bank Of Sweden Of Ashtabula	4506	6	–
The National Bank Of Ashtabula	5075	4	4
Athens			
The Athens National Bank	7744	5	5
The Bank Of Athens National Banking Association	10479	6	6
The First National Bank Of Athens	233	6	–
Baltimore			
The First National Bank Of Baltimore	7639	6	6
Barberton			
The American National Bank Of Barberton	5819	6	–
The First National Bank Of Barberton	5230	6	–
Barnesville			
The First National Bank Of Barnesville	911	4	5
The National Bank Of Barnesville	6621	6	–
The Peoples National Bank Of Barnesville	2908	6	–
Batavia			
The First National Bank Of Batavia	715	4	6
Batesville			
The First National Bank Of Batesville	2219	6	–
Beallsville			
The First National Bank Of Beallsville	7025	6	6
Bellaire			
Farmers And Merchants National Bank In Bellaire	13996	–	5
First National Bank In Bellaire	13914	–	6
The Farmers And Merchants National Bank Of Bellaire	7327	5	4
The First National Bank Of Bellaire	1944	5	5
Bellefontaine			
The Bellefontaine National Bank	1784	5	4
The Peoples National Bank In Bellefontaine	11726	6	–
The Peoples National Bank Of Bellefontaine	2480	6	–
Bellevue			
The First National Bank Of Bellevue	2302	5	5
Belmont			
The Belmont National Bank	6391	5	6
The First National Bank Of Belmont	4864	6	–
Belpre			
The First National Bank Of Belpre	8420	6	–
Berea			
The First National Bank Of Berea	2004	6	–
Bethel			
The First National Bank Of Bethel	5627	6	5
Bethesda			
The First National Bank Of Bethesda	5602	6	6
The Goshen National Bank Of Bethesda	14261	–	6
Beverly			
The First National Bank Of Beverly	133	5	–
Blanchester			
The First National Bank Of Blanchester	8588	6	6
Bluffton			
The Citizens National Bank Of Bluffton	11573	6	4
The First National Bank Of Bluffton	5626	6	–
Bowerston			
The First National Bank Of Bowerston	7486	6	6
Bowling Green			
The First National Bank Of Bowling Green	4045	6	–
Bradford			
The Bradford National Bank	14077	–	5
The First National Bank Of Bradford	9163	6	4
Bremen			
The First National Bank Of Bremen	9768	5	–
Bridgeport			
Bridgeport National Bank	6624	4	6
The Bridgeport National Bank	14050	–	6
The First National Bank Of Bridgeport	214	6	–

City, Bank	Ch. No.	L	S
Brookville			
The First National Bank Of Brookville	9553	6	–
Bryan			
The Citizens National Bank Of Bryan	13740	–	6
The Farmers National Bank Of Bryan	2474	4	5
The First National Bank In Bryan	13899	–	6
The First National Bank Of Bryan	237	4	5
Buckeye City			
The First National Bank Of Buckeye City	7631	6	–
Bucyrus			
The First National Bank Of Bucyrus	443	4	5
The Second National Bank Of Bucyrus	3274	2	4
Burton			
The First National Bank Of Burton	6249	6	5
Butler			
The First National Bank Of Butler	6515	6	–
Byesville			
The First National Bank Of Byesville	5641	6	6
Cadiz			
The Farmers And Mechanics National Bank Of Cadiz	2444	5	–
The First National Bank Of Cadiz	100	5	6
The Fourth National Bank Of Cadiz	4853	6	5
The Harrison National Bank Of Cadiz	1447	4	6
The Union National Bank And Trust Company Of Cadiz	100	–	6
The Union National Bank Of Cadiz	100	–	5
Caldwell			
The Citizens National Bank Of Caldwell	6458	6	5
The First National Bank Of Caldwell	13844	–	6
The Noble County National Bank In Caldwell	13154	6	6
The Noble County National Bank Of Caldwell	2102	6	–
Cambridge			
The Central National Bank At Cambridge	13905	–	6
The Central National Bank Of Cambridge	2872	5	5
The First National Bank Of Cambridge	141	6	–
The Guernsey National Bank Of Cambridge	1942	4	6
The National Bank Of Cambridge	6566	5	3
The Old National Bank Of Cambridge	2861	6	–
Camden			
The First National Bank Of Camden	8300	5	5
Canal Dover			
The Exchange National Bank Of Canal Dover	4293	6	–
The Exchange National Bank Of Dover	4293	5	5
The First National Bank Of Canal Dover	4331	6	–
The First National Bank Of Dover	4331	6	4
Canfield			
The Farmers National Bank Of Canfield	3654	6	5
Canton			
The City National Bank Of Canton	2489	4	–
The First National Bank Of Canton	76	4	3
Cardington			
The First National Bank Of Cardington	127	5	6
Carey			
The First National Bank Of Carey	6119	6	6
Carrollton			
First National Bank In Carrollton	11714	6	6
The First National Bank At Carrollton	13883	–	6
The First National Bank Of Carrollton	5396	6	–
Carthage			
The First National Bank Of Carthage	8488	6	–
Celina			
The First National Bank Of Celina	5523	5	5
Centerburg			
The First National Bank Of Centerburg	8182	6	–
Centreville			
The Centreville National Bank Of Thurman, Centreville	2181	5	–
Chardon			
Central National Bank Of Chardon	13569	–	5
The Central National Bank Of Chardon	13569	–	6
The First National Bank Of Chardon	4671	6	6
Chesterhill			
The First National Bank Of Chesterhill	5552	6	5
Cheviot			
The First National Bank Of Cheviot	8478	6	–
Chillicothe			
The Central National Bank Of Chillicothe	2993	5	5
The Chillicothe National Bank	1277	6	–
The Citizens National Bank Of Chillicothe	5634	6	6
The First National Bank Of Chillicothe	128	5	4
The Ross County National Bank Of Chillicothe	1172	5	5
Cincinnati			
The American National Bank Of Cincinnati	8438	6	–
The Atlas National Bank Of Cincinnati	3639	4	4
The Brotherhood Of Railway Clerks National Bank Of Cincin	12446	3	5
The Central National Bank Of Cincinnati	620	6	–
The Cincinnati National Bank	2922	6	–
The Citizens National Bank & Trust Company Of Cincinnati	2495	5	–
The Citizens National Bank Of Cincinnati	2495	1	–
The Commercial National Bank Of Cincinnati	1185	6	–
The Equitable National Bank Of Cincinnati	3707	6	–
The Exchange National Bank Of Cincinnati	2616	6	–
The Fidelity National Bank Of Cincinnati	3461	6	–
The Fifth National Bank Of Cincinnati	2798	3	–
The Fifth-Third National Bank Of Cincinnati	2798	2	–
The First National Bank Of Cincinnati	24	1	3
Cincinnati			
The Fourth National Bank Of Cincinnati	93	2	–
The German National Bank Of Cincinnati	2524	3	–
The Lincoln National Bank Of Cincinnati	2524	3	3
The Market National Bank Of Cincinnati	3642	4	–
The Merchants National Bank Of Cincinnati	844	4	–
The Metropolitan National Bank Of Cincinnati	2542	4	–
The National Bank Of Commerce	2315	6	–
The National Lafayette Bank Of Cincinnati	2315	5	–
The Ohio National Bank Of Cincinnati	630	6	–
The Ohio Valley National Bank Of Cincinnati	3606	5	–
The Queen City National Bank Of Cincinnati	2798	6	–
The Second National Bank Of Cincinnati	32	6	–
The Second National Bank Of Cincinnati	2664	3	3
The Third National Bank Of Cincinnati	20	6	–
The Third National Bank Of Cincinnati	2730	3	–
The Union National Bank Of Cincinnati	2549	6	–
Circleville			
The First National Bank Of Circleville	118	5	4
The Second National Bank Of Circleville	172	5	6
The Third National Bank Of Circleville	2817	6	6
Clarington			
The First National Bank Of Clarington	5762	6	6
Clarksville			
The Farmers National Bank Of Clarksville	7370	6	6
Cleveland			
Brotherhood Of Locomotive Engineers Co-Op N.B. Of Cleveland	11862	2	–
Central National Bank Of Cleveland	4318	5	5
Central National Bank Savings & Trust Co Of Cleveland	4318	4	–
Central United National Bank Of Cleveland	4318	–	1
Engineers National Bank Of Cleveland	11862	3	5
The American Exchange National Bank Of Cleveland	5090	6	–
The Bank Of Commerce National Association Of Cleveland	5194	4	–
The Bankers National Bank Of Cleveland	5805	6	–
The Central National Bank Of Cleveland	4318	4	–
The Century National Bank Of Cleveland	5350	6	–
The Cleveland National Bank	2956	5	–
The Coal And Iron National Bank Of Cleveland	5191	6	–
The Colonial National Bank Of Cleveland	5152	6	–
The Commercial National Bank Of Cleveland	807	6	–
The Euclid Avenue National Bank Of Cleveland	3545	5	–
The Euclid-Park National Bank Of Cleveland	3545	6	–
The First National Bank Of Cleveland	7	5	–
The First National Bank Of Cleveland	2690	2	–
The Market National Bank Of Cleveland	5678	6	–
The Mercantile National Bank Of Cleveland	3272	6	–
The Merchants National Bank Of Cleveland	773	5	–
The Metropolitan National Bank Of Cleveland	5653	6	–
The National Bank Of Commerce Of Cleveland	2662	6	–
The National City Bank Of Cleveland	786	4	3
The National Commercial Bank Of Cleveland	7487	4	–
The Northern National Bank Of Cleveland	11376	6	–
The Ohio National Bank Of Cleveland	1689	6	–
The Park National Bank Of Cleveland	5006	5	–
The Second National Bank Of Cleveland	13	6	–
The State National Bank Of Cleveland	3950	6	–
The Union National Bank Of Cleveland	3202	4	–
The Western Reserve National Bank Of Cleveland	4782	6	–
Union Commerce National Bank Of Cleveland	11141	6	–
Cleves			
The Cleves National Bank	13774	–	5
The Hamilton County National Bank Of Cleves	7456	6	6
Clyde			
The First National Bank Of Clyde	4197	6	–
College Corner			
The First National Bank Of College Corner	5277	6	–
Columbiana			
The First National Bank Of Columbiana	6296	6	–
Columbus			
First National Bank In Columbus	4443	5	–
The Central National Bank Of Columbus	9282	6	–
The City National Bank & Trust Company Of Columbus	7621	–	2
The City National Bank Of Columbus	7818	5	–
The City National Bank Of Commerce Of Columbus	7621	6	6
The Clinton National Bank Of Columbus	3610	6	–
The Commercial National Bank Of Columbus	2605	3	5
The Deshler National Bank Of Columbus	4579	5	–
The First National Bank Of Columbus	123	6	–
The Fourth National Bank Of Columbus	2423	4	–
The Franklin National Bank Of Columbus	599	6	–
Columbus			
The Hayden National Bank Of Columbus	4697	6	–
The Hayden-Clinton National Bank Of Columbus	4697	4	–
The Huntington National Bank Of Columbus	7745	3	2
The Merchants And Manufacturers National Bank Of Columbus	5029	6	–
The National Bank Of Commerce Of Columbus	4443	6	–
The National Bank Of Commerce Of Columbus	7621	6	–
The National Exchange Bank Of Columbus	591	6	–
The New First National Bank Of Columbus	4443	4	–
The Ohio National Bank Of Columbus	5065	3	1
The Union National Bank Of Columbus	7584	6	–
Conneaut			
The First National Bank Of Conneaut	3492	6	–
Convoy			
The First National Bank Of Convoy	8017	6	6
Coolville			
The Coolville National Bank	8175	6	6
Cortland			
The First National Bank Of Cortland	4772	6	–
Coshocton			
The Commercial National Bank Of Coshocton	6892	5	4
The Coshocton National Bank	5103	5	5
The First National Bank Of Coshocton	1920	6	–
Covington			
The Citizens National Bank Of Covington	5530	6	6
Crestline			
First National Bank In Crestline	13273	–	5
The First National Bank Of Crestline	5099	5	–
Cuyahoga Falls			
The First National Bank Of Cuyahoga Falls	378	6	–
Dalton			
The First National Bank Of Dalton	6372	6	6
Dayton			
The American National Bank & Trust Company Of Dayton	4054	6	–
The American National Bank Of Dayton	4054	6	–
The City National Bank And Trust Company Of Dayton	2874	6	6
The City National Bank Of Dayton	2874	5	–
The Dayton National Bank	898	5	–
The First National Bank Of Dayton	9	6	–
The Fourth National Bank Of Dayton	3821	5	–
The Merchants National Bank And Trust Company Of Dayton	1788	6	5
The Merchants National Bank Of Dayton	1788	4	–
The Second National Bank Of Dayton	10	6	–
The Teutonia National Bank Of Dayton	4054	5	–
The Third National Bank And Trust Company Of Dayton	2678	4	4
The Third National Bank Of Dayton	2678	4	–
The Winters National Bank And Trust Company Of Dayton	2604	4	3
The Winters National Bank Of Dayton	2604	3	–
Defiance			
The Defiance National Bank	1906	6	–
The First National Bank Of Defiance	4661	4	5
The Merchants National Bank Of Defiance	2516	4	6
The National Bank Of Defiance	13457	–	4
Delaware			
The Delaware County National Bank Of Delaware	853	5	–
The Delaware National Bank	7505	6	5
The First National Bank Of Delaware	243	4	5
Delphos			
The Delphos National Bank	2885	6	–
The First National Bank Of Delphos	274	6	–
The National Bank Of Delphos	6280	6	–
The Old National Bank Of Delphos	12196	6	6
Delta			
The Farmers National Bank Of Delta	5577	6	–
Delware			
The Delaware County National Bank Of Delaware	13535	–	3
Dennison			
The Dennison National Bank	6843	5	5
The First National Bank Of Dennison	13802	–	6
The Twin City National Bank Of Dennison	6836	6	–
Dillonvale			
First National Bank At Dillonvale	14011	–	6
The First National Bank Of Dillonvale	5618	5	5
Dresden			
The Dresden National Bank	6529	6	–
The First National Bank Of Dresden	5144	6	–
Dunkirk			
The First National Bank Of Dunkirk	6628	6	6
The Woodruff National Bank Of Dunkirk	6652	6	–
East Liverpool			
The Citizens National Bank Of East Liverpool	5098	5	–
The First National Bank Of East Liverpool	2146	4	4
The Potters National Bank Of East Liverpool	2544	3	5
East Palestine			
The First National Bank At East Palestine	13850	–	6
The First National Bank Of East Palestine	6593	6	6
Eaton			
The Eaton National Bank	7557	6	6
The First National Bank Of Eaton	530	6	–
The Preble County National Bank Of Eaton	3889	6	6
Elmore			
The First National Bank Of Elmore	6770	6	5
Elmwood Place			
The First National Bank Of Elmwood Place	6314	6	4

City, Bank	Ch. No.	L	S
Elyria			
First National Bank In Elyria	2863	6	–
The First National Bank Of Elyria	438	6	–
The National Bank Of Elyria	2863	6	–
Fairport Harbor			
The First National Bank Of Fairport Harbor	6068	6	–
Felicity			
The First National Bank Of Felicity	2882	6	–
Findlay			
The American National Bank Of Findlay	3729	4	–
The American-First National Bank Of Findlay	36	5	5
The Buckeye National Bank Of Findlay	3477	5	–
The Farmers National Bank Of Findlay	3477	6	–
The First National Bank And Trust Company Of Findlay	36	–	4
The First National Bank Of Findlay	36	6	–
Flushing			
The First National Bank Of Flushing	3177	6	–
Forest			
The First National Bank Of Forest	7518	6	5
Fostoria			
The First National Bank Of Fostoria	2831	5	6
The Union National Bank Of Fostoria	9192	6	4
Franklin			
The Farmers National Bank Of Franklin	2282	6	–
The First National Bank Of Franklin	738	6	–
The Franklin National Bank	5100	5	2
The Warren National Bank Of Franklin	8000	6	–
Fredericktown			
The First National Bank Of Fredericktown	5640	6	6
Freeport			
The Prairie Depot National Bank Of Freeport	11216	6	6
Fremont			
The First National Bank Of Fremont	5	4	5
The First National Bank Of Fremont	5	6	–
Galion			
The Citizens National Bank Of Galion	1984	4	6
The First National Bank Of Galion	419	4	5
The Galion National Bank	3581	6	–
Gallipolis			
The First National Bank Of Gallipolis	136	5	5
Garrettsville			
The First National Bank Of Garrettsville	2034	6	6
Geneva			
The First National Bank Of Geneva	153	6	–
The First National Bank Of Geneva	2719	6	6
Georgetown			
The First National Bank Of Georgetown	2705	5	6
The Peoples National Bank Of Georgetown	5996	6	3
Germantown			
The First National Bank Of Germantown	86	6	6
Gettysburg			
The Citizens National Bank Of Gettysburg	10058	6	6
Girard			
The First National Bank Of Girard	4884	6	6
Glouster			
The First National Bank Of Glouster	8423	6	–
Granville			
The First National Bank Of Granville	388	6	–
The First National Bank Of Granville	2496	6	–
Green Spring			
The First National Bank Of Green Spring	2037	6	–
Greenfield			
The First National Bank Of Greenfield	101	6	–
The Peoples National Bank Of Greenfield	10105	5	4
Greenville			
The Farmers National Bank Of Greenville	1092	6	4
The Greenville National Bank	7130	6	5
The Second National Bank Of Greenville	2992	6	5
Greenwich			
The First National Bank Of Greenwich	7001	6	5
Grove City			
The First National Bank Of Grove City	6827	6	6
Hamilton			
The First National Bank & Trust Company Of Hamilton	56	5	4
The First National Bank Of Hamilton	56	4	–
The Miami Valley National Bank Of Hamilton	3840	5	–
The Second National Bank Of Hamilton	829	4	5
Harrison			
The First National Bank Of Harrison	8228	6	6
Haviland			
The Farmers National Bank Of Haviland	10436	6	6
Hicksville			
The First National Bank Of Hicksville	4867	5	5
The Hicksville National Bank	5802	6	6
Higginsport			
The First National Bank Of Higginsport	9394	6	–
The First National Bank Of Winchester	9394	6	–
Hillsboro			
The Farmers And Traders National Bank Of Hillsboro	9243	6	3
Hillsborough			
The Citizens National Bank Of Hillsborough	2039	5	–
The First National Bank Of Hillsborough	787	6	–
The Hillsborough National Bank	787	6	–
The Merchants National Bank Of Hillsborough	2449	5	5
Hopedale			
The First National Bank Of Hopedale	6938	6	6
Hubbard			
The Hubbard National Bank	2389	6	–
Hudson			
The National Bank Of Hudson	9221	6	6
Huron			
The First National Bank Of Huron	4778	6	–
Ironton			
The Citizens National Bank Of Ironton	4336	5	6
The First National Bank Of Ironton	98	2	4
The Second National Bank Of Ironton	242	5	–
Jackson			
The First National Bank Of Jackson	1903	5	6
Jackson Center			
The First National Bank Of Jackson Center	8536	5	5
Jefferson			
The First National Bank Of Jefferson	427	6	–
The Second National Bank Of Jefferson	2026	6	–
Jewett			
The First National Bank Of Jewett	13150	–	5
Kalida			
The First National Bank Of Kalida	7074	6	–
Kansas			
The First National Bank Of Kansas	11598	6	6
Kent			
The Kent National Bank	652	5	5
Kenton			
The First Commercial National Bank Of Kenton	2500	–	6
The First National Bank Of Kenton	2500	5	5
The Kenton National Bank	3505	5	5
Kingston			
The First National Bank Of Kingston	9536	6	6
Kinsman			
The Kinsman National Bank	3077	6	–
La Rue			
The Campbell National Bank Of La Rue	6675	6	6
Lakewood			
The Peoples National Bank Of Lakewood	13715	–	5
Lancaster			
The Fairfield National Bank Of Lancaster	7517	5	4
The First National Bank Of Lancaster	137	6	–
The Hocking Valley National Bank Of Lancaster	1241	4	6
The Lancaster National Bank	9547	5	3
Lebanon			
Lebanon National Bank And Trust Company, Lebanon	2360	6	–
The Citizens National Bank And Trust Company Of Lebanon	4239	6	–
The Citizens National Bank Of Lebanon	4239	5	–
The Farmers And Merchants National Bank Of Lebanon	8507	6	–
The First National Bank Of Lebanon	1238	6	–
The Lebanon Citizens National Bank & Trust Co., Lebanon	2360	5	4
The Lebanon National Bank	2360	5	–
Leetonia			
The First National Bank Of Leetonia	3519	6	–
Leipsic			
The First National Bank Of Leipsic	6565	6	–
Lewisville			
The First National Bank Of Lewisville	8978	5	–
Lima			
The American National Bank Of Lima	5125	6	–
The First National Bank Of Lima	2035	5	–
The Lima National Bank	2859	6	–
The Merchants National Bank Of Lima	2497	6	–
The National Bank Of Lima	13767	–	5
The Ohio National Bank Of Lima	3772	6	–
The Old National Bank Of Lima	8701	6	–
The Old National City Bank Of Lima	8701	6	6
Lockland			
The First National Bank Of Lockland	4133	6	5
Lodi			
The Exchange National Bank Of Lodi	7017	6	–
The First National Bank Of Lodi	53	6	–
The Lodi National Bank	7017	6	–
The Peoples National Bank Of Lodi	10677	5	6
Logan			
First National Bank In Logan	7649	6	6
First-Rempel National Bank On Logan	7649	–	6
The First National Bank Of Logan	92	6	–
The National Bank Of Logan	7649	5	–
The Rempel National Bank Of Logan	9284	6	–
London			
The Central National Bank Of London	10373	5	4
The Madison National Bank Of London	1064	5	4
Lorain			
The First National Bank Of Lorain	2625	6	–
The National Bank Of Commerce Of Lorain	5371	5	4
Loudonville			
The First National Bank Of Loudonville	6657	6	–
Louisville			
The First National Bank Of Louisville	9630	6	–
Loveland			
The First National Bank Of Loveland	6816	6	–
The Loveland National Bank	6779	5	6
Lowell			
The First National Bank Of Lowell	5329	6	6
Lynchburg			
The First National Bank Of Lynchburg	11772	4	6
Madisonville			
The First National Bank Of Madisonville	8557	6	–
Malta			
The Malta National Bank	2052	6	5
Manchester			
The Farmers National Bank Of Manchester	9091	5	5
The Manchester National Bank	1982	5	–
Mansfield			
The Citizens National Bank & Trust Company Of Mansfield	2577	6	5
The Citizens National Bank Of Mansfield	2577	5	–
The Farmers National Bank Of Mansfield	800	6	–
The First National Bank Of Mansfield	436	5	–
The Richland National Bank Of Mansfield	480	6	–
Mantua			
The First National Bank Of Mantua	5370	6	5
Marietta			
The Central National Bank Of Marietta	5212	5	–
The Citizens National Bank Of Marietta	4164	4	5
The First National Bank Of Marietta	142	4	4
The German National Bank Of Marietta	5212	5	–
The Marietta National Bank	859	6	–
The New First National Bank Of Marietta	13971	–	3
Marion			
The City National Bank Of Marion	5650	6	–
The First National Bank Of Marion	287	6	–
The Marion National Bank	6308	5	6
The National City Bank And Trust Company Of Marion	11831	5	5
Mason			
The First National Bank Of Mason	7403	5	–
Massillon			
The First National Bank Of Massillon	216	4	4
The Merchants National Bank Of Massillon	4286	4	–
The Union National Bank Of Massillon	1318	4	5
Mc Connelsville			
The First National Bank Of Mc Connelsville	46	6	–
Mcarthur			
The Vinton County National Bank Of Mcarthur	2036	5	5
Mcconnelsville			
The Citizens National Bank Of Mcconnelsville	5259	4	5
The First National Bank Of Mcconnelsville	2712	4	5
Mechanicsburgh			
The Farmers National Bank Of Mechanicsburgh	2325	6	–
Medina			
The First National Bank Of Medina	2053	6	–
The Medina County National Bank Of Medina	5139	5	–
The Old Phoenix National Bank Of Medina	4842	6	5
The Phoenix National Bank Of Medina	2091	6	–
Mendon			
The First National Bank Of Mendon	9274	6	6
Miamisburg			
The Citizens National Bank Of Miamisburg	4822	6	–
The First National Bank Of Miamisburg	3876	5	5
Middleport			
The Citizens National Bank Of Middleport	8441	6	6
The First National Bank Of Middleport	2210	6	–
The Middleport National Bank	4472	6	–
Middletown			
The First & Merchants National Bank Of Middletown	2025	5	3
The First National Bank Of Middletown	1545	6	–
The Merchants National Bank Of Middletown	2025	6	–
Milford			
The Citizens National Bank Of Milford	8188	5	–
The Milford National Bank	3234	4	5
Millersburgh			
The First National Bank Of Millersburgh	1923	6	–
Minerva			
The First National Bank Of Minerva	1930	6	–
The First National Bank Of Minerva	5344	6	–
Mingo Junction			
The First National Bank Of Mingo Junction	5694	6	5
The Mingo National Bank Of Mingo Junction	14183	–	6
Monroe			
The Monroe National Bank	7947	6	5
Monroeville			
The First National Bank Of Monroeville	2438	6	–
Montpelier			
National Bank Of Montpelier	13912	–	5
The First National Bank Of Montpelier	5315	6	–
The Montpelier National Bank	5341	5	5
Morrow			
The First National Bank Of Morrow	8709	6	6
The Morrow National Bank	8741	6	5
Mount Gilead			
The First National Bank Of Mount Gilead	258	6	–
The Morrow County National Bank Of Mount Gilead	2459	6	–
The Mt. Gilead National Bank	6620	6	5
The National Bank Of Morrow County At Mount Gilead	5251	5	6
Mount Healthy			
The First National Bank Of Mt. Healthy	7661	6	5
Mount Orab			
The Brown County National Bank Of Mt. Orab	10692	6	6
Mount Pleasant			
The First National Bank Of Mount Pleasant	492	6	–
The Mount Pleasant National Bank	6640	6	–
The Peoples National Bank Of Mount Pleasant	6667	6	5
Mount Sterling			
The Citizens National Bank Of Mount Sterling	9095	5	–
The First National Bank Of Mt. Sterling	5382	4	–
The First-Citizens National Bank Of Mt. Sterling	5382	6	–
Mount Vernon			
Knox National Bank In Mt. Vernon	7638	6	5
The Farmers And Merchants National Bank Of Mount Vernon	7248	6	–
The First National Bank Of Mount Vernon	908	6	4
The Knox County National Bank Of Mount Vernon	1051	6	–

City, Bank	Ch. No.	L	S
Mount Vernon			
The Knox National Bank Of Mount Vernon	3328	6	–
The New Knox National Bank Of Mt. Vernon	7638	6	–
Mount Washington			
The First National Bank Of Mount Washington	9761	6	–
Napoleon			
The First National Bank Of Napoleon	1917	6	–
The First National Bank Of Napoleon	5218	4	6
Neffs			
The Neffs National Bank	9799	6	6
New Bremen			
The First National Bank Of New Bremen	7851	6	5
New Carlisle			
The First National Bank Of New Carlisle	6594	6	–
The New Carlisle National Bank	6594	–	6
New Concord			
The First National Bank Of New Concord	6976	6	6
New Holland			
The First National Bank Of New Holland	7187	5	5
New Lexington			
The Citizens National Bank Of New Lexington	6505	5	5
The First National Bank Of New Lexington	2056	6	–
The Peoples National Bank Of New Lexington	13596	–	4
New Lisbon			
The First National Bank Of New Lisbon	2203	6	–
New London			
The First National Bank Of New London	1981	6	–
The New London National Bank	4712	6	–
The Third National Bank Of New London	10101	5	6
New Matamoras			
The First National Bank Of New Matamoras	5999	6	6
New Paris			
The First National Bank Of New Paris	9211	6	6
New Philadelphia			
The Citizens National Bank Of New Philadelphia	1999	6	5
New Richmond			
The First National Bank Of New Richmond	1068	6	–
The New Richmond National Bank	7542	6	5
New Vienna			
The First National Bank Of New Vienna	10947	6	–
Newark			
The First National Bank Of Newark	858	2	5
The Franklin National Bank Of Newark	7787	4	–
The Park National Bank Of Newark	9179	4	5
The Peoples National Bank Of Newark	3191	6	–
Newcomerstown			
The First National Bank Of Newcomerstown	5262	5	4
Newton Falls			
The First National Bank Of Newton Falls	7391	6	–
Niles			
The City National Bank Of Niles	4977	6	–
The First National Bank Of Niles	4190	6	–
North Baltimore			
The First National Bank Of North Baltimore	4347	4	5
Norwalk			
The Citizens National Bank Of Norwalk	11275	4	1
The First National Bank Of Norwalk	215	4	–
The Norwalk National Bank	931	6	–
Norwood			
The First National Bank Of Norwood	6322	6	5
The Norwood National Bank	8505	4	–
Oak Harbor			
The First National Bank Of Oak Harbor	6632	6	5
Oberlin			
The Citizens National Bank Of Oberlin	2718	6	–
The First National Bank Of Oberlin	72	6	–
Okeana			
The First National Bank Of Okeana	9450	6	6
Orrville			
The First National Bank Of Orrville	6379	6	–
The National Bank Of Orrville	13742	–	6
The Orrville National Bank	6362	6	5
Osborn			
The First National Bank Of Osborn	9675	6	5
Ottawa			
The First National Bank Of Ottawa	7006	6	5
Oxford			
The First National Bank Of Oxford	4599	6	–
The Oxford National Bank	6059	5	3
Painesville			
First National Bank In Painesville	14232	–	6
The First National Bank Of Painesville	220	5	–
The Painesville National Bank	2842	6	–
The Painesville National Bank And Trust Company	13318	–	5
Pandora			
The First National Bank Of Pandora	11343	6	6
Paulding			
The First National Bank Of Paulding	5917	6	–
The Paulding National Bank	5862	6	5
Piketon			
Piketon National Bank	7039	5	6
Piqua			
The Citizens National Bank & Trust Company Of Piqua	1061	6	4
The Citizens National Bank Of Piqua	1061	6	–
The Piqua National Bank	1006	4	–
The Piqua National Bank And Trust Company, Piqua	1006	5	5
The Third National Bank Of Piqua	3750	6	–
Plain City			
The Farmers National Bank Of Plain City	5522	6	5
Plymouth			
The First National Bank Of Plymouth	1904	5	–
Plymouth			
The Peoples National Bank Of Plymouth	7035	6	6
Pomeroy			
The First National Bank Of Pomeroy	132	6	–
The Pomeroy National Bank	1980	6	5
Port Clinton			
National Bank Of Port Clinton	6227	6	5
The First National Bank Of Port Clinton	6227	6	–
The First National-Magruder Bank Of Port Clinton	6227	6	–
Portsmouth			
The Central National Bank Of Portsmouth	7781	4	6
The Farmers National Bank Of Portsmouth	1088	6	–
The First National Bank Of Portsmouth	68	2	3
The Iron National Bank Of Portsmouth	1948	6	–
The Kinney National Bank Of Portsmouth	1958	6	–
The National Bank Of Portsmouth	13832	–	4
The Portsmouth National Bank	935	5	–
The Security Central National Bank Of Portsmouth	7781	–	5
Powhatan Point			
The First National Bank Of Powhatan Point	7759	6	5
Quaker City			
The Quaker City National Bank	1989	4	5
Racine			
The First National Bank Of Racine	9815	6	6
Ravenna			
The First National Bank Of Ravenna	106	6	–
The Ravenna National Bank	6466	5	–
The Second National Bank Of Ravenna	350	4	5
Richwood			
The First National Bank Of Richwood	9199	5	6
Ripley			
The Citizens National Bank Of Ripley	3291	3	5
The Farmers National Bank Of Ripley	933	6	–
The First National Bank Of Ripley	289	6	–
The Ripley National Bank	2837	4	4
Rock Creek			
The First National Bank Of Rock Creek	7790	6	–
Rocky River			
The First National Bank Of Rocky River	12347	–	4
Roseville			
The First National Bank Of Roseville	5555	6	–
Sabina			
The First National Bank Of Sabina	8411	6	5
Saint Clairsville			
First National Bank In St. Clairsville	13922	–	4
The First National Bank Of St. Clairsville	315	4	4
The Second National Bank Of St. Clairsville	4993	5	5
Saint Marys			
The First National Bank Of St. Marys	4219	6	5
Saint Paris			
The Central National Bank Of Saint Paris	8127	5	5
The First National Bank Of Saint Paris	2488	4	6
Salem			
The Farmers National Bank Of Salem	973	4	5
The First National Bank Of Salem	43	6	–
The First National Bank Of Salem	2691	4	4
Sandusky			
The Citizens National Bank Of Sandusky	3141	6	–
The Commercial National Bank Of Sandusky	6455	6	–
The First National Bank Of Sandusky	16	6	–
The Moss National Bank Of Sandusky	2810	6	–
The Second National Bank Of Sandusky	210	6	–
The Third National Bank Of Sandusky	2061	5	–
The Third National Exchange Bank Of Sandusky	4792	6	6
Sardinia			
The First National Bank Of Sardinia	7800	5	6
Sardis			
The First National Bank Of Sardis	7711	6	–
Scio			
The Farmers And Producers National Bank Of Scio	5197	6	–
Senecaville			
The First National Bank Of Senecaville	7399	6	6
Seven Mile			
The Farmers National Bank Of Seven Mile	9518	6	5
Shelby			
The First National Bank Of Shelby	1929	4	5
Sidney			
The Citizens National Bank Of Sidney	7862	4	4
The First National Bank Of Sidney	257	6	–
The First National Exchange Bank Of Sidney	5214	4	4
Smithfield			
First National Bank At Smithfield	13171	6	6
The First National Bank Of Smithfield	501	4	–
Somerset			
The First National Bank Of Somerset	7237	6	–
Somerton			
The First National Bank Of Somerton	7984	6	–
Somerville			
The Somerville National Bank	9859	6	5
South Charleston			
The Farmers National Bank Of South Charleston	2754	6	–
The First National Bank Of South Charleston	171	6	–
Spring Valley			
The Spring Valley National Bank	7896	6	6
Springfield			
Farmers National Bank Of Springfield	9446	5	–
Lagonda National Bank Of Springfield	14105	–	4
Logonda-Citizens National Bank Of Springfield	2098	5	4
Springfield			
The Citizens National Bank Of Springfield	5160	3	–
The First National Bank And Trust Company Of Springfield	238	5	3
The First National Bank Of Springfield	238	3	–
The Lagonda National Bank Of Springfield	2098	4	–
The Mad River National Bank Of Springfield	1146	3	–
The Second National Bank Of Springfield	263	6	–
The Springfield National Bank	2620	4	–
Steubenville			
The Commercial National Bank Of Steubenville	5039	5	–
The First National Bank Of Steubenville	1164	6	–
The Jefferson National Bank Of Steubenville	1062	6	–
The National Exchange Bank & Trust Company Of Stuebenville	2160	5	4
The National Exchange Bank Of Steubenville	2160	4	–
The Peoples National Bank Of Steubenville	7688	6	5
The Steubenville National Bank	3310	6	–
Stockport			
The First National Bank Of Stockport	8042	5	5
Summerfield			
The First National Bank Of Summerfield	6662	6	6
Sycamore			
The First National Bank Of Sycamore	11383	5	5
Tiffin			
The City National Bank Of Tiffin	5427	5	5
The Commercial National Bank Of Tiffin	7795	4	4
The First National Bank Of Tiffin	900	6	–
The National Exchange Bank Of Tiffin	907	5	–
The Tiffin National Bank	3315	4	4
Tippecanoe City			
The Citizens National Bank Of Tippecanoe City	8839	6	5
The Tipp National Bank Of Tippecanoe City	3004	5	5
Toledo			
National Bank Of Toledo	14030	–	3
The Commercial National Bank Of Toledo	2296	6	–
The First National Bank Of Toledo	91	3	1
The Holcomb National Bank Of Toledo	4585	6	–
The Ketcham National Bank Of Toledo	3820	6	–
The Merchants National Bank Of Toledo	1895	4	–
The National Bank Of Commerce Of Toledo	3820	4	–
The National Bank Of Toledo	4585	6	–
The Northern National Bank Of Toledo	809	3	–
The Second National Bank Of Toledo	248	4	–
The Toledo National Bank	607	6	–
Toronto			
The First National Bank Of Toronto	8705	6	–
The National Bank Of Toronto	8826	6	5
Troy			
The First National Bank Of Troy	59	6	–
The First National Bank Of Troy	2727	4	–
The First Troy National Bank And Trust Company	3825	5	4
The Troy National Bank	3825	5	–
Uhrichsville			
The Farmers And Merchants National Bank Of Uhrichsville	2582	6	–
Upper Sandusky			
The Commercial National Bank Of Upper Sandusky	5448	6	–
The First National Bank Of Upper Sandusky	90	4	6
Urbana			
The Champaign National Bank Of Urbana	916	4	4
The Citizens National Bank Of Urbana	863	5	5
The National Bank Of Urbana	4805	5	–
The Third National Bank Of Urbana	2071	5	–
Utica			
The First National Bank Of Utica	7596	6	5
Van Wert			
The First National Bank Of Van Wert	422	5	5
The Van Wert National Bank	2628	5	5
Versailles			
The First National Bank Of Versailles	9336	6	5
Wadsworth			
The First National Bank Of Wadsworth	5828	6	4
The Wadsworth National Bank	5870	6	–
Wapakoneta			
The Auglaize National Bank Of Wapakoneta	9961	4	6
The First National Bank Of Wapakoneta	3157	5	3
The Peoples National Bank Of Wapakoneta	3535	6	4
Warren			
The First National Bank Of Warren	74	5	–
The New National Bank Of Warren	6289	6	–
The Second National Bank Of Warren	2479	5	3
The Trumbull National Bank Of Warren	1578	6	–
The Union National Bank Of Warren	6353	6	–
The Western Reserve National Bank Of Warren	3362	4	–
Washington			
The Midland National Bank Of Washington Court House	4763	5	–
Washington C H			
The Fayette County National Bank Of Washington	1972	5	–
The First National Bank Of Washington	284	6	–
Washington Court House			
The First National Bank Of Washington Court House	13490	–	2
Watertown			
The First National Bank Of Watertown	6943	6	6
Wauseon			
The First National Bank Of Wauseon	7091	5	6

City, Bank	Ch. No.	L	S
Waverly			
The First National Bank Of Waverly	5635	5	5
Waynesville			
The Waynesville National Bank	2220	4	4
Wellington			
The First National Bank Of Wellington	464	6	–
The First National Bank Of Wellington	2866	6	–
Wellston			
The First National Bank Of Wellston	3565	3	5
Wellsville			
The First National Bank Of Wellsville	1044	6	–
The Peoples National Bank Of Wellsville	6345	4	6
West Liberty			
The Logan National Bank Of West Liberty	2942	6	–
West Milton			
The First National Bank Of West Milton	9062	6	6
West Union			
The First National Bank Of West Union	9487	6	–
The National Bank Of Adams County Of West Union	13198	6	5
Westerville			
The First National Bank Of Westerville	7671	6	–
Weston			
The First National Bank Of Weston	6656	6	6
Williamsburg			
The First National Bank Of Williamsburg	9930	6	–
Williamsport			
The Farmers National Bank Of Williamsport	10267	5	5
Willoughby			
The First National Bank Of Willoughby	11994	5	6
Wilmington			
The Citizens National Bank Of Wilmington	8251	5	5
The Clinton County National Bank Of Wilmington	1997	4	–
The Clinton County Natl Bank & Trust Co. Of Wilmington	1997	5	4
The First National Bank Of Wilmington	365	5	5
Woodsfield			
The First National Bank Of Woodsfield	5414	5	6
Wooster			
The Citizens National Bank Of Wooster	7670	5	3
The National Bank Of Wooster	1912	6	–
The Wayne County National Bank Of Wooster	828	4	5
The Wooster National Bank	4657	6	–
Xenia			
The Citizens National Bank Of Xenia	2575	4	5
The First National Bank Of Xenia	369	6	–
The Second National Bank Of Xenia	277	6	–
The Xenia National Bank	2932	4	4
Youngstown			
The Commercial National Bank Of Youngstown	2482	3	4
The First National Bank Of Youngstown	3	2	1
The First National Bank Of Youngstown	3	5	–
The Mahoning National Bank Of Youngstown	2350	4	3
The Second National Bank In Youngstown	12332	6	6
The Second National Bank Of Youngstown	2217	5	–
The Union National Bank Of Youngstown	13586	–	3
The Wick National Bank Of Youngstown	4970	6	–
Zanesville			
The Citizens National Bank In Zanesville	5760	–	4
The Citizens National Bank Of Zanesville	2529	5	–
The Commercial National Bank Of Zanesville	5769	6	–
The First National Bank Of Zanesville	164	4	4
The Muskingum National Bank Of Zanesville	1230	6	–
The Old Citizens National Bank Of Zanesville	5760	4	5
The Second National Bank Of Zanesville	131	6	–
The Union National Bank Of Zanesville	4298	6	–

INDIAN TERRITORY

City, Bank	Ch. No.	L	S
Ada			
The Ada National Bank	5633	6	–
The Citizens National Bank Of Ada	7071	6	–
The First National Bank Of Ada	5620	6	–
Afton			
The First National Bank Of Afton	8790	6	–
Antlers			
The Antlers National Bank	7667	6	–
The Citizens National Bank Of Antlers	8082	6	–
Ardmore			
The Ardmore National Bank	5922	6	–
The Bankers National Bank Of Ardmore	8354	6	–
The City National Bank Of Ardmore	4723	6	–
The First National Bank Of Ardmore	4393	6	–
Atoka			
The Atoka National Bank	5791	6	–
The Citizens National Bank Of Atoka	7666	6	–
Bartlesville			
The American National Bank Of Bartlesville	7032	6	–
The Bartlesville National Bank	6258	6	–
The First National Bank Of Bartlesville	5310	6	–
Beggs			
The First National Bank Of Beggs	6868	6	–
Bennington			
The First National Bank Of Bennington	7099	6	–
Berwyn			
The First National Bank Of Berwyn	7209	6	–
Blanchard			
The First National Bank Of Blanchard	8702	6	–
Bokchito			
The Bokchito National Bank	7499	6	–
The First National Bank Of Bokchito	6683	6	–
Boswell			
The Boswell National Bank	8353	6	–
The First National Bank Of Boswell	7651	6	–
Boynton			
The First National Bank Of Boynton	6511	6	–
Bristow			
The First National Bank Of Bristow	6260	6	–
Broken Arrow			
The Arkansas Valley National Bank Of Broken Arrow	7600	6	–
The First National Bank Of Broken Arrow	7115	6	–
Byars			
The First National Bank Of Byars	7389	6	–
Caddo			
The Caddo National Bank	7368	6	–
The Choctaw National Bank Of Caddo	5246	6	–
Calvin			
The Citizens National Bank Of Calvin	7053	6	–
The First National Bank Of Calvin	6980	6	–
Centralia			
The First National Bank Of Centralia	7706	6	–
Checotah			
The First National Bank Of Checotah	5128	6	–
Chelsea			
The First National Bank Of Chelsea	5955	6	–
Chickasha			
The Chickasha National Bank	8203	6	–
The Citizens National Bank Of Chickasha	5547	6	–
The First National Bank Of Chickasha	5431	6	–
Claremore			
The First National Bank Of Claremore	4987	6	–
Coalgate			
The Coalgate National Bank	7321	6	–
The First National Bank Of Coalgate	5647	6	–
Colbert			
The First National Bank Of Colbert	7962	6	–
Collinsville			
The First National Bank Of Collinsville	6138	6	–
Comanche			
The Comanche National Bank	8366	6	–
The First National Bank Of Comanche	6299	6	–
Cornish			
The First National Bank Of Cornish	7420	6	–
Coweta			
The First National Bank Of Coweta	6879	6	–
Davis			
The First National Bank Of Davis	5298	6	–
The Merchants & Planters National Bank Of Davis	7442	6	–
Dewey			
The First National Bank Of Dewey	8270	6	–
Duncan			
The City National Bank Of Duncan	8616	6	–
The Duncan National Bank	7289	6	–
The First National Bank Of Duncan	5379	6	–
Durant			
The Choctaw-Chickasaw National Bank Of Durant	6928	6	–
The Durant National Bank	5590	6	–
The Farmers National Bank Of Durant	6928	6	–
The First National Bank Of Durant	5129	5	–
Eufaula			
The Eufaula National Bank	5967	6	–
The First National Bank Of Eufaula	5902	6	–
Fort Gibson			
The Farmers National Bank Of Fort Gibson	8079	6	–
The First National Bank Of Fort Gibson	6539	6	–
Fort Towson			
The First National Bank Of Fort Towson	8078	6	–
Francis			
The First National Bank Of Francis	7185	6	–
Hartshorne			
The First National Bank Of Hartshorne	7050	6	–
Haskell			
The First National Bank Of Haskell	7822	6	–
Henryetta			
The First National Bank Of Henryetta	6867	6	–
Holdenville			
The American National Bank Of Holdenville	7619	6	–
The First National Bank Of Holdenville	5270	6	–
The National Bank Of Commerce, Holdenville	6540	6	–
The National Bank Of Holdenville	5735	6	–
Hugo			
The First National Bank Of Hugo	6130	6	–
The Hugo National Bank	7747	6	–
Idabel			
The First National Bank Of Idabel	8486	6	–
Keota			
The First National Bank Of Keota	8177	6	–
Kiefer			
The First National Bank Of Kiefer	8553	6	–
Kingston			
The First National Bank Of Kingston	7893	6	–
Kiowa			
The First National Bank Of Kiowa	8638	6	–
Konawa			
The First National Bank Of Konawa	7633	6	–
The Konawa National Bank	8213	6	–
Lehigh			
The Lehigh National Bank	5755	6	–
The Merchants National Bank Of Lehigh	8189	6	–
Lindsay			
The Citizens National Bank Of Lindsay	6171	6	–
The First National Bank Of Lindsay	6171	6	–
The Lindsay National Bank	6710	6	–
Madill			
The City National Bank Of Madill	7723	6	–
The First National Bank Of Madill	5404	6	–
The Madill National Bank	6365	6	–
Mannsville			
The First National Bank Of Mannsville	6578	6	–
Marietta			
The Farmers National Bank Of Marietta	8278	6	–
The First National Bank Of Marietta	5345	6	–
The Marietta National Bank	5958	6	–
Marlow			
The First National Bank Of Marlow	5724	5	–
Miami			
The First National Bank Of Miami	5252	6	–
Milburn			
The First National Bank Of Milburn	7842	6	–
Mill Creek			
The First National Bank Of Mill Creek	7197	6	–
The Merchants & Planters National Bank Of Mill Creek	8546	6	–
Minco			
The First National Bank Of Minco	8644	6	–
Morris			
The First National Bank Of Morris	8876	6	–
Mounds			
The First National Bank Of Mounds	6263	6	–
Muldrow			
The First National Bank Of Muldrow	6717	6	–
Muscogee			
The First National Bank Of Muscogee	4385	4	–
Muskogee			
The City National Bank Of Muskogee	6911	6	–
The Commercial National Bank Of Muskogee	5236	6	–
Nowata			
The First National Bank Of Nowata	5401	6	–
The Nowata National Bank	6367	6	–
Oakland			
The Cotton National Bank Of Oakland	5404	6	–
Okemah			
The First National Bank Of Okemah	6477	6	–
The Okemah National Bank	7677	6	–
Okmulgee			
The Citizens National Bank Of Okmulgee	6241	6	–
The First National Bank Of Okmulgee	5418	6	–
The Okmulgee National Bank	6855	6	–
Owasso			
The First National Bank Of Owasso	7964	6	–
Pauls Valley			
The First National Bank Of Pauls Valley	5091	6	–
The National Bank Of Commerce Of Pauls Valley	6639	6	–
The Pauls Valley National Bank	7892	6	–
Porter			
The First National Bank Of Porter	7615	6	–
The Porter National Bank	8676	6	–
Porum			
The First National Bank Of Porum	8479	6	–
Poteau			
The First National Bank Of Poteau	7118	6	–
The National Bank Of Poteau	7104	6	–
Pryor Creek			
The First National Bank Of Pryor Creek	5546	6	–
Purcell			
The Chickasaw National Bank Of Purcell	4756	6	–
The Purcell National Bank	4636	6	–
The Union National Bank Of Purcell	7697	6	–
Quinton			
The First National Bank Of Quinton	6517	6	–
Ramona			
The First National Bank Of Ramona	7251	6	–
Ravia			
The First National Bank Of Ravia	7976	6	–
Roff			
The First National Bank Of Roff	5417	6	–
Rush Springs			
The First National Bank Of Rush Springs	8336	6	–
Ryan			
The First National Bank Of Ryan	5800	6	–
Sallisaw			
The First National Bank Of Sallisaw	5596	6	–
The Merchants National Bank Of Sallisaw	7571	6	–
Sapulpa			
The American National Bank Of Sapulpa	7788	6	–
The First National Bank Of Sapulpa	5951	6	–
South Mcalester			
The American National Bank Of South Mcalester	6230	6	–
The City National Bank Of South Mcalester	6406	6	–
The First National Bank Of Mcalester	5052	6	–
The First National Bank Of South Mcalester	5052	6	–
The State National Bank Of South Mcalester	5537	6	–
Spokogee			
The First National Bank Of Dustin	6804	6	–
The First National Bank Of Spokogee	6804	6	–
Sterrett			
The First National Bank Of Sterrett	7950	6	–
Stigler			
The American National Bank Of Stigler	7432	6	–
The First National Bank Of Stigler	7217	6	–
Stonewall			
The First National Bank Of Stonewall	7054	6	–
Stratford			
The First National Bank Of Stratford	8524	6	–
Sulphur			
The First National Bank Of Sulphur	5748	6	–
Tahlequah			
The Cherokee National Bank Of Tahlequah	6414	6	–
The First National Bank Of Tahlequah	5478	6	–
Talihina			
The First National Bank Of Talihina	7780	6	–
Terral			
The First National Bank Of Terral	7996	6	–
Tishomingo			
The American National Bank Of Tishomingo	7042	6	–

City, Bank	Ch. No.	L	S
Tishomingo			
The First National Bank Of Tishomingo	5809	6	–
Tulsa			
The Central National Bank Of Tulsa	8552	6	–
The City National Bank Of Tulsa	5732	6	–
The Farmers National Bank Of Tulsa	6669	6	–
The First National Bank Of Tulsa	5171	6	–
Tupelo			
The First National Bank Of Tupelo	8609	6	–
Tuttle			
The First National Bank Of Tuttle	8475	6	–
Vinita			
The Cherokee National Bank Of Vinita	5860	6	–
The Farmers National Bank Of Vinita	6602	6	–
The First National Bank Of Vinita	4704	5	–
The Vinita National Bank	5083	6	–
Wagoner			
The City National Bank Of Wagoner	7628	6	–
The First National Bank Of Wagoner	5016	6	–
The Wagoner National Bank	6048	6	–
Wapanucka			
The Farmers National Bank Of Wapanucka	5950	6	–
The First National Bank Of Wapanucka	5950	6	–
The Peoples National Bank Of Wapanucka	8137	6	–
Warner			
The First National Bank Of Warner	8809	6	–
Webbers Falls			
The First National Bank Of Webbers Falls	8024	6	–
Weleetka			
The First National Bank Of Weleetka	6324	6	–
The Weleetka National Bank	6689	6	–
Wetumka			
The American National Bank Of Wetumka	7724	6	–
Wetumpka			
The First National Bank Of Wetumpka	5935	6	–
Wewoka			
The Farmers National Bank Of Wewoka	8052	6	–
The First National Bank Of Wewoka	6254	6	–
Wilburton			
The First National Bank Of Wilburton	6890	6	–
Woodville			
The First National Bank Of Woodville	7707	6	–
Wynnewood			
The First National Bank Of Wynnewood	5126	6	–
The Southern National Bank Of Wynnewood	5731	6	–

OKLAHOMA TERRITORY

City, Bank	Ch. No.	L	S
Altus			
The City National Bank Of Altus	8775	6	–
Alva			
The Alva National Bank	6490	6	–
The Exchange National Bank Of Alva	5587	6	–
The First National Bank Of Alva	5587	6	–
Anadarko			
The Citizens National Bank Of Anadarko	6307	6	–
The First National Bank Of Anadarko	5905	6	–
The National Bank Of Anadarko	5923	6	–
Apache			
The First National Bank Of Apache	7127	6	–
Arapaho			
The First National Bank Of Arapaho	6257	6	–
Billings			
The First National Bank Of Billings	5960	5	6
Blackwell			
The Blackwell National Bank	6916	6	–
The First National Bank Of Blackwell	5460	6	–
The State National Bank Of Blackwell	7583	6	–
Buffalo			
The First National Bank Of Buffalo	8896	6	–
Carmen			
The Carmen National Bank	6844	6	–
The First National Bank Of Carmen	6719	6	–
Cashion			
The First National Bank Of Cashion	6161	6	–
Cement			
The First National Bank Of Cement	8144	6	–
Chandler			
The Chandler National Bank	6142	6	–
The First National Bank Of Chandler	5354	6	–
The Union National Bank Of Chandler	6269	6	–
Cherokee			
The First National Bank Of Cherokee	6677	6	–
Cleveland			
The Cleveland National Bank	7386	6	–
The First National Bank Of Cleveland	5911	6	–
Clinton			
The Clinton National Bank	6851	6	–
The First National Bank Of Clinton	6940	6	–
Cordell			
The City National Bank Of Cordell	6647	6	–
The First National Bank Of Cordell	6052	6	–
Cushing			
The Farmers National Bank Of Cushing	8730	6	–
The First National Bank Of Cushing	6893	6	–
Custer City			
The First National Bank Of Custer City	8727	6	–
Davenport			
The First National Bank Of Davenport	8668	6	–
Edmond			
The First National Bank Of Edmond	6156	6	–
El Dorado			
The First National Bank Of El Dorado	8126	6	–
El Reno			
The Citizens National Bank Of El Reno	5985	6	–
The First National Bank Of El Reno	4830	6	–
Elk City			
The Elk City National Bank	6164	6	–
The First National Bank Of Elk City	5766	6	–
Enid			
The Enid National Bank	8231	6	–
The First National Bank Of Enid	5335	6	–
Erick			
The First National Bank Of Erick	8010	6	–
Fairfax			
The Fairfax National Bank	8202	6	–
The First National Bank Of Fairfax	7972	6	–
Fairview			
The First National Bank Of Fairview	7117	6	–
Fort Sill			
The City National Bank Of Lawton	5753	6	–
The First National Bank Of Fort Sill	5753	6	–
Foss			
The First National Bank Of Foss	6736	6	–
Frederick			
The City National Bank Of Frederick	8206	6	–
The First National Bank Of Frederick	8140	6	–
Gage			
The First National Bank Of Gage	8543	6	–
Geary			
The First National Bank Of Geary	6163	6	–
Granite			
The First National Bank Of Granite	8342	6	–
Guthrie			
The Capitol National Bank Of Guthrie	4705	5	–
The Guthrie National Bank	4348	5	–
The National Bank Of Commerce Of Guthrie	7299	6	–
The National Bank Of Guthrie	4383	6	–
Guymon			
The First National Bank Of Guymon	8138	6	–
Harrison			
The First National Bank Of Harrison	6753	6	–
Hastings			
The First National Bank Of Hastings	8209	6	–
The National Bank Of Hastings	8210	6	–
Helena			
The First National Bank Of Helena	8349	6	–
Hennessey			
The First National Bank Of Hennessey	5473	6	–
The Hennessey National Bank	6111	6	–
Hobart			
The City National Bank Of Hobart	6267	6	–
The Farmers & Merchants National Bank Of Hobart	6358	6	–
The First National Bank Of Hobart	5954	6	–
The Hobart National Bank	5915	6	–
Hollis			
The First National Bank Of Hollis	8061	6	–
The Groves National Bank Of Hollis	8825	6	–
The Hollis National Bank	8056	6	–
Hominy			
The First National Bank Of Hominy	7927	6	–
Kaw City			
The First National Bank Of Kaw City	8577	6	–
Kingfisher			
The Farmers National Bank Of Kingfisher	6702	6	–
The First National Bank Of Kingfisher	5328	6	–
The Kingfisher National Bank	5740	6	–
The Peoples National Bank Of Kingfisher	5790	6	–
Lamont			
The First National Bank Of Lamont	7783	6	–
Lawton			
The First National Bank Of Lawton	5914	6	–
The Lawton National Bank	8375	6	–
Leger			
The Altus National Bank Of Leger	7159	6	–
The Altus National Bank, Altus	7159	6	–
The First National Bank Of Altus	6113	6	–
The First National Bank Of Leger	6113	6	–
Lexington			
The Farmers National Bank Of Lexington	7207	6	–
The First National Bank Of Lexington	5462	6	–
The Lexington National Bank	5462	6	–
Luther			
The National Bank Of Luther	8563	6	–
Mangum			
The City National Bank Of Mangum	7328	6	–
The First National Bank Of Mangum	5508	6	–
The Mangum National Bank	5811	6	–
Maud			
The First National Bank Of Maud	8294	6	–
Mcloud			
The First National Bank Of Mcloud	6660	6	–
Medford			
The First National Bank Of Medford	5796	6	–
Mountain View			
The First National Bank Of Mountain View	5656	6	–
Newkirk			
The Farmers National Bank Of Newkirk	8214	6	–
The First National Bank Of Newkirk	5272	6	–
Norman			
The City National Bank Of Norman	6450	6	–
The Cleveland County National Bank Of Norman	5612	6	–
The First National Bank Of Norman	5248	5	–
The National Bank Of Norman	7293	6	–
Okeene			
The First National Bank Of Okeene	5887	6	–
Oklahoma City			
The American National Bank Of Oklahoma City	5716	6	–
The Commercial National Bank Of Oklahoma City	6981	6	–
The First National Bank Of Oklahoma City	4402	6	–
The Oklahoma City National Bank	6678	6	–
The Oklahoma National Bank Of Oklahoma City	4770	6	–
The Security National Bank Of Oklahoma City	8472	6	–
The State National Bank Of Oklahoma City	4862	6	–
The Western National Bank Of Oklahoma City	5159	6	–
Olustee			
The Farmers National Bank Of Olustee	8754	6	–
The First National Bank Of Olustee	8316	6	–
Pawhuska			
The American National Bank Of Pawhuska	8313	6	–
Pawhuska			
The Citizens National Bank Of Pawhuska	7883	6	–
The First National Bank Of Pawhuska	5961	6	–
Pawnee			
The Arkansas Valley National Bank Of Pawnee	5492	6	–
The First National Bank Of Pawnee	5224	6	–
The Pawnee National Bank	7611	6	–
Perry			
The First National Bank Of Perry	6972	6	–
Ponca City			
The Farmers National Bank Of Ponca City	6061	6	–
The First National Bank Of Ponca City	5474	6	–
Pond Creek			
The First National Bank Of Pond Creek	6655	5	–
The National Bank Of Pond Creek	7103	6	–
Prague			
The First National Bank Of Prague	7177	6	–
The Prague National Bank	8159	6	–
Ralston			
The First National Bank Of Ralston	6232	6	–
Sayre			
The First National Bank Of Sayre	6058	6	–
Seiling			
The First National Bank Of Seiling	8615	6	–
Shattuck			
The First National Bank Of Shattuck	8687	6	–
Shawnee			
The First National Bank Of Shawnee	5095	6	–
The Oklahoma National Bank Of Shawnee	5875	6	–
The Shawnee National Bank	5115	6	–
The State National Bank Of Shawnee	6416	6	–
Stillwater			
The First National Bank Of Stillwater	5206	6	–
The National Bank Of Commerce Of Stillwater	5436	6	–
The Stillwater National Bank	5347	5	–
Stroud			
The First National Bank Of Stroud	6306	6	–
Taloga			
The First National Bank Of Taloga	7019	6	–
Tecumseh			
Farmers National Bank Of Tecumseh	7756	6	–
The First National Bank Of Tecumseh	5378	6	–
Temple			
The Farmers National Bank Of Temple	8310	6	–
The First National Bank Of Temple	6570	6	–
Texhoma			
The First National Bank Of Texhoma	8852	6	–
Thomas			
The First National Bank Of Thomas	7278	6	–
The Thomas National Bank	7771	6	–
Tonkawa			
The First National Bank Of Tonkawa	7444	6	–
The Tonkawa National Bank	8595	6	–
Verden			
The First National Bank Of Verden	8759	6	–
The National Bank Of Verden	8859	6	–
Wakita			
The First National Bank Of Wakita	5982	6	–
Walters			
The First National Bank Of Walters	6612	6	–
The Walters National Bank	7811	6	–
Wanette			
The First National Bank Of Wanette	6641	6	–
The State National Bank Of Wanette	8304	6	–
Watonga			
The First National Bank Of Watonga	5804	6	–
Waukomis			
The First National Bank Of Waukomis	7967	6	–
Waurika			
The Citizens National Bank Of Waurika	8715	6	–
The First National Bank Of Waurika	8744	6	–
The Waurika National Bank	8861	6	–
Weatherford			
The First National Bank Of Weatherford	5352	6	–
The German National Bank Of Weatherford	7238	6	–
The National Exchange Bank Of Weatherford	5758	6	–
Woodward			
The First National Bank Of Woodward	5575	6	–
Yukon			
The First National Bank Of Yukon	6159	6	–

OKLAHOMA

City, Bank	Ch. No.	L	S
Achille			
The Farmers And Merchants National Bank Of Achille	10380	6	6
The First National Bank Of Achille	10347	6	–
Ada			
The Ada National Bank	5633	6	–
The Citizens National Bank Of Ada	7071	6	–
The First National Bank In Ada	12591	–	4
The First National Bank Of Ada	5620	5	–
The Merchants And Planters National Bank Of Ada	10513	6	–
Addington			
The First National Bank Of Addington	10001	6	–
Afton			
The First National Bank Of Afton	10339	6	–
Alex			
The First National Bank Of Alex	10193	6	5
Allen			
The First National Bank Of Allen	9620	6	–
Altus			
Altus National Bank	12155	6	5
The City National Bank Of Altus	8775	6	–
The National Bank Of Commerce Of Altus	13756	–	5
Alva			
The Alva National Bank	6490	6	–
The First National Bank Of Alva	5587	5	6
Anadarko			
Anadarko National Bank, Anadarko	5923	6	–
The First National Bank Of Anadarko	5905	6	4

City, Bank	Ch. No.	L	S
Anadarko			
The National Bank Of Anadarko	5923	6	–
Antlers			
The Antlers National Bank	7667	6	–
The Citizens National Bank Of Antlers	8082	6	–
The First National Bank Of Antlers	7667	6	5
Apache			
The American National Bank Of Apache	12120	6	5
The First National Bank Of Apache	7127	5	5
Arapaho			
The First National Bank Of Arapaho	6257	6	–
Ardmore			
Exchange National Bank Of Ardmore	11093	5	4
First National Bank At Ardmore	13677	–	5
State National Bank Of Ardmore	10394	5	–
The Ardmore National Bank	5922	5	–
The Bankers National Bank Of Ardmore	8354	6	–
The City National Bank Of Ardmore	4723	6	–
The First National Bank In Ardmore	12472	–	5
The First National Bank Of Ardmore	4393	5	–
Atoka			
The American National Bank Of Atoka	8994	6	–
The Atoka National Bank	5791	6	–
Aylesworth			
The First National Bank Of Aylesworth	10385	6	–
Bartlesville			
First National Bank In Bartlesville	6258	6	4
The American National Bank Of Bartlesville	7032	6	–
The Bartlesville National Bank	6258	6	–
The First National Bank Of Bartlesville	5310	4	–
The Union National Bank Of Bartlesville	9567	5	3
Beggs			
The Farmers National Bank Of Beggs	10482	6	–
The First National Bank Of Beggs	6868	6	6
Bennington			
The Bennington National Bank	10343	6	–
The First National Bank Of Bennington	7099	5	6
Berwyn			
The First National Bank Of Berwyn	7209	6	6
Bixby			
The First National Bank Of Bixby	10467	6	–
Blackwell			
The Blackwell National Bank	6916	6	–
The First National Bank Of Blackwell	5460	4	5
The State National Bank Of Blackwell	7583	6	–
Blair			
First National Bank In Blair	12130	–	4
The First National Bank Of Blair	10368	6	–
Blanchard			
The First National Bank Of Blanchard	8702	6	5
Boise City			
The First National Bank Of Boise City	11084	6	–
Bokchito			
The Bokchito National Bank	7499	6	–
The First National Bank Of Bokchito	6683	6	–
The First National Bank Of Bokchito	9835	6	–
Boswell			
The Boswell National Bank	8353	6	–
The First National Bank Of Boswell	7651	6	–
The State National Bank Of Boswell	10363	6	–
Boynton			
The First National Bank Of Boynton	6511	6	5
Braggs			
The First National Bank Of Braggs	10437	4	–
Braman			
The First National Bank Of Braman	10003	6	5
Bristow			
The Bristow National Bank	10115	6	–
The First National Bank Of Bristow	6260	6	–
Broken Arrow			
The Arkansas Valley National Bank Of Broken Arrow	7600	6	–
The Citizens National Bank Of Broken Arrow	10255	6	–
The First National Bank Of Broken Arrow	7115	5	6
Broken Bow			
The First National Bank Of Broken Bow	10424	6	–
Buffalo			
The First National Bank Of Buffalo	8896	6	–
Byars			
The First National Bank Of Byars	7389	6	–
Caddo			
The Caddo National Bank	7368	6	–
The Security National Bank Of Caddo	10010	6	–
Calera			
The Calera National Bank	11182	5	–
Calvin			
The Calvin National Bank	10226	6	–
The First National Bank Of Calvin	6980	6	6
Canadian			
The First National Bank Of Canadian	9993	6	–
Carmen			
The Carmen National Bank	6844	6	–
The Carmen National Bank	10203	6	–
The First National Bank In Carmen	12498	6	5
Carnegie			
The First National Bank Of Carnegie	11763	6	6
Cashion			
The First National Bank Of Cashion	6161	6	–
Centralia			
The First National Bank Of Centralia	7706	6	–
Chandler			
The Chandler National Bank	6142	6	–
The First National Bank Of Chandler	5354	5	3
The Union National Bank Of Chandler	6269	5	4
Checotah			
The Commercial National Bank In Checotah	11920	6	–
The Commercial National Bank Of Checotah	10063	5	–
The First National Bank Of Checotah	5128	4	–
The Peoples National Bank Of Checotah	10051	5	5
Chelsea			
The First National Bank Of Chelsea	5955	6	6
Cherokee			
The Alfalfa County National Bank Of Cherokee	9008	6	–

City, Bank	Ch. No.	L	S
Cherokee			
The Farmers National Bank Of Cherokee	9884	5	–
The First National Bank Of Cherokee	6677	6	–
Chickasha			
Oklahoma National Bank Of Chickasha	9938	–	5
The Chickasha National Bank	8203	6	6
The Citizens National Bank Of Chickasha	5547	5	–
The Citizens-Farmers National Bank Of Chickasha	5547	–	5
The First National Bank Of Chickasha	5431	3	4
The Oklahoma National Bank Of Chickasha	9938	5	6
Claremore			
The First National Bank Of Claremore	4987	6	–
The National Bank Of Claremore	10117	5	5
Cleveland			
The Cleveland National Bank	7386	5	4
The First National Bank Of Cleveland	5911	4	4
Clinton			
The Clinton National Bank	6851	6	–
The First National Bank Of Clinton	6940	6	5
The Oklahoma State National Bank Of Clinton	9985	6	–
Coalgate			
The Coalgate National Bank	7321	6	–
The First National Bank Of Coalgate	5647	6	–
Colbert			
The First National Bank Of Colbert	10381	6	6
Collinsville			
The Collinsville National Bank	10280	6	–
The First National Bank Of Collinsville	6138	6	–
The First National Bank Of Collinsville	9965	6	–
Comanche			
The Comanche National Bank	8366	6	–
The First National Bank Of Comanche	6299	6	6
Commerce			
The First National Bank Of Commerce	10689	5	5
Cordell			
The Cordell National Bank	9971	6	–
The Farmers National Bank Of Cordell	9968	5	5
The First National Bank Of Cordell	6052	6	–
The State National Bank Of Cordell	9972	6	–
Coweta			
The First National Bank Of Coweta	6879	5	5
The National Bank Of Commerce Of Coweta	10031	6	–
Coyle			
The First National Bank Of Coyle	12148	5	5
Cushing			
The Farmers National Bank Of Cushing	8730	6	–
The Farmers National Bank Of Cushing	10332	6	6
The First National Bank Of Cushing	6893	5	3
Custer City			
The First National Bank Of Custer City	8727	5	5
The Peoples State National Bank Of Custer City	9981	6	–
Davenport			
The First National Bank Of Davenport	8668	6	–
Davidson			
The First National Bank Of Davidson	11654	6	–
Davis			
The First National Bank Of Davis	5298	6	5
The Merchants And Planters National Bank Of Davis	7442	6	–
Depew			
The State National Bank Of Depew	12104	–	5
Devol			
The First National Bank Of Devol	11535	6	–
Dewey			
The First National Bank Of Dewey	8270	5	5
The Security National Bank Of Dewey	9986	6	–
Duncan			
The City National Bank Of Duncan	8616	6	6
The Duncan National Bank	7289	6	–
The First National Bank Of Duncan	5379	6	–
The First National Bank Of Duncan	10244	6	–
The Security National Bank Of Duncan	12065	–	5
Durant			
The Durant National Bank	5590	4	–
The Durant National Bank In Durant	13018	–	4
The Farmers National Bank Of Durant	6928	6	–
The First National Bank In Durant	14005	–	6
The First National Bank Of Durant	5129	3	4
The State National Bank Of Durant	10538	6	–
Edmond			
The Citizens National Bank Of Edmond	10151	5	4
The First National Bank Of Edmond	6156	5	4
El Dorado			
The Farmers And Merchants National Bank Of El Dorado	8944	6	–
The First National Bank Of El Dorado	8126	6	–
The First National Bank Of El Dorado	9963	6	6
El Reno			
The Citizens National Bank Of El Reno	5985	4	1
The First National Bank Of El Reno	4830	4	4
Elk City			
The First National Bank Of Elk City	5766	6	–
The First National Bank Of Elk City	9952	5	5
Enid			
The Enid National Bank	10202	6	–
The First National Bank Of Enid	5335	6	–
The First National Bank Of Enid	9586	4	4
Erick			
First National Bank Of Erick	10875	6	5
Eufaula			
The Eufaula National Bank	5967	4	–
The First National Bank Of Eufaula	5902	4	–
The State National Bank Of Eufaula	10388	5	5
Fairfax			
The Fairfax National Bank	8202	5	–
The First National Bank Of Fairfax	7972	6	6
Fairview			
The Farmers And Merchants National Bank Of Fairview	9767	6	6
Foraker			
The First National Bank Of Foraker	10356	5	–

City, Bank	Ch. No.	L	S
Fort Gibson			
First National Bank In Fort Gibson	8079	–	5
The Citizens National Bank Of Fort Gibson	10561	5	–
The Farmers National Bank Of Fort Gibson	8079	6	–
The First National Bank Of Fort Gibson	6539	6	–
Fort Sill			
The City National Bank Of Lawton	5753	5	4
Fort Towson			
The First National Bank Of Fort Towson	8078	6	–
Francis			
The Francis National Bank	10454	6	–
Frederick			
First National Bank In Frederick	13760	–	5
The City National Bank Of Frederick	8206	6	–
The First National Bank Of Frederick	8140	5	5
The National Bank Of Commerce Of Frederick	10095	6	–
Geary			
The First National Bank Of Geary	6163	6	–
The First National Bank Of Geary	10020	6	5
Gotebo			
The First National Bank Of Gotebo	10389	5	–
Grandfield			
The First National Bank Of Grandfield	10006	6	–
Grove			
The First National Bank Of Grove	10119	6	–
Guthrie			
The First National Bank Of Guthrie	4348	3	4
The Guthrie National Bank	4348	5	–
The National Bank Of Commerce Of Guthrie	7299	6	–
Guymon			
The City National Bank Of Guymon	9964	6	6
The First National Bank Of Guymon	8138	5	5
Harrah			
The First National Bank Of Harrah	9980	6	6
Hartshorne			
The First National Bank Of Hartshorne	7050	4	–
The Hartshorne National Bank	11064	5	–
Haskell			
The First National Bank Of Haskell	7822	5	5
The Haskell National Bank	10160	6	–
Hastings			
First National Bank In Hastings	10094	6	–
The First National Bank Of Hastings	8209	6	–
The National Bank Of Hastings	8210	6	–
The National Bank Of Hastings	10094	6	–
Healdton			
The First National Bank Of Healdton	11018	6	–
Heavener			
The First National Bank Of Heavener	9888	6	6
The State National Bank Of Heavener	10239	6	6
Helena			
The Helena National Bank	12081	–	5
Hennessey			
The Farmers And Merchants National Bank Of Hennessey	10209	6	3
The First National Bank Of Hennessey	5473	5	4
Henryetta			
The First National Bank Of Henryetta	6867	5	–
The Miners National Bank Of Henryetta	10349	6	–
Hobart			
The City National Bank Of Hobart	6267	6	–
The City National Bank Of Hobart	10288	6	–
The Farmers And Merchants National Bank Of Hobart	6358	6	–
The First National Bank Of Hobart	5954	6	–
The Hobart National Bank	5915	6	–
Holdenville			
The American National Bank Of Holdenville	7619	6	–
The First National Bank Of Holdenville	5270	4	5
The State National Bank Of Holdenville	10013	6	–
Hollis			
First National Bank In Hollis	8825	5	–
The City National Bank Of Hollis	8825	6	–
The First National Bank Of Hollis	8061	6	–
The Groves National Bank Of Hollis	8825	6	–
The National Bank Of Commerce Of Hollis	10240	6	6
The State National Bank Of Hollis	10249	6	–
Hominy			
The First National Bank Of Hominy	7927	5	6
The National Bank Of Commerce Of Hominy	10002	6	5
Hugo			
The First National Bank Of Hugo	6130	6	–
The Hugo National Bank	7747	5	–
The National Bank Of Commerce At Hugo	12801	–	6
Hydro			
The Farmers National Bank Of Hydro	10442	6	–
The First National Bank Of Hydro	9944	6	5
Idabel			
The First National Bank Of Idabel	8486	6	–
The Idabel National Bank	11913	–	5
Kaw City			
First National Bank In Kaw City	10075	6	5
National Bank Of Kaw City	10402	5	5
The Farmers National Bank Of Kaw City	10075	6	–
Kenefic			
The First National Bank Of Kenefic	10104	6	–
Keota			
The First National Bank Of Keota	8177	6	–
The Keota National Bank	10298	6	–
Kingfisher			
The First National Bank Of Kingfisher	5328	5	5
The Peoples National Bank Of Kingfisher	9954	6	4
Kingston			
The First National Bank Of Kingston	9881	6	6
Kiowa			
The First National Bank Of Kiowa	8638	6	–
Konawa			
The First National Bank Of Konawa	7633	6	5
The Konawa National Bank	8213	6	–

City, Bank	Ch. No.	L	S
Lahoma			
The First National Bank Of Lahoma	9974	5	–
Lamont			
The First National Bank Of Lamont	7783	6	–
Lawton			
The American National Bank Of Lawton	12067	5	4
The First National Bank Of Lawton	5914	5	–
The Lawton National Bank	9962	6	–
Leger			
The First National Bank Of Altus	6113	6	6
Lehigh			
The Lehigh National Bank	5755	6	–
The Merchants National Bank Of Lehigh	8189	6	–
Lenapah			
The Lenapah National Bank	9951	6	–
Lexington			
The Farmers National Bank Of Lexington	7207	6	–
Lindsay			
The First National Bank Of Lindsay	6171	5	5
Lone Wolf			
The First National Bank Of Lone Wolf	10096	5	3
Luther			
The First National Bank Of Luther	8563	5	5
Madill			
The City National Bank Of Madill	7723	6	–
The First National Bank In Madill	13021	6	6
The Madill National Bank	6365	6	–
The Madill National Bank	10286	6	6
Mangum			
The City National Bank Of Mangum	7328	6	–
The First National Bank Of Mangum	5508	4	3
The Mangum National Bank	5811	5	6
Marietta			
The Farmers National Bank Of Marietta	8278	6	–
The First National Bank Of Marietta	5345	6	5
The Marietta National Bank	5958	5	6
Marlow			
The First National Bank In Marlow	12129	–	3
The First National Bank Of Marlow	5724	6	–
The National Bank Of Marlow	10205	6	6
The State National Bank Of Marlow	9946	5	5
Maud			
The First National Bank Of Maud	8294	6	6
Maysville			
The Farmers National Bank Of Maysville	10283	6	–
The First National Bank Of Maysville	8999	6	5
Mcalester			
The National Bank Of Mcalester	13770	–	4
Mcloud			
The First National Bank Of Mcloud	6660	6	6
Medford			
The First National Bank Of Medford	5796	5	5
Miami			
The First National Bank Of Miami	5252	3	3
The Ottawa County National Bank Of Miami	10019	4	–
Milburn			
The First National Bank Of Milburn	9920	5	–
Mill Creek			
The First National Bank Of Mill Creek	7197	5	5
The Merchants And Planters National Bank Of Mill Creek	8546	6	–
The Mill Creek National Bank	12188	6	–
Minco			
The First National Bank Of Minco	8644	6	6
Moore			
The First National Bank Of Moore	12035	6	5
Morris			
The First National Bank Of Morris	8876	6	–
The Morris National Bank	11932	6	–
Mounds			
The First National Bank Of Mounds	6263	5	–
Mountain View			
The First National Bank Of Mountain View	5656	5	5
Muldrow			
The First National Bank Of Muldrow	6717	6	–
The First National Bank Of Muldrow	9975	5	–
Mulhall			
The First National Bank Of Mulhall	9032	6	–
Muskogee			
The American National Bank Of Muskogee	9701	6	–
The Citizens National Bank Of Muskogee	12918	–	5
The Commercial National Bank In Muskogee	12890	5	3
The Commercial National Bank Of Muskogee	5236	3	–
The Exchange National Bank Of Muskogee	10321	4	–
The First National Bank And Trust Company Of Muskogee	4385	–	4
The First National Bank Of Muskogee	4385	3	–
The Muskogee National Bank	9023	4	–
The Muskogee-Security National Bank, Muskogee	12277	6	–
The Oklahoma National Bank Of Muskogee	10113	6	–
Nash			
The First National Bank Of Nash	11306	5	5
New Wilson			
The First National Bank Of New Wilson	10574	6	–
Newkirk			
The Eastman National Bank Of Newkirk	9011	5	5
The Farmers National Bank Of Newkirk	8214	6	–
The First National Bank Of Newkirk	5272	5	6
Noble			
The First National Bank Of Noble	9937	5	5
Norman			
The City National Bank In Norman	12157	–	6
The City National Bank Of Norman	6450	6	–
The Farmers National Bank Of Norman	7293	6	–
The First National Bank Of Norman	5248	5	4
The National Bank Of Norman	7293	6	–
The Security National Bank Of Norman	12036	–	5
Nowata			
The Commercial National Bank Of Nowata	9949	4	5
The First National Bank Of Nowata	5401	5	5
The Nowata National Bank	6367	6	–
The Producers National Bank Of Nowata	9948	6	–
Oakland			
The First National Bank Of Madill	5404	5	–
Okemah			
The First National Bank Of Okemah	6477	6	5
The Okemah National Bank	7677	4	4
Oklahoma City			
First National Bank In Oklahoma City	4862	3	–
The American National Bank Of Oklahoma City	5716	4	–
The Farmers National Bank Of Oklahoma City	9564	4	–
The First National Bank & Trust Company Of Oklahoma City	4862	–	1
The First National Bank Of Capitol Hill, Oklahoma City	9584	6	–
The Liberty National Bank Of Oklahoma City	11230	–	3
The Oklahoma City National Bank	6678	6	–
The Oklahoma Stock Yards National Bank Of Oklahoma City	9856	4	–
The Security National Bank Of Oklahoma City	8472	3	6
The State National Bank Of Oklahoma City	4862	4	–
The Western National Bank Of Oklahoma City	5159	5	–
Okmulgee			
The American National Bank Of Okmulgee	12048	6	–
The Citizens National Bank In Okmulgee	13751	–	6
The Citizens National Bank Of Okmulgee	6241	5	6
The Exchange National Bank Of Okmulgee	9947	6	–
The Farmers National Bank Of Okmulgee	9696	6	–
The First National Bank Of Okmulgee	5418	5	–
The Okmulgee National Bank	6855	6	–
Oktaha			
The First National Bank Of Oktaha	10015	6	–
Olustee			
The Farmers National Bank Of Olustee	8754	6	–
The First National Bank Of Olustee	8316	6	–
The First National Bank Of Olustee	9960	5	–
Owasso			
The First National Bank Of Owasso	7964	6	–
Pauls Valley			
The First National Bank Of Pauls Valley	5091	5	4
The National Bank Of Commerce Of Pauls Valley	6639	6	–
The Pauls Valley National Bank	7892	6	6
Pawhuska			
National Bank Of Commerce In Pawhuska	14304	–	6
The American National Bank Of Pawhuska	8313	6	6
The Citizens National Bank Of Pawhuska	7883	6	5
The Citizens-First National Bank Of Pawhuska	13527	–	4
The First National Bank Of Pawhuska	5961	4	6
The Liberty National Bank Of Pawhuska	11314	4	–
Pawnee			
The Arkansas Valley National Bank Of Pawnee	5492	6	–
The First National Bank Of Pawnee	5224	5	5
The Pawnee National Bank	7611	5	5
Perry			
First National Bank In Perry	14020	–	5
The First National Bank Of Perry	6972	5	5
Pocasset			
The First National Bank Of Pocasset	10960	5	6
Ponca City			
First National Bank In Ponca City	9801	5	5
The Farmers National Bank Of Ponca City	6061	6	–
The Farmers National Bank Of Ponca City	9801	6	–
The First National Bank At Ponca City	13891	–	5
The First National Bank Of Ponca City	5474	6	–
The Germania National Bank Of Ponca City	9616	6	–
Pond Creek			
Farmers National Bank Of Pond Creek	10005	6	–
First National Bank In Pond Creek	10005	6	6
The First National Bank Of Pond Creek	6655	6	–
The National Bank Of Pond Creek	7103	6	–
Porter			
The First National Bank Of Porter	7615	6	6
Porum			
The First National Bank Of Porum	8479	6	–
The National Bank Of Commerce Of Porum	10649	6	–
Poteau			
The First National Bank Of Poteau	7118	6	–
The National Bank Of Poteau	7104	6	–
Prague			
The First National Bank Of Prague	7177	5	5
The Prague National Bank	8159	5	5
Pryor Creek			
The American National Bank Of Pryor Creek	12117	–	5
The First National Bank Of Pryor Creek	5546	6	5
Purcell			
The Chickasaw National Bank Of Purcell	4756	5	–
The Mcclain County National Bank Of Purcell	12134	–	5
The Union National Bank Of Purcell	7697	6	–
Quinton			
The First National Bank Of Quinton	6517	6	6
Ralston			
The First National Bank Of Ralston	6232	5	6
Ringling			
The First National Bank Of Ringling	10548	4	5
Roff			
The Farmers And Merchants National Bank Of Roff	10172	6	–
The First National Bank Of Roff	5417	6	–
Rush Springs			
The First National Bank Of Rush Springs	8336	6	6
Ryan			
The First National Bank Of Ryan	5800	5	–
Sallsaw			
First National Bank In Sallisaw	7571	5	–
Sallisaw			
The Citizens National Bank Of Sallisaw	10474	5	–
The Farmers National Bank Of Sallisaw	9973	6	–
The First National Bank Of Sallisaw	5596	6	–
The Merchants National Bank Of Sallisaw	7571	6	–
Sand Springs			
The First National Bank Of Sand Springs	12079	5	–
Sapulpa			
The American National Bank Of Sapulpa	7788	5	5
The First National Bank Of Sapulpa	5951	5	–
Sasakwa			
The First National Bank Of Sasakwa	10314	6	–
Sayre			
The Beckham County National Bank Of Sayre	9976	6	6
The First National Bank Of Sayre	6058	6	–
The First National Bank Of Sayre	9959	5	6
Seiling			
The First National Bank Of Seiling	8615	6	6
Seminole			
The First National Bank Of Seminole	9514	6	5
Sentinel			
The First National Bank Of Sentinel	9995	5	–
Shattuck			
The First National Bank Of Shattuck	8687	6	–
The Shattuck National Bank	9987	6	6
Shawnee			
The Federal National Bank Of Shawnee	12339	6	5
The National Bank Of Commerce In Shawnee	12441	6	–
The National Bank Of Commerce Of Shawnee	9998	6	–
The Oklahoma National Bank Of Shawnee	5875	6	–
The Shawnee National Bank	5115	5	5
The State National Bank Of Shawnee	6416	4	5
Skiatook			
The First National Bank Of Skiatook	9969	6	–
The Oklahoma National Bank Of Skiatook	10464	6	–
Snyder			
The First National Bank Of Snyder	10317	6	–
The Kiowa National Bank Of Snyder	10311	6	–
Soper			
The First National Bank Of Soper	10366	6	–
South Mcalester			
The American National Bank Of Mcalester	6230	5	–
The City National Bank Of Mcalester	6406	5	–
The First National Bank Of Mcalester	5052	4	4
Spiro			
The First National Bank Of Spiro	9275	4	–
Spokogee			
The First National Bank Of Dustin	6804	6	–
Sterrett			
The First National Bank Of Sterrett	7950	5	–
Stigler			
The American National Bank Of Stigler	7432	6	–
The First National Bank Of Stigler	7217	5	6
Stillwater			
First National Bank Of Stillwater	5206	–	4
The First National Bank Of Stillwater	5206	6	–
The National Bank Of Commerce Of Stillwater	5436	6	–
The Stillwater National Bank	5347	6	6
Stilwell			
The First National Bank Of Stilwell	9970	5	6
Stonewall			
The First National Bank Of Stonewall	7054	5	–
Stratford			
The First National Bank Of Stratford	8524	4	5
Stroud			
The First National Bank Of Stroud	6306	6	6
Stuart			
The First National Bank Of Stuart	10007	6	–
The Liberty National Bank Of Stuart	11315	6	–
Sulphur			
Park National Bank Of Sulphur	9046	5	6
The First National Bank Of Sulphur	5748	6	–
Tahlequah			
The Central National Bank Of Tahlequah	10468	6	–
The First National Bank Of Tahlequah	5478	5	4
The Guaranty National Bank Of Tahlequah	11485	6	–
The Liberty National Bank Of Tahlequah	12089	5	–
Talihina			
The First National Bank Of Talihina	7780	6	–
Taloga			
The First National Bank Of Taloga	7019	5	–
Tecumseh			
Farmers National Bank Of Tecumseh	7756	6	–
The First National Bank Of Tecumseh	5378	6	–
The Tecumseh National Bank	10304	5	5
Temple			
The First National Bank Of Temple	6570	6	–
The Temple National Bank	9967	6	–
Terlton			
The First National Bank Of Terlton	9991	6	–
Terral			
The First National Bank Of Terral	7996	6	–
Texhoma			
The First National Bank Of Texhoma	8852	6	6
Thomas			
The First National Bank Of Thomas	7278	5	6
Tipton			
The First National Bank Of Tipton	11052	6	–

City, Bank	Ch. No.	L	S
Tishomingo			
The American National Bank Of Tishomingo	7042	6	–
The Farmers National Bank Of Tishomingo	10431	5	–
The First National Bank Of Tishomingo	5809	5	–
The Tishomingo National Bank	10012	6	–
Tonkawa			
The First National Bank In Tonkawa	11397	–	6
The First National Bank Of Tonkawa	7444	6	–
The Tonkawa National Bank	8595	5	–
Tulsa			
National Bank Of Tulsa	13679	–	4
The American National Bank Of Tulsa	10342	5	–
The Central National Bank And Trust Company Of Tulsa	8552	6	–
The Central National Bank Of Tulsa	8552	4	–
The Exchange National Bank Of Tulsa	9658	3	2
The Farmers National Bank Of Tulsa	6669	6	–
The First National Bank & Trust Company Of Tulsa	5171	–	3
The First National Bank Of Tulsa	5171	4	–
The Liberty National Bank Of Tulsa	10262	6	–
The National Bank Of Commerce Of Tulsa	9942	5	6
The Oklahoma National Bank Of Tulsa	9943	6	–
The Producers National Bank Of Tulsa	12042	4	5
The Security National Bank Of Tulsa	12043	6	–
The Union National Bank Of Tulsa	10906	5	–
Tupelo			
The Farmers National Bank Of Tupelo	10531	6	–
The First National Bank Of Tupelo	8609	6	–
Tuttle			
The First National Bank Of Tuttle	8475	6	–
Tyrone			
The First National Bank Of Tyrone	10032	6	5
Valliant			
The First National Bank Of Valliant	9992	6	–
Verden			
The First National Bank Of Verden	8759	6	–
The National Bank Of Verden	8859	6	6
Vian			
The First National Bank Of Vian	10573	5	6
Vinita			
The Cherokee National Bank Of Vinita	5860	6	–
The Farmers National Bank Of Vinita	6602	6	–
The First National Bank Of Vinita	4704	4	4
The Vinita National Bank	5083	5	–
Wagoner			
The City National Bank Of Wagoner	7628	6	–
The First National Bank Of Wagoner	5016	5	5
The Wagoner National Bank	6048	6	–
Wakita			
The First National Bank Of Wakita	5982	6	–
Walters			
The First National Bank Of Walters	6612	6	–
The Walters National Bank	7811	6	6
Walters National Bank	14108	–	6
Wanette			
The First National Bank Of Wanette	6641	6	6
The State National Bank Of Wanette	8304	6	–
Wapanucka			
The First National Bank Of Wapanucka	5950	6	–
The Peoples National Bank Of Wapanucka	8137	6	–
Warner			
The First National Bank Of Warner	8809	6	–
Washington			
The First National Bank Of Washington	10277	6	5
Watonga			
The First National Bank Of Watonga	5804	6	–
Waukomis			
The Waukomis National Bank	10227	5	5
Waurika			
The First National Bank Of Waurika	8744	6	5
The Waurika National Bank	8861	6	6
Waynoka			
The First National Bank Of Waynoka	9709	6	6
Weatherford			
The First National Bank Of Weatherford	5352	5	–
The German National Bank Of Weatherford	7238	6	–
The Liberty National Bank Of Weatherford	7238	6	5
Webbers Falls			
The First National Bank Of Webbers Falls	8024	6	–
Weleetka			
The First National Bank Of Weleetka	6324	6	–
Wellston			
The First National Bank Of Wellston	9983	6	–
The Wellston National Bank	12078	–	6
Westville			
The First National Bank Of Westville	10158	5	6
Wetumka			
The American National Bank Of Wetumka	7724	6	6
Wetumpka			
The First National Bank Of Wetumpka	5935	6	–
Wewoka			
The Farmers National Bank Of Wewoka	8052	6	6
The First National Bank Of Wewoka	6254	6	–
Wilburton			
The First National Bank Of Wilburton	6890	6	–
The Latimer County National Bank Of Wilburton	10170	6	–
Woodville			
The First National Bank Of Woodville	7707	6	–
Woodward			
The First National Bank Of Woodward	5575	5	6
Wynnewood			
The First National Bank Of Wynnewood	5126	4	5
The Southern National Bank Of Wynnewood	5731	5	6
Yale			
The First National Bank Of Yale	10014	6	6
Yukon			
The First National Bank Of Yukon	6159	6	5
The Yukon National Bank	10196	5	5

OREGON

City, Bank	Ch. No.	L	S
Albany			
The First National Bank Of Albany	2928	4	5
The Linn County National Bank Of Albany	4326	6	–
Arlington			
The Arlington National Bank	3918	6	–
The First National Bank Of Arlington	3676	6	–
Ashland			
The First National Bank Of Ashland	5747	5	4
The United States National Bank Of Ashland	9431	6	–
Astoria			
The Astoria National Bank	4403	5	–
The First National Bank Of Astoria	3486	6	6
The National Bank Of Commerce Of Astoria	13354	–	5
Athena			
The First National Bank Of Athena	4516	6	6
Baker City			
The Baker City National Bank, Baker City	4206	6	–
The Citizens National Bank Of Baker City	6768	4	6
The First National Bank Of Baker	2865	6	4
The First National Bank Of Baker City	2865	6	–
Bandon			
The First National Bank Of Bandon	9718	6	–
Bend			
The First National Bank Of Bend	9363	6	–
The Lumbermens National Bank Of Bend	13093	–	2
Burns			
The First National Bank Of Burns	6295	4	6
The Harney County National Bank Of Burns	8691	5	6
Canby			
First National Bank In Aurora	10619	–	6
The First National Bank Of Canby	10619	6	6
Canyon City			
The First National Bank Of Grant County At Canyon City	6491	6	–
Clatskanie			
First National Bank In Clatskanie	14001	–	6
Condon			
The Condon National Bank	8261	6	–
The First National Bank Of Condon	7059	6	3
Coquille			
The First National Bank Of Coquille	6849	6	6
Corvallis			
First National Bank Of Corvallis	4301	–	5
The Benton County National Bank Of Corvallis	8750	6	–
The First National Bank Of Corvallis	4301	5	–
Cottage Grove			
The First National Bank Of Cottage Grove	5642	6	6
Dallas			
The Dallas National Bank	7472	6	3
The First National Bank Of Dallas	7072	6	–
East Portland			
The First National Bank Of East Portland	3025	6	–
Elgin			
The First National Bank Of Elgin	6644	6	6
Enterprise			
The Wallowa National Bank Of Enterprise	3912	6	6
Eugene			
The United States National Bank Of Eugene	10345	6	5
Eugene City			
The Eugene National Bank Of Eugene City	3986	6	–
The First National Bank Of Eugene	3458	5	5
The First National Bank Of Eugene City	3458	6	–
Forest Grove			
The First National Bank Of Forest Grove	8036	5	4
The Forest Grove National Bank	8554	6	6
Gardiner			
The First National Bank Of Gardiner	10676	6	6
Grants Pass			
The First National Bank Of Southern Oregon At Grants Pass	4168	6	5
Harrisburg			
The First National Bank Of Harrisburg	9146	6	6
Heppner			
The First National Bank Of Heppner	3774	6	6
The National Bank Of Heppner	3953	6	–
Hermiston			
The First National Bank Of Hermiston	9281	6	6
Hillsboro			
The American National Bank Of Hillsboro	9923	6	–
The Commercial National Bank Of Hillsboro	9917	–	5
The First National Bank Of Hillsboro	3966	6	–
The Hillsboro National Bank	9917	6	–
Hood River			
The First National Bank Of Hood River	7272	6	4
Independence			
First National Bank Of Independence	3979	6	6
The First National Bank Of Independence	3972	6	–
The Independence National Bank	3979	6	–
Island City			
The First National Bank Of Island City	3313	6	–
Joseph			
The First National Bank Of Joseph	8048	6	–
Junction City			
The First National Bank Of Junction City	10218	5	6
Klamath Falls			
The American National Bank Of Klamath Falls	11801	6	5
The First National Bank Of Klamath Falls	7167	6	4
La Grande			
The Farmers And Traders National Bank	4452	6	–
The First National Bank Of La Grande	13602	–	3
The La Grande National Bank	3655	4	5
The United States National Bank Of La Grande	9314	5	5
Lakeview			
The Commercial National Bank Of Lakeview	11121	6	6
The First National Bank Of Lakeview	7244	5	6
Lebanon			
The First National Bank Of Lebanon	9127	6	6
The Lebanon National Bank	10164	6	6
Linnton			
The First National Bank Of Linnton	10534	6	–
Marshfield			
The First National Bank Of Coos Bay At Marshfield	7475	5	6
Mcminnville			
The First National Bank Of Mcminnville	3399	5	6
The Mcminnville National Bank	3857	6	–
The United States National Bank Of Mcminnville	9806	6	–
United States National Bank Of Mcminnville	3857	–	5
Medford			
Medford National Bank	13771	–	6
The First National Bank Of Medford	7701	4	4
The Medford National Bank	8236	5	6
Merrill			
The First National Bank Of Merrill	10056	6	6
Milton			
The First National Bank Of Milton	9201	6	–
Molalla			
The First National Bank Of Molalla	11271	–	6
Monmouth			
The First National Bank Of Monmouth	10071	6	6
Newberg			
The First National Bank Of Newberg	7537	6	6
United States National Bank Of Newburg	9358	6	4
North Bend			
The First National Bank Of North Bend	9328	6	6
Ontario			
Ontario National Bank	9348	–	4
The First National Bank Of Ontario	5822	6	6
The Ontario National Bank	9348	5	–
Oregon City			
The First National Bank Of Oregon City	8556	6	6
Paisley			
The Paisley National Bank	10432	6	6
Pendleton			
The American National Bank Of Pendleton	9228	5	–
The Commercial National Bank Of Pendleton	7301	6	–
The First Inland National Bank Of Pendleton	13576	–	4
The First National Bank Of Pendleton	2630	4	6
The National Bank Of Pendleton	4249	6	–
The Pendleton National Bank	3665	6	–
Portland			
Brotherhood Co-Operative National Bank Of Portland	12613	4	–
Brotherhood National Bank Of Portland	12613	–	6
Columbia National Bank Of Portland	12613	–	6
Lumbermens National Bank Of Portland	9180	5	–
The Ainsworth National Bank Of Portland	3402	6	–
The American National Bank Of Portland	12557	–	4
The Central National Bank Of Portland	13294	–	6
The Citizens National Bank Of Portland	13299	–	3
The Commercial National Bank Of Portland	3422	6	–
The First National Bank Of Portland	1553	3	1
The Merchants National Bank Of Portland	3536	6	–
The Northwestern National Bank Of Portland	10300	6	–
The Oregon National Bank Of Portland	3719	6	–
The Portland National Bank	3184	6	–
The United States National Bank Of Portland	4514	1	1
Prairie City			
The First National Bank Of Prairie City	9763	6	4
Prineville			
The First National Bank Of Prineville	3851	6	–
Redmond			
The First National Bank Of Redmond	11294	6	–
The Redmond National Bank	11302	6	–
Roseburg			
The Douglas National Bank Of Roseburg	9423	5	6
The First National Bank Of Roseburg	4624	6	–
The Roseburg National Bank	8955	6	–
Saint Helens			
The First National Bank Of St. Helens	11200	6	6
Saint Johns			
Peninsula National Bank Of Portland	10103	6	5
The First National Bank Of Saint Johns	9047	6	–
The Peninsula National Bank Of Saint Johns	10103	6	–
Salem			
First National Bank In Salem	3405	6	5
The Capital National Bank Of Salem	3405	5	–
The First National Bank Of Salem	2816	6	–
The United States National Bank Of Salem	9021	6	5
Scappoose			
The First National Bank Of Scappoose	10992	6	6
Sheridan			
The First National Bank Of Sheridan	8721	6	6
Silverton			
The First National Bank Of Silverton	11106	6	6
Springfield			
The First National Bank Of Springfield	8941	6	6

City, Bank	Ch. No.	L	S
Sumpter			
The First National Bank Of Sumpter	6547	6	–
The Dalles			
The Dalles National Bank, The Dalles	3534	6	–
The First National Bank Of The Dalles	3441	5	6
Tillamook			
The First National Bank Of Tillamook	8574	6	5
Union			
The First National Bank Of Union	2947	5	6
The Union National Bank	8387	6	–
Vale			
The First National Bank Of Vale	8528	6	–
The United States National Bank Of Vale	9496	5	–
Wallowa			
The Stockgrowers And Farmers National Bank Of Wallowa	9002	6	3
Wheeler			
The First National Bank Of Wheeler	12427	6	–

PENNSYLVANIA

City, Bank	Ch. No.	L	S
Adamsburg			
The First National Bank Of Beaver Springs At Adamsburg	5777	6	–
Addison			
The First National Bank Of Addison	6709	6	6
Akron			
The Akron National Bank	9364	6	6
Albion			
First National Bank At Albion	13871	–	6
The First National Bank Of Albion	9534	6	6
Alexandria			
The First National Bank Of Alexandria	11263	6	5
Aliquippa			
The Aliquippa National Bank	9902	6	–
Aliquippq			
The First National Bank Of Aliquippa	8590	6	6
Allegheny			
The Enterprise National Bank Of Allegheny	4991	6	–
The First National Bank Of Allegheny	198	5	–
The First National Bank Of Allegheny At Pittsburgh	198	6	–
The German National Bank Of Allegheny	2261	4	–
The National Bank Of America At Pittsburgh	2261	5	5
The Second National Bank Of Allegheny	776	5	–
The Second National Bank Of Allegheny, Pittsburgh	776	6	5
The Second National Bank Of Pittsburgh	776	–	6
The Third National Bank Of Allegheny	2235	6	–
Allentown			
The Allentown National Bank	1322	3	2
The First National Bank Of Allentown	161	5	–
The Merchants National Bank Of Allentown	6645	6	–
The Merchants National Bank Of Allentown	6645	–	6
The Merchants-Citizens Natl Bank & Trust Co Of Allentown	6645	6	6
The Second National Bank Of Allentown	373	5	5
Allenwood			
The Allenwood National Bank	11593	6	6
Altoona			
The First National Bank Of Altoona	247	6	4
The Second National Bank Of Altoona	2781	6	6
Ambler			
The First National Bank Of Ambler	3220	6	6
Ambridge			
The Ambridge National Bank	10839	6	6
The Economy National Bank Of Ambridge	13087	6	6
The First National Bank Of Ambridge	8459	6	
Annville			
The Annville National Bank	2384	6	5
Apollo			
The First National Bank Of Apollo	5723	6	6
Ardmore			
The Ardmore National Bank	9905	6	–
The Ardmore National Bank And Trust Company, Ardmore	9905	6	–
Arendtsville			
The National Bank Of Arendtsville	9139	6	6
Arnold			
The Arnold National Bank	11896	6	–
The National Deposit Bank Of Arnold	11896	6	6
Ashland			
The Ashland National Bank	5615	4	5
The Citizens National Bank Of Ashland	2280	5	5
The First National Bank Of Ashland	403	6	–
Ashley			
The First National Bank Of Ashley	8656	6	5
Aspinwall			
The First National Bank Of Aspinwall	8824	6	–
Atglen			
The Atglen National Bank	7056	6	5
Athens			
The Athens National Bank	5202	6	5
The Farmers National Bank Of Athens	4915	6	6
The First National Bank Of Athens	1094	6	–
Auburn			
The First National Bank Of Auburn	9240	6	–
Austin			
The First National Bank Of Austin	12562	6	6
Avella			
The Lincoln National Bank Of Avella	7854	6	6
Avoca			
The First National Bank Of Avoca	8494	5	5
Avondale			
The National Bank Of Avondale	4560	6	5
Avonmore			
The First National Bank Of Avonmore	7594	6	5
Bainbridge			
The First National Bank Of Bainbridge	9264	6	–
Bakerton			
The First National Bank Of Bakerton	11757	5	5
Bally			
The First National Bank Of Bally	9402	6	5
Bangor			
First National Bank In Bangor	14170	–	5
The First National Bank Of Bangor	2659	4	5
The Merchants National Bank Of Bangor	4513	5	5
Barnesboro			
The First National Bank Of Barnesboro	5818	6	5
Bath			
The First National Bank Of Bath	5444	6	5
Beaver			
The Beaver National Bank	5042	6	–
The First National Bank Of Beaver	3850	6	–
The Fort Mcintosh National Bank Of Beaver	8185	6	5
Beaver Falls			
First National Bank At Beaver Falls	14117	–	6
The Farmers National Bank Of Beaver Falls	4894	5	5
The First National Bank Of Beaver Falls	3356	5	5
Beaver Springs			
The First National Bank Of Beaver Springs	5777	6	6
Beaverdale			
The First National Bank Of Beaverdale	11317	6	6
Bedford			
First National Bank And Trust Company Of Bedford	3089	–	6
The First National Bank Of Bedford	3089	6	6
Beech Creek			
The Beech Creek National Bank	13205	6	6
Belle Vernon			
The First National Bank Of Belle Vernon	4850	4	5
Bellefonte			
The First National Bank Of Bellefonte	459	6	6
Belleville			
The Belleville National Bank	5306	6	5
The Farmers National Bank Of Belleville	10128	6	6
The Kishacoquillas Valley National Bank Of Belleville	10128	–	6
Bellevue			
The Bellevue National Bank	5509	6	–
The Citizens National Bank Of Bellevue	8761	6	–
Bellwood			
The First National Bank Of Bellwood	7356	6	6
Bendersville			
The Bendersville National Bank	9114	6	5
Benson			
The First National Bank Of Benson	7935	6	–
Bentleyville			
The Bentleyville National Bank	8196	6	–
The Citizens National Bank Of Bentleyville	13663	–	6
The Farmers And Miners National Bank Of Bentleyville	9058	6	6
The First National Bank Of Bentleyville	8196	6	–
Benton			
The Columbia County National Bank Of Benton	6328	6	6
Berlin			
The First National Bank Of Berlin	5823	6	6
The Philson National Bank Of Berlin	6512	6	5
Bernville			
The First National Bank Of Bernville	8913	6	6
Berwick			
The Berwick National Bank	6162	6	5
The First National Bank Of Berwick	568	6	6
Berwyn			
Berwyn National Bank	13999	–	6
The Berwyn National Bank	3945	6	6
Bethlehem			
The First National Bank And Trust Company Of Bethlehem	138	–	4
The First National Bank Of Bethlehem	138	5	5
The Lehigh Valley National Bank Of Bethlehem	2050	4	4
Big Run			
The Citizens National Bank Of Big Run	5667	6	6
Biglerville			
The Biglerville National Bank	7917	6	5
Birdsboro			
The First National Bank Of Birdsboro	3905	6	6
Black Lick			
The First National Bank Of Black Lick	8428	6	–
Blairsville			
Blairsville National Bank	13868	–	6
The Blairsville National Bank	4919	6	5
The First National Bank Of Blairsville	867	6	–
Bloomsburg			
The Bloomsburg National Bank	5211	5	–
The Farmers National Bank Of Bloomsburg	4543	6	6
The First National Bank Of Bloomsburg	293	6	5
Blossburg			
The Citizens National Bank And Trust Company Of Blossburg	13381	–	5
The Miners National Bank Of Blossburg	5007	6	–
Blue Ball			
The Blue Ball National Bank	8421	6	5
Blue Ridge Summit			
The First National Bank Of Blue Ridge Summit	12281	6	6
Bolivar			
The Bolivar National Bank	6135	6	6
The Citizens National Bank Of Bolivar	12355	6	6
Boswell			
The First National Bank Of Boswell	6603	6	6
Boyertown			
The Farmers National Bank And Trust Company Of Boyertown	2900	6	5
The Farmers National Bank Of Boyertown	2900	6	–
The National Bank And Trust Company Of Boyertown	2137	–	5
The National Bank Of Boyertown	2137	5	6
Braddock			
First National Bank Of Braddock	13866	–	5
Braddock			
The Braddock National Bank	2828	4	4
The First National Bank Of Braddock	2799	6	–
The Union National Bank Of Braddock	6796	6	–
Bradford			
The Bradford National Bank	2428	4	4
The Commercial National Bank Of Bradford	4199	6	5
The First National Bank Of Bradford	2470	6	–
Bridgeport			
The Bridgeport National Bank	8329	6	5
Bridgeville			
The First National Bank Of Bridgeville	6636	6	6
Bristol			
The Farmers National Bank Of Bucks County, Bristol	717	6	6
Brockwayville			
The First National Bank Of Brockway	5497	–	6
The First National Bank Of Brockwayville	5497	6	–
Brookville			
The First National Bank Of Brookville	897	6	–
The Jefferson County National Bank Of Brookville	2392	4	6
The National Bank Of Brookville	3051	6	6
Brownstown			
The Brownstown National Bank	9026	6	6
Brownsville			
The First National Bank Of Brownsville	135	6	–
The Monongahela National Bank Of Brownsville	648	5	6
The National Deposit Bank Of Brownsville	2457	6	6
The Second National Bank Of Brownsville	2673	6	6
Bruin			
The First National Bank Of Bruin	8919	6	6
Bryn Mawr			
The Bryn Mawr National Bank	3766	6	5
Burgettstown			
The Burgettstown National Bank	2408	6	–
The Washington National Bank Of Burgettstown	6944	6	6
Burnham			
The First National Bank Of Burnham	11257	6	6
Burnside			
The Burnside National Bank	11902	6	6
Butler			
The Butler County National Bank & Trust Co Of Butler	4374	–	6
The Butler County National Bank Of Butler	4374	4	5
The Farmers National Bank Of Butler	5391	6	–
The First National Bank Of Butler	309	6	–
The Merchants National Bank Of Butler	9814	6	–
Cairnbrook			
The First National Bank Of Cairnbrook	10704	6	6
California			
The First National Bank Of California	4622	5	6
Cambridge Springs			
The First National Bank Of Cambridge Springs	6533	6	–
The Springs National Bank Of Cambridge Springs	9430	6	–
The Springs-First National Bank Of Cambridge Springs	9430	6	5
Camp Hill			
The Camp Hill National Bank	12380	5	4
Canonsburg			
The First National Bank At Canonsburg	13813	–	3
The First National Bank Of Canonsburg	4570	6	6
Canton			
The Farmers National Bank Of Canton	9317	6	6
The First National Bank Of Canton	2505	5	5
Carbondale			
The First National Bank Of Carbondale	664	6	6
Carlisle			
The First National Bank Of Carlisle	21	6	–
The Merchants National Bank Of Carlisle	4444	6	–
Carmichaels			
The First National Bank Of Carmichaels	5784	6	6
Carnegie			
The Carnegie National Bank	6174	6	6
The Union National Bank Of Carnegie	12934	6	6
Carrolltown			
The First National Bank Of Carrolltown	5855	6	6
Cassandra			
The First National Bank Of Cassandra	12720	6	6
Castle Shannon			
The First National Bank Of Castle Shannon	9128	6	6
Catasauqua			
The Lehigh National Bank Of Catasauqua	8283	6	5
The National Bank Of Catasauqua	1411	5	5
Catawissa			
The Catawissa National Bank	7448	6	5
The First National Bank Of Catawissa	4548	5	6
Cecil			
First National Bank In Cecil	14094	–	6
The First National Bank Of Cecil	7076	6	4
Center Hall			
The First National Bank Of Center Hall	12192	6	6
Central City			
The Central City National Bank	11967	6	6
Centralia			
The First National Bank Of Centralia	9568	6	6
Chalfont			
The Chalfont National Bank	12582	–	6
Chambersburg			
The National Bank Of Chambersburg	593	5	4
The Valley National Bank Of Chambersburg	4272	5	4
Charleroi			
First National Bank In Charleroi	14123	–	6

City, Bank	Ch. No.	L	S
Charleroi			
The First National Bank Of Charleroi	4534	6	6
The National Bank Of Charleroi And Trust Company	13585	–	3
Chartiers			
The First National Bank Of Carnegie	4762	6	–
The First National Bank Of Chartiers	4762	6	–
Cheltenham			
The Cheltenham National Bank	12526	6	5
Cherry Tree			
The First National Bank Of Cherry Tree	7000	6	3
Chester			
The Chester National Bank	2904	4	5
The Delaware County National Bank Of Chester	355	4	3
The First National Bank Of Chester	332	4	3
The Pennsylvania National Bank Of Chester	6654	4	–
Christiana			
The Christiana National Bank	7078	6	5
The National Bank Of Christiana	2849	6	–
Clairton			
The Clairton National Bank	6495	6	–
Clarion			
The First National Bank Of Clarion	774	5	6
The Second National Bank Of Clarion	3044	6	–
Clarks Summit			
The Abington National Bank Of Clarks Summit	10383	6	6
Claysburg			
The First National Bank Of Claysburg	10232	6	6
Claysville			
The Farmers National Bank Of Claysville	9307	6	6
The First National Bank Of Claysville	4273	6	–
The National Bank Of Claysville	4255	6	6
Clearfield			
The Clearfield National Bank	4836	6	5
The County National Bank At Clearfield	13998	–	3
The County National Bank Of Clearfield	855	4	3
The Farmers And Traders National Bank Of Clearfield	8464	6	–
The First National Bank Of Clearfield	768	4	–
Clifton			
The First National Bank Of Clifton Heights	6275	6	6
Clifton Heights			
Clifton Heights National Bank	14122	–	6
Clintonville			
The First National Bank Of Clintonville	6948	6	–
The Peoples National Bank Of Clintonville	9154	6	6
Clymer			
The Clymer National Bank	9898	6	6
Coaldale			
Farmers National Bank And Trust Company Of Bedford	11188	6	5
The Broad Top National Bank Of Coaldale	11188	6	–
The Farmers National Bank Of Bedford	11188	6	–
The First National Bank Of Coaldale	9739	6	6
Coalport			
The First National Bank Of Coalport	6887	5	6
Coatesville			
The National Bank Of Chester Valley, Coatesville	575	5	–
The National Bank Of Coatesville	3990	6	6
Cochranton			
The First National Bank Of Cochranton	4971	5	5
Collegeville			
The Collegeville National Bank	8404	6	5
Columbia			
The Central National Bank Of Columbia	3873	5	4
The Columbia National Bank	641	6	–
The First National Bank Of Columbia	371	5	–
The First-Columbia National Bank	371	5	4
Confluence			
The First National Bank Of Confluence	5307	4	6
Conneaut Lake			
First National Bank At Conneaut Lake	13980	–	6
The First National Bank Of Conneaut Lake	6891	6	6
Conneautville			
First National Bank In Conneautville	12189	6	6
The Farmers National Bank Of Conneautville	13942	–	5
The First National Bank Of Conneautville	143	6	–
Connellsville			
The Citizens National Bank Of Connellsville	6452	6	6
The Colonial National Bank Of Connellsville	7445	5	–
The First National Bank Of Connellsville	2329	6	–
The National Bank And Trust Company Of Connellsville	13491	–	6
The Second National Bank Of Connellsville	4481	6	6
The Yough National Bank Of Connellsville	4861	6	–
Conshohocken			
The First National Bank Of Conshohocken	2078	5	5
The Tradesmen's National Bank Of Conshohocken	2671	6	–
Conyngham			
The Conyngham National Bank	13392	–	6
Coopersburg			
The First National Bank Of Coopersburg	9034	6	6
Coplay			
The Coplay National Bank	9113	5	4
Coraopolis			
The Coraopolis National Bank	5069	6	6
Corry			
The Citizens National Bank Of Corry	4479	5	5
Corry			
The Corry National Bank	569	6	–
The First National Bank Of Corry	605	6	–
The National Bank Of Corry	4823	6	6
Coudersport			
The First National Bank Of Coudersport	4948	6	6
Crafton			
The First National Bank Of Crafton	6010	6	6
Cresson			
The First National Bank Of Cresson	5768	6	6
Cressona			
The First National Bank Of Cressona	9318	6	5
Curwensville			
The Citizens National Bank Of Curwensville	6969	6	–
The Curwensville National Bank	7430	6	6
The First National Bank Of Curwensville	300	6	–
Dale			
The Dale National Bank	12967	6	6
Dallas			
The First National Bank Of Dallas	8164	6	6
Dallastown			
The First National Bank And Trust Company Of Dallastown	6648	–	5
The First National Bank Of Dallastown	6648	6	6
Danielsville			
The Danielsville National Bank	7931	6	6
Danville			
The Danville National Bank	1078	4	5
The First National Bank Of Danville	325	5	5
Darby			
The First National Bank Of Darby	4428	4	4
Dauphin			
The Dauphin National Bank	11512	6	6
Davidsville			
The First National Bank Of Davidsville	11407	6	6
Dawson			
The First National Bank Of Dawson	4673	5	5
Dayton			
The First National Bank Of Dayton	5742	6	6
Delmont			
The Peoples National Bank Of Delmont	9996	6	6
Delta			
The Delta National Bank	14201	–	6
The First National Bank Of Delta	4205	5	6
The Miles National Bank Of Delta	4367	6	–
The Peoples National Bank Of Delta	5198	6	5
Denver			
The Denver National Bank	6037	6	2
Derry			
First National Bank In Derry	12912	–	6
The First National Bank At Derry	13794	–	6
The First National Bank Of Derry	6756	6	–
Dickson City			
The Dickson City National Bank	9851	6	6
The Liberty National Bank Of Dickson City	12459	6	6
Dillsburg			
The Dillsburg National Bank	2397	6	5
Donora			
The First National Bank Of Donora	5835	6	6
The Union National Bank Of Donora	13644	–	3
Dover			
Dover National Bank	14049	–	6
The Dover National Bank	9362	6	6
Downington			
The First National Bank Of Downington	338	6	–
Downingtown			
The Downingtown National Bank	661	6	5
The Grange National Bank Of Chester County At Downingtown	8646	6	6
Doylestown			
The Doylestown National Bank	573	5	–
The Doylestown National Bank & Trust Company, Doylestown	573	6	5
Dry Run			
The Citizens National Bank Of Dry Run	10811	–	6
The Path Valley National Bank Of Dry Run	10811	–	6
Dublin			
The Dublin National Bank	13133	–	6
Dubois			
The Deposit National Bank Of Dubois	5019	5	3
The Dubois National Bank	7453	5	3
Dubois City			
The First National Bank Of Dubois City	2969	6	–
Dunbar			
The First National Bank Of Dunbar	7576	6	–
Duncannon			
The Duncannon National Bank	4142	5	4
The Peoples National Bank Of Duncannon	8778	6	6
Dunmore			
The First National Bank Of Dunmore	9868	6	5
Duquesne			
The First National Bank Of Duquesne	4730	6	5
Dushore			
The First National Bank Of Dushore	4505	6	6
East Berlin			
East Berlin National Bank	14091	–	6
The East Berlin National Bank	6878	6	6
East Brady			
The First National Bank Of East Brady	5321	6	–
The Peoples National Bank Of East Brady	5356	4	6
East Conemaugh			
The First National Bank Of East Conemaugh	6979	6	–
East Greenville			
The Perkiomen National Bank Of East Greenville	5166	6	6
East Mauch Chunk			
The Citizens National Bank Of East Mauch Chunk	8446	6	6
East Smithfield			
The First National Bank Of East Smithfield	10042	6	6
East Stroudsburg			
Monroe County National Bank Of East Stroudsburg	5578	–	6
Monroe County Natl Bank & Trust Co Of East Stroudsburg	5578	–	5
The East Stroudsburg National Bank	4011	6	6
The Monroe County National Bank Of East Stroudsburg	5578	6	–
Easton			
First National Bank And Trust Company Of Easton	1171	–	5
The Easton National Bank	1233	4	4
The First National Bank Of Easton	1171	3	–
The Northampton County National Bank Of Easton	2385	6	–
The Northampton National Bank Of Easton	5118	5	6
Ebensburg			
The American National Bank Of Ebensburg	6209	5	5
The First National Bank Of Ebensburg	5084	6	5
Economy			
The Peoples National Bank Of Economy	7528	6	–
Edenburg			
The Clarion County National Bank Of Edenburg	6182	6	3
Edinboro			
The First National Bank Of Edinboro	7312	6	6
Edwardsville			
Peoples National Bank Of Edwardsville	9862	6	5
The First National Bank Of Edwardsville	8633	6	–
Eldred			
The First National Bank Of Eldred	9416	6	6
Elizabeth			
The First National Bank Of Elizabeth	5114	6	–
Elizabethtown			
First National Bank And Trust Company Of Elizabethtown	3335	6	5
The Elizabethtown National Bank	3335	6	–
Elizabethville			
The First National Bank Of Elizabethville	5563	6	6
Elkins Park			
The Elkins Park National Bank	13030	–	6
Elkland			
The Pattison National Bank Of Elkland	5043	6	6
Ellsworth			
The National Bank Of Ellsworth	6929	5	6
Ellwood City			
The Citizens National Bank Of Ellwood City	11570	6	6
The Ellwood City National Bank	5899	6	–
The First National Bank Of Ellwood City	4818	6	6
The Peoples National Bank Of Ellwood City	8678	6	6
Elverson			
The Elverson National Bank	10775	6	6
Elysburg			
The First National Bank Of Elysburg	10837	6	6
Emaus			
The Emaus National Bank	7139	6	4
Emlenton			
The Farmers National Bank Of Emlenton	5481	6	6
The First National Bank Of Emlenton	4615	5	5
Emporium			
The First National Bank Of Emporium	3255	6	5
Ephrata			
The Ephrata National Bank	2515	5	5
The Farmers National Bank Of Ephrata	4923	5	5
Erie			
The First National Bank Of Erie	12	3	3
The Keystone National Bank Of Erie	535	6	–
The Marine National Bank Of Erie	870	5	4
The National Bank And Trust Company Of Erie	14219	–	6
The Second National Bank Of Erie	606	4	3
Etna			
The First National Bank Of Etna	6453	6	5
Evans City			
The Citizens National Bank Of Evans City	8854	6	6
Everett			
The First National Bank Of Everett	6220	6	6
Exchange			
The Farmers National Bank Of Exchange	8410	6	6
Exeter			
The First National Bank Of Exeter	13177	–	5
Export			
First National Bank Of Export	14051	–	6
The First National Bank Of Export	7624	6	6
Factoryville			
The First National Bank Of Factoryville	9130	6	6
Fairchance			
The First National Bank Of Fairchance	8245	6	6
Fairfield			
The First National Bank Of Fairfield	9256	6	5
Falls Creek			
The First National Bank Of Falls Creek	6384	6	5
Farrell			
The First National Bank Of Farrell	10415	6	–
Fawn Grove			
First National Bank Of Fawn Grove	9385	6	4
Fayette City			
The Fayette City National Bank	6800	6	–
The First National Bank Of Fayette City	5646	6	–
Finleyville			
The First National Bank Of Finleyville	6420	6	6
Fleetwood			
The First National Bank And Trust Company Of Fleetwood	8939	–	5
The First National Bank Of Fleetwood	8939	6	6
Fogelsville			
The Fogelsville National Bank	12975	–	6
Ford City			
The First National Bank And Trust Company Of Ford City	5130	6	6

City, Bank	Ch. No.	L	S
Ford City			
The First National Bank Of Ford City	5130	6	–
Forest City			
The Farmers And Miners National Bank Of Forest City	9248	6	6
The First And Farmers National Bank Of Forest City	14205	–	6
The First National Bank Of Forest City	5518	5	5
Frackville			
The First National Bank And Trust Company Of Frackville	7860	6	5
The First National Bank Of Frackville	7860	6	–
Franklin			
The First National Bank Of Franklin	189	5	–
The Lamberton National Bank Of Franklin	5221	5	4
The Venango National Bank Of Franklin	1176	6	–
Fredericksburg			
The First National Bank Of Fredericksburg	8783	6	6
Fredericktown			
The First National Bank Of Fredericktown	5920	6	6
Fredonia			
Fredonia National Bank	13884	–	6
The Fredonia National Bank	7471	6	6
Freedom			
The Freedom National Bank	5454	5	5
The Saint Clair National Bank Of Freedom	9543	6	–
Freeland			
The First National Bank Of Freeland	6175	5	6
Freeport			
The Farmers National Bank Of Freeport	7366	5	5
The First National Bank Of Freeport	2286	6	–
The First National Bank Of Freeport	13826	–	3
Fryburg			
The First National Bank Of Fryburg	9480	6	6
Galeton			
The First National Bank Of Galeton	7280	6	6
Gallitzin			
First National Bank At Gallitzin	14181	–	6
The First National Bank In Gallitzin	13533	–	6
The First National Bank Of Gallitzin	6442	6	6
Gap			
The Gap National Bank	2864	6	6
The Gap National Bank And Trust Company, Gap	2864	–	2
The Gap National Bank, Gap	2864	–	6
Garrett			
The First National Bank Of Garrett	6741	6	6
Genesee			
The First National Bank Of Genesee	9783	6	6
Gettysburg			
The First National Bank Of Gettysburg	311	6	4
The Gettysburg National Bank	611	3	4
Girard			
The First National Bank Of Girard	54	6	–
The National Bank Of Girard	7343	4	5
Girardville			
The First National Bank Of Girardville	4422	6	6
Glassport			
The Glassport National Bank	5708	6	–
Glen Campbell			
The First National Bank Of Glen Campbell	5204	5	1
Glen Lyon			
The Glen Lyon National Bank	13160	6	5
Glen Rock			
The First National Bank Of Glen Rock	435	6	–
Glenside			
The Glenside National Bank	9668	6	–
Goldsboro			
The First National Bank Of Goldsboro	9072	6	6
Grantham			
The Grantham National Bank	9727	6	–
Gratz			
The First National Bank Of Gratz	9473	6	6
Green Lane			
The First National Bank Of Green Lane	14214	–	5
The Green Lane National Bank	2131	6	–
The Valley National Bank Of Green Lane	9084	6	4
Greencastle			
The Citizens National Bank Of Greencastle	5857	6	6
The First National Bank Of Greencastle	1081	6	4
Greensburg			
First National Bank In Greensburg	14055	–	5
The Farmers National Bank Of Greensburg	1894	6	–
The Fifth National Bank Of Pittsburgh	1894	6	–
The First National Bank & Trust Company Of Greensburg	2558	–	6
The First National Bank Of Greensburg	2558	5	5
The Merchants And Farmers National Bank Of Greensburg	2562	4	6
The Westmoreland National Bank Of Greensburg	4974	6	–
Greenville			
The Greenville National Bank	2251	5	4
Grove City			
The First National Bank Of Grove City	5044	6	4
The Grove City National Bank	5501	5	5
The Peoples National Bank Of Grove City	5501	6	–
Halifax			
The Halifax National Bank	5601	5	5
Hallstead			
The First National Bank Of Hallstead	7702	6	6
Hamburg			
The First National Bank And Trust Company Of Hamburg	9028	6	5
The First National Bank Of Hamburg	9028	6	–
The National Bank Of Hamburg	14250	–	6
Hanover			
The First National Bank Of Hanover	187	5	5
Harleysville			
The Harleysville National Bank	9541	6	6
Harmony			
The Harmony National Bank	2335	6	–
Harrisburg			
The First National Bank Of Harrisburg	201	4	–
The Harrisburg National Bank	580	3	2
The Merchants National Bank Of Harrisburg	3713	6	–
Harrisville			
First National Bank In Harrisville	13812	–	5
The First National Bank Of Harrisville	6859	6	5
Hastings			
The First National Bank Of Hastings	11227	6	5
Hatboro			
The Hatboro National Bank	2253	6	6
Hatfield			
The Hatfield National Bank, Hatfield	13026	–	5
Hawley			
The First National Bank Of Hawley	6445	6	6
Hays			
The Hays National Bank	6507	6	5
Hazelhurst			
The Hazelhurst National Bank	8380	6	–
Hazleton			
The First National Bank Of Hazleton	3893	6	2
The Hazleton National Bank	4204	6	3
Hegins			
First National Bank Of Hegins	13994	–	6
The First National Bank Of Hegins	9107	6	5
Herminie			
The First National Bank Of Herminie	10188	6	6
Herndon			
The First National Bank Of Herndon	6049	6	6
The Herndon National Bank	13982	–	6
Hershey			
The Hershey National Bank	12688	–	4
Hickory			
The Farmers National Bank Of Hickory	7405	6	6
Highland Park			
The State Road National Bank Of Highland Park	13196	–	5
Hollidaysburg			
The Citizens National Bank Of Hollidaysburg	6874	6	6
The First National Bank Of Hollidaysburg	57	6	–
The First National Bank Of Hollidaysburg	2744	6	–
Homer City			
The Homer City National Bank	8855	6	6
Homestead			
The First National Bank Of Homestead	3829	6	4
The Homestead National Bank	5365	6	–
Honesdale			
The Honesdale National Bank	644	5	5
Honeybrook			
The First National Bank Of Honeybrook	1676	6	4
Hooversville			
The Citizens National Bank Of Hooversville	11413	6	6
The First National Bank Of Hooversville	6250	6	3
The Hooversville National Bank	14156	–	4
Hop Bottom			
The Hop Bottom National Bank	9647	6	5
Hopewell			
The Hopewell National Bank	9638	6	6
Houston			
The First National Bank Of Houston	5908	5	4
Houtzdale			
The First National Bank Of Houtzdale	6695	6	6
Howard			
The First National Bank Of Howard	9249	6	5
Hughesville			
The First National Bank Of Hughesville	3902	6	5
The Grange National Bank Of Lycoming County, Hughesville	8924	6	6
Hummelstown			
The Hummelstown National Bank	2022	6	5
Huntingdon			
The First National Bank Of Huntingdon	31	5	5
The Standing Stone National Bank Of Huntingdon	6090	5	–
The Union National Bank Of Huntingdon	4965	6	6
Union National Bank And Trust Company Of Huntingdon	4965	–	5
Hyndman			
The Hoblitzell National Bank Of Hyndman	6615	6	6
The National Bank Of South Pennsylvania At Hyndman	4063	6	–
Indiana			
First National Bank In Indiana	14098	–	4
The Citizens National Bank Of Indiana	7993	6	6
The First National Bank Of Indiana	313	5	4
Intercourse			
The First National Bank Of Intercourse	9216	4	2
Irvons			
The First National Bank Of Irvons	11115	6	6
Irwin			
The Citizens National Bank Of Irwin	5255	5	6
The First National Bank Of Irwin	4698	6	5
Jeannette			
The First National Bank Of Jeannette	4092	6	6
The Jeannette National Bank	5527	6	–
The Peoples National Bank Of Jeannette	7792	6	–
Jefferson			
Codorus National Bank In Jefferson	14071	–	6
The Codorus National Bank Of Jefferson	9660	6	6
The First National Bank Of Jefferson	11370	6	6
Jenkintown			
Citizens National Bank Of Jenkintown	12530	6	6
The Jenkintown National Bank	2249	5	–
Jermyn			
The First National Bank Of Jermyn	6158	6	5
Jerome			
The First National Bank Of Jerome	12029	6	6
Jersey Shore			
The Jersey Shore National Bank	1464	6	–
The National Bank Of Jersey Shore	6155	6	–
The Union National Bank Of Jersey Shore	13197	–	4
The Williamsport National Bank, Williamsport	1464	6	6
Williamsport National Bank, Williamsport	1464	–	6
Jessup			
The First National Bank Of Jessup	9600	6	5
Johnsonburg			
The Johnsonburg National Bank	4544	6	6
Johnstown			
The Cambria National Bank Of Johnstown	5059	6	–
The Citizens National Bank Of Johnstown	4212	6	–
The First National Bank Of Johnstown	51	6	–
The First National Bank Of Johnstown	2739	4	4
The Moxham National Bank Of Johnstown	12098	6	5
The National Bank Of Johnstown	10590	6	5
The Union National Bank Of Johnstown	7465	5	–
The United States National Bank Of Johnstown	5913	3	4
United States National Bank In Johnstown	13781	–	6
Juniata			
The First National Bank Of Juniata	8238	6	6
Kane			
The First National Bank Of Kane	5025	6	5
Kennett Square			
National Bank & Trust Company Of Kennett Square	2526	–	5
The National Bank Of Kennett Square	2526	4	6
Kingston			
The First National Bank Of Kingston	12921	–	6
The Kingston National Bank	14023	–	4
Kittanning			
The Farmers National Bank Of Kittanning	3104	4	4
The First National Bank Of Kittanning	69	6	–
The Mercfhants National Bank Of Kittanning	5073	5	5
The National Bank Of Kittanning	2654	6	–
The National Kittanning Bank	6127	6	5
Knoxville			
The First National Bank Of Knoxville	9978	6	6
Koppel			
First National Bank At Koppel	14070	–	6
The First National Bank Of Koppel	11938	6	6
Kutztown			
The Keystone National Bank Of Reading	1875	5	–
The Kutztown National Bank	5102	5	5
The National Bank Of Kutztown	1875	6	–
Laceyville			
The Grange National Bank Of Wyoming County At Laceyville	8845	6	5
Lake Ariel			
The First National Bank Of Lake Ariel	9886	6	5
Lancaster			
The Conestoga National Bank Of Lancaster	3987	6	4
The Farmers National Bank Of Lancaster	597	6	–
The First National Bank Of Lancaster	333	5	–
The Fulton National Bank Of Lancaster	2634	4	3
The Lancaster County National Bank Of Lancaster	683	6	3
The Northern National Bank Of Lancaster	3367	6	–
The Peoples National Bank Of Lancaster	3650	6	–
Landisville			
The First National Bank Of Landisville	9312	6	5
Langhorne			
The Peoples National Bank & Trust Company Of Langhorne	3063	6	6
The Peoples National Bank Of Langhorne	3063	6	–
Lansdale			
First National Bank Of Lansdale	430	6	–
The Citizens National Bank Of Lansdale	7735	5	–
The First National Bank Of Lansdale	430	–	5
Lansdowne			
The National Bank Of Lansdowne	13151	–	6
Lansford			
The Citizens National Bank Of Lansford	7051	6	6
The First National Bank Of Lansford	5234	6	6
Laporte			
The First National Bank Of Laporte	9528	6	6
Latrobe			
First National Bank In Latrobe	13700	–	6
The Citizens National Bank Of Latrobe	3910	6	–
The Commercial National Bank Of Latrobe	14133	–	5
The First National Bank Of Latrobe	3831	6	6
The Peoples National Bank Of Latrobe	5744	6	6
Lawrenceville			
The First National Bank Of Lawrenceville	9702	6	6
Le Raysville			
The First National Bank Of Le Raysville	6350	6	6
Lebanon			
Lebanon National Bank, Lebanon	680	–	6
The Farmers National Bank Of Lebanon	4979	6	–
The First National Bank Of Lebanon	240	5	5
The Lebanon National Bank	680	5	6
The Peoples National Bank Of Lebanon	4955	5	5
The Valley National Bank Of Lebanon	655	6	–
Leechburg			
The Farmers National Bank Of Leechburg	9290	6	6
The First National Bank Of Leechburg	5502	6	5

City, Bank	Ch. No.	L	S
Leesport			
The First National Bank Of Leesport	9495	6	5
Lehighton			
Citizens National Bank And Trust Company Of Lehighton	6531	6	5
The Citizens National Bank Of Lehighton	6531	6	–
The First National Bank Of Lehighton	2308	5	5
Lemasters			
The Lemasters National Bank	8405	6	–
The Peoples National Bank Of Lemasters	10950	6	6
Lemoyne			
West Shore National Bank Of Lemoyne	13494	–	5
Lewisburg			
The Lewisburg National Bank	745	5	5
The Union National Bank Of Lewisburg	784	6	6
Lewiston			
The Mifflin County National Bank Of Lewistown	1579	4	2
Lewistown			
The Citizens National Bank Of Lewistown	5289	6	5
The Russell National Bank Of Lewistown	10506	6	4
Liberty			
The Farmers National Bank Of Liberty	11127	6	6
Ligonier			
Ligonier National Bank	13432	–	5
The First National Bank In Ligonier	13658	–	6
The First National Bank Of Ligonier	6281	5	6
The National Bank Of Ligonier	6832	6	6
Lilly			
The First National Bank Of Lilly	8450	6	6
Lincoln			
The Lincoln National Bank	3198	6	6
Lititz			
Lititz Springs National Bank Of Lititz	9422	6	5
The Farmers National Bank Of Lititz	5773	6	6
The Lititz National Bank	2452	6	–
Littlestown			
The Littlestown National Bank	9207	6	5
Liverpool			
The First National Bank Of Liverpool	8326	6	5
Lock Haven			
The County National Bank Of Lock Haven	11692	6	–
The First National Bank Of Lock Haven	507	5	4
The Lock Haven National Bank	1273	6	–
Loganton			
The Loganton National Bank	9345	6	6
Loysville			
The First National Bank Of Loysville	11524	6	6
Luzerne			
The Luzerne National Bank	8921	6	5
Lykens			
The First National Bank Of Lykens	11062	5	5
Lyndora			
The Lyndora National Bank	8576	6	6
Madera			
The Madera National Bank	7400	6	6
Mahaffey			
The Mahaffey National Bank	7610	6	6
Mahanoy City			
The First National Bank Of Mahanoy City	567	5	5
The Union National Bank Of Mahanoy City	3997	5	5
Malvern			
The National Bank Of Malvern	3147	6	5
Manheim			
The Keystone National Bank Of Manheim	3635	6	5
The Manheim National Bank	912	5	4
Manor			
The Manor National Bank	6456	4	5
Mansfield			
First National Bank In Mansfield	13618	–	6
The First National Bank Of Mansfield	8810	6	6
The Grange National Bank Of Mansfield	8831	6	–
Mapleton			
The First National Bank Of Mapleton	11244	6	6
Marienville			
The Gold Standard National Bank Of Marienville	5727	4	5
Marietta			
The Exchange National Bank Of Marietta	10707	6	6
The First National Bank Of Marietta	25	6	–
The First National Bank Of Marietta	2710	4	3
Marion Center			
The Marion Center National Bank	7819	6	5
Mars			
The Mars National Bank	5599	6	5
Martinsburg			
The First National Bank Of Martinsburg	7974	6	6
Marysville			
The First National Bank Of Marysville	7353	6	5
Masontown			
The First National Bank Of Masontown	5441	6	6
The Masontown National Bank	6528	6	6
Mauch Chunk			
The First National Bank Of Mauch Chunk	437	6	–
The Linderman National Bank Of Mauch Chunk	2852	6	–
The Mauch Chunk National Bank	6534	4	4
The Second National Bank Of Mauch Chunk	469	4	–
Maytown			
The Maytown National Bank	9461	6	5
Mc Adoo			
The First National Bank Of Mc Adoo	8619	6	6
Mc Alisterville			
The Farmers National Bank Of Mc Alisterville	9526	6	2
Mc Clure			
The First National Bank Of Mc Clure	7769	6	6
Mc Connellsburg			
The First National Bank Of Mc Connellsburg	8083	6	6
Mc Donald			
The First National Bank Of Mc Donald	4752	6	6
The Peoples National Bank Of Mc Donald	5058	6	–
Mc Kees Rocks			
The First National Bank Of Mc Kees Rocks	5142	6	4
Mc Keesport			
The Citizens National Bank Of Mc Keesport	4876	6	–
The First National Bank Of Mc Keesport	2222	4	4
The National Bank Of Mc Keesport	4625	4	5
The Union National Bank Of Mc Keesport	7559	5	6
Mc Veytown			
The Mc Veytown National Bank	8773	6	6
Mcconnellsburg			
The Fulton County National Bank Of Mcconnellsburg	13765	–	6
Mckeesport			
The Union National Bank At Mckeesport	13967	–	6
Meadville			
First National Bank Of Meadville	4938	–	5
The First National Bank Of Meadville	115	6	–
The Merchants National Bank & Trust Company Of Meadville	871	–	6
The Merchants National Bank Of Meadville	871	6	6
The New First National Bank Of Meadville	4938	5	6
Mechanicsburg			
Mechanicsburg National Bank	8969	6	–
The First National Bank Of Mechanicsburg	380	4	–
The Second National Bank Of Mechanicsburg	326	5	5
Media			
The Charter National Bank Of Media	3666	6	–
The First National Bank Of Media	312	4	5
Mercer			
The Farmers And Mechanics National Bank Of Mercer	2256	6	5
The Farmers National Bank Of Mercer	13846	–	6
The First National Bank Of Mercer	392	6	4
The Mercer County National Bank Of Mercer	4909	6	–
Mercersburg			
The First National Bank Of Mercersburg	9330	6	6
Meshoppen			
The First National Bank Of Meshoppen	5429	6	5
Meyersdale			
The Citizens National Bank Of Meyersdale	5833	6	5
The First National Bank Of Meyersdale	2258	6	–
The Second National Bank Of Meyersdale	5801	6	6
Middleburgh			
The First National Bank Of Middleburgh	4156	5	5
Middletown			
The Citizens National Bank Of Middletown	7826	6	–
The National Bank Of Middletown	585	6	–
Midland			
The First National Bank Of Midland	8311	6	6
Midway			
The Midway National Bank	6626	6	6
Mifflinburg			
The First National Bank Of Mifflinburg	174	6	–
Mifflintown			
The First National Bank Of Mifflintown	4039	6	6
The Juniata Valley National Bank Of Mifflintown	5147	6	5
Mildred			
The First National Bank Of Mildred	9552	6	6
Milford			
The First National Bank Of Milford	5496	4	6
Millersburg			
The First National Bank Of Millersburg	2252	5	5
Millerstown			
The First National Bank Of Millerstown	7156	6	6
The German National Bank Of Millerstown	2241	6	–
Millersville			
The Millersville National Bank	9259	6	6
Millheim			
The Farmers National Bank And Trust Company Of Millheim	9511	6	4
The Farmers National Bank Of Millheim	9511	6	–
Millsboro			
The First National Bank Of Millsboro	7310	6	6
Millville			
The First National Bank Of Millville	5389	6	6
Milton			
First Milton National Bank, Milton	253	6	4
The First National Bank Of Milton	253	6	–
The Milton National Bank	711	5	–
Minersville			
The First National Bank Of Minersville	423	6	6
The Union National Bank Of Minersville	6131	6	5
Mocanaqua			
The First National Bank Of Mocanaqua	12349	6	6
Mohnton			
The Mohnton National Bank	8968	6	–
Monaca			
The Citizens National Bank Of Monaca	5879	5	6
The Monaca National Bank	5878	6	6
Monessen			
First National Bank And Trust Company Of Monessen	5253	6	6
The Citizens National Bank Of Monessen	11487	6	6
The First National Bank Of Monessen	5253	6	–
Monessen			
The Monessen National Bank	5253	6	–
The Peoples National Bank And Trust Company Of Monessen	5956	6	6
The Peoples National Bank Of Monessen	5956	5	–
Monongahela City			
The First National Bank Of Monongahela City	5968	5	5
Montgomery			
Farmers And Citizens National Bank Of Montgomery	8866	6	5
The First National Bank Of Montgomery	5574	6	6
Montoursville			
The First National Bank Of Montoursville	6997	6	5
Montrose			
The Farmers National Bank Of Montrose	6746	6	–
The First And Farmers National Bank & Trust Co. Of Montrose	2223	–	5
The First And Farmers National Bank Of Montrose	2223	–	–
The First National Bank Of Montrose	2223	6	–
Moscow			
The First National Bank Of Moscow	9340	6	5
Mount Carmel			
The First National Bank Of Mount Carmel	3980	5	5
The Union National Bank Of Mount Carmel	8393	5	5
Mount Holly Springs			
The First National Bank Of Mount Holly Springs	8493	6	5
Mount Jewett			
The Mount Jewett National Bank	7473	6	6
Mount Joy			
The First National Bank And Trust Company Of Mount Joy	667	–	5
The First National Bank Of Mount Joy	667	4	–
The Union National Mount Joy Bank	1516	5	5
Mount Morris			
The Farmers And Merchants National Bank Of Mount Morris	6983	6	–
Mount Pleasant			
The Citizens National Bank Of Mount Pleasant	4875	5	–
The Farmers And Merchants National Bank Of Mount Pleasant	4892	6	–
The First National Bank Of Mount Pleasant	386	5	5
The Peoples National Bank Of Mount Pleasant	9198	6	6
Mount Union			
The Central National Bank Of Mount Union	10206	5	5
The First National Bank Of Mount Union	6411	6	5
Mount Wolf			
The Union National Bank Of Mount Wolf	9361	6	5
Union National Bank In Mount Wolf	14121	–	6
Mountville			
The Mountville National Bank	3808	6	3
Muncy			
The Citizens National Bank Of Muncy	3480	6	5
The First National Bank Of Muncy	837	6	–
Munhall			
The First National Bank Of Munhall	8795	6	–
Myerstown			
The Farmers National Bank Of Myerstown	9752	6	–
The Myerstown National Bank	5241	5	5
Nanticoke			
The First National Bank Of Nanticoke	3955	6	5
The Miners National Bank Of Nanticoke	13524	–	5
The Nanticoke National Bank	7406	6	4
Natrona			
The First National Bank Of Natrona	5729	5	6
Nazareth			
The Nazareth National Bank	5077	5	–
The Nazareth National Bank & Trust Company, Nazareth	5077	–	5
The Second National Bank Of Nazareth	5686	4	5
Neffs			
The Neffs National Bank	12471	5	5
Nescopeck			
The Nescopeck National Bank, Nescopeck	12159	–	6
Nesquehoning			
The First National Bank Of Nesquehoning	10251	6	5
New Albany			
The First National Bank Of New Albany	8973	5	6
New Alexandria			
The New Alexandria National Bank	6580	6	6
New Berlin			
The First National Bank Of New Berlin	7897	5	6
New Bethlehem			
The Citizens National Bank Of New Bethlehem	5051	6	–
The First National Bank Of New Bethlehem	4978	6	5
New Bloomfield			
The First National Bank Of New Bloomfield	5133	5	4
New Brighton			
The National Bank Of Beaver County, New Brighton	632	6	–
The National Bank Of New Brighton	3259	6	–
The Old National Bank Of New Brighton	7395	5	6
The Union National Bank Of New Brighton	4549	5	5
New Castle			
First National Bank Of Lawrence County At New Castle	562	6	4
The Citizens National Bank Of New Castle	4676	5	5
The First National Bank Of New Castle	562	6	–
The National Bank Of Lawrence County At New Castle	1156	4	–
The Union National Bank Of New Castle	8503	6	6
New Cumberland			
The New Cumberland National Bank	7349	5	5

City, Bank	Ch. No.	L	S
New Florence			
New Florence National Bank	13907	–	6
The New Florence National Bank	10353	6	6
New Freedom			
First National Bank In New Freedom	13887	–	6
The First National Bank Of New Freedom	6715	6	6
New Haven			
The New Haven National Bank	6408	6	–
The Union National Bank Of Connellsville	6408	6	6
New Holland			
The Farmers National Bank & Trust Company Of New Holland	8499	–	5
The Farmers National Bank Of New Holland	8499	6	6
The New Holland National Bank	2530	5	6
New Hope			
The Solebury National Bank Of New Hope	11015	–	6
New Kensington			
The First National Bank Of New Kensington	4913	5	5
The Logan National Bank Of New Kensington	13571	–	3
The Union National Bank Of New Kensington	13084	6	6
New Milford			
The Grange Naional Bank Of Susquehanna County At New Milford	8960	6	6
New Salem			
The Delmont National Bank Of New Salem	5837	6	–
The First National Bank Of New Salem	6599	6	–
New Tripoli			
The New Tripoli National Bank	9656	6	5
New Wilmington			
The First National Bank Of New Wilmington	9554	6	6
Newfoundland			
The First National Bank Of Newfoundland	12911	–	6
Newport			
The Citizens National Bank Of Newport	7716	6	6
The First National Bank Of Newport	4917	5	5
The Perry County National Bank Of Newport	5245	6	–
Newtown			
The First National Bank And Trust Company Of Newtown	324	5	5
The First National Bank Of Newtown	324	5	–
Newville			
The Farmers National Bank Of Newville	9588	6	6
The First National Bank Of Newville	60	5	4
Nicholson			
The First National Bank Of Nicholson	7910	6	5
Norristown			
The First National Bank Of Norristown	272	5	–
The Montgomery National Bank Of Norristown	1148	5	5
The Peoples National Bank Of Norristown	2581	4	5
North Belle Vernon			
The Peoples National Bank Of North Belle Vernon	11995	6	6
North East			
The First National Bank Of North East	741	6	–
The First National Bank Of North East	4927	6	6
The National Bank Of North East	9149	6	6
North Girard			
The First National Bank Of North Girard	12363	6	6
North Wales			
The North Wales National Bank	4330	5	5
Northumberland			
The First National Bank Of Northumberland	566	5	–
The Northumberland National Bank	7005	6	5
Numidia			
The Valley National Bank Of Numidia	11981	–	6
Nuremburg			
The First National Bank Of Nuremburg	12563	6	6
Oakdale			
The First National Bank Of Oakdale	5327	4	5
Oakmont			
The First National Bank Of Oakmont	7642	6	5
Oil City			
Oil City National Bank, Oil City	14274	–	5
The First National Bank Of Oil City	173	6	5
The Lamberton National Bank Of Oil City	5565	4	–
The Oil City National Bank	5240	5	4
Oley			
The First National Bank Of Oley	8858	6	4
Olyphant			
First National Bank Of Olyphant	8806	5	–
The National Bank Of Olyphant	14079	–	6
Orbisonia			
The First National Bank Of Orbisonia	8985	6	–
The Orbisonia National Bank	10335	6	–
Orwigsburg			
The First National Bank & Trust Company Of Orwigsburg	4408	6	5
The First National Bank Of Orwigsburg	4408	4	–
Osceola			
The First National Bank Of Osceola, Osceola Mills	6501	6	6
Osceola Mills			
The Peoples National Bank Of Osceola Mills	11966	5	6
Oxford			
The Farmers National Bank Of Oxford	2906	6	5
The National Bank Of Oxford	728	5	4
Palmerton			
The First National Bank Of Palmerton	8930	5	4
Paoli			
The Paoli National Bank	12358	6	–
Parkers Landing			
The First National Bank Of Parkers Landing	6045	6	6
Parkesburg			
The Parkesburg National Bank	2464	5	–
Parnassus			
The Parnassus National Bank	7363	6	6
The Parnassus National Bank, New Kensington	7363	–	6
Patterson			
The Peoples National Bank Of Mifflin	9678	6	6
The Peoples National Bank Of Patterson	9678	6	–
Patton			
The First National Bank Of Patton	4857	6	4
The Grange National Bank Of Patton	8233	6	–
Peckville			
The Peckville National Bank	7785	6	6
Pen Argyl			
The First National Bank Of Pen Argyl	4352	5	5
The Pen Argyl National Bank	7710	6	5
Penbrook			
The National Bank Of Penbrook	12197	6	5
The Penbrook National Bank	9344	6	–
Pennsburg			
The Farmers National Bank Of Pennsburg	2334	5	5
The Perkiomen National Bank Of Pennsburg	2301	5	–
Perkasie			
The First National Bank Of Perkasie	5736	5	5
Perryopolis			
The First National Bank Of Perryopolis	6344	6	6
Petersburg			
The First National Bank Of Petersburg	10313	6	5
Philadelphia			
City National Bank Of Philadelphia	13180	–	4
Commercial National Bank & Trust Company Of Philadelphia	3604	–	4
Commercial National Bank Of Philadelphia	3604	–	5
Corn Exchange National Bank & Trust Company, Philadelphia	542	6	3
Mt. Airy National Bank & Trust Company In Philadelphia	13113	6	5
Mt. Airy National Bank In Philadelphia	13113	–	5
National Bank Of Germantown & Trust Company, Philadelphia	546	–	4
Overbrook National Bank Of Philadelphia	12573	6	6
The Bank Of North America, Philadelphia	602	2	–
The Broad Street National Bank Of Philadelphia	11539	4	–
The Centennial National Bank Of Philadelphia	2317	4	–
The Central National Bank Of Philadelphia	723	6	–
The Chestnut Street National Bank Of Philadelphia	3723	6	–
The City National Bank Of Philadelphia	543	6	–
The Commercial National Bank Of Pennsylvania	556	5	–
The Commonwealth National Bank Of Philadelphia	623	5	–
The Consolidation National Bank Of Philadelphia	561	5	–
The Corn Exchange National Bank Of Philadelphia	542	3	–
The Eighth National Bank Of Philadelphia	522	5	6
The Erie National Bank Of Philadelphia	13032	–	4
The Farmers And Mechanics National Bank Of Philadelphia	538	3	–
The First National Bank Of Philadelphia	1	5	–
The First National Bank Of Philadelphia	2731	2	1
The Fourth National Bank Of Philadelphia	286	6	–
The Fourth Street National Bank Of Philadelphia	3557	2	–
The Franklin National Bank Of Philadelphia	5459	4	–
The Girard National Bank Of Philadelphia	592	3	–
The Independence National Bank Of Philadelphia	3085	6	–
The Kensington National Bank Of Philadelphia	544	5	4
The Keystone National Bank Of Philadelphia	2291	6	–
The Manayunk National Bank Of Philadelphia	3604	5	–
The Manayunk-Quaker City National Bank Of Philadelphia	3604	5	–
The Manufacturers National Bank Of Philadelphia	557	5	–
The Market Street National Bank Of Philadelphia	3684	4	5
The Mechanics National Bank Of Philadelphia	610	4	–
The Merchants National Bank Of Philadelphia	2462	3	–
The National Bank Of Commerce Of Philadelphia	547	6	–
The National Bank Of Germantown, Philadelphia	546	4	–
The National Bank Of Mount Airy In Philadelphia	13113	6	–
The National Bank Of North Philadelphia	11908	6	–
The National Bank Of Northern Liberties	541	5	–
The National Bank Of Olney In Philadelphia	12931	6	5
The National Bank Of The Republic Of Philadelphia	1647	4	–
The National Deposit Bank Of Philadelphia	7929	5	–
The National Exchange Bank Of Philadelphia	755	6	–
The National Security Bank & Trust Co Of Philadelphia	1743	–	5
The National Security Bank Of Philadelphia	1743	3	–
The Ninth National Bank Of Philadelphia	3371	6	–
The North Broad National Bank Of Philadelphia	13325	–	5
The Northeast National Bank Of Philadelphia	13175	–	3
The Northern National Bank Of Philadelphia	4192	5	–
The Northwestern National Bank & Trust Co Of Philadelphia	3491	–	5
The Northwestern National Bank Of Philadelphia	3491	5	–
The Penn National Bank Of Philadelphia	540	5	6
The Philadelphia National Bank	539	2	1
The Produce National Bank Of Philadelphia	3507	6	–
The Quaker City National Bank Of Philadelphia	4050	4	–
The Queen Lane National Bank In Germantown	12860	5	–
The Second National Bank Of Philadelphia	213	5	5
The Seventh National Bank Of Philadelphia	413	6	–
The Sixth National Bank Of Philadelphia	352	5	5
The Southwark National Bank Of Philadelphia	560	5	–
The Southwestern National Bank Of Philadelphia	3498	6	6
The Spring Garden National Bank Of Philadelphia	3468	6	–
The Tenth National Bank Of Philadelphia	3423	4	–
The Textile National Bank Of Philadelphia	7522	4	4
The Third National Bank Of Philadelphia	234	5	–
The Tioga National Bank & Trust Company Of Philadelphia	13003	–	5
The Tradesmens National Bank Of Philadelphia	570	4	–
The Union National Bank Of Philadelphia	563	4	–
The Western National Bank Of Philadelphia	656	5	–
Tradesmens National Bank & Trust Company Of Philadelphia	570	5	3
Philipsburg			
The First National Bank Of Philipsburg	4832	5	5
The Moshannon National Bank Of Philipsburg	5066	5	6
The Philipsburg National Bank	4832	6	–
Phoenixville			
Farmers And Mechanics-National Bank Of Phoenixville	1936	–	5
The Farmers And Mechanics National Bank Of Phoenixville	1936	6	6
The National Bank Of Phoenixville	674	6	6
Picture Rocks			
The Picture Rocks National Bank	11643	6	6
Pine Grove			
The Pine Grove National Bank	8151	6	6
The Pine Grove National Bank & Trust Company, Pine Grove	8151	–	6
Pitcairn			
The First National Bank Of Pitcairn	5848	6	6
The Peoples National Bank Of Pitcairn	11892	6	6
Pittsburgh			
First National Bank At Pittsburgh	252	2	1
National Bank Of America In Pittsburgh	14271	–	4
The Allegheny National Bank Of Pittsburgh	722	6	
The American National Bank Of Pittsburgh	7581	6	–
The Bank Of Pittsburgh, National Association	5225	2	–
The Citizens National Bank Of Pittsburgh	619	6	–
The City National Bank Of Pittsburgh	2195	6	–
The Colonial National Bank Of Pittsburgh	6567	6	–
The Columbia National Bank Of Pittsburgh	4910	4	–
The Commercial National Bank Of Pittsburgh	2711	5	–
The Cosmopolitan National Bank Of Pittsburgh	6216	6	–
The Diamond National Bank Of Pittsburgh	2236	5	5
The Duquesne National Bank Of Pittsburgh	2278	3	5
The Exchange National Bank Of Pittsburgh	1057	2	5
The Farmers Deposit National Bank Of Pittsburgh	685	3	1
The Federal National Bank Of Pittsburgh	6023	4	–
The First National Bank Of Birmingham, Pittsburgh	926	5	6
The First National Bank Of Pittsburgh	48	5	–
The First National Bank Of Pittsburgh	2745	5	–
The First-Second National Bank Of Pittsburgh	252	3	–
The Forbes National Bank Of Pittsburgh	13153	–	4
The Fort Pitt National Bank Of Pittsburgh	2415	5	–
The Fourth National Bank Of Pittsburgh	432	5	–
The German National Bank Of Pittsburgh	757	3	–

City, Bank	Ch. No.	L	S
Pittsburgh			
The Highland National Bank Of Pittsburgh	12414	5	5
The Industrial National Bank Of Pittsburgh	6806	6	–
The Iron City National Bank Of Pittsburgh	675	5	–
The Keystone National Bank Of Pittsburgh	7560	5	–
The Liberty National Bank Of Pittsburgh	4339	5	–
The Lincoln National Bank Of Pittsburgh	4883	5	–
The Marine National Bank Of Pittsburgh	2237	4	–
The Mechanics National Bank Of Pittsburgh	700	6	–
The Mellon National Bank Of Pittsburgh	6301	1	1
The Merchants And Manufacturers National Bank Of Pittsburgh	613	4	–
The Metropolitan National Bank Of Pittsburgh	2279	5	–
The Monongahela National Bank Of Pittsburgh	3874	4	5
The National Bank Of Western Pennsylvania At Pittsburgh	4918	5	–
The Pennsylvania National Bank Of Pittsburgh	4222	4	6
The Peoples National Bank Of Pittsburgh	727	3	–
The Pitt National Bank Of Pittsburgh	13701	–	5
The Pittsburgh National Bank Of Commerce, Pittsburgh	668	4	–
The Republic National Bank Of Pittsburgh	6153	6	–
The Second National Bank Of Pittsburgh	252	5	–
The Smithfield National Bank Of Pittsburgh	2281	6	–
The Third National Bank Of Pittsburgh	291	4	5
The Tradesmens National Bank Of Pittsburgh	678	5	–
The Union National Bank Of Pittsburgh	705	4	4
The United States National Bank Of Pittsburgh	5017	5	–
The Washington National Bank Of Pittsburgh	6725	5	–
Western National Bank Of Pittsburgh	4918	5	–
Pittston			
The First National Bank Of Pittston	478	4	4
The Liberty National Bank Of Pittston	11865	6	5
Pleasant Unity			
The Pleasant Unity National Bank	6581	6	6
Plumer			
The First National Bank Of Plumer	854	6	–
Plumville			
The First National Bank Of Plumville	7887	6	6
Plymouth			
The First National Bank Of Plymouth	707	6	5
The Plymouth National Bank	6881	6	5
Point Marion			
The First National Bank Of Point Marion	6114	6	6
The Peoples National Bank Of Point Marion	9503	5	6
Port Allegany			
The Citizens National Bank Of Port Allegany	6066	6	–
Port Allegheny			
The First National Bank Of Port Allegheny	3877	6	6
Port Royal			
The First National Bank Of Port Royal	11369	6	6
The Port Royal National Bank	11373	6	4
Portage			
The First National Bank Of Portage	7367	6	6
Portland			
Portland National Bank	6665	5	6
The Portland National Bank	13606	–	5
Pottstown			
The Citizens National Bank & Trust Company Of Pottstown	4714	6	5
The Citizens National Bank Of Pottstown	4714	6	–
The National Bank Of Pottstown	608	4	4
The National Iron Bank Of Pottstown	3494	5	4
Pottsville			
The Government National Bank Of Pottsville	1152	5	–
The Merchants National Bank Of Pottsville	8964	6	5
The Miners' National Bank Of Pottsville	649	4	5
The Pennsylvania National Bank & Trust Co Of Pottsville	1663	6	5
The Pennsylvania National Bank Of Pottsville	1663	5	–
Providence			
The First National Bank Of Providence	521	6	–
Punxsutawney			
The County National Bank Of Punxsutawney	9863	6	6
The Farmers National Bank Of Punxsutawney	5965	6	–
The First National Bank Of Punxsutawney	3030	6	–
The Punxsutawney National Bank	5702	5	5
Quakertown			
The Merchants National Bank Of Quakertown	6465	6	6
The Quakertown National Bank	2366	4	5
Quarryville			
The Farmers National Bank Of Quarryville	8045	6	6
The Quarryville National Bank	3067	6	5
Ralston			
The First National Bank Of Ralston	9508	6	6
Reading			
Farmers National Bank And Trust Company Of Reading	696	6	4
Reading			
Penn Natinal Bank And Trust Company Of Reading	2899	–	5
The Commercial National Bank Of Reading	2473	6	–
The Farmers National Bank Of Reading	696	4	–
The First National Bank Of Reading	125	5	–
The National Union Bank Of Reading	693	5	–
The Penn National Bank Of Reading	2899	6	–
The Reading National Bank	4887	4	–
The Reading National Bank And Trust Company	4887	–	4
The Second National Bank Of Reading	2552	3	–
Rebersburg			
The Rebersburg National Bank	11789	6	6
Red Lion			
First National Bank And Trust Company Of Red Lion	5184	–	5
The Farmers And Merchants National Bank Of Red Lion	6708	5	5
The Red Lion First National Bank	5184	6	6
Reedsville			
The Reedsville National Bank	4538	5	5
Renova			
The First National Bank Of Renova	3763	6	6
Republic			
The First National Bank Of Republic	10466	6	6
Reynoldsville			
The Citizens National Bank Of Reynoldsville	6263	6	–
The First National Bank Of Reynoldsville	4908	5	5
The Peoples National Bank Of Reynoldsville	7620	6	5
Rices Landing			
The Rices Landing National Bank	7090	6	5
Richland			
The Richland National Bank	8344	6	6
Ridgway			
The Elk County National Bank Of Ridgway	5014	5	4
The Ridgway National Bank	5945	4	4
Ridley Park			
The Ridley Park National Bank	10847	6	5
Riegelsville			
The First National Bank Of Riegelsville	9202	6	6
Rimersburg			
The First National Bank Of Rimersburg	6676	6	3
The Rimersburg National Bank	6569	6	–
Ringtown			
The First National Bank Of Ringtown	6950	6	6
Roaring Spring			
First National Bank Of Roaring Spring	12304	–	5
Rochester			
The First National Bank Of Rochester	2977	6	6
The Peoples National Bank Of Rochester	7749	6	6
The Rochester National Bank	5170	6	–
Rockwood			
The Farmers And Merchants National Bank Of Rockwood	9769	6	6
The First National Bank Of Rockwood	5340	6	6
Rome			
The Farmers National Bank Of Rome	10246	6	5
Roscoe			
The First National Bank Of Roscoe	5495	6	6
Royersford			
The Home National Bank Of Royersford	4751	6	–
The National Bank Of Royersford	3551	6	5
Rural Valley			
The Peoples National Bank Of Rural Valley	13908	–	6
The Rural Valley National Bank	6083	6	6
Russellton			
The First National Bank Of Russellton	10493	6	6
Saegertown			
The First National Bank Of Saegertown	11910	6	6
Saint Marys			
The Saint Marys National Bank	6589	4	4
Saint Michael			
The Saint Michael National Bank	12588	–	6
Salisbury			
The First National Bank Of Salisbury	6106	6	5
Saltsburg			
The First National Bank Of Saltsburg	2609	5	5
Saxton			
The First National Bank Of Saxton	7229	6	6
Sayre			
The First National Bank Of Sayre	5666	6	5
The Merchants And Mechanics National Bank Of Sayre	5684	6	6
The National Bank Of Sayre	5684	6	–
Scenery Hill			
The First National Bank Of Scenery Hill	7262	6	3
Schaefferstown			
The First National Bank Of Schaefferstown	8962	6	6
Schellburg			
The First National Bank Of Schellburg	10666	6	6
The First National Bank Of Schellsburg	10666	–	6
Schuylkill Haven			
The First National Bank Of Schuylkill Haven	5216	5	–
The First Natl Bank & Trust Co Of Schuylkill Haven	5216	6	5
Schwenksville			
The National Bank & Trust Company Of Schwenksville	2142	–	5
The National Bank Of Schwenksville	2142	6	6
Scottdale			
First National Bank Of Scottdale	13772	–	6
The Broadway National Bank Of Scottdale	5974	5	6
The First National Bank Of Scottdale	4098	6	6
Scranton			
Scranton National Bank	13947	–	5
The First National Bank Of Scranton	77	6	–
The First National Bank Of Scranton	2697	4	2
Scranton			
The Peoples National Bank Of Scranton	8235	5	–
The Second National Bank Of Scranton	49	6	–
The Third National Bank Of Scranton	1946	4	6
The Traders National Bank Of Scranton	4183	3	6
The Union National Bank Of Scranton	8737	4	4
Third National Bank And Trust Company Of Scranton	1946	–	4
Selins Grove			
The First National Bank Of Selins Grove	357	5	4
Selinsgrove			
The Farmers National Bank Of Selinsgrove	8653	6	5
Sellersville			
The Sellersville National Bank	2667	5	5
Seven Valleys			
The Seven Valleys National Bank	9507	6	6
Seward			
The First National Bank Of Seward	11899	6	
Sewickley			
First National Bank In Sewickley	13699	–	6
The First National Bank Of Sewickley	4462	6	5
Shamokin			
National-Dime Bank Of Shamokin	6942	–	4
The First National Bank Of Shamokin	3045	6	–
The Market Street National Bank Of Shamokin	5625	5	5
The National Bank Of Shamokin	6942	5	5
The Northumberland County National Bank Of Shamokin	689	6	–
The West End National Bank Of Shamokin	12805	6	5
Sharon			
First National Bank In Sharon	13803	–	6
The First National Bank Of Sharon	1685	5	3
The Mc Dowell National Bank Of Sharon	8764	4	5
The Merchants And Manufacturers National Bank Of Sharon	6560	6	6
The Sharon National Bank	2244	6	–
Sharpsville			
The First National Bank Of Sharpsville	6829	6	4
The Sharpsville National Bank	7873	6	–
Sheffield			
The Sheffield National Bank	6193	5	5
Shenandoah			
The Citizens National Bank Of Shenandoah	9247	6	5
The First National Bank Of Shenandoah	3143	6	5
The Merchants National Bank Of Shenandoah	4546	4	6
The Miners National Bank Of Shenandoah	13619	–	3
Sheraden			
The First National Bank Of Sheraden	5977	6	–
Shickshinny			
The First National Bank Of Shickshinny	5573	6	5
Shingle House			
The First National Bank Of Shingle House	6799	6	6
Shippensburg			
The First National Bank Of Shippensburg	834	5	4
The Peoples National Bank Of Shippensburg	6946	6	6
Shippenville			
The First National Bank Of Shippenville	7874	6	6
Shoemakersville			
The First National Bank Of Shoemakersville	11841	6	5
Siegfried			
The Cement National Bank Of Siegfried	5227	5	–
The Cement National Bank Of Siegfried At Northampton	5227	5	5
Sipesville			
The First National Bank Of Sipesville	11849	6	6
Slatington			
The Citizens National Bank Of Slatington	6051	5	5
The National Bank Of Slatington	2293	4	5
Sligo			
Sligo National Bank, Sligo	8946	6	6
The Grange National Bank Of Clarion County At Sligo	8946	6	–
Slippery Rock			
The Citizens National Bank Of Slippery Rock	8724	6	–
The First National Bank Of Slippery Rock	6483	6	6
Smethport			
The Grange National Bank Of Mc Kean County At Smethport	8591	6	5
Smithfield			
The First National Bank Of Smithfield	6642	6	6
Smithton			
The First National Bank Of Smithton	5311	5	6
Somerfield			
The First National Bank Of Somerfield	8901	6	6
Somerset			
The Farmers National Bank Of Somerset	5452	5	6
The First National Bank Of Somerset	4100	5	5
The Peoples National Bank Of Somerset	13900	–	6
The Somerset County National Bank Of Somerset	4227	6	–
Souderton			
The Peoples National Bank Of Souderton	13251	–	5
The Union National Bank Of Souderton	2333	5	–
Union National Bank And Trust Company Of Souderton	2333	6	6
South Bethlehem			
The Bethlehem National Bank, Bethlehem	3961	6	5
The South Bethlehem National Bank	3961	6	–
South Fork			
The First National Bank Of South Fork	6573	6	6
Spangler			
The First National Bank Of Spangler	7181	6	5

City, Bank	Ch. No.	L	S
Spartansburg			
The Grange National Bank Of Spartansburg	9110	6	5
Spring City			
The National Bank And Trust Company Of Spring City	2018	6	4
The National Bank Of Spring City	2018	5	–
Spring Grove			
The First National Bank Of Spring Grove	6536	6	6
The Peoples National Bank Of Spring Grove	8141	6	6
The Spring Grove National Bank, Spring Grove	6536	–	6
Spring Mills			
The First National Bank Of Spring Mills	11213	6	4
Springdale			
The National Bank Of Springdale	8320	–	5
The Springdale National Bank	8320	5	4
Springville			
The First National Bank Of Springville	11393	6	6
State College			
The First National Bank Of State College	7511	5	5
The Peoples National Bank Of State College	12261	6	4
Steelton			
The Steelton National Bank	3599	6	–
Stewartstown			
The First National Bank Of Stewartstown	4665	6	5
The Peoples National Bank Of Stewartstown	6444	6	6
Stoneboro			
The First National Bank Of Stoneboro	6638	5	5
Stoystown			
The First National Bank At Stoystown	14089	–	6
The First National Bank Of Stoystown	5682	5	6
Strasburg			
The First National Bank Of Strasburg	42	5	6
The First National Bank Of Strasburg	2700	6	–
Strausstown			
Strausstown National Bank	13863	–	6
The Strausstown National Bank	10452	6	6
Stroudsburg			
The First National Bank Of Stroudsburg	2787	6	6
The First-Stroudsburg National Bank, Stroudsburg	3632	–	5
The Stroudsburg National Bank	3632	5	4
Summerville			
The Union National Bank Of Summerville	6739	6	6
Sunbury			
The First National Bank Of Sunbury	1237	3	2
The Sunbury National Bank	6877	6	–
Susquehanna			
The City National Bank Of Susquehanna	3144	5	6
The First National Bank Of Susquehanna	1053	5	6
Susquehanna Depot			
The First National Bank Of Susquehanna Depot	1053	5	–
Sutersville			
The First National Bank Of Sutersville	6270	6	6
Swarthmore			
The Swarthmore National Bank	7193	5	–
The Swarthmore National Bank & Trust Company, Swarthmore	7193	6	6
Swineford			
The First National Bank Of Swineford	7003	6	6
Swissvale			
The First National Bank Of Swissvale	6109	6	5
Sykesville			
First National Bank In Sykesville	14169	–	6
The First National Bank Of Sykesville	7488	6	6
Tamaqua			
The First National Bank Of Tamaqua	1219	5	5
The Tamaqua National Bank	7286	6	5
Tarentum			
First National Bank And Trust Company Of Tarentum	4453	6	6
First National Bank In Tarentum	13940	–	4
The First National Bank Of Tarentum	2285	6	–
The National Bank Of Tarentum	4453	6	–
The Peoples National Bank Of Tarentum	5351	4	4
Telford			
The Telford National Bank	9257	6	5
Terre Hill			
The Terre Hill National Bank	9316	6	6
Thompsontown			
The Farmers National Bank Of Thompsontown	10211	6	6
Three Springs			
The First National Bank Of Three Springs	10183	6	–
Timblin			
The First National Bank Of Timblin	11204	6	6
Tioga			
The Grange National Bank Of Tioga	8092	6	6
Tionesta			
The Citizens National Bank Of Tionesta	5040	6	6
The Forest County National Bank Of Tionesta	5038	5	6
Titusville			
The First National Bank Of Titusville	622	6	–
The Hyde National Bank Of Titusville	2466	6	–
The Roberts National Bank Of Titusville	2834	6	–
The Second National Bank Of Titusville	879	3	4
Topton			
The National Bank Of Topton	8223	6	5
The Topton National Bank	3358	6	–
Towanda			
The Citizens National Bank Of Towanda	2337	4	5
The First National Bank Of Towanda	39	4	5
Tower City			
The Tower City National Bank	6117	6	6
Tower City National Bank	14031	–	6
Trafford City			
The First National Bank Of Trafford	6962	–	6
The First National Bank Of Trafford City	6962	6	6
Tremont			
The First National Bank Of Tremont	797	6	–
The Tremont National Bank	6165	6	6
Trevorton			
The First National Bank Of Trevorton	7722	6	6
Troy			
The First National Bank Of Troy	4984	5	5
The Grange National Bank Of Bradford County At Troy	8849	5	6
Tunkhannock			
The Citizens National Bank Of Tunkhannock	6438	6	6
The Wyoming National Bank Of Tunkhannock	835	5	5
Turbotville			
The Turbotville National Bank	9803	6	6
Turtle Creek			
The First National Bank Of Turtle Creek	6574	6	6
The National Bank Of Turtle Creek	6568	6	–
Tyrone			
First Blair County National Bank Of Tyrone	4355	–	5
The Blair County National Bank & Trust Company Of Tyrone	6516	6	4
The Blair County National Bank Of Tyrone	6516	6	–
The Farmers And Merchants National Bank Of Tyrone	6499	6	6
The First National Bank Of Tyrone	4355	5	5
Ulster			
The First National Bank Of Ulster	9505	6	6
Ulysses			
The Grange National Bank Of Potter County At Ulysses	8739	6	6
Union City			
National Bank Of Union City	14093	–	6
The First National Bank Of Union Mills, Union City	110	6	–
The Home National Bank Of Union City	8879	6	6
The National Bank Of Union City	5131	6	6
Uniontown			
The First National Bank Of Uniontown	270	6	–
The National Bank Of Fayette County, Uniontown	681	4	3
The Second National Bank Of Uniontown	5034	6	3
The Uniontown National Bank And Trust Company	12500	5	6
Vanderbilt			
The First National Bank Of Vanderbilt	8190	6	6
Vandergrift			
The Citizens National Bank Of Vandergrift	7816	6	6
The First National Bank Of Vandergrift	5080	6	–
Verona			
The First National Bank Of Verona	4877	6	6
Volant			
The First National Bank Of Volant	11834	–	6
Wampum			
First National Bank In Wampum	14112	–	6
The First National Bank Of Wampum	6664	6	6
Warren			
The Citizens National Bank Of Warren	2226	4	5
The First National Bank Of Warren	520	5	5
The Warren National Bank	4879	3	3
Washington			
The Citizens National Bank Of Washington	3383	4	3
The Farmers And Mechanics National Bank Of Washington	4181	6	–
The First National Bank Of Washington	586	4	–
The Peoples National Bank Of Washington	9901	6	5
Waterford			
The Ensworth National Bank Of Waterford	10027	6	6
Watsontown			
The Farmers National Bank Of Watsontown	3459	5	5
The Watsontown National Bank	2483	5	6
Wayne			
The Main Line National Bank Of Wayne	12504	5	–
Waynesboro			
Citizens National Bank & Trust Company Of Waynesboro	5832	–	4
First National Bank & Trust Company In Waynesboro	11866	6	3
First National Bank In Waynesboro	11866	5	–
The Citizens National Bank Of Waynesboro	5832	4	–
The First National Bank Of Waynesboro	244	6	–
The Peoples National Bank Of Waynesboro	4445	5	–
The Union National Bank Of Waynesburg	13873	–	5
Waynesburg			
First National Bank And Trust Company Of Waynesburg	13134	–	5
The American National Bank Of Waynesburg	6105	6	–
The Citizens National Bank Of Waynesburg	4267	5	–
The Farmers And Drovers National Bank Of Waynesburg	839	6	–
The First National Bank Of Waynesburg	305	6	–
The Peoples National Bank Of Waynesburg	5085	5	–
Weatherly			
The First National Bank Of Weatherly	6108	6	5
Webster			
The First National Bank Of Webster	6937	6	–
Wehrum			
The First National Bank Of Wehrum	7112	6	–
Weissport			
The Weissport National Bank	10214	6	6
Wellsborough			
The First National Bank Of Wellsborough	328	5	5
The Wellsborough National Bank	3938	6	–
Wellsville			
The Wellsville National Bank	8498	6	6
Wernersville			
The Wernersville National Bank	8131	6	–
The Wernersville National Bank & Trust Co, Wernersville	8131	–	5
West Alexander			
The Citizens National Bank Of West Alexander	11993	6	6
The Peoples National Bank Of West Alexander	8954	6	5
The West Alexander National Bank	5948	5	–
West Chester			
National Bank Of Chester County & Trust Co, West Chester	552	–	3
The Farmers National Bank Of West Chester	2857	–	4
The First National Bank Of West Chester	148	4	4
The National Bank Of Chester County, West Chester	552	4	6
West Conshohocken			
The Peoples National Bank Of West Conshohocken	8890	6	–
West Elizabeth			
The First National Bank Of West Elizabeth	6373	6	–
West Greenville			
The First National Bank Of Greenville	249	6	4
The First National Bank Of West Greenville	249	6	–
West Grove			
The National Bank & Trust Company Of West Grove	2669	6	5
The National Bank Of West Grove	2669	6	–
West Middlesex			
The First National Bank Of West Middlesex	6913	6	6
West Newton			
The First National Bank Of West Newton	5010	6	6
West York			
The Industrial National Bank Of West York	8938	6	5
Westfield			
The Farmers And Traders National Bank Of Westfield	9513	6	6
Wilcox			
The Wilcox National Bank	12933	6	6
Wilkes Barre			
The First National Bank Of Wilkes Barre	2736	6	–
The Second National Bank Of Wilkes Barre	104	4	4
Wilkes-Barre			
Miners National Bank Of Wilkes-Barre	13852	–	3
The First National Bank Of Wilkes-Barre	30	4	3
The Luzerne County National Bank Of Wilkes-Barre	9235	6	–
The Wyoming National Bank Of Wilkes-Barre	732	5	4
Wilkinsburg			
The Central National Bank Of Wilkinsburg	5265	6	6
The First National Bank At Wilkinsburg	13823	–	5
The First National Bank Of Wilkinsburg	4728	6	4
Williamsburg			
First National Bank Of Williamsburg	14182	–	6
The Farmers And Merchants National Bank Of Williamsburg	9392	6	6
The First National Bank Of Williamsburg	6971	5	6
Williamsport			
The City National Bank Of Williamsport	2139	5	–
The First National Bank Of Williamsport	175	4	3
The Lumberman's National Bank Of Williamsport	734	6	–
The Lycoming National Bank Of Williamsport	2227	5	–
The Merchants National Bank Of Williamsport	3705	6	–
The West Branch National Bank Of Williamsport	1505	5	–
Wilmerding			
First National Bank Of Wilmerding	5000	6	2
The East Pittsburgh National Bank Of Wilmerding	5000	6	–
The Wilmerding National Bank Of Wilmerding	6325	6	–
Wilson			
The First National Bank Of Clairton	6794	6	6
The First National Bank Of Wilson	6794	6	–
Winburne			
The Bituminous National Bank Of Winburne	7334	5	6
Windber			
Citizens National Bank In Windber	14082	–	6
The Citizens National Bank Of Windber	6848	6	5
The Windber National Bank	5242	6	–
Windsor			
The First National Bank Of Windsor	12063	6	6
Woodlawn			
Aliquippa National Bank, Aliquippa	10951	6	5
The First National Bank Of Woodlawn	10951	6	–
Wrightsville			
The First National Bank Of Wrightsville	246	6	5
Wyalusing			
The First National Bank Of Wyalusing	5339	6	–
The National Bank Of Wyalusing	10606	6	6

City, Bank	Ch. No.	L	S
Wyoming			
The First National Bank Of Wyoming	8517	5	5
Yardley			
The Yardley National Bank	4207	6	6
Yardley National Bank	13950	–	6
York			
The Central National Bank & Trust Company Of York	9706		5
The Central National Bank Of York	9706	6	5
The Drovers And Mechanics National Bank Of York	2958	5	5
The Farmers National Bank Of York	2228	6	–
The First National Bank Of York	197	5	4
The Western National Bank Of York	2303	6	5
The York County National Bank Of York	694	4	4
The York National Bank	604	5	–
The York National Bank & Trust Company, York	604	6	4
York Springs			
The First National Bank Of York Springs	7856	6	5
Youngsville			
The First National Bank Of Youngsville	8165	6	5
Youngwood			
The First National Bank Of Youngwood	6500	6	6
Zelienople			
The First National Bank Of Zelienople	6141	6	6
The Peoples National Bank Of Zelienople	7409	6	5

PORTO RICO

City, Bank	Ch. No.	L	S
San Juan			
The First National Bank Of Porto Rico At San Juan	6484	3	–

RHODE ISLAND

City, Bank	Ch. No.	L	S
Anthony			
The Coventry National Bank Of Anthony	1161	6	–
Ashaway			
The Ashaway National Bank	1150	5	3
Bristol			
The First National Bank Of Bristol	1292	6	–
The National Eagle Bank Of Bristol	1562	6	–
Cumberland			
The Cumberland National Bank	1404	6	–
East Greenwich			
The Greenwich National Bank Of East Greenwich	1405	6	–
Greenville			
The National Exchange Bank Of Greenville	1498	4	–
Hopkinton			
The First National Bank Of Hopkinton	1054	4	–
Kingston			
The National Landholders Bank Of Kingston	1158	5	–
Newport			
The Aquidneck National Bank Of Newport	1546	5	–
The Aquidneck Natl Exchange Bank & Savings Co Of Newport	1546	5	2
The First National Bank Of Newport	1021	6	–
The National Bank Of Rhode Island Of Newport	1532	6	–
The National Exchange Bank Of Newport	1565	5	–
The Newport National Bank	1492	3	3
The Union National Bank Of Newport	2554	4	–
North Providence			
The Pacific National Bank Of North Providence	1616	5	–
The Pacific National Bank Of Pawtucket	1616	6	–
The Slater National Bank Of North Providence	856	4	–
The Slater National Bank Of Pawtucket	856	6	–
Pascoag			
The Pascoag National Bank	1512	5	–
Pawtucket			
The First National Bank Of Pawtucket	843	4	–
Phenix			
The Phenix National Bank	1460	6	–
Providence			
Rhode Island Hospital National Bank Of Providence	13901	–	1
The American National Bank Of Providence	1472	4	–
The Atlantic National Bank Of Providence	2913	6	–
The Blackstone Canal National Bank Of Providence	1328	2	2
The City National Bank Of Providence	1429	6	–
The Columbus National Bank Of Providence	13981	–	4
The Commercial National Bank Of Providence	1319	6	–
The Fifth National Bank Of Providence	1002	5	–
The First National Bank Of Providence	134	3	–
The Fourth National Bank Of Providence	772	4	–
The Globe National Bank Of Providence	1126	6	–
The Lime Rock National Bank Of Providence	1369	6	–
The Manufacturers National Bank Of Providence	1283	4	–
The Mechanics National Bank Of Providence	1007	3	2
The Merchants National Bank Of Providence	1131	2	–
The National Bank Of Commerce & Trust Co Of Providence	1366	–	3
The National Bank Of Commerce Of Providence	1366	3	5
The National Bank Of North America, Providence	1036	5	–
The National Eagle Bank Of Providence	1030	4	–
The National Exchange Bank Of Providence	1339	2	–
The Old National Bank Of Providence	1151	5	–
The Phenix National Bank Of Providence	948	2	2
The Providence National Bank	1302	2	2
The Rhode Island National Bank Of Providence	983	4	–
The Roger Williams National Bank Of Providence	1506	6	–
The Second National Bank Of Providence	565	5	–
The Third National Bank Of Providence	636	6	–
The Traders National Bank Of Providence	1396	6	–
The United National Bank Of Providence	5925	5	–
The Weybosset National Bank Of Providence	1173	5	–
Scituate			
The Scituate National Bank	1552	6	–
Slatersville			
The First National Bank Of Smithfield, Slatersville	1035	5	4
Wakefield			
The National Exchange Bank Of Wakefield	1554	6	–
The Wakefield National Bank	1206	6	–
Warren			
The First National Bank Of Warren	673	4	–
The National Hope Bank Of Warren	1008	5	–
The National Warren Bank Of Warren	1419	5	–
Warwick			
The Centreville National Bank Of Warwick, Centreville	1284	5	5
Westerly			
The National Niantic Bank Of Westerly	823	4	–
The National Phenix Bank Of Westerly	1169	6	–
The Washington National Bank Of Westerly	952	4	–
Wickford			
The Wickford National Bank	1592	5	–
Woonsocket			
The Citizens National Bank Of Woonsocket	970	5	–
The First National Bank Of Woonsocket	1402	6	–
The National Globe Bank Of Woonsocket	1423	5	–
The National Union Bank Of Woonsocket	1409	6	–
The Producers National Bank Of Woonsocket	1421	5	–
The Woonsocket National Bank	1058	6	–

SOUTH CAROLINA

City, Bank	Ch. No.	L	S
Abbeville			
The National Bank Of Abbeville	3421	6	–
Aiken			
The First National Bank Of Aiken	9650	5	–
Allendale			
The First National Bank Of Allendale	11111	6	–
Anderson			
The Citizens National Bank Of Anderson	9104	5	–
The National Bank Of Anderson	2072	6	–
Barnwell			
The First National Bank Of Barnwell	11287	6	–
Batesburg			
The Citizens National Bank Of Batesburg	10815	6	–
The First National Bank Of Batesburg	5595	4	5
Bennettsville			
The Planters National Bank Of Bennettsville	6385	4	6
Bishopville			
The First National Bank Of Bishopville	10263	5	6
Brunson			
The First National Bank Of Brunson	10832	5	–
Camden			
The First National Bank Of Camden	9083	3	4
Charleston			
Peoples-First National Bank Of Charleston	1621	3	4
The Atlantic National Bank Of Charleston	10708	4	–
The Bank Of Charleston National Banking Association	2044	2	–
The Commercial National Bank Of Charleston	10543	6	–
The First National Bank Of Charleston	1622	3	–
The Germania National Bank Of Charleston	10708	6	–
The Peoples National Bank Of Charleston	1621	2	–
The South Carolina National Bank Of Charleston	2044	3	2
Cheraw			
The First National Bank Of Cheraw	9342	6	–
Chester			
The National Bank Of Chester	1804	6	–
The National Exchange Bank Of Chester	8471	4	5
The Peoples National Bank Of Chester	10663	–	2
Clinton			
First National Bank Of Clinton	8041	5	5
Clio			
The First National Bank Of Clio	11153	6	–
Clover			
The First National Bank Of Clover	11439	6	5
Columbia			
The Carolina National Bank Of Columbia	1680	4	–
The Central National Bank Of Columbia	1765	6	–
The Columbia National Bank	12412	3	4
The First National Bank Of Columbia	13720	–	5
The Liberty National Bank Of South Carolina At Columbia	9687	4	–
The National Loan And Exchange Bank Of Columbia	6871	3	3
The National State Bank Of Columbia	10315	4	–
The Palmetto National Bank Of Columbia	8133	2	–
The Peoples National Bank Of Columbia	10597	5	–
The Union National Bank Of Columbia	9687	4	–
Conway			
The Conway National Bank	10536	5	5
The First National Bank Of Conway	9690	6	–
The Peoples National Bank Of Conway	10537	5	5
Darlington			
Carolina National Bank Of Darlington	9999	4	–
The Darlington National Bank	2512	6	–
Dillon			
The First National Bank Of Dillon	10908	6	–
Elloree			
The First National Bank Of Elloree	10679	5	6
Fairfax			
The First National Bank Of Fairfax	10979	6	–
Florence			
The First National Bank Of Florence	9747	4	–
Fort Mill			
The First National Bank Of Fort Mill	9941	6	6
Gaffney			
The First National Bank Of Gaffney	5064	5	6
The Merchants And Planters National Bank Of Gaffney	10655	4	3
The National Bank Of Gaffney	5064	6	–
Greenville			
The City National Bank Of Greenville	5004	5	–
The First National Bank Of Greenville	1935	5	4
The Fourth National Bank Of Greenville	9190	6	–
The National Bank Of Greenville	1935	4	–
The Norwood National Bank Of Greenville	8766	3	–
The Peoples National Bank Of Greenville	10635	6	3
The Woodside National Bank Of Greenville	11499	4	6
Greenwood			
National Loan & Exchange Bank Of Greenwood	7027	4	4
The First National Bank Of Greenwood	7027	6	–
Hartsville			
The First National Bank Of Hartsville	10137	6	–
Holly Hill			
The First National Bank Of Holly Hill	10680	6	6
Honea Path			
The National Bank Of Honea Path	12381	6	6
Lake City			
The Farmers And Merchants National Bank Of Lake City	10681	5	–
Lamar			
The Lamar National Bank	11080	6	–
Lancaster			
The First National Bank Of Lancaster	7858	5	–
Laurens			
The Enterprise National Bank Of Laurens	10605	6	–
The Laurens National Bank	10652	6	–
The National Bank Of Laurens	3540	6	–
Leesville			
The National Bank Of Leesville	9057	3	6
Lexington			
The Home National Bank Of Lexington	9296	4	6
Manning			
The First National Bank Of Manning	11155	6	–
Marion			
Marion National Bank	10085	4	3
Mullins			
The First National Bank Of Mullins	9876	5	6
Newberry			
The National Bank Of Newberry	1844	4	–
Norway			
The Farmers National Bank Of Norway	11189	6	–
Olanta			
The First National Bank Of Olanta	10748	6	–
Orangeburg			
The Edisto National Bank Of Orangeburg	10650	5	4
The First National Bank In Orangeburg	13918	–	6
The First National Bank Of Orangeburg	5269	6	–
The Orangeburg National Bank, Orangeburg	10674	5	–
The Peoples National Bank Of Orangeburg	10674	6	–
Prosperity			
The Peoples National Bank Of Prosperity	6994	6	–
Rock Hill			
The First National Bank Of Rock Hill	3616	6	–
The National Union Bank Of Rock Hill	5134	3	–
The Peoples National Bank Of Rock Hill	9407	4	3
Saint Matthews			
The St. Matthews National Bank	10651	6	–
Sharon			
The First National Bank Of Sharon	9533	4	5
Spartanburg			
The American National Bank Of Spartanburg	6658	4	5
The Central National Bank Of Spartanburg	4996	3	3
The Commercial National Bank Of Spartanburg	14211	–	1
The First National Bank Of Spartanburg	1848	3	4
The National Bank Of Spartanburg	1848	6	–
Springfield			
The First National Bank Of Springfield	10586	5	6
Sumter			
The City National Bank Of Sumter	10129	4	6
The First National Bank Of Sumter	3809	4	6
The National Bank Of South Carolina Of Sumter	10660	3	2
The National Bank Of Sumter	3082	6	–
The National Bank Of Sumter	10670	4	6
The Simonds National Bank Of Sumter	3809	6	–
Union			
The Citizens National Bank Of Union	9742	6	–
The Merchants And Planters National Bank Of Union	2060	6	–

City, Bank	Ch. No.	L	S
Wagener			
The First National Bank Of Wagener	10485	6	–
Walterboro			
The First National Bank Of Walterboro	9849	4	–
Whitmire			
The First National Bank Of Whitmire	6102	6	–
Winnsboro			
The Winnsboro National Bank	2087	6	–
Woodruff			
The First National Bank Of Woodruff	10593	6	–
Yorkville			
The First National Bank Of York	6931	6	–
The First National Bank Of Yorkville	6931	6	–

DAKOTA TERRITORY

City, Bank	Ch. No.	L	S
Aberdeen			
The Aberdeen National Bank	3326	6	–
The First National Bank Of Aberdeen	2980	6	–
The Northwestern National Bank Of Aberdeen	3932	6	–
Ashton			
The First National Bank Of Ashton	3437	6	–
Bismarck			
The Bismarck National Bank	2677	6	–
The Capital National Bank Of Bismarck	2986	6	–
The First National Bank Of Bismarck	2434	6	–
The Merchants National Bank Of Bismarck	3169	6	–
Brookings			
The First National Bank Of Brookings	3087	6	–
Canton			
The First National Bank Of Canton	2830	6	–
Casselton			
The First National Bank Of Casselton	2792	6	–
Chamberlain			
The First National Bank Of Chamberlain	2911	6	–
Clark			
The First National Bank Of Clark	3479	6	–
Columbia			
The First National Bank Of Columbia	3352	6	–
De Smet			
The First National Bank Of De Smet	3435	6	–
Deadwood			
The Deadwood National Bank	3552	6	–
The First National Bank Of Deadwood	2391	5	–
The Merchants National Bank Of Deadwood	2461	6	–
Dell Rapids			
The First National Bank Of Dell Rapids	3508	6	–
Devil's Lake			
The First National Bank Of Devil's Lake	3397	6	–
The Merchants National Bank Of Devil's Lake	3714	6	–
Doland			
The First National Bank Of Doland	3522	6	–
Fargo			
The Citizens National Bank Of Fargo	3602	6	–
The First National Bank Of Fargo	2377	6	–
The Red River Valley National Bank Of Fargo	2514	6	–
Grafton			
The First National Bank Of Grafton	2840	6	–
The Grafton National Bank	3096	6	–
Grand Forks			
The Citizens National Bank Of Grand Forks	2570	6	–
The First National Bank Of Grand Forks	2564	6	–
The Grand Forks National Bank	3301	6	–
The Second National Bank Of Grand Forks	3504	6	–
Hillsboro			
The First National Bank Of Hillsboro	3400	6	–
The Hillsboro National Bank	3411	6	–
Huron			
The Beadle County National Bank Of Huron	2989	6	–
The First National Bank Of Huron	2819	6	–
The Huron National Bank	3267	6	–
The National Bank Of Dakota, Huron	3636	6	–
Jamestown			
The First National Bank Of Jamestown	2578	6	–
The James River National Bank Of Jamestown	2580	6	–
The Jamestown National Bank	3331	6	–
Lakota			
The First National Bank Of Lakota	4143	6	–
Larimore			
The First National Bank Of Larimore	2854	6	–
Lisbon			
The First National Bank Of Lisbon	3669	6	–
Madison			
The Citizens National Bank Of Madison	3151	6	–
The First National Bank Of Madison	3149	6	–
The Madison National Bank	3597	6	–
Mandan			
The First National Bank Of Mandan	2585	6	–
Mayville			
The First National Bank Of Mayville	3673	6	–
Minot			
The First National Bank Of Minot	4009	6	–
Mitchell			
The First National Bank Of Mitchell	2645	6	–
The Mitchell National Bank	3578	6	–
Park River			
The First National Bank Of Park River	3436	6	–
Parker			
The First National Bank Of Parker	3675	6	–
Pembina			
The First National Bank Of Pembina	3438	6	–
Pierre			
The First National Bank Of Pierre	2941	6	–
The Pierre National Bank	4104	6	–
Plankinton			
The First National Bank Of Plankinton	3130	6	–
Rapid City			
The Black Hills National Bank Of Rapid City	3401	6	–
The First National Bank Of Rapid City	3237	6	–
Redfield			
The First National Bank Of Redfield	3398	6	–
Sioux Falls			
The Citizens National Bank Of Sioux Falls	3586	6	–
The Dakota National Bank Of Sioux Falls	2843	6	–
The First National Bank Of Sioux Falls	2465	6	–
The Minnehaha National Bank Of Sioux Falls	3393	6	–
The Sioux Falls National Bank	2823	6	–
Sturgis			
The First National Bank Of Sturgis	3739	6	–
Valley City			
The Farmers And Merchants National Bank Of Valley City	2650	6	–
The First National Bank Of Valley City	2548	6	–
Wahpeton			
The First National Bank Of Wahpeton	2624	6	–
The National Bank Of Wahpeton	4106	6	–
Watertown			
The Citizens National Bank Of Watertown	3349	6	–
The First National Bank Of Watertown	2935	6	–
The Watertown National Bank	3414	6	–
Yankton			
The First National Bank Of Yankton	2068	4	–

SOUTH DAKOTA

City, Bank	Ch. No.	L	S
Aberdeen			
First National Bank & Trust Company Of Aberdeen	2980	–	4
The Aberdeen National Bank	3326	3	–
The Dakota National Bank Of Aberdeen	8642	3	–
The First National Bank Of Aberdeen	2980	3	5
The Northwestern National Bank Of Aberdeen	3932	6	–
Alexandria			
The First National Bank Of Alexandria	5918	5	–
The Security National Bank Of Alexandria	10187	5	–
Arlington			
The First National Bank In Arlington	13286	–	5
The First National Bank Of Arlington	5916	4	–
Armour			
The First National Bank Of Armour	8012	6	–
Belle Fourche			
The First National Bank Of Belle Fourche	6561	4	6
Beresford			
The First National Bank Of Beresford	10813	4	4
Bridgewater			
The Farmers National Bank Of Bridgewater	7426	6	6
The First National Bank Of Bridgewater	6925	6	–
Bristol			
The First National Bank Of Bristol	8480	6	–
Britton			
First National Bank In Britton	13460	–	3
The First National Bank Of Britton	6073	5	6
Brookings			
The Farmers National Bank Of Brookings	6462	5	–
The First National Bank Of Brookings	3087	4	–
Canton			
The First National Bank Of Canton	2830	3	4
The National Bank Of Canton	4637	6	–
Carthage			
The First National Bank Of Carthage	10833	5	–
Castlewood			
The First National Bank Of Castlewood	6000	5	–
Centerville			
The First National Bank Of Centerville	5477	4	4
Chamberlain			
The Brule National Bank Of Chamberlain	8550	5	–
The Chamberlain National Bank	4282	6	–
The First National Bank And Trust Company Of Chamberlain	13483	–	3
The First National Bank Of Chamberlain	2911	6	–
The Whitbeck National Bank Of Chamberlain	9301	4	–
Clark			
The Clark County National Bank Of Clark	6409	5	5
The First National Bank Of Clark	3479	6	–
Clear Lake			
The Deuel County National Bank Of Clear Lake	12877	6	4
The First National Bank Of Clear Lake	6357	6	–
Colman			
The First National Bank Of Colman	6688	4	–
Custer			
The First National Bank Of Custer City	4448	6	–
Davis			
The First National Bank Of Davis	11457	6	6
De Smet			
The De Smet National Bank	5355	5	–
The First National Bank Of De Smet	3435	6	–
Deadwood			
The American National Bank Of Deadwood	4983	6	–
The Deadwood National Bank	3552	6	–
The First National Bank Of Deadwood	2391	3	3
The Merchants National Bank Of Deadwood	2461	6	–
Dell Rapids			
The First National Bank Of Dell Rapids	3508	3	–
The Home National Bank Of Dell Rapids	9693	3	5
Doland			
The First National Bank Of Doland	3522	6	–
The Merchants National Bank Of Redfield	3522	6	–
Egan			
The First National Bank Of Egan	7252	4	5
Elk Point			
The First National Bank Of Elk Point	5901	5	6
Elkton			
The First National Bank Of Elkton	6368	5	–
Emery			
The Security National Bank Of Emery	11812	5	5
Ethan			
The First National Bank Of Ethan	13549	–	6
Fairfax			
Farmers National Bank Of Fairfax	12325	4	–
The Farmers National Bank Of Fairfax	13302	–	5
The First National Bank Of Fairfax	8711	6	–
Flandreau			
The First National Bank Of Flandreau	5854	4	5
Fort Pierre			
The First National Bank Of Fort Pierre	4237	6	–
The Fort Pierre National Bank	9587	6	5
Frederick			
The First National Bank Of Frederick	8624	5	–
Freeman			
The First National Bank Of Freeman	6181	6	6
Garden City			
The Farmers National Bank Of Vienna	11558	6	3
Garretson			
The First National Bank Of Garretson	7755	6	–
Gary			
The First National Bank Of Gary	9393	6	4
The National Bank Of Gary	10846	6	6
Gettysburg			
Potter County National Bank Of Gettysburg	8776	–	6
The First National Bank Of Gettysburg	8776	5	6
Gregory			
The First National Bank Of Gregory	8600	6	–
The Gregory National Bank	9377	5	–
Groton			
The First National Bank Of Groton	7885	4	5
Hecla			
The First National Bank Of Hecla	9679	5	5
Henry			
The First National Bank Of Henry	10416	6	–
Highmore			
The First National Bank Of Highmore	7794	5	4
Hot Springs			
The First National Bank Of Hot Springs	4370	6	–
The Hot Springs National Bank	6339	6	–
The Peoples National Bank Of Hot Springs	9166	6	–
Howard			
The First National Bank Of Howard	6585	5	–
Hudson			
The First National Bank Of Hudson	7335	4	4
Huron			
The Beadle County National Bank Of Huron	2989	6	–
The City National Bank Of Huron	8781	6	–
The First National Bank Of Huron	2819	5	–
The Huron National Bank	3267	6	–
The National Bank Of Dakota, Huron	3636	6	–
The National Bank Of Huron	8841	4	4
Kennebec			
The First National Bank Of Kennebec	10098	5	–
Lake Norden			
The First National Bank & Trust Company Of Lake Norden	13221	–	5
The First National Bank Of Lake Norden	10714	6	–
Lake Preston			
The First National Bank Of Lake Preston	10758	6	–
Lead			
The First National Bank Of Lead	4631	4	3
Lemmon			
First National Bank In Lemmon	12857	–	4
New First National Bank In Lemmon	12857	6	–
The First National Bank Of Lemmon	9269	5	–
Letcher			
The First National Bank Of Letcher	9188	5	4
Madison			
The Citizens National Bank Of Madison	3151	6	–
The First National Bank Of Madison	3149	5	–
The Lake County National Bank Of Madison	10636	4	–
Mcintosh			
The First National Bank Of Mcintosh	9283	6	–
Midland			
The First National Bank Of Midland	10637	6	5
Milbank			
The Farmers And Merchants National Bank In Milbank	13407	–	4
The Farmers And Merchants National Bank Of Milbank	8698	5	6
The First National Bank Of Milbank	6473	4	–
The Merchants National Bank Of Milbank	8698	5	–
Miller			
The First National Bank Of Miller	6789	4	–
Mitchell			
The First National Bank Of Mitchell	2645	3	–
The Mitchell National Bank	3578	2	2
Western National Bank Of Mitchell	7455	4	–
Mobridge			
First National Bank In Mobridge	13467	–	4
The First National Bank Of Mobridge	10744	4	5
The Security National Bank Of Mobridge	11590	6	6
Morristown			
The First National Bank Of Morristown	9817	6	–
Mount Vernon			
The First National Bank Of Mount Vernon	7582	6	–

City, Bank	Ch. No.	L	S
Oldham			
The First National Bank Of Oldham	10256	4	–
The Oldham National Bank	12662	–	4
Onida			
The First National Bank Of Onida	11585	6	–
Parker			
The First National Bank Of Parker	3675	6	4
Parkston			
The First National Bank Of Parkston	7662	5	4
Pierre			
The First National Bank In Pierre	14252	–	5
The First National Bank Of Pierre	2941	3	3
The National Bank Of Commerce Of Pierre	4279	3	–
The Pierre National Bank	4104	3	3
Pukwana			
The First National Bank Of Pukwana	9958	4	4
Rapid City			
The Black Hills National Bank Of Rapid City	3401	6	–
The First National Bank Of Rapid City	3237	4	4
The Rapid City National Bank	14099	–	3
Redfield			
The American National Bank Of Redfield	8125	5	6
The First National Bank Of Redfield	3398	6	–
The German American National Bank Of Redfield	8125	6	–
The Redfield National Bank	6256	5	5
Saint Lawrence			
The First National Bank Of St. Lawrence	12547	4	6
Salem			
The First National Bank Of Salem	5898	4	–
The Mccook County National Bank Of Salem	12784	–	5
Scotland			
The First National Bank Of Scotland	7048	6	–
Selby			
The First National Bank Of Selby	9376	4	4
Sioux Falls			
Security National Bank And Trust Company Of Sioux Falls	10592	–	3
The American National Bank Of Sioux Falls	9915	6	–
The Dakota National Bank Of Sioux Falls	2843	6	–
The Minnehaha National Bank Of Sioux Falls	3393	6	–
The Security National Bank Of Sioux Falls	10592	3	–
The Sioux Falls National Bank	2823	6	–
The Union National Bank Of Sioux Falls	4629	6	–
Sisseton			
Citizens National Bank Of Sisseton	6395	5	–
The Citizens Security National Bank Of Sisseton	6395	6	5
The First National Bank Of Sisseton	5428	5	4
South Shore			
Farmers National Bank Of Estelline	11689	–	6
The First National Bank Of South Shore	7686	6	–
Spearfish			
The American National Bank Of Spearfish	8248	6	–
The First National Bank Of Spearfish	4874	6	–
Springfield			
The First National Bank Of Springfield	8942	6	–
Sturgis			
The Commercial National Bank Of Sturgis	6990	6	4
The First National Bank Of Sturgis	3739	6	–
Toronto			
The First National Bank Of Toronto	6381	6	–
Tyndall			
The First National Bank Of Tyndall	6792	3	3
Veblen			
The First National Bank Of Veblen	9858	6	–
Vermilion			
The First National Bank And Trust Company Of Vermilion	13346	–	4
The First National Bank Of Vermilion	4603	6	–
The Vermilion National Bank	7352	6	–
Vermillion			
First National Bank In Vermillion	13346	–	6
Viborg			
The Security National Bank Of Viborg	13589	–	4
Vienna			
The First National Bank Of Vienna	7597	6	–
Volga			
The First National Bank Of Volga	6099	5	5
Wakonda			
The First National Bank Of Wakonda	7968	6	–
Watertown			
Security National Bank Of Watertown	7504	4	–
The Citizens National Bank Of Watertown	3349	6	4
The First Citizens National Bank Of Watertown	2935	–	6
The First National Bank And Trust Company Of Watertown	2935	–	3
The First National Bank Of Watertown	2935	3	–
The Watertown National Bank	3414	6	–
Waubay			
The First National Bank Of Waubay	6124	6	–
Webster			
The Farmers And Merchants National Bank Of Webster	8559	4	4
The First National Bank Of Webster	6502	6	–
Wessington			
The First National Bank Of Wessington	8325	6	–
Wessington Springs			
The First National Bank Of Wessington Springs	6446	5	–
Wetonka			
The First National Bank Of Wetonka	11441	4	–
White			
The Farmers National Bank Of White	7134	6	–
The First National Bank Of White	6294	6	4
White Lake			
The First National Bank Of White Lake	8291	6	6
The United States National Bank Of White Lake	8332	6	–
White Rock			
The First National Bank Of White Rock	6185	6	5
The Roberts County National Bank Of Sisseton	6185	–	6
Wilmot			
The First National Bank Of Wilmot	11399	–	4
Winner			
The First National Bank Of Winner	11119	6	–
Woonsocket			
The Citizens National Bank Of Woonsocket	5946	5	–
The First National Bank Of Woonsocket	5946	6	–
Yankton			
The Dakota National Bank Of Yankton	9445	4	4
The First Dakota National Bank & Trust Company Of Yankton	2068	–	6
The First National Bank Of Yankton	2068	4	–
The Yankton National Bank	4613	6	–

TENNESSEE

City, Bank	Ch. No.	L	S
Athens			
The Citizens National Bank Of Athens	10735	5	6
The First National Bank Of Athens	3341	4	5
Bristol			
The First National Bank In Bristol	13640	–	5
The First National Bank Of Bristol	2167	6	–
The First National Bank Of Bristol	2796	3	5
The National Bank Of Bristol	2796	6	–
Brownsville			
The First National Bank Of Brownsville	6042	6	–
Camden			
The First National Bank Of Camden	8506	6	–
Cardiff			
The First National Bank Of Cardiff	4303	6	–
Carthage			
The First National Bank Of Carthage	7928	6	–
Centerville			
The Citizens National Bank Of Centerville	9827	6	–
The First National Bank Of Centerville	3288	6	6
Chattanooga			
Citizens National Bank Of Chattanooga	9176	6	–
The American National Bank Of Chattanooga	7817	6	–
The Chattanooga National Bank	3691	6	–
The City National Bank Of Chattanooga	1746	6	–
The Commercial National Bank Of Chattanooga	13746	–	4
The First National Bank Of Chattanooga	1606	2	2
The Fourth National Bank Of Chattanooga	4060	6	–
The Hamilton National Bank Of Chattanooga	7848	2	2
The Merchants National Bank Of Chattanooga	4456	6	–
The Third National Bank Of Chattanooga	2559	6	–
Clarksville			
The Clarksville National Bank	2720	5	6
The Farmers And Merchants National Bank Of Clarksville	3241	6	–
The First National Bank Of Clarksville	1603	4	5
Cleveland			
The Cleveland National Bank	1666	4	4
Coal Creek			
The First National Bank Of Coal Creek	10028	5	6
Columbia			
The First National Bank Of Columbia	1713	6	–
The Maury National Bank Of Columbia	4849	3	5
The Phoenix National Bank Of Columbia	7870	4	6
The Second National Bank Of Columbia	2568	6	–
Cookeville			
The Cookeville National Bank	9692	6	–
The First National Bank Of Cookeville	9667	5	6
Copperhill			
The First National Bank Of Polk County At Copperhill	9027	5	6
Covington			
The First National Bank Of Covington	10491	6	–
Crossville			
The First National Bank Of Crossville	9809	6	5
Dayton			
The American National Bank Of Dayton	5679	6	6
The First National Bank Of Dayton	4362	6	–
Dechard			
The First National Bank Of Franklin County At Decherd	7397	5	6
Dickson			
The Citizens National Bank Of Dickson	8292	6	6
The Dickson National Bank	10577	6	–
The First National Bank Of Dickson	6930	5	6
Doyle			
The First National Bank Of Doyle	10190	6	6
Ducktown			
The First National Bank Of Ducktown	9565	6	–
Dyersburg			
First-Citizens National Bank Of Dyersburg	5263	1	4
The First National Bank Of Dyersburg	5263	4	–
Elizabethton			
The First National Bank Of Elizabethton	9558	5	6
The Holston National Bank Of Elizabethton	10976	4	6
Erwin			
The Erwin National Bank	10583	–	6
The First National Bank Of Erwin	9720	6	–
Etowah			
The First National Bank Of Etowah	9162	6	6
Fayetteville			
Elk National Bank Of Fayetteville	8555	5	5
Fayetteville			
Farmers National Bank Of Fayetteville	10198	6	3
The Elk National Bank Of Fayetteville	3702	6	–
The First National Bank Of Fayetteville	2114	6	5
Union National Bank Of Fayetteville	13948	–	5
Franklin			
The Farmers National Bank Of Franklin	3062	6	–
The Harpeth National Bank Of Franklin	8443	5	5
The National Bank Of Franklin	1834	3	–
Gainesboro			
The First National Bank Of Gainesboro	5536	6	–
Gallatin			
First And Peoples National Bank Of Gallatin	5545	5	5
The First National Bank Of Gallatin	1707	6	–
The First National Bank Of Gallatin	4236	6	–
The Peoples National Bank Of Gallatin	5545	6	–
Greeneville			
The Citizens National Bank Of Greeneville	13482	–	6
The First National Bank Of Greeneville	4177	6	6
Harriman			
First National Bank In Harriman	12031	4	5
The First National Bank Of Harriman	4501	6	–
The Harriman National Bank	11915	5	6
The Manufacturers National Bank Of Harriman	4654	5	–
Hohenwald			
The First National Bank Of Hohenwald	11985	6	6
Huntland			
The First National Bank Of Huntland	8601	6	6
Huntsville			
The First National Bank Of Huntsville	10192	6	6
Jackson			
The First National Bank Of Jackson	2168	2	4
The National Bank Of Commerce Of Jackson	12790	6	5
The Second National Bank Of Jackson	3576	5	5
The Security National Bank Of Jackson	10334	6	6
Jefferson City			
The First National Bank Of Jefferson City	11479	6	6
Jellico			
The First National Bank Of Jellico	7665	6	5
The National Bank Of Jellico	7636	6	–
Johnson City			
The City National Bank Of Johnson City	6236	5	–
The First National Bank Of Johnson City	3951	6	–
The Hamilton National Bank Of Johnson City	13635	–	4
The Tennessee National Bank Of Johnson City	11839	4	5
The Unaka And City National Bank Of Johnson City	6236	3	4
The Unaka National Bank Of Johnson City	5888	4	–
Jonesboro			
The First National Bank Of Jonesboro	4715	6	6
Kenton			
The First National Bank Of Kenton	10404	6	–
Kingsport			
The First National Bank Of Kingsport	10842	6	5
Kingston			
The First National Bank Of Kingston	12319	6	6
Knoxville			
Holston-Union National Bank Of Knoxville	4648	5	5
Park National Bank Of Knoxville	2049	–	5
The American National Bank Of Knoxville	10327	5	–
The City And County National Bank Of Knoxville	3837	2	4
The East Tennessee National Bank Of Knoxville	2049	2	3
The First National Bank Of Knoxville	391	6	–
The Hamilton National Bank Of Knoxville	13539	–	3
The Holston National Bank Of Knoxville	4648	2	–
The Mechanics National Bank Of Knoxville	2658	4	–
The State National Bank Of Knoxville	4102	6	–
The Third National Bank Of Knoxville	3708	3	–
The Union National Bank Of Knoxville	10401	3	–
La Follette			
The First National Bank Of La Follette	7225	6	5
The National Bank Of La Follette	7225	6	–
The Peoples National Bank Of La Follette	12467	–	6
Lawrenceburg			
The First National Bank Of Lawrenceburg	6093	4	5
Lebanon			
The American National Bank Of Lebanon	5754	6	–
The Lebanon National Bank	8714	5	–
The National Bank Of Lebanon	1664	6	–
The Second National Bank Of Lebanon	1708	6	–
Lenoir City			
The First National Bank Of Lenoir City	8673	5	5
Lewisburg			
The First National Bank Of Lewisburg	8934	5	5
Lexington			
The First National Bank Of Lexington	12324	6	5
Linden			
The First National Bank Of Linden	10181	6	6
Loudon			
The First National Bank Of Loudon	12080	6	5
Lynnville			
The First National Bank Of Lynnville	8558	6	–
Manchester			
The First National Bank Of Manchester	5528	5	6
Martin			
The City National Bank Of Martin	9112	5	–
The First National Bank Of Martin	5617	6	–
Maryville			
The First National Bank Of Maryville	10542	5	6

City, Bank	Ch. No.	L	S
Mcminniville			
The First National Bank Of Mcminnville	2221	5	5
Mcminnville			
The American National Bank Of Mcminnville	7834	6	–
The National Bank Of Mcminnville	2221	6	–
The Peoples National Bank Of Mcminnville	2593	5	6
Memphis			
National Bank Of Commerce In Memphis	13681	–	6
Southern National Bank Of Memphis	12348	5	–
The Central-State National Bank Of Memphis	2127	4	–
The Continental National Bank Of Memphis	4307	6	–
The First National Bank Of Memphis	336	2	1
The Fourth National Bank Of Memphis	2096	6	–
The German National Bank Of Memphis	1636	6	–
The Memphis National Bank	3633	6	–
The Mercantile National Bank Of Memphis	10540	5	–
The Merchants National Bank Of Memphis	1407	6	–
The National Bank Of Commerce Of Memphis	5056	4	–
The National City Bank Of Memphis	9184	4	–
The State National Bank Of Memphis	2127	4	–
The Tennessee National Bank Of Memphis	1225	6	–
Union Planters National Bank And Trust Company Of Memphis	13349	–	1
Morristown			
City National Bank Of Morristown	8025	3	5
The First National Bank Of Morristown	3432	4	6
The Hamblen National Bank Of Morristown	8025	–	5
Mount Pleasant			
The First National Bank Of Mount Pleasant	9319	4	5
Murfreesboro			
The First National Bank Of Murfreesboro	1692	3	6
The Stones River National Bank Of Murfreesboro	2000	4	–
Nashville			
Broadway National Bank Of Nashville	9774	4	4
Fourth And First National Bank Of Nashville	1669	2	3
Tennessee-Hermitage National Bank Of Nashville	9532	5	6
The American National Bank Of Nashville	3032	2	1
The Commercial National Bank Of Nashville	3228	6	–
The Cumberland Valley National Bank Of Nashville	9659	5	–
The First National Bank Of Nashville	150	5	–
The Fourth National Bank Of Nashville	1669	3	–
The Hermitage National Bank Of Nashville	9532	6	–
The Mechanics National Bank Of Nashville	2200	6	–
The Merchants National Bank Of Nashville	2513	6	–
The Merchants National Bank Of Nashville	6729	6	–
The Second National Bank Of Nashville	771	6	–
The Third National Bank Of Nashville	1296	5	–
Third National Bank In Nashville	13103	–	3
Newport			
The First National Bank Of Newport	9632	5	6
Oliver Springs			
The Tri-County National Bank Of Oliver Springs	11998	6	6
Oneida			
The First National Bank Of Oneida	8039	6	6
The Scott County National Bank Of Oneida	8039	6	–
Paris			
The First National Bank Of Paris	9334	5	–
Petersburg			
The First National Bank Of Petersburg	10306	5	6
Pikeville			
The First National Bank Of Pikeville	10470	6	6
Pulaski			
The Citizens National Bank Of Pulaski	4679	6	–
The Giles National Bank Of Pulaski	1990	6	–
The National Bank Of Pulaski	1727	6	–
The National Peoples Bank Of Pulaski	6076	6	–
The Peoples National Bank Of Pulaski	2635	6	–
Ripley			
The First National Bank Of Ripley	10449	6	6
Rockwood			
The City National Bank Of Rockwood	12264	6	–
The First National Bank Of Rockwood	4169	6	6
The Rockwood National Bank	12257	6	6
Rogersville			
The Rogersville National Bank	4015	6	–
Russellville			
The First National Bank Of Russellville	10508	6	–
Savannah			
The First National Bank Of Savannah	8889	6	4
Selmer			
The First National Bank Of Selmer	8836	6	6
Shelbyville			
First National Bank Of Shelbyville	10785	–	4
The Farmers National Bank Of Shelbyville	10785	4	6
The National Bank Of Shelbyville	2198	6	–
The Peoples National Bank Of Shelbyville	3530	4	5
Smithville			
The First National Bank Of Smithville	13056	5	6
Smyrna			
The First National Bank Of Smyrna	9807	6	6
South Pittsburg			
The First National Bank Of South Pittsburg	3660	5	5
Sparta			
The American National Bank Of Sparta	7912	6	–
The First National Bank Of Sparta	3614	6	5
Spring City			
The First National Bank Of Spring City	9470	6	–
Springfield			
The First National Bank Of Springfield	12639	6	6
The Peoples National Bank Of Springfield	6189	6	–
The Springfield National Bank	2019	6	–
Sweetwater			
The First National Bank Of Sweetwater	11202	6	6
Tazewell			
The Claiborne National Bank Of Tazewell	7740	6	–
Tracy City			
The First National Bank Of Tracy City	7314	5	6
Trenton			
The Citizens National Bank Of Trenton	12438	5	5
The First National Bank Of Trenton	8406	6	–
Tullahoma			
The First National Bank Of Tullahoma	3107	6	6
The Traders National Bank Of Tullahoma	4020	6	5
Union City			
The Farmers And Merchants National Bank Of Union City	4442	6	–
The First National Bank Of Union City	3919	6	–
The Old National Bank Of Union City	9629	5	4
The Third National Bank Of Union City	9239	6	5
Wartrace			
The First National Bank Of Wartrace	9627	6	–
Waverly			
The Citizens National Bank Of Waverly	9331	6	–
The First National Bank Of Waverly	5963	6	–
Winchester			
The American National Bank Of Winchester	8631	6	–
The Farmers National Bank Of Winchester	8640	5	6
Woodbury			
The First National Bank Of Woodbury	9089	6	–

TEXAS

City, Bank	Ch. No.	L	S
Abilene			
The Abilene National Bank	33336	6	–
The American National Bank Of Abilene	7028	6	–
The Citizens National Bank In Abilene	13727	–	5
The Citizens National Bank Of Abilene	6476	6	6
The Commercial National Bank Of Abilene	7944	6	–
The Farmers And Merchants National Bank Of Abilene	4166	4	5
The First National Bank Of Abilene	3195	6	–
Alba			
The Alba National Bank	6896	6	6
Albany			
The Albany National Bank	5680	6	6
The First National Bank Of Albany	3248	6	5
Alpine			
State National Bank Of Alpine	12289	5	6
The First National Bank Of Alpine	7214	5	5
Alvarado			
The First National Bank Of Alvarado	3644	6	6
Alvin			
The First National Bank Of Alvin	7070	6	–
Alvord			
The Alvord National Bank	6067	6	–
The Farmers And Merchants National Bank Of Alvord	8071	6	–
Amarillo			
The Amarillo National Bank	4710	5	6
The First National Bank Of Amarillo	4214	4	5
The National Bank Of Commerce, Amarillo	6865	6	6
Anderson			
The First National Bank Of Anderson	7337	5	6
Angleton			
The First National Bank Of Angleton	14204		6
Anna			
The First National Bank Of Anna	12867	6	6
Annona			
The First National Bank Of Annona	7257	6	3
Anson			
The Farmers And Merchants National Bank Of Anson	8897	6	–
The First National Bank Of Anson	6091	6	6
Aransas Pass			
The First National Bank Of Aransas Pass	10274	6	4
Archer City			
The First National Bank Of Archer City	5711	6	–
Arlington			
The Arlington National Bank	7345	6	–
The Citizens National Bank Of Arlington	5806	6	–
Aspermont			
The First National Bank Of Aspermont	5786	6	4
Athens			
The Athens National Bank	6400	6	6
The First National Bank Of Athens	4278	5	6
Atlanta			
The Atlanta National Bank	7694	6	6
The First National Bank Of Atlanta	4922	5	6
Aubrey			
The First National Bank Of Aubrey	7495	6	–
Austin			
The American National Bank Of Austin	4322	3	4
The Austin National Bank	4308	3	4
The City National Bank Of Austin	3289	6	–
The First National Bank Of Austin	2118	6	–
The State National Bank Of Austin	2617	4	–
Avery			
The First National Bank Of Avery	10638	6	6
Bagwell			
The First National Bank Of Bagwell	10657	6	6
Bailey			
The First National Bank Of Bailey	12741	–	6
Baird			
The First National Bank Of Baird	3286	6	6
The Home National Bank Of Baird	5493	6	–
Ballinger			
The Ballinger National Bank	4193	6	–
The Citizens National Bank Of Ballinger	6757	6	–
The First National Bank Of Ballinger	3533	5	5
Bardwell			
The First National Bank Of Bardwell	10678	6	6
Barlett			
The Bartlett National Bank	7317	4	6
Bartlett			
The First National Bank Of Bartlett	5422	5	6
Bastrop			
The First National Bank Of Bastrop	4093	6	6
Bay City			
The Bay City National Bank	7753	6	–
The First National Bank Of Bay City	6062	6	5
Beaumont			
The American National Bank Of Beaumont	5825	4	–
The Beaumont National Bank	5201	6	–
The Citizens National Bank Of Beaumont	5841	6	–
The Commercial National Bank Of Beaumont	9357	6	–
The First National Bank Of Beaumont	4017	3	5
The Gulf National Bank Of Beaumont	6338	5	–
Beeville			
The Commercial National Bank Of Beeville	4866	5	5
The First National Bank Of Beeville	4238	6	5
Bellevue			
The First National Bank Of Bellevue	8672	6	4
Bells			
The First National Bank Of Bells	7524	6	6
Bellville			
The First National Bank Of Bellville	4241	5	5
Belton			
The Belton National Bank	3295	6	–
The Belton National Bank	7509	6	6
The Citizens National Bank Of Belton	4167	6	–
The Farmers National Bank Of Belton	13810	–	6
The First National Bank Of Belton	2735	6	–
The Peoples National Bank Of Belton	8518	6	3
Benjamin			
The First National Bank Of Benjamin	7669	6	–
Bertram			
The First National Bank Of Bertram	11519	6	–
Big Spring			
The First National Bank In Big Spring	13984	–	6
The First National Bank Of Big Spring	4306	5	6
The State National Bank Of Big Spring	12543	6	6
The West Texas National Bank Of Big Spring	6668	6	6
Blanco			
The Blanco National Bank	8134	6	3
Blooming Grove			
The Citizens National Bank Of Blooming Grove	7055	6	6
The First National Bank In Blooming Grove	13555	–	6
The First National Bank Of Blooming Grove	4768	6	–
Blossom			
The First National Bank Of Blossom	5733	6	–
Blum			
The First National Bank Of Blum	6069	6	–
Bogata			
The Bogata National Bank	10639	6	–
The First National Bank Of Bogata	10483	6	6
Bonham			
The Bonham National Bank	4540	6	–
The Fannan County National Bank Of Bonham	5146	5	–
The First National Bank Of Bonham	3094	5	–
Bonita			
The First National Bank Of Bonita	10163	6	–
Bowie			
The City National Bank Of Bowie	4785	4	6
The First National Bank Of Bowie	4265	5	6
The National Bank Of Bowie	8330	5	–
Brady			
The Brady National Bank	7827	4	6
The Commercial National Bank Of Brady	8573	6	4
The First National Bank Of Brady	4198	6	–
Breckenridge			
First National Bank In Breckenridge	14027	–	6
The First National Bank Of Breckenridge	7422	6	6
Brenham			
The Farmers National Bank In Brenham	13678	–	6
The Farmers National Bank Of Brenham	10860	6	3
The First National Bank Of Brenham	3015	4	4
Bridgeport			
The First National Bank Of Bridgeport	8731	6	6
Bronte			
The First National Bank Of Bronte	8641	6	–
Brownsville			
The First National Bank In Brownsville	12792	5	6
The First National Bank Of Brownsville	4577	4	–
The Merchants National Bank Of Brownsville	7002	5	6
The State National Bank Of Brownsville	12236	6	5
Brownwood			
Citizens National Bank At Brownwood	14273	–	6
First National Bank In Brownwood	4695	5	6
The Brownwood National Bank	4695	4	–
The Citizens National Bank In Brownwood	13588	–	3
The Citizens National Bank Of Brownwood	8312	5	6
The City National Bank Of Brownwood	4344	6	–
The Coggin National Bank Of Brownwood	9812	6	6
The First National Bank Of Brownwood	2937	6	–

City, Bank	Ch. No.	L	S
Brownwood			
The Merchants National Bank Of Brownwood	4344	6	–
Bryan			
The City National Bank Of Bryan	4070	5	5
The First National Bank Of Bryan	3446	5	5
The Merchants And Planters National Bank Of Bryan	4070	6	–
Buda			
The Farmers National Bank Of Buda	12241	6	–
Burkburnett			
First National Bank In Burkburnett	13668	–	3
The First National Bank Of Burkburnett	8706	5	5
Burnet			
The Burnet National Bank	6966	5	5
The First National Bank Of Burnet	3007	6	–
Byers			
The First National Bank Of Byers	8787	6	6
Bynum			
The First National Bank Of Bynum	10549	6	–
Caddo Mills			
The First National Bank Of Caddo Mills	9637	6	–
Caldwell			
The Caldwell National Bank	6607	6	6
The First National Bank Of Caldwell	6614	6	–
Calvert			
The First National Bank Of Calvert	3742	6	–
Cameron			
First National Bank In Cameron	13731	–	6
The Citizens National Bank Of Cameron	5484	4	5
The First National Bank Of Cameron	4086	6	5
Campbell			
The Campbell National Bank	7348	6	–
The Campbell National Exchange Bank	10473	6	–
Canadian			
The First National Bank Of Canadian	6826	6	–
Canton			
The First National Bank Of Canton	8891	6	6
Canyon			
The Canyon National Bank	7961	6	–
The First National Bank In Canyon	14090	–	4
The First National Bank Of Canyon	5238	5	6
The Stockmens National Bank Of Canyon	5238	6	–
Carthage			
The First National Bank Of Carthage	6197	6	6
The Merchants And Farmers National Bank Of Carthage	6152	6	–
Celeste			
The First National Bank Of Celeste	5324	5	6
Celina			
The First National Bank Of Celina	6046	6	–
Center			
The Farmers National Bank Of Center	7249	6	–
The First National Bank Of Center	5971	6	–
Center Point			
The First National Bank Of Center Point	6040	6	–
Childress			
The Childress National Bank	6024	6	–
The City National Bank Of Childress	5992	5	–
The First National Bank In Childress	12666	–	6
The First National Bank Of Childress	4571	6	–
Cisco			
The American National Bank Of Cisco	11357	6	–
The Citizens National Bank Of Cisco	6115	6	–
The First National Bank Of Cisco	4134	6	–
The Merchants And Farmers National Bank Of Cisco	7360	6	–
Clarendon			
The First National Bank Of Clarendon	5463	6	5
Clarksville			
First National Bank In Clarksville	13974	–	4
The City National Bank Of Clarksville	10643	6	–
The First National Bank Of Clarksville	3973	6	6
The Red River National Bank In Clarksville	13428	–	3
The Red River National Bank Of Clarksville	4982	5	6
Claude			
The First National Bank Of Claude	7123	6	4
Cleburne			
The Citizens National Bank Of Cleburne	6791	6	–
The City National Bank Of Cleburne	13107	6	4
The Farmers And Merchants National Bank Of Cleburne	4386	4	–
The First National Bank Of Cleburne	2982	6	–
The Home National Bank Of Cleburne	10411	5	–
The National Bank Of Cleburne	4035	5	–
Cleveland			
The First National Bank Of Cleveland	10276	6	6
Clifton			
The First National Bank Of Clifton	7245	5	–
Clyde			
The Clyde National Bank	8780	6	4
The First National Bank Of Clyde	8106	6	–
Coleman			
First Coleman National Bank Of Coleman	13595	–	2
The Coleman National Bank	4683	5	–
The First National Bank Of Coleman	3433	5	–
Collinsville			
The First National Bank Of Collinsville	6300	6	–
Colorado			
Colorado National Bank In Colorado	13562	–	6
The Citizens National Bank Of Colorado	4395	6	–
The City National Bank Of Colorado	5276	6	5
The Colorado National Bank	2801	6	6
The First National Bank Of Colorado	2893	6	–
The Peoples National Bank Of Colorado	4950	6	–
Comanche			
The Comanche National Bank	4246	5	5
The Farmers And Merchants National Bank Of Comanche	7105	5	–
The First National Bank Of Comanche	3561	5	–
Commerce			
The Commerce National Bank	4021	6	–
The First National Bank Of Commerce	4021	6	–
The Planters And Merchants National Bank Of Commerce	6224	6	–
Como			
The First National Bank Of Como	9931	6	–
Conroe			
First National Bank In Conroe	12809	–	5
The First National Bank Of Conroe	6394	6	–
Coolidge			
The First National Bank Of Coolidge	7231	5	5
Cooper			
The Delta National Bank Of Cooper	5533	5	6
The Farmers National Bank Of Cooper	10626	6	–
The First National Bank In Cooper	13046	–	6
The First National Bank Of Cooper	4500	6	–
Corpus Christi			
State National Bank Of Corpus Christi	12235	–	5
The City National Bank & Trust Company Of Corpus Christi	7668	6	6
The City National Bank Of Corpus Christi	7668	3	–
The Corpus Christi National Bank	4423	5	–
Corsicana			
The City National Bank Of Corsicana	3915	5	–
The Corsicana National Bank	3645	5	5
The First National Bank Of Corsicana	3506	4	4
The State National Bank Of Corsicana	11022	4	4
Cotulla			
Stockmens National Bank In Cotulla	14302	–	6
The Stockmens National Bank Of Cotulla	7243	6	6
Covington			
The First National Bank Of Covington	7147	6	–
Crandall			
The Citizens National Bank Of Crandall	5938	5	6
The First National Bank Of Crandall	5824	6	6
Crawford			
The First National Bank Of Crawford	10400	6	–
Cresson			
The Cresson National Bank	8965	6	–
Crockett			
The Farmers And Merchants National Bank Of Crockett	5953	6	–
The First National Bank Of Crockett	4684	5	6
Crosbyton			
The First National Bank Of Crosbyton	9989	6	6
Cross Plains			
The Farmers National Bank Of Cross Plains	8583	6	6
Crowell			
The First National Bank Of Crowell	6402	6	–
The Foard County National Bank Of Crowell	9178	6	–
Cuero			
Buchel National Bank In Cuero	14164	–	4
The Buchel National Bank Of Cuero	8562	6	4
The First National Bank Of Cuero	4140	6	–
Cumby			
The First National Bank Of Cumby	5719	6	–
Daingerfield			
The Citizens National Bank Of Daingerfield	7096	6	6
The National Bank Of Daingerfield	4701	6	5
Dalhart			
First National Bank In Dalhart	14199	–	6
The Dalhart National Bank	7977	6	–
The First National Bank Of Dalhart	6762	6	5
Dallas			
Dallas National Bank	11749	3	4
First National Bank In Dallas	3623	–	2
Mercantile National Bank At Dallas	13743	–	5
North Texas National Bank In Dallas	12736	3	4
Republic National Bank & Trust Company Of Dallas	12186	5	2
The American Exchange National Bank Of Dallas	3623	2	4
The American National Bank Of Dallas	3132	5	–
The Bankers And Merchants National Bank Of Dallas	4213	6	–
The Central National Bank Of Dallas	4127	6	–
The City National Bank Of Dallas	2455	1	4
The Commonwealth National Bank Of Dallas	8664	4	–
The Dallas National Bank	3008	6	–
The First National Bank Of Dallas	2157	6	–
The Fourth National Bank Of Dallas	3664	6	–
The Gaston National Bank Of Dallas	7113	6	–
The Mercantile National Bank In Dallas	12707	5	–
The Mercantile National Bank Of Dallas	4707	6	–
The Merchants National Bank Of Dallas	10331	6	–
The National Bank Of Commerce Of Dallas	3985	5	6
The National Bank Of Dallas	5078	6	–
The National Exchange Bank Of Dallas	3623	5	–
The Ninth National Bank Of Dallas	4415	6	–
The North Texas National Bank At Dallas	3834	6	–
The Republic National Bank Of Dallas	12186	4	–
The Security National Bank Of Dallas	10564	3	–
The Southwest National Bank Of Dallas	11996	4	–
The State National Bank Of Dallas	3664	6	–
The Tenison National Bank Of Dallas	10965	5	–
The Texas National Bank Of Dallas	7052	6	–
The Trinity National Bank Of Dallas	9341	6	–
The Union National Bank Of Dallas	9245	6	–
Dawson			
The First National Bank Of Dawson	10694	6	6
The Liberty National Bank Of Dawson	11239	5	6
De Kalb			
The First National Bank Of De Kalb	8449	6	–
De Leon			
The Farmers And Merchants National Bank Of De Leon	7553	6	3
The First National Bank Of De Leon	5660	6	–
Decatur			
The City National Bank Of Decatur	5665	5	–
Decatur			
The First National Bank In Decatur	13623	–	3
The First National Bank Of Decatur	2940	5	6
The Wise County National Bank Of Decatur	4116	6	–
Del Rio			
The Del Rio National Bank	7433	4	5
The First National Bank Of Del Rio	5294	4	6
Denison			
The Citizens National Bank Of Denison	12728	6	6
The First National Bank Of Denison	2099	6	–
The National Bank Of Denison	4447	4	–
The State National Bank Of Denison	3058	3	5
Denton			
The Denton County National Bank Of Denton	4708	5	6
The Exchange National Bank Of Denton	2949	5	–
The First National Bank Of Denton	2812	5	–
Deport			
The First National Bank Of Deport	6430	6	6
Detroit			
The First National Bank Of Detroit	4682	6	–
Devine			
The Adams National Bank Of Devine	7212	5	6
Dickens			
The First National Bank Of Dickens	8303	6	–
Dickinson			
The First National Bank Of Dickinson	12855	6	6
Dodd City			
The First National Bank Of Dodd City	5728	6	6
Dublin			
The Citizens National Bank Of Dublin	5836	5	–
The Dublin National Bank	4865	6	6
The First National Bank Of Dublin	4062	6	–
Eagle Lake			
The First National Bank Of Eagle Lake	7534	6	4
Eagle Pass			
The Border National Bank Of Eagle Pass	5181	4	–
The First National Bank Of Eagle Pass	4490	5	6
The Simpson National Bank Of Eagle Pass	5060	6	–
Eastland			
The American National Bank Of Eastland	11258	5	–
The City National Bank Of Eastland	7183	6	–
The Eastland National Bank	4466	6	–
Edgewood			
The First National Bank Of Edgewood	10624	5	6
Edinburg			
The First National Bank Of Edinburg	13315	–	2
Edna			
The Allen National Bank Of Edna	8123	6	–
El Campo			
The First National Bank Of El Campo	6112	5	4
El Dorado			
The First National Bank Of El Dorado	8575	6	6
El Paso			
El Paso National Bank	12769	5	4
The American National Bank Of El Paso	7530	6	–
The Border National Bank Of El Paso	10974	4	–
The City National Bank Of El Paso	7514	3	–
The Commercial National Bank Of El Paso	10140	6	–
The El Paso National Bank Of Texas	3608	6	–
The First National Bank Of El Paso	2532	1	4
The Lowdon National Bank Of El Paso	5239	6	–
The National Bank Of Commerce Of El Paso	9155	6	–
The National Exchange Bank Of El Paso	7075	6	–
The State National Bank Of El Paso	2521	4	4
Electra			
The First National Bank Of Electra	10050	6	–
Elgin			
The Elgin National Bank	8156	6	6
The First National Bank Of Elgin	4410	6	–
The First National Bank Of Giddings	4410	6	6
Emma			
The Citizens National Bank Of Crosbyton	8515	6	6
The First National Bank Of Emma	8515	6	–
Emory			
The First National Bank Of Emory	6814	6	6
Enloe			
The First National Bank Of Enloe	6271	6	–
Ennis			
Citizens National Bank In Ennis	13667	–	6
The Citizens National Bank Of Ennis	7331	5	3
The Ennis National Bank	2939	5	–
The First National Bank Of Ennis	12110	5	6
The Peoples National Bank Of Ennis	3532	6	–
Fabens			
The First National Bank Of Fabens	11700	–	6
Fairfield			
The First National Bank Of Fairfield	4291	6	–
Falfurrias			
The First National Bank In Falfurrias	14072	–	6
The First National Bank Of Falfurrias	11792	6	6
Falls City			
The Falls City National Bank	8606	5	6
Farmersville			
The Farmers And Merchants National Bank Of Farmersville	6011	6	–
The First National Bank Of Farmersville	3624	6	–
Farwell			
The First National Bank Of Farwell	8431	6	–
Fayetteville			
The Farmers National Bank Of Fayetteville	10954	5	6
Ferris			
The Citizens National Bank Of Ferris	6553	6	–
The Ferris National Bank	6376	6	6
Flatonia			
The First National Bank Of Flatonia	4179	6	–
Floresville			
First City National Bank Of Floresville	6320	–	4
The City National Bank Of Floresville	8519	5	6
The First National Bank Of Floresville	6320	5	6

City, Bank	Ch. No.	L	S
Floydada			
The First National Bank Of Floydada	7045	6	6
Follett			
The Follett National Bank	12101	6	6
Forney			
The City National Bank Of Forney	6078	6	6
The Farmers National Bank Of Forney	9369	5	6
The National Bank Of Forney	4014	6	–
Fort Stockton			
The First National Bank Of Fort Stockton	9848	6	6
Fort Worth			
Stockyards National Bank Of Fort Worth	6822	4	5
The American National Bank Of Fort Worth	4848	5	–
The City National Bank Of Fort Worth	2359	6	–
The Farmers And Mechanics National Bank Of Fort Worth	4004	4	–
The First National Bank Of Fort Worth	2349	3	–
The Fort Worth National Bank	3131	3	3
The Merchants National Bank Of Fort Worth	3631	6	–
The National Live Stock Bank Of Fort Worth	4946	6	–
The State National Bank Of Fort Worth	3221	5	–
The Texas National Bank Of Fort Worth	12371	3	6
The Traders National Bank Of Fort Worth	2689	5	–
The Western National Bank Of Fort Worth	7165	5	–
Franklin			
The First National Bank Of Franklin	7838	5	4
Frankston			
The First National Bank Of Frankston	7623	6	–
Freeport			
The Freeport National Bank	10420	5	6
Frisco			
The First National Bank Of Frisco	6346	6	–
Frost			
The First National Bank Of Frost	6968	6	6
The Frost National Bank	13507	–	4
Gainesville			
The First National Bank Of Gainesville	2836	5	–
The Gainesville National Bank	2802	6	–
The Lindsay National Bank Of Gainesville	6292	5	–
The Red River National Bank Of Gainesville	3229	6	–
Galveston			
The American National Bank Of Galveston	4321	4	–
The City National Bank Of Galveston	8899	4	3
The First National Bank Of Galveston	1566	4	4
The Galveston National Bank	4153	5	–
The Merchants National Bank Of Galveston	8068	6	–
The National Bank Of Texas, Galveston	1642	5	–
The United States National Bank Of Galveston	12475	3	3
Ganado			
The First National Bank Of Ganado	10076	6	–
Garland			
The Citizens National Bank Of Garland	7140	6	–
The First National Bank Of Garland	7140	6	6
The National Bank Of Garland	7989	6	–
The State National Bank Of Garland	7989	6	4
Gatesville			
The Citizens National Bank Of Gatesville	4388	6	–
The City National Bank Of Gatesville	4732	6	–
The Farmers National Bank Of Gatesville	8928	6	–
The First National Bank Of Gatesville	4097	6	5
The Gatesville National Bank	6150	6	6
George West			
The First National Bank Of George West	12919	6	6
Georgetown			
The First National Bank Of Georgetown	4294	6	3
Gilmer			
The Farmers And Merchants National Bank Of Gilmer	5741	4	6
The First National Bank Of Gilmer	5288	6	6
Glen Rose			
The First National Bank Of Glen Rose	5795	6	–
Goldthwaite			
The First National Bank Of Goldthwaite	4687	6	–
The Goldthwaite National Bank	6092	5	–
Goliad			
The Commercial National Bank Of Goliad	7548	6	–
The First National Bank Of Goliad	4565	5	5
Gonzales			
The Farmers National Bank Of Gonzales	8392	6	5
The Gonzales National Bank	6277	6	–
Gordon			
The First National Bank Of Gordon	5759	6	6
Goree			
The First National Bank Of Goree	8200	6	6
Gorman			
The First National Bank Of Gorman	7410	6	6
Graham			
First National Bank In Graham	4418	6	5
The Beckham National Bank Of Graham	4418	6	–
The First National Bank Of Graham	4391	6	–
The Graham National Bank	5897	6	6
Granbury			
The City National Bank Of Granbury	5808	5	–
The First National Bank Of Granbury	3727	4	5
Grand Saline			
The Citizens National Bank Of Grand Saline	8884	6	–
The First National Bank Of Grand Saline	5722	6	–
The National Bank Of Grand Saline	5696	6	–
The State National Bank Of Grand Saline	12745	6	5
Grandview			
The Farmers And Merchants National Bank Of Grandview	7269	5	–
The First National Bank Of Grandview	4389	6	6
Granger			
The First National Bank Of Granger	6361	6	6
The Granger National Bank	11642	6	6
Grapevine			
The Farmers National Bank Of Grapevine	8318	5	–
The Grapevine National Bank	5439	6	–
The Tarrant County National Bank Of Grapevine	12708	–	6
Greenville			
The City National Bank Of Greenville	5035	6	–
The Commercial National Bank Of Greenville	7510	4	–
The First National Bank Of Greenville	2998	5	–
The Greenville National Bank	3646	6	–
The Greenville National Exchange Bank	8581	3	5
The Hunt County National Bank Of Greenville	3016	6	–
Gregory			
The First National Bank Of Gregory	10241	5	6
Groesbeck			
Citizens National Bank In Groesbeck	14126	–	6
The Citizens National Bank Of Groesbeck	6461	6	6
The Groesbeck National Bank	4269	6	–
Groveton			
First National Bank In Groveton	14104	–	6
The First National Bank Of Groveton	6329	4	6
Gunter			
The First National Bank Of Gunter	6404	6	–
Hallettsville			
First National Bank Of Hallettsville	4338	5	5
The Lavaca County National Bank Of Hallettsville	4338	6	–
Hamilton			
The Hamilton National Bank	4451	5	6
Hamlin			
The Farmers And Merchants National Bank Of Hamlin	12700	–	6
The First National Bank Of Hamlin	8252	6	6
The Hamlin National Bank	8427	6	–
Harrisburg			
The Harrisburg National Bank Of Houston	12840	–	6
Haskell			
Haskell National Bank	14149	–	3
The Farmers National Bank Of Haskell	7825	6	–
The First National Bank Of Haskell	4333	6	–
The Haskell National Bank	4474	6	6
Hawley			
The First National Bank Of Hawley	8535	6	–
Hearne			
The First National Bank Of Hearne	4976	6	–
Hebbronville			
The First National Bank Of Hebbronville	12995	–	5
Hemphill			
First National Bank In Hemphill	13526	–	6
The First National Bank Of Hemphill	8526	6	6
Hempstead			
The Farmers National Bank Of Hempstead	4905	6	–
Henderson			
Citizens National Bank Of Henderson	13443	–	3
The Farmers And Merchants National Bank Of Henderson	6780	6	6
The First National Bank Of Henderson	6176	6	5
Henrietta			
The Farmers National Bank Of Henrietta	4068	6	–
The Henrietta National Bank	3022	6	–
Hereford			
The First National Bank Of Hereford	5604	5	6
The Hereford National Bank	5604	6	–
The Western National Bank Of Hereford	6812	6	6
Hico			
The First National Bank Of Hico	4366	6	–
The Hico National Bank, Hico	7157	6	6
Higgins			
First National Bank In Higgins	8249	–	6
The Citizens National Bank Of Higgins	8249	6	–
The First National Bank Of Higgins	8179	6	–
Hillsboro			
The Citizens National Bank Of Hillsboro	4900	4	5
The Farmers National Bank Of Hillsboro	3762	5	6
The Hill County National Bank Of Hillsboro	3046	6	–
The Sturgis National Bank Of Hillsboro	3786	5	–
Holland			
The First National Bank Of Holland	8008	6	6
Hondo			
The First National Bank Of Hondo	5765	5	6
Honey Grove			
First National Bank In Honey Grove	13416	–	5
The First National Bank Of Honey Grove	2867	5	6
The Planters National Bank Of Honey Grove	4112	6	–
The State National Bank Of Honey Grove	10617	6	–
Houston			
First National Bank In Houston	13683	–	3
Houston National Bank	9353	5	4
San Jacinto National Bank Of Houston	13925	–	4
South Texas Commercial National Bank Of Houston	10152	2	2
The American National Bank Of Houston	9226	6	–
The City National Bank Of Houston	13943	–	5
The Commercial National Bank Of Houston	3517	4	–
The First National Bank Of Houston	1644	1	3
The Guaranty National Bank Of Houston	12062	4	5
The Houston National Bank	4028	6	–
The Houston National Exchange Bank	9353	3	–
The Lumbermans National Bank Of Houston	8645	3	–
The Merchants National Bank Of Houston	5858	4	–
The National Bank Of Commerce Of Houston	10225	3	3
The National City Bank Of Houston	8288	5	–
The National Exchange Bank Of Houston	2092	5	–
The Planters And Mechanics National Bank Of Houston	4463	6	–
The Public National Bank & Trust Company Of Houston	12055	–	3
The Public National Bank Of Houston	12055	4	–
The Second National Bank Of Houston	8645	6	2
The South Texas National Bank Of Houston	4350	4	–
The State National Bank Of Houston	12070	4	3
The Union National Bank Of Houston	9712	3	1
Howe			
The Farmers National Bank Of Howe	5670	5	6
The First National Bank Of Howe	5681	6	–
Hubbard			
The Farmers National Bank Of Hubbard	7407	6	–
The First National Bank Of Hubbard	5008	5	6
Hughes Springs			
The First National Bank Of Hughes Springs	6922	6	6
Huntsville			
The First National Bank Of Huntsville	4208	6	6
The Gibbs National Bank Of Huntsville	4208	5	–
Hutto			
The Hutto National Bank	9625	6	6
Iowa Park			
The First National Bank Of Iowa Park	5589	6	6
Italy			
The Citizens National Bank Of Italy	6471	6	–
The First National Bank Of Italy	5663	4	6
Itasca			
The Citizens National Bank Of Itasca	4924	6	–
The First National Bank Of Itasca	4461	5	6
The Itasca National Bank	5749	4	6
Jacksboro			
The Citizens National Bank Of Jacksboro	5761	6	–
The First National Bank Of Jacksboro	4483	5	4
The Jacksboro National Bank	7814	6	6
Jacksonville			
The Citizens National Bank Of Jacksonville	6883	6	–
The First National Bank Of Jacksonville	5581	4	5
Jasper			
The Citizens National Bank Of Jasper	10478	–	6
The First National Bank Of Jasper	6134	6	–
Jayton			
The First National Bank Of Jayton	9845	6	6
Jefferson			
The Commercial National Bank Of Jefferson	8770	6	6
The National Bank Of Jefferson	1777	6	–
The State National Bank Of Jefferson	4721	6	–
Karnes City			
The City National Bank Of Karnes City	8565	6	–
The Karnes County National Bank Of Karnes City	5614	6	6
Kaufman			
The Citizens National Bank Of Kaufman	4492	6	–
The Farmers And Merchants National Bank Of Kaufman	10757	5	6
The First National Bank Of Kaufman	3836	5	6
Kemp			
The First National Bank Of Kemp	5932	5	6
Kenedy			
First Nichols National Bank Of Kenedy	12187	–	5
The First National Bank Of Kenedy	12182	6	6
The Kenedy National Bank	8013	6	–
Kerens			
First National Bank Of Kerens	13656	–	3
The First National Bank Of Kerens	7529	6	6
Kilgore			
The Kilgore National Bank	12698	6	5
Killeen			
The First National Bank Of Killeen	5750	5	–
Kingsbury			
The First National Bank Of Kingsbury	10266	6	–
Kingsville			
The First National Bank Of Kingsville	12968	6	5
Knox City			
The First National Bank Of Knox City	7953	6	6
Kosse			
The First National Bank Of Kosse	9205	6	–
Krum			
The First National Bank Of Krum	10418	6	–
La Coste			
The La Coste National Bank	10189	5	6
La Feria			
The First National Bank Of La Feria	12747	–	6
La Grange			
The First National Bank Of La Grange	3906	4	5
Ladonia			
The First National Bank Of Ladonia	4311	4	–
The Ladonia National Bank	5739	6	–
The Weldon National Bank Of Ladonia	4515	6	–
Lakeview			
The First National Bank Of Lakeview	12835	–	6
Lamesa			
The First National Bank Of Lamesa	11163	6	6
Lampasas			
The First National Bank Of Lampasas	3261	6	6
The Lampasas National Bank	5645	6	–
The Peoples National Bank Of Lampasas	7572	6	6
Lancaster			
The First National Bank Of Lancaster	11423	6	6
Laredo			
The First National Bank Of Laredo	2486	5	6
The Laredo National Bank	5001	4	5
The Milmo National Bank Of Laredo	2486	5	–
The Rio Grande National Bank Of Laredo	4146	6	–

City, Bank	Ch. No.	L	S
Leonard			
The First National Bank Of Leonard	5109	5	6
The Leonard National Bank	12382	6	6
Lewisville			
The First National Bank Of Lewisville	7144	6	6
Lindale			
The First National Bank Of Lindale	7956	6	–
Linden			
The First National Bank Of Linden	10476	–	4
Lipan			
The First National Bank Of Lipan	10598	6	6
Livingston			
The Citizens National Bank Of Livingston	6169	6	–
The First National Bank Of Livingston	6169	6	6
Llano			
The First National Bank Of Llano	4316	6	–
The Home National Bank Of Llano	7119	6	–
The Iron City National Bank Of Llano	4371	6	–
The Llano National Bank	5853	6	–
Lockhart			
First-Lockhart National Bank, Lockhart	13934	–	4
The First National Bank Of Lockhart	4030	5	6
The Lockhart National Bank	5491	6	6
Lockney			
The First National Bank Of Lockney	9126	6	6
The Lockney National Bank	9193	6	–
Lometa			
The First National Bank Of Lometa	10323	5	6
Lone Oak			
The Farmers National Bank Of Lone Oak	7657	6	–
The First National Bank Of Lone Oak	6605	6	–
Longview			
The Citizens National Bank Of Longview	6043	6	–
The First National Bank Of Longview	4077	6	5
The Rembert National Bank Of Longview	12411	5	5
Lorena			
The First National Bank Of Lorena	8621	6	–
Lott			
The First National Bank Of Lott	6223	5	6
Lovelady			
The First National Bank Of Lovelady	8742	6	6
Lubbock			
The Citizens National Bank Of Lubbock	8208	6	5
The First National Bank Of Lubbock	6195	6	–
The Lubbock National Bank	12683	–	5
Lufkin			
The Angelina County National Bank Of Lufkin	6009	6	–
The Lufkin National Bank	5797	5	5
Luling			
The First National Bank In Luling	13919	–	6
The First National Bank Of Luling	4266	6	–
Mabank			
The First National Bank Of Mabank	6422	6	6
Madisonville			
The First National Bank Of Madisonville	6356	6	6
Malakoff			
The First National Bank Of Malakoff	10403	6	6
Manor			
The Farmers National Bank Of Manor	7146	6	–
Mansfield			
The First National Bank Of Mansfield	7201	5	–
Marble Falls			
The First National Bank Of Marble Falls	4545	6	–
Marfa			
The Marfa National Bank	8674	5	5
Marlin			
Marlin-Citizens National Bank, Marlin	5606	–	6
The First National Bank Of Marlin	4706	5	5
The Marlin National Bank	5606	4	6
Marshall			
The First National Bank Of Marshall	3113	6	5
The Marshall National Bank	4101	5	5
The State National Bank Of Marshall	12703	5	5
Mart			
The Farmers And Merchants National Bank Of Mart	7546	6	3
The First National Bank Of Mart	5850	5	5
Mason			
The Citizens National Bank Of Mason	4378	6	–
The First National Bank Of Mason	4378	6	–
The German-American National Bank Of Mason	7098	6	–
The Mason National Bank, Mason	7098	5	5
Matador			
The First National Bank Of Matador	11002	–	5
Maud			
The Maud National Bank	10182	6	–
May			
The First National Bank Of May	8327	6	6
Mcgregor			
The Citizens National Bank Of Mcgregor	5504	6	–
The First National Bank Of Mcgregor	4076	5	6
The Mcgregor National Bank	7599	6	–
Mckinney			
Central National Bank Of Mckinney	14236	–	5
The Collin County National Bank Of Mckinney	2909	3	5
The First National Bank Of Mckinney	2729	5	6
Mclean			
The First National Bank Of Mclean	7413	6	–
Melissa			
The Melissa National Bank	10008	6	4
Memphis			
The First National Bank Of Memphis	6107	5	3
The Hall County National Bank Of Memphis	8005	5	5
Menard			
The First National Bank Of Menard	10044	6	–
Mercedes			
The First National Bank Of Mercedes	11879	5	6
Meridan			
The First National Bank Of Meridan	4016	6	–
Merit			
The First National Bank Of Merit	7378	6	6
Merkel			
The Farmers And Merchants National Bank Of Merkel	7481	6	6
The First National Bank Of Merkel	5661	6	–
The Merkel National Bank	7466	6	–
The Southern National Bank Of Merkel	10052	6	–
Mertzon			
The First National Bank Of Mertzon	9810	6	6
Mesquite			
The First National Bank Of Mesquite	6140	6	5
Mexia			
The Citizens National Bank Of Mexia	5697	6	–
The City National Bank Of Mexia	11964	6	5
The First National Bank Of Mexia	3014	6	–
The Prendergast-Smith National Bank Of Mexia	12190	–	5
Midland			
The First National Bank Of Midland	4368	6	6
The Midland National Bank, Midland	6410	6	5
Midlothian			
First National Bank In Midlothian	13670	–	6
The Farmers National Bank Of Midlothian	8568	6	–
The First National Bank Of Midlothian	7775	6	6
Miles			
The Miles National Bank	6935	6	–
The Runnels County National Bank Of Miles	7414	6	–
Millsap			
The First National Bank Of Millsap	12687	6	6
Mineola			
The First National Bank Of Mineola	5127	5	5
The Mineola National Bank	8037	6	–
Mineral Wells			
The City National Bank Of Mineral Wells	12734	6	5
The First National Bank Of Mineral Wells	5511	4	6
The State National Bank Of Mineral Wells	12669	5	5
Mission			
The First National Bank Of Mission	10090	5	6
Montague			
The First National Bank Of Montague	3165	6	–
Moody			
The First National Bank Of Moody	5774	6	5
Moore			
The Moore National Bank	8817	6	6
Morgan			
The First National Bank Of Morgan	6247	6	–
Moulton			
The First National Bank Of Moulton	5399	6	–
Mount Calm			
The First National Bank In Mount Calm	13669	–	6
The First National Bank Of Mount Calm	10297	6	6
Mount Pleasant			
The First National Bank Of Mount Pleasant	4722	5	–
The Merchants And Planters National Bank Of Mount Pleasant	6139	6	–
The State National Bank Of Mount Pleasant	6139	6	–
Mount Vernon			
The First National Bank Of Mount Vernon	5409	6	6
The Merchants And Planters National Bank Of Mount Vernon	7674	6	6
Munday			
The Citizens National Bank Of Munday	8215	6	–
The First National Bank Of Munday	7106	6	6
Nacogdoches			
The Commercial National Bank Of Nacogdoches	5991	6	–
The First National Bank Of Nacogdoches	4405	6	–
The Stone Fort National Bank Of Nacogdoches	6627	6	5
Naples			
The Morris County National Bank Of Naples	7194	6	5
The Naples National Bank	8585	5	–
Navasota			
The Citizens National Bank Of Navasota	5190	5	6
The First National Bank Of Navasota	4253	5	5
Nederland			
The First National Bank Of Nederland	6596	6	–
Nevada			
The First National Bank Of Nevada	5721	5	6
New Boston			
The First National Bank Of New Boston	5636	6	6
The New Boston National Bank	8522	6	6
New Braunfels			
The Comal National Bank Of New Braunfels	7924	6	–
The First National Bank Of New Braunfels	4295	5	6
Newcastle			
The First National Bank Of Newcastle	10472	6	6
Newsome			
The First National Bank Of Newsome	10661	6	–
Nixon			
The First National Bank Of Nixon	10682	6	–
Nocona			
The City National Bank Of Nocona	8610	6	–
The Farmers And Merchants National Bank Of Nocona	7617	6	2
The First National Bank Of Nocona	4621	6	–
The National Bank Of Nocona	5338	6	–
The Nocona National Bank, Nocona	5338	5	–
The Peoples National Bank Of Nocona	11959	–	6
Normangee			
The First National Bank Of Normangee	10275	6	6
North Fort Worth			
The Exchange National Bank Of North Fort Worth	8287	6	–
The Stockyards National Bank Of North Fort Worth	6822	6	–
Oakville			
The First National Bank Of Oakville	8807	6	–
Ochiltree			
The First National Bank Of Ochiltree	8769	6	–
The First National Bank Of Perryton	8769	6	6
The Ochiltree National Bank, Ochiltree	8911	6	–
Odessa			
The Citizens National Bank Of Odessa	8169	6	6
The First National Bank Of Odessa	13608	–	6
The Odessa National Bank	6410	6	–
The Western National Bank Of Odessa	8925	6	–
Olney			
The City National Bank Of Olney	12676	–	5
The First National Bank Of Olney	8982	5	5
Omaha			
The First National Bank Of Omaha	10426	6	–
Orange			
First National Bank In Orange	13661	–	6
The First National Bank Of Orange	4118	5	4
The Orange National Bank	6050	6	6
Ozona			
The Ozona National Bank	7748	6	6
Paducah			
The First National Bank Of Paducah	10230	6	6
Paint Rock			
The First National Bank Of Paint Rock	8306	6	–
Palestine			
The East Texas National Bank Of Palestine	12556	–	5
The First National Bank Of Palestine	3694	4	6
The Palestine National Bank	4436	6	–
The Royall National Bank Of Palestine	7170	4	5
Pampa			
The First National Bank Of Pampa	9142	6	6
Paris			
The American National Bank Of Paris	8542	4	5
The City National Bank Of Paris	4411	4	–
The First National Bank Of Paris	3638	4	4
The Paris National Bank	5079	6	–
Pearsall			
The Pearsall National Bank	6989	5	6
The Pearsall National Bank In Pearsall	13572	–	4
Pecos			
The First National Bank Of Pecos	8771	6	6
Petty			
The Citizens National Bank Of Petty	10647	6	–
The First National Bank Of Petty	5569	6	–
Pharr			
The First National Bank Of Pharr	10169	6	3
Pilot Point			
The Pilot Point National Bank	4777	6	6
Pittsburg			
The First National Bank Of Pittsburg	4863	6	6
The Pittsburg National Bank	7376	6	6
Plainview			
The Citizens National Bank Of Plainview	9081	6	–
The First National Bank Of Plainview	5475	6	6
The Third National Bank Of Plainview	9802	6	–
Plano			
The Farmers And Merchants National Bank Of Plano	5692	6	–
The First National Bank Of Plano	13511	–	6
The Plano National Bank	3764	5	6
Pleasanton			
The First National Bank Of Pleasanton	8103	6	6
Port Arthur			
The First National Bank Of Port Arthur	5485	5	5
Port Lavaca			
The First National Bank Of Port Lavaca	5367	5	–
Port Neches			
The First National Bank Of Port Neches	11799	6	6
Post			
The First National Bank Of Post	9485	–	6
Post City			
The First National Bank Of Post City	9485	6	6
Poth			
The First National Bank Of Poth	10320	6	6
Princeton			
The First National Bank Of Princeton	8611	6	–
Purdon			
The First National Bank Of Purdon	10927	6	6
Putnam			
The First National Bank Of Putnam	9749	6	–
Quanah			
The Citizens National Bank Of Quanah	9906	6	–
The City National Bank Of Quanah	4361	6	–
The First National Bank In Quanah	12307	6	6
The First National Bank Of Quanah	4144	6	–
The Quanah National Bank, Quanah	4571	6	–
The State National Bank Of Quanah	5972	6	–
Quinlan			
The First National Bank Of Quinlan	11970	5	–
Quitman			
The First National Bank Of Quitman	10646	6	–
Ranger			
The First National Bank Of Ranger	8072	6	–
Raymondville			
The First National Bank Of Raymondville	12789	–	6
Refugio			
The First National Bank Of Refugio	12462	–	6
Richmond			
The First National Bank Of Richmond	10350	5	6
Rio Grande			
The First National Bank Of Rio Grande	11591	6	6
Rising Star			
The First National Bank Of Rising Star	7906	6	6
Robert Lee			
The First National Bank Of Robert Lee	8659	6	–
Roby			
The First National Bank Of Roby	5865	6	–
Rockdale			
The First National Bank Of Rockdale	4175	6	6
Rockport			
The First National Bank Of Aransas Pass, Rockport	4438	6	–

City, Bank	Ch. No.	L	S
Rockport			
The First National Bank Of Rockport	4438	5	6
Rockwall			
The Citizens National Bank Of Rockwall	6679	6	–
The Farmers And Merchants National Bank Of Rockwall	4717	6	–
The Farmers National Bank Of Rockwall	8204	6	6
The First National Bank In Rockwall	13402	–	6
The First National Bank Of Rockwall	3890	6	–
The Rockwall County National Bank Of Rockwall	4911	6	–
The Rockwall National Bank	6703	6	–
Rogers			
The First National Bank Of Rogers	5704	6	6
Rosebud			
The First National Bank Of Rosebud	5513	6	5
The Planters National Bank Of Rosebud	8066	6	6
Rotan			
The First National Bank Of Rotan	8693	6	6
Roxton			
The First National Bank Of Roxton	5710	5	6
Royse			
The First National Bank Of Royse	6551	6	6
Rule			
The First National Bank Of Rule	8242	6	6
Runge			
The Runge National Bank	6522	6	–
Rusk			
The First National Bank Of Rusk	4346	5	–
Sabinal			
The Sabinal National Bank	7807	5	6
Saint Jo			
The Citizens National Bank Of Saint Jo	8402	5	6
The First National Bank Of Saint Jo	5325	5	5
San Angelo			
The Central National Bank Of San Angelo	10664	4	4
The Citizens National Bank Of San Angelo	4659	6	–
The Concho National Bank Of San Angelo	2767	5	–
The First National Bank Of San Angelo	2767	4	5
The Landon National Bank Of San Angelo	6807	6	–
The San Angelo National Bank	3260	5	6
The Western National Bank Of San Angelo	6807	6	–
San Antonio			
Bexar County National Bank Of San Antonio	14283	–	4
National Bank Of Commerce Of San Antonio	6956	4	3
The Alamo National Bank Of San Antonio	4525	3	3
The City National Bank Of San Antonio	5217	3	–
The Commercial National Bank Of San Antonio	12162	5	5
The Fifth National Bank Of San Antonio	4748	6	–
The Frost National Bank Of San Antonio	5179	3	3
The Groos National Bank Of San Antonio	10148	4	4
The Lockwood National Bank Of San Antonio	3738	4	–
The National Bank Of Fort Sam Houston At San Antonio	13578	–	3
The San Antonio National Bank	1657	3	5
The State National Bank Of San Antonio	10793	6	–
The Texas National Bank Of San Antonio	3298	6	–
The Traders National Bank Of San Antonio	2883	6	–
Woods National Bank Of San Antonio	7316	5	–
San Augustine			
The First National Bank Of San Augustine	6214	5	6
The San Augustine National Bank	6245	6	–
San Marcos			
The First National Bank Of San Marcos	3346	6	6
The Glover National Bank Of San Marcos	3344	6	–
The National Bank Of San Marcos	3344	6	–
The Wood National Bank Of San Marcos	3344	6	–
San Saba			
The First National Bank Of San Saba	7700	6	–
The San Saba National Bank	9781	6	–
Sanger			
The First National Bank Of Sanger	7886	6	6
The Sanger National Bank	8690	6	6
Santa Anna			
The First National Bank Of Santa Anna	8109	6	–
Santo			
The First National Bank Of Santo	8176	5	6
Savoy			
The First National Bank Of Savoy	7645	6	–
Schulenburg			
The First National Bank Of Schulenburg	8034	6	6
Schwertner			
The First National Bank Of Schwertner	10956	5	6
Sealy			
The Farmers National Bank Of Sealy	10398	6	–
The Sealy National Bank	6390	6	–
Seminole			
The Seminole National Bank	8465	6	–
Sequin			
The First National Bank Of Sequin	5097	5	4
Seymour			
The Davis National Bank Of Seymour	5904	6	–
The Farmers National Bank Of Seymour	7482	6	6
The First National Bank Of Seymour	4263	5	5
Shamrock			
The First National Bank Of Shamrock	7306	6	–
Sherman			
The Commercial National Bank Of Sherman	5864	5	–
The Commercial National Bank Of Sherman	10607	6	–
Sherman			
The Grayson County National Bank Of Sherman	5192	6	–
The Merchants And Planters National Bank Of Sherman	3159	3	3
Shiner			
The First National Bank Of Shiner	5628	3	6
Silverton			
The First National Bank Of Silverton	8816	6	6
Smithville			
The First National Bank Of Smithville	7041	6	6
Snyder			
Snyder National Bank	14270	–	6
The First National Bank Of Snyder	5580	6	–
The Snyder National Bank	7635	6	6
Sonora			
The First National Bank Of Sonora	5466	5	6
Sour Lake			
The Citizens National Bank Of Sour Lake	11021	6	6
The First National Bank Of Sour Lake	6810	6	–
The Sour Lake National Bank, Sour Lake	6856	6	–
Spur			
The City National Bank Of Spur	10703	6	6
The Spur National Bank	9611	5	6
Stamford			
The Citizens National Bank Of Stamford	7640	6	–
The First National Bank In Stamford	13598	–	3
The First National Bank Of Stamford	5560	5	6
Stanton			
The First National Bank Of Stanton	8094	6	6
The Home National Bank Of Stanton	9053	6	6
The Stanton National Bank	8112	6	–
Stephenville			
Farmers-First National Bank Of Stephenville	12730	5	5
The Erath County National Bank Of Stephenville	4081	6	–
The Farmers National Bank Of Stephenville	8054	6	–
The First National Bank Of Stephenville	4095	6	–
Sterling City			
The First National Bank Of Sterling City	9813	6	6
Stratford			
The First National Bank Of Stratford	8018	6	–
The Stratford National Bank	8018	6	–
Strawn			
The First National Bank Of Strawn	10229	6	6
The Strawn National Bank	12775	–	6
Sudan			
The First National Bank Of Sudan	12725	–	6
Sulphur Springs			
First National Bank In Sulphur Springs	12845	6	5
First National Bank Of Sulphur Springs	13653	–	6
The City National Bank Of Sulphur Springs	3989	5	5
The First National Bank Of Sulphur Springs	3466	6	–
Sweetwater			
The City National Bank Of Sweetwater	11468	6	–
The First National Bank Of Sweetwater	5781	5	–
Taft			
The First National Bank Of Taft	12309	6	6
Tahoka			
The First National Bank Of Tahoka	8597	6	6
Taylor			
First Taylor National Bank, Taylor	3027	–	6
The City National Bank Of Taylor	5275	5	5
The First National Bank Of Taylor	3027	5	5
The Taylor National Bank	3859	6	6
Teague			
The First National Bank Of Teague	8195	6	4
The Teague National Bank	13067	4	4
Temple			
The Bell County National Bank Of Temple	4404	6	
The City National Bank Of Temple	6317	6	6
The First National Bank Of Temple	3227	5	–
The Temple National Bank	3858	6	–
Terrell			
The American National Bank Of Terrell	4990	4	5
The First National Bank Of Terrell	3816	4	6
The Harris National Bank Of Terrell	4990	6	–
Texarkana			
The City National Bank Of Texarkana	7392	6	–
The First National Bank Of Texarkana	3065	6	–
The Interstate National Bank Of Texarkana	3998	6	–
The Texarkana National Bank	3785	4	3
Texas City			
The First National Bank Of Texas City	9936	6	6
The Texas City National Bank	10040	6	3
Thorndale			
The First National Bank Of Thorndale	5882	5	6
Thornton			
The First National Bank Of Thornton	8538	5	6
Throckmorton			
The First National Bank Of Throckmorton	6001	4	5
Timpson			
The First National Bank Of Timpson	6177	6	–
Tioga			
The First National Bank Of Tioga	7714	6	–
Tolar			
The First National Bank Of Tolar	8001	6	–
Tom Bean			
The First National Bank Of Tom Bean	11019	6	6
Toyah			
The First National Bank Of Toyah	8355	6	–
Trenton			
The First National Bank Of Trenton	5737	6	6
Trinity			
First National Bank Of Trinity	13706	–	3
The Trinity National Bank	10078	6	4
Troup			
The First National Bank Of Troup	6212	6	4
Tulia			
The First National Bank Of Tulia	6298	5	6
The Tulia National Bank	6298	6	–
Turnersville			
The First National Bank Of Turnersville	8843	6	–
Tyler			
The Citizens National Bank Of Tyler	5343	5	4
The City National Bank Of Tyler	4353	6	–
The Farmers And Merchants National Bank Of Tyler	7515	6	–
The First National Bank Of Tyler	3651	6	–
The Jester National Bank Of Tyler	6234	6	–
The Peoples National Bank Of Tyler	13110	4	5
The Tyler National Bank	4747	6	–
Uvalde			
The Commercial National Bank Of Uvalde	6831	5	6
The First National Bank Of Uvalde	4517	6	–
The Uvalde National Bank	5175	6	–
Valley Mills			
The First National Bank Of Valley Mills	9148	6	–
Valley View			
The First National Bank Of Valley View	7731	6	6
Van Alstyne			
The Farmers National Bank Of Van Alstyne	7016	6	–
The First National Bank Of Van Alstyne	4289	6	6
Velasco			
The Velasco National Bank	4662	6	–
Venus			
The Farmers And Merchants National Bank Of Venus	7798	6	–
The First National Bank Of Venus	5549	6	–
Vernon			
The First National Bank Of Vernon	4033	6	–
The Herring National Bank Of Vernon	7010	6	3
The State National Bank Of Vernon	4130	6	–
The Waggoner National Bank Of Vernon	5203	5	5
Victoria			
The First National Bank Of Victoria	4184	4	–
The Victoria National Bank	10360	3	3
Waco			
The American National Bank Of Waco	3901	6	–
The Central National Bank Of Waco	10220	6	–
The Central Texas Exchange National Bank Of Waco	10220	5	–
The Central Texas National Bank Of Waco	9828	6	–
The Citizens National Bank Of Waco	3135	4	4
The Exchange National Bank Of Waco	8818	6	–
The Farmers And Merchants National Bank Of Waco	4349	6	–
The First National Bank Of Waco	2189	3	3
The Liberty National Bank Of Waco	11140	5	5
The National City Bank Of Waco	6572	4	3
The Provident National Bank Of Waco	4309	6	–
The Waco National Bank	2189	6	–
Walnut Springs			
The First National Bank Of Walnut Springs	8130	6	–
Waxahachie			
Citizens National Bank In Waxahachie	13516	–	3
The Citizens National Bank Of Waxahachie	3212	5	6
The First National Bank Of Waxahachie	2974	6	–
The Waxahachie National Bank	4379	3	–
Weatherford			
The Citizens National Bank Of Weatherford	2723	5	5
The First National Bank Of Weatherford	2477	5	5
The Merchants And Farmers National Bank Of Weatherford	3975	6	–
Wellington			
The City National Bank Of Wellington	9805	6	–
The First National Bank In Wellington	13249	–	2
The First National Bank Of Wellington	8102	6	–
Weslaco			
The First National Bank Of Weslaco	12641	6	6
West			
The First National Bank Of West	5543	6	–
The National Bank Of West	8239	6	6
The West National Bank	13935	–	3
Wharton			
The First National Bank Of Wharton	4903	6	–
The Wharton National Bank	6313	6	–
Whitesboro			
The City National Bank Of Whitesboro	10634	6	6
The First National Bank Of Whitesboro	5847	5	6
The Whitesboro National Bank	10634	–	6
Whitewright			
The First National Bank Of Whitewright	4692	5	5
The Planters National Bank Of Whitewright	6915	5	6
Whitney			
First National Bank In Whitney	13649	–	6
The Citizens National Bank Of Whitney	7915	6	–
The First National Bank Of Whitney	7875	6	6
Wichita Falls			
The City National Bank Of Commerce Of Wichita Falls	4248	5	–
The City National Bank Of Wichita Falls	4248	5	–
The City National Bank Of Wichita Falls	4248	3	4
The First National Bank Of Wichita Falls	3200	4	3
The National Bank Of Commerce Of Wichita Falls	10547	6	–
The Panhandle National Bank Of Wichita Falls	3200	6	–
The Security National Bank Of Wichita Falls	11762	5	6
Wichita National Bank Of Wichita Falls	13676	–	5

City, Bank	Ch. No.	L	S
Wills Point			
The First National Bank Of Wills Point	5018	6	6
The Van Zandt County National Bank Of Wills Point	6071	6	–
Winfield			
The First National Bank Of Winfield	10488	6	–
Winnsboro			
The Farmers National Bank Of Winnsboro	6168	6	–
The First National Bank Of Winnsboro	5674	4	6
Wolfe City			
The Citizens National Bank Of Wolfe City	8178	6	–
The Wolfe City National Bank In Wolfe City	13199	–	4
The Wolfe City National Bank, Wolfe City	3984	5	–
Wortham			
The First National Bank Of Wortham	6686	6	6
Wylie			
The First National Bank Of Wylie	5483	6	–
Yoakum			
The First National Bank Of Yoakum	4363	6	–
The Yoakum National Bank	8694	5	5
Yorktown			
The First National Bank Of Yorktown	6987	5	5

UTAH TERRITORY

City, Bank	Ch. No.	L	S
Logan			
The First National Bank Of Logan	4670	6	–
Nephi			
The First National Bank Of Nephi	3537	6	–
Ogden			
The Commercial National Bank Of Ogden	3739	6	–
The First National Bank Of Ogden	2579	6	–
The Utah National Bank Of Ogden	2880	6	–
Park City			
The First National Bank Of Park City	4564	6	–
Provo City			
The First National Bank Of Provo City	2641	6	–
The National Bank Of Commerce, Provo City	4486	6	–
Salt Lake City			
The American National Bank Of Salt Lake City	4432	6	–
The Commercial National Bank Of Salt Lake City	4051	6	–
The Deseret National Bank Of Salt Lake City	2059	3	–
The First National Bank Of Utah	1695	6	–
The Miners National Bank Of Salt Lake City	1646	6	–
The National Bank Of The Republic At Salt Lake City	4310	6	–
The Salt Lake City National Bank Of Utah	1921	5	–
The Union National Bank Of Salt Lake City	3306	6	–
The Utah National Bank Of Salt Lake City	4341	6	–

UTAH

City, Bank	Ch. No.	L	S
Beaver City			
The First National Bank Of Beaver City	9119	6	–
Brigham City			
The First National Bank Of Brigham City	6036	4	6
Coalville			
The First National Bank Of Coalville	7696	4	4
Delta			
The First National Bank Of Delta	11529	6	–
Layton			
The First National Bank Of Layton	7685	6	4
Logan			
The First National Bank Of Logan	4670	4	3
Moab			
The First National Bank Of Moab	10925	5	3
Morgan			
The First National Bank Of Morgan	6958	5	6
Murray			
The First National Bank Of Murray	6558	5	4
Myton			
The First National Bank Of Myton	11702	6	–
Nephi			
The First National Bank Of Nephi	3537	4	–
The Nephi National Bank	8508	4	4
Ogden			
First National Bank Of Ogden	2597	6	2
First Security Bank Of Utah, National Association Ogden	2597	–	6
First Utah National Bank Of Ogden	2597	4	–
The Commercial National Bank Of Ogden	3139	4	–
The First & Utah National Bank Of Ogden	2597	5	–
The First National Bank Of Ogden	2597	3	–
The National Bank Of Commerce Of Ogden	7296	4	4
The Pingree National Bank Of Ogden	7296	5	–
The Utah National Bank Of Ogden	2880	4	–
Park City			
The First National Bank Of Park City	4564	4	–
Price			
The First National Bank Of Price	6012	4	3
Provo City			
The First National Bank Of Provo City	2641	6	–
Salt Lake City			
Security National Bank Of Salt Lake City	9652	–	3
The Commercial National Bank Of Salt Lake City	4051	5	–
The Continental National Bank Of Salt Lake City	9403	3	2
The Continental Nationl Bank & Trust Co Of Salt Lake City	9403	–	2
The Deseret National Bank Of Salt Lake City	2059	2	2
The First National Bank Of Salt Lake City	2059	–	2
The National Bank Of The Republic At Salt Lake City	4310	4	–
The National City Bank Of Salt Lake City	10308	5	–
The National Copper Bank Of Salt Lake City	9652	3	2
The Utah National Bank Of Salt Lake City	4341	4	–
The Utah State National Bank Of Salt Lake City	4341	3	2
Smithfield			
The Commercial National Bank Of Smithfield	10135	6	5
Spanish Fork			
The First National Bank Of Spanish Fork	9111	6	6

VERMONT

City, Bank	Ch. No.	L	S
Barre			
The National Bank Of Barre	2109	4	–
The Peoples National Bank Of Barre	7068	5	4
Barton			
The Barton National Bank	2290	6	–
Bellows Falls			
The National Bank Of Bellows Falls	1653	3	5
The Windham National Bank Of Bellows Falls	13894	–	5
Bennington			
The Bennington County National Bank Of Bennington	2395	3	–
The County National Bank Of Bennington	2395	5	5
The First National Bank Of Bennington	130	4	5
Bethel			
The National White River Bank Of Bethel	962	4	6
Bradford			
The Bradford National Bank	7267	6	4
Brandon			
The Brandon National Bank	404	5	5
The First National Bank Of Brandon	278	5	5
Brattleboro			
The First National Bank Of Brattleboro	470	6	–
The Peoples National Bank Of Brattleboro	2305	3	–
The Vermont National Bank Of Brattleboro	1430	4	–
Vermont-Peoples National Bank Of Brattleboro	1430	4	4
Bristol			
The First National Bank Of Bristol	6252	6	6
Burlington			
The First National Bank Of Burlington	861	6	–
The Howard National Bank & Trust Company Of Burlington	1698	–	4
The Howard National Bank Of Burlington	1698	3	5
The Merchants National Bank Of Burlington	1197	3	4
Castleton			
The Castleton National Bank	1598	6	–
Chelsea			
The First National Bank Of Chelsea	2120	6	–
The National Bank Of Orange County At Chelsea	4929	5	6
The Orange County National Bank Of Chelsea	1004	6	–
Chester			
The National Bank Of Chester	4380	6	6
Danville			
The Caledonia National Bank Of Danville	1576	4	5
Derby Line			
The National Bank Of Derby Line	1308	4	6
Enosburg Falls			
The Enosburg Falls National Bank	13986	–	6
The First National Bank Of Enosburg Falls	7614	6	6
Factory Point			
The Factory Point National Bank	3080	6	–
Fair Haven			
The Allen National Bank Of Fair Haven	2422	4	6
The First National Bank Of Fair Haven	344	4	5
Hyde Park			
The Lamoille County National Bank Of Hyde Park	1163	5	–
Irasburg			
The Irasburg National Bank Of Orleans At Irasburg	1541	6	–
Island Pond			
The Island Pond National Bank	4275	5	5
Jamaica			
The West River National Bank Of Jamaica	1564	6	–
Lyndon			
The National Bank Of Lyndon	1140	4	–
Lyndonville			
The Lyndonville National Bank	3158	5	–
Manchester			
The Battenkill National Bank Of Manchester	1488	6	–
Manchester Center			
The Factory Point National Bank Of Manchester Center	3080	5	5
Middlebury			
The National Bank Of Middlebury	1195	3	2
Middletown Springs			
The Gray National Bank Of Middletown Springs	3150	6	–
Montpelier			
The First National Bank Of Montpelier	748	4	5
The Montpelier National Bank	857	3	6
Newport			
The National Bank Of Newport	2263	5	5
North Bennington			
The First National Bank Of North Bennington	194	4	5
Northfield			
The Northfield National Bank	1638	5	6
Orwell			
The First National Bank Of Orwell	228	5	3
Poultney			
The Citizens National Bank Of Poultney	9824	5	5
The First National Bank In Poultney	13261	6	6
The First National Bank Of Poultney	2545	5	–
The National Bank Of Poultney	1200	6	–
The Poultney National Bank	14234	–	6
Proctorsville			
The National Black River Bank Of Proctorsville	1383	5	6
Richford			
The Richford National Bank	11615	5	6
Royalton			
The National Bank Of Royalton	1673	6	–
Rutland			
The Baxter National Bank Of Rutland	1700	4	–
The Central National Bank Of Rutland	1700	6	5
The Clement National Bank Of Rutland	2950	4	5
The Killington National Bank Of Rutland	2905	6	6
The Merchants National Bank Of Rutland	3311	6	–
The National Bank Of Rutland	1450	5	–
The Rutland County National Bank Of Rutland	820	4	5
Saint Albans			
The First National Bank Of Saint Albans	269	6	–
The Vermont National Bank Of Saint Albans	1583	6	–
The Welden National Bank In Saint Albans	13800	–	6
The Welden National Bank Of Saint Albans	3482	4	6
Saint Johnsbury			
The First National Bank Of St. Johnsbury	489	4	4
The Merchants National Bank Of St. Johnsbury	2295	4	5
Springfield			
The First National Bank Of Springfield	122	3	4
Swanton			
The Ferris National Bank Of Swanton	4258	6	–
The National Union Bank Of Swanton	1634	6	–
The Peoples National Bank Of Swanton	4943	6	–
Vergennes			
The Farmers National Bank Of Vergennes	2475	5	–
The National Bank Of Vergennes	1364	4	5
Waterbury			
The Waterbury National Bank	1462	6	–
Wells River			
The National Bank Of Newbury At Wells River	1406	3	4
The National Bank Of Newbury, Wells River	1406	4	–
West Randolph			
The Randolph National Bank Of Randolph	2274	6	–
The Randolph National Bank Of West Randolph	2274	6	–
White River Junction			
The First National Bank Of White River Junction	3484	5	4
The Hartford National Bank Of White River Junction	9108	6	–
The National Bank Of White River Junction	3484	5	–
Windsor			
The Ascutney National Bank Of Windsor	816	6	–
The State National Bank Of Windsor	7721	6	–
The Windsor National Bank	3257	6	–
Woodstock			
The Woodstock National Bank	1133	3	6

VIRGINIA

City, Bank	Ch. No.	L	S
Abingdon			
The First National Bank Of Abingdon	5150	3	6
The Peoples National Bank Of Abingdon	8819	5	–
Alexandria			
Alexandria National Bank	7093	4	4
The Citizens National Bank Of Alexandria	1716	4	4
The First National Bank Of Alexandria	651	5	5
Altavista			
The First National Bank Of Altavista	9295	6	5
Appalachia			
The First National Bank Of Appalachia	9379	6	4
Appomattox			
The Farmers National Bank Of Appomattox	11205	6	5
Ashland			
The First National Bank Of Ashland	11978	5	6
Bassett			
The First National Bank Of Bassett	11976	6	5
Bedford			
The Peoples National Bank Of Bedford	11328	6	6
Bedford City			
The First National Bank Of Bedford City	4257	6	–
Berryville			
The First National Bank Of Berryville	7338	6	6
Big Stone Gap			
The First National Bank Of Big Stone Gap	11765	6	6
Blackstone			
The First National Bank Of Blackstone	9224	4	5
Bristol			
The Dominion National Bank Of Bristol	4477	4	4
Broadway			
The First National Bank Of Broadway	6666	6	6

City, Bank	Ch. No.	L	S
Brookneal			
The First National Bank Of Brookneal	10835	6	–
The Peoples National Bank Of Brookneal	11960	6	–
Buchanan			
The Buchanan National Bank	9375	6	5
The First National Bank Of Buchanan	4460	6	–
Buena Vista			
The First National Bank Of Buena Vista	4314	6	–
The First National Bank Of Buena Vista	9890	6	6
The First National Bank Of Lexington	4314	6	5
Charlottesville			
National Bank And Trust Company At Charlottesville	10618	6	4
The Albemarle National Bank Of Charlottesville	9246	6	–
The Charlottesville National Bank	1468	6	–
The Citizens National Bank Of Charlottesville	1742	6	–
The Farmers And Merchants National Bank Of Charlottesville	11517	6	–
The Jefferson National Bank Of Charlottesville	6005	6	–
The National Bank Of Charlottesville	10618	4	–
The Peoples National Bank Of Charlottesville	2594	4	3
Chase City			
The First National Bank Of Chase City	9291	6	6
Chatham			
The First National Bank Of Chatham	10821	6	6
Chilhowie			
The National Bank Of Chilhowie	8875	6	5
Christiansburg			
The First National Bank Of Christiansburg	7937	6	4
Clarksville			
The First National Bank Of Clarksville	1658	6	–
Clifton Forge			
The Clifton Forge National Bank	9177	3	4
The First National Bank Of Clifton Forge	6008	3	5
Clintwood			
The Citizens National Bank Of Clintwood	8362	6	–
Coeburn			
The First National Bank Of Coeburn	6899	6	4
Covington			
The Citizens National Bank Of Covington	5326	4	5
The Covington National Bank	4503	4	5
Crewe			
The First National Bank Of Crewe	9455	5	5
The National Bank Of Crewe	14052	–	6
Culpeper			
The Culpeper National Bank	5591	5	5
The Farmers National Bank Of Culpeper	3570	6	–
The Second National Bank Of Culpeper	5394	4	5
Danville			
American National Bank And Trust Company Of Danville	9343	6	2
The American National Bank Of Danville	9343	4	–
The First National Bank Of Danville	1609	6	–
The First National Bank Of Danville	1985	5	5
The National Bank Of Danville	9475	5	–
The Planters National Bank Of Danville	1985	6	–
The Virginia National Bank Of Danville	10156	6	–
Dillwyn			
The First National Bank Of Dillwyn	11480	6	–
Emporia			
The Citizens National Bank Of Emporia	12240	6	6
The First National Bank Of Emporia	8688	6	6
The Planters National Bank Of Emporia	9732	6	–
Esmont			
The Esmont National Bank	8003	6	6
Fairfax			
The National Bank Of Fairfax	6389	5	6
Farmville			
The First National Bank Of Farmville	5603	5	5
The Peoples National Bank Of Farmville	9222	5	5
Ferrum			
The First National Bank Of Ferrum	12311	6	5
Flint Hill			
The First National Bank Of Flint Hill	11797	6	6
Fredericksburg			
The Conway, Gordon And Garnett Natl Bank Of Fredericksburg	5268	6	–
The National Bank Of Fredericksburg	1582	5	6
The Planters National Bank In Fredericksburg	13603	–	3
The Planters National Bank Of Fredericksburg	10325	5	4
Fries			
The First National Bank Of Fries	12290	6	6
Front Royal			
The Front Royal National Bank	2967	6	–
Galax			
The First National Bank Of Galax	8791	6	6
Gate City			
The First And Peoples National Bank Of Gate City	13502	–	6
The First National Bank Of Gate City	7208	6	6
The Peoples National Bank In Gate City	13502	–	6
The Peoples National Bank Of Gate City	7135	5	6
Gloucester			
The First National Bank Of Gloucester	10658	6	6
Gordonsville			
The National Bank Of Gordonsville	10287	6	6
Graham			
The American National Bank Of Graham	7734	6	–
The First National Bank Of Graham	7782	6	–
The Twin City National Bank Of Bluefield	7782	6	6
Grundy			
The First National Bank Of Grundy	11698	6	6
Hallwood			
The Hallwood National Bank	7659	5	6
Hamilton			
The Farmers And Merchants National Bank Of Hamilton	9861	6	6
Hampton			
The Citizens National Bank Of Hampton	13775	–	5
The First National Bank Of Hampton	6842	6	6
The Merchants National Bank Of Hampton	6778	5	5
Harrisonburg			
The First National Bank Of Harrisonburg	1572	5	5
The National Bank Of Harrisonburg	11694	5	5
The Rockingham National Bank Of Harrisonburg	5261	5	4
Herndon			
The National Bank Of Herndon	9635	6	4
Honaker			
The First National Bank Of Honaker	10252	6	6
Hopewell			
The National Bank Of Hopewell	10866	6	–
Hot Springs			
The Bath County National Bank Of Hot Springs	8722	3	6
Independence			
The Grayson County National Bank Of Independence	10834	6	5
Irvington			
The Lancaster National Bank Of Irvington	5290	6	6
Jonesville			
The Peoples National Bank Of Jonesville	8384	6	–
The Powell Valley National Bank Of Jonesville	9924	6	6
Kenbridge			
The First National Bank Of Kenbridge	12251	6	–
Lawrenceville			
The First National Bank Of Lawrenceville	9433	6	–
Lebanon			
The Citizens National Bank Of Lebanon	6886	6	–
The First National Bank Of Lebanon	6886	6	6
Leesburg			
The Loudoun National Bank Of Leesburg	1738	5	5
The Peoples National Bank Of Leesburg	3917	5	4
Lexington			
The Peoples National Bank Of Lexington	7173	6	5
Louisa			
The First National Bank Of Louisa	10968	5	–
Lovingston			
The First National Bank Of Nelson County At Lovingston	11957	6	5
Luray			
The First National Bank Of Luray	6031	6	5
The Page Valley National Bank Of Luray	6206	6	5
Lynchburg			
The American National Bank Of Lynchburg	7308	6	–
The First National Bank Of Lynchburg	1558	5	4
The Lynchburg National Bank	1522	3	–
The Lynchburg National Bank And Trust Company	1522	6	4
The National Exchange Bank Of Lynchburg	2506	4	–
The Peoples National Bank Of Lynchburg	2760	3	4
Manassas			
The National Bank Of Manassas	5032	5	6
The Peoples National Bank Of Manassas	6748	5	6
Manchester			
The Manchester National Bank	9663	6	–
The Manchester National Bank Of Richmond	9663	6	–
Marion			
The Marion National Bank	6839	5	6
The Peoples National Bank Of Marion	11718	6	–
Marshall			
Marshall National Bank And Trust Company	10253	6	5
The Marshall National Bank	10253	6	–
Martinsville			
The First National Bank Of Martinsville	7206	5	5
The Peoples National Bank Of Martinsville	9847	6	6
Monterey			
The First National Bank Of Highland At Monterey	9043	5	–
Mount Jackson			
The Mount Jackson National Bank	3209	4	5
Narrows			
The First National Bank Of Narrows	11444	6	6
New Castle			
The First National Bank Of New Castle	10993	6	6
New Market			
The First National Bank Of New Market	10568	6	–
Newport News			
The First National Bank Of Newport News	4635	4	5
The National Mechanics Bank Of Newport News	11364	6	–
The Newport News National Bank	6781	6	–
The Schmelz National Bank Of Newport News	11028	5	5
Norfolk			
National Bank Of Commerce Of Norfolk	9885	–	5
Norfolk National Bank Of Commerce & Trusts	6032	6	3
The City National Bank Of Norfolk	4743	6	–
The Exchange National Bank Of Norfolk	1137	6	–
The First National Bank Of Norfolk	271	6	–
The National Bank Of Commerce Of Norfolk	6032	3	–
The Norfolk National Bank	3368	2	–
The Peoples National Bank Of Norfolk	1704	6	–
Norfolk			
The Seaboard Citizens National Bank Of Norfolk	10194	3	2
The Seaboard National Bank Of Norfolk	10194	4	–
The Virginia National Bank Of Norfolk	9885	3	3
Norton			
The First National Bank Of Norton	6235	6	6
The National Bank Of Norton	9746	5	4
Onancock			
The First National Bank In Onancock	13878	–	6
The First National Bank Of Onancock	4940	6	6
Onley			
The Farmers And Merchants National Bank Of Onley	7258	5	6
Orange			
The American National Bank Of Orange	5532	6	–
The Citizens National Bank Of Orange	7150	4	4
The National Bank Of Orange	5438	6	5
Parksley			
The Parksley National Bank	6246	6	5
Pearisburg			
The First National Bank Of Pearisburg	8091	5	6
Petersburg			
First National Bank And Trust Company Of Petersburg	3515	–	4
The Citizens National Bank Of Petersburg	13792	–	6
The Commercial National Bank Of Petersburg	1769	6	–
The First National Bank Of Petersburg	1378	6	–
The Merchants National Bank Of Petersburg	1548	6	–
The National Bank Of Petersburg	3515	3	5
The Virginia National Bank Of Petersburg	7709	2	3
Phoebus			
The Old Point National Bank Of Phoebus	12267	6	6
Pocahontas			
The First National Bank Of Pocahontas	7847	6	–
Poquoson			
The First National Bank Of Poquoson	12092	6	6
Portsmouth			
American National Bank Of Portsmouth	11381	3	4
The First National Bank Of Portsmouth	9300	6	–
Pulaski			
The Peoples National Bank Of Pulaski	11387	5	4
The Pulaski National Bank	4071	5	5
Purcellville			
The Purcellville National Bank	6018	5	5
Quantico			
The First National Bank Of Quantico	12477	–	4
Radford			
The Farmers And Merchants National Bank Of Radford	11690	6	6
The First And Merchants National Bank Of Radford	6782	–	6
The First National Bank Of Radford	6782	6	6
Reedsville			
The Commonwealth National Bank Of Reedsville	10827	6	–
Richlands			
The First National Bank Of Richlands	10850	6	6
The Richlands National Bank	10857	6	6
Richmond			
National State And City Bank Of Richmond	8666	4	–
National State Bank Of Richmond	8666	6	–
The American National Bank Of Richmond	5229	2	–
The Broadway National Bank Of Richmond	10344	4	–
The Central National Bank Of Richmond	10080	2	2
The Farmers National Bank Of Richmond	1570	6	–
The First National Bank Of Richmond	1111	2	–
The Merchants National Bank Of Richmond	1754	5	–
The National Bank Of Virginia, Richmond	1125	4	–
The National Exchange Bank Of Richmond	1166	6	–
The Planters National Bank Of Richmond	1628	4	–
Roanoke			
The American National Bank Of Roanoke	10532	5	–
The Citizens National Bank Of Roanoke	4531	6	–
The City National Bank Of Roanoke	8152	5	–
The Colonial National Bank Of Roanoke	11817	5	–
The Colonial-American National Bank Of Roanoke	11817	–	3
The Commercial National Bank Of Roanoke	4026	6	–
The First National Bank Of Roanoke	2737	4	–
The First National Exchange Bank Of Roanoke	2737	4	3
The Liberty National Bank Of Roanoke	11191	6	–
The National Exchange Bank Of Roanoke	4027	4	–
The Peoples National Bank Of Roanoke	6798	6	–
The Roanoke National Bank	2907	6	–
Rocky Mount			
The First National Bank Of Rocky Mount	6685	6	–
The Peoples National Bank Of Rocky Mount	8984	4	5
Rosslyn			
The Arlington National Bank Of Rosslyn	8389	6	–
Round Hill			
The Round Hill National Bank	11569	6	6
Rural Retreat			
The First National Bank Of Rural Retreat	10061	6	6
Saint Paul			
St. Paul National Bank	8547	5	5
Salem			
The Farmers National Bank Of Salem	1824	5	5
Saltville			
The First National Bank Of Saltville	11265	6	5
Scottsville			
The Scottsville National Bank	5725	5	4

City, Bank	Ch. No.	L	S
South Boston			
Planters & Merchants First Natl Bank Of South Boston	8643	6	6
Planters And Merchants National Bank Of South Boston	8643	4	–
The Boston National Bank Of South Boston	8414	3	5
The First National Bank Of South Boston	5872	6	–
Stanley			
The Farmers And Merchants National Bank Of Stanley	10973	6	4
Staunton			
The Augusta National Bank Of Staunton	2269	5	5
The First National Bank Of Staunton	1585	6	–
The National Valley Bank Of Staunton	1620	3	4
The Staunton National Bank	6903	5	–
The Staunton National Bank And Trust Company	6903	6	5
Strasburg			
The First National Bank Of Strasburg	8746	–	6
The Massanutten National Bank Of Strasburg	8753	6	3
The Peoples National Bank Of Strasburg	8746	6	–
Stuart			
The First National Bank Of Stuart	11901	6	4
Suffolk			
National Bank Of Suffolk	9733	4	5
The First National Bank Of Suffolk	4047	6	–
Tazewell			
Tazewell National Bank	6123	6	5
The Farmers National Bank Of Tazewell	11533	6	6
Troutdale			
The First National Bank Of Troutdale	11990	6	6
Troutville			
The First National Bank Of Troutville	9764	6	6
Victoria			
The First National Bank Of Victoria	12183	6	6
Vienna			
The Vienna National Bank	11764	6	–
Vinton			
The First National Bank Of Vinton	11911	6	–
Warrenton			
The Fauquier National Bank Of Warrenton	6126	5	6
The Peoples National Bank Of Warrenton	9642	6	5
Washington			
The Rappahannock National Bank Of Washington	6443	6	6
Waverly			
The First National Bank Of Waverly	10914	6	–
Waynesboro			
The First National Bank Of Waynesboro	7587	6	5
The Waynesboro National Bank	9261	6	–
Winchester			
Farmers & Merchants Natl Bank & Trust Co Of Winchester	6084	5	5
The Farmers And Merchants National Bank Of Winchester	6084	3	–
The Shenandoah Valley National Bank Of Winchester	1635	4	4
Wise			
The First National Bank Of Wise	10611	6	6
Woodstock			
The Shenandoah National Bank Of Woodstock	5449	6	–
Wytheville			
The First National Bank Of Wytheville	9012	4	6
The First National Farmers Bank Of Wytheville	9012		4
Wythe County National Bank Of Wytheville	12599	–	6
Yorktown			
The First National Bank Of Yorktown	11554	5	5

WASHINGTON TERRITORY

City, Bank	Ch. No.	L	S
Colfax			
The First National Bank Of Colfax	3076	6	–
The Second National Bank Of Colfax	3119	6	–
Davenport			
The Big Bend National Bank Of Davenport	4002	6	–
Dayton			
The Columbia National Bank Of Dayton	2772	6	–
The First National Bank Of Dayton	2520	6	–
The National Bank Of Dayton	3799	6	–
Ellensburg			
The First National Bank Of Ellensburg	3037	6	–
Ellensburgh			
The Ellensburgh National Bank	3867	6	–
Goldendale			
The First National Bank Of Goldendale	4031	6	–
North Yakima			
The First National Bank Of North Yakima	3355	6	–
The Yakima National Bank Of North Yakima	3862	6	–
Oakesdale			
The First National Bank Of Oakesdale	4122	6	–
Olympia			
The First National Bank Of Olympia	3024	6	–
Pomeroy			
The First National Bank Of Pomeroy	3460	6	–
Port Townsend			
The First National Bank Of Port Townsend	2948	6	–
Seattle			
The Boston National Bank Of Seattle	4124	6	–
The First National Bank Of Seattle	2783	6	–
The Merchants National Bank Of Seattle	2985	6	–
The Puget Sound National Bank Of Seattle	2966	6	–
The Washington National Bank Of Seattle	4059	6	–
Sehome			
The Bellingham Bay National Bank Of Sehome	3976	6	–
Snohomish			
The First National Bank Of Snohomish	3887	6	–
Spokane Falls			
The Browne Natoinal Bank Of Spokane Falls	4025	6	–
The Citizens National Bank Of Spokane Falls	4005	6	–
The Exchange National Bank Of Spokane Falls	4044	6	–
The First National Bank Of Spokane Falls	2805	6	–
The Spokane National Bank Of Spokane Falls	3838	6	–
The Traders National Bank Of Spokane Falls	3409	6	–
Sprague			
The First National Bank Of Sprague	3528	6	–
Tacoma			
The Citizens National Bank Of Tacoma	4069	6	–
The Merchants National Bank Of Tacoma	3172	6	–
The National Bank Of Commerce Of Tacoma	3789	6	–
The Pacific National Bank Of Tacoma	3417	6	–
The Tacoma National Bank, New Tacoma	2924	6	–
The Washington National Bank Of Tacoma	4018	6	–
Vancouver			
The First National Bank Of Vancouver	3031	6	–
Walla Walla			
The Baker-Boyer National Bank Of Walla Walla	3956	6	–
The First National Bank Of Walla Walla	2380	6	–
Whatcom			
The First National Bank Of Whatcom	4099	6	–
Yakima			
The First National Bank Of Yakima	2876	6	–

WASHINGTON

City, Bank	Ch. No.	L	S
Aberdeen			
First National Bank In Aberdeen	11751	6	6
The Aberdeen National Bank	11751	6	–
The American National Bank Of Aberdeen	13091	6	5
The First National Bank Of Aberdeen	4407	6	–
The Grays Harbor National Bank Of Aberdeen	12704	5	4
The United States National Bank Of Aberdeen	9535	6	–
Anacortes			
The First National Bank Of Anacortes	4458	6	–
Bellingham			
The Bellingham National Bank	7474	5	5
The First National Bank Of Bellingham	7372	6	2
The Northwestern National Bank Of Bellingham	9070	6	6
Blaine			
The Blaine National Bank	4471	6	–
The First National Bank Of Blaine	4470	6	–
Bremerton			
The First National Bank Of Bremerton	9280	6	4
Brewster			
The First National Bank Of Brewster	9170	6	6
Burlington			
The Burlington National Bank	10648	6	–
The First National Bank Of Burlington	9808	6	6
Camas			
Clark County National Bank Of Vancouver	10686	–	6
The First National Bank Of Camas	10686	6	6
Centralia			
First National Bank In Centralia	13099	6	6
The First National Bank Of Centralia	4439	6	–
The United States National Bank Of Centralia	8736	6	–
Chehalis			
First National Bank In Chehalis	9389	6	5
The Chehalis National Bank	9389	6	–
The First National Bank Of Chehalis	4203	6	–
Cheney			
The First National Bank Of Cheney	4542	6	–
The National Bank Of Cheney	9080	6	–
The Security National Bank Of Cheney	9144	6	6
Chewelah			
The First National Bank Of Chewelah	8789	6	5
Clarkston			
The First National Bank Of Clarkston	6742	6	–
Cle Elum			
The First National Bank Of Cle Elum	10469	6	5
Colfax			
The Colfax National Bank	7095	4	5
The Farmers National Bank Of Colfax	10511	–	6
The First National Bank Of Colfax	3076	6	–
The Second National Bank Of Colfax	3119	6	–
Colton			
The First National Bank Of Colton	4788	6	–
Colville			
The First National Bank Of Colville	8104	6	6
Connell			
The Connell National Bank	8958	6	–
Conway			
The First National Bank Of Conway	11984	6	6
Davenport			
The Big Bend National Bank Of Davenport	4002	6	–
The Davenport National Bank	7527	6	–
Dayton			
The Broughton National Bank Of Dayton	9443	6	4
The Citizens National Bank Of Dayton	4473	6	–
The Columbia National Bank Of Dayton	2772	6	6
The Dayton National Bank	8090	6	–
East Stanwood			
The National Bank Of East Stanwood	13439	–	6
Ellensburg			
The National Bank Of Ellensburg	11045	6	6
The Washington National Bank Of Ellensburg	9079	6	4
Ellensburgh			
The Ellensburgh National Bank	3867	6	–
Ellensburgh			
The Kittitas Valley National Bank Of Ellensburgh	3867	6	–
Enumclaw			
The First National Bank Of Enumclaw	12114	–	6
Everett			
Citizens Security National Bank Of Everett	11693	–	5
Security National Bank Of Everett	11693	–	4
The American National Bank Of Everett	6053	6	–
The Everett National Bank	4738	6	–
The First National Bank Of Everett	4686	5	4
The Puget Sound National Bank Of Everett	4796	6	–
The Security National Bank Of Everett	11693	5	–
Fairhaven			
The Bennett National Bank Of New Whatcom	4171	6	–
The Citizens National Bank Of Fairhaven	5243	6	–
The Fairhaven National Bank	4387	6	–
The First National Bank Of Fairhaven	4171	6	–
Ferndale			
The First National Bank Of Ferndale	11667	–	6
Garfield			
The Garfield National Bank	9185	6	3
The State National Bank Of Garfield	12231	–	6
Gig Harbor			
The First National Bank Of Gig Harbor	13057	–	6
Goldendale			
The First National Bank Of Goldendale	4031	6	–
Harrington			
The First National Bank Of Harrington	9210	6	–
Hoquiam			
The First National Bank Of Hoquiam	4427	5	4
The Hoquiam National Bank	4390	6	–
Kelso			
The First National Bank Of Kelso	8639	4	6
Kennewick			
The First National Bank Of Kennewick	8948	6	6
Kent			
The First National Bank Of Kent	10174	6	6
The Kent National Bank	12217	–	6
Lind			
The First National Bank Of Lind	9101	6	6
Longview			
The First National Bank Of Longview	12392	–	5
Lynden			
The First National Bank Of Lynden	11808	6	6
Mabton			
The First National Bank Of Mabton	9757	6	–
Malden			
The First National Bank Of Malden	9351	6	–
Medical Lake			
The First National Bank Of Medical Lake	9030	6	6
Monroe			
The First National Bank Of Monroe	9372	6	6
The Monroe National Bank	9478	6	4
Montesano			
First National Bank In Montesano	5472	–	6
The First National Bank Of Montesano	4779	6	–
The Montesano National Bank	5472	6	6
Mount Vernon			
The First National Bank Of Mount Vernon	4529	6	–
The Mount Vernon National Bank	10602	6	–
The Skagit National Bank Of Mount Vernon	12154	–	6
Newport			
The First National Bank Of Newport	8828	6	–
North Yakima			
First National Bank Of Yakima	3355	6	6
The First National Bank Of North Yakima	3355	6	
The Yakima National Bank Of North Yakima	3862	6	–
The Yakima National Bank, Yakima	3862	6	6
Yakima First National Bank, Yakima	3355	–	3
Oakesdale			
The First National Bank Of Oakesdale	4122	6	–
The National Bank Of Oakesdale	9150	6	–
Odessa			
The First National Bank Of Odessa	9052	6	–
Okanogan			
The First National Bank Of Okanogan	9411	6	3
Olympia			
The Capital National Bank Of Olympia	4297	5	4
The First National Bank Of Olympia	3024	6	–
The Olympia National Bank	5652	6	–
Oroville			
The First National Bank Of Oroville	8279	6	–
Palouse			
The Farmers National Bank Of Palouse	9499	6	–
The National Bank Of Palouse	9499	6	–
The Security National Bank Of Palouse	12184	–	6
Palouse City			
The First National Bank Of Palouse City	4186	6	–
Pasco			
The First National Bank Of Pasco	9265	6	–
Pomeroy			
The Farmers National Bank Of Pomeroy	11416	6	6
The First National Bank Of Pomeroy	3460	6	–
Port Angeles			
First National Bank In Port Angeles	6074	6	4
The Cain National Bank Of Port Angeles	6074	6	–
The Citizens National Bank Of Port Angeles	6074	6	–
The First National Bank Of Port Angeles	4315	6	–
Port Townsend			
The American National Bank Of Port Townsend	13351	–	6
The First American National Bank Of Port Townsend	13351	–	6
The First National Bank Of Port Townsend	2948	6	6
The Port Townsend National Bank	4290	6	–

City, Bank	Ch. No.	L	S
Prosser			
The Benton County National Bank Of Prosser	9417	6	–
The First National Bank Of Prosser	7489	6	–
Pullman			
The First National Bank Of Pullman	4699	5	5
Puyallup			
The First National Bank Of Puyallup	4224	6	–
Quincy			
The First National Bank Of Quincy	9102	6	–
Raymond			
The First National Bank Of Raymond	11672	6	6
Reardan			
The First National Bank Of Reardan	13444	–	3
Ritzville			
The First National Bank Of Ritzville	5751	6	4
The Pioneer National Bank Of Ritzville	8743	6	–
Rosalia			
The Whitman County National Bank Of Rosalia	9273	6	6
Seattle			
Ballard First National Bank Of Seattle	13581	–	6
First National Bank Of Seattle	11280	–	1
First Seattle Dexter Horton National Bank, Seattle	11280	–	2
The Boston National Bank Of Seattle	4124	6	–
The Citizens National Bank Of Seattle	9662	6	–
The Commercial National Bank Of Seattle	4397	6	–
The Dexter Horton National Bank Of Seattle	9798	6	–
The Dexter Horton National Bank Of Seattle	11280	3	5
The First National Bank Of Seattle	2783	6	6
The Mercantile National Bank Of Seattle	9662	6	–
The Merchants National Bank Of Seattle	2985	6	–
The National Bank Of Commerce Of Seattle	4375	5	4
The National City Bank Of Seattle	10026	5	–
The Pacific National Bank Of Seattle	13230	5	3
The Puget Sound National Bank Of Seattle	2966	6	–
The Seattle National Bank	4229	3	–
The Union National Bank Of Seattle	11280	5	–
The University National Bank Of Seattle	12153	5	4
The Washington National Bank Of Seattle	4059	6	–
Sedro-Woolley			
The First National Bank Of Sedro-Woolley	7908	6	–
Sehome			
The Bellingham Bay National Bank Of New Whatsom	3976	6	–
The Bellingham Bay National Bank Of Sehome	3976	6	–
The Columbia National Bank Of New Whatcom	4351	6	–
The Columbia National Bank Of Sehome	4351	6	–
Slaughter			
The First National Bank Of Slaughter	4457	6	–
Snohomish			
The First National Bank Of Snohomish	3887	6	6
The Snohomish National Bank	4526	6	–
South Bend			
The First National Bank Of South Bend	4467	6	–
Spokane			
City National Bank Of Spokane	12418	6	–
The Brotherhoods Co-Operative National Bank Of Spokane	12418	5	–
The First National Bank Of Hillyard, Spokane	9182	6	6
The First National Trust And Savings Bank Of Spokane	13331	–	4
The National Bank Of Commerce Of Spokane	9589	6	–
The Old National Bank And Trust Company Of Spokane	4668	4	3
The Old National Bank Of Spokane	4668	2	–
Spokane Falls			
The Browne National Bank Of Spokane Falls	4025	6	–
The Citizens National Bank Of Spokane Falls	4005	6	–
The Exchange National Bank Of Spokane	4044	3	–
The Exchange National Bank Of Spokane Falls	4044	6	–
The First National Bank Of Spokane	2805	6	–
The Spokane National Bank Of Spokane Falls	3838	6	–
The Traders National Bank Of Spokane	3409	5	–
The Traders National Bank Of Spokane Falls	3409	6	–
The Washington National Bank Of Spokane Falls	4277	6	–
Sprague			
The Fidelity National Bank Of Spokane	3528	4	–
The First National Bank Of Sprague	3528	6	–
Stanwood			
The First National Bank Of Stanwood	11935	–	4
Sunnyside			
First National Bank Of Sunnyside	8481	6	–
The First National Bank Of Sunnyside	8481	–	6
Tacoma			
The Brotherhood Co-Operative National Bank Of Tacoma	12667	5	5
The Citizens National Bank Of Tacoma	4069	6	–
The Columbia National Bank Of Tacoma	4623	6	–
The Lumbermens National Bank Of Tacoma	6006	6	–
The Merchants National Bank Of Tacoma	3172	6	–
The National Bank Of Commerce Of Tacoma	3789	5	–
The National Bank Of Tacoma	3417	3	3
The National Bank Of The Republic, Tacoma	4426	6	–
The Pacific National Bank Of Tacoma	3417	4	–
Tacoma			
The Puget Sound National Bank Of Tacoma	12292	6	4
The Tacoma National Bank, Tacoma	2924	6	–
The Washington National Bank In The City Of Tacoma	12667	–	6
The Washington National Bank Of Tacoma	4018	6	–
Tonasket			
First National Bank In Tonasket	14166	–	6
The First National Bank Of Tonasket	10407	6	6
Toppenish			
The First National Bank Of Toppenish	7767	6	6
Vancouver			
The Citizens National Bank Of Vancouver	8987	6	–
The First National Bank Of Vancouver	3031	6	–
The United States National Bank Of Vancouver	9646	5	5
The Vancouver National Bank	6013	5	4
The Washington National Bank Of Vancouver	13137	–	5
Waitsburg			
The First National Bank Of Waitsburg	4681	6	–
The First National Bank Of Waitsburg	8895	6	6
Walla Walla			
The Baker-Boyer National Bank Of Walla Walla	3956	6	6
The First National Bank Of Walla Walla	2380	4	–
The Third National Bank Of Walla Walla	9068	6	–
Wapato			
The First National Bank Of Wapato	9129	6	6
Washtucna			
The First National Bank Of Washtucna	9054	6	–
Waterville			
The First National Bank Of Waterville	4532	6	–
Wenatchee			
The First National Bank Of Wenatchee	8064	5	3
Whatcom			
The First National Bank Of Whatcom	4099	6	–
White Salmon			
The First National Bank Of White Salmon	10000	6	–
Zillah			
The First National Bank Of Zillah	9576	6	6

WEST VIRGINIA

City, Bank	Ch. No.	L	S
Albright			
The First National Bank Of Albright	10480	6	4
Alderson			
The Alderson National Bank	9523	6	6
The First National Bank Of Alderson	5903	5	5
Anawalt			
The First National Bank Of Anawalt	10392	6	6
Ansted			
The Ansted National Bank	8904	5	6
Bayard			
The Bayard National Bank	11664	6	6
Beckley			
Beckley National Exchange Bank	10589	–	5
The Beckley National Bank	10589	6	5
The First National Bank Of Beckley	6735	6	–
The Peoples National Bank Of Beckley	9038	6	–
Belington			
The Belington National Bank	6634	6	–
The Citizens National Bank Of Belington	6618	6	–
The First National Bank Of Belington	6619	6	6
Berwind			
The Berwind National Bank	9909	6	–
Bluefield			
The American National Bank Of Bluefield, West Virginia	7734	6	–
The Bluefield National Bank	11109	6	4
The First National Bank Of Bluefield	4643	5	5
The Flat Top National Bank Of Bluefield	6674	4	5
The Flat Top National Bank Of Bluefield	11109	–	4
Buckhannon			
The Central National Bank Of Buckhannon	13646	–	5
The Traders National Bank Of Buckhannon	4760	5	6
Cameron			
The First National Bank Of Cameron	6020	5	5
Ceredo			
The First National Bank Of Ceredo	4775	5	5
Charles Town			
The National Citizens Bank Of Charles Town	7270	6	5
Charleston			
The Charleston National Bank	3236	2	2
The Citizens National Bank Of Charleston	4412	5	–
The First National Bank Of Charleston	1795	6	–
The First National Bank Of Jefferson At Charleston	1868	6	–
The Kanawha National Bank Of Charleston	4667	3	5
The National Bank Of Commerce Of Charleston	13509	–	4
The National City Bank Of Charleston	8569	5	–
Chester			
The First National Bank Of Chester	6984	6	6
Clark			
The Clark National Bank	10157	6	6
Clarksburg			
The Empire National Bank Of Clarksburg	7029	2	4
The Merchants National Bank Of West Virginia At Clarksburg	1530	4	4
The Traders National Bank Of Clarksburg	4569	5	–
The Union National Bank Of Clarksburg	7681	2	2
Clendenin			
The First National Bank Of Clendenin	7275	6	6
Davis			
The National Bank Of Davis	4828	6	6
Elkins			
Citizens National Bank Of Elkins	12483	6	6
The Elkins National Bank	4718	6	6
The Peoples National Bank Of Elkins	8376	6	5
The Randolph National Bank Of Elkins	7060	6	–
The Tygarts Valley National Bank Of Elkins	14002	–	3
Elm Grove			
The First National Bank And Trust Company Of Elm Grove	8983	6	6
The First National Bank Of Elm Grove	8983	6	–
Fairmont			
First National Bank In Fairmont	13811	–	4
The First National Bank Of Fairmont	961	4	–
The National Bank Of Fairmont	9462	2	3
The Peoples National Bank Of Fairmont	9645	3	5
The Union National Bank Of Fairmont	9645	–	5
Fairview			
The First National Bank Of Fairview	10219	5	6
Fayetteville			
The Fayette County National Bank Of Fayetteville	8345	6	6
The Fayetteville National Bank	5434	6	–
Friendly			
The First National Bank Of Friendly	5814	6	–
Gary			
Gary National Bank	13505	–	6
The Gary National Bank	8333	6	6
Glenville			
The First National Bank Of Glenville	5939	6	–
Gormania			
The First National Bank Of Gormania	8751	6	5
Grafton			
The First National Bank Of Grafton	2445	4	4
Griffithsville			
The Oil Field National Bank Of Griffithsville	10097	5	5
Hamlin			
The Lincoln National Bank Of Hamlin	8171	6	6
Harrisville			
The First National Bank Of Harrisville	6790	5	–
Hendricks			
The First National Bank Of Hendricks	7845	5	6
Hinton			
The Citizens National Bank Of Hinton	10348	6	5
The First National Bank Of Hinton	5562	4	3
The National Bank Of Summers Of Hinton	7998	5	4
Huntington			
The American National Bank Of Huntington	9598	5	–
The Commercial National Bank Of Huntington	4607	6	–
The First Huntington National Bank, Huntington	3106	2	2
The First National Bank Of Huntington	3106	2	–
The Huntington National Bank, Huntington	4607	3	–
The West Virginia National Bank Of Huntington	7359	5	–
Hurricane			
The Hurricane National Bank	11670	6	–
Iaeger			
The First National Bank Of Iaeger	11268	6	6
The Tug River National Bank Of Iaeger	12372	5	–
Kenova			
The First National Bank Of Kenova	9913	6	4
Keyser			
The First National Bank Of Keyser	6205	5	5
The National Bank Of Keyser	13831	–	5
Keystone			
The First National Bank Of Keystone	10369	6	6
Kimball			
The First National Bank Of Kimball	11502	6	6
The Kimball National Bank	13484	–	6
Kingwood			
The Kingwood National Bank	6332	6	–
The National Bank Of Kingwood	1608	6	
Logan			
The First National Bank Of Logan	8136	5	6
The Logan National Bank	8136	6	–
The National Bank Of Logan	13954	–	6
Madison			
Boone National Bank Of Madison	6510	–	5
The Madison National Bank	6510	5	–
Mannington			
The First National Bank Of Mannington	5012	5	5
Marlinton			
First National Bank In Marlinton	13783	–	6
The First National Bank Of Marlinton	6538	6	5
Martinsburg			
The Citizens National Bank Of Martinsburg	4811	4	4
The National Bank Of Martinsburg	1524	6	–
The Old National Bank Of Martinsburg	6283	5	3
The Peoples National Bank Of Martinsburg	2144	6	–
Matewan			
The Matewan National Bank	10370	6	5
Matoaka			
The First National Bank Of Matoaka	11264	6	–
The Matoaka National Bank	12839	6	5
Middlebourne			
The First National Bank Of Middlebourne	6170	5	6
Milton			
The Milton National Bank	12765	6	–
Monongah			
The First National Bank Of Monongah	7545	6	6
Montgomery			
The Merchants National Bank Of Montgomery	9740	6	4
The Montgomery National Bank	5691	4	4
Moorefield			
The South Branch Valley National Bank Of Moorefield	3029	5	4
Morgantown			
The Citizens National Bank Of Morgantown	5583	5	–

City, Bank	Ch. No.	L	S
Morgantown			
The Merchants National Bank Of West Virginia, Morgantown	1502	6	–
The Second National Bank Of Morgantown	2458	6	5
Moundsville			
First National Bank At Moundsville	14142	–	5
The First National Bank Of Moundsville	5717	5	5
Mount Hope			
The First National Bank Of Mount Hope	11049	6	6
New Cumberland			
The First National Bank Of New Cumberland	6582	6	–
New Martinsville			
The First National Bank Of New Martinsville	5266	4	6
Newburg			
The First National Bank Of Newburg	7626	5	6
Northfork			
The First Clark National Bank Of Northfork	8309	–	5
The First National Bank Of Northfork	8309	5	5
Oak Hill			
The Oak Hill National Bank	12075	5	5
Parkersburg			
The Citizens National Bank Of Parkersburg	2649	4	5
The Farmers And Mechanics National Bank Of Parkersburg	5320	5	–
The First National Bank Of Parkersburg	180	2	3
The Parkersburg National Bank	1427	4	4
The Peoples National Bank Of Parkersburg	13621	–	4
The Second National Bank Of Parkersburg	864	4	–
Parsons			
The First National Bank Of Parsons	9610	6	4
Pennsboro			
First Citizens National Bank Of Pennsboro	7191	–	5
The Citizens National Bank Of Pennsboro	7246	6	6
The First National Bank Of Pennsboro	7191	5	6
Peterstown			
The First National Bank Of Peterstown	9721	6	5
Philippi			
First National Bank In Philippi	14053	–	6
The Citizens National Bank Of Philippi	6377	5	5
The First National Bank Of Philippi	6302	5	6
Piedmont			
The Davis National Bank Of Piedmont	4088	6	5
The First National Bank Of Piedmont	3629	5	3
The National Bank Of Piedmont	1883	5	–
Pineville			
The Citizens National Bank Of Pineville	8749	6	–
The First National Bank Of Pineville	7672	6	6
Point Pleasant			
Citizens National Bank Of Point Pleasant	13231	–	4
The Merchants National Bank Of Point Pleasant	1504	4	–
The Merchants Natl Bank Of West Virginia At Point Pleasant	1504	5	–
The Point Pleasant National Bank	5701	5	5
Princeton			
The First National Bank Of Princeton	8219	5	6
Ravenswood			
The First National Bank Of Ravenswood	10759	–	6
Reedy			
The First National Bank Of Reedy	10285	6	3
Richwood			
Cherry River National Bank, Richwood	13627	–	4
The First National Bank Of Richwood	8434	5	6
Ripley			
The First National Bank Of Ripley	10762	6	6
Romney			
The First National Bank Of Romney	9766	6	4
Ronceverte			
The First National Bank Of Ronceverte	5280	5	5
The Ronceverte National Bank	6226	6	6
Rowlesburg			
The First National Bank Of Rowlesburg	9288	6	–
The Peoples National Bank Of Rowlesburg	10250	4	5
Salem			
The First National Bank Of Salem	7250	5	6
Shinnston			
The First National Bank Of Shinnston	9453	6	–
Sistersville			
The Farmers And Producers National Bank Of Sistersville	5028	5	–
The First National Bank Of Sistersville	5027	4	–
The Peoples National Bank Of Sistersville	6548	5	–
The Union National Bank Of Sistersville	5028	5	4
South Charleston			
The First National Bank Of South Charleston	11340	6	4
Spencer			
The First National Bank Of Spencer	10127	6	4
St. Albans			
The First National Bank Of St. Albans	9640	6	3
St. Marys			
The First National Bank Of St. Marys	5226	4	4
Sutton			
The First National Bank Of Sutton	6213	6	–
The Home National Bank Of Sutton	9604	5	4
Terra Alta			
The First National Bank Of Terra Alta	6999	5	5
Thurmond			
National Bank Of Thurmond	8998	5	6
Webster Springs			
The First National Bank Of Webster Springs	8360	6	6
The Webster Springs National Bank	14013	–	6
Welch			
Mcdowell County National Bank In Welch	13512	–	3
Mcdowell County National Bank Of Welch	9071	4	6
The First National Bank Of Welch	9048	6	6
Wellsburg			
The First National Bank Of Wellsburg	1387	6	–
The Wellsburg National Bank	1884	6	6
Wellsburg National Bank	14295	–	6
West Union			
First National Bank In West Union	13881	–	6
The First National Bank Of West Union	6424	6	5
Weston			
The National Exchange Bank Of Weston	1607	4	6
The Weston National Bank	13634	–	4
Wheeling			
The Citizens National Bank Of Wheeling	10455	6	–
The First National Bank Of Wheeling	360	6	–
The Merchants National Bank Of West Virginia, Wheeling	1343	6	–
The National Bank Of West Virginia, Wheeling	1424	3	2
The National Exchange Bank Of Wheeling	5164	2	2
The National Savings Bank Of Wheeling	1594	6	–
Williamson			
The First National Bank Of Williamson	6830	6	5
The National Bank Of Commerce Of Williamson	10067	5	4
Williamstown			
The Farmers And Mechanics National Bank Of Williamstown	11483	6	6
The Williamstown National Bank	6233	6	–
Winona			
The Winona National Bank	9850	6	6
Worthington			
The First National Bank Of Worthington	10450	6	6

WISCONSIN

City, Bank	Ch. No.	L	S
Alma			
The First National Bank Of Alma	8338	5	–
Antigo			
The First National Bank Of Antigo	5143	4	4
The Langlade National Bank Of Antigo	5942	4	4
Appleton			
First National Bank Of Appleton	1749	4	2
The Appleton National Bank	1650	6	–
The Citizens National Bank Of Appleton	4937	3	3
The Commercial National Bank Of Appleton	2565	3	–
The First National Bank Of Appleton	1749	3	–
The Manufacturers National Bank Of Appleton	1820	6	–
Ashland			
The Ashland National Bank	3196	5	5
The First National Bank Of Ashland	3590	5	–
The Northern National Bank Of Ashland	3607	4	4
The Union National Bank Of Ashland	13870	–	5
Baldwin			
The First National Bank Of Baldwin	10106	5	4
Bangor			
The First National Bank Of Bangor	13202	5	4
Baraboo			
First National Bank And Trust Company Of Baraboo	3609	–	5
The First National Bank Of Baraboo	2079	6	–
The First National Bank Of Baraboo	3609	4	5
Bayfield			
The First National Bank Of Bayfield	7158	5	5
Beaver Dam			
The American National Bank Of Beaver Dam	4602	4	4
The First National Bank Of Beaver Dam	3270	6	–
The German National Bank Of Beaver Dam	4602	4	–
The National Bank Of Beaver Dam	851	6	–
The Old National Bank Of Beaver Dam	7462	4	3
Beloit			
The Beloit National Bank	836	6	–
The Citizens National Bank Of Beloit	2407	6	–
The Firsts National Bank Of Beloit	2163	6	–
The Second National Bank Of Beloit	2725	5	5
Berlin			
The Berlin National Bank	4641	6	–
The First National Bank Of Berlin	400	6	–
The First National Bank Of Berlin	4620	2	3
Black River Falls			
The First National Bank Of Black River Falls	3897	4	5
Blair			
The First National Bank Of Blair	10667	5	6
Blanchardville			
The First National Bank Of Blanchardville	11114	5	5
Boscobel			
The First National Bank Of Boscobel	1771	6	–
Boyceville			
The First National Bank Of Boyceville	11128	6	–
Brillion			
The First National Bank Of Brillion	7224	5	3
Brodhead			
The First National Bank Of Brodhead	1710	6	–
Burlington			
The Burlington National Bank	11783	4	2
The First National Bank Of Burlington	1933	5	–
Campbellsport			
The First National Bank Of Campbellsport	6222	6	–
Cedarburg			
The First National Bank Of Cedarburg	1415	6	–
Chilton			
The Chilton National Bank	5933	4	4
Chippewa Falls			
The First National Bank Of Chippewa Falls	2125	3	3
Chippewa Falls			
The Lumbermen's National Bank Of Chippewa Falls	3778	5	3
Clintonville			
The First National Bank Of Clintonville	6273	3	4
Columbus			
The First National Bank Of Columbus	178	5	3
Crandon			
Crandon National Bank	12814	5	4
The First National Bank Of Crandon	9387	6	–
Cuba City			
The First National Bank Of Cuba City	5632	5	–
Dale			
The First National Bank Of Dale	8118	5	4
Darlington			
First National Bank At Darlington	14184	–	4
The Citizens National Bank Of Darlington	3308	4	4
The First National Bank Of Darlington	3161	3	4
De Pere			
The First National Bank Of De Pere	2133	6	–
The National Bank Of De Pere	6469	3	4
Deerfield			
The First National Bank Of Deerfield	11577	6	–
Delavan			
The National Bank Of Delavan	1248	6	–
Dodgeville			
The First National Bank Of Dodgeville	6698	4	3
Durand			
The First National Bank In Durand	13529	–	4
The First National Bank Of Durand	10791	5	5
The Security National Bank Of Durand	14095	–	6
Eagle River			
The First National Bank Of Eagle River	12124	6	4
Eau Claire			
The American National Bank And Trust Company Of Eau Clair	13645	–	3
The Eau Claire National Bank	2759	3	4
The First National Bank Of Eau Claire	2069	6	–
The Union National Bank Of Eau Claire	8281	2	2
Edgerton			
The First National Bank Of Edgerton	7040	4	3
The National Bank Of Edgerton	13932	–	6
Elkhorn			
The First National Bank Of Elkhorn	873	4	3
Evansville			
The First National Bank Of Evansville	1729	6	–
Fairchild			
The First National Bank Of Fairchild	7264	6	6
Fennimore			
The First National Bank In Fennimore	13599	–	5
The First National Bank Of Fennimore	9522	5	5
Fond Du Lac			
First-Fond Du Lac National Bank, Fond Du Lac	555	2	–
The Commercial National Bank Of Fond Du Lac	6015	2	2
The First National Bank Of Fond Du Lac	555	5	–
The First-Fond Du Lac National Bank, Fond Du Lac	555	–	2
The Fond Du Lac National Bank	3685	3	–
Fort Atkinson			
The First National Bank Of Fort Atkinson	157	4	4
Fort Howard			
The Mccartney National Bank Of Fort Howard	4783	5	–
The Mccartney National Bank Of Green Bay	4783	3	4
Fox Lake			
The First National Bank Of Fox Lake	426	5	–
Frederic			
The First National Bank Of Frederic	8491	6	5
Glenwood City			
The Farmers National Bank Of Glenwood City	11083	6	5
Grand Rapids			
The Citizens National Bank Of Grand Rapids	10330	3	–
The Citizens National Bank Of Wisconsin Rapids	10330	5	4
The First National Bank Of Grand Rapids	1998	3	–
The First National Bank Of Wisconsin Rapids	1998	4	2
The Wood County National Bank Of Grand Rapids	4639	2	–
The Wood County National Bank Of Wisconsin Rapids	4639	5	2
Grantsburg			
The First National Bank Of Grantsburg	8444	6	4
Green Bay			
Kellogg-Citizens National Bank Of Green Bay	2132	5	2
The Citizens National Bank Of Green Bay	3884	2	–
The City National Bank Of Green Bay	1009	6	–
The First National Bank Of Green Bay	874	6	–
The Kellogg National Bank Of Green Bay	2132	3	–
The National Bank Of Commerce Of Green Bay	1819	6	–
Hartford			
The First National Bank Of Hartford	8671	3	4
Hayward			
The First National Bank Of Hayward	7831	6	–
Hudson			
The First National Bank Of Hudson	95	4	4
Hurley			
The First National Bank Of Hurley	4304	6	–
The Hurley National Bank	11594	5	4
Janesville			
The First National Bank Of Janesville	83	6	–
The First National Bank Of Janesville	2748	4	3
The Rock County National Bank Of Janesville	749	4	4
Jefferson			
The National Bank Of Jefferson	1076	6	–

City, Bank	Ch. No.	L	S
Kaukauna			
The First National Bank Of Kaukauna	3641	4	5
Kenosha			
The First National Bank Of Kenosha	212	4	3
United States National Bank And Trust Company Of Kenosha	12351	6	4
United States National Bank Of Kenosha	12351	4	–
La Crosse			
The Batavian National Bank Of La Crosse	7347	3	3
The First National Bank Of La Crosse	1313	6	–
The La Crosse National Bank	2344	1	–
The National Bank Of La Crosse	5047	2	2
The Union National Bank Of La Crosse	3412	6	–
Ladysmith			
The First National Bank Of Ladysmith	5535	6	–
The Ladysmith National Bank	7966	6	–
The Pioneer National Bank Of Ladysmith	11826	5	4
Lake Geneva			
The Farmers National Bank Of Lake Geneva	5592	5	4
The First National Bank Of Lake Geneva	3125	4	4
Lancaster			
The First National Bank Of Lancaster	7007	6	–
Madison			
The Commercial National Bank Of Madison	9153	3	3
The First National Bank Of Madison	144	3	1
Manawa			
The First National Bank Of Manawa	8710	3	5
Manitowoc			
First National Bank In Manitowoc	4975	4	3
The First National Bank Of Manitowoc	852	6	–
The National Bank Of Manitowoc	4975	3	–
Marinette			
The First National Bank Of Marinette	4123	4	4
The Stephenson National Bank Of Marinette	4137	3	3
Marion			
First National Bank In Marion	14130	–	6
The First National Bank Of Marion	12286	5	4
Marshfield			
The American National Bank Of Marshfield	5437	4	3
The Citizens National Bank Of Marshfield	14125	–	5
The First National Bank Of Marshfield	4573	4	4
Mayville			
The First National Bank Of Mayville	10653	6	5
Medford			
The First National Bank Of Medford	5695	4	2
Menasha			
The First National Bank Of Menasha	3724	3	3
The National Bank Of Menasha	1714	6	–
Menominie			
The First National Bank Of Menominie	2851	2	2
Merrill			
The Citizens National Bank Of Merrill	10176	3	3
The First National Bank Of Merrill	3704	6	–
The National Bank Of Merrill	4736	6	–
Milwaukee			
Bay View National Bank Of Milwaukee	12816	–	5
First Wisconsin National Bank Of Milwaukee	2715	1	1
Marine National Exchange Bank Of Milwaukee	5458	–	1
Sixth Wisconsin National Bank Of Milwaukee	12628	4	4
The Central National Bank Of Milwaukee	4816	6	–
The First National Bank Of Milwaukee	64	6	–
The First National Bank Of Milwaukee	2715	1	–
The Germania National Bank Of Milwaukee	6853	3	–
The Grand And Sixth National Bank Of Milwaukee	12628	5	–
The Marine National Bank Of Milwaukee	5458	1	3
The Mechanics National Bank Of Milwaukee	12816	4	5
The Merchants National Bank Of Milwaukee	1438	6	–
The Milwaukee National Bank Of Wisconsin	1017	4	–
The National Bank Of Commerce Of Milwaukee	6853	2	2
The National City Bank Of Milwaukee	1483	6	–
The National Exchange Bank Of Milwaukee	1003	2	3
The Northwestern National Bank Of Milwaukee	12564	3	5
The Wisconsin National Bank Of Milwaukee	4817	2	–
Mineral Point			
The First National Bank Of Mineral Point	3203	6	–
Mondovi			
The First National Bank Of Mondovi	5779	5	4
Monroe			
The First National Bank Of Monroe	230	3	3
Neenah			
The First National Bank Of Neenah	1602	6	4
The Manufacturers National Bank Of Neenah	2603	4	–
The National Bank Of Neenah	1602	6	–
The National Manufacturers Bank Of Neenah	6034	4	4
Neillsville			
First National Bank Of Neillsville	9606	–	3
The First National Bank At Neillsville	14200	–	5
The First National Bank Of Neillsville	9606	4	–
New London			
The First National Bank Of New London	5013	5	5
New Richmond			
The First National Bank Of New Richmond	11412	5	5
Niagara			
The First National Bank Of Niagara	11051	6	5
Oconomowoc			
The First National Bank Of Oconomowoc	5505	3	4
The Oconomowoc National Bank	13616	–	4
Oconto			
The Citizens National Bank Of Oconto	5521	4	4
The Oconto National Bank	3541	4	4
Omro			
The First National Bank Of Omro	5566	6	–
Oregon			
The First National Bank Of Oregon	10620	5	5
Oshkosh			
First National Bank In Oshkosh	6604	4	2
The City National Bank Of Oshkosh	9347	3	2
The Commercial National Bank Of Oshkosh	1568	6	–
The Commercial National Bank Of Oshkosh	5557	3	–
The First National Bank Of Oshkosh	218	6	–
The German National Bank Of Oshkosh	4196	6	–
The National Bank Of Oshkosh	2877	6	–
The National Union Bank Of Oshkosh	4508	4	–
The Old Commercial National Bank Of Oshkosh	6604	3	–
The Old National Bank Of Oshkosh	6604	4	–
The Oshkosh National Bank	13806	–	3
The Union National Bank Of Oshkosh	1787	6	–
Park Falls			
The First National Bank Of Park Falls	10489	5	4
Peshtigo			
The Peshtigo National Bank	5658	6	5
Phillips			
First National Bank In Phillips	13487	–	3
The First National Bank Of Phillips	7434	5	5
Platteville			
The First National Bank Of Platteville	4650	4	4
Port Washington			
The First National Bank Of Port Washington	9419	5	3
Portage			
The First National Bank Of Portage	4234	4	4
Prescott			
The First National Bank Of Prescott	10522	6	5
Princeton			
Farmers-Merchants National Bank In Princeton	13904	–	5
The First National Bank Of Princeton	5978	5	–
Racine			
First National Bank And Trust Company Of Racine	457	–	2
The American National Bank Of Racine	10938	6	–
The First National Bank Of Racine	457	4	–
The Manufacturers National Bank Of Racine	1802	5	–
The Union National Bank Of Racine	2557	6	–
Rhinelander			
The First National Bank Of Rhinelander	4312	4	4
The Oneida National Bank Of Rhinelander	11646	4	4
Rib Lake			
The First National Bank Of Rib Lake	6711	5	4
Rice Lake			
The First National Bank Of Rice Lake	6663	5	3
Richland Center			
The First National Bank Of Richland Center	7901	5	–
Rio			
The First National Bank Of Rio	8632	6	6
Ripon			
The American National Bank Of Ripon	4305	4	5
The First National Bank Of Ripon	425	3	2
The German National Bank Of Ripon	4305	2	–
The Ripon National Bank	3146	6	–
River Falls			
The First National Bank Of River Falls	7087	6	–
Saint Croix Falls			
The First National Bank Of Saint Croix Falls	11526	6	–
Seymour			
The First National Bank Of Seymour	6575	4	4
Shawano			
The First National Bank Of Shawano	5469	3	4
The German-American National Bank Of Shawano	6403	4	–
The Wisconsin National Bank Of Shawano	6403	4	5
Sheboygan			
The First National Bank Of Sheboygan	2123	6	–
The Security National Bank Of Sheboygan	11150	–	3
Sheboygan Falls			
The Dairymen's National Bank Of Sheboygan Falls	5947	6	–
Shullsburg			
The First National Bank Of Shullsburg	4055	4	5
Soldiers Grove			
The First National Bank Of Soldiers Grove	13308	–	5
South Milwaukee			
The South Milwaukee National Bank	4893	6	–
Sparta			
The Farmers National Bank Of Sparta	11463	5	4
The First National Bank Of Sparta	1115	6	–
Stevens Point			
The Citizens National Bank Of Stevens Point	4912	3	3
The First National Bank Of Stevens Point	3001	3	3
Stone Lake			
The First National Bank Of Stone Lake	10322	5	5
Stoughton			
The Citizens National Bank Of Stoughton	9304	5	5
The First National Bank Of Stoughton	5222	3	5
Superior			
The First National Bank Of Superior	2653	6	–
The United States National Bank Of Superior	9140	5	2
Tigerton			
First National Bank In Tigerton	14150	–	4
The First National Bank Of Tigerton	5446	4	4
Viroqua			
The First National Bank Of Viroqua	8529	5	4
Watertown			
The Merchants National Bank Of Watertown	9003	3	3
The Wisconsin National Bank Of Watertown	1010	4	5
Waukesha			
The Farmers National Bank Of Waukesha	1159	6	–
The National Exchange Bank Of Waukesha	2647	3	4
The Waukesha National Bank	1086	4	3
Waupaca			
First National Bank Of Waupaca	14063	–	5
Old National Bank Of Waupaca	4424	–	6
The First National Bank Of Waupaca	4414	5	–
The National Bank Of Waupaca	4424	5	–
The Old National Bank Of Waupaca	4424	3	–
The Waupaca County National Bank Of Waupaca	4414	6	–
Waupun			
The First National Bank Of Waupun	3391	6	–
The National Bank Of Waupun	7898	4	5
Wausau			
American National Bank Of Wausau	4744	4	3
The First National Bank Of Wausau	2820	3	1
The National German-American Bank Of Wausau	4744	3	–
Wautoma			
The First National Bank Of Wautoma	7136	6	–
Wauwatosa			
First National Bank Of Wauwatosa	8689	5	4
West Allis			
The First National Bank Of West Allis	6908	4	4
West Bend			
The First National Bank Of West Bend	11060	5	3
West Superior			
The First National Bank Of The City Of Superior	3926	4	2
The First National Bank Of West Superior	3926	6	–
The Keystone National Bank Of Superior, West Superior	4399	6	–
The Northwestern National Bank Of Superior, West Superior	4878	6	–
The Superior National Bank Of West Superior	4680	6	–
Weyauwega			
The First National Bank Of Weyauwega	7470	4	5
Whitewater			
The Citizens National Bank Of Whitewater	2925	6	–
The First National Bank Of Whitewater	124	4	4

WYOMING TERRITORY

City, Bank	Ch. No.	L	S
Buffalo			
The First National Bank Of Buffalo	3299	6	–
Cheyenne			
The Cheyenne National Bank	3416	6	–
The First National Bank Of Cheyenne	1800	5	–
The Stock Growers National Bank Of Cheyenne	2652	6	–
Douglas			
The First National Bank Of Douglas	3556	6	–
Laramie City			
The Albany County National Bank Of Laramie City	3615	6	–
The Laramie National Bank Of Laramie City	2518	6	–
The Wyoming National Bank Of Laramie City	2110	4	–
Rawlins			
The First National Bank Of Rawlins	4320	6	–
Rock Springs			
The First National Bank Of Rock Springs	3920	6	–
Sundance			
The First National Bank Of Sundance	4343	6	–

WYOMING

City, Bank	Ch. No.	L	S
Basin			
The First National Bank Of Basin	10858	6	–
Buffalo			
The First National Bank Of Buffalo	3299	4	3
Casper			
The Casper National Bank	6850	3	3
The Citizens National Bank Of Casper	11683	5	–
The National Bank Of Commerce Of Casper	11490	6	–
The Stockmen's National Bank Of Casper	7083	4	–
The Wyoming National Bank Of Casper	10533	3	2
Cheyenne			
The American National Bank Of Cheyenne	11380	3	2
The Cheyenne National Bank	3416	6	–
The Citizens National Bank Of Cheyenne	8089	4	–
The First National Bank Of Cheyenne	1800	3	–
The Stock Growers National Bank Of Cheyenne	2652	2	–
Cody			
The First National Bank Of Cody	7319	5	4
The Shoshone National Bank Of Cody	8020	5	4
Douglas			
The Douglas National Bank	8087	4	4
The First National Bank Of Douglas	3556	4	3
Evanston			
The Evanston National Bank	8612	4	3
The First National Bank Of Evanston	8534	6	3
Green River			
First National Bank Of Green River	10698	4	2
Greybull			
The First National Bank Of Greybull	10810	5	5

City, Bank	Ch. No.	L	S
Guernsey			
The First National Bank Of Guernsey	5295	6	–
Kemmerer			
The First National Bank Of Kemmerer	5480	3	2
Lander			
The First National Bank Of Lander	4720	3	4
Laramie			
The First National Bank Of Laramie	4989	4	2
Laramie City			
The Albany County National Bank Of Laramie City	3615	5	–
The Albany National Bank, Laramie	3615	4	2
The Laramie National Bank Of Laramie	2518	6	–
The Laramie National Bank Of Laramie City	2518	6	–
The Wyoming National Bank Of Laramie	2110	6	–
The Wyoming National Bank Of Laramie City	2110	6	–
Lovell			
The First National Bank Of Lovell	10844	–	3
Lusk			
The First National Bank Of Lusk	11390	6	–
Manville			
The First National Bank Of Manville	11352	6	–
Meeteetse			
The First National Bank Of Meeteetse	6340	5	5
Newcastle			
The First National Bank Of Newcastle	7198	6	–
Powell			
The First National Bank Of Powell	10265	6	4
The Powell National Bank	10565	5	–
Rawlins			
The First National Bank Of Rawlins	4320	3	2
The Rawlins National Bank	5413	4	2
The Stockgrowers National Bank Of Rawlins	9557	4	–
Rock River			
The First National Bank Of Rock River	11342	6	–
Rock Springs			
The First National Bank Of Rock Springs	3920	5	–
The Rock Springs National Bank	4755	3	2
Saratoga			
The First National Bank Of Saratoga	8961	5	–
Sheridan			
The First National Bank Of Sheridan	4604	4	2
The Sheridan National Bank	8275	4	–
Shoshoni			
The First National Bank Of Shoshoni	7978	6	–
The Wind River National Bank Of Shoshoni	8232	6	–
Sundance			
The First National Bank Of Sundance	4343	6	–
Thermopolis			
First National Bank In Thermopolis	12638	5	4
The First National Bank Of Thermopolis	5949	5	–
Torrington			
The First National Bank Of Torrington	9289	6	–
Wheatland			
The First National Bank Of Wheatland	8432	6	–
Worland			
The First National Bank Of Worland	8253	6	–

Small Size Notes

United States Notes

When the switch to the smaller, current size U.S. currency was made in July, 1929, the United States Notes (Legal Tender Notes), bearing red Treasury seals and serial numbers, were included, although denominations were pared back to $1, $2, $5 and $100.

The Red Seal $1 is especially popular with collectors in that it was issued only in one series (1928) and in fewer than two million notes. The 1928 $1 Legal Tenders were principally released in Puerto Rico more than 20 years after the notes had been printed. Star notes of the type are especially sought-after and command a strong premium, even in circulated grades.

The small size U.S. Note remained current in the $2 denomination until July, 1965, and in the $5 value until November, 1967. The last issue of Red Seal $100s was in 1968, though the denomination remains technically current.

The obligation for small size U.S. Notes began in Series 1928 as: "This note is a legal tender at its face value for all debts public and private except duties on imports and interest on the public debt." Under terms of the Act of May 12, 1933, the clause was amended to read: "This note is a legal tender at its face value for all debts public and private." Beginning in Series 1963, it was changed to: "This note is legal tender for all debts, public and private."

Gold Certificates

With the rest of the U.S. currency, the change to smaller notes in 1929 affected the Gold Certificates. Most noticably, the type lost its distinguishing gold-colored back design as the general configuration of the notes was standardized in all types. The seal and serial numbers continued in gold ink. Among the small size notes, Gold Certificate denominations continued from $10-$10,000, nominally intended for circulation, and even included the $100,000 Gold Certificate of Series 1934, for use in fiscal channels. Like the $100, $1,000 and $10,000 gold notes of Series 1934, the $100,000s were never released to general circulation and may not be legally held by collectors.

Likewise, Series 1928A Gold Certificates were printed in denominations of $10, $20 and $100, though never released.

The small size gold notes were a short series, cut off by the Gold Reserve Act of 1933, which required the surrender of all Gold Certificates (a restriction which was lifted in 1964). For practical purposes the collectibility of the type is thus limited to the Series 1928 notes in the $10, $20, $50 and $100 denominations, which are currently in strong demand in uncirculated condition. Star notes are especially in demand.

Silver Certificates

From the 1929 release date of the small size U.S. currency issues, until Silver Certificate legislation was abolished by a Congressional Act on June 4, 1963, small size Silver Certificates, distinguished by their blue Treasury seal and serial number, were issued in denominations of $1, $5, and $10.

The earliest small size silver notes were redeemable for "One Silver Dollar," (or the appropriate number) as had been the large size issues. A change in the redemption clause, however, was made with the Silver Purchase Act of 1934, which specified the certificates be redeemable for silver dollars or silver bullion. At that time the wording on the notes was changed to read: "One Dollar in Silver." In March, 1964, by order of the Secretary of the Treasury, redemption in silver dollars was halted, and on June 24, 1968, redemption in silver bullion was also discontinued. Like all U.S. currency issued since 1861, Silver Certificates retain their status as legal tender, though today they are convertible only into current U.S. Federal Reserve Notes.

Federal Reserve Notes

Virtually the only type of U.S. paper money encountered in circulation today is the Federal Reserve Note, in denominations of $1-$100.

Authorization continued in the small size period for FRNs to be issued in denominations from $5-$10,000. With the demise of the Silver Certificate $1 bill in 1963, that denomination was moved into the FRN realm. The Bicentennial in 1976 led to the re-introduction of the $2 note, which had last been issued as a United States Note in 1966, in the guise of a green-seal Federal Reserve Note.

No Federal Reserve Note of denomination higher than $100 has been printed since 1945, and since 1969 all notes of $500 and higher face value have been actively retired as they are turned into the Federal Reserve System.

Federal Reserve Bank Notes

The small size Federal Reserve Bank Notes were an emergency currency issue authorized March 9, 1933, to inject cash into the economy to combat heavy withdrawals from the Federal Reserve System in the first months of that year.

FRBNs in the small size were printed on currency stock prepared for the regular Series 1929 National Currency. Changes consisted of overprinting several elements. The President (and sometimes Cashier) title at the bottom of the notes was obliterated, and replaced with Governor, and the appropriate signatures of those Federal Reserve Bank officers engraved. There are, however, three exceptions to the Cashier-Governor combination on the small size FRBNs. On the notes of the Chicago bank, the signatures are those of the Assistant Deputy Governor and Governor; for New York, the signature of the Deputy Governor replaces that of the Cashier, and in the St. Louis district, the Controller signed instead of the Cashier.

In the places where the National Bank's charter number would have been imprinted, the proper district letter of the issuing bank appears in heavy black block type. At top of the note, near the obligation, a line was added to read: "or by like deposit of other securities."

Like the regular National Bank Notes of the small size era, the Treasury seal and serial number on the Federal Reserve Bank Notes are in brown ink.

Collector demand for this type has been almost non-existant until recent years. Now, however, the true rarity of some banks and denominations ($5-$100), especially in star notes, is being appreciated.

WWII Emergency Notes

Emergency conditions during World War II brought about several interesting and collectible varieties of small size U.S. currency.

North African Invasion Notes

When U.S. armed forces hit the beaches of North Africa in 1942 to begin the advance into Axis-held Europe from the south, special currency was issued to the troops which could be easily identified and demonitized in the event of military reverses and the capture of large quantities of the cash.

The notes were normal Silver Certificates, with blue serial numbers, but with Treasury seals printed in yellow. All bearing the Julian-Morgenthau signature combination, the $1 denominations were issued in Series 1935A, the $5s in Series 1934A and $10s in Series 1934 and 1934A. The 1934 $10 notes are quite scarce, especially as star notes.

Hawaii Overprints

As an economic defense precaution against Japanese invasion and occupation of Hawaii, specially marked U.S. currency was issued there in July, 1942, to replace other types in circulation. Distinguished by brown seal and serial numbers, and by "HAWAII" overprints on face and back, such notes could have been declared worthless in the event large numbers of them were captured.

The $1 notes used as emergency currency were Silver Certificates of Series 1935A, while $5s, $10s, and $20s were overprinted examples of San Francisco-district Federal Reserve Notes; the $5s in Series 1934 and '34A, the $10s in Series 1934A only, and the $20s in Series 1934 and '34A. All notes bear the Julian-Morgenthau combination.

By late October, 1944, the emergency monetary conditions were declared ended, and normal currency returned to use in Hawaii, and the Hawaii-overprinted notes went on to do further duty during the occupation of formerly Japanese-held islands in the Pacific.

R & S Experimentals

To test different types of security paper during World War II, when it was not known whether supplies of normal U.S. bank note paper could be maintained, an experimental run of notes was produced using normal, and a new special paper.

Notes on the special paper were overprinted with a large red S in the lower right corner, while a control group on regular paper was printed with a large red R in the same location. Exactly 1,184,000 of each type were released to circulation, all Silver Certificates bearing Series 1935A designation and the Julian-Morgenthau signature combination. The tests proved to be inconclusive, so no change in bank note paper resulted, but collectors were left with an interestingly variety that is especially challenging in uncirculated condition, and truly rare in star note form.

Because unscrupulous persons have applied phony R and S overprints to regular Series 1935A $1 Silver Certificates in an effort to pass them off as the higher-value experimental issue, collectors should be aware of the serial number ranges of the genuine issues. Serial numbers for the genuine R notes run from S70884001C through S72068000C; while those for the S notes are S73884001C through S75068000C.

U. S. Small Size Currency Valuations

Note: National Bank Notes issued between 1929-1935 will be found in a separate section, Pages 38-129.

One Dollar

United States Notes

KL#	Series	Signatures	Fine	VF	CU
1444	1928	Woods-Wooden	10.00	20.00	45.00
1444☆	1928	Woods-Wooden	—	—	2750.

Silver Certificates

KL#	Series	Signatures	Fine	VF	CU
1445	1928	Tate-Mellon	3.50	5.00	14.00
1445☆	1928	Tate-Mellon	—	—	75.00
1446	1928-A	Woods-Mellon	3.00	4.00	9.00
1446☆	1928-A	Woods-Mellon	—	—	40.00
1447	1928-B	Woods-Mills	3.00	6.00	12.50
1447☆	1928-B	Woods-Mills	—	—	75.00
1448	1928-C	Woods-Woodin	50.00	95.00	450.
1448☆	1928-C	Woods-Woodin	—	—	1000.

KL#	Series	Signatures	Fine	VF	CU
1449	1928-D	Julian-Woodin	40.00	80.00	275.
1449☆	1928-D	Julian-Woodin	—	—	1000.
1450	1928-E	Julian-Morgenthau	200.	300.	975.
1450☆	1928-E	Julian-Morgenthau	—	—	5000.
1451	1934	Julian-Morgenthau	2.25	4.00	17.50
1451☆	1934	Julian-Morgenthau	—	—	200.

KL#	Series	Signatures	Fine	VF	CU
1452	1935	Julian-Morgenthau	2.25	2.75	10.00
1452☆	1935	Julian-Morgenthau	6.75	8.00	100.
1453	1935-A	Julian Morgenthau	—	—	4.00
1453☆	1935-A	Julian-Morgenthau	—	—	17.50
1454	1935-B	Julian-Vinson	—	3.00	5.50
1454☆	1935-B	Julian-Vinson	—	3.00	50.00
1455	1935-C	Julian-Snyder	—	2.00	4.00
1455☆	1935-C	Julian-Snyder	—	2.00	20.00
1456	1935 D	Clark-Snyder	—	—	4.00
1456☆	1935-D	Clark-Snyder	—	—	7.50
1457	1935-E	Priest-Humphrey	—	—	3.50
1457☆	1935-E	Priest-Humphrey	—	—	7.50
1458	1935-F	Priest-Anderson	—	—	3.50
1458☆	1935-F	Priest-Anderson	—	—	7.50
1459	1935-G	Smith-Dillon	—	—	3.50
1459☆	1935-G	Smith-Dillon	—	—	6.00

KL#	Series	Signatures	Fine	VF	CU
1460	1935-G	Smith-Dillon (with motto)	—		5.00
1460☆	1935-G	Smith-Dillon (with motto)	—	—	15.00
1461	1935-H	Granahan-Dillon	—	—	4.00
1461☆	1935-H	Granahan-Dillon	—	—	10.00
1462	1957	Priest-Anderson	—	—	2.50
1462☆	1957	Priest-Anderson	—	—	4.00
1463	1957-A	Smith-Dillon	—	—	2.50
1463☆	1957-A	Smith-Dillon	—	—	3.50
1464	1957-B	Granahan-Dillon	—	—	2.50
1464☆	1957-B	Granahan-Dillon	—	—	3.00

Federal Reserve Notes

Series 1963 Granahan-Dillon

KL#	Bank	XF	CU
1465	Boston	—	3.00
1465☆	Boston	—	4.00
1466	New York	—	3.00
1466☆	New York	—	10.00
1467	Philadelphia	—	3.00
1467☆	Philadelphia	—	5.00
1468	Cleveland	—	3.00
1468☆	Cleveland	—	50.00
1469	Richmond	—	3.00
1469☆	Richmond	—	5.00
1470	Atlanta	—	3.00
1470☆	Atlanta	—	5.00
1471	Chicago	—	3.00
1471☆	Chicago	—	4.00
1472	St. Louis	—	3.00
1472☆	St. Louis	—	4.00
1473	Minneapolis	—	3.00
1473☆	Minneapolis	—	4.00
1474	Kansas City	—	3.00
1474☆	Kansas City	—	4.00
1475	Dallas	—	3.00
1475☆	Dallas	—	4.00
1476	San Francisco	—	3.00
1476☆	San Francisco	—	5.00

Series 1963-A Granahan-Fowler

KL#	Bank	XF	CU
1477	Boston	—	3.00
1477☆	Boston	—	10.00
1478	New York	—	3.00
1478☆	New York	—	3.50
1479	Philadelphia	—	3.00
1479☆	Philadelphia	—	3.50
1480	Cleveland	—	3.00
1480☆	Cleveland	—	3.50
1481	Richmond	—	3.00
1481☆	Richmond	—	3.50
1482	Atlanta	—	3.00
1482☆	Atlanta	—	5.00
1483	Chicago	—	3.00
1483☆	Chicago	—	3.50
1484	St. Louis	—	3.00
1484☆	St. Louis	—	3.50
1485	Minneapolis	—	3.00
1485☆	Minneapolis	—	3.50
1486	Kansas City	—	3.00
1486☆	Kansas City	—	4.00
1487	Dallas	—	3.00
1487☆	Dallas	—	25.00
1488	San Francisco	—	3.00
1488☆	San Francisco	—	3.50

Series 1963-B Granahan-Barr

KL#	Bank	XF	CU
1490	New York	—	3.00
1490☆	New York	—	3.50
1493	Richmond	—	3.00
1493☆	Richmond	—	5.00
1495	Chicago	—	3.00
1495☆	Chicago	—	3.50
1498	Kansas City	—	3.00
1498☆	Kansas City		None Printed
1500	San Francisco	—	3.00
1500☆	San Francisco	—	3.50

Series 1969 Elston-Kennedy

KL#	Bank	XF	CU
1501	Boston	—	2.50
1501☆	Boston	—	3.00
1502	New York	—	2.50
1502☆	New York	—	3.00
1503	Philadelphia	—	2.50
1503☆	Philadelphia	—	25.00
1504	Cleveland	—	2.50
1504☆	Cleveland	—	5.00
1505	Richmond	—	2.50
1505☆	Richmond	—	5.00
1506	Atlanta	—	2.50
1506☆	Atlanta	—	4.00
1507	Chicago	—	2.50
1507☆	Chicago	—	4.00
1508	St. Louis	—	2.50
1508☆	St. Louis	—	3.00
1509	Minneapolis	—	2.50
1509☆	Minneapolis	—	3.00
1510	Kansas City	—	2.50
1510☆	Kansas City	—	3.00
1511	Dallas	—	2.50
1511☆	Dallas	—	5.00
1512	San Francisco	—	2.50
1512☆	San Francisco	—	5.00

Series 1969-A Kabis-Kennedy

KL#	Bank	XF	CU
1513	Boston	—	2.50
1513☆	Boston	—	3.00
1514	New York	—	2.50
1514☆	New York	—	3.00
1515	Philadelphia	—	2.50
1515☆	Philadelphia	—	3.00
1516	Cleveland	—	2.50
1516☆	Cleveland	—	3.00
1517	Richmond	—	2.50
1517☆	Richmond	—	3.00
1518	Atlanta	—	2.50
1518☆	Atlanta	—	3.00
1519	Chicago	—	2.50
1519☆	Chicago	—	3.00
1520	St. Louis	—	2.50
1520☆	St. Louis	—	4.00
1521	Minneapolis	—	2.50
1521☆	Minneapolis	—	5.00
1522	Kansas City	—	2.50
1522☆	Kansas City	—	3.00
1523	Dallas	—	2.50
1523☆	Dallas		None Printed
1524	San Francisco	—	2.50
1524☆	San Francisco	—	3.00

Series 1969-B Kabis-Connally

KL#	Bank	XF	CU
1525	Boston	—	2.50
1525☆	Boston	—	3.50
1526	New York	—	2.50
1526☆	New York	—	5.00
1527	Philadelphia	—	2.50
1527☆	Philadelphia	—	4.00
1528	Cleveland	—	2.50
1528☆	Cleveland	—	3.50
1529	Richmond	—	2.50
1529☆	Richmond	—	3.50
1530	Atlanta	—	2.50
1530☆	Atlanta	—	3.50
1531	Chicago	—	2.50
1531☆	Chicago	—	4.00
1532	St. Louis	—	2.50
1532☆	St. Louis	—	3.50
1533	Minneapolis	—	2.50
1533☆	Minneapolis	—	3.50
1534	Kansas City	—	2.50
1534☆	Kansas City	—	3.50
1535	Dallas	—	2.50
1535☆	Dallas	—	4.00
1536	San Francisco	—	2.50
1536☆	San Francisco	—	5.00

Series 1969-C Banuelos-Connally

KL#	Bank	XF	CU
1538	New York	—	2.00
1538☆	New York		None Printed
1540	Cleveland	—	2.00
1540☆	Cleveland	—	5.00
1541	Richmond	—	2.00
1541☆	Richmond	—	5.00
1542	Atlanta	—	2.00
1542☆	Atlanta	—	3.00
1543	Chicago	—	2.00
1543☆	Chicago	—	25.00
1544	St. Louis	—	2.00
1544☆	St. Louis	—	5.00
1545	Minneapolis	—	2.00
1545☆	Minneapolis	—	5.00
1546	Kansas City	—	2.00
1546☆	Kansas City	—	3.00
1547	Dallas	—	2.00
1547☆	Dallas	—	5.00
1548	San Francisco	—	2.00
1548☆	San Francisco	—	5.00

Series 1969-D Banuelos-Shultz

KL#	Bank	XF	CU
1561	Boston	—	2.00
1561☆	Boston	—	3.50
1562	New York	—	2.00
1562☆	New York	—	3.00
1563	Philadelphia	—	2.00
1563☆	Philadelphia	—	3.50
1564	Cleveland	—	2.00
1564☆	Cleveland	—	3.00
1565	Richmond	—	2.00
1565☆	Richmond	—	3.00
1566	Atlanta	—	2.00
1566☆	Atlanta	—	3.00
1567	Chicago	—	2.00
1567☆	Chicago	—	25.00
1568	St. Louis	—	2.00
1568☆	St. Louis	—	3.00
1569	Minneapolis	—	2.00
1569☆	Minneapolis		None Printed
1570	Kansas City	—	2.00
1570☆	Kansas City	—	3.00
1571	Dallas	—	2.00
1571☆	Dallas	—	3.00
1572	San Francisco	—	2.00
1572☆	San Francisco	—	3.00

Series 1974 Neff-Simon

KL#	Bank	XF	CU
1573	Boston	—	2.00
1573☆	Boston	—	25.00
1574	New York	—	2.00
1574☆	New York	—	25.00
1575	Philadelphia	—	2.00
1575☆	Philadelphia	—	3.50
1576	Cleveland	—	2.00
1576☆	Cleveland	—	3.50
1577	Richmond	—	2.00
1577☆	Richmond	—	3.50
1578	Atlanta	—	2.00
1578☆	Atlanta	—	25.00
1579	Chicago	—	2.00
1579☆	Chicago	—	25.00
1580	St. Louis	—	2.00
1580☆	St. Louis	—	3.50
1581	Minneapolis	—	2.00
1581☆	Minneapolis	—	5.00
1582	Kansas City	—	2.00
1582☆	Kansas City	—	25.00
1583	Dallas	—	2.00
1583☆	Dallas	—	25.00
1584	San Francisco	—	2.00
1584☆	San Francisco	—	3.50

Series 1977 Morton-Blumenthal

KL#	Bank	XF	CU
1585	Boston	—	2.00
1585☆	Boston	—	25.00
1586	New York	—	2.00
1586☆	New York	—	25.00
1587	Philadelphia	—	2.00
1587☆	Philadelphia	—	25.00
1588	Cleveland	—	2.00
1588☆	Cleveland	—	25.00
1589	Richmond	—	2.00
1589☆	Richmond	—	25.00
1590	Atlanta	—	2.00
1590☆	Atlanta	—	25.00
1591	Chicago	—	2.00
1591☆	Chicago	—	25.00
1592	St. Louis	—	2.00
1592☆	St. Louis	—	25.00
1593	Minneapolis	—	2.00
1593☆	Minneapolis	—	5.00
1594	Kansas City	—	2.00
1594☆	Kansas City	—	25.00
1595	Dallas	—	2.00
1595☆	Dallas	—	25.00
1596	San Francisco	—	2.00
1596☆	San Francisco	—	25.00

Series 1977-A Morton-Miller

KL#	Bank	XF	CU
1597	Boston	—	2.00
1597☆	Boston	—	25.00
1598	New York	—	2.00
1598☆	New York	—	25.00
1599	Philadelphia	—	2.00
1599☆	Philadelphia	—	25.00
1600	Cleveland	—	2.00
1600☆	Cleveland	—	25.00
1601	Richmond	—	2.00
1601☆	Richmond	—	25.00
1602	Atlanta	—	2.00
1602☆	Atlanta	—	25.00
1603	Chicago	—	2.00
1603☆	Chicago	—	3.50
1604	St. Louis	—	2.00
1604☆	St. Louis	—	25.00
1605	Minneapolis	—	2.00
1605☆	Minneapolis	—	25.00
1606	Kansas City	—	2.00
1606☆	Kansas City	—	25.00
1607	Dallas	—	2.00
1607☆	Dallas	—	25.00
1608	San Francisco	—	2.00
1608☆	San Francisco	—	25.00

Series 1981 Buchanan-Regan

KL#	Bank	XF	CU
3500	Boston	—	2.00
3500☆	Boston	—	2.50
3501	New York	—	2.00
3501☆	New York	—	2.50
3502	Philadelphia	—	2.50
3502☆	Philadelphia	—	10.00
3503	Cleveland	—	2.00
3503☆	Cleveland	—	2.50
3504	Richmond	—	2.00
3504☆	Richmond	—	2.50
3505	Atlanta	—	2.00
3505☆	Atlanta	—	2.50
3506	Chicago	—	2.00
3506☆	Chicago	—	2.50
3507	St. Louis	—	2.00
3507☆	St. Louis	—	10.00
3508	Minneapolis	—	2.00
3508☆	Minneapolis	—	10.00
3509	Kansas City	—	2.00
3509☆	Kansas City	—	2.50
3510	Dallas	—	2.00
3510☆	Dallas	—	2.50
3511	San Francisco	—	2.00
3511☆	San Francisco	—	2.50

Series 1981-A Ortega-Regan

KL#	Bank	XF	CU
3600	Boston	—	2.00
3600☆	Boston	—	2.50
3601	New York	—	2.00
3601☆	New York	—	2.50
3602	Philadelphia	—	2.00
3602☆	Philadelphia	—	2.50
3603	Cleveland	—	2.00
3603☆	Cleveland	—	2.50
3604	Richmond	—	2.00
3604☆	Richmond	—	2.50
3605	Atlanta	—	2.00
3605☆	Atlanta	—	2.50
3606	Chicago	—	2.00
3606☆	Chicago	—	2.50
3607	St. Louis	—	2.00
3607☆	St. Louis	—	2.50
3608	Minneapolis	—	2.00
3608☆	Minneapolis	—	2.50
3609	Kansas City	—	2.00
3609☆	Kansas City	—	2.50
3610	Dallas	—	2.00
3610☆	Dallas	—	2.50
3611	San Francisco	—	2.00
3611☆	San Francisco	—	2.50

Series 1985 Ortega-Baker

KL#	Bank	XF	CU
3700	Boston	—	(Current)
3700☆	Boston	—	—
3701	New York	—	(Current)
3701☆	New York	—	—
3702	Philadelphia	—	(Current)
3702☆	Philadelphia	—	—
3703	Cleveland	—	(Current)
3703☆	Cleveland	—	—
3704	Richmond	—	(Current)
3704☆	Richmond	—	—
3705	Atlanta	—	(Current)
3705☆	Atlanta	—	—
3706	Chicago	—	(Current)
3706☆	Chicago	—	—
3707	St. Louis	—	(Current)
3707☆	St. Louis	—	—
3708	Minneapolis	—	(Current)
3708☆	Minneapolis	—	—
3709	Kansas City	—	(Current)
3709☆	Kansas City	—	—
3710	Dallas	—	(Current)
3710☆	Dallas	—	—
3711	San Francisco	—	(Current)
3711☆	San Francisco	—	—

Hawaii Emergency Silver Certificates

KL#	Series	Signatures	Fine	VF	CU
1609	1935-A	Julian-Morgenthau	6.00	7.00	35.00
1609☆	1935-A	Julian-Morgenthau	—	—	400.

North Africa Emergency Silver Certificates

KL#	Series	Signatures	Fine	VF	CU
1610	1935-A	Julian-Morgenthau	7.75	10.00	50.00
1610☆	1935-A	Julian-Morgenthau	—	—	400.

1935A Experimental Issue Silver Certificates

KL#	Type	Fine	VF	CU
1611	$1 Red "R"	14.00	20.00	175.
1611☆	$1 Red "R"	—	—	—
1612	$1 Red "S"	12.00	15.00	150.
1612☆	$1 Red "S"	—	—	—

Two Dollars United States Notes

KL#	Series	Signatures	Fine	VF	CU
1613	1928	Tate-Mellon	7.50	12.50	30.00
1613☆	1928	Tate-Mellon	—	—	175.
1614	1928-A	Woods-Mellon	15.00	30.00	135.
1614☆	1928-A	Woods-Mellon	—	—	350.
1615	1928-B	Woods-Mills	65.00	120.	425.
1615☆	1928-B	Woods-Mills	—	—	700.
1616	1928-C	Julian-Morgenthau	5.00	7.50	50.00
1616☆	1928-C	Julian-Morgenthau	—	—	350.
1617	1928-D	Julian-Morgenthau	4.00	7.50	15.00
1617☆	1928-D	Julian-Morgenthau	—	—	50.00
1618	1928-E	Julian-Vinson	6.00	15.00	40.00
1618☆	1928-E	Julian-Vinson	—	—	1000.
1619	1928-F	Julian-Snyder	4.50	6.50	10.00
1619☆	1928-F	Julian-Snyder	—	—	35.00
1620	1928-G	Clark-Snyder	4.00	6.00	12.50
1620☆	1928-G	Clark-Snyder	—	—	40.00
1621	1953	Priest-Humphrey	3.25	4.50	6.00
1621☆	1953	Priest-Humphrey	—	—	12.50
1622	1953-A	Priest-Anderson	3.25	4.50	5.00
1622☆	1953-A	Priest-Anderson	—	—	10.00
1623	1953-B	Smith-Dillon	3.25	4.50	5.00
1623☆	1953-B	Smith-Dillon	—	—	10.00
1624	1953-C	Granahan-Dillon	3.25	4.50	5.00
1624☆	1953-C	Granhan-Dillon	—	—	10.00
1625	1963	Granahan-Dillon	2.75	3.50	4.00
1625☆	1963	Granhan-Dillon	—	—	10.00
1626	1963-A	Granhan-Fowler	2.75	3.50	4.50
1626☆	1963-A	Granhan-Fowler	—	—	10.00

Fedcral Reserve Notes

Series 1976 Neff-Simon

KL#	Bank	XF	CU
1627	Boston	—	3.50
1627☆	Boston	—	4.00
1628	New York	—	3.50
1628☆	New York	—	4.00
1629	Philadelphia	—	3.50
1629☆	Philadelphia	—	4.00
1630	Cleveland	—	3.50
1630☆	Cleveland	—	4.00
1631	Richmond	—	3.50
1631☆	Richmond	—	4.00
1632	Atlanta	—	3.50
1632☆	Atlanta	—	4.00

KL#	Bank	XF	CU
1633	Chicago	—	3.50
1633☆	Chicago	—	4.00
1634	St. Louis	—	3.50
1634☆	St. Louis	—	4.00
1635	Minneapolis	—	3.50
1635☆	Minneapolis	—	4.00
1636	Kansas City	—	3.50
1636☆	Kansas City	—	4.00
1637	Dallas	—	3.50
1637☆	Dallas	—	4.00
1638	San Francisco	—	3.50
1638☆	San Francisco	—	4.00

Five Dollars
United States Notes

KL#	Series	Signatures	Fine	VF	CU
1639	1928	Woods-Mellon	6.00	8.00	20.00
1639☆	1928	Woods-Mellon	6.00	8.00	200.
1640	1928-A	Woods-Mills	12.00	13.00	40.00
1640☆	1928-A	Woods-Mills	—	—	400.
1641	1928-B	Julian-Morgenthau	8.00	9.00	18.00
1641☆	1928-B	Julian-Morgenthau	—	—	125.
1642	1928-C	Julian-Morgenthau	7.00	10.00	20.00
1642☆	1928-C	Julian-Morgenthau	—	—	75.00
1643	1928-D	Julian-Vinson	10.00	16.50	100.
1643☆	1928-D	Julian-Vinson	—	—	300.
1644	1928-E	Julian-Snyder	7.00	9.50	17.00
1644☆	1928-E	Julian-Snyder	—	—	80.00
1645	1928-F	Clark-Snyder	7.00	8.50	18.00
1645☆	1928-F	Clark-Snyder	—	—	100.
1646	1953	Priest-Humphrey	7.00	8.50	12.50
1646☆	1953	Priest-Humphrey	—	—	75.00
1647	1953-A	Priest-Anderson	7.00	7.50	10.00
1647☆	1953-A	Priest-Anderson	—	—	25.00
1648	1953-B	Smith-Dillon	6.50	7.50	10.00
1648☆	1953-B	Smith-Dillon	—	—	20.00
1649	1953-C	Granahan-Dillon	6.50	7.50	12.00
1649☆	1953-C	Granahan-Dillon	—	—	20.00
1650	1963	Granahan-Dillon	6.00	7.50	10.00
1650☆	1963	Granahan-Dillon	—	—	15.00

Silver Certificates

KL#	Series	Signatures	Fine	VF	CU
1651	1934	Julian-Morgenthau	—	8.00	18.00
1651☆	1934	Julian-Morgenthau	—	—	50.00
1652	1934-A	Julian-Morgenthau	—	8.00	12.50
1652☆	1934-A	Julian-Morgenthau	—	—	35.00
1653	1934-B	Julian-Vinson	—	10.00	25.00
1653☆	1934-B	Julian-Morgenthau	—	—	100.
1654	1934 C	Julian-Snyder	—	8.00	14.00
1654☆	1934-C	Julian-Snyder	—	—	30.00
1655	1934-D	Clark-Snyder	—	8.00	12.50
1655☆	1934-D	Clark-Snyder	—	—	25.00
1656	1953	Priest-Humphrey	—	—	12.50
1656☆	1953	Priest-Humphrey	—	—	25.00
1657	1953-A	Priest-Anderson	—	—	12.50
1657☆	1953-A	Priest-Anderson	—	—	20.00
1658	1953-B	Smith-Dillon	—	—	12.50
1658☆	1953-B	Smith-Dillon	—	—	350.

Federal Reserve Bank Notes

KL#	Series	District	Fine	VF	CU
1659	1929	Boston	7.50	15.00	55.00
1660	1929	New York	7.50	12.00	50.00
1661	1929	Philadelphia	7.50	15.00	60.00
1662	1929	Cleveland	7.50	12.00	50.00
1664	1929	Atlanta	7.50	15.00	90.00
1665	1929	Chicago	7.50	10.00	50.00
1666	1929	St. Louis	90.00	150.	325.
1667	1929	Minneapolis	10.00	25.00	150.
1668	1929	Kansas City	7.50	12.00	65.00
1669	1929	Dallas	8.00	15.00	60.00
1670	1929	San Francisco	450.	750.	2000.

Federal Reserve Notes

KL#	Bank	XF	CU
1671	Boston	—	35.00
1672	New York	—	35.00
1673	Philadelphia	—	35.00
1674	Cleveland	—	35.00
1675	Richmond	—	35.00
1676	Atlanta	—	35.00
1677	Chicago	—	35.00
1678	St. Louis	—	35.00
1679	Minneapolis	—	35.00
1680	Kansas City	—	35.00
1681	Dallas	—	35.00
1682	San Francisco	—	35.00

Series 1928-A Woods-Mellon

KL#	Bank	XF	CU
1683	Boston	—	35.00
1684	New York	—	35.00
1685	Philadelphia	—	35.00
1686	Cleveland	—	35.00
1687	Richmond	—	35.00
1688	Atlanta	—	35.00
1689	Chicago	—	35.00
1690	St. Louis	—	35.00
1691	Minneapolis	—	35.00
1692	Kansas City	—	35.00
1693	Dallas	—	35.00
1694	San Francisco	—	35.00

Series 1928-B Woods-Mellon

KL#	Bank	XF	CU
1695	Boston	—	35.00
1696	New York	—	35.00
1697	Philadelphia	—	35.00
1698	Cleveland	—	35.00
1699	Richmond	—	35.00
1700	Atlanta	—	35.00
1701	Chicago	—	35.00
1702	St. Louis	—	35.00
1703	Minneapolis	—	35.00
1704	Kansas City	—	35.00
1705	Dallas	—	35.00
1706	San Francisco	—	35.00

Series 1928-C Woods-Mills

KL#	Bank	XF	CU
1707	Boston	200.	375.
1708	New York	200.	375.
1709	Philadelphia	200.	375.
1710	Cleveland	200.	375.
1711	Richmond	200.	375.
1712	Atlanta	200.	375.
1713	Chicago	200.	375.
1714	St. Louis	200.	375.
1715	Minneapolis	200.	375.
1716	Kansas City	200.	375.
1717	Dallas	200.	375.
1718	San Francisco	200.	375.

Series 1928-D Woods-Woodin

KL#	Bank	XF	CU
1724	Atlanta	225.	575.

Series 1934 Julian-Morgenthau

KL#	Bank	XF	CU
1731	Boston	—	20.00
1732	New York	—	20.00
1733	Philadelphia	—	20.00
1734	Cleveland	—	20.00
1735	Richmond	—	20.00
1736	Atlanta	—	20.00
1737	Chicago	—	20.00
1738	St. Louis	—	20.00
1739	Minneapolis	—	20.00
1740	Kansas City	—	20.00
1741	Dallas	—	20.00
1742	San Francisco	—	20.00

Series 1934-A Julian-Morgenthau

KL#	Bank	XF	CU
1743	Boston	—	20.00
1744	New York	—	20.00
1745	Philadelphia	—	20.00
1746	Cleveland	—	20.00
1747	Richmond	—	20.00
1748	Atlanta	—	20.00
1749	Chicago	—	20.00
1750	St. Louis	—	20.00
1754	San Francisco	—	20.00

Series 1934-B Julian-Vinson

KL#	Bank	XF	CU
1755	Boston	—	30.00
1756	New York	—	30.00
1757	Philadelphia	—	30.00
1758	Cleveland	—	30.00
1759	Richmond	—	30.00
1760	Atlanta	—	30.00
1761	Chicago	—	30.00
1762	St. Louis	—	30.00
1763	Minneapolis	—	30.00
1764	Kansas City	—	30.00
1766	San Francisco	—	30.00

Series 1934-C Julian-Snyder

KL#	Bank	XF	CU
1767	Boston	—	20.00
1768	New York	—	20.00
1769	Philadelphia	—	20.00
1770	Cleveland	—	20.00
1771	Richmond	—	20.00
1772	Atlanta	—	20.00
1773	Chicago	—	20.00
1774	St. Louis	—	20.00
1775	Minneapolis	—	20.00
1776	Kansas City	—	20.00
1777	Dallas	—	20.00
1778	San Francisco	—	20.00

Series 1934-D Clark-Snyder

KL#	Bank	XF	CU
1779	Boston	—	14.00
1780	New York	—	14.00
1781	Philadelphia	—	14.00
1782	Cleveland	—	14.00
1783	Richmond	—	14.00
1784	Atlanta	—	14.00
1785	Chicago	—	14.00
1786	St. Louis	—	14.00
1787	Minneapolis	—	14.00
1788	Kansas City	—	14.00
1789	Dallas	—	14.00
1790	San Francisco	—	14.00

Series 1950 Clark-Snyder

KL#	Bank	XF	CU
1791	Boston	—	20.00
1791★	Boston	—	27.50
1792	New York	—	20.00
1792★	New York	—	22.50
1793	Philadelphia	—	20.00
1793★	Philadelphia	—	25.00
1794	Cleveland	—	20.00
1794★	Cleveland	—	25.00
1795	Richmond	—	20.00
1795★	Richmond	—	25.00
1796	Atlanta	—	20.00
1796★	Atlanta	—	25.00
1797	Chicago	—	20.00
1797★	Chicago	—	22.50
1798	St. Louis	—	20.00
1798★	St. Louis	—	27.50
1799	Minneapolis	—	20.00
1799★	Minneapolis	—	30.00
1800	Kansas City	—	20.00
1800★	Kansas City	—	27.50
1801	Dallas	—	20.00
1801★	Dallas	—	27.50
1802	San Francisco	—	20.00
1802★	San Francisco	—	25.00

Series 1950-A Priest-Humphrey

KL#	Bank	XF	CU
1803	Boston	—	16.00
1803★	Boston	—	21.50
1804	New York	—	16.00
1804★	New York	—	20.00
1805	Philadelphia	—	16.00
1805★	Philadelphia	—	21.50
1806	Cleveland	—	16.00
1806★	Cleveland	—	21.50
1807	Richmond	—	16.00
1807★	Richmond	—	20.00
1808	Atlanta	—	16.00
1808★	Atlanta	—	20.00
1809	Chicago	—	16.00
1809★	Chicago	—	20.00
1810	St. Louis	—	16.00
1810★	St. Louis	—	22.00
1811	Minneapolis	—	16.00
1811★	Minneapolis	—	25.00
1812	Kansas City	—	16.00
1812★	Kansas City	—	22.50
1813	Dallas	—	16.00
1813★	Dallas	—	22.50
1814	San Francisco	—	16.00
1814★	San Francisco	—	21.00

Series 1950-B Priest-Anderson

KL#	Bank	XF	CU
1815	Boston	—	16.00
1815★	Boston	—	18.50
1816	New York	—	16.00
1816★	New York	—	18.50
1817	Philadelphia	—	16.00
1817★	Philadelphia	—	18.50
1818	Cleveland	—	16.00
1818★	Cleveland	—	18.50
1819	Richmond	—	16.00
1819★	Richmond	—	18.50
1820	Atlanta	—	16.00
1820★	Atlanta	—	18.50
1821	Chicago	—	16.00
1821★	Chicago	—	18.50
1822	St. Louis	—	16.00
1822★	St. Louis	—	18.50
1823	Minneapolis	—	16.00
1823★	Minneapolis	—	19.00
1824	Kansas City	—	16.00
1824★	Kansas City	—	18.00
1825	Dallas	—	16.00
1825★	Dallas	—	17.50
1826	San Francisco	—	16.00
1826★	San Francisco	—	17.50

Series 1950-C Smith-Dillon

KL#	Bank	XF	CU
1827	Boston	—	15.00
1827★	Boston	—	17.00
1828	New York	—	15.00
1828★	New York	—	17.00
1829	Philadelphia	—	15.00
1829★	Philadelphia	—	17.00
1830	Cleveland	—	15.00
1830★	Cleveland	—	17.00

KL#	Bank	XF	CU
1831	Richmond	—	15.00
1831★	Richmond	—	17.00
1832	Atlanta	—	15.00
1832★	Atlanta	—	17.00
1833	Chicago	—	15.00
1833★	Chicago	—	17.00
1834	St. Louis	—	15.00
1834★	St. Louis	—	17.50
1835	Minneapolis	—	15.00
1835★	Minneapolis	—	18.50
1836	Kansas City	—	15.00
1836★	Kansas City	—	17.50
1837	Dallas	—	15.00
1837★	Dallas	—	20.00
1838	San Francisco	—	15.00
1838★	San Francisco	—	17.50

Series 1950-D Granahan-Dillon

KL#	Bank	XF	CU
1839	Boston	—	15.00
1839★	Boston	—	17.00
1840	New York	—	15.00
1840★	New York	—	17.00
1841	Philadelphia	—	15.00
1841★	Philadelphia	—	17.00
1842	Cleveland	—	15.00
1842★	Cleveland	—	17.00
1843	Richmond	—	15.00
1843★	Richmond	—	17.00
1844	Atlanta	—	15.00
1844★	Atlanta	—	17.00
1845	Chicago	—	15.00
1845★	Chicago	—	17.00
1846	St. Louis	—	15.00
1846★	St. Louis	—	17.00
1847	Minneapolis	—	15.00
1847★	Minneapolis	—	17.50
1848	Kansas City	—	15.00
1848★	Kansas City	—	17.00
1849	Dallas	—	15.00
1849★	Dallas	—	17.50
1850	San Francisco	—	15.00
1850★	San Francisco	—	17.00

Series 1950-E Granahan-Fowler

KL#	Bank	XF	CU
1852	New York	—	20.00
1852★	New York	—	22.50
1853	Chicago	—	20.00
1853★	Chicago	—	22.50
1854	San Francisco	—	20.00
1854★	San Francisco	—	22.50

Series 1963 Granahan-Dillon

KL#	Bank	XF	CU
1855	Boston	—	14.00
1855★	Boston	—	17.50
1856	New York	—	14.00
1856★	New York	—	16.00
1857	Philadelphia	—	14.00
1857★	Philadelphia	—	17.00
1858	Cleveland	—	14.00
1858★	Cleveland	—	16.50
1859	Atlanta	—	14.00
1859★	Atlanta	—	16.00
1860	Chicago	—	14.00
1860★	Chicago	—	16.00
1861	St. Louis	—	14.00
1861★	St. Louis	—	16.00
1861A	Kansas City	—	14.00
1861A★	Kansas City	—	19.00
1862	Dallas	—	14.00
1862★	Dallas	—	17.50
1863	San Francisco	—	14.00
1863★	San Francisco	—	16.00

Series 1963-A Granahan-Fowler

KL#	Bank	XF	CU
1864	Boston	—	12.00
1864★	Boston	—	14.00
1865	New York	—	12.00
1865★	New York	—	14.00
1866	Philadelphia	—	12.00
1866★	Philadelphia	—	14.00
1867	Cleveland	—	12.00
1867★	Cleveland	—	14.00
1868	Richmond	—	12.00
1868★	Richmond	—	14.00
1869	Atlanta	—	12.00
1869★	Atlanta	—	14.00
1870	Chicago	—	12.00
1870★	Chicago	—	14.00
1871	St. Louis	—	12.00
1871★	St. Louis	—	14.00
1872	Minneapolis	—	12.00
1872★	Minneapolis	—	14.00
1873	Kansas City	—	12.00
1873★	Kansas City	—	14.00
1874	Dallas	—	12.00
1874★	Dallas	—	15.00
1875	San Francisco	—	12.00
1875★	San Francisco	—	14.00

Series 1969 Elston-Kennedy

KL#	Bank	XF	CU
1876	Boston	—	10.00
1876★	Boston	—	12.00
1877	New York	—	10.00
1877★	New York	—	12.00
1878	Philadelphia	—	10.00
1878★	Philadelphia	—	12.00
1879	Cleveland	—	10.00
1879★	Cleveland	—	12.00
1880	Richmond	—	10.00
1880★	Richmond	—	12.00
1881	Atlanta	—	10.00
1881★	Atlanta	—	12.00
1882	Chicago	—	10.00
1882★	Chicago	—	12.00
1883	St. Louis	—	10.00
1883★	St. Louis	—	12.00
1884	Minneapolis	—	10.00
1884★	Minneapolis	—	12.00
1885	Kansas City	—	10.00
1885★	Kansas City	—	12.00
1886	Dallas		10.00
1886★	Dallas	—	12.00
1887	San Francisco	—	10.00
1887★	San Francisco	—	12.00

Series 1969-A Kabis-Connally

KL#	Bank	XF	CU
1888	Boston	—	10.00
1888★	Boston	—	12.00
1889	New York	—	10.00
1889★	New York	—	12.00
1890	Philadelphia	—	10.00
1890★	Philadelphia	—	12.00
1891	Cleveland	—	10.00
1891★	Cleveland	—	12.00
1892	Richmond	—	10.00
1892★	Richmond	—	12.00
1893	Atlanta	—	10.00
1893★	Atlanta	—	12.00
1894	Chicago	—	10.00
1894★	Chicago	—	12.00
1895	St. Louis	—	10.00
1895★	St. Louis	—	12.00
1896	Minneapolis	—	10.00
1896★	Minneapolis	—	12.00
1897	Kansas City	—	10.00
1897★	Kansas City	—	12.00
1898	Dallas	—	10.00
1898★	Dallas	—	12.00
1899	San Francisco	—	10.00
1899★	San Francisco	—	12.00

Series 1969-B Banuelos-Connally

KL#	Bank	XF	CU
1900	Boston	—	9.00
1900★	Boston		None Printed
1901	New York	—	9.00
1901★	New York	—	11.00
1902	Philadelphia	—	9.00
1902★	Philadelphia		None Printed
1903	Cleveland	—	9.00
1903★	Cleveland		None Printed
1904	Richmond	—	9.00
1904★	Richmond	—	11.00
1905	Atlanta	—	9.00
1905★	Atlanta	—	11.00
1906	Chicago	—	9.00
1906★	Chicago	—	12.50
1907	St. Louis	—	9.00
1907★	St. Louis		None Printed
1908	Minneapolis	—	9.00
1908★	Minneapolis		None Printed
1909	Kansas City	—	9.00
1909★	Kansas City	—	11.00
1910	Dallas	—	9.00
1910★	Dallas		None Printed
1911	San Francisco	—	9.00
1911★	San Francisco	—	11.00

Series 1969-C Banuelos-Shultz

KL#	Bank	XF	CU
1912	Boston	—	9.00
1912★	Boston	—	11.00
1913	New York	—	9.00
1913★	New York	—	11.00
1914	Philadelphia	—	9.00
1914★	Philadelphia	—	11.00
1915	Cleveland	—	9.00
1915★	Cleveland	—	11.00
1916	Richmond	—	9.00
1916★	Richmond	—	11.00
1917	Atlanta	—	9.00
1917★	Atlanta	—	11.00
1918	Chicago	—	9.00
1918★	Chicago		None Printed
1919	St. Louis	—	9.00
1919★	St. Louis	—	11.00
1920	Minneapolis	—	9.00
1920★	Minneapolis		None Printed
1921	Kansas City	—	9.00
1921★	Kansas City	—	11.00
1922	Dallas	—	9.00
1922★	Dallas	—	11.00
1923	San Francisco	—	9.00
1923★	San Francisco	—	11.00

Series 1974 Neff-Simon

KL#	Bank	XF	CU
1924	Boston	—	9.00
1924★	Boston	—	25.00
1925	New York	—	9.00
1925★	New York	—	25.00
1926	Philadelphia	—	9.00
1926★	Philadelphia	—	10.00
1927	Cleveland	—	9.00
1927★	Cleveland	—	—
1928	Richmond	—	9.00
1928★	Richmond	—	11.00
1929	Atlanta	—	9.00
1929★	Atlanta	—	11.00
1930	Chicago	—	9.00
1930★	Chicago	—	25.00
1931	St. Louis	—	9.00
1931★	St. Louis	—	11.00
1932	Minneapolis	—	9.00
1932★	Minneapolis	—	11.00
1933	Kansas City	—	9.00
1933★	Kansas City	—	25.00
1934	Dallas	—	9.00
1934★	Dallas	—	25.00
1935	San Francisco	—	9.00
1935★	San Francisco	—	25.00

Series 1977 Morton-Blumenthal

KL#	Bank	XF	CU
1936	Boston	—	7.50
1936★	Boston	—	25.00
1937	New York	—	7.50
1937★	New York	—	25.00
1938	Philadelphia	—	7.50
1938★	Philadelphia	—	10.00
1939	Cleveland	—	7.50
1939★	Cleveland	—	25.00
1940	Richmond	—	7.50
1940★	Richmond	—	25.00
1941	Atlanta	—	7.50
1941★	Atlanta	—	25.00
1942	Chicago	—	7.50
1942★	Chicago	—	25.00
1943	St. Louis	—	7.50
1943★	St. Louis	—	25.00
1944	Minneapolis	—	7.50
1944★	Minneapolis		None Printed
1945	Kansas City	—	7.50
1945★	Kansas City	—	25.00
1946	Dallas	—	7.50
1946★	Dallas	—	25.00
1947	San Francisco	—	7.50
1947★	San Francisco	—	25.00

Series 1977-A Morton-Miller

KL#	Bank	XF	CU
1948	Boston	—	7.50
1948★	Boston	—	25.00
1949	New York	—	7.50
1949★	New York	—	25.00
1950	Philadelphia	—	7.50
1950★	Philadelphia	—	25.00
1951	Cleveland	—	7.50
1951★	Cleveland	—	25.00
1952	Richmond	—	7.50
1952★	Richmond	—	25.00
1953	Atlanta	—	7.50
1953★	Atlanta	—	25.00
1954	Chicago	—	7.50
1954★	Chicago	—	25.00
1955	St. Louis	—	7.50
1955★	St. Louis	—	25.00
1956	Minneapolis	—	7.50
1956★	Minneapolis	—	25.00
1957	Kansas City	—	7.50
1957★	Kansas City	—	25.00
1958	Dallas	—	7.50
1958★	Dallas	—	25.00
1959	San Francisco	—	7.50
1959★	San Francisco	—	25.00

Series 1981 Buchanan-Regan

KL#	Bank	XF	CU
3512	Boston	—	6.00
3512★	Boston	—	7.50
3513	New York	—	6.00
3513★	New York	—	7.50
3514	Philadelphia	—	6.00
3514★	Philadelphia	—	7.50
3515	Cleveland	—	6.00
3515★	Cleveland	—	7.50
3516	Richmond	—	6.00
3516★	Richmond	—	7.50
3517	Atlanta	—	6.00
3517★	Atlanta	—	7.50
3518	Chicago	—	6.00
3518★	Chicago	—	7.50
3519	St. Louis	—	6.00
3519★	St. Louis	—	7.50
3520	Minneapolis	—	6.00
3520★	Minneapolis	—	7.50
3521	Kansas City	—	6.00
3521★	Kansas City	—	7.50
3522	Dallas	—	6.00
3522★	Dallas	—	7.50
3523	San Francisco	—	6.00
3523★	San Francisco	—	7.50

Series 1981-A Ortega-Regan

KL#	Bank	XF	CU
3612	Boston	—	6.00
3612★	Boston	—	7.50
3613	New York	—	6.00
3613★	New York	—	7.50
3614	Philadelphia	—	6.00
3614★	Philadelphia	—	7.50
3615	Cleveland	—	6.00
3615★	Cleveland	—	7.50
3616	Richmond	—	6.00
3616★	Richmond	—	7.50
3617	Atlanta	—	6.00
3617★	Atlanta	—	7.50
3618	Chicago	—	6.00
3618★	Chicago	—	7.50
3619	St. Louis	—	6.00
3619★	St. Louis	—	7.50
3620	Minneapolis	—	6.00
3620★	Minneapolis	—	7.50
3621	Kansas City	—	6.00
3621★	Kansas City	—	7.50
3622	Dallas	—	6.00
3622★	Dallas	—	7.50
3623	San Francisco	—	6.00
3623★	San Francisco	—	7.50

Series 1985 Ortega-Baker

KL#	Bank	XF	CU
3712	Boston	—	(Current)
3712★	Boston	—	—
3713	New York	—	(Current)
3713★	New York	—	—
3714	Philadelphia	—	(Current)
3714★	Philadelphia	—	—
3715	Cleveland	—	(Current)
3715★	Cleveland	—	—
3716	Richmond	—	(Current)
3716★	Richmond	—	—
3717	Atlanta	—	(Current)
3717★	Atlanta	—	—
3718	Chicago	—	(Current)
3718★	Chicago	—	—
3719	St. Louis	—	(Current)
3719★	St. Louis	—	—
3720	Minneapolis	—	(Current)
3720★	Minneapolis	—	—
3721	Kansas City	—	(Current)
3721★	Kansas City	—	—
3722	Dallas	—	(Current)
3722★	Dallas	—	—
3723	San Francisco	—	(Current)
3723★	San Francisco	—	—

Hawaii Emergency Federal Reserve Notes

KL#	Series	Signatures	Fine	VF	CU
1960	1934	Julian-Morgenthau	12.50	30.00	125.
1960☆	1934	Julian-Morgenthau	—	—	500.
1961	1934-A	Julian-Morgenthau	9.50	22.00	100.
1961☆	1934-A	Julian-Morgenthau	—	—	300.

North Africa Emergency Silver Certificates

KL#	Series	Signatures	Fine	VF	CU
1962	1934-A	Julian-Morgenthau	10.00	16.00	100.
1962☆	1934-A	Julian-Morgenthau	—	—	175.

Ten Dollars Gold Certificates

KL#	Series	Signatures	Fine	VF	CU
1963	1928	Woods-Mellon	20.00	35.00	200.
1963☆	1928	Woods-Mellon	—	—	500.

Silver Certificates

KL#	Series	Signatures	Fine	VF	CU
1964	1933	Julian-Woodin	875.	1400.	4500.
1965	1933-A	Julian-Morgenthau	—	—	Unique
1966	1934	Julian-Morgenthau	—	18.00	40.00
1966☆	1934	Julian-Morgenthau	—	—	75.00
1967	1934-A	Julian-Morgenthau	—	18.00	45.00
1967☆	1934-A	Julian-Morgenthau	—	—	90.00
1968	1934-B	Julian-Vinson	25.00	80.00	725.
1968☆	1934-B	Julian-Vinson	—	—	1500.
1969	1934-C	Julian-Snyder	—	14.00	27.50
1969☆	1934-C	Julian-Snyder	—	—	40.00
1970	1934-D	Clark-Snyder	—	14.00	30.00
1970☆	1934-D	Clark-Snyder	—	—	40.00
1971	1953	Priest-Humphrey	12.00	15.00	35.00
1971☆	1953	Priest-Humphrey	—	—	60.00
1972	1953-A	Priest-Anderson	12.00	15.00	100.
1972☆	1953-A	Priest-Anderson	—	—	60.00
1973	1953-B	Smith-Dillon	12.00	17.00	35.00

Federal Reserve Bank Notes

KL#	Series	District	Fine	VF	CU
1974	1929	Boston	11.50	20.00	50.00
1975	1929	New York	11.50	15.00	42.50
1976	1929	Philadelphia	11.00	18.00	55.00
1977	1929	Cleveland	11.00	18.00	45.00
1978	1929	Richmond	11.50	22.00	75.00
1979	1929	Atlanta	11.50	22.00	55.00
1980	1929	Chicago	11.00	18.00	45.00
1981	1929	St. Louis	11.00	18.00	55.00
1982	1929	Minneapolis	11.50	20.00	70.00
1983	1929	Kansas City	11.50	20.00	60.00
1984	1929	Dallas	250.	400.	1500.
1985	1929	San Francisco	11.50	22.00	75.00

Federal Reserve Notes

Series 1928 Tate-Mellon

KL#	Bank	XF	CU
1986	Boston	—	42.50
1987	New York	—	42.50
1988	Philadelphia	—	42.50

KL#	Bank	XF	CU
1989	Cleveland	—	42.50
1990	Richmond	—	42.50
1991	Atlanta	—	42.50
1992	Chicago	—	42.50
1993	St. Louis	—	42.50
1994	Minneapolis	—	42.50
1995	Kansas City	—	42.50
1996	Dallas	—	42.50
1997	San Francisco	—	42.50

Series 1928-A Woods-Mellon

KL#	Bank	XF	CU
1998	Boston	—	35.00
1999	New York	—	35.00
2000	Philadelphia	—	35.00
2001	Cleveland	—	35.00
2002	Richmond	—	35.00
2003	Atlanta	—	35.00
2004	Chicago	—	35.00
2005	St. Louis	—	35.00
2006	Minneapolis	—	35.00
2007	Kansas City	—	35.00
2008	Dallas	—	35.00
2009	San Francisco	—	35.00

Series 1928-B Woods-Mellon

KL#	Bank	XF	CU
2010	Boston	—	22.00
2011	New York	—	22.00
2012	Philadelphia	—	22.00
2013	Cleveland	—	22.00
2014	Richmond	—	22.00
2015	Atlanta	—	22.00
2016	Chicago	—	22.00
2017	St. Louis	—	22.00
2018	Minneapolis	—	22.00
2019	Kansas City	—	22.00
2020	Dallas	—	22.00
2021	San Francisco	—	22.00

Series 1928-C Woods-Mills

KL#	Bank	XF	CU
2022	New York	30.00	90.00
2023	Cleveland	30.00	90.00
2024	Richmond	30.00	90.00
2025	Atlanta	30.00	90.00
2026	Chicago	30.00	90.00

Series 1934 Julian-Morgenthau

KL#	Bank	XF	CU
2027	Boston	—	27.50
2028	New York	—	27.50
2029	Philadelphia	—	27.50
2030	Cleveland	—	27.50
2031	Richmond	—	27.50
2032	Atlanta	—	27.50
2033	Chicago	—	27.50
2034	St. Louis	—	27.50
2035	Minneapolis	—	27.50
2036	Kansas City	—	27.50
2037	Dallas	—	27.50
2038	San Francisco	—	27.50

Series 1934-A Julian-Morgenthau

KL#	Bank	XF	CU
2039	Boston	—	23.50
2040	New York	—	23.50
2041	Philadelphia	—	23.50
2042	Cleveland	—	23.50
2043	Richmond	—	23.50
2044	Atlanta	—	23.50
2045	Chicago	—	23.50
2046	St. Louis	—	23.50
2047	Minneapolis	—	23.50
2048	Kansas City	—	23.50
2049	Dallas	—	23.50
2050	San Francisco	—	23.50

Series 1934-B Julian-Vinson

KL#	Bank	XF	CU
2051	Boston	—	25.00
2052	New York	—	25.00
2053	Philadelphia	—	25.00
2054	Cleveland	—	25.00
2055	Richmond	—	25.00
2056	Atlanta	—	25.00
2057	Chicago	—	25.00
2058	St. Louis	—	25.00
2059	Minneapolis	—	25.00
2060	Kansas City	—	25.00
2061	Dallas	—	25.00
2062	San Francisco	—	25.00

Series 1934-C Julian-Snyder

KL#	Bank	XF	CU
2063	Boston	—	20.00
2064	New York	—	20.00
2065	Philadelphia	—	20.00
2066	Cleveland	—	20.00
2067	Richmond	—	20.00
2068	Atlanta	—	20.00
2069	Chicago	—	20.00
2070	St. Louis	—	20.00
2071	Minneapolis	—	20.00
2072	Kansas City	—	20.00
2073	Dallas	—	20.00
2074	San Francisco	—	20.00

Series 1934-D Clark-Snyder

KL#	Bank	XF	CU
2075	Boston	—	20.00
2076	New York	—	20.00
2077	Philadelphia	—	20.00
2078	Cleveland	—	20.00
2079	Richmond	—	20.00
2080	Atlanta	—	20.00
2081	Chicago	—	20.00
2082	St. Louis	—	20.00
2083	Minneapolis	—	20.00
2084	Kansas City	—	20.00
2085	Dallas	—	20.00
2086	San Francisco	—	20.00

Series 1950 Clark-Snyder

KL#	Bank	XF	CU
2087	Boston	—	25.00
2087☆	Boston	—	30.00
2088	New York	—	25.00
2088☆	New York	—	30.00
2089	Philadelphia	—	25.00
2089☆	Philadelphia	—	30.00
2090	Cleveland	—	25.00
2090☆	Cleveland	—	30.00
2091	Richmond	—	25.00
2091☆	Richmond	—	30.00
2092	Atlanta	—	25.00
2092☆	Atlanta	—	30.00
2093	Chicago	—	25.00
2093☆	Chicago	—	30.00
2094	St. Louis	—	25.00
2094☆	St. Louis	—	30.00
2095	Minneapolis	—	25.00
2095☆	Minneapolis	—	35.00
2096	Kansas City	—	25.00
2096☆	Kansas City	—	27.50
2097	Dallas	—	25.00
2097☆	Dallas	—	35.00
2098	San Francisco	—	25.00
2098☆	San Francisco	—	27.50

Series 1950-A Priest-Humphrey

KL#	Bank	XF	CU
2099	Boston	—	20.00
2099☆	Boston	—	25.00
2100	New York	—	20.00
2100☆	New York	—	25.00
2101	Philadelphia	—	20.00
2101☆	Philadelphia	—	25.00
2102	Cleveland	—	20.00
2102☆	Cleveland	—	25.00
2103	Richmond	—	20.00
2103☆	Richmond	—	25.00
2104	Atlanta	—	20.00
2104☆	Atlanta	—	25.00
2105	Chicago	—	20.00
2105☆	Chicago	—	25.00
2106	St. Louis	—	20.00
2106☆	St. Louis	—	25.00
2107	Minneapolis	—	20.00
2107☆	Minneapolis	—	35.00
2108	Kansas City	—	20.00
2108☆	Kansas City	—	25.00
2109	Dallas	—	20.00
2109☆	Dallas	—	25.00
2110	San Francisco	—	20.00
2110☆	San Francisco	—	25.00

Series 1950-B Priest-Anderson

KL#	Bank	XF	CU
2111	Boston	—	20.00
2111☆	Boston	—	22.50
2112	New York	—	20.00
2112☆	New York	—	22.50
2113	Philadelphia	—	20.00
2113☆	Philadelphia	—	22.50
2114	Cleveland	—	20.00
2114☆	Cleveland	—	22.50
2115	Richmond	—	20.00
2115☆	Richmond	—	22.50
2116	Atlanta	—	20.00
2116☆	Atlanta	—	22.50
2117	Chicago	—	20.00
2117☆	Chicago	—	22.50
2118	St. Louis	—	20.00
2118☆	St. Louis	—	22.50
2119	Minneapolis	—	20.00
2119☆	Minneapolis	—	22.50
2120	Kansas City	—	20.00
2120☆	Kansas City	—	22.50
2121	Dallas	—	20.00
2121☆	Dallas	—	22.50
2122	San Francisco	—	20.00
2122☆	San Francisco	—	22.50

Series 1950-C Smith-Dillon

KL#	Bank	XF	CU
2123	Boston	—	18.00
2123★	Boston	—	20.00
2124	New York	—	18.00
2124★	New York	—	20.00
2125	Philadelphia	—	18.00
2125★	Philadelphia	—	20.00
2126	Cleveland	—	18.00
2126★	Cleveland	—	20.00
2127	Richmond	—	18.00
2127★	Richmond	—	20.00
2128	Atlanta	—	18.00
2128★	Atlanta	—	20.00
2129	Chicago	—	18.00
2129★	Chicago	—	20.00
2130	St. Louis	—	18.00
2130★	St. Louis	—	20.00
2131	Minneapolis	—	18.00
2131★	Minneapolis	—	20.00
2132	Kansas City	—	18.00
2132★	Kansas City	—	20.00
2133	Dallas	—	18.00
2133★	Dallas	—	20.00
2134	San Francisco	—	18.00
2134★	San Francisco	—	20.00

Series 1950-D Granahan-Dillon

KL#	Bank	XF	CU
2135	Boston	—	18.00
2135★	Boston	—	20.00
2136	New York	—	18.00
2136★	New York	—	20.00
2137	Philadelphia	—	18.00
2137★	Philadelphia	—	20.00
2138	Cleveland	—	18.00
2138★	Cleveland	—	25.00
2139	Richmond	—	18.00
2139★	Richmond	—	20.00
2140	Atlanta	—	18.00
2140★	Atlanta	—	20.00
2141	Chicago	—	18.00
2141★	Chicago	—	20.00
2142	St. Louis	—	18.00
2142★	St. Louis	—	20.00
2144	Kansas City	—	18.00
2144★	Kansas City	—	20.00
2145	Dallas	—	18.00
2145★	Dallas	—	20.00
2146	San Francisco	—	18.00
2146★	San Francisco	—	20.00

Series 1950-E Granahan-Fowler

KL#	Bank	XF	CU
2147	New York	—	20.00
2147★	New York	—	25.00
2148	Chicago	—	20.00
2148★	Chicago	—	25.00
2149	San Francisco	—	20.00
2149★	San Francisco	—	35.00

Series 1963 Granahan-Dillon

KL#	Bank	XF	CU
2150	Boston	—	18.00
2151	New York	—	18.00
2152	Philadelphia	—	18.00
2153	Cleveland	—	18.00
2154	Richmond	—	18.00
2155	Atlanta	—	18.00
2156	Chicago	—	18.00
2157	St. Louis	—	18.00
2159	Kansas City	—	18.00
2160	Dallas	—	18.00
2161	San Francisco	—	18.00

Series 1963-A Granahan-Fowler

KL#	Bank	XF	CU
2162	Boston	—	18.00
2162★	Boston	—	20.00
2163	New York	—	18.00
2163★	New York	—	20.00
2164	Philadelphia	—	18.00
2164★	Philadelphia	—	20.00
2165	Cleveland	—	18.00
2165★	Cleveland	—	20.00
2166	Richmond	—	18.00
2166★	Richmond	—	20.00
2167	Atlanta	—	18.00
2167★	Atlanta	—	20.00
2168	Chicago	—	18.00
2168★	Chicago	—	20.00
2169	St. Louis	—	18.00
2169★	St. Louis	—	20.00
2170	Minneapolis	—	18.00
2170★	Minneapolis	—	20.00
2171	Kansas City	—	18.00
2171★	Kansas City	—	20.00
2172	Dallas	—	18.00
2172★	Dallas	—	20.00
2173	San Francisco	—	18.00
2173★	San Francisco	—	20.00

Series 1969 Elston-Kennedy

KL#	Bank	XF	CU
2174	Boston	—	18.00
2174★	Boston	—	20.00
2175	New York	—	18.00
2175★	New York	—	20.00
2176	Philadelphia	—	18.00
2176★	Philadelphia	—	20.00
2177	Cleveland	—	18.00
2177★	Cleveland	—	20.00
2178	Richmond	—	18.00
2178★	Richmond	—	20.00
2179	Atlanta	—	18.00
2179★	Atlanta	—	20.00
2180	Chicago	—	18.00
2180★	Chicago	—	20.00
2181	St. Louis	—	18.00
2181★	St. Louis	—	20.00
2182	Minneapolis	—	18.00
2182★	Minneapolis	—	22.00
2183	Kansas City	—	18.00
2183★	Kansas City	—	20.00
2184	Dallas	—	18.00
2184★	Dallas	—	20.00
2185	San Francisco	—	18.00
2185★	San Francisco	—	20.00

Series 1969-A Kabis-Connally

KL#	Bank	XF	CU
2186	Boston	—	16.00
2186★	Boston	—	17.50
2187	New York	—	16.00
2187★	New York	—	17.50
2188	Philadelphia	—	16.00
2188★	Philadelphia	—	17.50
2189	Cleveland	—	16.00
2189★	Cleveland	—	17.50
2190	Richmond	—	16.00
2190★	Richmond	—	20.00
2191	Atlanta	—	16.00
2191★	Atlanta	—	20.00
2192	Chicago	—	16.00
2192★	Chicago	—	17.50
2193	St. Louis	—	16.00
2193★	St. Louis	—	20.00
2194	Minneapolis	—	16.00
2194★	Minneapolis		None Printed
2195	Kansas City	—	16.00
2195★	Kansas City		None Printed
2196	Dallas	—	16.00
2196★	Dallas	—	20.00
2197	San Francisco	—	16.00
2197★	San Francisco	—	17.50

Series 1969-B Banuelos-Connally

KL#	Bank	XF	CU
2198	Boston	—	16.00
2198★	Boston		None Printed
2199	New York	—	16.00
2199★	New York	—	17.00
2200	Philadelphia	—	16.00
2200★	Philadelphia		None Printed
2201	Cleveland	—	16.00
2201★	Cleveland		None Printed
2202	Richmond	—	16.00
2202★	Richmond	—	20.00
2203	Atlanta	—	16.00
2203★	Atlanta	—	20.00
2204	Chicago	—	16.00
2204★	Chicago	—	17.00
2205	St. Louis	—	16.00
2205★	St. Louis	—	17.00
2206	Minneapolis	—	16.00
2206★	Minneapolis		None Printed
2207	Kansas City	—	16.00
2207★	Kansas City	—	20.00
2208	Dallas	—	16.00
2208★	Dallas		None Printed
2209	San Francisco	—	16.00
2209★	San Francisco	—	20.00

Series 1969-C Banuelos-Shultz

KL#	Bank	XF	CU
2210	Boston	—	16.00
2210★	Boston	—	17.00
2211	New York	—	16.00
2211★	New York	—	17.00
2212	Philadelphia	—	16.00
2212★	Philadelphia	—	17.00
2213	Cleveland	—	16.00
2213★	Cleveland	—	17.00
2214	Richmond	—	16.00
2214★	Richmond	—	17.00
2215	Atlanta	—	16.00
2215★	Atlanta	—	17.00
2216	Chicago	—	16.00
2216★	Chicago	—	17.00
2217	St. Louis	—	16.00
2217★	St. Louis	—	17.00
2218	Minneapolis	—	16.00
2218★	Minneapolis	—	17.00
2219	Kansas City	—	16.00
2219★	Kansas City	—	17.00

KL#	Bank	XF	CU
2220	Dallas	—	16.00
2220☆	Dallas	—	17.00
2221	San Francisco	—	16.00
2221☆	San Francisco	—	17.00

Series 1974 Neff-Simon

KL#	Bank	XF	CU
2222	Boston	—	14.00
2222☆	Boston	—	25.00
2223	New York	—	14.00
2223☆	New York	—	25.00
2224	Philadelphia	—	14.00
2224☆	Philadelphia	—	15.00
2225	Cleveland	—	14.00
2225☆	Cleveland	—	15.00
2226	Richmond	—	14.00
2226☆	Richmond	—	15.00
2227	Atlanta	—	14.00
2227☆	Atlanta	—	15.00
2228	Chicago	—	14.00
2228☆	Chicago	—	25.00
2229	St. Louis	—	14.00
2229☆	St. Louis	—	15.00
2230	Minneapolis	—	14.00
2230☆	Minneapolis	—	25.00
2231	Kansas City	—	14.00
2231☆	Kansas City	—	15.00
2232	Dallas	—	14.00
2232☆	Dallas	—	15.00
2233	San Francisco	—	14.00
2233☆	San Francisco	—	15.00

Series 1977 Morton-Blumenthal

KL#	Bank	XF	CU
2234	Boston	—	14.00
2234☆	Boston	—	25.00
2235	New York	—	14.00
2235☆	New York	—	25.00
2236	Philadelphia	—	14.00
2236☆	Philadelphia	—	25.00
2237	Cleveland	—	14.00
2237☆	Cleveland	—	25.00
2238	Richmond	—	14.00
2238☆	Richmond	—	25.00
2239	Atlanta	—	14.00
2239☆	Atlanta	—	25.00
2240	Chicago	—	14.00
2240☆	Chicago	—	25.00
2241	St. Louis	—	14.00
2241☆	St. Louis	—	26.00
2242	Minneapolis	—	14.00
2242☆	Minneapolis	—	25.00
2243	Kansas City	—	14.00
2243☆	Kansas City	—	25.00
2244	Dallas	—	14.00
2244☆	Dallas	—	15.00
2245	San Francisco	—	14.00
2245☆	San Francisco	—	25.00

Series 1977-A Morton-Miller

KL#	Bank	XF	CU
2246	Boston	—	14.00
2246☆	Boston	—	25.00
2247	New York	—	14.00
2247☆	New York	—	25.00
2248	Philadelphia	—	14.00
2248☆	Philadelphia	—	25.00
2249	Cleveland	—	14.00
2249☆	Cleveland	—	25.00
2250	Richmond	—	14.00
2250☆	Richmond	—	25.00
2251	Atlanta	—	14.00
2251☆	Atlanta	—	15.00
2252	Chicago	—	14.00
2252☆	Chicago	—	25.00
2253	St. Louis	—	14.00
2253☆	St. Louis	—	25.00
2254	Minneapolis	—	14.00
2254☆	Minneapolis	—	25.00
2255	Kansas City	—	14.00
2255☆	Kansas City	—	25.00
2256	Dallas	—	14.00
2256☆	Dallas	—	25.00
2257	San Francisco	—	14.00
2257☆	San Francisco	—	25.00

Series 1981 Buchanan-Regan

KL#	Bank	XF	CU
3524	Boston	—	12.50
3524☆	Boston	—	20.00
3525	New York	—	12.50
3525☆	New York	—	20.00
3526	Philadelphia	—	12.50
3526☆	Philadelphia	—	20.00
3527	Cleveland	—	12.50
3527☆	Cleveland	—	20.00
3528	Richmond	—	12.50
3528☆	Richmond	—	20.00
3529	Atlanta	—	12.50
3529☆	Atlanta	—	20.00
3530	Chicago	—	12.50

KL#	Bank	XF	CU
3530☆	Chicago	—	20.00
3531	St. Louis	—	12.50
3531☆	St. Louis	—	20.00
3532	Minneapolis	—	12.50
3532☆	Minneapolis	—	20.00
3533	Kansas City	—	12.50
3533☆	Kansas City	—	20.00
3534	Dallas	—	12.50
3534☆	Dallas	—	20.00
3535	San Francisco	—	12.50
3535☆	San Francisco	—	20.00

Series 1981-A Ortega-Regan

KL#	Bank	XF	CU
3624	Boston	—	12.50
3624☆	Boston	—	20.00
3625	New York	—	12.50
3625☆	New York	—	20.00
3626	Philadelphia	—	12.50
3626☆	Philadelphia	—	20.00
3627	Cleveland	—	12.50
3627☆	Cleveland	—	20.00
3628	Richmond	—	12.50
3628☆	Richmond	—	20.00
3629	Atlanta	—	12.50
3629☆	Atlanta	—	20.00
3630	Chicago	—	12.50
3630☆	Chicago	—	20.00
3631	St. Louis	—	12.50
3631☆	St. Louis	—	20.00
3632	Minneapolis	—	12.50
3632☆	Minneapolis	—	20.00
3633	Kansas City	—	12.50
3633☆	Kansas City	—	20.00
3634	Dallas	—	12.50
3634☆	Dallas	—	20.00
3635	San Francisco	—	12.50
3635☆	San Francisco	—	20.00

Series 1985 Ortega-Baker

3724	Boston	—	(Current)
3724☆	Boston	—	—
3725	New York	—	(Current)
3725☆	New York	—	—
3726	Philadelphia	—	(Current)
3726☆	Philadelphia	—	—
3727	Cleveland	—	(Current)
3727☆	Cleveland	—	—
3728	Richmond	—	(Current)
3728☆	Richmond	—	—
3729	Atlanta	—	(Current)
3729☆	Atlanta	—	—
3730	Chicago	—	(Current)
3730☆	Chicago	—	—
3731	St. Louis	—	(Current)
3731☆	St. Louis	—	—
3732	Minneapolis	—	(Current)
3732☆	Minneapolis	—	—
3733	Kansas City	—	(Current)
3733☆	Kansas City	—	—
3734	Dallas	—	(Current)
3734☆	Dallas	—	—
3735	San Francisco	—	(Current)
3735☆	San Francisco	—	—

Hawaii Emergency Federal Reserve Notes

KL#	Series	Signatures	Fine	VF	CU
2258	1934-A	Julian-Morgenthau	18.00	25.00	235.
2258☆	1934-A	Julian-Morgenthau	—	—	400.

North Africa
Silver Certificates

KL#	Series	Signatures	Fine	VF	CU
2259	1934	Julian-Morgenthau	450.	1000.	6500.
2259☆	1934	Julian-Morgenthau	—	—	Unique
2260	1934-A	Julian-Morgenthau	15.00	19.50	125.
2260☆	1934-A	Julian-Morgenthau	—	—	200.

Twenty Dollars
Gold Certificates

KL#	Series	Signatures	Fine	VF	CU
2261	1928	Woods-Mellon	25.00	35.00	125.
2261☆	1928	Woods-Mellon	—	—	350.

Federal Reserve Bank Notes

KL#	Series	District	Fine	VF	CU
2262	1929	Boston	—	—	70.00
2263	1929	New York	—	—	60.00
2264	1929	Philadelphia	—	—	60.00
2265	1929	Cleveland	—	—	60.00
2266	1929	Richmond	—	—	60.00
2267	1929	Atlanta	—	—	60.00
2268	1929	Chicago	—	—	60.00
2269	1929	St. Louis	—	—	60.00
2270	1929	Minneapolis	—	—	60.00
2271	1929	Kansas City	—	—	80.00
2272	1929	Dallas	—	25.00	450.
2273	1929	San Francisco	—	25.00	125.

Federal Reserve Notes

Series 1928 Tate-Mellon

KL#	Bank	XF	CU
2274	Boston	—	50.00
2275	New York	—	50.00
2276	Philadelphia	—	50.00
2277	Cleveland	—	50.00
2278	Richmond	—	50.00
2279	Atlanta	—	50.00
2280	Chicago	—	50.00
2281	St. Louis	—	50.00
2282	Minneapolis	—	50.00
2283	Kansas City	—	50.00
2284	Dallas	—	50.00
2285	San Francisco	—	50.00

Series 1928-A Woods-Mellon

KL#	Bank	XF	CU
2286	Boston	—	50.00
2287	New York	—	50.00
2288	Philadelphia	—	50.00
2289	Cleveland	—	50.00
2290	Richmond	—	50.00
2291	Atlanta	—	50.00
2292	Chicago	—	50.00
2293	St. Louis	—	50.00
2294	Kansas City	—	50.00
2295	Dallas	—	50.00

Series 1928-B Woods-Mellon

KL#	Bank	XF	CU
2296	Boston	—	35.00
2297	New York	—	35.00
2298	Philadelphia	—	35.00
2299	Cleveland	—	35.00
2300	Richmond	—	35.00
2301	Atlanta	—	35.00
2302	Chicago	—	35.00
2303	St. Louis	—	35.00
2304	Minneapolis	—	35.00
2305	Kansas City	—	35.00
2306	Dallas	—	35.00
2307	San Francisco	—	35.00

Series 1928-C Woods-Mills

KL#	Bank	XF	CU
2308	Chicago	75.00	300.
2309	San Francisco	75.00	300.

Series 1934 Julian-Morgenthau

KL#	Bank	XF	CU
2310	Boston	—	40.00
2311	New York	—	40.00
2312	Philadelphia	—	40.00
2313	Cleveland	—	40.00
2314	Richmond	—	40.00
2315	Atlanta	—	40.00
2316	Chicago	—	40.00
2317	St. Louis	—	40.00
2318	Minneapolis	—	40.00
2319	Kansas City	—	40.00
2320	Dallas	—	40.00
2321	San Francisco	—	40.00

Series 1934-A Julian-Morgenthau

KL#	Bank	XF	CU
2322	Boston	—	40.00
2323	New York	—	40.00
2324	Philadelphia	—	40.00
2325	Cleveland	—	40.00
2326	Richmond	—	40.00
2327	Atlanta	—	40.00
2328	Chicago	—	40.00
2329	St. Louis	—	40.00
2330	Minneapolis	—	40.00
2331	Kansas City	—	40.00
2332	Dallas	—	40.00
2333	San Francisco	—	40.00

Series 1934-B Julian-Vinson

KL#	Bank	XF	CU
2334	Boston	—	40.00
2335	New York	—	40.00
2336	Philadelphia	—	40.00
2337	Cleveland	—	40.00
2338	Richmond	—	40.00
2339	Atlanta	—	40.00
2340	Chicago	—	40.00
2341	St. Louis	—	40.00
2342	Minneapolis	—	40.00
2343	Kansas City	—	40.00
2344	Dallas	—	40.00
2345	San Francisco	—	40.00

Series 1934-C Julian-Snyder

KL#	Bank	XF	CU
2346	Boston	—	40.00
2347	New York	—	40.00
2348	Philadelphia	—	40.00
2349	Cleveland	—	40.00
2350	Richmond	—	40.00
2351	Atlanta	—	40.00
2352	Chicago	—	40.00

KL#	Bank	XF	CU
2353	St. Louis	—	40.00
2354	Minneapolis	—	40.00
2355	Kansas City	—	40.00
2356	Dallas	—	40.00
2357	San Francisco	—	40.00

Series 1934-D Clark-Snyder

KL#	Bank	XF	CU
2358	Boston	—	37.50
2359	New York	—	37.50
2360	Philadelphia	—	37.50
2361	Cleveland	—	37.50
2362	Richmond	—	37.50
2363	Atlanta	—	37.50
2364	Chicago	—	37.50
2365	St. Louis	—	37.50
2366	Minneapolis	—	37.50
2367	Kansas City	—	37.50
2368	Dallas	—	37.50
2369	San Francisco	—	37.50

Series 1950 Clark-Snyder

KL#	Bank	XF	CU
2370	Boston	—	35.00
2371	New York	—	35.00
2372	Philadelphia	—	35.00
2373	Cleveland	—	35.00
2374	Richmond	—	35.00
2375	Atlanta	—	35.00
2376	Chicago	—	35.00
2377	St. Louis	—	35.00
2378	Minneapolis	—	35.00
2379	Kansas City	—	35.00
2380	Dallas	—	35.00
2381	San Francisco	—	35.00

Series 1950-A Priest-Humphrey

KL#	Bank	XF	CU
2382	Boston	—	30.00
2383	New York	—	30.00
2384	Philadelphia	—	30.00
2385	Cleveland	—	30.00
2386	Richmond	—	30.00
2387	Atlanta	—	30.00
2388	Chicago	—	30.00
2389	St. Louis	—	30.00
2390	Minneapolis	—	30.00
2391	Kansas City	—	30.00
2392	Dallas	—	30.00
2393	San Francisco	—	30.00

Series 1950-B Priest-Anderson

KL#	Bank	XF	CU
2394	Boston	—	30.00
2395	New York	—	30.00
2396	Philadelphia	—	30.00
2397	Cleveland	—	30.00
2398	Richmond	—	30.00
2399	Atlanta	—	30.00
2400	Chicago	—	30.00
2401	St. Louis	—	30.00
2402	Minneapolis	—	30.00
2403	Kansas City	—	30.00
2404	Dallas	—	30.00
2405	San Francisco	—	30.00

Series 1950-C Smith-Dillon

KL#	Bank	XF	CU
2406	Boston	—	30.00
2407	New York	—	30.00
2408	Philadelphia	—	30.00
2409	Cleveland	—	30.00
2410	Richmond	—	30.00
2411	Atlanta	—	30.00
2412	Chicago	—	30.00
2413	St. Louis	—	30.00
2414	Minneapolis	—	30.00
2415	Kansas City	—	30.00
2416	Dallas	—	30.00
2417	San Francisco	—	30.00

Series 1950-D Granahan-Dillon

KL#	Bank	XF	CU
2418	Boston	—	32.00
2419	New York	—	32.00
2419A	Philadelphia	—	32.00
2420	Cleveland	—	32.00
2421	Richmond	—	32.00
2422	Atlanta	—	32.00
2423	Chicago	—	32.00
2424	St. Louis	—	32.00
2424A	Minneapolis	—	32.00
2425	Kansas City	—	32.00
2426	Dallas	—	32.00
2427	San Francisco	—	32.00

Series 1950-E Granahan-Fowler

KL#	Bank	XF	CU
2428	New York	—	32.00
2429	Chicago	—	32.00
2430	San Francisco	—	32.00

Series 1963 Granahan-Dillon

KL#	Bank	XF	CU
2431	Boston	—	30.00
2432	New York	—	30.00
2433	Cleveland	—	30.00
2434	Richmond	—	30.00
2435	Atlanta	—	30.00
2436	Chicago	—	30.00
2437	St. Louis	—	30.00
2438	Kansas City	—	30.00
2439	Dallas	—	30.00
2440	San Francisco	—	30.00

Series 1963-A Granahan-Fowler

KL#	Bank	XF	CU
2441	Boston	—	30.00
2441★	Boston	—	34.00
2442	New York	—	30.00
2442★	New York	—	34.00
2443	Philadelphia	—	30.00
2443★	Philadelphia	—	34.00
2444	Cleveland	—	30.00
2444★	Cleveland	—	34.00
2445	Richmond	—	30.00
2445★	Richmond	—	34.00
2446	Atlanta	—	30.00
2446★	Atlanta	—	34.00
2447	Chicago	—	30.00
2447★	Chicago	—	34.00
2448	St. Louis	—	30.00
2448★	St. Louis	—	34.00
2449	Minneapolis	—	30.00
2449★	Minneapolis	—	34.00
2450	Kansas City	—	30.00
2450★	Kansas City	—	34.00
2451	Dallas	—	30.00
2451★	Dallas	—	34.00
2452	San Francisco	—	30.00
2452★	San Francisco	—	34.00

Series 1969 Elston-Kennedy

KL#	Bank	XF	CU
2453	Boston	—	30.00
2453★	Boston	—	34.00
2454	New York	—	30.00
2454★	New York	—	34.00
2455	Philadelphia	—	30.00
2455★	Philadelphia	—	34.00
2456	Cleveland	—	30.00
2456★	Cleveland	—	34.00
2457	Richmond	—	30.00
2457★	Richmond	—	34.00
2458	Atlanta	—	30.00
2458★	Atlanta	—	34.00
2459	Chicago	—	30.00
2459★	Chicago	—	34.00
2460	St. Louis	—	30.00
2460★	St. Louis	—	36.00
2461	Minneapolis	—	30.00
2461★	Minneapolis	—	36.00
2462	Kansas City	—	30.00
2462★	Kansas City	—	34.00
2463	Dallas	—	30.00
2463★	Dallas	—	36.00
2464	San Francisco	—	30.00
2464★	San Francisco	—	34.00

Series 1969-A Kabis-Connally

KL#	Bank	XF	CU
2465	Boston	—	30.00
2465★	Boston		None Printed
2466	New York	—	30.00
2466★	New York	—	34.00
2467	Philadelphia	—	30.00
2467★	Philadelphia		None Printed
2468	Cleveland	—	30.00
2468★	Cleveland	—	36.00
2469	Richmond	—	30.00
2469★	Richmond	—	34.00
2470	Atlanta	—	30.00
2470★	Atlanta		None Printed
2471	Chicago	—	30.00
2471★	Chicago	—	34.00
2472	St. Louis	—	30.00
2472★	St. Louis	—	36.00
2473	Minneapolis	—	30.00
2473★	Minneapolis		None Printed
2474	Kansas City	—	30.00
2474★	Kansas City		None Printed
2475	Dallas	—	30.00
2475★	Dallas	—	36.00
2476	San Francisco	—	30.00
2476★	San Francisco	—	34.00

Series 1969-B Banuelos-Connally

KL#	Bank	XF	CU
2477	New York	—	30.00
2477☆	New York	—	35.00
2478	Cleveland	—	30.00
2478☆	Cleveland		None Printed
2479	Richmond	—	30.00
2479☆	Richmond		None Printed
2480	Atlanta	—	30.00
2480☆	Atlanta	—	35.00
2481	Chicago	—	30.00
2481☆	Chicago	—	34.00
2482	St. Louis	—	30.00
2482☆	St. Louis		None Printed
2483	Minneapolis	—	30.00
2483☆	Minneapolis		None Printed
2484	Kansas City	—	30.00
2484☆	Kansas City	—	35.00
2485	Dallas	—	30.00
2485☆	Dallas		None Printed
2486	San Francisco	—	30.00
2486☆	San Francisco	—	35.00

Series 1969-C Banuelos-Shultz

KL#	Bank	XF	CU
2487	Boston	—	30.00
2487☆	Boston	—	32.00
2488	New York	—	30.00
2488☆	New York	—	32.00
2489	Philadelphia	—	30.00
2489☆	Philadelphia	—	32.00
2490	Cleveland	—	30.00
2490☆	Cleveland	—	32.00
2491	Richmond	—	30.00
2491☆	Richmond	—	32.00
2492	Atlanta	—	30.00
2492☆	Atlanta	—	32.00
2493	Chicago	—	30.00
2493☆	Chicago	—	32.00
2494	St. Louis	—	30.00
2494☆	St. Louis	—	32.00
2495	Minneapolis	—	30.00
2495☆	Minneapolis	—	32.00
2496	Kansas City	—	30.00
2496☆	Kansas City	—	32.00
2497	Dallas	—	30.00
2497☆	Dallas	—	32.00
2498	San Francisco	—	30.00
2498☆	San Francisco	—	32.00

Series 1974 Neff-Simon

KL#	Bank	XF	CU
2499	Boston	—	30.00
2499☆	Boston	—	35.00
2500	New York	—	30.00
2500☆	New York	—	50.00
2501	Philadelphia	—	30.00
2501☆	Philadelphia	—	32.00
2502	Cleveland	—	30.00
2502☆	Cleveland	—	50.00
2503	Richmond	—	30.00
2503☆	Richmond	—	50.00
2504	Atlanta	—	30.00
2504☆	Atlanta	—	32.00
2505	Chicago	—	30.00
2505☆	Chicago	—	50.00
2506	St. Louis	—	30.00
2506☆	St. Louis	—	32.00
2507	Minneapolis	—	30.00
2507☆	Minneapolis	—	32.00
2508	Kansas City	—	30.00
2508☆	Kansas City	—	50.00
2509	Dallas	—	30.00
2509☆	Dallas	—	50.00
2510	San Francisco	—	30.00
2510☆	San Francisco	—	50.00

Series 1977 Morton-Blumenthal

KL#	Bank	XF	CU
2511	Boston	—	24.00
2511☆	Boston	—	50.00
2512	New York	—	24.00
2512☆	New York	—	50.00
2513	Philadelphia	—	24.00
2513☆	Philadelphia	—	50.00
2514	Cleveland	—	24.00
2514☆	Cleveland	—	50.00
2515	Richmond	—	24.00
2515☆	Richmond	—	50.00
2516	Atlanta	—	24.00
2516☆	Atlanta	—	50.00
2517	Chicago	—	24.00
2517☆	Chicago	—	50.00
2518	St. Louis	—	24.00
2518☆	St. Louis	—	50.00
2519	Minneapolis	—	24.00
2519☆	Minneapolis	—	50.00
2520	Kansas City	—	24.00
2520☆	Kansas City	—	50.00
2521	Dallas	—	24.00
2521☆	Dallas	—	50.00
2522	San Francisco	—	24.00
2522☆	San Francisco	—	50.00

Series 1981 Buchanan-Regan

KL#	Bank	XF	CU
3536	Boston	—	22.50
3536☆	Boston	—	40.00
3537	New York	—	22.50
3537☆	New York	—	40.00
3538	Philadelphia	—	22.50
3538☆	Philadelphia	—	40.00
3539	Cleveland	—	22.50
3539☆	Cleveland	—	40.00
3540	Richmond	—	22.50
3540☆	Richmond	—	40.00
3541	Atlanta	—	22.50
3541☆	Atlanta	—	40.00
3542	Chicago	—	22.50
3542☆	Chicago	—	40.00
3543	St. Louis	—	22.50
3543☆	St. Louis	—	40.00
3544	Minneapolis	—	22.50
3544☆	Minneapolis	—	40.00
3545	Kansas City	—	22.50
3545☆	Kansas City	—	40.00
3546	Dallas	—	22.50
3546☆	Dallas	—	40.00
3547	San Francisco	—	22.50
3547☆	San Francisco	—	40.00

Series 1981-A Ortega-Regan

KL#	Bank	XF	CU
3636	Boston	—	22.50
3636☆	Boston	—	40.00
3637	New York	—	22.50
3637☆	New York	—	40.00
3638	Philadelphia	—	22.50
3638☆	Philadelphia	—	40.00
3639	Cleveland	—	22.50
3639☆	Cleveland	—	40.00
3640	Richmond	—	22.50
3640☆	Richmond	—	40.00
3641	Atlanta	—	22.50
3641☆	Atlanta	—	40.00
3642	Chicago	—	22.50
3642☆	Chicago	—	40.00
3643	St. Louis	—	22.50
3643☆	St. Louis	—	40.00
3644	Minneapolis	—	22.50
3644☆	Minneapolis	—	40.00
3645	Kansas City	—	22.50
3645☆	Kansas City	—	40.00
3646	Dallas	—	22.50
3646☆	Dallas	—	40.00
3647	San Francisco	—	22.50
3647☆	San Francisco	—	40.00

Series 1985 Ortega-Baker

3736	Boston	—	(Current)
3736☆	Boston	—	—
3737	New York	—	(Current)
3737☆	New York	—	—
3738	Philadelphia	—	(Current)
3738☆	Philadelphia	—	—
3739	Cleveland	—	(Current)
3739☆	Cleveland	—	—
3740	Richmond	—	(Current)
3740☆	Richmond	—	—
3741	Atlanta	—	(Current)
3741☆	Atlanta	—	—
3742	Chicago	—	(Current)
3742☆	Chicago	—	—
3743	St. Louis	—	(Current)
3743☆	St. Louis	—	—
3744	Minneapolis	—	(Current)
3744☆	Minneapolis	—	—
3745	Kansas City	—	(Current)
3745☆	Kansas City	—	—
3746	Dallas	—	(Current)
3746☆	Dallas	—	—
3747	San Francisco	—	(Current)
3747☆	San Francisco	—	—

Hawaii Emergency Federal Reserve Notes

KL#	Series	Signatures	Fine	VF	CU
2523	1934	Julian-Morgenthau	50.00	95.00	750.
2523☆	1934	Julian-Morgenthau	—	—	1500.
2524	1934-A	Julian-Morgenthau	22.50	32.50	350.
2524☆	1934-A	Julian-Morgenthau	—	—	2000.

Fifty Dollars Gold Certificates

KL#	Series	Signatures	Fine	VF	CU
2525	1928	Woods-Mellon	55.00	90.00	550.
2525☆	1928	Woods-Mellon	—	—	—

Federal Reserve Bank Notes

KL#	Series	District	Fine	VF	CU
2526	1929	New York	—	—	125.
2527	1929	Cleveland	—	—	125.
2528	1929	Chicago	—	—	125.
2529	1929	Minneapolis	—	—	175.
2530	1929	Kansas City	—	—	135.
2531	1929	Dallas	—	—	325.
2532	1929	San Francisco	—	—	200.

Federal Reserve Notes

Series 1928 Woods-Mellon

KL#	Bank	XF	CU
2533	Boston	—	120.
2534	New York	—	120.
2535	Philadelphia	—	120.
2536	Cleveland	—	120.
2537	Richmond	—	120.
2538	Atlanta	—	120.
2539	Chicago	—	120.
2540	St. Louis	—	120.
2541	Minneapolis	—	120.
2542	Kansas City	—	120.
2543	Dallas	—	120.
2544	San Francisco	—	120.

Series 1928-A Woods-Mellon

KL#	Bank	XF	CU
2545	Boston	—	100.
2546	New York	—	100.
2547	Philadelphia	—	100.
2548	Cleveland	—	100.
2549	Richmond	—	100.
2550	Atlanta	—	100.
2551	Chicago	—	100.
2552	St. Louis	—	100.
2553	Minneapolis	—	100.
2554	Kansas City	—	100.
2555	Dallas	—	100.
2556	San Francisco	—	100.

Series 1934 Julian-Morgenthau

KL#	Bank	XF	CU
2557	Boston	—	85.00
2558	New York	—	85.00
2559	Philadelphia	—	85.00
2560	Cleveland	—	85.00
2561	Richmond	—	85.00
2562	Atlanta	—	85.00
2563	Chicago	—	85.00
2564	St. Louis	—	85.00
2565	Minneapolis	—	85.00
2566	Kansas City	—	85.00
2567	Dallas	—	85.00
2568	San Francisco	—	85.00

Series 1934-A Julian-Morgenthau

KL#	Bank	XF	CU
2569	Boston	—	80.00
2570	New York	—	80.00
2571	Cleveland	—	80.00
2572	Richmond	—	80.00
2573	Atlanta	—	80.00
2574	Chicago	—	80.00
2575	St. Louis	—	80.00
2576	Minneapolis	—	80.00
2577	Kansas City	—	80.00
2578	Dallas	—	80.00
2579	San Francisco	—	80.00

Series 1934-B Julian-Vinson

KL#	Bank	XF	CU
2580	Philadelphia	—	95.00
2581	Cleveland	—	95.00
2582	Richmond	—	95.00
2583	Atlanta	—	95.00
2584	Chicago	—	95.00
2585	St. Louis	—	95.00
2586	Minneapolis	—	95.00
2587	Kansas City	—	95.00
2588	Dallas	—	95.00
2589	San Francisco	—	95.00

Series 1934-C Julian-Snyder

KL#	Bank	XF	CU
2590	Boston	—	85.00
2591	New York	—	85.00
2592	Philadelphia	—	85.00
2593	Cleveland	—	85.00
2594	Richmond	—	85.00
2595	Atlanta	—	85.00
2596	Chicago	—	85.00

KL#	Bank	XF	CU
2597	St. Louis	—	85.00
2598	Minneapolis	—	85.00
2599	Kansas City	—	85.00
2600	Dallas	—	85.00

Series 1934-D Clark-Snyder

KL#	Bank	XF	CU
2601	Boston	—	77.50
2602	New York	—	77.50
2603	Philadelphia	—	77.50
2604	Richmond	—	77.50
2605	Atlanta	—	77.50
2606	Chicago	—	77.50
2607	Dallas	—	77.50

Series 1950 Clark-Snyder

KL#	Bank	XF	CU
2608	Boston	—	72.50
2609	New York	—	72.50
2610	Philadelphia	—	72.50
2611	Cleveland	—	72.50
2612	Richmond	—	72.50
2613	Atlanta	—	72.50
2614	Chicago	—	72.50
2615	St. Louis	—	72.50
2616	Minneapolis	—	72.50
2617	Kansas City	—	72.50
2618	Dallas	—	72.50
2619	San Francisco	—	72.50

Series 1950-A Priest-Humphrey

KL#	Bank	XF	CU
2620	Boston	—	70.00
2621	New York	—	70.00
2622	Philadelphia	—	70.00
2623	Cleveland	—	70.00
2624	Richmond	—	70.00
2625	Atlanta	—	70.00
2626	Chicago	—	70.00
2627	St. Louis	—	70.00
2628	Kansas City	—	70.00
2629	Dallas	—	70.00
2630	San Francisco	—	70.00

Series 1950-B Priest-Anderson

KL#	Bank	XF	CU
2631	Boston	—	65.00
2632	New York	—	65.00
2633	Philadelphia	—	65.00
2634	Cleveland	—	65.00
2635	Richmond	—	65.00
2636	Chicago	—	65.00
2637	St. Louis	—	65.00
2638	Kansas City	—	65.00
2639	Dallas	—	65.00
2640	San Francisco	—	65.00

Series 1950-C Smith-Dillon

KL#	Bank	XF	CU
2641	Boston	—	67.50
2642	New York	—	67.50
2643	Philadelphia	—	67.50
2644	Cleveland	—	67.50
2645	Richmond	—	67.50
2646	Chicago	—	67.50
2647	St. Louis	—	67.50
2648	Minneapolis	—	67.50
2649	Kansas City	—	67.50
2650	Dallas	—	67.50
2651	San Francisco	—	67.50

Series 1950-D Granahan-Dillon

KL#	Bank	XF	CU
2652	Boston	—	60.00
2653	New York	—	60.00
2654	Philadelphia	—	60.00
2655	Cleveland	—	60.00
2656	Richmond	—	60.00
2657	Atlanta	—	60.00
2658	Chicago	—	60.00
2659	St. Louis	—	60.00
2660	Minneapolis	—	60.00
2661	Kansas City	—	60.00
2662	Dallas	—	60.00
2663	San Francisco	—	60.00

Series 1950-E Granahan-Fowler

KL#	Bank	XF	CU
2664	New York	—	60.00
2665	Chicago	—	60.00
2666	San Francisco	—	60.00

Series 1963-A Granahan-Fowler

KL#	Bank	XF	CU
2667	Boston	—	60.00
2667★	Boston	—	85.00
2668	New York	—	60.00
2668★	New York	—	85.00
2669	Philadelphia	—	60.00
2669★	Philadelphia	—	85.00
2670	Cleveland	—	60.00
2670★	Cleveland	—	85.00
2671	Richmond	—	60.00
2671★	Richmond	—	85.00
2672	Atlanta	—	60.00
2672★	Atlanta	—	85.00
2673	Chicago	—	60.00
2673★	Chicago	—	85.00
2674	St. Louis	—	60.00
2674★	St. Louis	—	90.00
2675	Minneapolis	—	60.00
2675★	Minneapolis	—	90.00
2676	Kansas City	—	60.00
2676★	Kansas City	—	100.
2677	Dallas	—	60.00
2677★	Dallas	—	90.00
2678	San Francisco	—	60.00
2678★	San Francisco	—	85.00

Series 1969 Elston-Kennedy

KL#	Bank	XF	CU
2679	Boston	—	55.00
2679★	Boston		None Printed
2680	New York	—	55.00
2680★	New York	—	75.00
2681	Philadelphia	—	55.00
2681★	Philadelphia	—	80.00
2682	Cleveland	—	55.00
2682★	Cleveland	—	75.00
2683	Richmond	—	55.00
2683★	Richmond	—	90.00
2684	Atlanta	—	55.00
2684★	Atlanta		None Printed
2685	Chicago	—	55.00
2685★	Chicago	—	75.00
2686	St. Louis	—	55.00
2686★	St. Louis		None Printed
2687	Minneapolis	—	55.00
2687★	Minneapolis		None Printed
2688	Kansas City	—	55.00
2688★	Kansas City	—	90.00
2689	Dallas	—	55.00
2689★	Dallas	—	90.00
2690	San Francisco	—	55.00
2690★	San Francisco	—	75.00

Series 1969-A Kabis-Connally

KL#	Bank	XF	CU
2691	Boston	—	55.00
2691★	Boston	—	75.00
2692	New York	—	55.00
2692★	New York	—	75.00
2693	Philadelphia	—	55.00
2693★	Philadelphia		None Printed
2694	Cleveland	—	55.00
2694★	Cleveland		None Printed
2695	Richmond	—	55.00
2695★	Richmond	—	75.00
2696	Atlanta	—	55.00
2696★	Atlanta	—	75.00
2697	Chicago	—	55.00
2697★	Chicago	—	75.00
2698	St. Louis	—	55.00
2698★	St. Louis		None Printed
2699	Minneapolis	—	55.00
2699★	Minneapolis		None Printed
2700	Kansas City	—	55.00
2700★	Kansas City		None Printed
2701	Dallas	—	55.00
2701★	Dallas	—	75.00
2702	San Francisco	—	55.00
2702★	San Francisco	—	75.00

Series 1969-B Banuelos-Connally

KL#	Bank	XF	CU
2703	Boston	—	55.00
2704	New York	—	55.00
2705	Richmond	—	55.00
2706	Atlanta	—	55.00
2707	Chicago	—	55.00
2708	Dallas	—	55.00
2708★	Dallas	—	—

Series 1969-C Banuelos-Shultz

KL#	Bank	XF	CU
2709	Boston	—	55.00
2709★	Boston	—	60.00
2710	New York	—	55.00
2710★	New York	—	60.00
2711	Philadelphia	—	55.00
2711★	Philadelphia	—	60.00
2712	Cleveland	—	55.00
2712★	Cleveland	—	60.00

KL#	Bank	XF	CU
2713	Richmond	—	55.00
2713☆	Richmond	—	60.00
2714	Atlanta	—	55.00
2714☆	Atlanta	—	60.00
2715	Chicago	—	55.00
2715☆	Chicago	—	60.00
2716	St. Louis	—	55.00
2716☆	St. Louis	—	60.00
2717	Minneapolis	—	55.00
2717☆	Minneapolis	—	60.00
2718	Kansas City	—	55.00
2718☆	Kansas City	—	60.00
2719	Dallas	—	55.00
2719☆	Dallas	—	60.00
2720	San Francisco	—	55.00
2720☆	San Francisco	—	60.00

Series 1974 Neff-Simon

KL#	Bank	XF	CU
2721	Boston	—	55.00
2721☆	Boston	—	65.00
2722	New York	—	55.00
2722☆	New York	—	65.00
2723	Philadelphia	—	55.00
2723☆	Philadelphia	—	65.00
2724	Cleveland	—	55.00
2724☆	Cleveland	—	65.00
2725	Richmond	—	55.00
2725☆	Richmond	—	65.00
2726	Atlanta	—	55.00
2726☆	Atlanta	—	—
2727	Chicago	—	55.00
2727☆	Chicago	—	65.00
2728	St. Louis	—	55.00
2728☆	St. Louis	—	65.00
2729	Minneapolis	—	55.00
2729☆	Minneapolis	—	65.00
2730	Kansas City	—	55.00
2730☆	Kansas City	—	65.00
2731	Dallas	—	55.00
2731☆	Dallas	—	65.00
2732	San Francisco	—	55.00
2732☆	San Francisco	—	65.00

Series 1977 Morton-Blumenthal

KL#	Bank	XF	CU
2733	Boston	—	55.00
2733☆	Boston	—	100.
2734	New York	—	55.00
2734☆	New York	—	100.
2735	Philadelphia	—	55.00
2735☆	Philadelphia	—	100.
2736	Cleveland	—	55.00
2736☆	Cleveland	—	100.
2737	Richmond	—	55.00
2737☆	Richmond	—	100.
2738	Atlanta	—	55.00
2738☆	Atlanta	—	100.
2739	Chicago	—	55.00
2739☆	Chicago	—	100.
2740	St. Louis	—	55.00
2740☆	St. Louis	—	100.
2741	Minneapolis	—	55.00
2741☆	Minneapolis	—	100.
2742	Kansas City	—	55.00
2742☆	Kansas City	—	100.
2743	Dallas	—	55.00
2743☆	Dallas	—	100.
2744	San Francisco	—	55.00
2744☆	San Francisco	—	100.

Series 1981 Buchanan-Regan

KL#	Bank	XF	CU
3548	Boston	—	55.00
3548*	Boston	—	75.00
3549	New York	—	55.00
3549*	New York	—	75.00
3550	Philadelphia	—	55.00
3550*	Philadelphia	—	75.00
3551	Cleveland	—	55.00
3551*	Cleveland	—	75.00
3552	Richmond	—	55.00
3552*	Richmond	—	75.00
3553	Atlanta	—	55.00
3553*	Atlanta	—	75.00
3554	Chicago	—	55.00
3554*	Chicago	—	75.00
3555	St. Louis	—	55.00
3555*	St. Louis	—	75.00
3556	Minneapolis	—	55.00
3556*	Minneapolis	—	75.00
3557	Kansas City	—	55.00
3557*	Kansas City	—	75.00
3558	Dallas	—	55.00
3558*	Dallas	—	75.00
3559	San Francisco	—	55.00
3559*	San Francisco	—	75.00

Series 1981-A Ortega-Regan

KL#	Bank	XF	CU
3648	Boston	—	55.00
3648☆	Boston	—	75.00
3649	New York	—	55.00
3649☆	New York	—	75.00
3650	Philadelphia	—	55.00
3650☆	Philadelphia	—	75.00
3651	Cleveland	—	55.00
3651☆	Cleveland	—	75.00
3652	Richmond	—	55.00
3652☆	Richmond	—	75.00
3653	Atlanta	—	55.00
3653☆	Atlanta	—	75.00
3654	Chicago	—	55.00
3654☆	Chicago	—	75.00
3655	St. Louis	—	55.00
3655☆	St. Louis	—	75.00
3656	Minneapolis	—	55.00
3656☆	Minneapolis	—	75.00
3657	Kansas City	—	55.00
3657☆	Kansas City	—	75.00
3658	Dallas	—	55.00
3658☆	Dallas	—	75.00
3659	San Francisco	—	55.00
3659☆	San Francisco	—	75.00

Series 1985 Ortega-Baker

KL#	Bank	XF	CU
3748	Boston	—	(Current)
3748☆	Boston	—	—
3749	New York	—	(Current)
3749☆	New York	—	—
3750	Philadelphia	—	(Current)
3750☆	Philadelphia	—	—
3751	Cleveland	—	(Current)
3751☆	Cleveland	—	—
3752	Richmond	—	(Current)
3752☆	Richmond	—	—
3753	Atlanta	—	(Current)
3753☆	Atlanta	—	—
3754	Chicago	—	(Current)
3754☆	Chicago	—	—
3755	St. Louis	—	(Current)
3755☆	St. Louis	—	—
3756	Minneapolis	—	(Current)
3756☆	Minneapolis	—	—
3757	Kansas City	—	(Current)
3757☆	Kansas City	—	—
3758	Dallas		(Current)
3758☆	Dallas	—	—
3759	San Francisco	—	(Current)
3759☆	San Francisco	—	—

One Hundred Dollars United States Notes

KL#	Series	Signatures	Fine	VF	CU
2745	1966	Granahan-Fowler	—	115.	175.
2745☆	1966	Granahan-Fowler	—	—	220.
2746	1966-A	Elston-Kennedy	—	120.	300.

Gold Certificates

KL#	Series	Signatures	Fine	VF	CU
2747	1928	Woods-Mellon	110.	150.	650.
2747★	1928	Woods-Mellon	—	—	850.

Federal Reserve Bank Notes

KL#	Series	District	Fine	VF	CU
2749	1929	New York	—	—	200.
2751	1929	Cleveland	—	—	220.
2752	1929	Richmond	—	—	240.
2754	1929	Chicago	—	—	200.
2756	1929	Minneapolis	—	—	200.
2757	1929	Kansas City	110.	125.	275.
2758	1929	Dallas	110.	125.	450.

Federal Reserve Notes

Series 1928 Woods-Mellon

KL#	Bank	XF	CU
2760	Boston	—	180.
2761	New York	—	180.
2762	Philadelphia	—	180.
2763	Cleveland	—	180.
2764	Richmond	—	180.
2765	Atlanta	—	180.
2766	Chicago	—	180.
2767	St. Louis	—	180.
2768	Minneapolis	—	180.
2769	Kansas City	—	180.
2770	Dallas	—	180.
2771	San Francisco	—	180.

Series 1928-A Woods-Mellon

KL#	Bank	XF	CU
2772	Boston	—	185.
2773	New York	—	185.
2774	Philadelphia	—	185.
2775	Cleveland	—	185.
2776	Richmond	—	185.
2777	Atlanta	—	185.
2778	Chicago	—	185.
2779	St. Louis	—	185.
2780	Minneapolis	—	185.
2781	Kansas City	—	185.
2782	Dallas	—	185.
2783	San Francisco	—	185.

Series 1934 Julian-Morgenthau

KL#	Bank	XF	CU
2784	Boston	—	175.
2785	New York	—	175.
2786	Philadelphia	—	175.
2787	Cleveland	—	175.
2788	Richmond	—	175.
2789	Atlanta	—	175.
2790	Chicago	—	175.
2791	St. Louis	—	175.
2792	Minneapolis	—	175.
2793	Kansas City	—	175.
2794	Dallas	—	175.
2795	San Francisco	—	175.

Series 1934-A Julian-Morgenthau

KL#	Bank	XF	CU
2784A	Boston	—	175.
2785A	New York	—	175.
2786A	Philadelphia	—	175.
2787A	Cleveland	—	175.
2788A	Richmond	—	175.
2789A	Atlanta	—	175.
2790A	Chicago	—	175.
2791A	St. Louis	—	175.
2792A	Minneapolis	—	175.
2793A	Kansas City	—	175.
2794A	Dallas	—	175.
2795A	San Francisco	—	175.

Series 1934-B Julian-Vinson

KL#	Bank	XF	CU
2796	Boston	—	175.
2797	Philadelphia	—	175.
2798	Cleveland	—	175.
2799	Richmond	—	175.
2800	Atlanta	—	175.
2801	Chicago	—	175.
2802	St. Louis	—	175.
2803	Minneapolis	—	175.
2804	Kansas City	—	175.
2805	Dallas	—	175.

Series 1934-C Julian-Snyder

KL#	Bank	XF	CU
2806	Boston	—	160.
2807	New York	—	160.
2808	Philadelphia	—	160.
2809	Cleveland	—	160.
2810	Atlanta	—	160.
2811	Chicago	—	160.
2812	St. Louis	—	160.
2813	Minneapolis	—	160.
2814	Kansas City	—	160.
2815	Dallas	—	160.
2816	San Francisco	—	160.

Series 1934-D Clark-Snyder

KL#	Bank	XF	CU
2817	New York	—	175.
2818	Philadelphia	—	175.
2819	Atlanta	—	175.
2820	Chicago	—	175.
2821	St. Louis	—	175.
2822	Dallas	—	175.

Series 1950 Clark-Snyder

KL#	Bank	XF	CU
2823	Boston	—	140.
2824	New York	—	140.
2825	Philadelphia	—	140.
2826	Cleveland	—	140.
2827	Richmond	—	140.
2828	Atlanta	—	140.
2829	Chicago	—	140.
2830	St. Louis	—	140.
2831	Minneapolis	—	140.
2832	Kansas City	—	140.
2833	Dallas	—	140.
2834	San Francisco	—	140.

Series 1950-A Priest-Humphrey

KL#	Bank	XF	CU
2835	Boston	—	130.
2836	New York	—	130.
2837	Philadelphia	—	130.
2838	Cleveland	—	130.
2839	Richmond	—	130.
2840	Atlanta	—	130.
2841	Chicago	—	130.
2842	St. Louis	—	130.
2843	Minneapolis	—	130.
2844	Kansas City	—	130.
2845	Dallas	—	130.
2846	San Francisco	—	130.

Series 1950-B Priest-Anderson

KL#	Bank	XF	CU
2847	Boston	—	130.
2848	New York	—	130.
2849	Philadelphia	—	130.
2850	Cleveland	—	130.
2851	Richmond	—	130.
2852	Atlanta	—	130.
2853	Chicago	—	130.
2854	St. Louis	—	130.
2855	Minneapolis	—	130.
2856	Kansas City	—	130.
2857	Dallas	—	130.
2858	San Francisco	—	130.

Series 1950-C Smith-Dillon

KL#	Bank	XF	CU
2859	Boston	—	135.
2860	New York	—	135.
2861	Philadelphia	—	135.
2862	Cleveland	—	135.
2863	Richmond	—	135.
2864	Atlanta	—	135.
2865	Chicago	—	135.
2866	St. Louis	—	135.
2867	Minneapolis	—	135.
2868	Kansas City	—	135.
2869	Dallas	—	135.
2870	San Francisco	—	135.

Series 1950-D Granahan-Dillon

KL#	Bank	XF	CU
2871	Boston	—	135.
2872	New York	—	135.
2873	Philadelphia	—	135.
2874	Cleveland	—	135.
2875	Richmond	—	135.
2876	Atlanta	—	135.
2877	Chicago	—	135.
2878	St. Louis	—	135.
2879	Minneapolis	—	135.
2880	Kansas City	—	135.
2881	Dallas	—	135.
2882	San Francisco	—	135.

Series 1950-E Granahan-Fowler

KL#	Bank	XF	CU
2883	New York	—	135.
2884	Chicago	—	135.
2885	San Francisco	—	135.

Series 1963-A Granahan-Fowler

KL#	Bank	XF	CU
2886	Boston	—	125.
2886☆	Boston	—	130.
2887	New York	—	125.
2887☆	New York	—	130.
2888	Philadelphia	—	125.
2888☆	Philadelphia	—	130.
2889	Cleveland	—	125.
2889☆	Cleveland	—	130.
2890	Richmond	—	125.
2890☆	Richmond	—	130.
2891	Atlanta	—	125.
2891☆	Atlanta	—	130.
2892	Chicago	—	125.
2892☆	Chicago	—	130.
2893	St. Louis	—	125.
2893☆	St. Louis	—	130.
2894	Minneapolis	—	125.
2894☆	Minneapolis	—	130.
2895	Kansas City	—	125.
2895☆	Kansas City	—	130.
2896	Dallas	—	125.
2896☆	Dallas	—	130.
2897	San Francisco	—	125.
2897☆	San Francisco	—	130.

Series 1969 Elston-Kennedy

KL#	Bank	XF	CU
2898	Boston	—	120.
2898☆	Boston	—	130.
2899	New York	—	120.
2899☆	New York	—	130.
2900	Philadelphia	—	120.
2900☆	Philadelphia	—	130.
2901	Cleveland	—	120.
2901☆	Cleveland	—	135.
2902	Richmond	—	120.
2902☆	Richmond	—	130.
2903	Atlanta	—	120.
2903☆	Atlanta	—	130.
2904	Chicago	—	120.
2904☆	Chicago	—	130.
2905	St. Louis	—	120.
2905☆	St. Louis	—	135.
2906	Minneapolis	—	120.
2906☆	Minneapolis	—	135.
2907	Kansas City	—	120.
2907☆	Kansas City	—	130.
2908	Dallas	—	120.
2908☆	Dallas	—	130.
2909	San Francisco	—	120.
2909☆	San Francisco	—	130.

Series 1969-A Kabis-Connally

KL#	Bank	XF	CU
2898A	Boston	—	115.
2898A☆	Boston	—	125.
2899A	New York	—	115.
2899A☆	New York	—	125.
2900A	Philadelphia	—	115.
2900A☆	Philadelphia	—	125.
2901A	Cleveland	—	115.
2901A☆	Cleveland	—	125.
2902A	Richmond	—	115.
2902A☆	Richmond	—	125.
2903A	Atlanta	—	115.
2903A☆	Atlanta	—	125.
2904A	Chicago	—	115.
2904A☆	Chicago	—	125.
2905A	St. Louis	—	115.
2905A☆	St. Louis	—	135.
2906A	Minneapolis	—	115.
2906A☆	Minneapolis		None Printed
2907A	Kansas City	—	115.
2907A☆	Kansas City		None Printed
2908A	Dallas	—	115.
2908A☆	Dallas	—	125.
2909A	San Francisco	—	115.
2909A☆	San Francisco	—	125.

Series 1969-C Banuelos-Shultz

KL#	Bank	XF	CU
2910	Boston	—	110.
2910☆	Boston	—	125.
2911	New York	—	110.
2911☆	New York	—	125.
2912	Philadelphia	—	110.
2912☆	Philadelphia	—	125.
2913	Cleveland	—	110.
2913☆	Cleveland	—	125.
2914	Richmond	—	110.
2914☆	Richmond	—	125.
2915	Atlanta	—	110.
2915☆	Atlanta	—	125.
2916	Chicago	—	110.
2916☆	Chicago	—	125.
2917	St. Louis	—	110.
2917☆	St. Louis	—	125.
2918	Minneapolis	—	110.
2918☆	Minneapolis	—	125.
2919	Kansas City	—	110.
2919☆	Kansas City	—	125.
2920	Dallas	—	110.
2920☆	Dallas	—	125.
2921	San Francisco	—	110.
2921☆	San Francisco	—	125.

Series 1974 Neff-Simon

KL#	Bank	XF	CU
2922	Boston	—	110.
2922☆	Boston	—	120.
2923	New York	—	110.
2923☆	New York	—	120.
2924	Philadelphia	—	110.
2924☆	Philadelphia	—	120.
2925	Cleveland	—	110.
2925☆	Cleveland	—	120.
2926	Richmond	—	110.
2926☆	Richmond	—	120.
2927	Atlanta	—	110.
2927☆	Atlanta	—	120.
2928	Chicago	—	110.
2928☆	Chicago	—	120.
2929	St. Louis	—	110.
2929☆	St. Louis	—	120.
2930	Minneapolis	—	110.
2930☆	Minneapolis	—	120.
2931	Kansas City	—	110.
2931☆	Kansas City	—	120.
2932	Dallas	—	110.
2932☆	Dallas	—	120.
2933	San Francisco	—	110.
2933☆	San Francisco	—	120.

Series 1977 Morton-Blumenthal

KL#	Bank	XF	CU
2934	Boston	—	110.
2934☆	Boston	—	125.
2935	New York	—	110.
2935☆	New York	—	125.
2936	Philadelphia	—	110.
2936☆	Philadelphia	—	125.
2937	Cleveland	—	110.
2937☆	Cleveland	—	125.
2938	Richmond	—	110.
2938☆	Richmond	—	125.
2939	Atlanta	—	110.
2939☆	Atlanta	—	115.
2940	Chicago	—	110.
2940☆	Chicago	—	125.
2941	St. Louis	—	110.
2941☆	St. Louis	—	125.
2942	Minneapolis	—	110.
2942☆	Minneapolis	—	125.
2943	Kansas City	—	110.
2943☆	Kansas City	—	125.
2944	Dallas	—	110.
2944☆	Dallas	—	125.
2944A	San Francisco	—	110.
2944A☆	San Francisco	—	125.

Series 1981 Buchanan-Regan

KL#	Bank	XF	CU
3560	Boston	—	105.00
3560☆	Boston	—	125.00
3561	New York	—	105.00
3561☆	New York	—	125.00
3562	Philadelphia	—	105.00
3562☆	Philadelphia	—	125.00
3563	Cleveland	—	105.00
3563☆	Cleveland	—	125.00
3564	Richmond	—	105.00
3564☆	Richmond	—	125.00
3565	Atlanta	—	105.00
3565☆	Atlanta	—	125.00
3566	Chicago	—	105.00
3566☆	Chicago	—	125.00
3567	St. Louis	—	105.00
3567☆	St. Louis	—	125.00
3568	Minneapolis	—	105.00
3568☆	Minneapolis	—	125.00
3569	Kansas City	—	105.00
3569☆	Kansas City	—	125.00
3570	Dallas	—	105.00
3570☆	Dallas	—	125.00
3571	San Francisco	—	105.00
3571☆	San Francisco	—	125.00

Series 1981-A Ortega-Regan

KL#	Bank	XF	CU
3660	Boston	—	105.00
3660☆	Boston	—	125.00
3661	New York	—	105.00
3661☆	New York	—	125.00
3662	Philadelphia	—	105.00
3662☆	Philadelphia	—	125.00
3663	Cleveland	—	105.00
3663☆	Cleveland	—	125.00
3664	Richmond	—	105.00
3664☆	Richmond	—	125.00
3665	Atlanta	—	105.00
3665☆	Atlanta	—	125.00
3666	Chicago	—	105.00
3666☆	Chicago	—	125.00
3667	St. Louis	—	105.00
3667☆	St. Louis	—	125.00
3668	Minneapolis	—	105.00
3668☆	Minneapolis	—	125.00
3669	Kansas City	—	105.00
3669☆	Kansas City	—	125.00
3670	Dallas	—	105.00
3670☆	Dallas	—	125.00
3671	San Francisco	—	105.00
3671☆	San Francisco	—	125.00

Series 1985 Ortega-Baker

KL#	Bank	XF	CU
3760	Boston	—	(Current)
3760☆	Boston	—	—
3761	New York	—	(Current)
3761☆	New York	—	—
3762	Philadelphia	—	(Current)
3762☆	Philadelphia	—	—
3763	Cleveland	—	(Current)
3763☆	Cleveland	—	—
3764	Richmond	—	(Current)
3764☆	Richmond	—	—
3765	Atlanta	—	(Current)
3765☆	Atlanta	—	—
3766	Chicago	—	(Current)
3766☆	Chicago	—	—
3767	St. Louis	—	(Current)
3767☆	St. Louis	—	—
3768	Minneapolis	—	(Current)
3768☆	Minneapolis	—	—
3769	Kansas City	—	(Current)
3769☆	Kansas City	—	—
3770	Dallas	—	(Current)
3770☆	Dallas	—	—
3771	San Francisco	—	(Current)
3771☆	San Francisco	—	—

Five Hundred Dollars Gold Certificates

KL#	Series	Signatures	Fine	VF	CU
2945	1928	Woods-Mellon	575.	750.	2000.

Federal Reserve Notes

Series 1928 Woods-Mellon

KL#	Bank	XF	CU
2946	Boston	575.	750.
2947	New York	575.	750.
2948	Philadelphia	575.	750.
2949	Cleveland	575.	750.
2950	Richmond	575.	750.
2951	Atlanta	575.	750.
2952	Chicago	575.	750.
2953	St. Louis	575.	750.
2954	Minneapolis	575.	750.
2955	Kansas City	575.	750.
2956	Dallas	575.	750.
2957	San Francisco	575.	750.

Series 1934 Julian-Morgenthau

KL#	Bank	XF	CU
2958	Boston	575.	750.
2959	New York	575.	750.
2960	Philadelphia	575.	750.
2961	Cleveland	575.	750.
2962	Richmond	575.	750.
2963	Atlanta	575.	750.
2964	Chicago	575.	750.
2965	St. Louis	575.	750.
2966	Minneapolis	575.	750.
2967	Kansas City	575.	750.
2968	Dallas	575.	750.
2969	San Francisco	575.	750.

Series 1934-A Julian-Morgenthau

KL#	Bank	XF	CU
2971	New York	550.	700.
2972	Philadelphia	550.	700.
2973	Cleveland	550.	700.
2974	Richmond	550.	700.
2975	Chicago	550.	700.
2976	St. Louis	550.	700.
2977	Minneapolis	550.	700.
2978	Kansas City	550.	700.
2979	Dallas	550.	700.
2980	San Francisco	550.	700.

Series 1934-B Julian-Vinson

KL#	Bank	XF	CU
2981	Atlanta	1500.	3500.

Series 1934-C Julian-Snyder

KL#	Bank	XF	CU
2982	Boston	1250.	2000.
2983	New York	1500.	2500.

One Thousand Dollars Gold Certificates

KL#	Series	Signatures	Fine	VF	CU
2984	1928	Woods-Mellon	1150.	1500.	3500.

Federal Reserve Notes

Series 1928 Woods-Mellon

KL#	Bank	XF	CU
2985	Boston	1075.	1250.
2986	New York	1075.	1250.
2987	Philadelphia	1075.	1250.
2988	Cleveland	1075.	1250.
2989	Richmond	1075.	1250.
2990	Atlanta	1075.	1250.
2991	Chicago	1075.	1250
2992	St. Louis	1075.	1250.
2993	Minneapolis	1075.	1250.
2994	Kansas City	1075.	1250.
2995	Dallas	1075.	1250.
2996	San Francisco	1075.	1250.

Series 1934 Julian-Morgenthau

KL#	Bank	XF	CU
2997	Boston	1075.	1250.
2998	New York	1075.	1250.
2999	Philadelphia	1075.	1250.
3000	Cleveland	1075.	1250.
3001	Richmond	1075.	1250.
3002	Atlanta	1075.	1250.
3003	Chicago	1075.	1250.
3004	St. Louis	1075.	1250.
3005	Minneapolis	1075.	1250.
3006	Kansas City	1075.	1250.
3007	Dallas	1075.	1250.
3008	San Francisco	1075.	1250.

Series 1934-A Julian-Morgenthau

KL#	Bank	XF	CU
3009	Boston	1075.	1250.
3010	New York	1075.	1250.
3011	Philadelphia	1075.	1250.
3012	Cleveland	1075.	1250.
3013	Richmond	1075.	1250.
3014	Atlanta	1075.	1250.
3015	Chicago	1075.	1250.
3016	St. Louis	1075.	1250.
3017	Minneapolis	1075.	1250.
3018	Kansas City	1075.	1250.
3019	San Francisco	1075.	1250.

Series 1934-C Julian-Snyder

KL#	Bank	XF	CU
3020	Boston	2000.	3000.
3021	New York	2000.	3000.

Five Thousand Dollars Gold Certificates

KL#	Series	Signatures	Fine	VF	CU
3022	1928	Woods-Mellon	—	—	6000.

Federal Reserve Notes

Series 1928 Woods-Mellon

KL#	Bank	XF	CU
3023	Boston	5250.	6000.
3024	New York	5250.	6000.
3025	Cleveland	5250.	6000.
3026	Richmond	5250.	6000.
3027	Atlanta	5250.	6000.
3028	Chicago	5250.	6000.
3029	Kansas City	5250.	6000.
3030	Dallas	5250.	6000.
3031	San Francisco	5250.	6000.

Series 1934 Julian-Morgenthau

KL#	Bank	XF	CU
3032	Boston	5250.	6000.
3033	New York	5250.	6000.
3034	Philadelphia	5250.	6000.
3035	Cleveland	5250.	6000.
3036	Richmond	5250.	6000.
3037	Atlanta	5250.	6000.
3038	Chicago	5250.	6000.
3039	St. Louis	5250.	6000.
3040	Kansas City	5250.	6000.
3041	Dallas	5250.	6000.
3042	San Francisco	5250.	6000.

Series 1934-A Julian-Morgenthau

KL#	Bank	XF	CU
3043	St. Louis	6500.	7500.

Series 1934-B

KL#	Bank	XF	CU
3044	Boston	5500.	6500.
3045	New York	5500.	6500.

Ten Thousand Dollars
Gold Certificates

KL#	Series	Signatures	Fine	VF	CU
3046	1928	Woods-Mellon	—	—	15,000.

Federal Reserve Notes

Series 1928 Woods-Mellon

KL#	Bank	XF	CU
3047	Boston	11,500.	12,500.
3048	New York	11,500.	12,500.
3049	Cleveland	11,500.	12,500.
3050	Richmond	11,500.	12,500.
3051	Atlanta	11,500.	12,500.
3052	Chicago	11,500.	12,500.
3053	St. Louis	11,500.	12,500.
3054	Minneapolis	11,500.	12,500.
3055	Kansas City	11,500.	12,500.
3056	Dallas	11,500.	12,500.
3057	San Francisco	11,500.	12,500.

Series 1934 Julian-Morgenthau

KL#	Bank	XF	CU
3058	Boston	11,500.	12,500.
3059	New York	11,500.	12,500.
3060	Philadelphia	11,500.	12,500.
3061	Cleveland	11,500.	12,500.
3062	Richmond	11,500.	12,500.
3063	Atlanta	11,500.	12,500.
3064	Chicago	11,500.	12,500.
3065	St. Louis	11,500.	12,500.
3066	Kansas City	11,500.	12,500.
3067	Dallas	11,500.	12,500.
3068	San Francisco	11,500.	12,500.

Series 1934-A Julian-Morgenthau

KL#	Bank	XF	CU
3069	Chicago	12,500.	15,000.

Series 1934-B Julian-Vinson

KL#	Bank	XF	CU
3070	New York	15,000.	17,500.

Paper Coin Substitutes of the Civil War

The collector's first encounter with U.S. Postage and Fractional Currency invariably provokes two questions: What is it? Why was it?

The first question is easily answered. Postage and Fractional Currency is genuine paper money of the United States issued during the 1862-1875 period in denominations of 3, 5, 10, 15, 25 and 50 cents.

Why paper money in denominations of less than the familiar dollar unit was required in commerce is less easily answered. The causes of this unusual issue of official "paper coins" at a time when people still demanded coins of high intrinsic value can only be found in the jumble of cause and effect that has been the catalyst of numismatic history from time immemorial.

It would be convenient to state, as has frequently been done, that within a few days of the outbreak of the Civil War all of the gold, silver and copper coins in circulation disappeared due to the desire of the timid to save something of universal value from the threatened wreck of the Union, and of the avaricious to hoard something which would possibly increase in value. Undoubtedly, fear and greed acted at once to trigger the hoarding instinct in some individuals, but on the whole, such an observation seems to be overdrawn. Contemporary newspaper accounts make little mention of a serious coin shortage until early in 1862.

There was no pervading fear in the North that the armed forces of the Confederacy would prevail and shatter the Union for all time. If anything, the tendency was to underestimate the power and tenacity of the South.

It would appear that the initial hoarding of hard money was caused by little more than an ingrained distrust of paper money, an attitude more than justified by the nation's experience with non-metallic currency up to that time. The Yankee worker, whose livelihood was completely bound to the money earned tending the lathes and forges of the industrialized North, simply felt more secure when his paper wages had been converted to gold and silver. Consequently, he gave a cool reception to "Greenbacks," which could not be redeemed for either gold or silver and were suspiciously regarded as "faith paper." The reception grew progressivly colder as the flood of paper dollars increased.

This practically expressed preference for coins inevitably depreciated Greenbacks in terms of the gold standard. Gold coins commanded a premium of three percent over U.S. and state paper money in January, 1862, the month following the general suspension of specie payment by banks and the Federal Treasury; six percent in June, 1862; 15 percent in July, and 32 percent by the end of 1862. Thereafter the depreciation of Greenbacks accelerated, until at one point in 1864 it required $285 in paper to purchase $100 in gold. The distrust of the Government's fiat paper was also maintained by the snowballing national debt, which reached its high-point of the war — $2.8 billion — in 1865.

A monetary situation whereby gold commanded a substantial premium over a like face value of paper dollars swiftly drove gold coins from commercial channels, effectively removing the United States from a gold standard. It also created a favorable condition for the exporting of silver coins, which disappeared from the marketplace, but at a less precipitous pace than gold.

In 1858 Canada had adopted a decimal system of coinage with a dollar unit similar to that of the United States. In lieu of a sufficient quantity of decimal coinage of British origin, Canada unofficially adopted the coinage of the United States and used it widely in domestic trade. The West Indies and many Latin American countries also imported large quantities of U.S. silver coinage for domestic use. Disappearance of gold from American trade channels and the willingness of foreign users of U.S. silver coins to pay for them with gold combined to produce a legal and highly profitable bullion trade which speculators and bankers found irresistible.

The discounting of Greenbacks in terms of gold enabled the exchange of paper money for silver coins, which were then exchanged for gold in Canada, the West Indies or Latin America. The gold was then returned to the United States, where it was used to purchase more Greenbacks at the metal's high premium rate. A safer round-robin to riches can hardly be imagined. Even in times of national crisis, pragmatic profit taking will attract more adherents than an idealistic consideration for the national good. During the last week of June and the first week of July, 1862, more than $25 million in subsidiary coins vanished from circulation in the North. The shortage of silver coins, particularly in the eastern United States, would not be relieved until the summer of 1876.

Illogically, the Philadelphia Mint continued a small but steady production of silver coins during the 1860s, although they were of no use to the nation's economy. Bullion dealers obtained them directly from the Mint and sped them abroad. In 1863, the entire production of silver coins was exported.

The withdrawal of subsidiary silver coins in the summer of 1862 all but paralyzed the institutions and practice of everyday commerce. The smallest denominations of official money available were discounted $5 Legal Tender Notes and the copper-nickel cents which had been fed into circulation in great quantities to retire demonitized Spanish silver coins and the large copper cents.

When first forced upon the public in 1857, the copper-nickel cent, which was intrinsically worth about 60 percent of face value, had been considered a nuisance; it was regularly discounted three percent and more in large transactions. But with the disappearance of silver coins, the ugly duckling became the belle of the ball. The erstwhile nuisance became the only alternative to walking, or going without a newspaper, or buying a pound of pomegranctes and receiving change in kumquats and quince. Cents were bundled in bags of 25, 50 and 100 in a hopeless attempt to bridge the gap between the 1-cent piece and the $5 bill. By March, 1863, the lowly cent commanded a premium of 20 percent, but few could be found.

The disappearance of nearly all official coinage from trade channels resulted in an outpouring of private emergency monies, some hoary with tradition, others as new and untried as the inspiration which gave them form. State bank notes of $1 and $2 denominations were cut into fractional parts. Other banks issued notes in denominations of $1.25, $1.50 and $1.75. Eastern cities issued their own fractional notes. Merchants, reviving a practice prevalent during the coin shortages of 1837 and 1857, made change in their own promissory notes or "shinplasters," which were notes of small value, redeemable in merchandise at the issuer's place of business. Unscrupulous merchants made change with their own notes even when they had sufficient specie on hand, knowing that the notes were not likely to be presented for redemption by other than their regular neighborhood customers. In like manner, private issues of the eminently collectible Civil War tokens began.

Most novel of the emergency monies called into use was the common postage stamp. The use of postage stamps as a low denomination medium of exchange was not a success, but it led directly to the issuing of the highly successful Postage and Fractional Currency series.

First issued by the Federal Government in 1847, by the time the Civil War began, the adhesive postage stamp had become a well-established part of the public routine. Inasmuch as they were of official origin, had a constant value throughout the country and were easily obtained, consideration of postage stamps as a medium of exchange for coin-deprived people was inevitable. In early July, 1862, Horace Greeley, publisher of the politically influential New York *Tribune,* suggested that stamps pasted on a half sheet of paper, with the other half folded over the stamps to afford them protection from wear, would make an excellent coin substitute. Other newspapers quickly endorsed the proposal, as did the coin-starved public.

Although there were surely those who attempted to do so, fragile, gummed stamps could not be carried loose in pocket or purse without soon becoming a crumpled, stuck-together, totally useless blob of colored paper.

Methods of affording the stamps a degree of protection were quickly devised. They were pasted on sheets of light vellum paper — with or without a protective flap — which also bore an advertising message and a large numeral indicating the total face value of the stamps. Stamps were also encased in small envelopes, on the outside of which was printed the value of the contents and an advertising message.

It soon became apparent that both methods of preparing stamps for the role of emergency money had as many drawbacks as advantages. Pasting the stamps on sheets of paper did not provide them sufficient protection from wear. Those enclosed in envelopes were better protected, but the method of protection provided an opportunity for petty larceny which wasn't neglected. Few recipients had the time to check the contents of each envelope to determine if it contained the proper denominational total of stamps, or if the stamps were unused, or if rectangles of colored paper had been substituted for the stamps.

The method of stamp packaging which best satisfied the dual requirements of visibility and protection was patented on Aug. 12, 1862, by a New England inventor named John Gault, who encased a single postage stamp in a round brass frame (25 mm in diameter) with a clear mica frontpiece through which the stamp could be viewed. The reverse of this case bore the advertising message of the participating merchant who purchased a quantity of Gault's "encased postage stamps" as a means of giving his customers the precise change required by their purchases.

Stamps encased by Gault were the 1-, 3-, 5-, 10-, 12-, 24-, 30-, and 90-cent denominations of the Series of 1861-1869. That series also contains a 2-cent and a 15-cent stamp, but the 2-cent stamp wasn't issued until July 6, 1863, and the 15-cent value came along on June 17, 1866.

But for the eventual authorization of Postage and Fractional Currency, Gault's encased postage stamps would probably have become the chief means of "spending" postage stamps, although they, too, had their disadvantages. The protective mica shield was easily cracked, and the encased stamps cost the distributing merchant the face value of the stamps, plus about two cents per holder. In view of the 20 percent premium existing on official coins, the additional two cents was of little consequence in the instance of the higher denomination stamps, but in the case of the popular one-cent stamp, it meant an expenditure of three cents for every one-cent encased postage stamp obtained from Gault for monetary use.

The timing of the initiation of Gault's encased stamps also worked against their quantity distribution. At the time of their appearance in midsummer of 1862, the Postmaster General, Montgomery Blair, was still not reconciled to the idea of using postage stamps for money, and was doing his utmost to prevent quantity sales of stamps to anyone desiring them for coinage purposes.

All methods of using stamps for money that had been employed prior to July 17, 1862, suffered the ultimate disadvantage of being illegal, with the consequence that the holder of the stamps could neither redeem them at the post office nor exchange them for Treasury notes.

On that date, however, President Lincoln signed into law a measure proposed in self-defense by Treasury Secretary Salmon P. Chase, providing that "postage and other stamps of the United States" were to be receivable for all dues to the U.S. and were to be redeemable at any "designated depository" in sums less that $5. The law also prohibited the issue by "any private corporation, banking association, firm, or individual" of any note or token for a sum less than $5 — a provision that was widely ignored as the private sector continued its efforts to overcome a coin shortage in the face of which the Government seemed helpless.

The new law was not without its problems of practicality, either. The post office, already facing a stamp shortage before the gummed bits of paper had been declared legal tender, now had the almost impossible task of providing sufficient stamps for postal use as well as "coinage" use.

In addition, there was the problem of who would redeem nearly exhausted specimens of stamps which had been circulating for some time. Blair refused to take them in trade for new stamps and the Treasury would not exchange them for paper money because they hadn't issued them in the first place.

Blair's obstinacy ultimately melted before the heat of public pressure, and he agreed to redeem the masses of soiled and stuck-together stamps, but he continued to insist that the actual intent of the poorly-written law had been for the Treasury Department to print and distribute special stamps that would bear a general resemblance to postage stamps, but would be of a different design. A compromise was finally worked out whereby the Treasury Department would sell and redeem specially marked stamps which the post office would also accept for postage. Blair agreed to print the special stamps for the Treasury.

Before the stamps could be printed, a further decision was made to issue them in a larger, more convenient size, and to print them on a heavier, ungummed paper. Credit for the final form in which Postage Currency appeared is given to Gen. F.E. Spinner, Treasurer of the United States. Spinner pasted unused postage stamps on small sheets of Treasury security paper of uniform size, signed his name to some of them and passed them out to his friends as samples of currency. Congress responded to Spinner's suggestion by authorizing the printing of reproductions of postage stamps on Treasury paper in arrangements patterned after Spinner's models. In this form, the "stamps" ceased to be stamps; they became, in effect, fractional Government promissory notes, a development not authorized by the initial enabling legislation of July 17, 1862. Nonetheless, the notes would be issued without legal authorization until passage of the Act of March 3, 1863, which provided for the issuing of fractional notes by the Federal Government.

Five issues of Postage and Fractional Currency in the total amount of $369 million were printed and released to circulation between Aug. 21, 1862, and Feb. 15, 1876, when a flood of silver from the Comstock Lode drove down silver bullion prices, reducing the intrinsic value of silver coins to a point below face value, thereby insuring that they would remain in circulation. The silver price drop further augmented the supply of circulating silver by triggering a flow back to the United States — where they could be exchanged for their greater face value — of the hundreds of millions of silver coins which had been exported to Canada, the West Indies and Latin America since 1862.

Congressional Acts of Jan. 14, 1875, and April 17, 1876, provided for the redemption of Postage and Fractional Currency in silver coins, and all but about $1.8 million worth was returned to the Treasury for redemption. The outstanding notes remain legal tender and can purchase their face value equivalent in goods and services today.

FIRST ISSUE
August 21, 1862 - May 27, 1863
Denominations: 5¢, 10¢, 25¢, 50¢

The First Issue of U.S. Government stamp money is the only one of the five issues to be identified by name as Postage Currency. The initial printing of the First Issue was released through Army paymasters on Aug. 1, 1862, and was provided for general circulation a few weeks later.

Although it is a moot point, Postage Currency probably constitutes an illegal issue of fractional notes. Rather than being strictly "postage and other stamps of the United States," and despite being "receivable for postage stamps at any U.S. post office," Postage Currency took the form of reproductions of postage stamps printed on paper which carried the promise of the United States to exchange the currency for United States Notes, which gave Postage Currency the attributes of a promissory note, a development beyond the intent of the enabling Act of July 17, 1862.

The stamps reproduced on Postage Currency are the brown (sometimes buff) five-cent stamp of the Series of 1861, bearing the portrait of Thomas Jefferson, and the green ten-cent stamp of the same series, with George Washington's portrait. The 25- and 50-cent denominations bear multiple reproductions of the appropriate stamp. Various colors of paper were used in printing the four notes of the First Issue, but the color does not influence the collector value of the individual note. Faces of the notes are printed in a color approximating the color of the genuine postage stamp, backs are all printed in black.

An interesting feature of the First Issue is the existence of notes with both perforated and straight edges. Apparently, the idea of perforated Postage Currency was a carry-over from the postage stamp printing process and was discarded when the demand for Postage Currency exceeded the capacity of the perforating machines.

Inasmuch as the Bureau of Engraving and Printing had not yet been established, contracts for printing of the First Issue were awarded to private bank note printing companies. The National Bank Note Company printed the face, the American Bank Note Company, the back. The ABNC monogram appears on the backs of some notes.

Total value of Postage Currency issued was more than $20 million.

SECOND ISSUE
October 10, 1863 - February 23, 1867
Denominations: 5¢, 10¢, 25¢, 50¢

The Second Issue of a fractional currency, authorized by Congress on March 3, 1863, all but discarded the concept of postage stamp money. Notes continued to be "receivable for all United States postage stamps," but the identity of the notes was changed from Postage Currency to Fractional Currency, and the notes of the Second Issue did not bear a reproduction of a postage stamp, although the portrait of George Washington on all notes of this issue is the same as that appearing on the 24-cent stamp of the Series of 1861. The Second Issue was made necessary by the ease with which notes of the First Issue had been counterfeited.

All Second Issue notes have a slate-colored face with bronze oval surcharge centered on the portrait of Washington. Back of the 5-cent note is brown; the 10-cent, green; the 25-cent, violet, and the 50-cent note, red or reddish-orange. All backs have a large, bronze numerical outline overprinted.

Some specimen notes of this issue (and of the Third Issue) were printed on paper watermarked "C.S.A." in block letters, for Confederate States of America. The paper, made in England for the printing of Confederate States paper money, was contraband seized from a captured blockade runner.

First Issue notes had been printed by the National Bank Note Company of New York and the American Bank Note Company of New York — which were one concern in all respects but name — at a cost which the Treasury Department thought excessive. The Act of July 11, 1863, instructed the Treasury Department to undertake the printing of its own currency.

Although the primary purpose of Second Issue notes was to retire and replace First Issue notes, they were issued in excess of the requirement, to a total value of $23 million.

THIRD ISSUE
December 5, 1864 - August 16, 1869
Denominations: 3¢, 5¢, 10¢, (15¢ essay), 25¢, 50¢

Authorized by the Act of June 30, 1864, the Third Issue of Fractional Currency was necessitated by an increased demand for the low denomination notes and by the continuing counterfeiting of earlier issues. Counterfeits of the Second Issue were of better quality and even more numerous than those of the First Issue had been.

Third Issue notes provide the greatest number of varieties of any issue of Postage or Fractional Currency. Among these are varieties of paper, different colors of backs, ornamental and numerical value surcharges (or none at all), autographed or printed signatures, no signatures, and multiple designs for a single denomination.

In regard to varieties, the 10-cent note is particularly interesting. Through an oversight, the word CENTS does not appear anywhere on the note. The Third Issue varieties are too extensive to be within the scope of these remarks, but they are indicated and priced in the listing which follows.

The Act of June 30, 1864, contained a provision which, by amending the Act of March 3, 1863, authorized the Secretary of the Treasury to determine the form and denominations of Fractional Currency, the means by which it would be made, and the terms of note redemption. This authority permitted Secretary Chase to issue a 3-cent note to facilitate purchase of the new 3-cent first-class postage stamp. Need for the small note was eventually eliminated by the issue of nickel three-cent coins under the Act of March 3, 1865.

Little events can have lasting repercussions, as exemplified by the story of the 5-cent note of the Third Issue. Without the knowledge or authority of his superiors, Spencer M. Clark, then superintendent of the National Currency Bureau, had his likeness put on the 5-cent note of the Third Issue. Clark's presumptive act so angered Congress that a law was enacted April 7, 1866, prohibiting the placing of the likeness of a living person upon any "bonds, securities, notes, Fractional or Postal Currency of the United States." However, the wording of the law did not prohibit the likeness of a living person if the plate for the intended item had already been prepared. Consequently, Clark's portrait didn't disappear from the nation's currency until the passage of May 17, 1866, legislation which authorized the issue of a nickel 5-cent piece and prohibited the issue of any note with a denomination of less than 10 cents.

Likewise unaffected were the Third Issue 25-cent note bearing the portrait of William Fessenden, and the 50-cent note portraying F.E. Spinner, "The Father of Fractional Currency." The only note affected by the legislation was a proposed 15-cent denomination bearing the portraits of Generals Grant and Sherman, for which the plate had not yet been completed. This note was printed only as an essay, and in uniface form, with face and back being printed on separate pieces of paper.

All of the Third Issue notes were produced by the Treasury Department. Total face value was in excess of $86 million.

POSTAGE AND FRACTIONAL CURRENCY SHIELD

The Postage and Fractional Currency Shield was one of the measures by which the Treasury Department sought to overcome and prevent the wide-spread counterfeiting of Fractional Currency notes.

The shields consisted of a type set of the first three issues of Postage and Fractional Currency mounted on a heavy cardboard shield surmounted by an eagle and 13 stars. Size of the framed unit was 24 by 28 inches. The shields were made available to banks and other commercial institutions in 1866-67 to provide them with a file of genuine notes to use as a reference when checking suspect notes. Those qualified to receive the shield paid face value for the notes ($4.66), plus a presumed transportation charge, for a total cost believed to be $7.50.

The 39 closely-trimmed notes (20 faces and 19 backs) mounted on the shield are specimen notes printed on one side only. They include the scarce 15-cent Sherman/Grant essays and the two faces of the 3-cent note, which are distinguished by dark and light backgrounds to Washington's portrait. The shields upon which the notes were pasted are known in gray, pink and green, with gray being the most common.

Although the shields were produced in a quantity believed to be in excess of 4,500, it is presumed that fewer than 200 remain intact, with many of those folded, faded or water-stained. Apparently demand for the shields was less than the Treasury Department had anticipated and the surplus shields were carelessly stored — by common account in an old shed behind the Treasury Building. The number of intact shields was further reduced by early collectors who obtained them solely to secure the scarcer notes, which they removed from the shield.

FOURTH ISSUE
July 14, 1869 - February 16, 1875
Denominations: 10¢, 15¢, 25¢, 50¢

The Fourth Issue of Fractional Currency continued the refinements evident in the Second and Third Issues, and further diminished the pretense of stamp money with which the five issues of fractional notes were launched. The unaesthetic bronze overprintings were eliminated, and an improved type of paper — containing silk fibers — was used.

Three of the six designs (there are three different 50-cent notes) comprising the Fourth Issue make no mention of "stamps." Allegorical art claimed a greater role in note design than before; the 10-cent note bearing a representation of Liberty, and the 15-cent note, a representation of Columbia. The 25-cent and the trio of 50-cent notes bear definitive male portraits.

The Fourth Issue was produced outside the Treasury Department while the BEP experimented with new dry-printing operations that only succeeded in destroying nearly every hydraulic press the Government owned. Combined with increased demand for Legal Tender notes, the Treasury was forced to job out the production of the Fourth Issue Fractionals to the National and American Bank Note Companies.

The total value of the Fourth Issue was more than $166 million.

FIFTH ISSUE
February 26, 1874 - February 15, 1876
Denominations: 10¢, 25¢, 50¢

The Fifth Issue of Fractional Currency was short and simple, consisting of but three notes, each of a different design. Why a change of design was thought necessary at that time is unclear, but the decision may reflect the Treasury Department's continuing disenchantment with the cost of notes produced by the two New York bank note firms.

Faces of the Fifth Issue were printed by the Bureau of Engraving and Printing, the backs by the Columbian Bank Note Company of Washington, D.C., and Joseph R. Carpenter of Philadelphia. Printing of this issue was terminated when the appropriations for the printing of Fractional Currency were exhausted.

Noteworthy varieties of the Fifth Issue include the green seal 10-cent note and the "long key" and "short key" 10-and 25-cent notes. All notes have faces printed in black, with green backs. All carry printed signatures.

Fifth Issue notes were printed to the total value of nearly $63 million, bringing the total value of all Postage and Fractional Currency issued to about $369 million, of which an estimated $1.8 million remains outstanding.

Fractional Currency Valuations

(Editor's Note: With this edition, a number of Fractional Currency listings have been dropped which had appeared in earlier editions of this catalog. These listings include varieties which have never been authenticated, or which Fractional Currency experts now agree to be merely color changes caused by aging of ink or paper.

(The Krause-Lemke numbers of the deleted listings are: 3280, 3330, 3335, 3339 and 3346.)

First Issue "Postage Currency"

5 CENTS

KL#	Date Description	VG	VF	Unc
3209	17.7.1862. Brown. One 5 cent Jefferson stamp at center. Perf. edges; ANBC's monogram on back.	6.50	12.50	120.
3210	Perf. edges; back w/o ANBC's monogram.	8.00	15.00	150.
3211	Straight edges; ABNC's monogram on back.	5.00	7.50	50.00
3212	Straight edges; back w/o ABNC's monogram.	10.00	20.00	175.

10 CENTS

KL#	Date Description	VG	VF	Unc
3213	17.7.1862. Green. One 10 cent Washington stamp at center. Perf. edges; ABNC's monogram on back.	6.50	14.00	140.
3214	Perf. edges; back w/o ABNC's monogram.	6.50	14.00	160.
3215	Straight edges; ABNC's monogram on back.	5.00	7.50	60.00
3216	Straight edges; back w/o ABNC's monogram.	12.00	25.00	200.

25 CENTS

KL#	Date Description	VG	VF	Unc
3217	17.7.1862. Brown. Horizontal row of five 5 cent Jefferson stamps. Perf. edges; ABNC's monogram on back.	10.00	20.00	170.
3218	Perf. edges; back w/o ABNC's monogram.	10.00	25.00	250.
3219	Straight edges; ABNC's monogram on back.	6.50	7.50	70.00
3220	Straight edges; back w/o ABNC's monogram.	13.00	26.00	280.

50 CENTS

KL#	Date Description	VG	VF	Unc
3221	17.7.1862. Green. Horizontal row of five 10 cent Washington stamps. #12 perf. edges; ABNC's monogram on back.	12.50	25.00	225.
3222	#14 perf. edges; ABNC's monogram on back.	—	Rare	—
3223	Perf. edges; back w/o ABNC's monogram.	20.00	40.00	300.
3224	Straight edges; ABNC's monogram on back.	6.50	10.00	100.
3225	Straight edges; back w/o ABNC's monogram.	20.00	30.00	350.

Second Issue

5 CENTS

All notes have oval bronze ovpt. on face around head of Washington at center and bronze number(s) on back.

KL#	Date	Description	VG	VF	Unc
3226	3.3.1863.	W/o ovpt., on back.	6.50	9.00	70.00
3227		W/ovpt: "18-63" on back.	6.50	9.00	70.00
3228		W/ovpt: "18-63" and "S" on back.	10.00	13.50	100.
3229		W/ovpt: "18-63" and "R-1" on back.	10.00	20.00	275.

10 CENTS

KL#	Date	Description	VG	VF	Unc
3230		W/o ovpt. on back.	7.50	10.00	75.00
3231		W/ovpt: "18-63" on back.	7.50	12.00	80.00
3232		W/ovpt: "18-63" and "S" on back.	8.50	15.00	90.00
3233		W/ovpt: "18-63" and "1" on back.	20.00	45.00	275.
3234		W/ovpt: "0-63" on back.	500.	1200.	2000.
3235		W/ovpt: "18-63" and "T-1" on back.	10.00	18.00	220.

25 CENTS

KL#	Date	Description	VG	VF	Unc
3236	3.3.1863.	W/o ovpt. on back.	7.50	10.00	110.
3237		W/ovpt: "18-63" on back.	12.50	15.00	130.
3238		W/ovpt: "18-63" and "A" on back.	12.50	15.00	140.
3239		W/ovpt: "18-63" and "S" on back.	12.50	15.00	120.
3240		W/ovpt: "18-63" and "1" on back.	Reported, not confirmed		
3241		W/ovpt: "18-63" and "2" on back.	15.00	25.00	130.
3242		W/ovpt: "18-63" and "T-1" on back.	9.00	15.00	245.
3243		W/ovpt: "18-63" and "T-2" on back.	9.00	15.00	245.
3244		W/ovpt: "18-63" and "S-2" on back.	Reported, not confirmed		

50 CENTS

KL#	Date	Description	VG	VF	Unc
3245	3.3.1863.	W/ovpt: "18-63" on back.	12.50	20.00	250.
3246		W/ovpt: "18-63" and "A" on back.	10.00	18.00	215.
3247		W/ovpt: "18-63" and "I" on back.	10.00	18.00	215.
3248		W/ovpt: "18-63" and "0-1" on back.	15.00	25.00	225.
3249		W/ovpt: "18-63" and "R-2" on back.	17.50	30.00	250.
3250		W/ovpt: "18-63" and "T-1" on back.	17.00	30.00	225.
3251		W/ovpt: "18-63" and "T" on back.	Reported, not confirmed		

Third Issue

3 CENTS

KL#	Date	Description	VG	VF	Unc
3252	3.3.1863.	Portrait of Washington at center with light background.	10.00	12.50	65.00
3253		Portrait with dark background.	10.00	15.00	135.

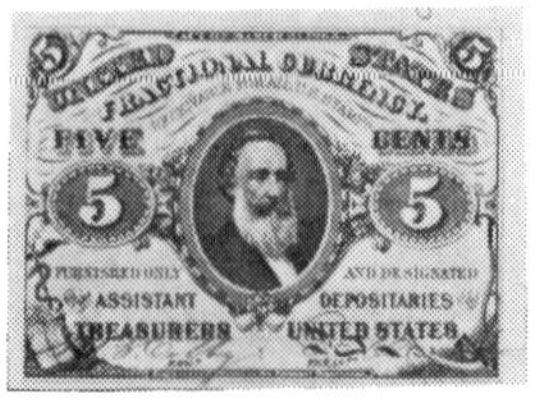

5 CENTS

KL#	Date	Description	VG	VF	Unc
3254	3.3.1863.	Portrait of Clark at center. Red back.	7.50	15.00	140.
3255		With 'a' on face.	9.00	18.00	150.
3256		Green back.	5.00	7.50	70.00
3257		With 'a' on face.	7.00	10.00	80.00

10 CENTS

KL#	Date	Description	VG	VF	Unc
3258	3.3.1863.	Portrait of Washington at center; bronze 10's in each corner. Small sign: Colby-Spinner. Red back.	7.50	13.00	145.
3259		With '1' on face.	9.00	15.00	165.

KL#	Date	Description	VG	VF	Unc
3260		Large autographed sign: Colby-Spinner.	12.00	18.00	200.
3261		Large autographed sign: Jeffries-Spinner.	17.00	22.00	250.
3262		Green back w/printed sign: Colby-Spinner.	5.00	10.00	50.00
3263		Green back. Large autographed sign: Colby-Spinner.	—	Rare	—
3264		With '1" on face.	6.00	12.00	60.00

25 CENTS

KL#	Date	Description	VG	VF	Unc
3265	3.3.1863.	Portrait of Fessenden at center. Red back.	7.50	15.00	150.
3266		Small 'a' on face.	9.00	18.00	170.

KL#	Date Description	VG	VF	Unc
3267	Large 'a' on face.	9.00	18.00	170.
3268	Green back.	6.50	10.00	75.00
3269	Small 'a' on face.	8.00	12.00	80.00
3270	Large 'a' on face.	8.00	12.00	80.00
3271	W/ovpt: "M-2-6-5" on back. (Fiber paper).	10.00	20.00	300.
3272	'a' on face; ovpt: "M-2-6-5" on back. (Fiber paper).	14.00	30.00	325.
3273	Solid bronze ornamental ovpt. on face. (Fiber paper).	250.	450.	1250.
3274	Solid bronze ornamental ovpt. and 'a' on face. (Fiber paper).	400.	800.	2000.

50 CENTS

KL#	Date Description	VG	VF	Unc
3275	3.3.1863. Portrait of General Spinner at center; small sign: Colby-Spinner. W/ovpt: 'A-2-6-5' and 50, red back.	14.00	25.00	265.
3276	With '1' and 'a' on face.	25.00	75.00	500.
3277	With '1' on face.	20.00	50.00	265.
3278	With 'a' on face.	20.00	50.00	275.
3279	Large sign: Colby-Spinner.	15.00	25.00	265.
3281	Sign: Allison-Spinner.	20.00	40.00	375.
3282	Sign: Allison-New.	600.00	1250.	3000.

KL#	Date Description	VG	VF	Unc
3283	Multiple 50's in green back.	15.00	20.00	210.
3284	With '1' and 'a' on face.	22.50	50.00	395.
3285	With '1' on face.	15.00	25.00	195.
3286	With 'a' on face.	17.00	30.00	215.
3287	W/ovpt: 'A-2-6-5' on back.	20.00	40.00	295.
3288	With '1' and 'a' on face.	30.00	160.	1200.
3289	With '1' on face.	20.00	50.00	325.
3290	With 'a' on face.	22.50	80.00	350.

KL#	Date Description	VG	VF	Unc
3291	Face similar to #1324. Redesigned green back.	16.00	25.00	260.
3292	With '1' and 'a' on face.	25.00	50.00	425.
3293	With '1' on face.	18.00	30.00	270.
3294	With 'a' on face.	18.00	35.00	290.

KL#	Date Description	VG	VF	Unc
3295	3.3.1863. Red back. Small sign.	16.00	31.50	365.
3296	With '1' and 'a' on face.	50.00	160.	1500.
3297	With '1' on face.	16.00	45.00	350.

KL#	Date Description	VG	VF	Unc
3298	With 'a' on face.	20.00	50.00	400.
3299	W/ovpt: 'A-2-6-5' on back.	16.00	45.00	300.
3300	With '1' and 'a' on face.	50.00	350.	1500.
3301	With '1' on face.	16.00	50.00	375.
3302	With 'a' on face.	20.00	50.00	400.
3303	With small sign. Ovpt: 'S-2-6-4' on back.	750.	2000.	4000.
3304	With '1' and 'a' on face.	—	Rare	—
3305	With '1' on face.	1000.	2750.	5000.
3306	With 'a' on face.	1250.	3000.	5500.

KL#	Date Description	VG	VF	Unc
3307	Red back. Large autographed sign.	19.00	32.00	395.

KL#	Date Description	VG	VF	Unc
3308	Large autographed sign. w/ovpt: 'A-2-6-5' on back.	21.00	40.00	425.
3309	Large autographed sign. w/ovpt: 'S-2-6-4' on back.	32.50	160.	1400.
3310	Green back.	16.00	30.00	350.
3311	With '1' and 'a' on face.	65.00	150.	850.
3312	With '1' on face.	16.00	30.00	400.
3313	With 'a' on face.	18.00	35.00	420.
3314	W/ovpt: 'A-2-6-5' on back compactly spaced.	18.00	30.00	400.
3315	With '1' and 'a' on face.	35.00	175.	700.
3316	With '1' on face.	18.00	30.00	350.
3317	With 'a' on face.	22.50	40.00	400.
3318	W/ovpt: 'A-2-6-5' on back widely spaced.	22.50	45.00	425.
3319	With '1' and 'a' on face.	90.00	225.	1500.
3321	With 'a' on face.	27.50	60.00	475.
3322	W/ovpt: 'A-2-6-5' on back. Fibre paper.	20.00	40.00	485.
3323	With '1' and 'a' on face. Fibre paper.	50.00	325.	1000.
3324	With '1' on face. Fibre paper.	25.00	45.00	575.
3325	With 'a' on face. Fibre paper.	30.00	60.00	675.
3326	W/ovpt: 'S-2-6-4' on back. Fibre paper.	2000.	3500.	7500.

Fourth Issue

10 CENTS

KL#	Date Description	VG	VF	Unc
3327	3.3.1863. Bust of Liberty at left; 40mm red seal. Wtmkd. paper with pink silk fibres.	4.75	7.50	45.00
3328	Unwtmkd. Paper with pink silk fibres.	4.75	9.00	50.00
3329	Bluish right side of face, paper with violet silk fibres.	4.75	9.00	50.00
3331	38mm red seal; bluish right side of face.	4.75	11.00	50.00

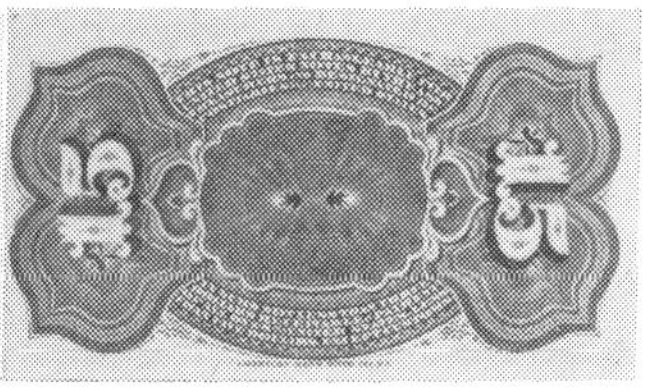

15 CENTS

KL#	Date Description	VG	VF	Unc
3332	3.3.1863. Bust of Columbia at left; 40mm red seal. Wtmk. paper with pink silk fibres.	12.50	16.50	145.
3333	Unwtmkd. paper with pink silk fibres.	12.50	18.00	150.
3334	Bluish right side of face. Paper with violet silk fibres.	15.00	20.00	165.
3336	38mm red seal; bluish right side of face.	12.50	18.00	150.

25 CENTS

KL#	Date	Description	VG	VF	Unc
3337	3.3.1863.	Portrait of Washington at left; 40mm red seal. Wtmkd. paper with pink silk fibres.	6.50	9.00	75.00
3338		Unwtmkd. paper with pink silk fibres.	6.50	9.00	80.00
3340		Bluish right side of face. Paper with violet silk fibres.	6.50	9.00	80.00
3342		38mm red seal; bluish right side of face.	6.50	9.00	80.00

50 CENTS

KL#	Date	Description	VG	VF	Unc
3343	3.3.1863.	Portrait of Lincoln at right. Wtmkd. paper with silk fibres.	17.50	25.00	200.
3344		Unwtmkd. paper with pink silk fibres.	17.50	25.00	200.

KL#	Date	Description	VG	VF	Unc
3345	3.3.1863.	Portrait of Stanton at left; red seal.	12.00	15.00	125.

KL#	Date	Description	VG	VF	Unc
3347	3.3.1863.	Portrait of Dexter at left; green seal.	9.00	12.50	100.

Fifth Issue, Series of 1874/1875 SHIELD VARIETIES

Long thin solid key

Short thick outlined key

10 CENTS

KL#	Date	Description	VG	VF	Unc
3348	1874.	Portrait of Meredith at left. Green seal with long key.	5.00	7.50	65.00
3349		Red seal with long key.	4.75	6.50	30.00
3350		Red seal with short key.	4.75	6.50	30.00

25 CENTS

KL#	Date	Description	VG	VF	Unc
3351	1874.	Portrait of Walker at left. Red seal with long key.	4.75	6.50	35.00
3352		Red seal with short key.	4.75	6.50	35.00

50 CENTS

KL#	Date	Description	VG	VF	Unc
3353		Portrait of Crawford at left, pink paper.	7.00	9.00	50.00
3357		Portrait of Crawford at left, white paper.	7.00	9.00	50.00

Proofs and Specimens

All examples are printed uniface with wide or narrow margins. Some notes have 'SPECIMEN' printed in bronze on the blank side. Specimens and proofs of the 4th and 5th issues are extremely rare.

KL#	Denomination	Description	VG	VF	Unc
3252SP	**3 CENTS**	Third Issue			
	a. Face with narrow margins, light background.		—	—	95.00
	b. Face with wide margins, light background.		—	Rare	—
	c. Back with narrow margins.		—	—	60.00
	d. Back with wide margins.		—	—	120.
3253SP	**3 CENTS**				
	a. Face with narrow margins, dark background.		—	—	60.00
	b. Face with wide margins, dark background.		—	—	130.
	c. Back with narrow margins.		—	—	60.00
	d. Back with wide margins.		—	—	120.
3212SP	**5 CENTS**	First Issue			
	a. Face with narrow margins.		—	—	55.00
	b. Face with wide margins.		—	—	150.
	c. Back with narrow margins.		—	—	50.00
	d. Back with wide margins.		—	—	140.
3226SP	**5 CENTS**	Second Issue			
	a. Face with narrow margins.		—	—	70.00
	b. Face with wide margins.		—	—	150.
	c. Back with narrow margins.		—	—	55.00
	d. Back with wide margins.		—	—	125.

KL#	Denomination	Description	VG	VF	Unc
3254SP	**5 CENTS**	Third Issue.			
	a. Face with narrow margins.		—	—	55.00
	b. Face with wide margins.		—	—	130.
	c. Red back with narrow margins.		—	—	50.00
	d. Red back with wide margins.		—	—	115.
3256SP	**5 CENTS**				
	a. Face with narrow margins.		—	—	55.00
	b. Face with wide margins.		—	—	130.
	c. Green back with narrow margins.		—	—	50.00
	d. Green back with wide margins.		—	—	115.
3216SP	**10 CENTS**	First issue.			
	a. Face with narrow margins.		—	—	50.00
	b. Face with wide margins.		—	—	145.
	c. Back with narrow margins.		—	—	45.00
	d. Back with wide margins.		—	—	125.
3230SP	**10 CENTS**	Second issue.			
	a. Face with narrow margins.		—	—	75.00
	b. Face with wide margins.		—	—	150.
	c. Back with narrow margins.		—	—	65.00
	d. Back with wide margins.		—	—	125.
3258SP	**10 CENTS**	Third issue, small sign: Colby-Spinner.			
	a. Face with narrow margins.		—	—	55.00
	b. Face with wide margins.		—	—	140.
	c. Red back with narrow margins.		—	—	50.00
	d. Red back with wide margins.		—	—	140.
3260SP	**10 CENTS**	Large sign: Colby-Spinner.			
	a. Face with narrow margins.		—	—	75.00
	b. Face with wide margins.		—	—	175.
	c. Red back with narrow margins.		—	—	50.00
	d. Red back with wide margins.		—	—	140.
3261SP	**10 CENTS**	Sign: Jeffries-Spinner.			
	a. Face with narrow margins.		—	—	155.
	b. Face with wide margins.		—	—	1000.
	c. Red back with narrow margins.		—	—	50.00
	d. Red back with wide margins.		—	—	140.
3262SP	**10 CENTS**				
	a. Face with narrow margins.		—	—	155.
	b. Face with wide margins.		—	—	140.
	c. Green back with narrow margins.		—	—	50.00
	d. Green back with wide margins.		—	—	140.
3453SP	**15 CENTS**	Portraits of Grant at right and Sherman at left; small sign: Colby-Spinner.			
	a. Face with narrow margins.		—	—	190.
	b. Face with wide margins.		—	—	350.
	c. Green back with narrow margins.		—	—	150.
	d. Green back with wide margins.		—	—	210.
3454SP	**15 CENTS**	Large sign: Colby-Spinner.			
	a. Face with narrow margins.		—	—	1100.
	b. Face with wide margins.		—	Rare	—
	c. Red back with narrow margins.		—	—	150.
	d. Red back with wide margins.		—	—	210.
3455SP	**15 CENTS**	Sign: Jeffries-Spinner.			
	a. Face with narrow margins.		—	—	220.
	b. Face with wide margins.		—	—	350.
	c. Red back with narrow margins.		—	—	150.
	d. Red back with wide margins.		—	—	210.
3456SP	**15 CENTS**	Sign: Allison-Spinner.			
	a. Face with narrow margins.		—	—	250.
	b. Face with wide margins.		—	—	400.
	c. Red back with narrow margins.		—	—	150.
	d. Red back with wide margins.		—	—	210.
3457SP	**15 CENTS**	W/o any signatures.			
	a. Face with narrow margins.		—	Rare	—
	b. Face with wide margins.		—	Rare	—
	c. Red back with narrow margins		—	—	150.
	d. Red back with wide margins.		—	—	210.
3220SP	**25 CENTS**	First issue.			
	a. Face with narrow margins.		—	—	80.00
	b. Face with wide margins.		—	—	175.
	c. Back with narrow margins.		—	—	70.00
	d. Back with wide margins.			—	165.
3236SP	**25 CENTS**	Second issue.			
	a. Face with narrow margins.		—	—	75.00
	b. Face with wide margins.		—	—	195.
	c. Back with narrow margins.		—	—	65.00
	d. Back with wide margins.		—	—	180.
3265SP	**25 CENTS**	Third issue.			
	a. Face with narrow margins.		—	—	60.00
	b. Face with wide margins.		—	—	165.
	c. Red back with narrow margins.		—	—	55.00
	d. Red back with wide margins.		—	—	150.
3268SP	**25 CENTS**				
	a. Face with narrow margins.		—	—	60.00
	b. Face with wide margins.		—	—	165.
	c. Green back with narrow margins.		—	—	55.00
	d. Green back with wide margins.		—	—	155.
3225SP	**50 CENTS**	First issue.			
	a. Face with narrow margins.		—	—	90.00
	b. Face with wide margins.		—	—	220.
	c. Back with narrow margins.		—	—	80.00
	d. Back with wide margins.		—	—	200.
3245SP	**50 CENTS**	Second issue, no surcharge.			
	a. Face with narrow margins.		—	—	80.00
	b. Face with wide margins.		—	—	265.
	c. Back with narrow margins.		—	—	70.00
	d. Back with wide margins.		—	—	200.
3275SP	**50 CENTS**	Third issue, small sign: Colby-Spinner.			
	a. Face with narrow margins.		—	—	85.00
	b. Face with wide margins.		—	—	180.
	c. Red back with narrow margins.		—	—	75.00
	d. Red back with wide margins.		—	—	180.

KL#	Denomination	Description	VG	VF	Unc
3279SP	**50 CENTS**	Large sign: Colby-Spinner.			
	a. Face with narrow margins.		—	—	110.
	b. Face with wide margins.		—	—	250.
	c. Red back with narrow margins.		—	—	75.00
	d. Red back with wide margins.		—	—	180.
3281SP	**50 CENTS**	Sign: Allison-Spinner.			
	a. Face with narrow margins.		—	Rare	—
	b. Face with wide margins.		—	Rare	—
	c. Red back with narrow margins.		—	—	75.00
	d. Red back with wide margins.		—	—	150.
3282SP	**50 CENTS**	Sign: Jeffries-Spinner.			
	a. Face with narrow margins.		—	—	150.
	b. Face with wide margins.		—	—	3000.
	c. Red back with narrow margins.		—	—	75.00
	d. Red back with wide margins.		—	—	180.
3283SP	**50 CENTS**	Small sign: Colby-Spinner.			
	a. Face with narrow margins.		—	—	85.00
	b. Face with wide margins.		—	—	180.
	c. Green back with narrow margins.		—	—	75.00
	d. Green back with wide margins.		—	—	185.
3291SP	**50 CENTS**	Small sign: Colby-Spinner.			
	a. Face with narrow margins.		—	—	85.00
	b. Face with wide margins.		—	—	180.
	c. Green back with narrow margins.		—	—	1750.
	d. Green back with wide margins.		—	—	5000.
3295SP	**50 CENTS**	Small sign: Colby-Spinner.			
	a. Face with narrow margins.		—	—	85.00
	b. Face with wide margins.		—	—	220.
	c. Red back with narrow margins.		—	—	75.00
	d. Red back with wide margins.		—	—	180.
3307SP	**50 CENTS**	Large sign: Colby-Spinner.			
	a. Face with narrow margins.		—	—	110.
	b. Face with wide margins.		—	—	250.
	c. Red back with narrow margins.		—	—	75.00
	d. Red back with wide margins.		—	—	180.
3309SP	**50 CENTS**	Sign: Jeffries-Spinner.			
	a. Face with narrow margins.		—	—	150.
	b. Face with wide margins.		—	Rare	—
	c. Red back with narrow margins.		—	—	75.00
	d. Red back with wide margins.		—	—	180.
3310SP	**50 CENTS**	Small sign: Colby-Spinner.			
	a. Face with narrow margins.		—	—	85.00
	b. Face with wide margins.		—	—	220.
	c. Green back with narrow margins.		—	—	75.00
	d. Green back with wide margins.		—	—	185.

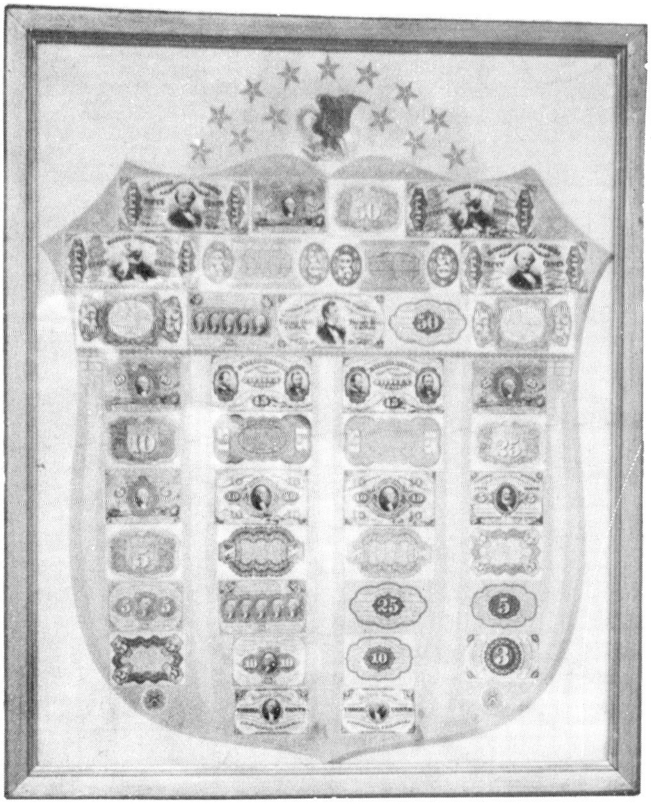

Currency Shields

Produced by the Treasury Dept. in 1866-67 for sale to banks to aid in detection of counterfeit notes. These shields consist of 39 specimens of the first, second and third issues. Mounted in a picture frame.

KL#	Date	Description	VG	VF	Unc
3354		Gray background.	—	—	2750.
3355		Pink background.	—	—	6000.
3356		Green background.	—	Rare	—

Encased Postage Stamps

By Len Glazer

Encased postage has always been among the most elusive of American numismatic items to collect, and consequently, among the most rewarding. With their natural appeal to numismatists, philatelists, and collectors of antique advertising media, demand has also been strong. This competition for scarce items, especially so in high grades of preservation, has meant a steady upward price progression that also makes Encased Postage Stamps desirable from an investment viewpoint.

While a complete set — by denomination, merchant and major variety — of Encased Postage has never been formed and likely never will be, it is entirely within the grasp of the determined numismatist to assemble a collection that is "complete" within self-set boundries; that is, be denomination, by merchant, by type of merchant (medicinal, dry goods, etc.), by locality of issue, or by any other criteria.

(Encased Postage Stamp photographs in this section are provided through the courtesy of Kagin's.)

While not generally collected along with the Gault encased postage stamps, the so-called Feuchtwanger rectangular encasement is a contemporary, though unsuccessful, competitor.

Approximately 31x61mm, with a brass frame and no mica cover for the stamps, this item is generally found with a trio of 3-cent postage stamps; a face value of nine cents. The item is also found with other quantities of 3-cent stamps, though the originality of these other denominations is questionable.

Naturally, since the stamps are easily replaced, their condition has little bearing on the value.

KL#	VF
EPS300	395.00

Grading

Three factors must be considered in the grading of Encased Postage Stamps: the case itself, the enclosed stamp and the protective mica.

For the listings which follow, generally accepted standards for coin grading have been used to grade the cases. The accepted standards for grading unused U.S. postage stamps have been considered for that element. For the mica, terminology is that which has been in use since the collecting of Encased Postage Stamps began.

In referring to the price listing that follows, it should be made clear that unlike coins or stamps, which are bought and sold on the basis of generally accepted grading standards, Encased Postage Stamps are sold on the individual merits of the piece involved. This is the result of the many and varied states of preservation of each of the three main elements — case, stamp and mica — of these items.

The valuations quoted refer basically to the condition of the case. If the condition of the stamp and mica are consistent in their own way with that of the case, the valuations can be considered accurate at the time of this catalog's issue. If, however, either the stamp or the mica is significantly better or worse than the case, the value of the item as a whole may be more or less than the figure quoted.

Assume, for example, that a piece with a VF case holds a stamp that is Extremely Fine, protected by a piece of mica which is crazed (see mica grading). The stamp is obviously better than the case, and the crazed mica is also quite nice, though not perfect. The value of such a piece is definitely higher than the quoted VF price, and may be closer to the XF valuation.

Grading of Case

NEW — A condition unknown among Encased Postage Stamps. While there do, indeed, exist specimens which show no wear traces of circulation on the case, the condition of the stamp and/or mica will always contain some imperfection which prevents the accurate description of any Encased Postage Stamp as "New."

ABOUT NEW — The highest grade in which Encased Postage can practically be collected. Just a touch of rubbing on the case, which may or may not still retain some original silvering, if so issued.

EXTREMELY FINE — Higher than average grade, with a bit of noticeable wear on the case; still a very nice piece.

VERY FINE — The average grade for collectible Encased Postage Stamps. The case shows definite wear, but little or no flatness of the embossed lettering. Most catalog values are based on this grade.

FINE — A worn, but acceptable, piece. Generally the lowest undamaged or collectible grade of untampered Encased Postage, since the items did not circulate long enough to attain any greater degree of wear.

Grading of Stamp

In their usage with Encased Postage, stamps are generally described in one of the following degrees of brightness. Since the paper was protected by the mica, the only measurement of the state of preservation of the stamp can be the degree to which it was subjected to the fading effects of sunlight or other causes.

FULLY BRIGHT — A stamp that is 100% as vivid as the day it was issued.

NEAR FULL BRIGHT — Perhaps a spot or two of less than perfect brightness.

BRIGHT — A stamp which has lost some of its original color, but is still sharp and always acceptable.

TONED — A stamp which has darkened with age or exposure to light and other elements.

DULL or FADED — A stamp which has lost much of its color; the lowest generally collectable condition for an undamaged item.

Grading of Mica

Because it is a natural silicate mineral, mica of flawless, perfect quality probably does not exist in connection with its use in Encased Postage Stamps. Collectors are warned that only "perfect" mica generally encountered is acetate which has been used to repair a damaged Encased Postage Stamp. Upon close examination, some flaw can be found on virtually every mica piece used in this manner.

NEARLY PERFECT — The highest degree of preservation for a mica encasement.

CRAZED — Fine cracks in the surface on the surface, or between the thin natural layers of mica. Separation beginning in its early stages. None of the crazing fully breaks the mica, exposing the stamp.

CRACKED — A break in the mica through to the stamp, but with no piece of the mica missing.

CHIPPED — A breaking of only the upper layer or layers of mica, with the chip or chips missing, though the mica beneath remains intact and the stamp protected.

BROKEN — A break in all layers of the mica, with some missing and the stamp exposed. The degree of broken or missing mica should be described.

Other Terms

Two other terms which the collector of Encased Postage will encounter also bear definition.

RIBBED FRAME — Some varieties of Encased Postage are known with cases which have fine parallel lines on the face (stamp side) of the metal case.

SILVERING — Many Encased Postage Stamps were issued with a thin silver wash on the case, to enhance their resemblance to the disappearing silver coinage of the day. More research is needed to determine which issues came with silvering, which came without and which, if any, were issued both ways. Since the silver wore off very quickly, even many high grade pieces have no traces of the original finish. A piece with a high percentage of silvering remaining is worth a premium, but those with just a trace of silver are not; though it is generally mentioned when describing an item for sale.

Rarity Ratings

When dealing with the relative rarity of Encased Postage Stamps, the collector must realize that all are scarce in terms of numismatic collectibles. Even the most common variety "Take Ayer's Pills" may not be easy to locate on the market at any given time.

Following years of study of major collections and auction offerings, and conversations with other specialists, the following table of rarity lists each piece in what we believe to be its correct order, and broken into six categories of rarity. While there may be some disagreement as to order within category, we believe most knowledgeable specialists will agree with the listing.

VERY RARE
1. Arthur M. Claflin
2. B. F. Miles
3. John W. Norris
4. Pearce, Tolle & Holton

RARE
5. White the Hatter
6. Sands' Ale
7. S. Steinfeld
8. Dougan
9. N.G. Taylor & Co.
10. Ellis McAlpin & Co.
11. L.C. Hopkins & Co.
12. Aerated Bread

VERY SCARCE
13. F. Buhl & Co.
14. Weir & Larminie
15. Lord & Taylor
16. H.A. Cook
17. Bailey & Co.

SCARCE
18. Schapker & Bussing
19. G.G. Evans
20. John Shillito & Co.
21. Mendum's Wine Emporium
22. North America Life Insurance Co.

COMMON
23. Tremont House
24. Joseph L. Bates
25. Kirkpatrick & Gault
26. Irving House
27. Brown's Bronchial Troches
28. Burnett's Cocoaine
29. J. Gault
30. Burnett's Cooking Extracts
31. Drake's Plantation Bitters

MOST COMMON
32. Take Ayer's Pills
33. Ayer's Cathartic Pills
34. Ayer's Sarsaparilla

Aerated Bread Co., New York

KL#	Denom.	Fine	VF	XF
EPS1	1¢	800.00	1250.	1750.

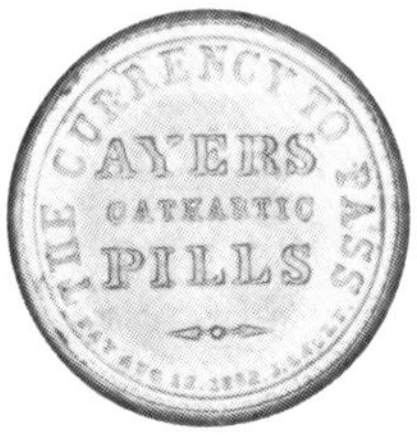

Ayer's Cathartic Pills (Long arrows variety)

KL#	Denom.	Fine	VF	XF
EPS2	3¢	100.00	175.00	250.00
EPS3	5¢	125.00	275.00	350.00
EPS4	10¢	250.00	500.00	650.00

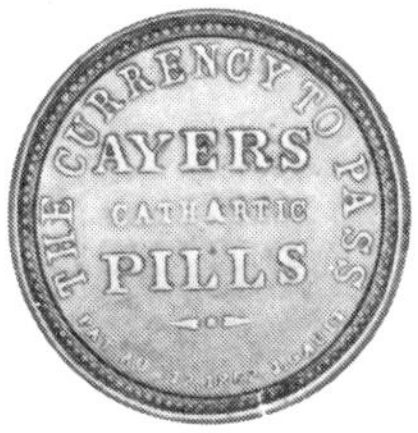

(Short arrows variety)

KL#	Denom.	Fine	VF	XF
EPS5	1¢	150.00	225.00	300.00
EPS6	3¢	100.00	175.00	250.00
EPS7	5¢	125.00	275.00	350.00
EPS8	10¢	200.00	350.00	500.00
EPS9	12¢	300.00	550.00	1000.
EPS10	24¢	1200.	2000.	3000.
EPS11	30¢	1500.	3000.	4000.

Take Ayer's Pills

KL#	Denom.	Fine	VF	XF
EPS12	1¢	150.00	250.00	325.00
EPS13	3¢	100.00	150.00	225.00
EPS14	5¢	125.00	250.00	350.00
EPS15	10¢	175.00	375.00	500.00
EPS16	12¢	300.00	550.00	1000.
EPS17	90¢	2500.	5000.	9000.

Ayer's Sarsaparilla (Small Ayer's)

KL#	Denom.	Fine	VF	XF
EPS18	1¢	600.00	1250.	1850.
EPS19	3¢	350.00	550.00	750.00
EPS20	10¢	600.00	1250.	1850.
EPS21	12¢	700.00	1400.	2000.

(Medium Ayer's)

KL#	Denom.	Fine	VF	XF
EPS22	1¢	150.00	225.00	300.00
EPS23	3¢	100.00	175.00	225.00
EPS24	5¢	150.00	225.00	300.00
EPS25	10¢	175.00	300.00	450.00
EPS26	12¢	300.00	550.00	1000.
EPS27	24¢	1200.	2000.	3000.
EPS28	30¢	1500.	3000.	4000.
EPS29	90¢	2500.	5000.	9000.

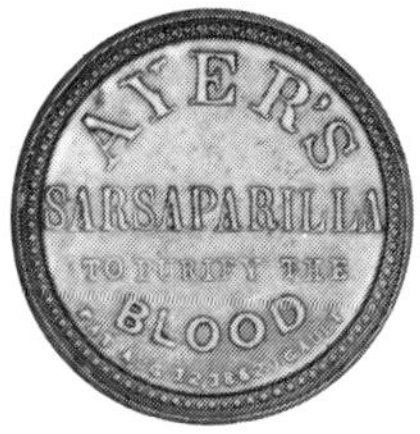

(Large Ayer's)

KL#	Denom.	Fine	VF	XF
EPS30	3¢	275.00	400.00	750.00
EPS31	10¢	450.00	700.00	1000.

Bailey & Co., Philadelphia

KL#	Denom.	Fine	VF	XF
EPS32	1¢	375.00	550.00	1000.
EPS33	3¢	375.00	550.00	1000.
EPS34	5¢	375.00	550.00	1000.
EPS35	10¢	400.00	600.00	1250.
EPS36	12¢	1000.	1500.	2500.

Joseph L. Bates "Fancy Goods," Boston
Fancygoods One Word

KL#	Denom.	Fine	VF	XF
EPS41	1¢	150.00	225.00	300.00
EPS42	3¢	300.00	450.00	650.00
EPS43	10¢	200.00	375.00	600.00

Joseph L. Bates Fancy Goods Two Words

KL#	Denom.	Fine	VF	XF
EPS37	1¢	150.00	225.00	300.00
EPS38	3¢	200.00	375.00	550.00
EPS39	10¢	200.00	375.00	600.00
EPS40	12¢	300.00	550.00	1000.

Brown's Bronchial Troches

KL#	Denom.	Fine	VF	XF
EPS44	1¢	225.00	375.00	550.00
EPS45	3¢	175.00	300.00	400.00
EPS46	5¢	175.00	300.00	400.00
EPS47	10¢	250.00	375.00	500.00
EPS48	12¢	600.00	1000.	1400.

F. Buhl & Co., Detroit

KL#	Denom.	Fine	VF	XF
EPS49	1¢	400.00	650.00	1100.
EPS50	3¢	400.00	700.00	1250.
EPS51	5¢	400.00	650.00	1100.
EPS52	10¢	450.00	700.00	1250.
EPS53	12¢	750.00	1500.	2000.

Burnett's Cocoaine Kalliston

KL#	Denom.	Fine	VF	XF
EPS54	1¢	150.00	250.00	375.00
EPS55	3¢	125.00	175.00	275.00
EPS56	5¢	150.00	300.00	425.00
EPS57	10¢	200.00	400.00	550.00
EPS58	12¢	300.00	550.00	1000.
EPS59	24¢	1500.	2000.	3000.
EPS60	30¢	1750.	3000.	4000.
EPS61	90¢	2500.	5000.	9000.

Burnett's Cooking Extracts

(Plain frame)

KL#	Denom.	Fine	VF	XF
EPS62	1¢	150.00	250.00	375.00
EPS63	3¢	125.00	225.00	325.00
EPS64	5¢	150.00	250.00	375.00
EPS65	10¢	200.00	375.00	550.00
EPS66	12¢	300.00	550.00	1000.
EPS67	24¢	1500.	2000.	3000.
EPS68	30¢	1750.	3000.	4000.
EPS69	90¢	2500.	5000.	9000.

(Ribbed frame)

KL#	Denom.	Fine	VF	XF
EPS70	10¢	350.00	650.00	800.00

A.M. Claflin, Hopkinton, R.I.

KL#	Denom.	Fine	VF	XF
EPS71	1¢	3000.	4000.	6000.
EPS72	3¢	3000.	4000.	6000.
EPS73	5¢	3000.	4000.	6000.
EPS74	12¢	3000.	5000.	7500.

H.A. Cook, Evansville, Ind.

KL#	Denom.	Fine	VF	XF
EPS75	5¢	350.00	650.00	1300.
EPS76	10¢	300.00	600.00	1250.

Dougan, New York

KL#	Denom.	Fine	VF	XF
EPS77	1¢	800.00	1500.	2500.
EPS78	3¢	800.00	1500.	2500.
EPS79	5¢	800.00	1500.	2500.
EPS80	10¢	1000.	2000.	3000.

Drake's Plantation Bitters, New York

KL#	Denom.	Fine	VF	XF
EPS81	1¢	175.00	225.00	300.00
EPS82	3¢	125.00	200.00	275.00
EPS83	5¢	200.00	300.00	400.00
EPS84	10¢	225.00	375.00	550.00
EPS85	12¢	300.00	550.00	1000.
EPS86	24¢	1500.	2500.	3000.
EPS87	30¢	2000.	3000.	4000.
EPS88	90¢	2750.	5500.	9000.

Ellis, McAlpin & Co., Cincinnati

KL#	Denom.	Fine	VF	XF
EPS89	1¢	600.00	1250.	1850.
EPS90	3¢	600.00	1250.	1750.
EPS91	5¢	600.00	1250.	1750.
EPS92	10¢	600.00	1250.	1750.
EPS93	12¢	800.00	1500.	2250.
EPS94	24¢	1200.	2000.	3000.

G.G. Evans, Philadelphia

KL#	Denom.	Fine	VF	XF
EPS95	1¢	400.00	700.00	1000.
EPS96	3¢	400.00	700.00	1000.
EPS97	5¢	450.00	750.00	1250.
EPS98	10¢	450.00	750.00	1250.

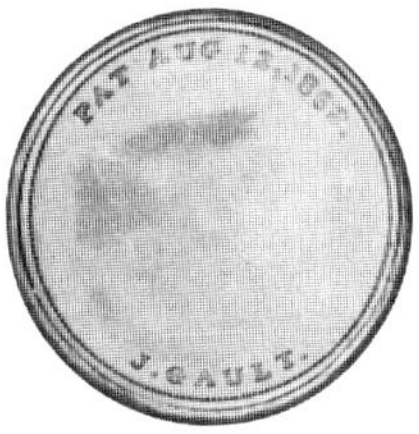

J. Gault

(Plain frame)

KL#	Denom.	Fine	VF	XF
EPS99	1¢	150.00	225.00	300.00
EPS100	2¢	—	12,000.	—
		(Three known)		
EPS101	3¢	150.00	250.00	350.00
EPS102	5¢	150.00	250.00	375.00
EPS103	10¢	200.00	300.00	500.00
EPS104	12¢	300.00	550.00	1000.
EPS105	24¢	1250.	2000.	3000.
EPS106	30¢	1500.	3000.	4000.
EPS107	90¢	2500.	5000.	9000.

(Ribbed frame)

KL#	Denom.	Fine	VF	XF
EPS108	1¢	400.00	700.00	1000.
EPS109	3¢	400.00	700.00	1000.
EPS110	5¢	275.00	450.00	600.00
EPS111	10¢	300.00	550.00	700.00
EPS112	12¢	500.00	800.00	1500.
EPS113	24¢	1500.	2750.	3500.
EPS114	30¢	1750.	3000.	4000.

L. C. Hopkins & Co., Cincinnati

KL#	Denom.	Fine	VF	XF
EPS115	1¢	700.00	1250.	1750.
EPS116	3¢	700.00	1250.	1750.
EPS117	5¢	800.00	1500.	2250.
EPS118	10¢	700.00	1250.	1750.

Irving House, N.Y. (Hunt & Nash)

(Plain frame)

KL#	Denom.	Fine	VF	XF
EPS119	1¢	150.00	250.00	350.00
EPS120	3¢	150.00	250.00	350.00
EPS121	5¢	400.00	700.00	1000.
EPS122	10¢	200.00	300.00	450.00
EPS123	12¢	300.00	550.00	1000.
EPS124	24¢	1250	2000.	3000.
EPS125	30¢	1500.	3000.	4000.

(Ribbed frame)

KL#	Denom.	Fine	VF	XF
EPS126	1¢	400.00	700.00	1000.
EPS127	3¢	400.00	700.00	1000.
EPS128	5¢	250.00	425.00	550.00
EPS129	10¢	350.00	550.00	750.00
EPS130	12¢	500.00	800.00	1500.
EPS131	24¢	1500.	2750.	3500.

Kirkpatrick & Gault, New York

KL#	Denom.	Fine	VF	XF
EPS132	1¢	150.00	225.00	300.00
EPS133	3¢	125.00	200.00	275.00
EPS134	5¢	175.00	300.00	400.00
EPS135	10¢	200.00	300.00	500.00
EPS136	12¢	300.00	550.00	1000.
EPS137	24¢	1250.	2000.	3000.
EPS138	30¢	1500.	3000.	4000.
EPS139	90¢	2500.	5000.	9000.

Lord & Taylor, New York

KL#	Denom.	Fine	VF	XF
EPS140	1¢	400.00	650.00	1250.
EPS141	3¢	400.00	650.00	1250.
EPS142	5¢	400.00	650.00	1250.
EPS143	10¢	400.00	700.00	1500.
EPS144	12¢	800.00	1500.	2000.
EPS145	24¢	1500.	2500.	3500.
EPS146	30¢	2000.	4000.	5000.
EPS147	90¢	4000.	7500.	9000.

Mendum's Family Wine Emporium, New York

(Plain frame)

KL#	Denom.	Fine	VF	XF
EPS148	1¢	250.00	350.00	500.00
EPS149	3¢	350.00	500.00	800.00
EPS150	5¢	300.00	450.00	600.00
EPS151	10¢	300.00	450.00	700.00
EPS152	12¢	650.00	1250.	1750.

(Ribbed frame)

KL#	Denom.	Fine	VF	XF
EPS153	10¢	400.00	700.00	1000.

B. F. Miles, Peoria

KL#	Denom.	Fine	VF	XF
EPS154	5¢	1500.	2500.	4500.

John W. Norris, Chicago

KL#	Denom.	Fine	VF	XF
EPS155	1¢	1000.	1750.	3000.
EPS156	3¢	1000.	1750.	3000.
EPS157	5¢	1000.	1750.	3000.
EPS158	10¢	1000.	1750.	3000.

North America Life Insurance Co., New York

(Straight "Insurance")

KL#	Denom.	Fine	VF	XF
EPS159	1¢	175.00	250.00	350.00
EPS160	3¢	175.00	250.00	350.00
EPS161	10¢	200.00	375.00	600.00
EPS162	12¢	450.00	1000.	1500.

(Curved "Insurance")

(Trial Piece)

KL#	Denom.	Fine	VF	XF
EPS163	1¢	175.00	250.00	350.00
EPS164	10¢	300.00	500.00	750.00

Pearce, Tolle & Holton, Cincinnati

KL#	Denom.	Fine	VF	XF
EPS165	1¢	1000.	1750.	3000.
EPS166	3¢	1000.	1750.	3000.
EPS167	5¢	1000.	1750.	3000.
EPS168	10¢	1100.	2000.	3500.

Sands' Ale

KL#	Denom.	Fine	VF	XF
EPS169	5¢	800.00	1500.	2500.
EPS170	10¢	1000.	1750.	2750.
EPS171	30¢	2000.	3500.	5000.

Schapker & Bussing, Evansville, Ind.

KL#	Denom.	Fine	VF	XF
EPS172	1¢	400.00	700.00	1000.
EPS173	3¢	225.00	350.00	600.00
EPS174	5¢	450.00	750.00	1250.
EPS175	10¢	450.00	750.00	1250.
EPS176	12¢	500.00	1250.	1750.

John Shillito & Co., Cincinnati

KL#	Denom.	Fine	VF	XF
EPS177	1¢	400.00	700.00	1000.
EPS178	3¢	250.00	350.00	600.00
EPS179	5¢	250.00	350.00	600.00
EPS180	10¢	275.00	425.00	750.00
EPS181	12¢	500.00	1250.	1750.

S. Steinfeld, New York

KL#	Denom.	Fine	VF	XF
EPS182	1¢	1000.	1600.	2500.
EPS183	10¢	1000.	1600.	2500.
EPS184	12¢	1000.	1750.	2750.

N. G. Taylor & Co., Philadelphia

KL#	Denom.	Fine	VF	XF
EPS185	1¢	800.00	1250.	1750.
EPS186	3¢	800.00	1250.	1750.
EPS187	5¢	800.00	1500.	2000.
EPS188	10¢	800.00	1250.	1750.

Tremont House (Gage Brothers & Drake), Chicago

KL#	Denom.	Fine	VF	XF
EPS189	1¢	150.00	225.00	300.00
EPS190	5¢	150.00	300.00	375.00
EPS191	10¢	200.00	325.00	450.00
EPS192	12¢	350.00	600.00	1250.

Weir & Larminie, Montreal

KL#	Denom.	Fine	VF	XF
EPS193	1¢	450.00	750.00	1250.
EPS194	3¢	400.00	700.00	1000.
EPS195	5¢	500.00	800.00	1500.
EPS196	10¢	400.00	600.00	1000.

White the Hatter, New York

KL#	Denom.	Fine	VF	XF
EPS197	1¢	800.00	1500.	2500.
EPS198	3¢	800.00	1500.	2500.
EPS199	5¢	900.00	1750.	3000.
EPS200	10¢	800.00	1500.	2500.

Postage Stamp Envelopes

By R.B. White

The introduction to these pages gives the background of the financial times preceeding the introduction of Fractional Currency. In mid-1862 hard money was fast disappearing from circulation and postage stamps were pressed into service as a means of making small change.

The Postmaster General in his December report of 1862 said: "In the first quarter of the current year, ending September 20th, the number of stamps issued to postmasters was one hundred and four million dollars; there were calls for about two hundred millions, which would have been nearly sufficient to meet the usual demands for the year. This extraordinary demand arose from the temporary use of these stamps as a currency for the public in lieu of the smaller denominations of specie, and ceased with the introduction of the so-called 'postal currency.'"

But stamps were ill-suited for the wear and tear of commerce and at least in the early part of this period, the post office refused to exchange them for new issues. Before Gault produced his "encased postage" or the die-sinkers had produced their "copperheads" (more commonly now known as Civil War Tokens), a few enterprising printers produced small envelops, usually about 30 x 60 mm, labeled with the value of the stamps contained and usually with an advertising message either for themselves or for some local merchant. This was mainly confined to the larger cities of the east. New York City had by far the most pieces, but Brooklyn, Albany, Cincinnati and Jersey City are also represented. A few were reported to have circulated in Philadelphia, but this has not yet been confirmed.

The New York Central Railroad issued a slightly different version. The only example seen being a piece of stiff card with two slots by which the stamp or stamps are captured.

Some of these envelopes have the denomination altered, one being reported that was raised from 75¢ to 90¢. Other envelopes were left blank and the value of the stamps enclosed written in by hand.

The issues of J. Leach, stationer and printer in New York City, are by far the most common. They have been seen in three distinct types with multiple denominations within the types. In an article in *The Numismatist,* May, 1920. Henry R. Drowne made the first listing of these pieces. He reported that Leach had issued some 25 varieties.

Drowne also reported that these pieces "were variously printed with black, blue, red and green ink on white, amber, lemon, pink, orange, violet, blue, pale green, buff, manilla and brown paper." Red and blue ink on white paper was the most popular combination. Wood cuts and electrotypes were employed in the manufacture. One single piece bears a picture, of Washington. All of the envelopes show evidence of having been hastily made and printed.

In the listings which follow, spaces have been left in the numbering system to accomodate future finds. No claim is made that the list is complete. Most of the pieces listed by Drowne have not been seen. His cursory listings did not give details of values or types. Where Drowne listed "two types" and one or both have not been seen, two numbers have been assigned and notation made.

These pieces are all extremely rare. The most common probably having no more than half a dozen existent pieces. The pricing thus reflects the rarity of the firm name and the desirability of the legend and value. Drowne reported that the 25¢ denomination is "by far the most common, about half as many are for 50¢, and a quarter for 10¢ and 75¢." All prices are for the envelope only; stamps may be included but there is really no way of knowing that they are original with the envelopes. Any stamps will increase the total value by their own philatelic value. A total of 93 different numbers are listed here; it is doubtful that 500 pieces total of all types still exist.

In the numbering system, a first number is assigned for each firm name or known type within that firm. The second number of the system is the stated value of the envelope in cents; "hc" following the second number means the value was hand changed to this new value, in such cases the "hc" is followed by another number which was the original value of the envelope.

POSTAGE STAMP ENVELOPES

KL#	Name, address and notations	Value
1-?	H. Armstrong, Hosiery, Laces, etc	
	140 6th Ave, NYC	275.
3-?	Arthur, Gregory & Co., Stationer	
	39 Nassau St. NYC	250.
3-?	Same	250.
5-?	Bergen & Trippe, Stationer	
	114 Nassau St, NYC	250.
7-?	Berlin & Jones, Stationer	
	134 Williams St, NYC	250.

KL#	Name, address and notations	Value
9-15	Joseph Bryan, Clothing	
	214 Fulton St, Brooklyn	300.
9-50	Same	250.
11-?	G.C. Brown, Tobacco	
	669 Broadway, NYC	250.
13-?	P.D. Braisted, Jr. Billiards	
	14-16 4th Ave, NYC	250.
15-25	John M. Burnett, Stationer	
	51 William St, NYC	250.
15-50hc50		250.
15-50	Same	250.
17-?	Chas. T. Chickhaus, Tobacco	
	176 Broadway, NYC	300.
19-?	Clarry & Reilley, Stationer	
	12-14 Spruce St, NYC	300.

KL#	Name, address and notations	Value
21-50	B.F. Corlies & Macy, Stationer	
	33 Nassau St, NYC	300.
23-?	Crook & Duff, Bar-Lunch-Dining	
	39-40 Park Row, NYC	350.
25-?	Cutter Tower & Co, Stationer	
	128 Nassau St, NYC	250.
27-25	T.R. Dawley, Stationer	
	Read & Centre Sts, NYC	250.
27-?	Same	250.
27-?	Same	250.
29-?	Mad A. Doubet, Importer	
	697 & 951 Broadway, NYC	300.
31-?	Francis Duffy, Oysters & Dining	
	239-241 8th Ave, NYC	300.
33-25	Embree, Stationer	
	130 Grand St, NYC	250.
34-50	Jno. C. Force	
	Brooklyn	350.
35-?	Fox's Old Bowery Theatre	
	NYC	350.
37-?	German Opera	
	485 Broadway, NYC	350.

KL#	Name, address and notations	Value
39-75	Gould's Dining Rooms	
	35 Nassau St, NYC	250.
40-50	Arthur Gregory	
	NYC	350.

KL#	Name, address and notations	Value
41-?	Harlem & NY Navigation Co	
	Sylvan Shore & Sylvan Grove, NYC	250.
	If marked "LEGAL CURRENCY"	450.
43-5	Harpel, Printers	
	Cincinnati	300.
45-10	Irving House, Hotel	
	Broadway & 12th St, NYC	250.
47-?	James, Hatter	
	525 Broadway, NYC	250.
49-?	Hamilton Johnston, Stationer	
	545 Broadway, NYC	200.
	with Washington portrait	500.
51-25	C.O. Jones, Stationer	
	76 Cedar St, NYC	250.
53-?	Kaiser & Waters, Stationer	
	104 Fulton St, NYC	250.
55-60	Kavanagh & Freeman, Billards	
	10th & Broadway, NYC	300.
57-25	Lansingh's Gent's Furnishings	
57-50	Albany	250.
59-10	J. Leach, Stationer	
	86 Nassau St, NYC	200.
	Type I, Value in central diamond, most	
	common type	200.
59-15		250.
59-20		200.
59-25		200.
59-30		250.
59-50		200.
59-75		400.

KL#	Name, address and notations	Value
60-25	As Above	
	Type II, Eagle between "U" and "S"	200.
60-50		200.
61-25	As above	
	Type III, Large central oval with	
	denomination	200.

KL#	Name, address and notations	Value
62-25	As above	
	Type IV, denomination between flags	200.
71-?	D.W. Lee, Stationer	
	82 Nassau St, NYC	200.
71-?	Same	200.
73-?	Macoy & Herwig, Stationers	
	112-114 Broadway, NYC	250.
75-?	Hy Maillards, Confectionery	
	621 Broadway, NYC	250.
77-?	Frank McElroy, Stationers	
	113 Nassau St, NYC	250.
79-?	Mercantile Dining Room - B. Letson	
	256 Broadway, NYC	250.
81-10	Metropolitan Hotel	
	NYC	250.
83-?	Miller & Grant, Importers, Laces	
	703 Broadway, NYC	300.
85-?	W.H. Murphy (by D. Murphy's Sons)	
	(Stationers, 372 Pearl St, NYC	250.
87-?	Wm. Murphy, Stationer	
	438 Canal St, NYC	250.
89-25	National Express Co.	
	74 Broadway, NYC	350.
91-?	New Bowery Theatre, J.W. Lingard	
	NYC	300.
91-?	Same	300.
93-20	New York Central Railraod (N.Y.C.R.R.)	
	NYC	300.
95-?	N.Y. Consolidated Stage Co.	
	NYC	300.
97-?	Niblos Garden - Wm Wheatley	
	(Edwin Forrest) NYC	300.
99-?	Same except Ravel Troup	
	NYC	300.
101-10	Nixon's Cremorne Garden,	
	Palace of Music	
	14th and 6th Ave, NYC	300.
101-25hc10		300.

KL#	Name, address and notations	Value
101-25		300.
101-?	Postal type hand stamp appears to	
	read "NI(XON'S) CREMORNE" (Note:	
	This item was listed as KL#153-? in the	
	First edition).	300.
103-?	Chris O'Neills, Liquors	
	Hudson Ave, Brooklyn	250.
	If "UNCLE SAM'S CHANGE"	350.
105-?	Oyster Bay House	
	553 Broadway, NYC	250.
107-?	The Oyster House	
	604 Broadway, NYC	250.
109-?	Pettit & Crook's Dining Rooms	
	136 Water St, NYC	250.
	If "UNCLE SAM'S CHANGE"	350.
111-50	Pomroy's	
	699 Broadway, NYC	250.
113-50	Power, Bogardus & Co., Steamship Line	
	Pier 34, No. River, NYC	275.
115-?	S. Raynor, Stationer	
	118 William St, NYC	250.

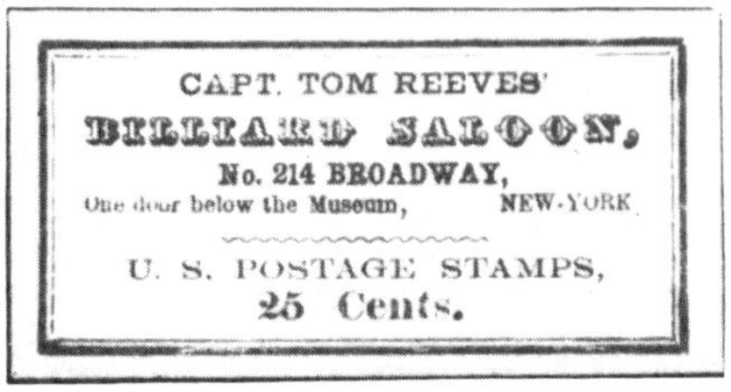

KL#	Name, address and notations	Value
117-25	Capt. Tom Reeves, Billards	
	214 Broadway, NYC	350.
119-25	Revere House	
	604-608 Broadway, NYC	250.
121-?	Thomas Richardson,	
	Chop Steak & Oyster House	
	66 Maiden Lane, NYC	250.
122-50	E.M. Riggin, Sanford House	
	336 Delaware Ave., Pine St. Wharf,	
	Philadelphia	250.
123-25	Wm Robins, Envelopes	
	51 Ann St, NYC	200.
123-?	Same	200.
125-?	R. Scovel, Stationer	
	26 Nassau St, NYC	250.
	If "GOV'T CURRENCY"	350.
125-?	Same	250.
127-25	C.C. Shelley, Stationer	
	68 Barclay St, NYC	250.
129-10	H. Smith, Stationer	
	137 Williams St, NYC	200.
129-25	Same	200.
129-?	Same	200.
130-25	Snow & Hapgood	
	22 Court St., Boston	250.
131-?	Sonneborn, Stationer	
	130 Nassau St., NYC	250.
131-?	Same	250.
133-25	Taylor's Hotel	
	Exchange Place, Jersey City	300.
135-?	Dion Thomas, Stationer	
	142 Nassau St, NYC	300.
137-25	R.D. Thompson, Stationer	
	104 Fulton St, NYC	250.
139-25	G.W. & S. Turney	
	77 Chatham St, NYC	250.
140-?	S.C. Upham	
	403 Chestnut St., Phil.	250.
141-?	James Wiley, Wines & Liquors	
	307 Broadway, NYC	250.

PIECES WITH NO COMPANY NAME

KL#	Name, address and notations	Value
151-25	Blank - marked by hand	
	Envelope perhaps hand made	200.
155-25	U.S. POSTAGE STAMPS 25 CENTS	200.
157-25	"UNITED STATES POSTAGE STAMPS"	
	in oval	200.

A single hoard of these pieces consisting of a "cigar box full" is known to exist but it has not been seen or cataloged. A small group is known to have been lost in a fire some years ago. The author is indebted to Jackson Storm and to the Chase Bank Collection for some of the illustrations, and to Gene Hessler for some of the photography.

Error Notes

By Alan Herbert, J. Frederick Bart and Harry Jones

Considering the more than four billion pieces of U.S. paper money which the Bureau of Engraving and Printing currently produces each year, the miniscule number of error notes which reach the public are a tribute to the BEP's workmanship and quality control — and the reason that U.S. paper money errors enjoy significant popularity (and in many cases, premium value) within the numismatic hobby.

The following listings of major categories of currency errors have been produced to allow the non-specialist to quickly and easily determine the value of any paper money error based on the way it looks. Since, in the final analysis, the value of an error note is usually based on how different it looks from a normal note, no attempt has been made to delve into the technical causes of the errors. While it often requires a familiarity with currency production processes at the Bureau of Engraving and Printing to adequately understand how an error occured or escaped detection, such knowledge is only necessary for the error-variety specialist. These listings will generally answer the most important question in the mind of the non-collector or casual collector who encounters an error note: "What's it worth?"

The listings in this catalog are a simplification of the computerized "Paper Money Cataloging System" developed by consultant Alan Herbert to classify paper money errors and printing varieties.

Error note listings are arranged in the same sequence in which modern U.S. paper money is printed: face printing, back printing, overprinting, cutting.

Wherever possible, valuations for error notes have been provided in up to three grades of preservation. All values quoted are for current, or recent, small size U.S. paper money issues. **Values quoted are in addition to the face value of the note.** As a general rule, paper money errors are most avidly collected in the lower denominations, since few collectors are willing to tie up their money in high-denomination notes. Thus, contrary to expectation, a high denomination or rare note valuable in its own right will not often draw any premium as an error, and may in fact be reduced in value because of a lack of collector demand. It should also be noted that for many types of error notes, there is little demand for notes in circulated condition. In such cases, a dash will be used in the circulated grade columns to indicate little, if any, premium over face value.

Because "star" notes (notes with an open-center 5-pointed star in place of a serial number suffix letter) are printed to replace notes that have been misprinted or damaged in production, they carry a premium value when they are encountered with printing errors. Many collectors also attach special value to error notes which exhibit the red crayon marks (easily faked) or special stickers which Bureau of Engraving and Printing inspectors use to tag unfit notes for destruction.

Some error notes, especially the more spectacular varieties, cannot be evaluated in a catalog listing such as this. Their value must be determined on an individual basis, between buyer and seller. Such listings will be indicated in these pages with a series of dashes in all condition columns.

Multiple Errors

Because of the nature of the note-printing process, one malfunction of the press, one problem with the paper, or one human error will occasionally manifest itself in the form of notes which exhibit two or more distinct types of error. While most such notes are usually caught in the stringent inspection procedure, they are sometimes found in circulation.

The value of such multiple-error notes cannot be computed by simply adding the values of each error represented on the note; rather, it must be determined on an individual basis.

Large-size Note Errors

Paper money errors on large-size U.S. paper money are much scarcer and more valuable than the same type of printing mishap on current-size currency.

Because quantities of notes produced in the period before 1928 were much lower than today, and the printing processes were slower and less mechanical, the chances of errors occuring and escaping undetected were much smaller than is now the case. Additionally, since there were few collectors of paper money, and fewer collectors of error notes in the period when the "saddleblankets" were current, those error notes which did reach circulation were not likely to be saved as collector's items.

The value of large-size currency errors is usually several times the value of the same error on a small-size note. Again, however, specific value must be determined on an individual basis.

National Currency Errors

While the number of extra printing processes associated with the production of National Bank Notes, such as affixing individual bank names and charter numbers, created extra opportunities for mistakes to be made, all National Currency error notes can be considered extremely rare.

For much of their circulation period, the signatures of the bank officials had to be hand-affixed and the notes were individually cut from the sheets by hand. In effect, they were subject to a second "inspection" at the issuing bank, after they had left the Bureau of Engraving and Printing.

National Currency errors are probably unique in that their value is most often determined by the bank of issue, rather than the type of error. Thus, while all National Bank Note errors are in great demand, those from particularly rare banks or from popularly-collected states will be in greater demand. Naturally, the value of every National Bank Note error is highly individual.

Fake Error Notes

Some types of currency errors naturally lend themselves to fakery. The addition or removal of ink to simulate a genuine printing error is a relatively simple process which the collector must continually bear in mind when confronted with what appears to be an error note.

The collector's best defense against being stuck with a phony error is to either acquire a working knowledge of the printing process and the mishaps which can occur, or to deal with reputable specialists in this area.

Not all apparent error notes which are not genuine can be traced to intentionally deceptive practices. Current U.S. notes are often enocuntered, for example, with backs that are some shade of blue or yellow. Since it can be unequivacably stated that the no modern U.S. paper money has yet been printed with the wrong color of ink — either face or back — all such color variations occurred after the currency reached circulation. The change of the green ink to blue or yellow can usually be traced to the application of bleach or alkali to a note — often when a note mistakenly goes through the washing machine.

First (Back) Printing

This division includes all of the errors that occur during the first printing, the back of current U.S. paper money, including those which result in some or all of the back design being printed on the face of the note.

Missing Back Printing: Any note which has failed to receive the first printing and is completely blank on the back. Usually the result of two sheets going through the press at the same time.

	VG	VF	Unc.
Missing Back Printing	75.00	125.00	225.00

Incomplete Printing, Unprinted: Any note which has had a portion of the back design left unprinted. Often another part of the same currency sheet becomes folded and intercepts the printing. In other cases, a foreign object, such as other paper, marker strips, tape, wrapping material, etc., comes between the printing plate and the paper. Value depends on whether the foreign object is recovered with the note, and on the size and location of the unprinted area. **Note:** Beware of fake errors created by erasing portions of the printing.

	VG	VF	Unc.
Incomplete Printing, with foreign object	—	—	200.00+
Incomplete Printing, without foreign object	7.50+	15.00+	25.00+

Incomplete Printing, Insufficient Ink: A note which displays missing, weak or irregular printing of the back due to a lack of ink or less than the normal amount of ink. May be caused by a "board break" or other defects in the system which presses paper onto the inked printing plate, as well as by problems with the ink or inking operation, itself.

	VG	VF	Unc.
Insufficient Ink, one or more small spots	5.00	10.00	30.00
Insufficient Ink, 25-50% of back	10.00	15.00	50.00
Insufficient Ink, 50% or more of back	15.00	25.00	65.00
Insufficient Ink, 100% of back	25.00	45.00	110.00

Ink Stain or Smear: Areas of ink of the normal color (though the density may vary) deposited on the back of the note at some point in the printing process, or ink which has been smeared while still wet. Value depends on the size, number and location of the defect. A minimum of one inch in width is necessary for the defect to be considered "large."

	VG	VF	Unc.
Ink Stain or Smear, small	2.00	5.00	10.00
Ink Stain or Smear, medium or several small	5.00	8.00	15.00
Ink Stain or Smear, large	8.00	15.00	40.00

Offset Printing, Back to Face: An ink impression of all or part of the back design transferred by some part of the printing press in a mirror-image to the face of the note. Values depend on the percentage of the whole design that is transferred and the darkness (the darker the better) of the ink impression. Values quoted here are for dark offset impressions at or about the percentages indicated.

	VG	VF	Unc.
Offset Printing, Back to Face, less than 25%	3.00	5.00	15.00
Offset Printing, Back to Face, 25-50%	4.50	7.50	30.00
Offset Printing, Back to Face, 50-75%	5.00	10.00	40.00
Offset Printing, Back to Face, 75-95%	10.00	15.00	65.00
Offset Printing, Back to Face, 100%	20.00	40.00	125.00

Double Printing on Back: A note which has been fed through the printing press twice, and shows two complete printed images of the back design.

	VG	VF	Unc.
Double Printing on Back	125.00	275.00	675.00

Partial Double Printing on Back: A note which shows doubling of a portion of the back design or partial overlapping image due to a loose plate or other printing press malfunction.

	VG	VF	Unc.
Partial Double Printing on Back:	50.00	80.00	275.00

Back Printing Out of Register: Notes which have the back printed out of normal centered position due to faulty feed of the note paper through the printing press or faulty adjustment of press alignment. Front of the note will be properly centered.

	VG	VF	Unc.
Back Printing Out of Register, unequal margins	2.00	3.00	10.00

Back Printing Out of Register, adjoining note shows	5.00	7.50	25.00+

Second (Face) Printing

In the current U.S. currency printing process at the Bureau of Engraving and Printing, 32-note sheets which have received the back printing are then printed with the face design. This section includes those printing varieties and errors which occur during this stage of note production. In recent years, the face design has included the engraved signatures of the Treasurer of the United States and Secretary of the Treasury, but earlier small size U.S. currency, depending on series, had the signatures as part of the overprint, along with the Treasury seal and serial numbers.

Missing Face Printing: Any note which has failed to receive the face printing and exhibits only the overprinting on the front of the note. Usually the result of two sheets going through the press at the same time.

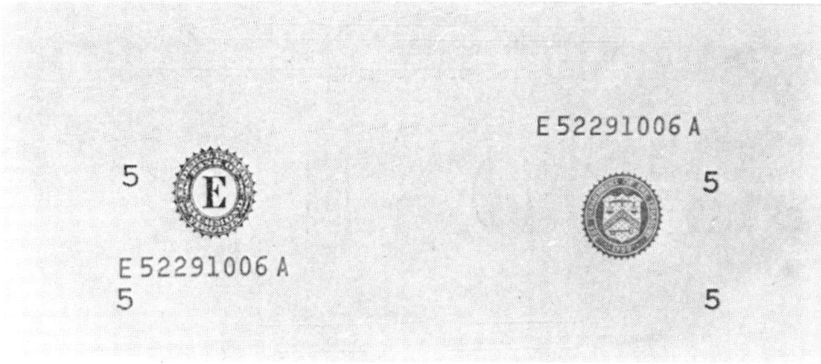

	VG	VF	Unc.
Missing Face Printing	150.00	250.00	450.00

Incomplete Printing, Unprinted: Any note which has had a portion of the face design left unprinted. Often another part of the same currency sheet becomes folded and intercepts the printing. In other cases, a foreign object, such as other paper, marker strips, tape, wrapping material (in one case, a Band-Aid), etc., comes between the printing plate and the paper. Value depends on whether the foreign object is recovered with the note, and on the size and location of the unprinted area. **Note:** Beware of fake errors created by erasing portions of the printing.

	VG	VF	Unc.
Incomplete Printing, with foreign object	—	—	300.00+

Incomplete Printing, without foreign object	15.00+	25.00+	40.00+

Incomplete Printing, Insufficient Ink: A note which displays missing, weak or irregular printing of the face design due to a lack of ink or less than the normal amount of ink. May be caused by a "board break" or other defects of the system which presses paper onto the inked printing plate, as well as by problems with the ink or inking operation, itself.

	VG	VF	Unc.
Insufficient Ink, one or more small spots	5.00	10.00	25.00
Insufficient Ink, 25-50% of face	10.00	15.00	40.00
Insufficient Ink, 50% or more of face	15.00	25.00	75.00
Insufficient Ink, 100% of face	25.00	45.00	125.00

Ink Stain or Smear: Areas of ink of the normal color (though the density may vary) deposited on the face of the note at some point in the printing process, or ink that has been smeared while still wet. Value depends on the size, number and location of the defect. A minimum of one inch in width is necessary for the defect to be considered "large."

	VG	VF	Unc.
Ink Stain or Smear, small	2.00	4.00	10.00
Ink Stain or Smear, medium or several small	5.00	10.00	20.00
Ink Stain or Smear, large	10.00	20.00	50.00

Offset Printing, Face to Back: An ink impression of all or part of the face design transferred by some part of the printing press in a mirror-image to the back of the note. Values depend on the percentage of the whole design that is transferred and the darkness (the darker the better) of the ink impression. Values quoted here are for dark offset impressions at or about the percentages indicated.

	VG	VF	Unc.
Offset Printing, Face to Back, less than 25%	2.00	4.00	20.00
Offset Printing, Face to Back, 25-50%	4.50	7.50	30.00
Offset Printing, Face to Back, 50-75%	5.00	10.00	40.00
Offset Printing, Face to Back, 75-95%	10.00	15.00	60.00
Offset Printing, Face to Back, 100%	15.00	25.00	75.00

Double Printing on Face: A note which has been fed through the printing press twice, and shows two complete images of the face design.

	VG	VF	Unc.
Double Printing on Face	200.00	300.00	1000.00

Partial Double Printing on Face: A note which shows doubling of a portion of the face design or partial overlapping image due to a loose plate or other printing press malfunction.

	VG	VF	Unc.
Partial Double Printing on Face	50.00	75.00	200.00

Face Printing Out of Register: A note that has the face printed out of normal centered position due to faulty feed of the note paper through the printing press or faulty adjustment of press alignment. Back of the note will be properly centered.

	VG	VF	Unc.
Face Printing Out of Register, unequal margins	2.00	5.00	12.50

Face Printing Out of Register, adjoining note shows	3.00	7.50	25.00+

Inverted Face: Since the back is printed first, it is used as a reference to determine an inversion error. Such notes are printed with the face upside down in relation to the back.

	VG	VF	Unc.
Inverted Face	50.00	75.00	200.00

Mismatched Denominations. A note printed with one denomination on the back and a different denomination on the face. Often called the "King" of paper money errors.

	VG	VF	Unc.
Mismatched Denominations	1250.	2250.	4000.

Third (Overprint) Printing

This section includes all of the errors that occur during the third printing, the application of the overprinting. On current U.S. paper money, that includes the green Treasury seal and serial numbers, and the black Federal Reserve District seal and Federal Reserve District designation numbers in the four corners of the interior of the note's face design. Earlier notes also included the Treasury officials' engraved signatures as part of the overprinting.

Completely Missing Overprint: Any note which failed to receive the complete overprint; i.e., all overprint elements are missing. Usually the result of two sheets going through the overprinting press at the same time.

	VG	VF	Unc.
Completely Missing Overprint	40.00	75.00	250.00

Incomplete Overprint, Unprinted: Any note which has had one or more of the overprint elements left unprinted. Often another part of the same currency sheet becomes folded and intercepts the printing. In other cases a foreign object, such as other paper, marker strips, tape, wrapping material (in one case, a Band-Aid), etc., comes between the printing plate and the paper. Value depends on whether the foreign object is recovered with the note, and how many of the overprint elements are missing. On current notes, because the overprint is applied in a two-color printing process, it is possible for a note to receive only one set of elements (green or black), with the intercepting paper falling off in between.

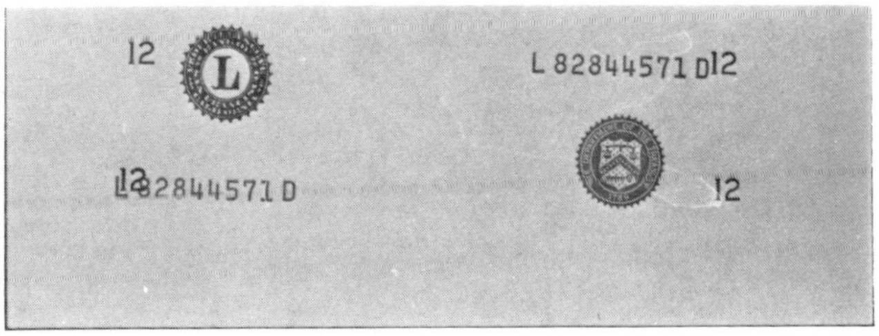

	VG	VF	Unc.
Incomplete Overprint, with foreign object	—	—	500.00+
Incomplete Overprint, without foreign object	20.00	40.00	90.00+

Incomplete Printing, Insufficient Ink: A note which displays missing, weak or irregular printing of the overprint elements due to a lack of ink or less than the normal amount of ink.

	VG	VF	Unc.
Incomplete Printing, Insufficient Ink	5.00	10.00	30.00+

Ink Stain or Smear: Areas of ink of the normal color (though the density may vary) deposited on the face of the note at some point in the printing process, or ink that has been smeared while still wet. Value depends on the size, number and location of the defect. A minimum of one inch in width is necessary for the defect to be considered "large."

	VG	VF	Unc.
Ink Stain or Smear, small	2.00	3.00	5.00
Ink Stain or Smear, medium or several small	4.00	6.00	10.00
Ink Stain or Smear, large	5.00	10.00	25.00

Offset Printing, Overprint to Back: An ink impression of all or part of the overprint transferred by the overprinting press in a mirror-image to the back of a subsequently-printed note. Value depends on the number of overprint elements thus transferred and the darkness (the darker the better) of the ink impression. Values quoted here are for dark offset impressions at or about the percentages indicated.

	VG	VF	Unc.
Offset Printing, Overprint to Back, 25-50%	8.00	15.00	40.00
Offset Printing, Overprint to Back, 50-75%	12.00	20.00	60.00
Offset Printing, Overprint to Back, 100%	50.00	100.00	225.00

Double Printing of Overprint: A note which has been fed through the overprinting press twice, and shows two complete printed images of the overprint elements.

	VG	VF	Unc.
Double Printing of Overprint	200.00	350.00	550.00+

Partial Double Printing of Overprint: A note which shows doubling of a portion of the overprint elements, or a partial overlapping image of the overprint design due to a loose plate or other overprinting press malfunction.

	VG	VF	Unc.
Partial Double Printing of Overprint	50.00	100.00	225.00

Overprinting Out of Register: A note which has had the third printing out of position on the face of the note, due to faulty sheet feed or faulty adjustment of the press alignment. As a rule, notes have no premium value unless the overprint is far enough out of alignment to overlap some portion of the face design not normally touched. The further out of alignment, the more valuable the error note.

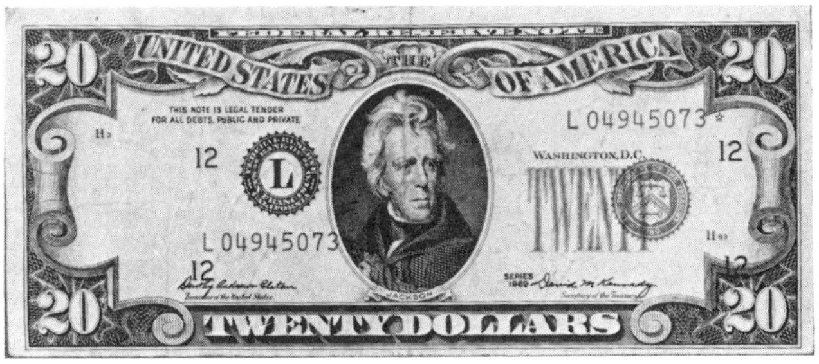

	VG	VF	Unc.
Overprint Out of Register Into Design, slightly	5.00	10.00	25.00
Overprint Out of Register Into Design, significantly	10.00	20.00	50.00
Overprint Out of Register, adjoining overprint shows	25.00	50.00	250.00

Inverted Overprint: A note on which the overprinting is upside-down in relation to the face design; the result of a sheet of notes being fed into the overprinting press at a 180-degree rotation from normal.

	VG	VF	Unc.
Inverted Overprint	45.00	75.00	125.00

Overprint on Back: A note which has the overprint applied to the back; the result of sheets being fed into the overprinting press with the wrong wide up, or the sheet being folded during the overprinting process.

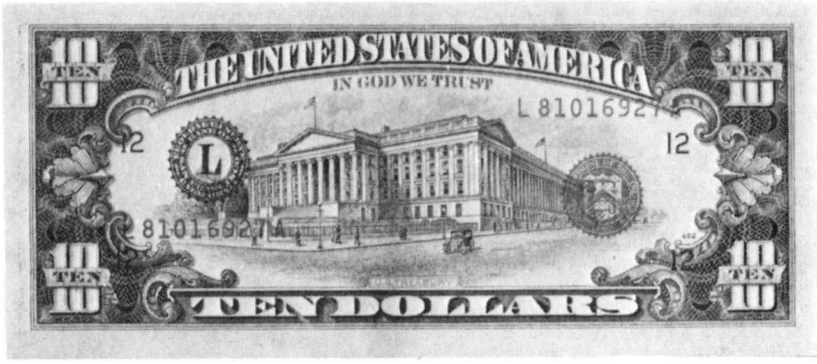

	VG	VF	Unc.
Overprint on Back, normal position	35.00	65.00	150.00
Overprint on Back, inverted	100.00	150.00	250.00

	VG	VF	Unc.
Overprint on Back, at angle	65.00	100.00	200.00

Mismatched Serial Numbers: A note on which the serial numbers are not the same; the result of the serial numbering block being incorrectly set, or one or more digits becoming stuck during overprinting.

	VG	VF	Unc.
Mismatched Serial Numbers, one digit	10.00	20.00	50.00
Mismatched Serial Numbers, two digits	30.00	50.00	100.00
Mismatched Serial Numbers, three or more digits	45.00	60.00	150.00
Mismatched Serial Numbers, prefix or suffix letter	50.00	100.00	200.00

Turned Digit: A note which has one or more of digits of the serial number partially visible, the result of the digit being stuck in the numbering block during the overprinting process.

	VG	VF	Unc.
Turned Digit	1.00	2.00	10.00

Hawaii, North Africa, "R" & "S" Notes: Because of the popularity of the several World War II era emergency and experimental currency issues, and the relative rarity of error notes among these issues, the values of overprinting errors on these types are highly individual and negotiable.

Paper, Folding & Cutting

Some of the most dramatic paper money errors occur during the printing process when a sheet of bank note paper becomes folded in the printing press at some stage of the operation. This generally causes areas of the notes which would normally be printed to be left blank, and/or other areas to receive ink where it would not normally be found. Similarly, when a malfunction occurs during the cutting of the sheets into individual notes, the results can be spectacular. On all but the most minor and commonly encountered paper, folding and cutting errors, values for such notes is largely dependent on the size and area affected.

Paper Errors: Paper in the principal ingredient in a bank note, and defects in the paper itself often result in significant error notes, printed on paper that may be defective, damaged during production or printing, marked or otherwise spoiled. Values are based on the size and prominence of the defect.

	VG	VF	Unc.
Printed on Torn Paper, small tear	5.00	10.00	25.00+

	VG	VF	Unc.
Printed on Torn Paper, medium or several small tears	15.00	30.00	65.00+

	VG	VF	Unc.
Printed on Torn Paper, large tear	25.00	50.00	75.00+
Printed on Scrap of Torn Paper	—	—	200.00+
Printed on Faulty (Marked, Split, etc.) Paper	5.00	10.00	25.00+

Interior Fold: A note which shows the result of a folded sheet within the dimensions of a normal note is classed as an interior fold. They are generally smaller and less dramatic than exterior folds.

	VG	VF	Unc.
Interior Fold, single	1.00	2.00	5.00
Interior Fold, two	3.00	5.00	10.00

Interior Fold, several	5.00	10.00	25.00+

Exterior Fold: A fold anywhere on the sheet may affect one or more of the notes and will affect the size and shape of printed and unprinted areas, and where the printing is located if out of normal position. Often when being cut, a portion of the sheet outside the normal margins of the note will remain attached to the note (the piece is sometimes referred to as a "butterfly"). Value depends on the fold and cut, and increases sharply with the size of the affected area.

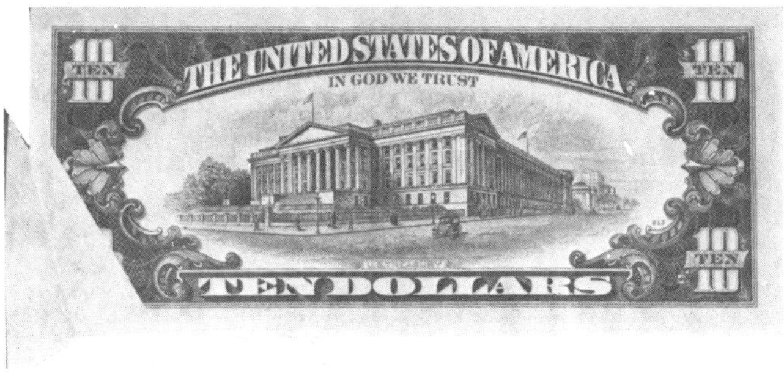

	VG	VF	Unc.
Exterior Fold, minor extra paper and corresponding blank area	10.00	25.00	75.00+
Exterior Fold, significant extra paper and corresponding blank area	30.00	75.00	175.00+

Exterior Fold, very large extra paper and corresponding blank area	75.00	150.00	200.00+

Cutting Errors: Malfunctions in the cutting operating, whereby hundreds or thousands of sheets of bank notes are cut at a time will result in notes which are poorly centered on both sides. Generally, unless part of another note shows, there is little premium value. Notes which exhibit about half of each of two notes are the most valuable.

	VG	VF	Unc.
Cut Out of Register, minor	7.50	15.00	65.00+
Cut Out of Register, major	75.00	150.00	300.00+
Scrap of Torn or Cut Paper Attached to Note	5.00	10.00	20.00+

Fake Cutting Errors

Collectors should be aware of the existence of fake cutting error notes created by unscrupulous persons from the uncut sheets of U.S. paper money now being sold to the public. Any Series 1976 $2 Federal Reserve Note with a star suffix, or any Series 1981 or later $1 FRN with serial number of 99 840 001 or higher that exhibits a cutting error should be viewed with suspicion. At least one advertisment has appeared in a national "gossip" tabloid offering such notes for sale.

Military Payment Certificates

Military Payment Certificates (MPC) were special currency issued by the U.S. Armed Forces between the end of World War II and 1973.

Their issue to and use by military and certain civilian personnel in lieu of regular U.S. currency was designed to minimize black market trafficking in occupied areas and around U.S. military installations. The various series of MPC replaced each other with no advance warning, and the scrip, exchangeable only by those to whom its issue was authorized, could become worthless overnight. This discouraged its acceptance by unauthorized local civilians.

Given the low rate of military pay during most of this period and the fact the no MPC retains any redemption value, it is no wonder that high denomination notes in uncirculated condition are rare in many of the series.

MPC replacement notes, analogous to star notes in regular U.S. currency, are designated by the lack of a suffix letter in the serial number. They are especially sought-after by collectors.

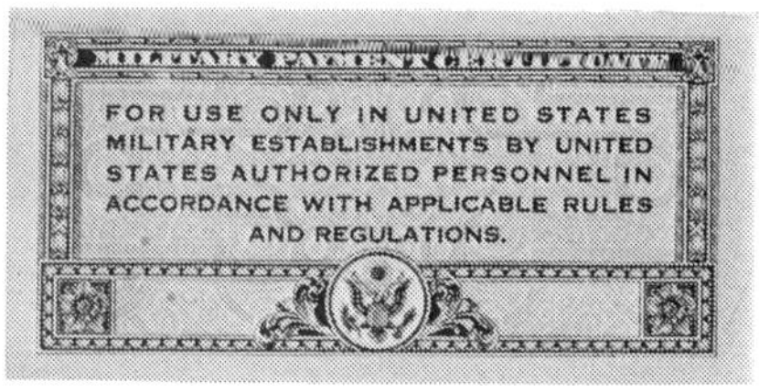

SERIES 461

Issued: European Theater, Sept. 16, 1946; Pacific Theater, Sept. 30, 1946
Withdrawn: March 10, 1947
Areas of Use: Austria, Belgium, England, France, Germany, Greece, Hungary, Iceland, Italy, Japan, Korea, Morocco, Philippines, Ryukyus, Scotland, Trieste, Yugoslavia

KL#	Denomination	Fine	VF	XF	Unc
M1	5 CENTS	1.50	6.00	11.50	60.00
	r. Replacement A-	16.50	32.50	90.00	200.00
M2	10 CENTS	1.50	6.00	13.00	65.00
	r. Replacement A-	15.00	30.00	50.00	200.00
M3	25 CENTS	2.00	10.00	25.00	110.00
	r. Replacement A-	—	—	—	—
M4	50 CENTS	4.00	15.00	25.00	115.00
	r. Replacement A-	—	—	—	—
M5	1 DOLLAR	3.00	6.00	10.00	100.00
	r. Replacement A-	87.50	175.00	—	—
M6	5 DOLLARS	15.00	25.00	45.00	250.00
	r. Replacement A-	—	—	—	—
M7	10 DOLLARS	17.50	25.00	45.00	250.00
	r. Replacement A-	100.00	200.00	—	—

SERIES 471

Issued: March 10, 1947
Withdrawn: March 22, 1948
Areas of Use: Austria, Belgium, England, France, Germany, Greece, Hungary, Iceland, Italy,

Japan, Korea, Morocco, Philippines, Ryukyus, Scotland, Trieste, Yugoslavia

KL#	Denomination	Fine	VF	XF	Unc
M8	5 CENTS	4.00	8.00	15.00	80.00
	r. Replacement B-	—	—	—	—
M9	10 CENTS	3.50	7.00	12.00	70.00
	r. Replacement B-	100.00	200.00	400.00	550.00
M10	25 CENTS	5.00	12.50	27.50	125.00
	r. Replacement B-	—	—	—	—
M11	50 CENTS	10.00	20.00	45.00	200.00
	r. Replacement B-	—	—	—	—
M12	1 DOLLAR	8.00	15.00	40.00	175.00
	r. Replacement B-	—	—	—	—
M13	5 DOLLARS	1000.	1500.	2500.	5000.
	r. Replacement B-	—	—	—	—
M14	10 DOLLARS	200.00	300.00	650.00	2000.
	r. Replacement B-	—	—	—	—

SERIES 472

Issued: March 22, 1948
Withdrawn: June 20, 1951
Areas of Use: Austria, Belgium, England, France, Germany, Greece, Hungary, Iceland, Italy, Japan, Korea, Morocco, Philippines, Ryukyus, Scotland, Trieste, Yugoslavia

#M15-M21 blue unpt. and seal of the United States at ctr.

KL#	Denomination	Fine	VF	XF	Unc
M15	5 CENTS	.40	1.00	1.50	3.50
	r. Replacement C-	7.50	15.00	70.00	120.00
M16	10 CENTS	2.00	4.00	10.00	50.00
	r. Replacement C-	11.50	22.50	100.00	180.00
M17	25 CENTS	4.00	8.00	12.50	80.00
	r. Replacement C-	—	—	—	—
M18	50 CENTS	5.00	10.00	15.00	100.00
	r. Replacement C-	10.00	20.00	90.00	170.00
M19	1 DOLLAR	4.00	10.00	20.00	150.00
	r. Replacement C-	18.50	37.50	170.00	300.00
M20	5 DOLLARS	75.00	185.00	475.00	1500.
	r. Replacement C-	—	—	—	—
M21	10 DOLLARS	25.00	90.00	200.00	1100.
	r. Replacement C-	—	—	—	—

SERIES 481

Issued: June 20, 1951
Withdrawn: May 25, 1954
Areas of Use: Austria, Belgium, England, France,

Germany, Greece, Hungary, Iceland, Italy, Japan, Korea, Morocco, Philippines, Ryukyus, Scotland, Trieste, Yugoslavia

KL#	Denomination	Fine	VF	XF	Unc
M22	5 CENTS	1.00	2.00	4.00	20.00
	r. Replacement D-	25.00	50.00	—	—
M23	10 CENTS	1.00	2.00	3.00	21.00
	r. Replacement D-	10.00	20.00	35.00	—
M24	25 CENTS	1.50	4.00	10.00	50.00
	r. Replacement D-	30.00	60.00	—	—
M25	50 CENTS	5.00	10.00	20.00	95.00
	r. Replacement D-	—	—	—	—
M26	1 DOLLAR	6.00	15.00	25.00	160.00
	r. Replacement D-	—	—	—	—

NOTE: #M26 exists with the position # at r. or l; the l. variety is worth 10 percent more.

KL#	Denomination	Fine	VF	XF	Unc
M27	5 DOLLARS	50.00	125.00	240.00	1000.
	r. Replacement D-	—	—	—	—
M28	10 DOLLARS	40.00	100.00	200.00	825.00
	r. Replacement D-	—	—	—	—

SERIES 521

Issued: May 25, 1954
Withdrawn: May 27, 1958
Areas of Use: Austria, Belgium, England, France, Germany, Greece, Hungary, Iceland, Italy, Japan, Korea, Morocco, Philippines, Ryukyus, Scotland, Trieste, Yugoslavia

KL#	Denomination	Fine	VF	XF	Unc
M29	5 CENTS	.75	2.00	5.00	18.50
	r. Replacement E-	50.00	100.00	—	—
M30	10 CENTS	.75	2.00	5.00	20.00
	r. Replacement E-	32.50	65.00	—	—
M31	25 CENTS	1.50	4.00	8.50	45.00
	r. Replacement E-	25.00	50.00	—	—
M32	50 CENTS	3.00	6.50	12.50	90.00
	r. Replacement E-	—	—	—	—
M33	1 DOLLAR	6.00	10.00	18.00	120.00
	r. Replacement E-	87.50	175.00	—	—
M34	5 DOLLARS	180.00	295.00	475.00	2000.
	r. Replacement E-	375.00	750.00	—	—
M35	10 DOLLARS	150.00	200.00	300.00	1100.
	r. Replacement E-	—	—	—	—

SERIES 541

Issued: May 27, 1958
Withdrawn: May 26, 1961
Areas of Use: Cyprus, England, France, Germany, Iceland, Northern Ireland, Italy, Japan, Korea, Morocco, Philippines, Ryukyus, Scotland

KL#	Denomination	Fine	VF	XF	Unc
M36	5 CENTS	.75	1.00	1.50	5.00
	r. Replacement F-	10.00	20.00	—	—
M37	10 CENTS	1.00	1.25	2.00	20.00
	r. Replacement F-	10.00	20.00	60.00	100.00
M38	25 CENTS	1.50	4.00	7.00	25.00
	r. Replacement F-	50.00	100.00	150.00	200.00
M39	50 CENTS	2.00	5.00	10.00	70.00
	r. Replacement F-	7.50	15.00	35.00	100.00
M40	1 DOLLAR	8.00	20.00	40.00	200.00
	r. Replacement F-	20.00	40.00	150.00	275.00
M41	5 DOLLARS	850.00	1000.	1500.	2500.
	r. Replacement F-	—	—	—	—
M42	10 DOLLARS	200.00	400.00	850.00	2500.
	r. Replacement F-	—	—	—	—

SERIES 591

Issued: May 26, 1961
Withdrawn: Pacific, Jan. 6, 1964; Europe, Jan. 13, 1946
Areas of Use: Cyprus, Iceland, Japan, Korea, Philippines

KL#	Denomination	Fine	VF	XF	Unc
M43	5 CENTS	1.50	3.00	6.50	50.00
	r. Replacement G-	17.50	35.00	80.00	150.00
M44	10 CENTS	1.50	3.00	7.50	60.00
	r. Replacement G-	—	—	—	—
M45	25 CENTS	10.00	15.00	30.00	150.00
	r. Replacement G-	—	—	—	—
M46	50 CENTS	15.00	30.00	45.00	375.00
	r. Replacement G-	—	—	—	—
M47	1 DOLLAR	12.50	25.00	45.00	250.00
	r. Replacement G-	100.00	200.00	—	—
M48	5 DOLLARS	600.00	900.00	1250.	2750.
	r. Replacement G-	—	—	—	—
M49	10 DOLLARS	200.00	350.00	575.00	1300.
	r. Replacement G-	100.00	200.00	750.00	—

SERIES 611

Issued: Jan. 6, 1964
Withdrawn: April 28, 1969
Areas of Use: Cyprus, Japan, Korea, Libya

KL#	Denomination	Fine	VF	XF	Unc
M50	5 CENTS	.75	1.50	2.50	9.00
	r. Replacement H-	6.50	12.50	20.00	65.00
M51	10 CENTS	1.00	2.50	3.50	12.00
	r. Replacement H-	5.00	10.00	17.50	65.00
M52	25 CENTS	1.25	2.50	5.00	25.00
	r. Replacement H-	100.00	200.00	—	—
M53	50 CENTS	3.75	7.50	12.50	55.00
	r. Replacement H-	—	—	—	—
M54	1 DOLLAR	3.75	6.00	14.00	70.00
	r. Replacement H-	20.00	40.00	60.00	100.00
M55	5 DOLLARS	100.00	175.00	250.00	600.00
	r. Replacement H-	115.00	225.00	275.00	725.00
M56	10 DOLLARS	37.50	75.00	175.00	550.00
	r. Replacement H-	50.00	100.00	175.00	600.00

SERIES 641

Issued: Aug. 31, 1965
Withdrawn: Oct. 21, 1968
Areas of Use: Vietnam

KL#	Denomination	Fine	VF	XF	Unc
M57	5 CENTS	.15	.35	.60	2.50
	r. Replacement J-	3.50	7.00	12.00	50.00
M58	10 CENTS	.15	.40	.65	2.75
	r. Replacement J-	5.00	10.00	18.00	30.00

KL#	Denomination	Fine	VF	XF	Unc
M59	25 CENTS	.25	.50	1.00	4.75
	r. Replacement J-	5.00	10.00	35.00	125.00
M60	50 CENTS	.75	1.25	2.50	8.00
	r. Replacement J-	35.00	70.00	100.00	175.00
M61	1 DOLLAR	1.75	2.25	4.00	22.50
	r. Replacement J-	55.00	110.00	160.00	275.00
M62	5 DOLLARS	25.00	35.00	60.00	180.00
	r. Replacement J-	—	—	—	—
M63	10 DOLLARS	20.00	40.00	65.00	250.00
	r. Replacement J-	50.00	100.00	175.00	350.00

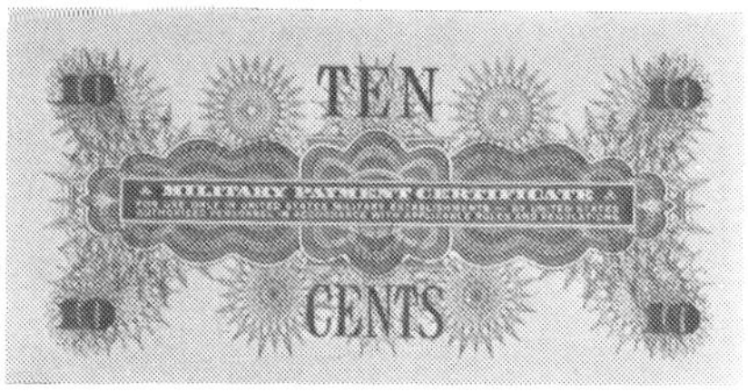

SERIES 661

Issued: Oct. 21, 1968
Withdrawn: Aug. 11, 1969
Areas of Use: Vietnam

KL#	Denomination	Fine	VF	XF	Unc
M64	5 CENTS	.25	.50	.75	2.00
	r. Replacement B-	30.00	60.00	100.00	175.00
M65	10 CENTS	.25	.50	.75	2.25
	r. Replacement B-	27.50	55.00	90.00	160.00
M66	25 CENTS	.40	.85	1.75	5.50
	r. Replacement B-	30.00	60.00	100.00	175.00
M67	50 CENTS	.50	1.25	2.50	8.00
	r. Replacement B-	75.00	150.00	250.00	400.00
M68	1 DOLLAR	.75	1.50	3.75	6.50
	r. Replacement B-	15.00	30.00	45.00	75.00
M69	5 DOLLARS	1.25	2.50	4.00	10.00
	r. Replacement B-	60.00	120.00	200.00	350.00

KL#	Denomination	Fine	VF	XF	Unc
M70	10 DOLLARS	125.00	200.00	300.00	800.00
	r. Replacement B-	200.00	350.00	600.00	1200.
M71	20 DOLLARS	75.00	125.00	200.00	600.00
	r. Replacement B-	—	—	—	—

SERIES 651

Issued: April 28, 1969
Withdrawn: Japan, May 19, 1969; Libya, June 11, 1969; Korea, Nov. 19, 1973
Areas of Use: Japan, Korea, Libya
NOTE: Similar to Series 641 except for colors and the addition of a "Minuteman" at left on face.

KL#	Denomination	Fine	VF	XF	Unc
M72A	5 CENTS				(One known)
M72B	10 CENTS				(One known)
M72C	25 CENTS				(One known)
M72D	50 CENTS	1500.	2500.	3500.	6000.

NOTE: 5 pieces known of #M72D.

KL#	Denomination	Fine	VF	XF	Unc
M72E	1 DOLLAR	1.50	3.00	5.00	25.00
	r. Replacement A-	—	—	—	—
M73	5 DOLLARS	25.00	35.00	75.00	250.00
M74	10 DOLLARS	21.00	50.00	75.00	280.00
	r. Replacement A-	75.00	150.00	250.00	400.00

SERIES 681

Issued: Aug. 11, 1969
Withdrawn: Oct. 7, 1970
Areas of Use: Vietnam

KL#	Denomination	Fine	VF	XF	Unc
M75	5 CENTS	.25	.50	.75	2.00
	r. Replacement C-	7.50	15.00	25.00	40.00
M76	10 CENTS	.25	.55	1.00	3.00
	r. Replacement C-	7.50	15.00	25.00	40.00
M77	25 CENTS	.35	.75	1.75	6.00
	r. Replacement C-	—	—	—	—
M78	50 CENTS	.50	1.25	2.00	7.00
	r. Replacement C-	17.50	35.00	60.00	100.00
M79	1 DOLLAR	1.00	1.50	2.50	10.00
	r. Replacement C-	10.00	20.00	50.00	100.00
M80	5 DOLLARS	2.00	3.50	5.00	20.00
	r. Replacement C-	37.50	75.00	125.00	300.00
M81	10 DOLLARS	7.50	15.00	30.00	150.00
	r. Replacement C-	50.00	100.00	200.00	—
M82	20 DOLLARS	7.50	15.00	35.00	140.00
	r. Replacement C-	40.00	80.00	100.00	300.00

SERIES 692

Issued: Oct. 7, 1970
Withdrawn: Fractional denominations, June 1, 1971; dollar denominations, March 15, 1973
Areas of Use: Vietnam

KL#	Denomination	Fine	VF	XF	Unc
M83	5 CENTS	.75	1.00	1.60	5.00
	r. Replacement E-	12.50	25.00	50.00	100.00
M84	10 CENTS	.75	1.00	1.60	6.50
	r. Replacement E-	12.50	25.00	50.00	100.00
M85	25 CENTS	1.00	2.00	3.50	15.00
	r. Replacement E-	18.50	37.50	75.00	150.00
M86	50 CENTS	1.60	2.25	3.75	17.00
	r. Replacement E-	16.50	31.50	62.50	125.00
M87	1 DOLLAR	2.50	3.50	6.50	22.50
	r. Replacement E-	12.50	25.00	50.00	100.00
M88	5 DOLLARS	35.00	45.00	75.00	150.00
	r. Replacement E-	—	—	—	—
M89	10 DOLLARS	100.00	140.00	190.00	475.00
	r. Replacement E-	—	—	—	—
M90	20 DOLLARS	75.00	100.00	170.00	450.00
	r. Replacement E-	62.50	135.00	275.00	750.00

Catalog Number Cross-reference

The catalog number cross-reference charts on these pages will allow the user of the *Standard Catalog of U.S. Paper Money* to reconcile the Friedberg (*Paper Money of the United States,* by Robert Friedberg) catalog numbering system with the Krause-Lemke (KL) numbering.

Since not every currency item appears in both catalog, dashes will be used in the appropriate column to indicate that catalog contains no listing for the item.

In the pages immediately following, the appropriate Friedberg number is cross-referenced to the Krause-Lemke number. Following that, the Krause-Lemke number is cross-referenced to Friedberg numbers, giving the user the ability to immediately identify any piece of U.S. currency by either catalog number.

Permission is hereby given for the free use of the Krause-Lemke catalog numbering system by any newspaper, magazine or other periodical and also by any currency dealer for use in advertisements, direct mail offerings, fixed price lists or auction catalogs. Such permission is granted only when proper acknowledgement of the source is made by the user. Such acknowledgement may be in the form of the title of this catalog, the names of the authors, or both. Written permission is required for the commercial use of this numbering system.

KL	Fr.	KL	Fr.	KL	Fr.	KL	Fr.	KL	Fr.	KL	Fr.
1	17	66	713	132	251	198	68	264	836	330	782
2	17-A	67	714	133	252	199	69	265	837	331	783
3	16	68	715	134	253	200	70	266	838	332	784
4	16-A	69	716	135	254	201	71	267	839	333	785
5	18	70	717	136	255	202	72	268	840	334	786
6	19	71	718	137	256	203	73	269	841	335	787
7	20	72	719	138	257	204	74	270	842	336	790
8	21	73	720	139	258	205	75	271	843	337	791
9	22	74	721	140	353	206	76	272	844	338	792
10	23	75	722	141	354	207	77	273	845	339	794
11	24	76	723	142	355	208	78	274	846	340	795
12	25	77	724	143	356	209	79	275	847	341	796
13	26	78	725	144	357	210	80	276	848	342	797
14	27	79	726	145	358	211	81	277	849	343	798
15	28	80	727	146	747	212	82	278	850	344	799
16	29	81	728	147	748	213	83	279	851	345	803
17	30	82	729	148	749	214	84	280	852	346	804
18	31	83	730	149	750	215	85	281	853	347	807
19	32	84	731	150	751	216	86	282	854	348	809
20	33	85	732	151	752	217	87	283	855	349	8-A
21	34	86	733	152	753	218	88	284	856	350	8
22	35	87	734	153	754	219	89	285	857	351	6-A
23	36	88	735	154	755	220	90	286	858	352	6
24	37	89	736	155	756	221	91	287	859	353	7-A
25	37-A	90	737	156	757	222	92	288	860	354	7
26	38	91	738	157	758	223	1136	289	861	355	10-A
27	39	92	739	158	759	224	1137	290	862	356	10
28	40	93	740	159	760	225	1138	291	863	357	9-A
29	215	94	741	160	761	226	1139	292	864	358	9
30	216	95	742	161	762	227	1140	293	865	359	93
31	217	96	743	162	763	228	1141	294	866	360	94
32	218	97	744	163	764	229	259	295	867	361	95-A
33	219	98	745	164	765	230	260	296	868	362	96
34	220	99	746	165	766	231	261	297	869	363	97
35	221	100	41	166	767	232	262	298	870	364	98
36	222	101	41-A	167	768	233	263	299	871	365	99
37	223	102	42	168	769	234	264	300	872	366	100
38	224	103	43	169	770	235	265	301	873	367	101
39	225	104	44	170	771	236	266	302	874	368	102
40	226	105	45	171	772	237	267	303	875	369	103
41	226-A	106	46	172	773	238	268	304	876	370	104
42	227	107	47	173	774	239	269	305	877	371	105
43	228	108	48	174	775	240	270	306	878	372	106
44	229	109	49	175	776	241	271	307	879	373	107
44A	—	110	50	176	777	242	272	308	880	374	108
45	230	111	51	177	778	243	273	309	881	375	109
46	231	112	52	178	779	244	274	310	882	376	110
47	232	113	53	179	780	245	275	311	883	377	111
48	233	114	54	180	3-A	246	276	312	884	378	112
49	234	115	55	181	3	247	277	313	885	379	113
50	235	116	56	182	1-A	248	278	314	886	380	114
51	236	117	57	183	1	249	279	315	887	381	115
52	237	118	58	184	2-A	250	280	316	888	382	116
53	238	119	59	185	2	251	281	317	889	383	117
54	239	120	60	186	5-A	252	282	318	890	384	118
55	347	121	240	187	5	253	359	319	891	385	119
56	348	122	241	188	4-A	254	360	320	788	386	120
57	349	123	242	189	4	255	361	321	789	387	121
58	350	124	243	190	61	256	362	322	793	388	122
59	351	125	244	191	62	257	363	323	800	389	123
60	352	126	245	192	63	258	364	324	801	390	190
61	708	127	246	193	63-A	259	365	325	802	391	190-A
62	709	128	247	194	64	260	832	326	805	392	190-B
63	710	129	248	195	65	261	833	327	806	393	196
64	711	130	249	196	66	262	834	328	808	394	213
65	712	131	250	197	67	263	835	329	781	395	214

KL	Fr.	KL	Fr.	KL	Fr.	KL	Fr.	KL	Fr.	KL	Fr.
396	1142	487	936	579	309	670	150	760	1049	851	1078
397	1143	488	937	580	310	671	151	761	1050	852	1079
398	1144	489	938	581	311	672	152	762	1051	853	1080
399	1145	490	939	582	312	673	153	763	1052	854	1081
400	1146	491	940	583	313	674	154	764	1053	855	1082
401	1147	492	941	584	314	675	155	765	1054	856	1083
402	1148	493	942	585	315	676	156	766	1055	857	1084
403	1149	494	943	586	316	677	157	767	1056	858	1085
404	1150	495	944	587	317	678	158	768	1057	859	1086
405	1151	496	945	588	318	679	159	769	1058	860	1087
406	1151-A	497	946	589	319	680	160	770	1059	861	1088
407	284	498	947	590	320	681	161	771	1060	862	1089
408	283	499	948	591	321	682	162	772	1061	863	1090
409	285-A	500	949	592	322	683	163	773	1062	864	1091
410	284-A	501	950	593	372	684	164	774	1063	865	1092
411	286	502	951	594	373	685	192	775	1064	866	1093
412	287	503	811	595	374	686	192-A	776	1065	867	1094
413	288	504	813	596	375	687	192-B	777	1066	868	1095
414	289	505	816	597	375-A	688	198	778	1067	869	1096
415	290	506	817	598	952	688A	—	779	1068	870	1097
416	291	507	818	599	953	689	203	780	1069	871	1098
417	292	508	819	600	954	690	207	781	1070	872	1099
418	293	509	820	601	955	691	212	782	1071	873	1100
419	294	510	821	602	956	692	212-D	783	831	874	1101
420	295	511	810	603	957	693	1189	784	165	875	1102
421	296	512	812	604	958	694	1188	785	166	876	1103
422	297	513	814	605	959	695	1190	786	167	877	1104
423	298	514	815	606	960	696	1191	787	168	878	1105
424	299	515	13-A	607	961	697	1192	788	169	879	1106
425	300	516	13	608	962	698	1193	789	170	880	1107
426	301	517	11-A	609	963	699	1194	790	171	881	1108
427	302	518	11	610	964	700	1195	791	172	882	1109
428	303	519	12-A	611	965	701	1196	792	173	883	1110
429	304	520	12	612	966	702	1197	793	174	884	1111
430	366	521	14-A	613	967	703	1198	794	175	885	1112
431	367	522	14	614	968	704	1199	795	176	886	1113
432	368	523	124	615	969	705	1200	796	177	887	1114
433	369	524	125	616	970	706	1160	797	178	888	1115
434	370	526	126	617	971	707	1161	798	179	889	1116
435	371	526	127	618	972	708	324-C	799	180	890	1117
436	1167	527	128	619	973	709	324	800	181	891	1118
437	1168	528	129	620	974	710	324-A	801	182	892	1119
438	1169	529	130	621	975	711	325	802	193	893	1120
439	1170	530	131	622	976	712	326	803	193-A	894	1121
440	1171	531	132	623	977	713	327	804	193-B	895	1122
441	1172	532	133	624	978	714	328	805	199	896	1123
442	1173	533	134	625	979	715	329	805A	—	897	1124
443	892	534	135	626	980	716	330	806	204	898	1125
444	893	535	136	627	981	717	331	807	208	899	1126
445	894	536	137	628	982	718	332	808	212-A	900	1127
446	895	537	138	629	983	719	333	809	212-E	901	1128
447	896	538	139	630	984	720	334	810	1166-C	902	1129
448	897	539	140	631	985	721	335	811	1166-H	903	1130
449	898	540	141	632	986	722	376	812	1166-M	904	1131
450	899	541	142	633	987	723	1012	813	1202	904A	183-A
451	900	542	143	634	988	724	1013	814	1201	905	183-B
452	901	543	144	635	989	725	1014	815	1203	906	183-C
453	902	544	145	636	990	726	1015	816	1204	907	184
454	903	545	146	637	991	727	1016	817	1205	908	185-A
455	904	546	147	638	992	728	1017	818	1206	909	185-B
456	905	547	191	639	993	729	1018	819	1207	910	185-C
457	906	548	191-A	640	994	730	1019	820	1208	911	185-D
458	907	549	197	641	995	731	1020	821	1209	912	185-E
459	908	550	1166-B	642	996	732	1021	822	1210	913	185-F
460	909	551	1175	643	997	733	1022	823	1211	914	185-G
461	910	552	1174	644	998	734	1023	824	1212	915	185-H
462	911	553	1176	645	999	735	1024	825	1213	916	185-I
463	912	554	1177	646	1000	736	1025	826	1214	917	185-J
464	913	555	1178	647	1001	737	1026	827	1215	918	185-K
465	914	556	1179	648	1002	738	1027	828	1162	919	185-L
466	915	557	1180	649	1003	739	1028	829	1163	920	185-M
467	916	558	1181	650	1004	740	1029	830	1164	921	185-N
468	917	559	1182	651	1005	741	1030	831	1165	922	194
469	918	560	1183	652	1006	742	1031	832	1166	923	194-A
470	919	561	1184	653	1007	743	1032	833	337-B	924	194-B
471	920	562	1185	654	1008	744	1033	834	337	925	200
472	921	563	1186	655	1009	745	1034	836	338	925A	—
473	922	564	1187	656	1010	746	1035	837	339	926	205
474	923	566	1152	657	1011	747	1036	838	340	927	209
475	924	567	1154	658	822	748	1037	839	341	928	212-B
476	925	568	1155	659	822-A	749	1038	840	342	929	212-F
477	926	569	1159-A	660	824	750	1039	841	343	930	1166-D
478	927	570	1156	661	826	751	1040	842	344	931	1166-I
479	928	571	1153	662	827	752	1041	843	377	932	1166-N
480	929	572	1157	663	828	753	1042	844	378	937	1216
481	930	573	1158	664	829	754	1043	845	1072	938	1216-A
482	931	574	1159	665	830	755	1044	846	1073	939	1216-B
483	932	575	305	666	823	756	1045	847	1074	940	1217
484	933	576	307	667	825	757	1046	848	1075	944-948	345-A
485	934	577	306	668	148	758	1047	849	1076	949	345-B
486	935	578	308	669	149	759	1048	850	1077	950	345-C

KL	Fr.
951	345-D
952-965	1132
966	186-A
967	186-B
968	186-C
969	186-D
970	187-A
971	187-B
972	187-C
973	187-D
974	187-E
975	187-F
976	187-G
977	187-H
978	187-I
979	187-J
980	187-K
981	187-L
982	195
983	195-A
984	201
984A	—
985	206
986	210
987	212-C
988	212-G
989	1166-E
990	1166-J
991	1166-O
992	1218-A
993	1218
994	1218-B
995	1218-C
996	1218-D
997	1218-E
998	1218-F
999	1218-G
1000-1005	1219
1006	1220
1007-1009	346-A
1010	346-B
1011	346-C
1012	346-D
1013	346-E
1014	379-A
1015	379-B
1016	379-C
1017	379-D
1018-1032	1133
1036	654
1044	202
1045	211
1045A	—
1046	1166-F
1047	1166-K
1049	1221-A
1050	1221
1051	1221-B
1052	1221-C
1053	1221-D
1054	1221-E
1055	1221-F
1056	1221-G
1057	1221-H
1058	1221-I
1059	1221-J
1059A	1222
1059B	1222-A
1059C	1222-B
1060-1067	1134
1068	1166-G
1069	1166-L
1071	1223-A
1072	1223
1073	1223-B
1074	1223-C
1075	1223-D
1076	1223-E
1077	1223-F
1078	1223-G
1078A	1224
1078B	1224-A
1078C	1224-B
1079	1225
1080-1085	1135
1086	380
1087	381
1088	382
1089	383
1090	384
1091	385
1092	386

KL	Fr.
1093	387
1094	388
1095	389
1096	390
1097	391
1098	392
1099	393
1100	394
1101	397
1102	398
1103	399
1104-1105	401
1106	402
1107	403
1108	404
1109	405
1110	406
1111	406-A
1112	407
1113	408
1114	466
1115	467
1116	468
1117	469
1118	470
1119	471
1120	472
1121	473
1122	474
1123	475
1124	476
1125	477
1126	478
1127	532
1128	533
1129	533-A
1130	534
1131	535
1132	536
1133	537
1134	538
1135	538-B
1136	573
1137	573-A
1138	574
1139	574-A
1140	575
1141	575-A
1142	575-B
1143	587
1144	588
1145	589
1146	590
1147	591
1148	592
1149	593
1150	594
1151	595
1152	596
1153	597
1154	597-A
1155	598
1156	599
1157	600
1158	601
1159	602
1160	603
1161	604
1162	605
1163	606
1164	607
1165	608
1166	609
1167	610
1168	611
1169	612
1170	1800-1
1171	1800-2
1172	409
1173	412
1174	413
1175	414
1176	416
1177	417
1178	418
1179	419
1180	420
1181	421
1182	422
1183	423
1184	423-A
1185	479

KL	Fr.
1186	480
1187	481
1188	482
1189	483
1190	484
1191	485
1192	486
1193	487
1194	488
1195	489
1196	490
1197	491
1198	492
1199	539
1200	540
1201	541
1202	542
1203	543
1204	544
1205	545
1206	546
1207	547
1208	548
1209	576
1210	576-A
1211	576-B
1212	577
1213	578
1214	579
1215	579-B
1216	613
1217	614
1218	615
1219	616
1220	617
1221	618
1222	619
1223	620
1224	621
1225	622
1226	623
1227	623-A
1228	624
1229	625
1230	626
1231	627
1232	628
1233	629
1234	630
1235	631
1236	632
1237	633
1238	634
1239	635
1240	636
1241	637
1242	638
1243	1801-1
1244	1801-2
1245	424
1246	427
1247	428
1248	429
1249	431
1250	432
1251	433
1252	434
1253	435
1254	436
1255	437
1256	438
1257	439
1258	493
1259	494
1260	495
1261	496
1262	497
1263	498
1264	499
1265	500
1266	501
1267	502
1268	503
1269	504
1270	505
1271	506
1272	549
1273	550
1274	551
1275	552
1276	553
1277	554

KL	Fr.
1278	555
1279	556
1280	557
1281	580
1282	580-A
1283	580-B
1284	581
1285	582
1286	583
1287	584
1288	584-A
1289	585
1290	639
1291	640
1292	641
1293	642
1294	643
1295	644
1296	645
1297	646
1298	647
1299	648
1300	649
1301	649-A
1302	650
1303	651
1304	652
1305	653
1307	655
1308	656
1309	657
1310	658
1311	659
1312	660
1313	661
1314	662
1315	663
1316	663-A
1317	1802-1
1318	1802-2
1319	440
1320	442
1321	443
1322	444
1323	444-A
1324	445
1325	446
1326	447
1327	448
1328	449
1329	450
1330	451
1331	507
1332	508
1333	509
1334	510
1335	511
1336	512
1337	513
1338	514
1339	515
1340	516
1341	517
1342	518
1343	518-A
1344	558
1345	559
1346	560
1347	561
1348	562
1349	563
1350	564
1351	565
1352	586
1353	664
1354	665
1355	666
1356	667
1357	668
1358	669
1359	670
1360	671
1361	672
1362	673
1363	674
1364	674-A
1365	675
1366	676
1367	677
1368	678
1369	679
1370	679-A

KL	Fr.
1371	680
1372	681
1373	682
1374	683
1375	684
1376	685
1377	685-A
1378	1803-1
1379	1803-2
1380	452
1381	454
1382	455
1383	456
1384	457
1385	458
1386	459
1387	460
1388	461
1389	462
1390	462-A
1391	463
1392	519
1393	520
1394	521
1395	522
1396	523
1397	524
1398	525
1399	526
1400	527
1401	528
1401A	529
1402	530
1403	531
1404	566
1405	567
1406	568
1407	569
1408	570
1409	571
1410	572
1411	572-A
1412	586-A
1413	686
1414	687
1415	688
1416	689
1417	690
1418	691
1419	692
1420	693
1421	694
1422	695
1423	696
1424	697
1425	698
1426	699
1427	700
1428	701
1429	702
1430	702-A
1431	703
1432	704
1433	705
1434	706
1435	707
1436	707-A
1437	1804-1
1438	1804-2
1439-1441	464
1442-1443	465
1444	1500
1445	1600
1446	1601
1447	1602
1448	1603
1449	1604
1450	1605
1451	1606
1452	1607
1453	1608
1454	1611
1455	1612
1456	1613
1457	1614
1458	1615
1459	1616
1460	1617
1461	1618
1462	1619
1463	1620
1464	1621

KL	Fr.
1465	1900-A
1466	1900-B
1467	1900-C
1468	1900-D
1469	1900-E
1470	1900-F
1471	1900-G
1472	1900-H
1473	1900-I
1474	1900-J
1475	1900-K
1476	1900-L
1477	1901-A
1478	1901-B
1479	1901-C
1480	1901-D
1481	1901-E
1482	1901-F
1483	1901-G
1484	1901-H
1485	1901-I
1486	1901-J
1487	1901-K
1488	1901-L
1490	1902-B
1493	1902-E
1495	1902-G
1498	1902-J
1500	1902-L
1501	1903-A
1502	1903-B
1503	1903-C
1504	1903-D
1505	1903-E
1506	1903-F
1507	1903-G
1508	1903-H
1509	1903-I
1510	1903-J
1511	1903-K
1512	1903-L
1513	1904-A
1514	1904-B
1515	1904-C
1516	1904-D
1517	1904-E
1518	1904-F
1519	1904-G
1520	1904-H
1521	1904-I
1522	1904-J
1523	1904-K
1524	1904-L
1525	1905-A
1526	1905-B
1527	1905-C
1528	1905-D
1529	1905-E
1530	1905-F
1531	1905-G
1532	1905-H
1533	1905-I
1534	1905-J
1535	1905-K
1536	1905-L
1538	1906-B
1540	1906-D
1541	1906-E
1542	1906-F
1543	1906-G
1544	1906-H
1545	1906-I
1546	1906-J
1547	1906-K
1548	1906-L
1561	1907-A
1562	1907-B
1563	1907-C
1564	1907-D
1565	1907-E
1566	1907-F
1567	1907-G
1568	1907-H
1569	1907-I
1570	1907-J
1571	1907-K
1572	1907-L
1573	1908-A
1574	1908-B
1575	1908-C
1576	1908-D
1577	1908-E

KL	Fr.	KL	Fr.	KL	Fr.	KL	Fr.	KL	Fr.	KL	Fr.
1578	1908-F	1670	1850-L	1785	1960-G	1876	1969-A	1967	1702	2058	2007-H
1579	1908-G	1671	1950-A	1786	1960-H	1877	1969-B	1968	1703	2059	2007-I
1580	1908-H	1672	1950-B	1787	1960-I	1878	1969-C	1969	1704	2060	2007-J
1581	1908-I	1673	1950-C	1788	1960-J	1879	1969-D	1970	1705	2061	2007-K
1582	1908-J	1674	1950-D	1789	1960-K	1880	1969-E	1971	1706	2062	2007-L
1583	1908-K	1675	1950-E	1790	1960-L	1881	1969-F	1972	1707	2063	2008-A
1584	1908-L	1676	1950-F	1791	1961-A	1882	1969-G	1973	1708	2064	2008-B
1585	1909-A	1677	1950-G	1792	1961-B	1883	1969-H	1974	1860-A	2065	2008-C
1586	1909-B	1678	1950-H	1793	1961-C	1884	1969-I	1975	1860-B	2066	2008-D
1587	1909-C	1679	1950-I	1794	1961-D	1885	1969-J	1976	1860-C	2067	2008-E
1588	1909-D	1680	1950-J	1795	1961-E	1886	1969-K	1977	1860-D	2068	2008-F
1589	1909-E	1681	1950-K	1796	1961-F	1887	1969-L	1978	1860-E	2069	2008-G
1590	1909-F	1682	1950-L	1797	1961-G	1888	1970-A	1979	1860-F	2070	2008-H
1591	1909-G	1683	1951-A	1798	1961-H	1889	1970-B	1980	1860-G	2071	2008-I
1592	1909-H	1684	1951-B	1799	1961-I	1890	1970-C	1981	1860-H	2072	2008-J
1593	1909-I	1685	1951-C	1800	1961-J	1891	1970-D	1982	1860-I	2073	2008-K
1594	1909-J	1686	1951-D	1801	1961-K	1892	1970-E	1983	1860-J	2074	2008-L
1595	1909-K	1687	1951-E	1802	1961-L	1893	1970-F	1984	1860-K	2075	2009-A
1596	1909-L	1688	1951-F	1803	1962-A	1894	1970-G	1985	1860-L	2076	2009-B
1597	1910-A	1689	1951-G	1804	1962-B	1895	1970-H	1986	2000-A	2077	2009-C
1598	1910-B	1690	1951-H	1805	1962-C	1896	1970-I	1987	2000-B	2078	2009-D
1599	1910-C	1691	1951-I	1806	1962-D	1897	1970-J	1988	2000-C	2079	2009-E
1600	1910-D	1692	1951-J	1807	1962-E	1898	1970-K	1989	2000-D	2080	2009-F
1601	1910-E	1693	1951-K	1808	1962-F	1899	1970-L	1990	2000-E	2081	2009-G
1602	1910-F	1694	1951-L	1809	1962-G	1900	1971-A	1991	2000-F	2082	2009-H
1603	1910-G	1695	1952-A	1810	1962-H	1901	1971-B	1992	2000-G	2083	2009-I
1604	1910-H	1696	1952-B	1811	1962-I	1902	1971-C	1993	2000-H	2084	2009-J
1605	1910-I	1697	1952-C	1812	1962-J	1903	1971-D	1994	2000-I	2085	2009-K
1606	1910-J	1698	1952-D	1813	1962-K	1904	1971-E	1995	2000-J	2086	2009-L
1607	1910-K	1699	1952-E	1814	1962-L	1905	1971-F	1996	2000-K	2087	2010-A
1608	1910-L	1700	1952-F	1815	1963-A	1906	1971-G	1997	2000-L	2088	2010-B
1609	2300	1701	1952-G	1816	1963-B	1907	1971-H	1998	2001-A	2089	2010-C
1610	2306	1702	1952-H	1817	1963-C	1908	1971-I	1999	2001-B	2090	2010-D
1611	1609	1703	1952-I	1818	1963-D	1909	1971-J	2000	2001-C	2091	2010-E
1612	1610	1704	1952-J	1819	1963-E	1910	1971-K	2001	2001-D	2092	2010-F
1613	1501	1705	1952-K	1820	1963-F	1911	1971-L	2002	2001-E	2093	2010-G
1614	1502	1706	1952-L	1821	1963-G	1912	1972-A	2003	2001-F	2094	2010-H
1615	1503	1710	1953-D	1822	1963-H	1913	1972-B	2004	2001-G	2095	2010-I
1616	1504	1712	1953-F	1823	1963-I	1914	1972-C	2005	2001-H	2096	2010-J
1617	1505	1718	1953-L	1824	1963-J	1915	1972-D	2006	2001-I	2097	2010-K
1618	1506	1724	1954-F	1825	1963-K	1916	1972-E	2007	2001-J	2098	2010-L
1619	1507	1731	1955-A	1826	1963-L	1917	1972-F	2008	2001-K	2099	2011-A
1620	1508	1732	1955-B	1827	1964-A	1918	1972-G	2009	2001-L	2100	2011-B
1621	1509	1733	1955-C	1828	1964-B	1919	1972-H	2010	2002-A	2101	2011-C
1622	1510	1734	1955-D	1829	1964-C	1920	1972-I	2011	2002-B	2102	2011-D
1623	1511	1735	1955-E	1830	1964-D	1921	1972-J	2012	2002-C	2103	2011-E
1624	1512	1736	1955-F	1831	1964-E	1922	1972-K	2013	2002-D	2104	2011-F
1625	1513	1737	1955-G	1832	1964-F	1923	1972-L	2014	2002-E	2105	2011-G
1626	1514	1738	1955-H	1833	1964-G	1924	1973-A	2015	2002-F	2106	2011-H
1627	1935-A	1739	1955-I	1834	1964-H	1925	1973-B	2016	2002-G	2107	2011-I
1628	1935-B	1740	1955-J	1835	1964-I	1926	1973-C	2017	2002-H	2108	2011-J
1629	1935-C	1741	1955-K	1836	1964-J	1927	1973-D	2018	2002-I	2109	2011-K
1630	1935-D	1742	1955-L	1837	1964-K	1928	1973-E	2019	2002-J	2110	2011-L
1631	1935-E	1743	1957-A	1838	1964-L	1929	1973-F	2020	2002-K	2111	2012-A
1632	1935-F	1744	1957-B	1839	1965-A	1930	1973-G	2021	2002-L	2112	2012-B
1633	1935-G	1745	1957-C	1840	1965-B	1931	1973-H	2022	2003-B	2113	2012-C
1634	1935-H	1746	1957-D	1841	1965-C	1932	1973-I	2023	2003-D	2114	2012-D
1635	1935-I	1747	1957-E	1842	1965-D	1933	1973-J	2024	2003-E	2115	2012-E
1636	1935-J	1748	1957-F	1843	1965-E	1934	1973-K	2025	2003-F	2116	2012-F
1637	1935-K	1749	1957-G	1844	1965-F	1935	1973-L	2026	2003-G	2117	2012-G
1638	1935-L	1750	1957-H	1845	1965-G	1936	1974-A	2027	2004-A	2118	2012-H
1639	1525	1754	1957-L	1846	1965-H	1937	1974-B	2028	2004-B	2119	2012-I
1640	1526	1755	1958-A	1847	1965-I	1938	1974-C	2029	2004-C	2120	2012-J
1641	1527	1756	1958-B	1848	1965-J	1939	1974-D	2030	2004-D	2121	2012-K
1642	1528	1757	1958-C	1849	1965-K	1940	1974-E	2031	2004-E	2122	2012-L
1643	1529	1758	1958-D	1850	1965-L	1941	1974-F	2032	2004-F	2123	2013-A
1644	1530	1759	1958-E	1852	1966-B	1942	1974-G	2033	2004-G	2124	2013-B
1645	1531	1760	1958-F	1853	1966-G	1943	1974-H	2034	2004-H	2125	2013-C
1646	1532	1761	1958-G	1854	1966-L	1944	1974-I	2035	2004-I	2126	2013-D
1647	1533	1762	1958-H	1855	1967-A	1945	1974-J	2036	2004-J	2127	2013-E
1648	1534	1763	1958-I	1856	1967-B	1946	1974-K	2037	2004-K	2128	2013-F
1649	1535	1764	1958-J	1857	1967-C	1947	1974-L	2038	2004-L	2129	2013-G
1650	1536	1766	1958-L	1858	1967-D	1948	1975-A	2039	2006-A	2130	2013-H
1651	1650	1767	1959-A	1859	1967-F	1949	1975-B	2040	2006-B	2131	2013-I
1652	1651	1768	1959-B	1860	1967-G	1950	1975-C	2041	2006-C	2132	2013-J
1653	1652	1769	1959-C	1861	1967-H	1951	1975-D	2042	2006-D	2133	2013-K
1654	1653	1770	1959-D	1861A	1967-J	1952	1975-E	2043	2006-E	2134	2013-L
1655	1654	1771	1959-E	1862	1967-K	1953	1975-F	2044	2006-F	2135	2014-A
1656	1655	1772	1959-F	1863	1967-L	1954	1975-G	2045	2006-G	2136	2014-B
1657	1656	1773	1959-G	1864	1968-A	1955	1975-H	2046	2006-H	2137	2014-C
1658	1657	1774	1959-H	1865	1968-B	1956	1975-I	2047	2006-I	2138	2014-D
1659	1850-A	1775	1959-I	1866	1968-C	1957	1975-J	2048	2006-J	2139	2014-E
1660	1850-B	1776	1959-J	1867	1968-D	1958	1975-K	2049	2006-K	2140	2014-F
1661	1850-C	1777	1959-K	1868	1968-E	1959	1975-L	2050	2006-L	2141	2014-G
1662	1850-D	1778	1959-L	1869	1968-F	1960	2301	2051	2007-A	2142	2014-H
1664	1850-F	1779	1960-A	1870	1968-G	1961	2302	2052	2007-B	2144	2014-J
1665	1850-G	1780	1960-B	1871	1968-H	1962	2307	2053	2007-C	2145	2014-K
1666	1850-H	1781	1960-C	1872	1968-I	1963	2400	2054	2007-D	2146	2014-L
1667	1850-I	1782	1960-D	1873	1968-J	1964	1700	2055	2007-E	2147	2015-B
1668	1850-J	1783	1960-E	1874	1968-K	1965	1700-A	2056	2007-F	2148	2015-G
1669	1850-K	1784	1960-F	1875	1968-L	1966	1701	2057	2007-G	2149	2015-L

KL	Fr.	KL	Fr.	KL	Fr.	KL	Fr.	KL	Fr.	KL	Fr.
2150	2016A	2242	2023-I	2333	2055-L	2423	2063-G	2513	2072-C	2603	2106-C
2151	2016-B	2243	2023-J	2334	2056-A	2424	2063-H	2514	2072-D	2604	2106-E
2152	2016-C	2244	2023-K	2335	2056-B	2424A	2063-I	2515	2072-E	2605	2106-F
2153	2016-D	2245	2023-L	2336	2056-C	2425	2063-J	2516	2072-F	2606	2106-G
2154	2016-E	2246	2024-A	2337	2056-D	2426	2063-K	2517	2072-G	2607	2106-K
2155	2016-F	2247	2024-B	2338	2056-E	2427	2063-L	2518	2072-H	2608	2107-A
2156	2016-G	2248	2024-C	2339	2056-F	2428	2064-B	2519	2072-I	2609	2107-B
2157	2016-H	2249	2024-D	2340	2056-G	2429	2064-G	2520	2072-J	2610	2107-C
2159	2016-J	2250	2024-E	2341	2056-H	2430	2064-L	2521	2072-K	2611	2107-D
2160	2016-K	2251	2024-F	2342	2056-I	2431	2065-A	2522	2072-L	2612	2107-E
2161	2016-L	2252	2024-G	2343	2056-J	2432	2065-B	2523	2304	2613	2107-F
2162	2017-A	2253	2024-H	2344	2056-K	2433	2065-D	2524	2305	2614	2107-G
2163	2017-B	2254	2024-I	2345	2056-L	2434	2065-E	2525	2404	2615	2107-H
2164	2017-C	2255	2024-J	2346	2057-A	2435	2065-F	2526	1880-B	2616	2107-I
2165	2017-D	2256	2024-K	2347	2057-B	2436	2065-G	2527	1880-D	2617	2107-J
2166	2017-E	2257	2024-L	2348	2057-C	2437	2065-H	2528	1880-G	2618	2107-K
2167	2017-F	2258	2303	2349	2057-D	2438	2065-J	2529	1880-I	2619	2107-L
2168	2017-G	2259	2308	2350	2057-E	2439	2065-K	2530	1880-J	2620	2108-A
2169	2017-H	2260	2309	2351	2057-F	2440	2065-L	2531	1880-K	2621	2108-B
2170	2017-I	2261	2402	2352	2057-G	2441	2066-A	2532	1880-L	2622	2108-C
2171	2017-J	2262	1870-A	2353	2057-H	2442	2066-B	2533	2072-L	2623	2108-D
2172	2017-K	2263	1870-B	2354	2057-I	2443	2066-C	2534	2100-A	2624	2108-E
2173	2017-L	2264	1870-C	2355	2057-J	2444	2066-D	2535	2100-B	2625	2108-F
2174	2018-A	2265	1870-D	2356	2057-K	2445	2066-E	2536	2100-C	2626	2108-G
2175	2018-B	2266	1870-E	2357	2057-L	2446	2066-F	2537	2100-D	2627	2108-H
2176	2018-C	2267	1870-F	2358	2058-A	2447	2066-G	2538	2100-E	2628	2108-J
2177	2018-D	2268	1870-G	2359	2058-B	2448	2066-H	2539	2100-F	2629	2108-K
2178	2018-E	2269	1870-H	2360	2058-C	2449	2066-I	2540	2100-G	2630	2108-L
2179	2018-F	2270	1870-I	2361	2058-D	2450	2066-J	2541	2100-H	2631	2109-A
2180	2018-G	2271	1870-J	2362	2058-E	2451	2066-K	2542	2100-I	2632	2109-B
2181	2018-H	2272	1870-K	2363	2058-F	2452	2066-L	2543	2100-J	2633	2109-C
2182	2018-I	2273	1870-L	2364	2058-G	2453	2067-A	2544	2100-K	2634	2109-D
2183	2018-J	2274	2050-A	2365	2058-H	2454	2067-B	2545	2100-L	2635	2109-E
2184	2018-K	2275	2050-B	2366	2058-I	2455	2067-C	2546	2101-A	2636	2109-G
2185	2018-L	2276	2050-C	2367	2058-J	2456	2067-D	2547	2101-B	2637	2109-H
2186	2019-A	2277	2050-D	2368	2058-K	2457	2067-E	2548	2101-C	2638	2109-J
2187	2019-B	2278	2050-E	2369	2058-L	2458	2067-F	2549	2101-D	2639	2109-K
2188	2019-C	2279	2050-F	2370	2059-A	2459	2067-G	2550	2101-E	2640	2109-L
2189	2019-D	2280	2050-G	2371	2059-B	2460	2067-H	2551	2101-F	2641	2110-A
2190	2019-E	2281	2050-H	2372	2059-C	2461	2067-I	2552	2101-G	2642	2110-B
2191	2019-F	2282	2050-I	2373	2059-D	2462	2067-J	2553	2101-H	2643	2110-C
2192	2019-G	2283	2050-J	2374	2059-E	2463	2067-K	2554	2101-I	2644	2110-D
2193	2019-H	2284	2050-K	2375	2059-F	2464	2067-L	2555	2101-J	2645	2110-E
2194	2019-I	2285	2050-L	2376	2059-G	2465	2068-A	2556	2101-K	2646	2110-G
2195	2019-J	2286	2051-A	2377	2059-H	2466	2068-B	2557	2101-L	2647	2110-H
2196	2019-K	2287	2051-B	2378	2059-I	2467	2068-C	2558	2102-A	2648	2110-I
2197	2019-L	2288	2051-C	2379	2059-J	2468	2068-D	2559	2102-B	2649	2110-J
2198	2020-A	2289	2051-D	2380	2059-K	2469	2068-E	2560	2102-C	2650	2110-K
2199	2020-B	2290	2051-E	2381	2059-L	2470	2068-F	2561	2102-D	2651	2110-L
2200	2020-C	2291	2051-F	2382	2060-A	2471	2068-G	2562	2102-E	2652	2111-A
2201	2020-D	2292	2051-G	2383	2060-B	2472	2068-H	2563	2102-F	2653	2111-B
2202	2020-E	2293	2051-H	2384	2060-C	2473	2068-I	2564	2102-G	2654	2111-C
2203	2020-F	2294	2051-J	2385	2060-D	2474	2068-J	2565	2102-H	2655	2111-D
2204	2020-G	2295	2051-K	2386	2060-E	2475	2068-K	2566	2102-I	2656	2111-E
2205	2020-H	2296	2052-A	2387	2060-F	2476	2068-L	2567	2102-J	2657	2111-F
2206	2020-I	2297	2052-B	2388	2060-G	2477	2069-B	2568	2102-K	2658	2111-G
2207	2020-J	2298	2052-C	2389	2060-H	2478	2069-D	2569	2102-L	2659	2111-H
2208	2020-K	2299	2052-D	2390	2060-I	2479	2069-E	2570	2103-A	2660	2111-I
2209	2020-L	2300	2052-E	2391	2060-J	2480	2069-F	2571	2103-B	2661	2111-J
2210	2021-A	2301	2052-F	2392	2060-K	2481	2069-G	2572	2103-D	2662	2111-K
2211	2021-B	2302	2052-G	2393	2060-L	2482	2069-H	2573	2103-E	2663	2111-L
2212	2021-C	2303	2052-H	2394	2061-A	2483	2069-I	2574	2103 F	2664	2112-B
2213	2021-D	2304	2052-I	2395	2061-B	2484	2069-J	2575	2103-G	2665	2112-G
2214	2021-E	2305	2052-J	2396	2061-C	2485	2069-K	2576	2103-H	2666	2112-L
2215	2021-F	2306	2052-K	2397	2061-D	2486	2069-L	2577	2103-I	2667	2113-A
2216	2021-G	2307	2052-L	2398	2061-E	2487	2070-A	2578	2103-J	2668	2113-B
2217	2021-H	2308	2053-G	2399	2061-F	2488	2070-B	2579	2103-K	2669	2113-C
2218	2021-I	2309	2053-L	2400	2061-G	2489	2070-C	2580	2103-L	2670	2113-D
2219	2021-J	2310	2054-A	2401	2061-H	2490	2070-D	2581	2104-C	2671	2113-E
2220	2021-K	2311	2054-B	2402	2061-I	2491	2070-E	2582	2104-D	2672	2113-F
2221	2021-L	2312	2054-C	2403	2061-J	2492	2070-F	2583	2104-E	2673	2113-G
2222	2022-A	2313	2054-D	2404	2061-K	2493	2070-G	2584	2104-F	2674	2113-H
2223	2022-B	2314	2054-E	2405	2061-L	2494	2070-H	2585	2104-G	2675	2113-I
2224	2022-C	2315	2054-F	2406	2062-A	2495	2070-I	2586	2104-H	2676	2113-J
2225	2022-D	2316	2054-G	2407	2062-B	2496	2070-J	2587	2104-I	2677	2113-K
2226	2022-E	2317	2054-H	2408	2062-C	2497	2070-K	2588	2104-J	2678	2113-L
2227	2022-F	2318	2054-I	2409	2062-D	2498	2070-L	2589	2104-K	2679	2114-A
2228	2022-G	2319	2054-J	2410	2062-E	2499	2071-A	2589	2104-L	2680	2114-B
2229	2022-H	2320	2054-K	2411	2062-F	2500	2071-B	2590	2105-A	2681	2114-C
2230	2022-I	2321	2054-L	2412	2062-G	2501	2071-C	2591	2105-B	2682	2114-D
2231	2022-J	2322	2055-A	2413	2062-H	2502	2071-D	2592	2105-C	2683	2114-E
2232	2022-K	2323	2055-B	2414	2062-I	2503	2071-E	2593	2105-D	2684	2114-F
2233	2022-L	2324	2055-C	2415	2062-J	2504	2071-F	2594	2105-E	2685	2114-G
2234	2023-A	2325	2055-D	2416	2062-K	2505	2071-G	2595	2105-F	2686	2114-H
2235	2023-B	2326	2055-E	2417	2062-L	2506	2071-H	2596	2105-G	2687	2114-I
2236	2023-C	2327	2055-F	2418	2063-A	2507	2071-I	2597	2105-H	2688	2114-J
2237	2023-D	2328	2055-G	2419	2063-B	2508	2071-J	2598	2105-I	2689	2114-K
2238	2023-E	2329	2055-H	2419A	2063-C	2509	2071-K	2599	2105-J	2690	2114-L
2239	2023-F	2330	2055-I	2420	2063-D	2510	2071-L	2600	2105-K	2691	2115-A
2240	2023-G	2331	2055-J	2421	2063-E	2511	2072-A	2601	2106-A	2692	2115-B
2241	2023-H	2332	2055-K	2422	2063-F	2512	2072-B	2602	2106-B	2693	2115-C

KL	Fr.	KL	Fr.	KL	Fr.	KL	Fr.	KL	Fr.	KL	Fr.
2694	2115-D	2787	2152-D	2869	2160-K	2947	2200-B	3039	2221-H	3268	1294
2695	2115-E	2787A	2153-D	2870	2160-L	2948	2200-C	3040	2221-J	3269	1295
2696	2115-F	2788	2152-E	2871	2161-A	2949	2200-D	3041	2221-K	3270	1296
2697	2115-G	2788A	2153-E	2872	2161-B	2950	2200-E	3042	2221-L	3271	1297
2698	2115-H	2789	2152-F	2873	2161-C	2951	2200-F	3043	2222-H	3272	1298
2699	2115-I	2789A	2153-F	2874	2161-D	2952	2200-G	3044	2223-A	3273	1299
2700	2115-J	2790	2152-G	2875	2161-E	2953	2200-H	3045	2223-B	3274	1300
2701	2115-K	2790A	2153-G	2876	2161-F	2954	2200-I	3046	2411	3275	1324
2702	2115-L	2791	2152-H	2877	2161-G	2955	2200-J	3047	2230-A	3276	1325
2703	2116-A	2791A	2153-H	2878	2161-H	2956	2200-K	3048	2230-B	3277	1326
2704	2116-B	2792	2152-I	2879	2161-I	2957	2200-L	3049	2230-D	3278	1327
2705	2116-E	2792A	2153-I	2880	2161-J	2958	2201-A	3050	2230-E	3279	1328
2706	2116-F	2793	2152-J	2881	2161-K	2959	2201-B	3051	2230-F	3281	1329
2707	2116-G	2793A	2153-J	2882	2161-L	2960	2201-C	3052	2230-G	3282	1330
2708	2116-K	2794	2152-K	2883	2162-B	2961	2201-D	3053	2230-H	3283	1331
2709	2117-A	2794A	2153-K	2884	2162-G	2962	2201-E	3054	2230-I	3284	1332
2710	2117-B	2795	2152-L	2885	2162-L	2963	2201-F	3055	2230-J	3285	1333
2711	2117-C	2795A	2153-L	2886	2163-A	2964	2201-G	3056	2230-K	3286	1334
2712	2117-D	2796	2154-A	2887	2163-B	2965	2201-H	3057	2230-L	3287	1335
2713	2117-E	2797	2154-C	2888	2163-C	2966	2201-I	3058	2231-A	3288	1336
2714	2117-F	2798	2154-D	2889	2163-D	2967	2201-J	3059	2231-B	3289	1337
2715	2117-G	2799	2154-E	2890	2163-E	2968	2201-K	3060	2231-C	3290	1338
2716	2117-H	2800	2154-F	2891	2163-F	2969	2201-L	3061	2231-D	3291	1339
2717	2117-I	2801	2154-G	2892	2163-G	2971	2202-B	3062	2231-E	3292	1340
2718	2117-J	2802	2154-H	2893	2163-H	2972	2202-C	3063	2231-F	3293	1341
2719	2117-K	2803	2154-I	2894	2163-I	2973	2202-D	3064	2231-G	3294	1342
2720	2117-L	2804	2154-J	2895	2163-J	2974	2202-E	3065	2231-H	3295	1343
2721	2118-A	2805	2154-K	2896	2163-K	2975	2202-G	3066	2231-J	3296	1344
2722	2118-B	2806	2155-A	2897	2163-L	2976	2202-H	3067	2231-K	3297	1345
2723	2118-C	2807	2155-B	2898	2164-A	2977	2202-I	3068	2231-L	3298	1346
2724	2118-D	2808	2155-C	2898A	2165-A	2978	2202-J	3069	2232-G	3299	1347
2725	2118-E	2809	2155-D	2899	2164-B	2979	2202-K	3070	2233-B	3300	1348
2726	2118-F	2810	2155-F	2899A	2165-B	2980	2202-L	3209	1228	3301	1349
2727	2118-G	2811	2155-G	2900	2164-C	2981	2203-F	3210	1229	3302	1350
2728	2118-H	2812	2155-H	2900A	2165-C	2982	2204-A	3211	1230	3303	1351
2729	2118-I	2813	2155-I	2901	2164-D	2983	2204-B	3212	1231	3304	1352
2730	2118-J	2814	2155-J	2901A	2165-D	2984	2408	3213	1240	3305	1353
2731	2118-K	2815	2155-K	2902	2164-E	2985	2210-A	3214	1241	3306	1354
2732	2118-L	2816	2155-L	2902A	2165-E	2986	2210-B	3215	1242	3307	1355
2733	2119-A	2817	2156-B	2903	2164-F	2987	2210-C	3216	1243	3308	1356
2734	2119-B	2818	2156-C	2903A	2165-F	2988	2210-D	3217	1279	3309	1357
2735	2119-C	2819	2156-F	2904	2164-G	2989	2210-E	3218	1280	3310	1358
2736	2119-D	2820	2156-G	2904A	2165-G	2990	2210-F	3219	1281	3311	1359
2737	2119-E	2821	2156-H	2905	2164-H	2991	2210-G	3220	1282	3312	1360
2738	2119-F	2822	2156-K	2905A	2165-H	2992	2210-H	3221	1310	3313	1361
2739	2119-G	2823	2157-A	2906	2164-I	2993	2210-I	3222	1310-A	3314	1362
274J	2119-L	2824	2157-B	2906A	2165-I	2994	2210-J	3223	1311	3315	1363
2740	2119-H	2825	2157-C	2907	2164-J	2995	2210-K	3224	1312	3316	1364
2741	2119-I	2826	2157-D	2907A	2165-J	2996	2210-L	3225	1313	3317	1365
2742	2119-J	2827	2157-E	2908	2164-K	2997	2211-A	3226	1232	3318	1366
2743	2119-K	2828	2157-F	2908A	2165-K	2998	2211-B	3227	1233	3319	1367
2745	1550	2829	2157-G	2909	2164-L	2999	2211-C	3228	1234	3320	1368
2746	1551	2830	2157-H	2909A	2165-L	3000	2211-D	3229	1235	3321	1369
2747	2405	2831	2157-I	2910	2166-A	3001	2211-E	3230	1244	3322	1370
2749	1890-B	2832	2157-J	2911	2166-B	3002	2211-F	3231	1245	3323	1371
2751	1890-D	2834	2157-K	2912	2166-C	3003	2211-G	3232	1246	3324	1372
2752	1890-E	2835	2157-L	2913	2166-D	3004	2211-H	3233	1247	3325	1373
2754	1890-G	2835	2158-A	2914	2166-E	3005	2211-I	3234	1248	3326	1373-A
2756	1890-I	2836	2158-B	2915	2166-F	3006	2211-J	3235	1249	3327	1257
2757	1890-J	2837	2158-C	2916	2166-G	3007	2211-K	3236	1283	3328	1258
2758	1890-K	2838	2158-D	2917	2166-H	3008	2211-L	3237	1284	3329	1259
2760	2150-A	2839	2158-E	2918	2166-I	3009	2212-A	3238	1285	3330	1260
2761	2150-B	2840	2158-F	2919	2166-J	3010	2212-B	3239	1286	3331	1261
2762	2150-C	2841	2158-G	2920	2166-K	3011	2212-C	3240	1287	3332	1267
2763	2150-D	2842	2158-H	2921	2166-L	3012	2212-D	3241	1288	3333	1268
2764	2150-E	2843	2158-I	2922	2167-A	3013	2212-E	3242	1289	3334	1269
2765	2150-F	2844	2158-J	2923	2167-B	3014	2212-F	3243	1290	3335	1270
2766	2150-G	2845	2158-K	2924	2167-C	3015	2212-G	3244	1290-A	3336	1271
2767	2150-H	2846	2158-L	2925	2167-D	3016	2212-H	3245	1314	3337	1301
2768	2150-I	2847	2159-A	2926	2167-E	3017	2212-I	3246	1316	3338	1302
2769	2150-J	2848	2159-B	2927	2167-F	3018	2212-J	3247	1317	3339	1302-A
2770	2150-K	2849	2159-C	2928	2167-G	3019	2212-L	3248	1318	3340	1303
2771	2150-L	2850	2159-D	2929	2167-H	3020	2213-A	3249	1320	3341	1305
2772	2151-A	2851	2159-E	2930	2167-I	3021	2213-B	3250	1321	3342	1307
2773	2151-B	2852	2159-F	2931	2167-J	3022	2410	3251	1322	3343	1374
2774	2151-C	2853	2159-G	2932	2167-K	3023	2220-A	3252	1226	3344	1375
2775	2151-D	2854	2159-H	2933	2167-L	3024	2220-B	3253	1227	3345	1376
2776	2151-E	2855	2159-I	2934	2168-A	3025	2220-D	3254	1236	3346	1377
2777	2151-F	2856	2159-J	2935	2168-B	3026	2220-E	3255	1237	3347	1379
2778	2151-G	2857	2159-K	2936	2168-C	3027	2220-F	3256	1238	3348	1264
2779	2151-H	2858	2159-L	2937	2168-D	3028	2220-G	3257	1239	3349	1265
2780	2151-I	2859	2160-A	2938	2168-E	3029	2220-J	3258	1251	3350	1266
2781	2151-J	2860	2160-B	2939	2168-F	3030	2220-K	3259	1252	3351	1308
2782	2151-K	2861	2160-C	2940	2168-G	3031	2220-L	3260	1253	3352	1309
2783	2151-L	2862	2160-D	2941	2168-H	3032	2221-A	3261	1254	3353	1380
2784	2152-A	2863	2160-E	2942	2168-I	3033	2221-B	3262	1255	3353A	1381
2784A	2153-A	2864	2160-F	2943	2168-J	3034	2221-C	3263	1255-A	3354	1382
2785	2152-B	2865	2160-G	2944	2168-K	3035	2221-D	3264	1256	3355	1383
2785A	2153-B	2866	2160-H	2945	2168-L	3036	2221-E	3265	1291	3356	1383-A
2786	2152-C	2867	2160-I	2945	2407	3037	2221-F	3266	1292	3500	1911-A
2786A	2153-C	2868	2160-J	2946	2200-A	3038	2221-G	3267	1293	3501	1911-B

KL	Fr.
3502	1911-C
3503	1911-D
3504	1911-E
3505	1911-F
3506	1911-G
3507	1911-H
3508	1911-I
3509	1911-J
3510	1911-K
3511	1911-L
3512	1976-A
3513	1976-B
3514	1976-C
3515	1976-D
3516	1976-E
3517	1976-F
3518	1976-G
3519	1976-H
3520	1976-I
3521	1976-J
3522	1976-K
3523	1976-L
3524	2025-A
3525	2025-B
3526	2025-C
3527	2025-D
3528	2025-E
3529	2025-F
3530	2025-G
3531	2025-H
3532	2025-I
3533	2025-J
3534	2025-K
3535	2025-L
3536	—
3537	—
3538	—
3539	—
3540	—
3541	—
3542	—
3543	—
3544	—
3545	—
3546	—
3547	—
3548	—
3549	—
3550	—
3551	—
3552	—
3553	—
3554	—
3555	—
3556	—
3557	—
3558	—
3559	—
3560	—
3561	—
3562	—
3563	—
3564	—
3565	—
3566	—
3567	—
3568	—
3569	—
3570	—
3571	—
3600	—
3601	—
3602	—
3603	—
3604	—
3605	—
3606	—
3607	—
3608	—
3609	—
3610	—
3611	—
3612	—
3613	—
3614	—
3615	—
3616	—
3617	—
3618	—
3619	—
3620	—
3621	—
3622	—
3623	—
3624	—
3625	—
3626	—
3627	—
3628	—
3629	—
3630	—
3631	—
3632	—
3633	—
3634	—
3635	—
3636	—
3637	—
3638	—
3639	—
3640	—
3641	—
3642	—
3643	—
3644	—
3645	—
3646	—
3647	—
3648	—
3649	—
3650	—
3651	—
3652	—
3653	—
3654	—
3655	—
3656	—
3657	—
3658	—
3659	—
3660	—
3661	—
3662	—
3663	—
3664	—
3665	—
3666	—
3667	—
3668	—
3669	—
3670	—
3671	—
3700	—
3701	—
3702	—
3703	—
3704	—
3705	—
3706	—
3707	—
3708	—
3709	—
3710	—
3711	—
3712	—
3713	—
3714	—
3715	—
3716	—
3717	—
3718	—
3719	—
3720	—
3721	—
3722	—
3723	—
3724	—
3725	—
3726	—
3727	—
3728	—
3729	—
3730	—
3731	—
3732	—
3733	—
3734	—
3735	—
3736	—
3737	—
3738	—
3739	—
3740	—
3741	—
3742	—
3743	—
3744	—
3745	—
3746	—
3747	—
3748	—
3749	—
3750	—
3751	—
3752	—
3753	—
3754	—
3755	—
3756	—
3757	—
3758	—
3759	—
3760	—
3761	—
3762	—
3763	—
3764	—
3765	—
3766	—
3767	—
3768	—
3769	—
3770	—
3771	—
M1	—
M2	—
M3	—
M4	—
M5	—
M6	—
M7	—
M8	—
M9	—
M10	—
M11	—
M12	—
M13	—
M14	—
M15	—
M16	—
M17	—
M18	—
M19	—
M20	—
M21	—
M22	—
M23	—
M24	—
M25	—
M26	—
M27	—
M28	—
M29	—
M30	—
M31	—
M32	—
M33	—
M34	—
M35	—
M36	—
M37	—
M38	—
M39	—
M40	—
M41	—
M42	—
M43	—
M44	—
M45	—
M46	—
M47	—
M48	—
M49	—
M50	—
M51	—
M52	—
M53	—
M54	—
M55	—
M56	—
M57	—
M58	—
M59	—
M60	—
M61	—
M62	—
M63	—
M64	—
M65	—
M66	—
M67	—
M68	—
M69	—
M70	—
M71	—
M72	—
M73	—
M74	—
M75	—
M76	—
M77	—
M78	—
M79	—
M80	—
M81	—
M82	—
M83	—
M84	—
M85	—
M86	—
M87	—
M88	—
M89	—
M90	—
EPS1	EP-1
EPS2	EP-32A
EPS3	EP-60A
EPS4	EP-96A
EPS5	EP-2
EPS6	EP-32
EPS7	EP-60
EPS8	EP-96
EPS9	EP-135
EPS10	EP-159B
EPS11	EP-172B
EPS12	EP-3
EPS13	EP-33
EPS14	EP-61
EPS15	EP-97
EPS16	EP-136
EPS17	EP-183A
EPS18	EP-4
EPS19	EP-34
EPS20	EP-98
EPS21	EP-137A
EPS22	EP-4A
EPS23	EP-34A
EPS24	EP-63
EPS25	EP-98A
EPS26	EP-137
EPS30	EP-34B
EPS31	EP-98B
EPS32	EP-5
EPS33	EP-36
EPS34	EP-64
EPS35	EP-100
EPS36	EP-138
EPS37	EP-6
EPS38	EP-37
EPS39	EP-101
EPS40	EP-139
EPS41	EP-6A
EPS42	EP-37A
EPS43	EP-102A
EPS44	EP-7
EPS45	EP-38
EPS46	EP-67
EPS47	EP-103
EPS48	EP-140
EPS49	EP-8
EPS50	EP-38A
EPS51	EP-68
EPS52	EP-104
EPS53	EP-141
EPS54	EP-9
EPS55	EP-39
EPS56	EP-69
EPS57	EP-105
EPS58	EP-142
EPS59	EP-163
EPS60	EP-175
EPS61	EP-184
EPS62	EP-10
EPS63	EP-40
EPS64	EP-70
EPS65	EP-106
EPS66	EP-143
EPS67	EP-164
EPS68	EP-176
EPS69	EP-184A
EPS70	EP-107
EPS71	EP-11
EPS72	EP-40A
EPS73	EP-71
EPS74	EP-144
EPS75	EP-72
EPS76	EP-108
EPS77	EP-12
EPS78	EP-41
EPS79	EP-73
EPS80	EP-109
EPS81	EP-13
EPS82	EP-42
EPS83	EP-74
EPS84	EP-110
EPS85	EP-145
EPS86	EP-165
EPS87	EP-177
EPS88	EP-185
EPS89	EP-13A
EPS90	EP-43
EPS91	EP-76
EPS92	EP-112
EPS93	EP-146
EPS94	EP-166
EPS95	EP-14
EPS96	EP-44
EPS97	EP-76A
EPS98	EP-113
EPS99	EP-16
EPS100	EP-31
EPS101	EP-46
EPS102	EP-78
EPS103	EP-116
EPS104	EP-148
EPS105	EP-167
EPS106	EP-178
EPS107	EP-186
EPS108	EP-17
EPS109	EP-47
EPS110	EP-79
EPS111	EP-117
EPS112	EP-149
EPS113	EP-168
EPS114	EP-179
EPS115	EP-17A
EPS116	EP-48
EPS117	EP-80
EPS118	EP-117A
EPS119	EP-18
EPS120	EP-49
EPS121	EP-81
EPS122	EP-118
EPS123	EP-150
EPS124	EP-169
EPS125	EP-180
EPS127	EP-49A
EPS128	EP-82
EPS129	EP-119
EPS130	EP-151
EPS131	EP-170
EPS132	EP-19
EPS133	EP-50
EPS134	EP-83
EPS135	EP-120
EPS136	EP-152
EPS137	EP-171
EPS138	EP-181
EPS139	EP-187
EPS140	EP-20
EPS141	EP-51
EPS142	EP-84
EPS143	EP-121
EPS144	EP-153
EPS145	EP-172
EPS146	EP-182
EPS147	EP-188
EPS148	EP-21
EPS149	EP-52
EPS150	EP-85
EPS151	EP-122
EPS152	EP-154
EPS153	EP-123
EPS154	EP-86
EPS155	EP-23
EPS156	EP-52A
EPS157	EP-87
EPS158	EP-124
EPS159	EP-24
EPS160	EP-53
EPS161	EP-125
EPS162	EP-155
EPS163	EP-24A
EPS164	EP-125A
EPS165	EP-24B
EPS166	EP-54
EPS167	EP-89
EPS168	EP-127
EPS169	EP-90
EPS170	EP-128
EPS171	EP-183
EPS172	EP-25
EPS173	EP-55
EPS174	EP-91
EPS175	EP-129
EPS176	EP-157
EPS177	EP-26
EPS178	EP-56
EPS179	EP-92
EPS180	EP-130
EPS181	EP-158
EPS182	EP-27
EPS183	EP-131
EPS184	EP-159
EPS185	EP-28
EPS186	EP-57
EPS187	EP-93A
EPS188	EP-132
EPS189	EP-15
EPS190	EP-77
EPS191	EP-114
EPS192	EP-147
EPS193	EP-29
EPS194	EP-58
EPS195	EP-94
EPS196	EP-133
EPS197	EP-30
EPS198	EP-59
EPS199	EP-95
EPS200	EP-134
EPS300	—

Fr.	KL	Fr.	KL	Fr.	KL	Fr.	KL	Fr.	KL	Fr.	KL
1	183	73	203	163	683	212-D	692	297	422	378	844
1-A	182	74	204	164	684	212-E	809	298	423	379-A	1014
2	185	75	205	165	784	212-F	929	299	424	379-B	1015
2-A	184	76	206	166	785	212-G	988	300	425	379-C	1016
3	181	77	207	167	786	213	394	301	426	379-D	1017
3-A	180	78	208	168	787	214	395	302	427	380	1086
4	189	79	209	169	788	215	29	303	428	381	1087
4-A	188	80	210	170	789	216	30	304	429	382	1088
5	187	81	211	171	790	217	31	305	575	383	1089
5-A	186	82	212	172	791	218	32	306	577	384	1090
6	352	83	213	173	792	219	33	307	576	385	1091
6-A	351	84	214	174	793	220	34	308	578	386	1092
7	354	85	215	175	794	221	35	309	579	387	1093
7-A	353	86	216	176	795	222	36	310	580	388	1094
8	350	87	217	177	796	223	37	311	581	389	1095
8-A	349	88	218	178	797	224	38	312	582	390	1096
9	358	89	219	179	798	225	39	313	583	391	1097
9-A	357	90	220	180	799	226	40	314	584	392	1098
10	356	91	221	181	800	226-A	41	315	585	393	1099
10-A	355	92	222	182	801	227	42	316	586	394	1100
11	518	93	359	183-A	904A	228	43	317	587	397	1101
11-A	517	94	360	183-B	905	229	44	318	588	398	1102
12	520	95-A	361	183-C	906	230	45	319	589	399	1103
12-A	519	96	362	184	907	231	46	320	590	401	1104-1105
13	516	97	363	185-A	908	232	47	321	591	402	1106
13-A	515	98	364	185-B	909	233	48	322	592	403	1107
14	522	99	365	185-C	910	234	49	324	709	404	1108
14-A	521	100	366	185-D	911	235	50	324-A	710	405	1109
16	3	101	367	185-E	912	236	51	324-C	708	406	1110
16-A	4	102	368	185-F	913	237	52	325	711	406-A	1111
17	1	103	369	185-G	914	238	53	326	712	407	1112
17-A	2	104	370	185-H	915	239	54	327	713	408	1113
18	5	105	371	185-I	916	240	121	328	714	409	1172
19	6	106	372	185-J	917	241	122	329	715	412	1173
20	7	107	373	185-K	918	242	123	330	716	413	1174
21	8	108	374	185-L	919	243	124	331	717	414	1175
22	9	109	375	185-M	920	244	125	332	718	416	1176
23	10	110	376	185-N	921	245	126	333	719	417	1177
24	11	111	377	186-A	966	246	127	334	720	418	1178
25	12	112	378	186-B	967	247	128	335	721	419	1179
26	13	113	379	186-C	968	248	129	337	834	420	1180
27	14	114	380	186-D	969	249	130	337-B	833	421	1181
28	15	115	381	187-A	970	250	131	338	836	422	1182
29	16	116	382	187-B	971	251	132	339	837	423	1183
30	17	117	383	187-C	972	252	133	340	838	423-A	1184
31	18	118	384	187-D	973	253	134	341	839	424	1245
32	19	119	385	187-E	974	254	135	342	840	427	1246
33	20	120	386	187-F	975	255	136	343	841	428	1247
34	21	121	387	187-G	976	256	137	344	842	429	1248
35	22	122	388	187-H	977	257	138	345-A	944-948	431	1249
36	23	123	389	187-I	978	258	139	345-B	949	432	1250
37	24	124	523	187-J	979	259	229	345-C	950	433	1251
37-A	25	125	524	187-K	980	260	230	345-D	951	434	1252
38	26	126	526	187-L	981	261	231	346-A	1007-1009	435	1253
39	27	127	526	190	390	262	232	346-B	1010	436	1254
40	28	128	527	190-A	391	263	233	346-C	1011	437	1255
41	100	129	528	190-B	392	264	234	346-D	1012	438	1256
41-A	101	130	529	191	547	265	235	346-E	1013	439	1257
42	102	131	530	191-A	548	266	236	347	55	440	1319
43	103	132	531	192	685	267	237	348	56	442	1320
44	104	133	532	192-A	686	268	238	349	57	443	1321
45	105	134	533	192-B	687	269	239	350	58	444	1322
46	106	135	534	193	802	270	240	351	59	444-A	1323
47	107	136	535	193-A	803	271	241	352	60	445	1324
48	108	137	536	193-B	804	272	242	353	140	446	1325
49	109	138	537	194	922	273	243	354	141	447	1326
50	110	139	538	194-A	923	274	244	355	142	448	1327
51	111	140	539	194-B	924	275	245	356	143	449	1328
52	112	141	540	195	982	276	246	357	144	450	1329
53	113	142	541	195-A	983	277	247	358	145	451	1330
54	114	143	542	196	393	278	248	359	253	452	1380
55	115	144	543	197	549	279	249	360	254	454	1381
56	116	145	544	198	688	280	250	361	255	455	1382
57	117	146	545	199	805	281	251	362	256	456	1383
58	118	147	546	200	925	282	252	363	257	457	1384
59	119	148	668	201	984	283	408	364	258	458	1385
60	120	149	669	202	1044	284	407	365	259	459	1386
61	190	150	670	203	689	284-A	410	366	430	460	1387
62	191	151	671	204	806	285-A	409	367	431	461	1388
63	192	152	672	205	926	286	411	368	432	462	1389
63-A	193	153	673	206	985	287	412	369	433	462-A	1390
64	194	154	674	207	690	288	413	370	434	463	1391
65	195	155	675	208	807	289	414	371	435	464	1439-1441
66	196	156	676	209	927	290	415	372	593	465	1442-1443
67	197	157	677	210	986	291	416	373	594	466	1114
68	198	158	678	211	1045	292	417	374	595	467	1115
69	199	159	679	212	691	293	418	375	596	468	1116
70	200	160	680	212-A	808	294	419	375-A	597	469	1117
71	201	161	681	212-B	928	295	420	376	722	470	1118
72	202	162	682	212-C	987	296	421	377	843	471	1119

Fr.	KL
472	1120
473	1121
474	1122
475	1123
476	1124
477	1125
478	1126
479	1185
480	1186
481	1187
482	1188
483	1189
484	1190
485	1191
486	1192
487	1193
488	1194
489	1195
490	1196
491	1197
492	1198
493	1258
494	1259
495	1260
496	1261
497	1262
498	1263
499	1264
500	1265
501	1266
502	1267
503	1268
504	1269
505	1270
506	1271
507	1331
508	1332
509	1333
510	1334
511	1335
512	1336
513	1337
514	1338
515	1339
516	1340
517	1341
518	1342
518-A	1343
519	1392
520	1393
521	1394
522	1395
523	1396
524	1397
525	1398
526	1399
527	1400
528	1401
529	1401A
530	1402
531	1403
532	1127
533	1128
533-A	1129
534	1130
535	1131
536	1132
537	1133
538	1134
538-B	1135
539	1199
540	1200
541	1201
542	1202
543	1203
544	1204
545	1205
546	1206
547	1207
548	1208
549	1272
550	1273
551	1274
552	1275
553	1276
554	1277
555	1278
556	1279
557	1280
558	1344
559	1345
560	1346
561	1347
562	1348
563	1349
564	1350
565	1351
566	1404
567	1405
568	1406
569	1407
570	1408
571	1409
572	1410
572-A	1411
573	1136
573-A	1137
574	1138
574-A	1139
575	1140
575-A	1141
575-B	1142
576	1209
576-A	1210
576-B	1211
577	1212
578	1213
579	1214
579-B	1215
580	1281
580-A	1282
580-B	1283
581	1284
582	1285
583	1286
584	1287
584-A	1288
585	1289
586	1352
586-A	1412
587	1143
588	1144
589	1145
590	1146
591	1147
592	1148
593	1149
594	1150
595	1151
596	1152
597	1153
597-A	1154
598	1155
599	1156
600	1157
601	1158
602	1159
603	1160
604	1161
605	1162
606	1163
607	1164
608	1165
609	1166
610	1167
611	1168
612	1169
613	1216
614	1217
615	1218
616	1219
617	1220
618	1221
619	1222
620	1223
621	1224
622	1225
623	1226
623-A	1227
624	1228
625	1229
626	1230
627	1231
628	1232
629	1233
630	1234
631	1235
632	1236
633	1237
634	1238
635	1239
636	1240
637	1241
638	1242
639	1290
640	1291
641	1292
642	1293
643	1294
644	1295
645	1296
646	1297
647	1298
648	1299
649	1300
649-A	1301
650	1302
651	1303
652	1304
653	1305
654	1036
655	1307
656	1308
657	1309
658	1310
659	1311
660	1312
661	1313
662	1314
663	1315
663-A	1316
664	1353
665	1354
666	1355
667	1356
668	1357
669	1358
670	1359
671	1360
672	1361
673	1362
674	1363
674-A	1364
675	1365
676	1366
677	1367
678	1368
679	1369
679-A	1370
680	1371
681	1372
682	1373
683	1374
684	1375
685	1376
685-A	1377
686	1413
687	1414
688	1415
689	1416
690	1417
691	1418
692	1419
693	1420
694	1421
695	1422
696	1423
697	1424
698	1425
699	1426
700	1427
701	1428
702	1429
702-A	1430
703	1431
704	1432
705	1433
706	1434
707	1435
707-A	1436
708	61
709	62
710	63
711	64
712	65
713	66
714	67
715	68
716	69
717	70
718	71
719	72
720	73
721	74
722	75
723	76
724	77
725	78
726	79
727	80
728	81
729	82
730	83
731	84
732	85
733	86
734	87
735	88
736	89
737	90
738	91
739	92
740	93
741	94
742	95
743	96
744	97
745	98
746	99
747	146
748	147
749	148
750	149
751	150
752	151
753	152
754	153
755	154
756	155
757	156
758	157
759	158
760	159
761	160
762	161
763	162
764	163
765	164
766	165
767	166
768	167
769	168
770	169
771	170
772	171
773	172
774	173
775	174
776	175
777	176
778	177
779	178
780	179
781	329
782	330
783	331
784	332
785	333
786	334
787	335
788	320
789	321
790	336
791	337
792	338
793	322
794	339
795	340
796	341
797	342
798	343
799	344
800	323
801	324
802	325
803	345
804	346
805	326
806	327
807	347
808	328
809	348
810	511
811	503
812	512
813	504
814	513
815	514
816	505
817	506
818	507
819	508
820	509
821	510
822	658
822-A	659
823	666
824	660
825	667
826	661
827	662
828	663
829	664
830	665
831	783
832	260
833	261
834	262
835	263
836	264
837	265
838	266
839	267
840	268
841	269
842	270
843	271
844	272
845	273
846	274
847	275
848	276
849	277
850	278
851	279
852	280
853	281
854	282
855	283
856	284
857	285
858	286
859	287
860	288
861	289
862	290
863	291
864	292
865	293
866	294
867	295
868	296
869	297
870	298
871	299
872	300
873	301
874	302
875	303
876	304
877	305
878	306
879	307
880	308
881	309
882	310
883	311
884	312
885	313
886	314
887	315
888	316
889	317
890	318
891	319
892	443
893	444
894	445
895	446
896	447
897	448
898	449
899	450
900	451
901	452
902	453
903	454
904	455
905	456
906	457
907	458
908	459
909	460
910	461
911	462
912	463
913	464
914	465
915	466
916	467
917	468
918	469
919	470
920	471
921	472
922	473
923	474
924	475
925	476
926	477
927	478
928	479
929	480
930	481
931	482
932	483
933	484
934	485
935	486
936	487
937	488
938	489
939	490
940	491
941	492
942	493
943	494
944	495
945	496
946	497
947	498
948	499
949	500
950	501
951	502
952	598
953	599
954	600
955	601
956	602
957	603
958	604
959	605
960	606
961	607
962	608
963	609
964	610
965	611
966	612
967	613
968	614
969	615
970	616
971	617
972	618
973	619
974	620
975	621
976	622
977	623
978	624
979	625
980	626
981	627
982	628
983	629
984	630
985	631
986	632

Fr.	KL	Fr.	KL	Fr.	KL	Fr.	KL	Fr.	KL	Fr.	KL
987	633	1077	850	1165	831	1222	1059A	1310	3221	1527	1641
988	634	1078	851	1166	832	1222-A	1059B	1310-A	3222	1528	1642
989	635	1079	852	1166-B	550	1222-B	1059C	1311	3223	1529	1643
990	636	1080	853	1166-C	810	1223	1072	1312	3224	1530	1644
991	637	1081	854	1166-D	930	1223-A	1071	1313	3225	1531	1645
992	638	1082	855	1166-E	989	1223-B	1073	1314	3245	1532	1646
993	639	1083	856	1166-F	1046	1223-C	1074	1316	3246	1533	1647
994	640	1084	857	1166-G	1068	1223-D	1075	1317	3247	1534	1648
995	641	1085	858	1166-H	811	1223-E	1076	1318	3248	1535	1649
996	642	1086	859	1166-I	931	1223-F	1077	1320	3249	1536	1650
997	643	1087	860	1166-J	990	1223-G	1078	1321	3250	1550	2745
998	644	1088	861	1166-K	1047	1224	1078A	1322	3251	1551	2746
999	645	1089	862	1166-L	1069	1224-A	1078B	1324	3275	1600	1445
1000	646	1090	863	1166-M	812	1224-B	1078C	1325	3276	1601	1446
1001	647	1091	864	1166-N	932	1225	1079	1326	3277	1602	1447
1002	648	1092	865	1166-O	991	1226	3252	1327	3278	1603	1448
1003	649	1093	866	1167	436	1227	3253	1328	3279	1604	1449
1004	650	1094	867	1168	437	1228	3209	1329	3281	1605	1450
1005	651	1095	868	1169	438	1229	3210	1330	3282	1606	1451
1006	652	1096	869	1170	439	1230	3211	1331	3283	1607	1452
1007	653	1097	870	1171	440	1231	3212	1332	3284	1608	1453
1008	654	1098	871	1172	441	1232	3226	1333	3285	1609	1611
1009	655	1099	872	1173	442	1233	3227	1334	3286	1610	1612
1010	656	1100	873	1174	552	1234	3228	1335	3287	1611	1454
1011	657	1101	874	1175	551	1235	3229	1336	3288	1612	1455
1012	723	1102	875	1176	553	1236	3254	1337	3289	1613	1456
1013	724	1103	876	1177	554	1237	3255	1338	3290	1614	1457
1014	725	1104	877	1178	555	1238	3256	1339	3291	1615	1458
1015	726	1105	878	1179	556	1239	3257	1340	3292	1616	1459
1016	727	1106	879	1180	557	1240	3213	1341	3293	1617	1460
1017	728	1107	880	1181	558	1241	3214	1342	3294	1618	1461
1018	729	1108	881	1182	559	1242	3215	1343	3295	1619	1462
1019	730	1109	882	1183	560	1243	3216	1344	3296	1620	1463
1020	731	1110	883	1184	561	1244	3230	1345	3297	1621	1464
1021	732	1111	884	1185	562	1245	3231	1346	3298	1650	1651
1022	733	1112	885	1186	563	1246	3232	1347	3299	1651	1652
1023	734	1113	886	1187	564	1247	3233	1348	3300	1652	1653
1024	735	1114	887	1188	694	1248	3234	1349	3301	1653	1654
1025	736	1115	888	1189	693	1249	3235	1350	3302	1654	1655
1026	737	1116	889	1190	695	1251	3258	1351	3303	1655	1656
1027	738	1117	890	1191	696	1252	3259	1352	3304	1656	1657
1028	739	1118	891	1192	697	1253	3260	1353	3305	1657	1658
1029	740	1119	892	1193	698	1254	3261	1354	3306	1700	1964
1030	741	1120	893	1194	699	1255	3262	1355	3307	1700-A	1965
1031	742	1121	894	1195	700	1255-A	3263	1356	3308	1701	1966
1032	743	1122	895	1196	701	1256	3264	1357	3309	1702	1967
1033	744	1123	896	1197	702	1257	3327	1358	3310	1703	1968
1034	745	1124	897	1198	703	1258	3328	1359	3311	1704	1969
1035	746	1125	898	1199	704	1259	3329	1360	3312	1705	1970
1036	747	1126	899	1200	705	1260	3330	1361	3313	1706	1971
1037	748	1127	900	1201	814	1261	3331	1362	3314	1707	1972
1038	749	1128	901	1202	813	1264	3348	1363	3315	1708	1973
1039	750	1129	902	1203	815	1265	3349	1364	3316	1800-1	1170
1040	751	1130	903	1204	816	1266	3350	1365	3317	1800-2	1171
1041	752	1131	904	1205	817	1267	3332	1366	3318	1801-1	1243
1042	753	1132	952-965	1206	818	1268	3333	1367	3319	1801-2	1244
1043	754	1133	1018-1032	1207	819	1269	3334	1368	3320	1802-1	1317
1044	755	1134	1060-1067	1208	820	1270	3335	1369	3321	1802-2	1318
1045	756	1135	1080-1085	1209	821	1271	3336	1370	3322	1803-1	1378
1046	757	1136	223	1210	822	1279	3217	1371	3323	1803-2	1379
1047	758	1137	224	1211	823	1280	3218	1372	3324	1804-1	1437
1048	759	1138	225	1212	824	1281	3219	1373	3325	1804-2	1438
1049	760	1139	226	1213	825	1282	3220	1373-A	3326	1850-A	1659
1050	761	1140	227	1214	826	1283	3236	1374	3343	1850-B	1660
1051	762	1141	228	1215	827	1284	3237	1375	3344	1850-C	1661
1052	763	1142	396	1216	937	1285	3238	1376	3345	1850-D	1662
1053	764	1143	397	1216-A	938	1286	3239	1377	3346	1850-F	1664
1054	765	1144	398	1216-B	939	1287	3240	1379	3347	1850-G	1665
1055	766	1145	399	1217	940	1288	3241	1380	3353	1850-H	1666
1056	767	1146	400	1218	993	1289	3242	1381	3353A	1850-I	1667
1057	768	1147	401	1218-A	992	1290	3243	1382	3354	1850-J	1668
1058	769	1148	402	1218-B	994	1290-A	3244	1383	3355	1850-K	1669
1059	770	1149	403	1218-C	995	1291	3265	1383-A	3356	1850-L	1670
1060	771	1150	404	1218-D	996	1292	3266	1500	1444	1860-A	1974
1061	772	1151	405	1218-E	997	1293	3267	1501	1613	1860-B	1975
1062	773	1151-A	406	1218-F	998	1294	3268	1502	1614	1860-C	1976
1063	774	1152	566	1218-G	999	1295	3269	1503	1615	1860-D	1977
1064	775	1153	571	1219	1000-1005	1296	3270	1504	1616	1860-E	1978
1065	776	1154	567	1220	1006	1297	3271	1505	1617	1860-F	1979
1066	777	1155	568	1221	1050	1298	3272	1506	1618	1860-G	1980
1067	778	1156	570	1221-A	1049	1299	3273	1507	1619	1860-H	1981
1068	779	1157	572	1221-B	1051	1300	3274	1508	1620	1860-I	1982
1069	780	1158	573	1221-C	1052	1301	3337	1509	1621	1860-J	1983
1070	781	1159	574	1221-D	1053	1302	3338	1510	1622	1860-K	1984
1071	782	1159-A	569	1221-E	1054	1302-A	3339	1511	1623	1860-L	1985
1072	845	1160	706	1221-F	1055	1303	3340	1512	1624	1870-A	2262
1073	846	1161	707	1221-G	1056	1305	3341	1513	1625	1870-B	2263
1074	847	1162	828	1221-H	1057	1307	3342	1514	1626	1870-C	2264
1075	848	1163	829	1221-I	1058	1308	3351	1525	1639	1870-D	2265
1076	849	1164	830	1221-J	1059	1309	3352	1526	1640	1870-E	2266

Fr.	KL
1870-F	2267
1870-G	2268
1870-H	2269
1870-I	2270
1870-J	2271
1870-K	2272
1870-L	2273
1880-B	2526
1880-D	2527
1880-G	2528
1880-I	2529
1880-J	2530
1880-K	2531
1880-L	2532
1890-B	2749
1890-D	2751
1890-E	2752
1890-G	2754
1890-I	2756
1890-J	2757
1890-K	2758
1900-A	1465
1900-B	1466
1900-C	1467
1900-D	1468
1900-E	1469
1900-F	1470
1900-G	1471
1900-H	1472
1900-I	1473
1900-J	1474
1900-K	1475
1900-L	1476
1901-A	1477
1901-B	1478
1901-C	1479
1901-D	1480
1901-E	1481
1901-F	1482
1901-G	1483
1901-H	1484
1901-I	1485
1901-J	1486
1901-K	1487
1901-L	1488
1902-B	1490
1902-E	1493
1902-G	1495
1902-J	1498
1902-L	1500
1903-A	1501
1903-B	1502
1903-C	1503
1903-D	1504
1903-E	1505
1903-F	1506
1903-G	1507
1903-H	1508
1903-I	1509
1903-J	1510
1903-K	1511
1903-L	1512
1904-A	1513
1904-B	1514
1904-C	1515
1904-D	1516
1904-E	1517
1904-F	1518
1904-G	1519
1904-H	1520
1904-I	1521
1904-J	1522
1904-K	1523
1904-L	1524
1905-A	1525
1905-B	1526
1905-C	1527
1905-D	1528
1905-E	1529
1905-F	1530
1905-G	1531
1905-H	1532
1905-I	1533
1905-J	1534
1905-K	1535
1905-L	1536
1906-B	1538
1906-D	1540
1906-E	1541
1906-F	1542

Fr.	KL
1906-G	1543
1906-H	1544
1906-I	1545
1906-J	1546
1906-K	1547
1906-L	1548
1907-A	1561
1907-B	1562
1907-C	1563
1907-D	1564
1907-E	1565
1907-F	1566
1907-G	1567
1907-H	1568
1907-I	1569
1907-J	1570
1907-K	1571
1907-L	1572
1908-A	1573
1908-B	1574
1908-C	1575
1908-D	1576
1908-E	1577
1908-F	1578
1908-G	1579
1908-H	1580
1908-I	1581
1908-J	1582
1908-K	1583
1908-L	1584
1909-A	1585
1909-B	1586
1909-C	1587
1909-D	1588
1909-E	1589
1909-F	1590
1909-G	1591
1909-H	1592
1909-I	1593
1909-J	1594
1909-K	1595
1909-L	1596
1910-A	1597
1910-B	1598
1910-C	1599
1910-D	1600
1910-E	1601
1910-F	1602
1910-G	1603
1910-H	1604
1910-I	1605
1910-J	1606
1910-K	1607
1910-L	1608
1911-A	3500
1911-B	3501
1911-C	3502
1911-D	3503
1911-E	3504
1911-F	3505
1911-G	3506
1911-H	3507
1911-I	3508
1911-J	3509
1911-K	3510
1911-L	3511
1935-A	1627
1935-B	1628
1935-C	1629
1935-D	1630
1935-E	1631
1935-F	1632
1935-G	1633
1935-H	1634
1935-I	1635
1935-J	1636
1935-K	1637
1935-L	1638
1950-A	1671
1950-B	1672
1950-C	1673
1950-D	1674
1950-E	1675
1950-F	1676
1950-G	1677
1950-H	1678
1950-I	1679
1950-J	1680
1950-K	1681
1950-L	1682

Fr.	KL
1951-A	1683
1951-B	1684
1951-C	1685
1951-D	1686
1951-E	1687
1951-F	1688
1951-G	1689
1951-H	1690
1951-I	1691
1951-J	1692
1951-K	1693
1951-L	1694
1952-A	1695
1952-B	1696
1952-C	1697
1952-D	1698
1952-E	1699
1952-F	1700
1952-G	1701
1952-H	1702
1952-I	1703
1952-J	1704
1952-K	1705
1952-L	1706
1953-D	1710
1953-F	1712
1953-L	1718
1954-F	1724
1955-A	1731
1955-B	1732
1955-C	1733
1955-D	1734
1955-E	1735
1955-F	1736
1955-G	1737
1955-H	1738
1955-I	1739
1955-J	1740
1955-K	1741
1955-L	1742
1957-A	1743
1957-B	1744
1957-C	1745
1957-D	1746
1957-E	1747
1957-F	1748
1957-G	1749
1957-H	1750
1957-L	1754
1958-A	1755
1958-B	1756
1958-C	1757
1958-D	1758
1958-E	1759
1958-F	1760
1958-G	1761
1958-H	1762
1958-I	1763
1958-J	1764
1958-L	1766
1959-A	1767
1959-B	1768
1959-C	1769
1959-D	1770
1959-E	1771
1959-F	1772
1959-G	1773
1959-H	1774
1959-I	1775
1959-J	1776
1959-K	1777
1959-L	1778
1960-A	1779
1960-B	1780
1960-C	1781
1960-D	1782
1960-E	1783
1960-F	1784
1960-G	1785
1960-H	1786
1960-I	1787
1960-J	1788
1960-K	1789
1960-L	1790
1961-A	1791
1961-B	1792
1961-C	1793
1961-D	1794
1961-E	1795
1961-F	1796

Fr.	KL
1961-G	1797
1961-H	1798
1961-I	1799
1961-J	1800
1961-K	1801
1961-L	1802
1962-A	1803
1962-B	1804
1962-C	1805
1962-D	1806
1962-E	1807
1962-F	1808
1962-G	1809
1962-H	1810
1962-I	1811
1962-J	1812
1962-K	1813
1962-L	1814
1963-A	1815
1963-B	1816
1963-C	1817
1963-D	1818
1963-E	1819
1963-F	1820
1963-G	1821
1963-H	1822
1963-I	1823
1963-J	1824
1963-K	1825
1963-L	1826
1964-A	1827
1964-B	1828
1964-C	1829
1964-D	1830
1964-E	1831
1964-F	1832
1964-G	1833
1964-H	1834
1964-I	1835
1964-J	1836
1964-K	1837
1964-L	1838
1965-A	1839
1965-B	1840
1965-C	1841
1965-D	1842
1965-E	1843
1965-F	1844
1965-G	1845
1965-H	1846
1965-I	1847
1965-J	1848
1965-K	1849
1965-L	1850
1966-B	1852
1966-G	1853
1966-L	1854
1967-A	1855
1967-B	1856
1967-C	1857
1967-D	1858
1967-F	1859
1967-G	1860
1967-H	1861
1967-J	1861A
1967-K	1862
1967-L	1863
1968-A	1864
1968-B	1865
1968-C	1866
1968-D	1867
1968-E	1868
1968-F	1869
1968-G	1870
1968-H	1871
1968-I	1872
1968-J	1873
1968-K	1874
1968-L	1875
1969-A	1876
1969-B	1877
1969-C	1878
1969-D	1879
1969-E	1880
1969-F	1881
1969-G	1882
1969-H	1883
1969-I	1884
1969-J	1885
1969-K	1886

Fr.	KL
1969-L	1887
1970-A	1888
1970-B	1889
1970-C	1890
1970-D	1891
1970-E	1892
1970-F	1893
1970-G	1894
1970-H	1895
1970-I	1896
1970-J	1897
1970-K	1898
1970-L	1899
1971-A	1900
1971-B	1901
1971-C	1902
1971-D	1903
1971-E	1904
1971-F	1905
1971-G	1906
1971-H	1907
1971-I	1908
1971-J	1909
1971-K	1910
1971-L	1911
1972-A	1912
1972-B	1913
1972-C	1914
1972-D	1915
1972-E	1916
1972-F	1917
1972-G	1918
1972-H	1919
1972-I	1920
1972-J	1921
1972-K	1922
1972-L	1923
1973-A	1924
1973-B	1925
1973-C	1926
1973-D	1927
1973-E	1928
1973-F	1929
1973-G	1930
1973-H	1931
1973-I	1932
1973-J	1933
1973-K	1934
1973-L	1935
1974-A	1936
1974-B	1937
1974-C	1938
1974-D	1939
1974-E	1940
1974-F	1941
1974-G	1942
1974-H	1943
1974-I	1944
1974-J	1945
1974-K	1946
1974-L	1947
1975-A	1948
1975-B	1949
1975-C	1950
1975-D	1951
1975-E	1952
1975-F	1953
1975-G	1954
1975-H	1955
1975-I	1956
1975-J	1957
1975-K	1958
1975-L	1959
1976-A	3512
1976-B	3513
1976-C	3514
1976-D	3515
1976-E	3516
1976-F	3517
1976-G	3518
1976-H	3519
1976-I	3520
1976-J	3521
1976-K	3522
1976-L	3523
2000-A	1986
2000-B	1987
2000-C	1988
2000-D	1989
2000-E	1990

Fr.	KL
2000-F	1991
2000-G	1992
2000-H	1993
2000-I	1994
2000-J	1995
2000-K	1996
2000-L	1997
2001-A	1998
2001-B	1999
2001-C	2000
2001-D	2001
2001-E	2002
2001-F	2003
2001-G	2004
2001-H	2005
2001-I	2006
2001-J	2007
2001-K	2008
2001-L	2009
2002-A	2010
2002-B	2011
2002-C	2012
2002-D	2013
2002-E	2014
2002-F	2015
2002-G	2016
2002-H	2017
2002-I	2018
2002-J	2019
2002-K	2020
2002-L	2021
2003-B	2022
2003-D	2023
2003-E	2024
2003-F	2025
2003-G	2026
2004-A	2027
2004-B	2028
2004-C	2029
2004-D	2030
2004-E	2031
2004-F	2032
2004-G	2033
2004-H	2034
2004-I	2035
2004-J	2036
2004-K	2037
2004-L	2038
2006-A	2039
2006-B	2040
2006-C	2041
2006-D	2042
2006-E	2043
2006-F	2044
2006-G	2045
2006-H	2046
2006-I	2047
2006-J	2048
2006-K	2049
2006-L	2050
2007-A	2051
2007-B	2052
2007-C	2053
2007-D	2054
2007-E	2055
2007-F	2056
2007-G	2057
2007-H	2058
2007-I	2059
2007-J	2060
2007-K	2061
2007-L	2062
2008-A	2063
2008-B	2064
2008-C	2065
2008-D	2066
2008-E	2067
2008-F	2068
2008-G	2069
2008-H	2070
2008-I	2071
2008-J	2072
2008-K	2073
2008-L	2074
2009-A	2075
2009-B	2076
2009-C	2077
2009-D	2078
2009-E	2079
2009-F	2080

Fr.	KL
2009-G	2081
2009-H	2082
2009-I	2083
2009-J	2084
2009-K	2085
2009-L	2086
2010-A	2087
2010-B	2088
2010-C	2089
2010-D	2090
2010-E	2091
2010-F	2092
2010-G	2093
2010-H	2094
2010-I	2095
2010-J	2096
2010-K	2097
2010-L	2098
2011-A	2099
2011-B	2100
2011-C	2101
2011-D	2102
2011-E	2103
2011-F	2104
2011-G	2105
2011-H	2106
2011-I	2107
2011-J	2108
2011-K	2109
2011-L	2110
2012-A	2111
2012-B	2112
2012-C	2113
2012-D	2114
2012-E	2115
2012-F	2116
2012-G	2117
2012-H	2118
2012-I	2119
2012-J	2120
2012-K	2121
2012-L	2122
2013-A	2123
2013-B	2124
2013-C	2125
2013-D	2126
2013-E	2127
2013-F	2128
2013-G	2129
2013-H	2130
2013-I	2131
2013-J	2132
2013-K	2133
2013-L	2134
2014-A	2135
2014-B	2136
2014-C	2137
2014-D	2138
2014-E	2139
2014-F	2140
2014-G	2141
2014-H	2142
2014-J	2144
2014-K	2145
2014-I	2146
2015-B	2147
2015-G	2148
2015-L	2149
2016-B	2151
2016-C	2152
2016-D	2153
2016-E	2154
2016-F	2155
2016-G	2156
2016-H	2157
2016-J	2159
2016-K	2160
2016-L	2161
2016A	2150
2017-A	2162
2017-B	2163
2017-C	2164
2017-D	2165
2017-E	2166
2017-F	2167
2017-G	2168
2017-H	2169
2017-I	2170
2017-J	2171
2017-K	2172

Fr.	KL
2017-L	2173
2018-A	2174
2018-B	2175
2018-C	2176
2018-D	2177
2018-E	2178
2018-F	2179
2018-G	2180
2018-H	2181
2018-I	2182
2018-J	2183
2018-K	2184
2018-L	2185
2019-A	2186
2019-B	2187
2019-C	2188
2019-D	2189
2019-E	2190
2019-F	2191
2019-G	2192
2019-H	2193
2019-I	2194
2019-J	2195
2019-K	2196
2019-L	2197
2020-A	2198
2020-B	2199
2020-C	2200
2020-D	2201
2020-E	2202
2020-F	2203
2020-G	2204
2020-H	2205
2020-I	2206
2020-J	2207
2020-K	2208
2020-L	2209
2021-A	2210
2021-B	2211
2021-C	2212
2021-D	2213
2021-E	2214
2021-F	2215
2021-G	2216
2021-H	2217
2021-I	2218
2021-J	2219
2021-K	2220
2021-L	2221
2022-A	2222
2022-B	2223
2022-C	2224
2022-D	2225
2022-E	2226
2022-F	2227
2022-G	2228
2022-H	2229
2022-I	2230
2022-J	2231
2022-K	2232
2022-L	2233
2023-A	2234
2023-B	2235
2023-C	2236
2023-D	2237
2023-F	2238
2023-F	2239
2023-G	2240
2023-H	2241
2023-I	2242
2023-J	2243
2023-K	2244
2023-L	2245
2024-A	2246
2024-B	2247
2024-C	2248
2024-D	2249
2024-E	2250
2024-F	2251
2024-G	2252
2024-H	2253
2024-I	2254
2024-J	2255
2024-K	2256
2024-L	2257
2025-A	3524
2025-B	3525
2025-C	3526
2025-D	3527
2025-E	3528

Fr.	KL
2025-F	3529
2025-G	3530
2025-H	3531
2025-I	3532
2025-J	3533
2025-K	3534
2025-L	3535
2050-A	2274
2050-B	2275
2050-C	2276
2050-D	2277
2050-E	2278
2050-F	2279
2050-G	2280
2050-H	2281
2050-I	2282
2050-J	2283
2050-K	2284
2050-L	2285
2051-A	2286
2051-B	2287
2051-C	2288
2051-D	2289
2051-E	2290
2051-F	2291
2051-G	2292
2051-H	2293
2051-J	2294
2051-K	2295
2052-A	2296
2052-B	2297
2052-C	2298
2052-D	2299
2052-E	2300
2052-F	2301
2052-G	2302
2052-H	2303
2052-I	2304
2052-J	2305
2052-K	2306
2052-L	2307
2053-G	2308
2053-L	2309
2054-A	2310
2054-B	2311
2054-C	2312
2054-D	2313
2054-E	2314
2054-F	2315
2054-G	2316
2054-H	2317
2054-I	2318
2054-J	2319
2054-K	2320
2054-L	2321
2055-A	2322
2055-B	2323
2055-C	2324
2055-D	2325
2055-E	2326
2055-F	2327
2055-G	2328
2055-H	2329
2055-I	2330
2055-J	2331
2055-K	2332
2055-L	2333
2056-A	2334
2056-B	2335
2056-C	2336
2056-D	2337
2056-E	2338
2056-F	2339
2056-G	2340
2056-H	2341
2056-I	2342
2056-J	2343
2056-K	2344
2056-L	2345
2057-A	2346
2057-B	2347
2057-C	2348
2057-D	2349
2057-E	2350
2057-F	2351
2057-G	2352
2057-H	2353
2057-I	2354
2057-J	2355
2057-K	2356

Fr.	KL
2057-L	2357
2058-A	2358
2058-B	2359
2058-C	2360
2058-D	2361
2058-E	2362
2058-F	2363
2058-G	2364
2058-H	2365
2058-I	2366
2058-J	2367
2058-K	2368
2058-L	2369
2059-A	2370
2059-B	2371
2059-C	2372
2059-D	2373
2059-E	2374
2059-F	2375
2059-G	2376
2059-H	2377
2059-I	2378
2059-J	2379
2059-K	2380
2059-L	2381
2060-A	2382
2060-B	2383
2060-C	2384
2060-D	2385
2060-E	2386
2060-F	2387
2060-G	2388
2060-H	2389
2060-I	2390
2060-J	2391
2060-K	2392
2060-L	2393
2061-A	2394
2061-B	2395
2061-C	2396
2061-D	2397
2061-E	2398
2061-F	2399
2061-G	2400
2061-H	2401
2061-I	2402
2061-J	2403
2061-K	2404
2061-L	2405
2062-A	2406
2062-B	2407
2062-C	2408
2062-D	2409
2062-E	2410
2062-F	2411
2062-G	2412
2062-H	2413
2062-I	2414
2062-J	2415
2062-K	2416
2062-L	2417
2063-A	2418
2063-B	2419
2063-C	2419A
2063-D	2420
2063-E	2421
2063-F	2422
2063-G	2423
2063-H	2424
2063-I	2424A
2063-J	2425
2063-K	2426
2063-L	2427
2064-B	2428
2064-G	2429
2064-L	2430
2065-A	2431
2065-B	2432
2065-D	2433
2065-E	2434
2065-F	2435
2065-G	2436
2065-H	2437
2065-J	2438
2065-K	2439
2065-L	2440
2066-A	2441
2066-B	2442
2066-C	2443
2066-D	2444

Fr.	KL
2066-E	2445
2066-F	2446
2066-G	2447
2066-H	2448
2066-I	2449
2066-J	2450
2066-K	2451
2066-L	2452
2067-A	2453
2067-B	2454
2067-C	2455
2067-D	2456
2067-E	2457
2067-F	2458
2067-G	2459
2067-H	2460
2067-I	2461
2067-J	2462
2067-K	2463
2067-L	2464
2068-A	2465
2068-B	2466
2068-C	2467
2068-D	2468
2068-E	2469
2068-F	2470
2068-G	2471
2068-H	2472
2068-I	2473
2068-J	2474
2068-K	2475
2068-L	2476
2069-B	2477
2069-D	2478
2069-E	2479
2069-F	2480
2069-G	2481
2069-H	2482
2069-I	2483
2069-J	2484
2069-K	2485
2069-L	2486
2070-A	2487
2070-B	2488
2070-C	2489
2070-D	2490
2070-E	2491
2070-F	2492
2070-G	2493
2070-H	2494
2070-I	2495
2070-J	2496
2070-K	2497
2070-L	2498
2071-A	2499
2071-B	2500
2071-C	2501
2071-D	2502
2071-E	2503
2071-F	2504
2071-G	2505
2071-H	2506
2071-I	2507
2071-J	2508
2071-K	2509
2071-L	2510
2072-A	2511
2072-B	2512
2072-C	2513
2072-D	2514
2072-E	2515
2072-F	2516
2072-G	2517
2072-H	2518
2072-I	2519
2072-J	2520
2072-K	2521
2072-L	2522
2072-L2533	
2100-A	2534
2100-B	2535
2100-C	2536
2100-D	2537
2100-E	2538
2100-F	2539
2100-G	2540
2100-H	2541
2100-I	2542
2100-J	2543
2100-K	2544

Fr.	KL
2100-L	2545
2101-A	2546
2101-B	2547
2101-C	2548
2101-D	2549
2101-E	2550
2101-F	2551
2101-G	2552
2101-H	2553
2101-I	2554
2101-J	2555
2101-K	2556
2101-L	2557
2102-A	2558
2102-B	2559
2102-C	2560
2102-D	2561
2102-E	2562
2102-F	2563
2102-G	2564
2102-H	2565
2102-I	2566
2102-J	2567
2102-K	2568
2102-L	2569
2103-A	2570
2103-B	2571
2103-D	2572
2103-E	2573
2103-F	2574
2103-G	2575
2103-H	2576
2103-I	2577
2103-J	2578
2103-K	2579
2103-L	2580
2104-C	2581
2104-D	2582
2104-E	2583
2104-F	2584
2104-G	2585
2104-H	2586
2104-I	2587
2104-J	2588
2104-K	2589
2104-L	2589
2105-A	2590
2105-B	2591
2105-C	2592
2105-D	2593
2105-E	2594
2105-F	2595
2105-G	2596
2105-H	2597
2105-I	2598
2105-J	2599
2105-K	2600
2106-A	2601
2106-B	2602
2106-C	2603
2106-E	2604
2106-F	2605
2106-G	2606
2106-K	2607
2107-A	2608
2107-B	2609
2107-C	2610
2107-D	2611
2107-E	2612
2107-F	2613
2107-G	2614
2107-H	2615
2107-I	2616
2107-J	2617
2107-K	2618
2107-L	2619
2108-A	2620
2108-B	2621
2108-C	2622
2108-D	2623
2108-E	2624
2108-F	2625
2108-G	2626
2108-H	2627
2108-J	2628
2108-K	2629
2108-L	2630
2109-A	2631
2109-B	2632
2109-C	2633

Fr.	KL	Fr.	KL	Fr.	KL	Fr.	KL	Fr.	KL	Fr.	KL
2109-D	2634	2118-D	2724	2156-B	2817	2164-J	2907	2210-C	2987	2308	2259
2109-E	2635	2118-E	2725	2156-C	2818	2164-K	2908	2210-D	2988	2309	2260
2109-G	2636	2118-F	2726	2156-F	2819	2164-L	2909	2210-E	2989	2400	1963
2109-H	2637	2118-G	2727	2156-G	2820	2165-A	2898A	2210-F	2990	2402	2261
2109-J	2638	2118-H	2728	2156-H	2821	2165-B	2899A	2210-G	2991	2404	2525
2109-K	2639	2118-I	2729	2156-K	2822	2165-C	2900A	2210-H	2992	2405	2747
2109-L	2640	2118-J	2730	2157-A	2823	2165-D	2901A	2210-I	2993	2407	2945
2110-A	2641	2118-K	2731	2157-B	2824	2165-E	2902A	2210-J	2994	2408	2984
2110-B	2642	2118-L	2732	2157-C	2825	2165-F	2903A	2210-K	2995	2410	3022
2110-C	2643	2119-A	2733	2157-D	2826	2165-G	2904A	2210-L	2996	2411	3046
2110-D	2644	2119-B	2734	2157-E	2827	2165-H	2905A	2211-A	2997	EP-1	EPS1
2110-E	2645	2119-C	2735	2157-F	2828	2165-I	2906A	2211-B	2998	EP-2	EPS5
2110-G	2646	2119-D	2736	2157-G	2829	2165-J	2907A	2211-C	2999	EP-3	EPS12
2110-H	2647	2119-E	2737	2157-H	2830	2165-K	2908A	2211-D	3000	EP-4	EPS18
2110-I	2648	2119-F	2738	2157-I	2831	2165-L	2909A	2211-E	3001	EP-4A	EPS22
2110-J	2649	2119-G	2739	2157-J	2832	2166-A	2910	2211-F	3002	EP-5	EPS32
2110-K	2650	2119-H	2740	2157-K	2834	2166-B	2911	2211-G	3003	EP-6	EPS37
2110-L	2651	2119-I	2741	2157-L	2835	2166-C	2912	2211-H	3004	EP-6A	EPS41
2111-A	2652	2119-J	2742	2158-A	2835	2166-D	2913	2211-I	3005	EP-7	EPS44
2111-B	2653	2119-K	2743	2158-B	2836	2166-E	2914	2211-J	3006	EP-8	EPS49
2111-C	2654	2119-L	274J	2158-C	2837	2166-F	2915	2211-K	3007	EP-9	EPS54
2111-D	2655	2150-A	2760	2158-D	2838	2166-G	2916	2211-L	3008	EP-10	EPS62
2111-E	2656	2150-B	2761	2158-E	2839	2166-H	2917	2212-A	3009	EP-11	EPS71
2111-F	2657	2150-C	2762	2158-F	2840	2166-I	2918	2212-B	3010	EP-12	EPS77
2111-G	2658	2150-D	2763	2158-G	2841	2166-J	2919	2212-C	3011	EP-13	EPS81
2111-H	2659	2150-E	2764	2158-H	2842	2166-K	2920	2212-D	3012	EP-13A	EPS89
2111-I	2660	2150-F	2765	2158-I	2843	2166-L	2921	2212-E	3013	EP-14	EPS95
2111-J	2661	2150-G	2766	2158-J	2844	2167-A	2922	2212-F	3014	EP-15	EPS189
2111-K	2662	2150-H	2767	2158-K	2845	2167-B	2923	2212-G	3015	EP-16	EPS99
2111-L	2663	2150-I	2768	2158-L	2846	2167-C	2924	2212-H	3016	EP-17	EPS108
2112-B	2664	2150-J	2769	2159-A	2847	2167-D	2925	2212-I	3017	EP-17A	EPS115
2112-G	2665	2150-K	2770	2159-B	2848	2167-E	2926	2212-J	3018	EP-18	EPS119
2112-L	2666	2150-L	2771	2159-C	2849	2167-F	2927	2212-L	3019	EP-19	EPS132
2113-A	2667	2151-A	2772	2159-D	2850	2167-G	2928	2213-A	3020	EP-20	EPS140
2113-B	2668	2151-B	2773	2159-E	2851	2167-H	2929	2213-B	3021	EP-21	EPS148
2113-C	2669	2151-C	2774	2159-F	2852	2167-I	2930	2220-A	3023	EP-23	EPS155
2113-D	2670	2151-D	2775	2159-G	2853	2167-J	2931	2220-B	3024	EP-24	EPS159
2113-E	2671	2151-E	2776	2159-H	2854	2167-K	2932	2220-D	3025	EP-24A	EPS163
2113-F	2672	2151-F	2777	2159-I	2855	2167-L	2933	2220-E	3026	EP-24B	EPS165
2113-G	2673	2151-G	2778	2159-J	2856	2168-A	2934	2220-F	3027	EP-25	EPS172
2113-H	2674	2151-H	2779	2159-K	2857	2168-B	2935	2220-G	3028	EP-26	EPS177
2113-I	2675	2151-I	2780	2159-L	2858	2168-C	2936	2220-J	3029	EP-27	EPS182
2113-J	2676	2151-J	2781	2160-A	2859	2168-D	2937	2220-K	3030	EP-28	EPS185
2113-K	2677	2151-K	2782	2160-B	2860	2168-E	2938	2220-L	3031	EP-29	EPS193
2113-L	2678	2151-L	2783	2160-C	2861	2168-F	2939	2221-A	3032	EP-30	EPS197
2114-A	2679	2152-A	2784	2160-D	2862	2168-G	2940	2221-B	3033	EP-31	EPS100
2114-B	2680	2152-B	2785	2160-E	2863	2168-H	2941	2221-C	3034	EP-32	EPS6
2114-C	2681	2152-C	2786	2160-F	2864	2168-I	2942	2221-D	3035	EP-32A	EPS2
2114-D	2682	2152-D	2787	2160-G	2865	2168-J	2943	2221-E	3036	EP-33	EPS13
2114-E	2683	2152-E	2788	2160-H	2866	2168-K	2944	2221-F	3037	EP-34	EPS19
2114-F	2684	2152-F	2789	2160-I	2867	2168-L	2945	2221-G	3038	EP-34A	EPS23
2114-G	2685	2152-G	2790	2160-J	2868	2200-A	2946	2221-H	3039	EP-34B	EPS30
2114-H	2686	2152-H	2791	2160-K	2869	2200-B	2947	2221-J	3040	EP-36	EPS33
2114-I	2687	2152-I	2792	2160-L	2870	2200-C	2948	2221-K	3041	EP-37	EPS38
2114-J	2688	2152-J	2793	2161-A	2871	2200-D	2949	2221-L	3042	EP-37A	EPS42
2114-K	2689	2152-K	2794	2161-B	2872	2200-E	2950	2222-H	3043	EP-38	EPS45
2114-L	2690	2152-L	2795	2161-C	2873	2200-F	2951	2223-A	3044	EP-38A	EPS50
2115-A	2691	2153-A	2784A	2161-D	2874	2200-G	2952	2223-B	3045	EP-39	EPS55
2115-B	2692	2153-D	2785A	2161-E	2875	2200-H	2953	2230-A	3047	EP-40	EPS63
2115-C	2693	2153-C	2786A	2161-F	2876	2200-I	2954	2230-B	3048	EP-40A	EPS72
2115-D	2694	2153-D	2787A	2161-G	2877	2200-J	2955	2230-D	3049	EP-41	EPS78
2115-E	2695	2153-E	2788A	2161-H	2878	2200-K	2956	2230-E	3050	EP-42	EPS82
2115-F	2696	2153-F	2789A	2161-I	2879	2200-L	2957	2230-F	3051	EP-43	EPS90
2115-G	2697	2153-G	2790A	2161-J	2880	2201-A	2958	2230-G	3052	EP-44	EPS96
2115-H	2698	2153-H	2791A	2161-K	2881	2201-B	2959	2230-H	3053	EP-46	EPS101
2115-I	2699	2153-I	2792A	2161-L	2882	2201-C	2960	2230-I	3054	EP-47	EPS109
2115-J	2700	2153-J	2793A	2162-B	2883	2201-D	2961	2230-J	3055	EP-48	EPS116
2115-K	2701	2153-K	2794A	2162-G	2884	2201-E	2962	2230-K	3056	EP-49	EPS120
2115-L	2702	2153-L	2795A	2162-L	2885	2201-F	2963	2230-L	3057	EP-49A	EPS127
2116-A	2703	2154-A	2796	2163-A	2886	2201-G	2964	2231-A	3058	EP-50	EPS133
2116-B	2704	2154-C	2797	2163-B	2887	2201-H	2965	2231-B	3059	EP-51	EPS141
2116-E	2705	2154-D	2798	2163-C	2888	2201-I	2966	2231-C	3060	EP-52	EPS149
2116-F	2706	2154-E	2799	2163-D	2889	2201-J	2967	2231-D	3061	EP-52A	EPS156
2116-G	2707	2154-F	2800	2163-E	2890	2201-K	2968	2231-E	3062	EP-53	EPS160
2116-K	2708	2154-G	2801	2163-F	2891	2201-L	2969	2231-F	3063	EP-54	EPS166
2117-A	2709	2154-H	2802	2163-G	2892	2202-B	2971	2231-G	3064	EP-55	EPS173
2117-B	2710	2154-I	2803	2163-H	2893	2202-C	2972	2231-H	3065	EP-56	EPS178
2117-C	2711	2154-J	2804	2163-I	2894	2202-D	2973	2231-J	3066	EP-57	EPS186
2117-D	2712	2154-K	2805	2163-J	2895	2202-E	2974	2231-K	3067	EP-58	EPS194
2117-E	2713	2155-A	2806	2163-K	2896	2202-G	2975	2231-L	3068	EP-59	EPS198
2117-F	2714	2155-B	2807	2163-L	2897	2202-H	2976	2232-G	3069	EP-60	EPS7
2117-G	2715	2155-C	2808	2164-A	2898	2202-I	2977	2233-B	3070	EP-60A	EPS3
2117-H	2716	2155-D	2809	2164-B	2899	2202-J	2978	2300	1609	EP-61	EPS14
2117-I	2717	2155-F	2810	2164-C	2900	2202-K	2979	2301	1960	EP-63	EPS24
2117-J	2718	2155-G	2811	2164-D	2901	2202-L	2980	2302	1961	EP-64	EPS34
2117-K	2719	2155-H	2812	2164-E	2902	2203-F	2981	2303	2258	EP-67	EPS46
2117-L	2720	2155-I	2813	2164-F	2903	2204-A	2982	2304	2523	EP-68	EPS51
2118-A	2721	2155-J	2814	2164-G	2904	2204-B	2983	2305	2524	EP-69	EPS56
2118-B	2722	2155-K	2815	2164-H	2905	2210-A	2985	2306	1610	EP-70	EPS64
2118-C	2723	2155-L	2816	2164-I	2906	2210-B	2986	2307	1962	EP-71	EPS73

Fr.	KL
EP-72	EPS75
EP-73	EPS79
EP-74	EPS83
EP-76	EPS91
EP-76A	EPS97
EP-77	EPS190
EP-78	EPS102
EP-79	EPS110
EP-80	EPS117
EP-81	EPS121
EP-82	EPS128
EP-83	EPS134
EP-84	EPS142
EP-85	EPS150
EP-86	EPS154
EP-87	EPS157
EP-89	EPS167
EP-90	EPS169
EP-91	EPS174
EP-92	EPS179
EP-93A	EPS187
EP-94	EPS195
EP-95	EPS199
EP-96	EPS8
EP-96A	EPS4
EP-97	EPS15
EP-98	EPS20
EP-98A	EPS25
EP-98B	EPS31
EP-100	EPS35
EP-101	EPS39
EP-102A	EPS43
EP-103	EPS47
EP-104	EPS52
EP-105	EPS57
EP-106	EPS65
EP-107	EPS70
EP-108	EPS76
EP-109	EPS80
EP-110	EPS84
EP-112	EPS92
EP-113	EPS98
EP-114	EPS191
EP-116	EPS103
EP-117	EPS111
EP-117A	EPS118
EP-118	EPS122
EP-119	EPS129
EP-120	EPS135
EP-121	EPS143
EP-122	EPS151
EP-123	EPS153
EP-124	EPS158
EP-125	EPS161
EP-125A	EPS164
EP-127	EPS168
EP-128	EPS170
EP-129	EPS175
EP-130	EPS180
EP-131	EPS183
EP-132	EPS188
EP-133	EPS196
EP-134	EPS200
EP-135	EPS9
EP-136	EPS16
EP-137	EPS26
EP-137A	EPS21
EP-138	EPS36
EP-139	EPS40
EP-140	EPS48
EP-141	EPS53
EP-142	EPS58
EP-143	EPS66
EP-144	EPS74
EP-145	EPS85
EP-146	EPS93
EP-147	EPS192
EP-148	EPS104
EP-149	EPS112
EP-150	EPS123
EP-151	EPS130
EP-152	EPS136
EP-153	EPS144
EP-154	EPS152
EP-155	EPS162
EP-157	EPS176
EP-158	EPS181
EP-159	EPS184
EP-159B	EPS10
EP-163	EPS59

Fr.	KL
EP-164	EPS67
EP-165	EPS86
EP-166	EPS94
EP-167	EPS105
EP-168	EPS113
EP-169	EPS124
EP-170	EPS131
EP-171	EPS137
EP-172	EPS145
EP-172B	EPS11
EP-175	EPS60
EP-176	EPS68
EP-177	EPS87
EP-178	EPS106
EP-179	EPS114
EP-180	EPS125
EP-181	EPS138
EP-182	EPS146
EP-183	EPS171
EP-183A	EPS17
EP-184	EPS61
EP-184A	EPS69
EP-185	EPS88
EP-186	EPS107
EP-187	EPS139
EP-188	EPS147